AIR AND WATER POLLUTION CONTROL ENGINEERING

AIR AND WATER POLLUTION CONTROL ENGINEERING

Prof. D N Ghosh BChE, MS, PhD
Former Professor and Head
Chemical Engineering Department
Jadavpur University, Kolkata

Prof. S K Ghosh BChE, MChE, MS
Former Process Engineering Consultant
Harzog-Hart Corporation, USA
Brown & Root, USA
BE & K Inc., USA

New Central Book Agency (P) Ltd
LONDON
HYDERABAD ERNAKULAM BHUBANESWAR
DELHI KOLKATA PUNE GUWAHATI

NCBA

REGD OFFICE

8/1 Chintamoni Das Lane, Kolkata 700 009, India
ncbapvtltd@eth.net

OVERSEAS

NCBA (UK) Ltd, 149 Park Avenue North, Northampton, NN3 2HY, UK
ncbauk@yahoo.com

EXPORT

NCBA Exports Pvt. Ltd, 212 Shahpur Jat, New Delhi 110 049
ncbaexports@ncbaindia.com

BRANCHES

208B Peacock Lane, Shahpur Jat
New Delhi 110 049
ncbadel@ncbapvtltd.com

House No. 3-1-315, 1st Floor
Nimboliadda, Kachiguda, **Hyderabad** 500 027
ncbahydb@ncbapvtltd.com

Shop Nos. 3 & 4, Vinayak Towers
681/B Budhwar Peth, Appa Balwant Chowk
Pune 411 002
ncbapune@ncbapvtltd.com

GSS Shopping Complex, 1st Floor
Opposite College Post Office, Convent Road
Ernakulam 682 035
ncbaernk@ncbapvtltd.com

Shop No. 15, Bharati Towers, Ground Floor
Forest Park, **Bhubaneswar** 751 001
ncbabub@ncbapvtltd.com

Radhamayee Complex (Second Floor)
Opp. SBI, Panbazar, Jaswanta Road
Guwahati 781 001
ncbaguwahati@ncbapvtltd.com

AIR AND WATER POLLUTION CONTROL ENGINEERING • Prof. D N Ghosh, Prof. S K Ghosh

First Published: July 2012

PUBLISHER AND TYPESETTER
New Central Book Agency (P) Ltd
8/1 Chintamoni Das Lane, Kolkata 700 009

PRINTER
New Central Book Agency (P) Ltd
Web-Offset Division, Dhulagarh, Sankrail, Howrah

COVER DESIGNER
Soumen Paul

COVER PRINTER
Liba Graphics, Kolkata

TECHNICAL EDITOR
Dipan Roy

PROJECT TEAM
Somenath Ganguly, Pradip Baidya, and Prabhat Jas

ISBN 978 81 7381 754 0

Price: ₹ 750.00

CONTENTS

Preface xiii-xv

List of Tables xvii-xviii

List of Illustrations xix-xxi

1. INTRODUCTION **1-7**

1.1 Biosphere 2

1.2 Human Activity, Biosphere and Ecology 2

1.3 Food Chain, Food Web 4

1.4 Waste Handling, Treatment and Disposal 5

1.5 Pollution Regulation Approach 6

1.6 Pollution Control Legislation 7

2. THE ATMOSPHERE **8-35**

2.1 Atmospheric Pressure 8

2.2 Atmospheric Temperature and Composition 8

2.2.1 Atmospheric Temperature 8

2.2.2 Atmospheric Chemical Composition 10

2.3 Air Pollutants 11

2.3.1 Classification of Air Pollutants 11

2.4 Sources of Atmospheric Pollutants 13

2.5 Effects of Atmospheric Pollutants 14

2.5.1 Effects on Atmospheric Properties 14

2.5.2 Effects on Vegetation 20

2.5.3 Effects on Animals 21

2.5.4 Effects on Human Beings 21

2.5.5 Effects on Land and Water Bodies 24

2.5.6 Effects on Materials 24

2.6 Atmospheric Chemistry 25

2.6.1 Tropospheric Reactions 25

2.6.2 Stratospheric Reactions 28

2.7 Material Balance and Mass Conservation in the Troposphere 29

2.7.1 The Hydrological Cycle 29

2.7.2 The Oxygen Cycle 29

2.7.3 The Nitrogen Cycle 31

2.7.4 The Carbon Cycle 31

2.7.5 The Sulphur Cycle 31

3. **AIR POLLUTANT MONITORING** **36-44**

3.1 Sampling 36

3.1.1 Sampling Train 37

3.1.2 Stack Sampling 38

3.1.3 Ambient Air Sampling 38

3.2 Particulate Monitoring 38

3.3 Gaseous Pollutants Monitoring 39

3.3.1 In Situ Analysis 40

3.3.1.1 Instrumental Methods 40

3.3.1.2 Chemical Methods 42

3.4 Sample Collection and Analysis at Convenience 43

4. **GAS-BORNE POLLUTANT ABATEMENT METHODS** **45-121**

4.1 Pollutant Classification and Treatment Methods 47

4.2 Particulate Abatement Devices 49

4.2.1 Gravity Settler 50

4.2.2 Inertial Separator 57

4.2.3 Centrifugal Separator 59

4.2.4 Filters 67

4.2.4.1 Gravel Filter 67

4.2.4.2 Fabric Filter 67

4.2.5 Electrostatic Precipitator (ESP) 71

4.2.6 Scrubbers 78

4.2.6.1 Plate Columns 80

4.2.6.2 Packed Scrubbers 80

4.2.6.3 Fiber Bed 80

4.2.6.4 Spray Contactors 81

4.3 Removal of Liquid Droplets and Mists 82

4.4 Cooling and Condensation 84

4.5 Absorption of Gaseous Pollutants 87

4.5.1 Absorption Theory 87

4.5.2 Absorption Equipment 89

4.5.3 Packed Tower Design Approach 90

4.5.3.1 Required Solvent Rate 91

4.5.3.2 Column Diameter 91

4.5.3.3 Column Height 92

4.5.3.4 Pressure Drop Across a Packed Tower 92

4.6 Adsorption of Gaseous Pollutants 92

4.6.1 Fixed Bed Adsorber Design Approach 94

4.7 Chemical Treatment of Gaseous Pollutants 101
4.7.1 Thermal Incineration 101
4.7.2 Catalytic Incineration 104
4.7.3 Bio-Oxidation 106
4.8 Disposal of a Gaseous Effluent 106
4.8.1 Actual Plume Profile 107
4.8.2 Stack Design Approach 111
4.8.2.1 Stack Height Estimation 111
4.8.2.2 Empirical Approach 111
4.8.2.3 Semi-empirical Approach 111
4.8.2.4 Pollutant Concentration Profile in a Plume 112
4.8.2.5 Plume Rise Correlations 115
4.8.2.6 Estimation of Stack Cross-Sectional Area / Diameter and Stack Pressure Drop 117
4.8.3 Plume Dust Deposition 120

5. ABATEMENT OF SOME SPECIFIC GASEOUS POLLUTANTS 122-143

5.1 Abatement of Sulphur Dioxide (SO_2) 122
5.1.1 Dry Processes 123
5.1.1.1 Dry Throwaway Process—Limestone/Dolomite Process 123
5.1.1.2 Dry Recovery Processes 123
5.1.2 Wet Processes 126
5.1.2.1 Wet Throwaway Processes 126
5.1.2.2 Wet Recovery Processes 128
5.2 Abatement of Hydrogen Sulphide (H_2S) 132
5.2.1 Dry Process 132
5.2.2 Wet Processes 133
5.3 Abatement of Nitrogenous Compounds 135
5.3.1 Abatement of Basic Compounds 135
5.3.2 Abatement of Acidic Compounds/Oxides 136
5.4 Abatement of Fluorine and Fluorides 138
5.5 Abatement of Chlorine and Chlorides 138
5.6 Abatement of Carbon Monoxide 139
5.7 Abatement of VOCs (Volatile Organic Compounds) 139
5.7.1 Physical Methods 139
5.7.1.1 Condensation 139
5.7.1.2 Absorption 140
5.7.1.3 Adsorption 140
5.7.2 Combustion Based Processes 141
5.7.2.1 Non-Catalytic Combustion Processes 141
5.7.2.2 Catalytic Combustion Process 142

	5.8	VOC Emission From Other Sources	142
		5.8.1 Fugitive Emissions	142
		5.8.2 Flare Stack Emission	143
	5.9	Abatement of Odorous Compounds	143
6.	**WATER POLLUTION**		**144-153**
	6.1	Water Pollutants, Their Sources and Effects	147
		6.1.1 Pollutant Classification	147
		6.1.2 Sources of Water Pollutants	148
		6.1.3 Effects of Water-borne Pollutants	148
	6.2	Tolerance Limits of Pollutants in Treated Effluents	150
7.	**WATER POLLUTION MONITORING**		**154-164**
	7.1	Sampling	154
	7.2	Sample Preservation	155
	7.3	Analysis	155
	7.4	Process Outlines for Estimation of Some Common Pollutant Attributes	156
		7.4.1 Total Residue	156
		7.4.2 Dissolved Residue	156
		7.4.3 Fixed Solids and Volatile Solids	156
		7.4.4 Suspended Solids	156
		7.4.5 Fixed Suspended Solids	156
		7.4.6 Turbidity	157
		7.4.7 Colour	157
		7.4.8 Odour	157
		7.4.9 Conductivity	157
		7.4.10 Hardness	158
		7.4.11 Alkalinity	158
		7.4.12 pH	158
		7.4.13 Temperature	158
		7.4.14 Oils, Fats and Greases	158
		7.4.15 Dissolved Oxygen	159
		7.4.16 Biochemical Oxygen Demand (BOD)	160
		7.4.17 Chemical Oxygen Demand (COD)	162
		7.4.18 Plant Nutrients	162
		7.4.18.1 Nitrogen Estimation	162
		7.4.18.2 Phosphorous Estimation	163
		7.4.19 Bacteriological Assessment	163
		7.4.20 Bioassay	163

8. WATER-BORNE POLLUTANT CLASSIFICATION, TREATMENT TECHNIQUES AND CONTROL STRATEGY **165-169**

8.1 Treatment Techniques 166

8.2 Control Strategy 169

9. WATER-BORNE POLLUTANT ABATEMENT METHODS **170-297**

9.1 Primary Treatment 174

9.1.1 Screening 175

9.1.2 Grit Removal 176

9.1.2.1 Rectangular Cross-section Grit Chamber Design Approach 177

9.1.2.2 Trapezoidal Cross-section Grit Chamber Design Approach 179

9.1.2.3 Hydrocyclone 187

9.2 Thickening/Sedimentation 187

9.2.1 Design of a Rectangular Tank for Sedimentation of Discrete Particles at Low Concentration 190

9.2.2 Design of a Rectangular Tank for Sedimentation of Flocculant Particles at a Low Concentration 193

9.2.3 Design of a Circular Sedimentation Tank 195

9.3 Air Floatation 199

9.3.1 Induced Air Floatation (IAF) Process 199

9.3.2 Dissolved Air Floatation (DAF) Process 199

9.3.2.1 Vacuum Floatation 200

9.3.2.2 Dissolved Air Floatation 200

9.3.3 Floatation Unit Design Approach 201

9.3.3.1 Absorber Design 201

9.3.3.2 Floatation Tank Design 203

9.4 Filtration 203

9.4.1 Granular Bed Filters 204

9.4.2 Rotary Filters 205

9.5 Coagulation and Flocculation 206

9.6 Removal of Oils and Greases 208

9.6.1 Removal of Free Oils and Greases 208

9.6.2 Removal of Emulsified Oil 209

9.7 Secondary Treatment 211

9.8 Fundamentals of Microbes 211

9.8.1 Microbial Interaction in Waste Water Treatment 215

9.8.2 Microbe Physiology 216

9.8.3 Enzymatic Kinetics 218

9.8.4 Microbial Growth Process 221

9.8.5 Cell Growth Kinetics 223

9.9 Aerobic Treatment of Waste Water 225
9.9.1 Aerobic Lagoon 227
9.9.2 Completely Mixed Aerated Lagoon 228
9.9.2.1 Design Approach 228
9.9.2.2 CMAL Oxygen Demand 230
9.9.3 Activated Sludge Unit 234
9.9.3.1 Activated Sludge Unit Design Approach 239
9.9.3.2 Activated Sludge Reactor Oxygen Demand Estimation 241
9.9.4 Trickling Filter 245
9.9.4.1 Trickling Filter Design Approach 246
9.9.5 Rotating Biological Contractor (RBC) 250
9.9.5.1 RBC Design Approach 252
9.10 Anaerobic Treatment of Waste Water 256
9.10.1 Anaerobic Treatment Units 258
9.10.2 Facultative Lagoon 258
9.10.3 Anaerobic Lagoon 259
9.10.4 Septic Tank 259
9.10.5 Imhoff Tank 260
9.10.6 Anaerobic Digester/Reactor 262
9.10.6.1 Suspended Growth Units 262
9.10.6.2 Up-flow Anaerobic Sludge Blanket Reactor 265
9.10.6.3 Attached Growth Units 265
9.10.6.3.1 Anaerobic Filter Reactor 266
9.10.6.3.2 Expanded Bed and Fluidized Bed Anaerobic Reactor 266
9.10.6.4 Anaerobic Digester Design Approach 267
9.11 Tertiary Treatment 270
9.11.1 Filtration 271
9.11.2 Air/Steam Stripping 272
9.11.3 Biological Processes 274
9.11.3.1 Biological Treatment of Nitrogenous Compounds 274
9.11.3.2 Nitrification Process 274
9.11.3.3 Denitrification Process 276
9.11.3.4 Biological Phosphorous Removal 279
9.11.4 Adsorption 280
9.11.4.1 Process Description 281
9.11.4.2 Carbon Regeneration 282
9.11.5 Membrane Separation Processes 282
9.11.5.1 Process Description 283
9.11.5.2 Membrane Configuration and Geometry 286

9.11.6 Ion Exchange Process 288
9.11.7 Precipitation 294
9.11.8 Oxidation and Reduction 294
9.11.9 Disinfection 295

10. ABATEMENT OF SOME SPECIFIC WATER-BORNE POLLUTANTS 298-315

10.1 Arsenic (As) 298
10.2 Cadmium (Cd) 299
10.3 Chromium (Cr) 300
10.3.1 Hexavalent Chromium 300
10.3.2 Trivalent Chromium 301
10.4 Cyanide 301
10.5 Fluoride 302
10.6 Heavy Metals 304
10.7 Mercury (Hg) 305
10.8 Nutrients 307
10.8.1 Nitrogen Removal 307
10.8.2 Phosphorous Removal 309
10.9 Phenol 311
10.10 Volatile Organic Compounds (VOCs) 312
10.11 Pesticides 315

APPENDICES

Appendix I : A Brief Guideline for Preparation of Environmental Impact Assessment Report 317-318

Appendix II : Salient Features of Pollution Control Acts and Rules in India 318-321

Appendix IIIA : Maximum Permissible Limits of Discharge from Some Specific Industries 322-353

Appendix IIIB : National Ambient Air Quality Standards in India 354-355

REFERENCES 357-360

INDEX 361-366

PREFACE

For over a hundred years, the rapid industrialization of developed and developing nations without paying any heed to adequate pollution monitoring and control efforts has finally started taking its toll on our current ecological balance. That—as well as the explosive growth of (human) population—are the two main factors that have resulted in the present state of global pollution level. As a consequence of this pollution, we see several drastic changes in our ecosystem. Our overall weather pattern is changing rapidly—we see heavy rainfall occurring in places where earlier semi-desert conditions prevailed; sweet water-bodies have become fouled due to discharge of untreated/partially treated waste water and acid rain. As a result of the above, not only are flora and fauna getting affected, even the oceans are becoming more polluted by the day.

The developed countries have long been adopting stringent measures for pollution control by shutting down highly polluting industrial operations. However, such operations and processes are now being relocated to developing countries, where very little pollution control measures are being implemented to address the issue. In order to mitigate this, the time has come for the developing countries to frame strict pollution control norms and to set up agencies for enforcing the industries to abide by those established norms.

In currently available open literature, considerable amount of information is available about the various types of pollutants that are likely to emanate from the different types of industrial processes/operations; their effects on the ecosystems; their monitoring and abatement methods. Published information about pollution control norms already established by the developed countries is also available. However, there is no text currently available that consolidates all this varying information and presents a lucid text on pollutants and their treatments, the laws and regulations governing their emission norms and methods of abatements.

The purpose of this book is to do just that. It collects, collates and consolidates available information related to

1. the pollutants that are likely to be produced from the different types of industrial processes/operations,
2. the effects of the pollutants resulting from industrial activities on the ecosystems,
3. the pollutant monitoring methods,
4. the Pollution Control Acts and Rules in India,
5. the prescribed maximum permissible limits of discharge from some specific industries in India,
6. the gas-borne and water-borne pollution abatement methods,
7. the methods for abatement of some specific pollutants which need special attention.

This book is intended for use as a textbook for any Undergraduate or Postgraduate curriculum of Environmental, Chemical and Civil Engineering discipline in India today. In addition, professionals can also use this book to guide them through the intricacies of the Indian Pollution Control Acts and Rules or to confirm the data available in supplier specifications or use it to prepare EIA reports. This book is also a valuable reference to understand the pitfalls of the industrial gas and water-borne pollutant treatment processes.

This book is organized in such a fashion that one may study it sequentially or study the chapters selectively. The chapters are sufficiently independent to enable one to study a chapter of one's choice without having to look up the previous chapter(s).

There are ten chapters and here is a brief preview of each :

1. **Introduction :** It provides an overview of ecology, ecosystems, wastes, pollutants, effects of pullutants, pollution control approach and the Indian Pollution Control Acts frame over the years.
2. **The Atmosphere :** It describes the temperature and pressure profile; the composition and structure of the different strata of the atmosphere. The effects of the gas-borne pollutants (which are released into the atmosphere) on the local and global ecosystem are also discussed.
3. **Air Pollutant Monitoring :** The procedure for sampling gaseous effluents and the monitoring methods of particulate and gaseous pollutants are covered in this chapter.
4. **Gas-borne Pollutant Abatement Methods :** This chapter deals with the classification of gas-borne pollutants and their treatment methods. The devices used for abatement of particulate (solid and liquid), vapour and gaseous pollutants and their limitations have also been described. The design procedures of the major devices have been elaborated and illustrated with the help of worked-out examples. Stack design procedure has also been enumerated.
5. **Abatement of Some Specific Gaseous Pollutants :** The abatement methods of some specific gaseous pollutants—which need special attention—have been detailed.
6. **Water Pollution :** Waste water borne pollutants have been classified; their sources and effects have been enumerated. The tolerance limits of pollutants in treated effluent have been listed.
7. **Water Pollution Monitoring :** The sampling procedures of waste water and sample preservation techniques have been discussed. The procedures for estimation of some common pollutant attributes have been outlined.
8. **Water-borne Pollutants :** The treatment techniques have been classified and control strategy has been discussed.
9. **Water-borne Pollutant Abatement Methods :** Primary treatment methods for removal of suspended matter have been discussed at length and the equipment design procedures have been elaborated. Some worked out examples have also been included. Secondary treatment methods for removal of organic impurities in waste water have been discussed. The microbes being the causative factor of secondary treatment, their fundamentals, physiology, growth process have been discussed. Various aerobic and anaerobic units for treatment of waste water, their working principles and design procedures have been detailed. The advantages and limitations of the different types of units have been discussed. A few worked out examples related to equipment design have been incorporated. Tertiary treatment methods for removal of inorganic impurities and other residual pollutants including pathogens have been discussed.
10. **Abatement of Some Specific Water-borne Pollutants :** Abatement processes for removal of some specific harmful pollutants which need selective treatment have been dealt with at length. Their effects on human beings and their tolerance limits in potable water have been listed.

A list of references has also been included in this book for the enquiring minds.

In summary, this book is an extensive treatise on the abatement of gas-borne and water-borne pollutants emanating from industrial units and on current rules and regulations governing pollution control in India.

Other highlights of the book that make it both unique and a must and easy read for any student or professional alike are :

1. a chronological listing and brief outline of Indian Pollution Control Acts and Rules,
2. design procedures of major pollution control equipment for treatment of waste gases and waste water,

3. several worked out mathematical examples on equipment design that can come in very handy for preliminary sizing of any equipment,
4. the sources, toxic effects and abatement processes of all major gas-borne and water-borne pollutants released from industrial units today.

These are just a few of the many advantages of the book, thus making it ideal for professionals in all walks of life in this field. As a textbook, it may be used to cover more than one course—it will be just as effective for a course on the sources of gas-borne pollutants, their effects, their monitoring and abatement methods including equipment design procedure (by covering chapters 2, 3, 4 and 5) as it will be for a course on waste water borne pollutants, their sources and effects, monitoring methods, abatement processes and major equipment design procedures (chapters 6, 7, 8, 9 and 10). An abridged course on gas-borne and water-borne pollution abatement can be taught by covering chapters 3, 4, 7 and 9.

We are confident that this book will be very popular amongst students, teachers and professionals alike due to its coverage and detailed research.

The authors acknowledge that information has been collated and incorporated in this book from open literature, some of which are listed under references. Information has also been obtained from WHO publications, the Gazette of India, and U.S. Environmental Pollution Agency (EPA) publications.

Saraswati Puja
28 January 2012
Kolkata

Prof. D N Ghosh
Prof. S K Ghosh

LIST OF TABLES

Table		
2.1	Average Composition of Tropospherical Dry Air	11
2.2	Sources of Emission of Some Common Airborne Pollutants	13
2.3	Plant Injury Threshold of Some Gaseous Pollutants	21
2.4	TLV and Biological Effects of Some Common Gaseous Pollutants	23
2.5	Primary and Secondary Sinks of Some Common Gaseous Pollutants	26
3.1	Some Pollutant Specific Gas Chromatograph Detectors	40
3.2	Some Techniques for Monitoring Specific Pollutants	40
3.3	Bubbler Liquid Composition and Analytical Approaches Used for Estimation of Some Common Gaseous Pollutants	44
3.4	Merits and Demerits of Instrumental and Chemical Methods for Analysis of Gaseous Pollutants	44
4.1	Basic Information Required for Designing a Gaseous Pollutant Abatement System	46
4.2	Classification of Gas-borne Pollutant Treatment Methods	47
4.3	Waste Gas Treatment Methods and Their Areas of Application	48
4.4	Different Treatment Methods for Removal of a Specific Type of Gas-borne Pollutant	49
4.5	Relative Dimensions of the Different Portions of Standard Cyclones	60
4.6	Typical Cyclone Pressure Drop	62
4.7	Characteristics of Filter Fabrics	69
4.8	Air to Cloth Ratio	71
4.9	Typical Drift Velocity of Some Specific Particles	74
4.10	Normal Range of Variation of Parameter Values of Plate Type Commercial ESPs	77
4.11	Scrubber Classification	79
4.12	Performance and Pertinent Data of Scrubbers	82
4.13	Indirect Contact Exchanger Coolant Selection Guidelines	85
4.14	Typical Values of Individual Heat Transfer Coefficient	87
4.15	Qualitative Atmospheric Stability Designations	110
4.16	Numerical Values of Coefficients and Exponents Related to Eq. (4.71)	115
5.1	Approximate Sludge Composition of Limestone and Lime System	127
6.1	Annual Water Consumption Pattern and Availability in India (km^3)	145
6.2	Water Consumption Rate of Some Specific Indian Industries	145
6.3	WHO Guideline Values for Chemicals that are of Health Significance in Drinking Water	150
7.1	Oxygen Solubility in Fresh Water from Atmospheric Air	159
8.1	Classification of the Waste Water Treatment Techniques Based on Their Causative Factors	166
8.2	Treatment Techniques, Basic Purpose and Consequent Pollutant Removal	167

Table

9.1	Rack Clearance and Angle	175
9.2	Typical Parameters of Rectangular and Circular Sedimentation Tanks	197
9.3	Classification of Protists	212
9.4	Classification of Microbes	217
9.5	Classification of Chemo-heterotrophs based on their Optimum Temperature Range	217
9.6	Typical Value of Mixed Culture Kinetic Parameters for Aerobic Waste Water Treatment around 20°C	225
9.7	Basic Features of Aerobic Treatment Units	226
9.8	Design and Performance Parameters of Aerobic Lagoons	227
9.9	Design and Performance Parameters of Aerated Lagoons (CMAL)	232
9.10	Design and Performance Parameters Ranges of Activated Sludge Units	243
9.11	Design and Performance Parameters of Trickling Filters	249
9.12	Some Inorganic Anaerobic Process Inhibitors	258
9.13	Tertiary Treatment Methods and their Effectiveness	271
9.14	Design and Performance Parameters of Denitrification Reactors	277
9.15	Characteristics of Polymeric Membrane Based Separation Processes	287
10.1	Phosphate Precipitation Reactions	310

LIST OF ILLUSTRATIONS

Figure

1.1	Human Activities, Wastes and Pollution	3
1.2	Energy Flow and Food Chain	4
1.3	Population Pyramid	5
2.1	Pressure and Temperature Distribution in the Atmosphere	9
2.2	Tropospheric Temperature Profile	17
2.3	A Typical Wind Rose for Kolkata City	20
2.4	The Hydrological Cycle	30
2.5	The Oxygen Cycle	32
2.6	The Nitrogen Cycle	33
2.7	The Carbon Cycle	34
2.8	The Sulfur Cycle	35
3.1	A Schematic Diagram of a Sample Train	37
3.2	Stauscheibe/Reverse Type Pitot Tube Assembly	39
4.1	General Treatment Sequence of a Waste Gas Stream	48
4.2	Sketches of Gravity Settlers	50
4.3	Sketches of Some Types of Intertial Separators	58
4.4	Sketch of a Standard Cyclone	60
4.5	Cyclone Efficiency vs dpi/d_{50}	61
4.6	Schematic Diagram of a Gravel Filter	68
4.7	Schematic Diagram of a Bag Filter	72
4.8	Schematic Diagram of a Pair of Parallel Plates (ESP)	74
4.9	Schematic Representation of Some Types of Wet Scrubbers	83
4.10	Shell and Tube Cooler-Condenser	86
4.11	Schematic Diagram of a Packed Bed Absorber	90
4.12	Schematic Diagram Showing Progressive Saturation of an Adsorbent Bed	94
4.13	Adsorbate Concentration at Adsorber Exit vs Time	95
4.14	Typical Equilibrium Curve and Operating Line of a Fixed Bed Adsorber	97
4.15	H_{OG} for a Fix-Bed Adsorption	98
4.16	Schematic Representation of a Flare Stack	103
4.17	Schematic Diagram of a Catalytic Incinerator	105
4.18	Plume Profile Development under Ideal Condition with Ground Reflection	107
4.19A-G	Sketches of Plume Profile Corresponding to various Atmospheric Stability Conditions	108
4.20A	Horizontal Dispersion Coefficient (σ) as a Function of Downwind Distance from the Stack Base	113

Figure

4.20B	Vertical Dispersion Coefficient (σ_2) as a Function of Downwind Distance from the Stack Base	114
4.21	Dust Deposition Factor (Bosanquet et al)	121
7.1	Dependence of BOD_{20} on Incubation Period	161
8.1	Water-borne Pollutant Classification	165
8.2	A Broad Scheme for Treatment of an Industrial Plant Effluent	169
9.1	Schematic Sketch of an Equalisation Basin	173
9.2	Sketch of a Limestone Neutralizer	174
9.3A	Proportional Weir	177
9.3B	Sutro Weir	177
9.4	Trapezoidal Grit Chamber	180
Ex. 9.2	Trapezoidal Grit Chamber	186
9.5	Schematic Diagram of a Hydrocyclone	187
9.6	Sketch of a Settling Column for Studying Suspension Settling Characteristics	188
9.7	Rectangular Sedimentation Tank	189
9.8	Circular Sedimentation Tank	190
9.9	P vs V Plot	192
9.10	Isopercent Removal Plot	194
9.11	Detention Time and Overflow Rate vs Percent Removal R	195
9.12	Settling Curve for a Low Concentration Suspension	196
Ex. 9.3	Circular Thickener	198
9.13	Dissolved Air Floatation—Full Flow Unit	200
9.14	Dissolved Air Floatation—Partial Flow Unit	201
9.15	Dissolved Air Floatation—Recycle Flow Unit	202
9.16	Granular Filter Bed	205
9.17	Grease Trap	209
9.18	API Gravity Oil—Water Separator	210
9.19A	Prokaryotic Cell	212
9.19B	Eukaryotic Cell	213
9.20	Plots for Evaluation of Kinetic Parameters K_m and V_m	220
9.21	Typical Growth Process of Organisms During a Batch Operation	221
9.22	Schematic Representation of Aerobic Lagoon Reactions	227
9.23	Schematic Sketch of a CMAL	228
9.24	Schematic Representation of Activated Sludge Process	234
9.25	Different Types of Activated Sludge Units	236
9.26	Oxidation Ditch with Sludge Recycle	237
9.27	A Schematic Diagram of an Activated Sludge Unit	238
9.28	Diagram of a Trickling Filter	246

Figure

9.29	RBC Units Connected in Series	252
9.30	Graphical Approach for Solution of Eq. 9.88	254
Ex. 9.7	Multistage R.B.C.	256
9.31	Representation of Waste Water Treatment—Anaerobic Process	257
9.32	Two-Chamber Septic Tank	260
9.33	Imhoff Tank	261
9.34	Different Types of Anaerobic Reactors	263
9.35	Single Stage Anaerobic Digester	264
9.36	Two Stage Anaerobic Digester with Sludge Recycle	265
9.37	Two Stage Anaerobic Digester without Sludge Recycle	268
9.38	Countercurrent Packed Air—Stripping Column	273
9.39	Single Stage Nitrification—Denitrification Process	278
9.40	Two Stage Nitrification—Denitrification Process	278
9.41	Biological Phosphorous Removal—Basic Process	279
9.42	Biological Process for Simultaneous Removal of Phosphorous and Nitrogen	280
9.43	Schematic Diagram of an Electrodialyser	285
9.44	Alternative Arrangements of Two-Bed Ion Exchangers	293

CHAPTER 1

Introduction

Since the dawn of civilization, human activity is aimed at producing/procuring materials useful to human beings. But all such activities produce some materials, other than the desired products, which have very limited use or no use at all. These materials are referred to as by-products or wastes. To be more specific, by-products have less economic value compared to that of the desired products, whereas wastes have no market value at the place where it is produced. Co-production of wastes cannot be avoided altogether, but can be minimized by modifying the production processes.

> ***Wastes** are materials or effects produced during a process, which do not have any utility to the producer.*

Much before the industrial revolution, human activity was confined to hunting and agriculture. At that period, population was rather small and the quantity of wastes was small too. Moreover, the wastes, because of their natural organic constituents, used to undergo bacterial decay without causing too much of a problem. However, even in those days, epidemics used to occur owing to improper disposal of wastes.

As time passed, population increased and their demand for consumables increased. To meet the demand man started producing more agricultural produce, products based on domesticated animals as well as some manufactured goods. As a result, the quality of waste changed and the quantity increased. Some of the wastes, generated from the manufacturing processes were non-degradable by bacteria and some were harmful. However, during this period the manufacturing processes used to depend mainly on human and animal muscle power and hence the scale of operation was low. Consequently, the volume of manufacturing process based waste generation was not that large.

When man discovered ways and means of converting the potential energy of fossil fuels to mechanical energy, the industrial revolution got started. It became possible to operate larger and larger machines and produce larger quantities of manufactured goods at a cheaper price. With progressive industrialization, people started earning more and more and the demand for manufactured goods, as well as other consumables increased. This led to more industrialization and more waste generation. To meet both the domestic as well as the industrial energy need, large quantities of fossil fuels have been utilized over the years and are still being utilized today. Not only fossil fuels but also nuclear fuels are being used these days to meet the ever-increasing energy needs of man. A considerable amount of waste is being generated on account of energy production apart from the waste generated on account of the manufacturing processes.

1.1 Biosphere

The by-products produced and wastes generated as a result of domestic and industrial activities of man are partly re-used and partly discarded either pre-treated or without any treatment. The discarded wastes are either dumped on land or discharged into water bodies or vented into the atmosphere. These are the spaces where living beings are present. All of these spaces put together is referred to as the biosphere. The biosphere, made up of a biotic community and an abiotic environment, is a 16 km thick layer, constituting about a 10 km deep hydrosphere, a thin crust of the earth's surface and about a 6 km thick layer of the atmosphere, adjacent to the earth's surface.

> ***Biosphere*** *is the fragile layer on and around the earth, made up of the water bodies, the earth's crust and a portion of the atmosphere. It sustains life, and living organisms dwell here.*
>
> ***Biotic Community*** *means all the flora and fauna, including micro-organisms, that is, all the living organisms co-existing in the different parts of the biosphere and in the entire biosphere.*
>
> ***Abiotic Environment*** *is the sum total of the physical factors and chemical surroundings which interact with the biotic community associated with it.*

1.2 Human Activity, Biosphere and Ecology

Human activity leading to waste generation and pollution is shown schematically in Fig. 1.1. The waste produced may be in different state of aggregation, such as solid particles, particles suspended in a fluid, dissolved solutes, vapour and gas.

Some of the wastes, discharged into the biosphere are directly or indirectly harmful to some living species or other, or to the entire biotic community. These wastes are referred to as pollutants. The biotic community is made up of all the living beings : the tiniest members being microbes and the largest members being certain species of whales and trees. Man is the most important member of this community. He is responsible for causing pollution and he is capable of combating pollution.

Man has realized rather recently that his existence on earth is neither independent of the other living beings nor of the abiotic environment. It has also dawned on him that nature (the biosphere) cannot assimilate all the wastes generated by him. Pollution resulting from his activities, particularly from industrial activities has now reached a staggering magnitude. This not only concerns the developed countries, but it is also causing anxiety to the developing countries.

This realization has led man to study the inter-relation (dependence) between the different living beings and their surrounding environment. The environment is made up of land, water, air and the physical factors in the immediate vicinity of a biotic community. This branch of study is known as ecology.

> ***Pollutants** are those wastes, which cause adverse effects on the biotic community of an ecosystem by interfering with the growth or health or comfort of different species. In a narrow sense, Pollutants are those substances or effects, which are produced as a result of natural processes and or human activities, that are harmful to man directly or indirectly or prejudicial to his amenities and property.*
>
> ***Ecology** is a branch of science, which deals with the distribution, and the population of living beings and their dependence and interaction with surrounding environment.*

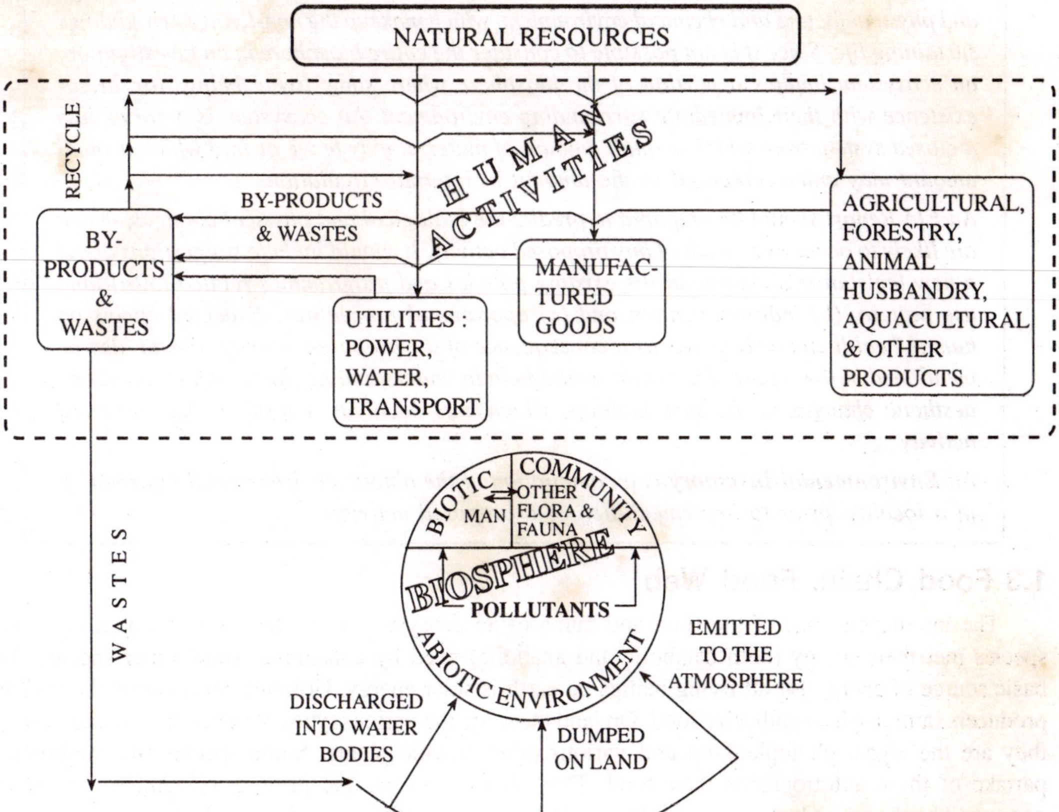

Fig. 1.1 : Human Activities, Wastes and Pollution.

The composition of the biotic community is not uniform throughout the biosphere. The different species making up a community, and the population of each species in a locality, depend on the local abiotic environment, including the weather.

Pollutants, discharged in a locality, affect the biotic community in the neighbourhood immediately after the discharge and may affect the entire biotic community in the long run. Hence, for ecological studies selected portions of the biosphere (termed as ecosystems) are considered at a time, and the effects of pollutants (which are likely to be discharged as a result of a proposed activity) on the local flora and fauna of these ecosystems are investigated. Such studies are known as "Environment Impact Assessment" (EIA). The aspects, which need examination, for preparation of an EIA report depend on the activity being planned.

Prior to carrying out an activity which is likely to affect an ecosystem, it is desirable to take a stock of the local environment, that is, to prepare an environmental inventory.

Based on the environmental inventory, and the EIA Report, an Environmental Impact Statement (EIS) is prepared to highlight the environmental changes expected as a result of a proposed activity. It is to be presented in a specified format as laid down by the national/state/local authority that finally decides about the implementation of the activity.

A brief guideline for an EIA report preparation is given in **Appendix—I.**

An ***Ecosystem*** *in the broadest sense, is the entire biosphere with all the living beings and physical factors and chemical environment, which makeup the non-living surroundings sustaining life. Since it is not possible to consider the entire biosphere in an investigation, an ecosystem implies a portion of the biosphere where some living beings are in co-existence with their immediate surrounding environment. An ecosystem is more or less a closed system from which a small amount of material may leave or into which a small amount may enter compared to the amount in internal circulation.*

An EIA Report should be prepared to predict the biological and physical changes, which are likely to occur as a result of any proposed activity. It should include suggestions about a new legislation/a change in the existing policies and programmes related to (a) land use pattern, (b) industrialization and (c) operational procedures. Expected effects on human health and well-being, as a consequence of the proposed activity, should also be mentioned in the report. The report would help in understanding the social, cultural and aesthetic changes in the surroundings, which may occur as a result of the proposed activity.

An ***Environmental Inventory*** *is a compilation of the abiotic environmental information in a locality, prior to implementation of a proposed activity.*

1.3 Food Chain, Food Web

The interdependence of the flora and fauna of an ecosystem is evident from the fact that some species met their energy (both catabolic and anabolic) need by consuming some other species. The basic source of energy for all living beings on earth is solar energy. Utilizing this energy, the primary producers (autotrophs) synthesize food. On land these are the various types of vegetation, while in water they are the algae, phytoplankton and various other aquatic plants. Some species (the herbivores) partake of these autotrophs as their food. These herbivores are the primary consumers, which are consumed by the secondary consumers (the carnivores). Some bigger carnivores (the tertiary consumers) live on the smaller ones. This energy flow pattern, from species to species, is schematically shown in Fig. 1.2.

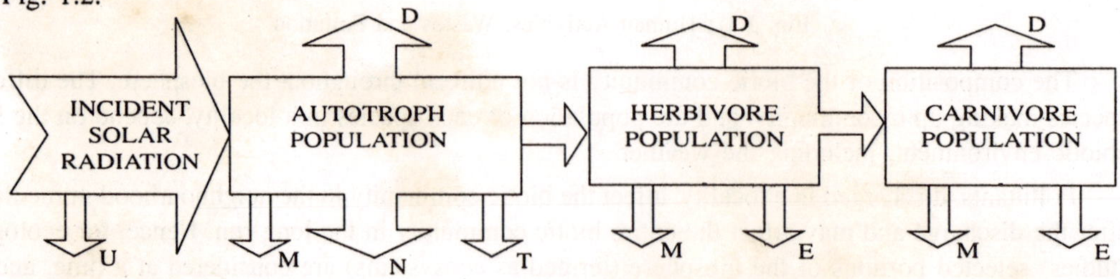

D—Energy lost due to decomposition.
E—Energy lost as EXCRETA.
M—Energy lost on Account of Metabolic Activity.
N—Unutilized Energy.
T—Energy lost due to Transpiration.
U—Energy not utilized by the Primary Producer.

Fig. 1.2 : Energy Flow and Food Chain.

In a simplified way, the sequential dependence of a species of a higher trophic level on another of a lower trophic level for food, is termed as the "food chain". However, the dependence pattern is a complex one and a better term to represent the situation is "food web", as many species take in, as food, species of different trophic levels.

The efficiency of assimilation of energy is higher at a lower trophic level and lower at a higher trophic level. Because of this, the population and the total mass of a species of lower trophic level are much larger than that of the immediate higher trophic level. The population structure is termed as "population pyramid", as shown in Fig. 1.3.

P.P. Primary Producer

P.C. Primary Consumer

S.C. Secondary Consumer

T.C. Tertiary Consumer

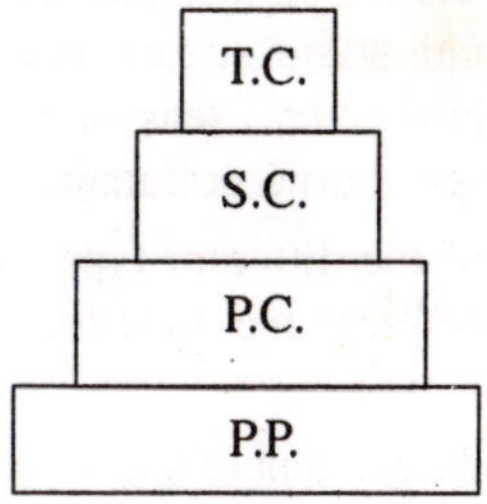

Fig. 1.3 : Population Pyramid.

> *The **food chain** is an idealized concept of trophic dependence of one species on another. Classically, it is considered that, the producer, i.e., the species belonging to the plant kingdom (termed as autotroph) synthesize food to meet their nutrition requirement by utilizing carbon dioxide, water and sunlight. All other species, directly or indirectly, live on the autotrophs. The herbivores (animals belonging to the next higher trophic level) live on autotrophs. Similarly, the carnivores belonging to the third trophic level live on the herbivores.*
>
> *The **food web** : In reality, a species of a specific trophic level is dependent on several species belonging to different trophic levels for its nourishment. Because of such food habits, a complex relation exists between the different species as consumer and consumed. The actual complex food habit of different species in an ecosystem is termed as the food web. As a consequence of food chain/food web, once a pollutant gets absorbed in a species, it is transmitted to the other species of the higher trophic levels.*

1.4 Waste Handling, Treatment and Disposal

The waste generated as a result of human activities very often contains pollutants. Pollutant bearing wastes need to be handled and treated properly and finally disposed off. Pollutant-free wastes having some market value can be disposed off without any difficulty. However, those (pollutant-free wastes) having no market value need to be handled and disposed carefully as they are likely to cause nuisance.

The handling, treatment and disposal methods of a waste depend on its state of aggregation. A gaseous waste stream would have a large volume even when its mass is relatively small. Because of this fact a waste gas stream cannot be stored but has to be let out to the immediate surrounding of its source. On its release to the atmosphere it is carried away in the downwind direction and the pollutants present, if any, start diffusing towards the earths surface and thereby affect the ecosystem. Hence, it is essential to treat a waste gas stream in order to reduce its pollutant content prior to its release to the atmosphere. Release of an untreated waste gas may affect not only the ecosystem in the neighbourhood of its point of release but also those of the distant places within a short time.

The effects of the different types of airborne pollutants on the atmosphere, living beings and man-made structures are discussed in Chapter 2. The different methods for treatment of a waste gas stream for abatement of pollutants are discussed in Chapters 4 and 5.

Handling and treatment of a liquid waste stream can be carried out more conveniently as its volume would be much less compared to a gaseous waste stream having the same mass. A low volume liquid waste stream may be stored for some time before its treatment but care should be taken that it does not percolate the earth's surface and thereby contaminate ground water. Care should also be taken that an untreated liquid waste stream does not flow into the neighbouring surface water bodies and ultimately runs into rivers, seas and oceans. Liquid-borne pollutants take longer time to migrate compared to the gas-borne pollutants.

The effects of the different types of pollutants present in a liquid waste stream are discussed in Chapter 6. The different methods for treatment of liquid wastes containing pollutants are discussed in Chapter 9.

Handling and treatment of solid waste are little easier compared to those of waste gases and liquids as solid waste cannot spread on their own. Waste solid may be stored for some time at its point of origin prior to its treatment. However, special care needs to be taken for storage of solid wastes containing combustible/putrescible/ toxic constituents. Storage of solid wastes having innocuous constituents only needs proper care as those may get air-borne or get carried away by rain water and thereby cause nuisance in the neighbourhood.

1.5 Pollution Regulation Approach

Since the beginning of the industrial revolution, man has started discovering/synthesizing and producing new chemicals. The rate of discover/synthesis of new chemicals and their production are gaining momentum and the process is accelerating. The aim of these endeavours is to make his life more comfortable. However, some of these chemicals are toxic to the flora and fauna and even to man himself. When some of those chemicals get spilled or when some are discharged/discarded after use they cause immense harm to the entire biotic community including man. This is happening not only in the developed countries where these chemicals are produced and used in large quantities but also in the developing countries which are using them, even if they are not producing those themselves.

Several accidents have taken place and subsequent investigations have revealed that man cannot allow the process of pollution to continue unabated, as his own survival is at stake. At the same time, man has become so accustomed to use the synthetic materials that he cannot refrain from producing and using them.

To prevent the ever spiralling pollution from getting totally out of hand, the following preventive steps have envisaged :

1. To set specific limits to pollutant emission and keep strict vigil so that the manufacturers and the users operate within these limits. This can be achieved by treating the liquid effluents, waste gas streams and solid wastes prior to their discharge.
2. To modify the existing processes so as to eliminate/reduce production of the toxic and polluting by-products and wastes.
3. To develop lesser toxic/polluting chemicals as a replacement of the more toxic/ polluting chemicals being produced and used now.
4. To try to develop suitable use of the waste products.

1.6 Pollution Control Legislation

There is neither an universally accepted pollution emission standard, nor a programme for phasing out the toxic and highly polluting chemicals. This lack of a unified approach is due to differences in viewpoints stemming from varied economic considerations. Each country is formulating her own pollution control standards and her own programme, for tackling pollution. Efforts are also being made to regulate production and use of hazardous chemicals.

In India the first pollution control act was framed as far back as 1860. Since then, various acts have been enacted to make the regulations more effective as well as to spell out the obligations of the industrial units towards pollution abatement.

The major Indian Pollution Control acts and rules are listed below and their salient features are given in Appendix—II.

LIST OF MAJOR INDIAN POLLUTION CONTROL ACTS AND RULES

Indian Penal Code, 1860

The Bengal Smoke Nuisance Act, 1905

The Factories Act, 1948

The Gujarat Smoke Nuisance Act, 1963

The Water (Prevention and Control of Pollution) Act, 1974

The Water Cess Act, 1977

The Water Cess Rules, 1978

The Air (Prevention and Control of Pollution) Act, 1981

The Environment (Protection) Act, 1986

The Hazardous Wastes Rules, 1989

Though the Acts and Rules of 1860, 1905 and 1948 were framed with good intentions, those were not implemented for various reasons, including lack of enforcing machinery and lack of sense of moral obligation and social consciousness of the industrial magnets.

Since 1974, a series of comprehensive and well-knit acts and rules have been enacted to spell out, in unambiguous terms, the obligations of industries and others, as well as about the constitution of the enforcement machinery and its power to inspect, to obtain information and to collect samples.

As provided in the acts, competent bodies (Central/State) have laid down limits and standards of pollutant emission from some specific industries/sources. These are listed in Appendix IIIA. In Appendix IIIB, the Ambient Air Quality Standards in India are listed.

CHAPTER 2

The Atmosphere

The earth is surrounded by a gaseous envelope, which extends from the earth's surface to an altitude of about 10,000 km. This gaeous layer is referred to as the earth's atmosphere. 97% of its mass lies within a height of about 29 km. The portion of the atmosphere, which is close to the earth's surface, is a part of the biosphere.

2.1 Atmospheric Pressure

The atmosphere is not homogeneous in its composition. Its temperature is not uniform. The atmospheric pressure, which is due to its static head, decreases with the increase in altitude. It is maximum at the sea level. Its average value at the sea level is equivalent to the pressure exerted by a 76 cm mercury (Hg) column, which is referred to as 1 atmosphere (atm). The exact value of the atmospheric pressure at a location depends on its altitude as well as on the weather condition at that location at that point of time. The average pressure at an altitude of about 16 km is around 7.6 cm of Hg and and at an altitude of about 32 km it is around 0.76 cm of Hg.

2.2 Atmospheric Temperature and Composition

The atmosphere is considered to be made up of different layers. The average thickness of these layers depends on the criterion chosen for their classification. The criteria chosen for classification are : temperature, chemical composition and physico-chemical properties

2.2.1 Atmospheric Temperature

Based on the atmospheric temperature profile, the atmosphere is classified into four regions. The layer next to the earth's surface is called the troposphere. Its thickness ranges between 8 to 16 km depending upon the season and the latitude of a place. Its temperature decreases progressively with height and becomes minimum at the 'tropopause', where the next layer stratosphere starts. Under 'normal' condition the decrease in temperature in the troposphere is 0.64°C per 100 m increase in altitude. This is termed as the lapse rate. The theoretical lapse rate (considering adiabatic expansion of dry air) is –1°C/100 m. Because of this temperature gradient there is vertical convective movement of air within this layer. Most of the water vapour present in the atmosphere is confined in this layer.

The major constituents of the troposphere being oxygen (O_2) and nitrogen (N_2), it cannot absorb solar radiation. During the day it receives heat from the earth's surface by convection. (The earth's surface absorbs solar radiation during the day, as a result its temperature becomes higher than that of the troposphere). At night as the earth's surface cools because of radiation to the space, its temperature becomes less than that of the troposphere. Consequently it (the earth's surface) receives heat from the lower part of the troposphere. As a result the temperature profile in the troposphere changes at night and temperature inversion takes place.

The stratosphere, starting at the tropopause, extends to a height of about 50 km and ends at the stratopause. In this layer the temperature increases with altitude but the rate of increase is slow. The warming of the stratosphere is mainly due to absorption of ultraviolet solar radiation by the ozone molecules of the stratosphere.

As the temperature gradient is not favourable in the stratosphere, convective motion is virtually absent here. Consequently once some gaseous components reach this layer from the troposphere by diffusion they continue to reside there till they are transformed due to chemical reactions.

The layer above the stratosphere is known as the mesosphere, which is about 35 km thick. This layer ends at the mesopause, where the layer known as the thermosphere starts. In the mesosphere the temperature decreases with increase in altitude and becomes less than –100°C at the mesopause.

The thermosphere, which starts at the mesopause, extends up to the end of atmosphere. In this layer the temperature goes on increasing with the altitude indefinitely

Figure 2.1 shows schematically vertical pressure and temperature distribution in the atmosphere.

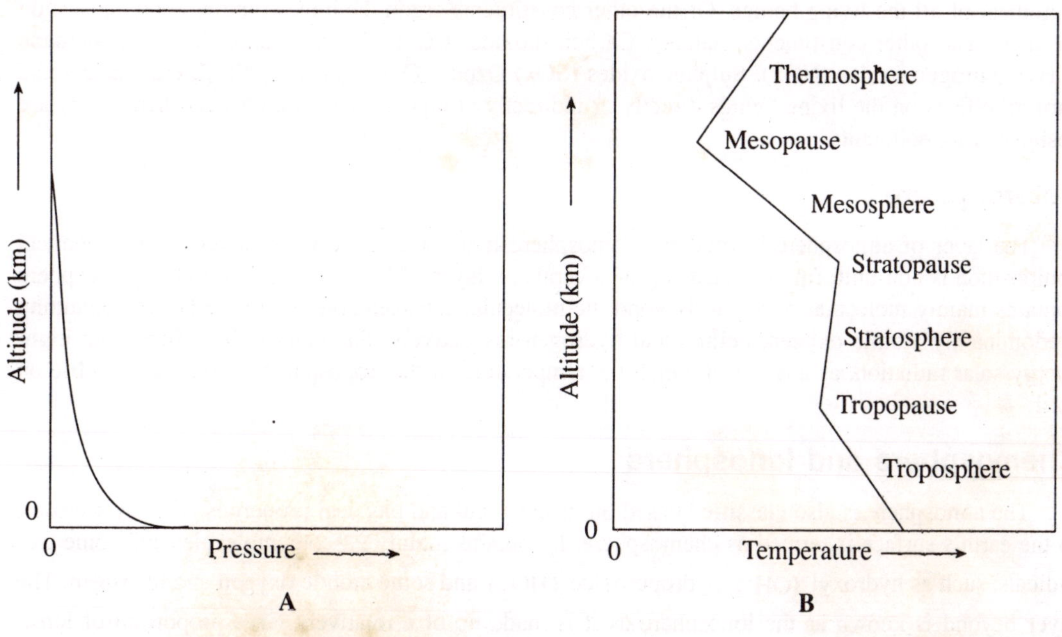

Fig. 2.1 : Pressure and Temperature Distribution in the Atmosphere.

A. Vertical Pressure Distribution

B. Vertical Temperature Distribution

2.2.2 Atmospheric Chemical Composition

Chemical composition of the atmosphere is not the same all through. The layer adjacent to the earth's surface is somewhat homogeneous in composition and hence this layer is termed as the homosphere. It includes the troposphere, the stratosphere and the mesosphere and extends up to an altitude of about 100 km. A sub-layer relatively rich in ozone exists in the upper part of the stratosphere and the lower part of the mesosphere. The layer is referred to the ozone layer. It shields the earth from the ultraviolet solar radiation. The concentration of ozone in the troposphere is normally low, about 0.02 to 0.08 ppmv, whereas that in the ozone layer may be more than 5 ppmv.

Macro-scale movement of air parcels tends to homogenize the atmosphere, whereas molecular diffusion tends to segregate the atmospheric constituents on the basis of molecular weight. Well above 100 km altitude molecular diffusion becomes dominant, as a result the concentration of the lighter (lower, molecular weight) gases increases at higher altitude.

Homosphere

The composition of ambient air, particularly, in the troposphere, depends on whether it is clean or polluted. The concentration of one of the constituents, namely, water vapour depends on the season, as well as on the location of the place.

The major constituents of tropospherical air are nitrogen and oxygen. There are several minor constituents. In Table 2.1. an average composition of the tropospherical dry air is listed.

Of the different constituents of ambient air, oxygen is highly reactive. It is essential for all living beings, as well as for some industrial processes. Even though nitrogen is less reactive, it is an important ingredient of all the living beings. Of the other constituents argon, helium, krypton, neon and xenon are inert. The other constituents, namely, Carbon dioxide (CO_2), Carbon monoxide (CO), Methane (CH_4), Nitrogen oxides (NOx), Sulphur oxides (SOx) Ozone (O_3) Ammonia (NH_3), etc., have some harmful effects on the living beings directly or indirectly at higher concentrations and hence they are designated as pollutants.

Heterosphere

The layer of atmosphere beyond the homosphere is termed as the heterosphere as its chemical composition is non-uniform. It is made up of several sub-layers. The layer adjacent to the homosphere contains mainly molecular nitrogen. Beyond the molecular nitrogen layer there are layers containing predominantly atomic oxygen, helium and hydrogen respectively. The heterosphere filters out high-energy solar radiation, as a result of which the temperature of the troposphere is conducive to life on earth

Chemosphere and Ionosphere

The atmosphere is also classified based on its chemical and physical properties. The layer closest to the earth's surface is termed as chemosphere. It contains mainly gaseous molecules and some free radicals, such as hydroxyl (OH'), hydroperoxide (HO_2') and some atomic oxygen and hydrogen. The layer beyond is known as the ionosphere as it is made up of a relatively large proportion of ions.

Table 2.1 : Average Composition of Tropospherical Dry Air

Component	Concentration	
Nitrogen	78.09	vol %
Oxygen	20.95	,,
Argon	0.93	,,
Carbon dioxide	350	ppmv
Neon	18	,,
Helium	5.2	,,
Methane	1.5	,,
Krypton	1.0	,,
Xenon	0.08	,,
Hydrogen	0.5	,,
Carbon monoxide	120	ppbv
Sulphur dioxide	0.2	,,
Nitric oxide (NO)	0.01–0.6	,,
Nitrogen dioxide (NO_2)	0.1–1	,,
Ozone	20–80	,,
Ammonia	1 – 6	,,
Hydrogen sulphide (H_2S)	0.2	,,

2.3 Air Pollutants

Particulate matter (both liquid and solid) and some gases, which when present in air in large enough quantities so as to cause deleterious effects on living beings directly or indirectly or bring about undesirable changes in the surroundings are termed as air pollutants. The list of air pollutants is a long one. It is becoming longer as newer chemicals are being commercially produced and we are becoming more knowledgeable about their harmful physico-chemical properties.

Some of the pollutants are produced by nature and some are produced as a result of domestic, agricultural and industrial activities of man. Such pollutants are referred to as **primary pollutants.** Some of the primary pollutants when present in the atmosphere react among themselves and thereby produce some other harmful chemicals. These chemicals are termed as **secondary pollutants.**

2.3.1 Classification of Air Pollutants

Pollutants present in the atmosphere may be classified into two groups depending on their physical state, namely, particulate and gaseous. The particulate pollutants are further classified as viable and non-viable. Based on their size both the viable and non-viable particulate pollutants are further sub-classified as detailed hereunder.

Viable Particulate Pollutants

The largest sized air-borne viable particulate pollutants are plant fragments, seeds and micro-fauna, which are larger than 100 μm in size. The smallest sized are viruses having diameter as small as

0.015 μm. Viable particles having intermediate size are bacteria, fungi, algae, protozoa, spores and pollen grains. The larger viable particles are of natural origin. But the presence of microbes and their density in ambinet air depend on the environmental condition created by man. Ambient air in the vicinity of land and water bodies having putrefying organic matter would have a higher density of microbial population

Non-Viable Particulate Pollutants

The non-viable particulate pollutants may be either liquid or solid. The terminology is normally associated with non-viable particles present in air and there connotations are as follows :

Fog denotes a high concentration of very fine water droplets suspended in air, resulting from condensation of moisture in air due to fall in air temperature at night

Mist and Sprays may result from natural processes as well as due to industrial operations. These are liquid droplets having diameter in the range of 0.1 to 5000 μm dispersed in air. Gas emitted from gas-liquid contacting devices often carries entrained liquid droplets which are referred to as mist. Spraying devices produce fine liquid droplets, some of which may escape to the atmosphere unless steps are taken to prevent their escape.

The term **Haze** signifies the presence of fine dust, mist and gaseous pollutants in the atmosphere which reduce visibility.

Smoke is produced as a result of incomplete combustion of organics (solid, liquid and gas). It contains fine solid particles (unburnt) suspended in the flue gas. The particles are rather small in size, ranging from less than 0.01 μm to 1 μm diameter.

Smog is a mixture of smoke and fog. It is more stable than fog.

Dusts are air-borne fine solid particles. Industrial operations such as size reductioin, detonation, pneumatic conveying, screening, loading and unloading of granular and powdery materials and polishing produce particles in the size range of 1 to 1000 μm. Dust particles do not diffuse in air but settle out due to gravity.

Fly ash is entrained ash particles in a flue gas resulting from combustion of powdered solid fuels. Fly ash particles may be finer than 1 μm.

Fumes are finely divided solid particles that result from condensation of a vapour. Fumes are generally produced during sublimation, distillation and molten metal processing. The particle sizes of fumes range from 0.1 to 1 μm.

Aerosols are small particles, either solid or liquid, suspended in a gas. The aerosol particle size ranges from 0.01 to 100 μm. They are of two types, namely **dispersion aerosol and condensation aerosol.**

Dispersion aerosol is formed during operations like grinding, solid-liquid atomization and conveying of powders. The particles are coarse and may be individual or slightly aggregated.

Condensation aerosol is produced when supersaturated vapours condense or when air-borne gases react chemically to form non-viable particles. Individual particles may be less than 1 μm in size. A large number of these particles may combine to form loose aggregates.

Gaseous Pollutants

Gaseous pollutants are classified as primary and secondary pollutants. Primary pollutants are those, which are directly emitted from natural sources or are produced as a result of human activity. Some of the common pollutants of this group are Carbon monoxide (CO), Carbon dioxide (CO_2), Sulphur dioxide (SO_2), Hydrogen sulphide (H_2S), Nitrogen oxides (NO, NO_2, N_2O), Ammonia

(NH_3), hydrocarbons and other volatile organic compounds. Secondary pollutants are those, which are produced as a result of interaction between the primary pollutants under favourable atmospheric conditions. Some of the common pollutants, which belong to this group, are Ozone (O_3), Hydrogen peroxide (H_2O_2), Peroxyacetyl nitrate (PAN), aldehydes (such as formaldehyde) and organic hydroperoxides.

2.4 Sources of Atmospheric Pollutants

Pollutants are emitted to the atmosphere as a result of natural processes as well as due to human activity. The sources of some common pollutant are tabulated in Table 2.2. It should be pointed out here that the list is not a complete one.

Natural sources of emission are oceans, volcanoes, swamps, biologically decaying organic matter, desert and semi-desert areas, forests and forest fires, lightning, etc.

Human activities, which give rise to air-borne pollutants, are domestic, transport, agricultural and industrial. The major industrial sources are fossil fuel combustors, mines, quarries, metallurgical and metal processing industries, chemical processing industries; food, biochemical and pharmaceutical industries.

Table 2.2 : Sources of Emission of Some Common Airborne Pollutants

Sources	Pollutants
Oceans	Sea water spray containing dissolved salt, CO_2, H_2S, CH_4
Volcanoes	Solid particles, SO_2, H_2S, HCl, CO_2 CO, H_2S, NH_3
Decaying vegetables and	CO, CH_4, CO_2, H_2S, NH_3
animal residues	Mercaptans.
Desert and semi-desert areas	Mainly solid particles.
Forests	Organic compounds, such as turpentines.
Forest Fires	CO, CO_2, aldehydes, soots.
Lightning	NO (Nitrogen Oxide)
Fossil fuel combustors both	Solid Particles, CO, CO_2, SO_2, NOx,
mobile and stationary	hydrocarbons, aldehydes.
Mines and quarries	Solid Particles, CO, SO_2, hydrocarbons
Metallurgical and Metal processing industries :	
(a) Ore sintering	Solid Particles, CO, CO_2, SO_2
(b) Ore roasting	Solid Particles, CO, CO_2, SO_2
(c) Pig Iron & Steel	Solid Particles, CO, CO_2, SO_2, NO_x,
(d) Foundries	Solid Particles, CO, CO_2, SO_2, NO_x, hydrocarbons
(e) Non-ferrous Metals	Solid Particles, CO, CO_2, SO_2, NO_x,

Contd.

Table 2.2 (Contd.)

Chemical & Allied process industries : (a) Petroleum refinery, Petrochemicals and polymer industries	H_2S, SO_2, CO, CO_2, NO_x Hydrocarbons and other volatile organic compounds (VOCs)
(b) Acid Manufacturing :	
(i) Sulphuric acid	Acid mist, SO_2, NO_x.
(ii) Nitric acid	NO_x, acid mist.
(iii) Hydrochloric acid	Cl_2, acid mist.
(iv) Phosphoric acid	Fluorine compounds, acid mist, solid particles.
(c) Alkali Manufacturing :	
(i) Caustic-Chlorine	Salt dust, Cl_2, HCl, Hg.
(ii) Soda ash	NH_3, CO_2.
(d) Fertilizer Industries :	
(i) Nitrogen	NH_3, CO_2, NOx.
(ii) Phosphate	Fluorine Compounds, solid particles.
(e) Pulp and Paper	H_2S, mercaptans, SO_2, NO_x, turpentine, Cl_2, ClO_2, Solid particles.
(f) Organic Chemical and Pharmaceutical Industries :	Mainly volatile organic compounds.
Agricultural Activities :	
(a) Slash burning	CO, CO_2, hydrocarbons, soot.
(b) Fertilizer and pesticide sprays	Particles of fertilizers and pesticides.
(c) Decaying farm wastes	NH_3, H_2S, CO, CO_2, mercaptans.

2.5 Effects of Atmospheric Pollutants

Atmospheric pollutants affect ecosystems in various ways. The effects are manifested by bringing about some changes in an ecosystem directly or indirectly. The overall effects may be classified as hereunder :

I. Effects on atmospheric properties
II. Effects on vegetations
III. Effects on animals
IV. Effects on human beings
V. Effects on land and water bodies
VI. Effects on materials.

2.5.1 Effects on Atmospheric Properties

The atmospheric properties of the troposphere get affected considerably due to the presence of pollutants and those of the stratosphere to some extent.

The properties of the other layers (mesosphere and thermosphere) remain almost unaffected, as pollutants are virtually not present there.

A. Tropospheric Effects

The gaseous and particulate pollutants which are directly emitted into the troposphere due to natural as well as human activity affect the following properties of the troposphere :

(i) Visibility, (ii) Fog and haze formation,
(iii) Precipitation, (iv) Solar radiation incidence,
(v) Temperature, (vi) Wind direction and velocity.

(i) Visibility

When a beam of light passes through air its intensity decreases due to absorption and scattering by the molecules of gases present in air as well as by the suspended particles (particularly by the sub-micron sized ones) present in air.

The major constituents of air, namely, oxygen, and nitrogen do not absorb or scatter light, but the pollutant gas molecules and suspended particles (both liquid and solid) do. The extent of absorption and scattering is dependent on the specific pollutants present and their concentration. Decreased intensity of light as a result of absorption and scattering decreases visibility.

Nitrogen dioxide and aerosols strongly absorb visible light in the blue–green wave length range and produce a yellow-brown haze. Ozone absorbs at wave lengths below 3200 Å.

Hygroscopic particles present in air picks up moisture from air as the humidity increase and consequently reduce the visibility further. At a humidity of 70% R. H. and less the effect is not that marked, but above 70% R. H. the effect is considerable.

Visibility being dependent on the concentration of the gaseous pollutants and suspended particles is influenced by the wind speed. With the increase in wind speed upto about 24 kmph the visibility improves as the pollutant concentration decreases due to dispersion. But at higher wind speed, due to scouring effect the concentration of solid particles (dust) increases in air. This leads to more scattering, and consequently visibility becomes poorer.

(ii) Fog and Haze Formation

Polluted air having a large number of suspended particles is conducive to fog formation under favourable condition. Normally air is unsaturated with water vapour. When air temperature decreases (at night) it may become saturated and with further decrease in temperature air may become supersaturated with water vapour. Under such condition a suspension of fine water droplets in air, that is, a fog is formed. Fine suspended solid particles present in air serve as condensation nuclei. If the number of particles be large, the water droplets formed would be small in size and the fog would be more stable. Such a fog would be more effective in scattering light and thereby reduce visibility. If fewer suspended particles be present in air the water droplets would be larger in size, hence the resulting fog would be less stable.

When a large number of tiny solid particles are present in air, they absorb and scatter light. This results in reduced visibility. Such a situation is termed as haze. Fine solid particles may get suspended in air due to high wind velocity and or due to emission from industrial units as well as due to aerosol formation.

(iii) Precipitation

When the relative humidity (RH) in air becomes sufficiently high the nucleating particles get 'activated' and condensation of water vapour in atmosphere is initiated. The mechanism by which the cloud condensation nuclei (CCN) act is not known; however, it is known that hygroscopic and water soluble particles are more effective as CCN.

The sources of CCN may be natural processes as well as industrial operations. The CCN emitted fom industrial sources supplement the natural CCN.

Once the process of condensation is initiated further development would depend on the number and size of the droplets in a cloud. If there are a larger number of smaller droplets, those would not agglomerate easily and hence there would be less precipitation. If the number of CCN be relatively fewer, the size of droplets produced would be larger which would coalesce more readily and thereby would cause more precipitation. The precipitation may be either dry (snow) or wet (rain) depending upon the ambient air temperature.

(iv) Solar Radiation Incidence

Pollutants present in air interfere with the incidence of solar radiation on the earth's surface by scattering and absorbing the incoming radiation. Solid and liquid particles generally scatter the incoming radiation whereas the gaseous pollutants and aerosols absorb radiation. Absorption occurs at specific wave lengths depending upon the pollutants present. For example, nitrogen dioxide absorbs radiation in the wave length range of 3600–4000 Å, whereas ozone absorbs at wave lengths below 3200 Å.

Due to scattering and absorption of incoming solar radiation by air-borne pollutants less energy would reach the earth's surface resulting in lower surface temperature. The energy absorbed by gaseous pollutants is released to the atmosphere as heat which causes rise in tropospheric temperature.

Cloud cover also reduces incidence of solar radiation on the earth's Surface.

(v) Temperature

During the daytime solar radiation reaches the earth's surface, a part of which is absorbed. Subsequently the ground transfers a portion of the absorbed radiation to the tropospheric air by re-radiation and convection. At higher altitude of the troposphere the flux due to re-radition and convection is less. Consequently the air temprature is less. The variation of temperature with altitude in the troposphere is also due to the decrease in atmospheric pressure with altitude. This decrease is due to adiabatic expansion of 'air packets' as they move upward because of convection.

The intensity of solar radiation at a place in the ground level depends on the angle of incidence, which in turn depends on the time of the day (relative to sun rise) as well as on the season. On a cloudless day and the air free from pollutants, the intensity is maximum at mid-day when the sun is overhead. When pollutants are present at a higher concentration in air, and there is cloud cover, the solar intensity is less. Variation of solar intensity results in changing the normal tropospheric temperature profile.

The ground receives solar radiation and re-radiates a part of it during the daytime but at night it re-radiates only. Hence the ground temperature decreases gradually after sunset and after some point of time it becomes less than that of air above it. This situation is termed as **'inversion'**. Normally after sunrise the ground starts receiving solar energy and its temperature increases gradually, which results in the disappearance of the inversion condition. However, when pollutants are present in air at higher concentration the state of inversion may continue for a longer period even after sunrise because of lesser incidence of solar radiation. In severely polluted atmosphere the inversion may continue for days together.

Vertical convective movement of air in the troposphere occurs due to its negative temperature gradient. Such movement helps in dispersing the pollutants. The factors mentioned earlier affects the 'normal' tropospheric temperature gradient and thereby interferes with the pollutant dispersion process.

The tropospheric temperature profile patterns under different atmospheric conditions are shown in Fig. 2.2.

It should be noted here that the atmospheric condition is termed as 'stable' when it resists the vertical convective movement.

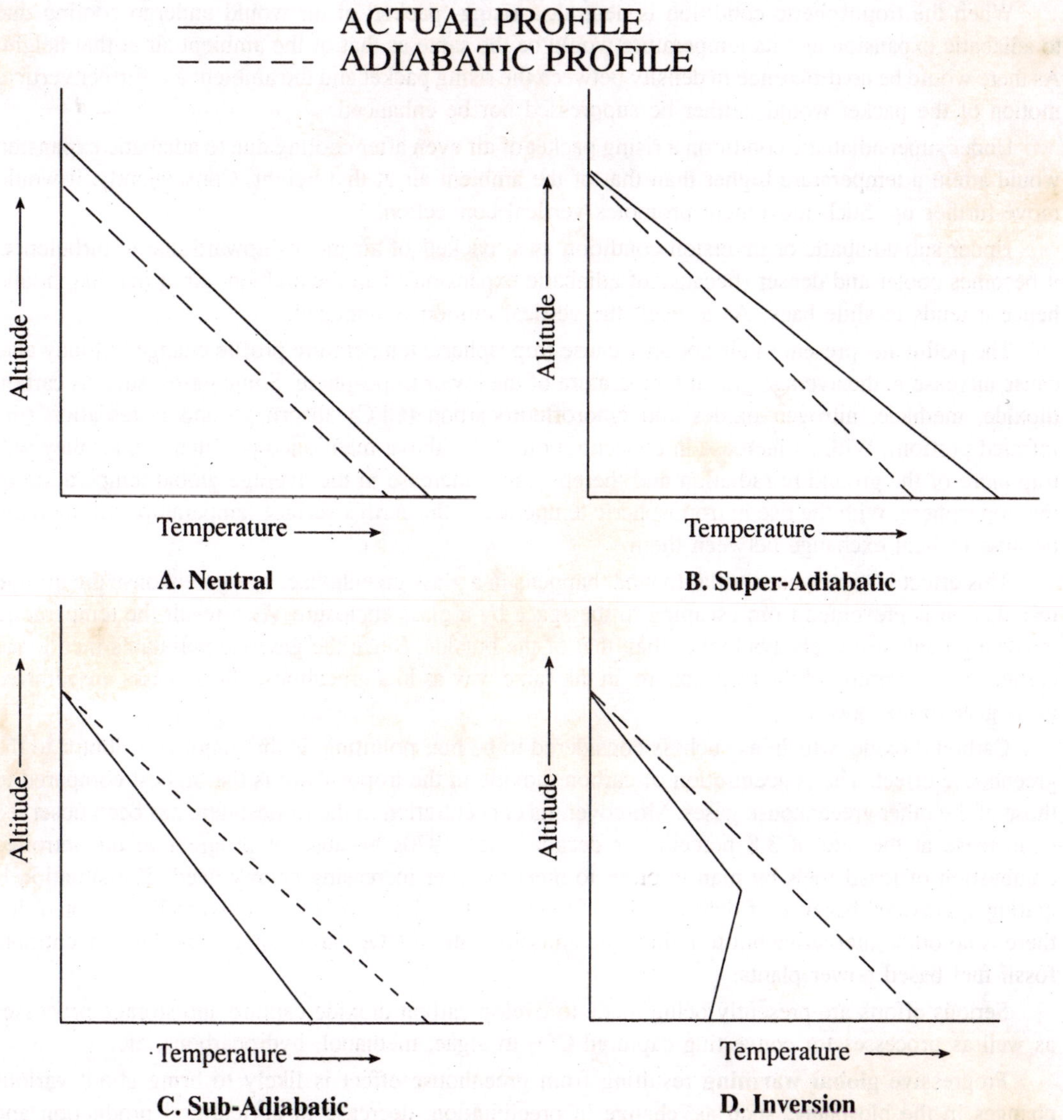

Fig. 2.2 : Tropospheric Temperature Profile.

A. Neutral : The lapse rate is nearly identical to the dry adiabatic lapse rate. Such a condition prevails on days of moderate solar incedence. When some vertical air movement takes place the situation is referred to as neutral stable.

B. Super-Adiabatic : The lapse sate is more than that of the dry adiabatic. On days of strong solar incidence such a condition is observed.

C. Sub-Adiabatic : The lapse rate is less than that of the dry adiabatic. It happens on days of slight solar incidence. When very little vertical air movement takes place the condition is termed as slightly stable.

D. Inversion : Air temperature increases with height up to some altitude and then decreases. Such a situation may occur at late night. Stable inversion occurs when there is no vertical air movement below the break.

When the tropospheric condition is neutral, a rising 'packet' of air would undergo cooling due to adiabatic expansion and its temperature would be the same as that of the ambient air at that height. As there would be no difference in density between the rising packet and the ambient air, further vertical motion of the packet would neither be suppressed nor be enhanced.

Under super adiabatic condition a rising packet of air even after cooling due to adiabatic expansion would attain a temperature higher than that of the ambient air at that height. Consequently, it would move further up. Such movement promotes vertical convection.

Under sub-adiabatic or inversion condition as a 'packet' of air moves upward due to turbulence, it becomes cooler and denser (because of adiabatic expansion) than the ambient air at that height and hence it tends to slide back. As a result the vertical motion is impeded.

The pollutants present in air not only cause tropospheric temperature profile change but may also cause increase in the average global temperature of the lower troposphere. Some gases, such as carbon dioxide, methane, nitrogen oxides and chlorofluorocarbon (CFC) absorb ground re-radiation (the infrared portion). With an increase in concentration of the above-mentioned pollutants in air they will trap more of the ground re-radiation and thereby cause increase in the average global temperature of the troposphere. With the rise in tropospheric temperature, the earth's surface temperature will increase because of heat exchange between them.

This effect is somewhat similar to what happens in a glass greenhouse. In a greenhouse the ground re-radiation is prevented from escaping to the space by a glass enclosure. As a result the temperature inside a greenhouse is always higher than that of the outside. Since the gaseous pollutants mentioned earlier cause warming of the troposphere, in the same way as in a greenhouse, those gases are referred to as **greenhouse gases**.

Carbon dioxide, which, as such, is considered to be non-polluting, is the major contributor to the greenhouse effect. The concentration of carbon dioxide in the troposphere is the highest compared to those of the other greeenhouse gases. Moreover, its concentration in the troposphere has been observed to increase at the rate of 3.8 percent per decade since 1970s because of progressive uncontrolled combustion of fossil fuels by man in order to meet his ever-increasing energy need. The situation is getting aggravated because of deforestation. In view of the above, it is now universally accepted that there is no other alternative but to reduce the emission rate of CO_2 particularly from the conventional fossil fuel based power plants.

Serious efforts are presently being made to dvelop carbon dioxide capture and storage processes as well as processes for converting captured CO_2 to algae, methanol, hydrocarbons, etc.

Progressive **global warming** resulting from greenhouse effect is likely to bring about various changes in the biosphere, such as, change in precipitation, decrease in agricultural production and melting of some of the permanent ice packs. If some of the permanent ice packs (glaciers and polar ice) melt, then the ocean level will increase, as a result of which the low-lying costal areas of the earth would be inundated.

In order to save the earth (the only habitat of man) from not so far away catastrophic situation, the representatives from 160 countries met in Kyoto in 1997 to frame a protocol, which is known as **Kyoto Protocol**. The objective of the protocol is to make an all out effort to reduce the rate of emission of the 'greenhouse gases'. The target fixed is to reduce the rate of emission progressively, so that by 2012 their concentration in the atmosphere would be 5.2% less than that in 1990. However, because of non-endorsement of the protocol by some of the developed countries there is every doubt that the target would be realized.

(vi) Wind Direction and Velocity

Wind is generally defined as air movement in the horizontal direction. Vertical movement of air is referred to as updraft or downdraft.

The factors which influence motion of air in the horizontal direction are :

(i) the pressure gradient,

(ii) the Coriolis force, and

(iii) the frictional force.

The pressure gradient occurs mainly due to uneven rate of heating of land and ocean. Normally during the daytime the land mass gets heated quickly whereas the ocean heats up slowly. As a consequence, pressure gradient develops from ocean to land and sea breeze blows landward. At night land cools quickly compared to the ocean and land breeze blows seaward.

The wind speed depends on the magnitude of the pressure gradient, which in turn is influenced by the intensity of solar radiation, pollutant concentration in air, cloud cover and local topography.

The Coriolis force is caused by the rotation of the earth around its axis. This force deflects wind towards the right and it is proportional to the wind speed.

The frictional force opposes movement of air. This force is maximum at the earth's surface, hence the wind speed at any instant of time is the minimum at the ground level and it increases with the altitude. The wind speed is generally measured at meteorological stations at a height of 10 m. The speed at any other height is calculated using the relation

$$\frac{U_h}{U_{10}} = \left(\frac{h}{10}\right)^n, \tag{2.1}$$

Where U_h = wind speed at a height of h in m,

U_{10} = wind speed at a height of 10 m,

n = an exponent, a positive fraction, 0.5 or less. Its numerical value depends on the atmospheric stability and the local features including its relief (nature and man made topography). In the absence of any specific information the following values may be taken depending on the weather condition :

n = 0.2 for unstable conditions,

= 0.25 for neutral conditions, and

= 0.5 for stable conditions.

The wind speed may be expreseed in the unit of m/s or kmph.

The meteorological stations not only report wind speed but also its direction throughout the year. Such data are often presented graphically. Both the frequency and speed of wind in all possible directions (8 to 16) are drawn to a scale normally for a period of one year. Such a diagram is termed as a **wind rose**. Figure 2.3 shows a typical wind rose for Kolkata City.

The length of a bar segment of a wind rose represents its frequency from a particular direction, while the width/shade of the same represents the range of wind speed from that direction. Such a diagram is accompanied by a scale for the wind speed.

From the discussion so far it is apparent that the prime factor which gives rise to wind is the pressure gradient arising out of unequal heating and cooling of land and ocean. The other factors, which influence wind speed and direction, are the weather condition, the season, the ocean current, etc.

It should be noted here that high wind speed helps to disperse particulate matter and gaseous pollutants, but too high a wind speed scours dusts (during dry season) and thereby increases the solid particle concentration in air.

Particulate matter and gaseous pollutants when present in air at a relatively higher concentration interfere with the incidence of solar radian to the ground, as a result of which the wind speed is adversely affected. This in turn retards the process of dispersal of pollutants.

2.5.2 Effects on Vegetation

The pollutants present in the troposphere affect vegetation in three different ways : (i) by attacking the cells of the different parts of plants, (ii) by interacting with enzymes present in plants and (iii) by interfering with the photosynthesis process. The effects may be visible or invisible.

The visible injuries to plants may be acute or chronic. Acute injuries occur when plants are exposed to a higher concentration of pollutants. The cell membranes may get ruptured due to chemical actions of gaseous pollutants resulting in loss of cell content and finally cell death. Pollutants such as SO_2, O_3, PAN bring about such changes. Pollutants like SO_2, NH_3, O_3, fluorides, and PAN affect chlorophyll, which is the key component for photosynthesis. As a result the leaves wither. Abnormal growth of leaves and stems are induced by ethylene and herbicides.

Chronic visible injuries occur due to prolonged and repeated exposure of plants to pollutants at a relatively low concentration.

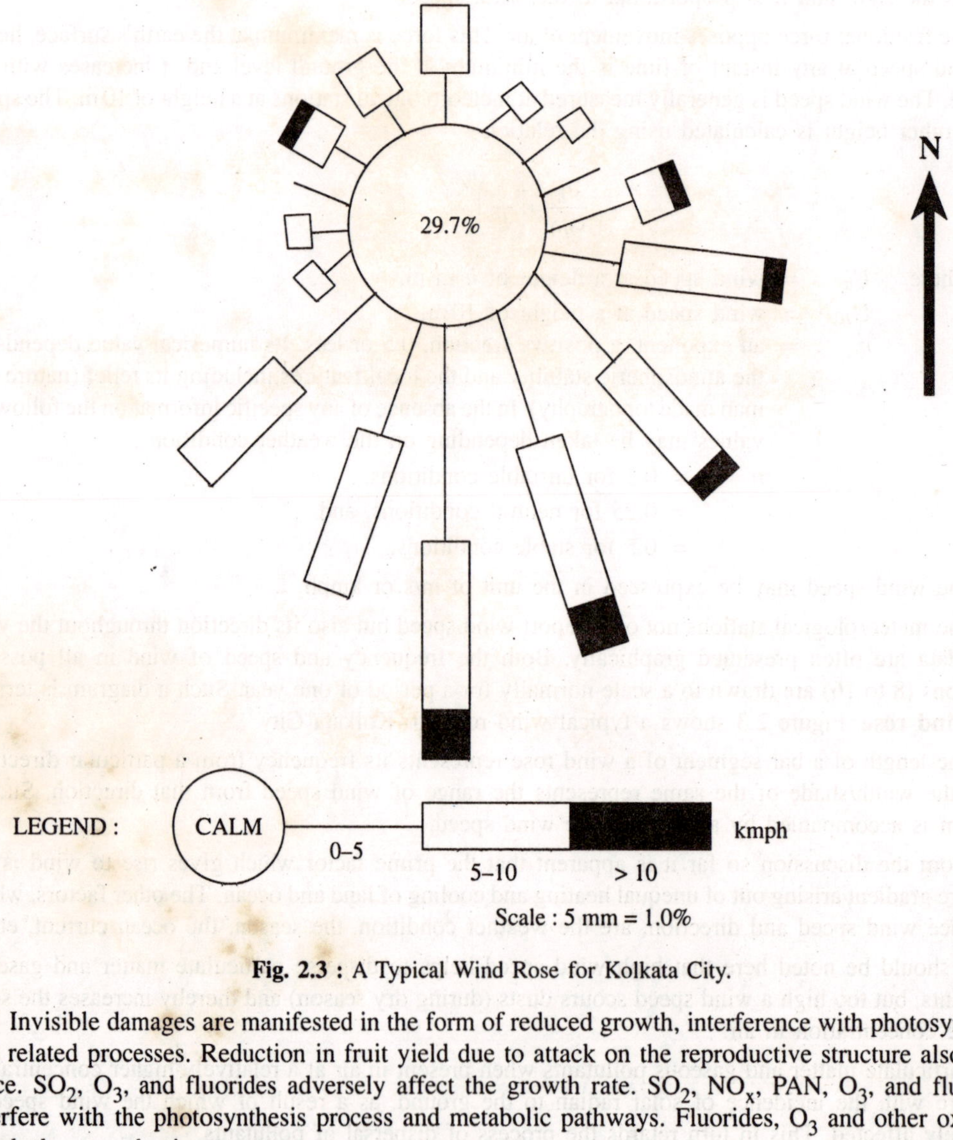

Fig. 2.3 : A Typical Wind Rose for Kolkata City.

Invisible damages are manifested in the form of reduced growth, interference with photosynthesis and related processes. Reduction in fruit yield due to attack on the reproductive structure also takes place. SO_2, O_3, and fluorides adversely affect the growth rate. SO_2, NO_x, PAN, O_3, and fluorides interfere with the photosynthesis process and metabolic pathways. Fluorides, O_3 and other oxidants attack the reproductive structure.

Dust particles interfere with the photosynthesis process by covering leaf surfaces and also by blocking the stomatas.

The extent of damage to vegetation in polluted atmosphere depends on the plant species, the specific pollutants present, their concentration and the duration of exposure.

The injury threshold concentrations of some common pllutants are listed in Table 2.3.

Table 2.3 : Plant Injury Threshold of Some Gaseous Pollutants

Pollutant	Threshold Concentration in ppmv.
SO_2	0.3
O_3	0.03
PAN [$CH_3C(O)O_2N_2$]	0.01
NO_2	2.5
F_2	0.01
Cl_2	0.1
C_2H_4	0.05
NH_3	20
H_2S	20

2.5.3 Effects on Animals

Fish and domestic animals get affected when they ingest toxic chemicals and heavy metals.

Domestic animals may get affected in the same way as human beings by inhaling air-borne gaseous pollutants and particles. Heavy metals, such as arsenic, lead, molybdenum, mercury and their compounds are emitted during industrial processes, like roasting, smelting, steel making, etc. These may accumulate on vegetation and forages which when consumed by herbivores may affect them. Man may get affected by consuming milk and meat of the affected herbivores.

2.5.4 Effects on Human Beings

Air-borne gaseous pollutants and suspended particles affect human health and may produce various types of physiological effects. Common pollutants, such as CO, SO_2, NOx, hydrocarbons and particulates are directly emitted from industrial sources, whereas, O_3, PAN, and some other oxidants are produced due to secondary reactions. Various other toxic chemicals are emitted and are present in the surroundings of the places where those chemicals are produced, used or handled. The biological/physiological effects of some of the above mentioned pollutants are briefly discussed hereunder and are summarized in Table 2.4.

(i) Effects of Carbon monoxide (CO)

CO is a colourless and odourless gas. It affects by combining with haemoglobin (Hb) in blood. Haemoglobin carries O_2 from the respiratory system to the different parts of human body and removes CO_2 from those places by forming unstable complexes with O_2 and CO_2.

The affinity of CO towards haemoglobin is more than that for oxygen. As a result when CO is breathed in, it forms a relatively more stable complex (COHb, carboxyhaemoglobin) with haemoglobin; consequently the oxygen carrying and CO_2 removal capacity of blood, decrease. The level of COHb complex in the blood of a person depends on CO concentration in air as well as on the duration of exposure of an individual. If about 0.5 to 2% of the total haemoglobin is complexed with CO there would not be much effect. However, with increasing concentration of COHb in blood, progressively manifested symptoms are headache, dizziness, nausea, vomiting, difficulty in breathing, collapse, unconsciousness and death.

The reaction between CO and haemoglobin being a reversible one when a person leaves a polluted area with a non-lethal dose of CO he breathes out CO and recovers. CO does not leave any permanent effect.

The global average concentration of CO in air is about 0.1 ppmv. Its threshold limit is 50 ppmv. At a concentration of 1000 ppmv or more it is fatal.

(ii) Effects of Sulphur dioxide (SO_2)

SO_2 combines with water in the respiratory system to produce sulphurous acid (H_2SO_3) which irritates conjunctiva, upper respiratory tract and throat resulting in airway resistance. When inhaled at a concentration of 5 ppmv or more for about 10 minutes or so the pulse and breathing rate increase. Symptoms such as nasopharyngitis and coughing develop on prolonged exposure. SO_2 combined with benzo (α) pyrene (C_2OH_{12}), a product of incomplete combustion, causes pulmonary cancer. The global average concentration of SO_2 is 0.0002 ppmv. Its threshold limit is 2 ppmv. At a concentration level of 500 ppmv it is fatal.

(iii) Effects of NO_x

Nitric oxide (NO) and nitrogen dioxide are the major nitrogen oxides present in air. Of these two NO is less toxic. Like CO, NO combines with haemoglobin and thereby interferes with the oxygen transfer process. NO gets oxidized to NO_2 which on inhalation is converted to nitrous acid (HNO_2) and nitric acid (NHO_3) in the lungs. These exert toxic effects on the deep lungs and peripherial airway. At a lower concentration of NO_x, the eyes, throat and lungs get irritated. Regular exposure at 10-40 ppmv concentration may cause distention of lungs and scarring of pulmonary tissues. Continued exposure at 500 ppmv or more would lead to death.

The threshold value of NO_2 is 5 ppmv.

(iv) Effects of Ammonia (NH_3)

NH_3 is a colourless gas with a pungent odour. It is an irritant to skin, respiratory tract, mucous membranes and eyes. At higher concentrations it corrodes tissues and causes laryngeal and bronchial spasm and edema. At a concentration of about 5 ppmv it can be detected by its pungent smell. At concentration around 150-200 ppmv it causes general discomfort and tears in the eyes. When a person is exposed to about 2000 ppmv concentration of ammonia, suffers from burns and skin blisters and progressively experiences serious edema, asphyxia and finally death.

(v) Effects of Hydrogen Sulphide (H_2S)

H_2S is a colourless gas with a rottern egg smell. It may cause eye irritation at a concentration of about 100 ppmv. Inhalation of H_2S at a higher concentration irritates the entire respiration tract.

(vi) Effects of Chlorine (Cl_2)

Cl_2 is a greenish yellow gas with a characteristic pungent smell. It irritates eyes, skin and the respiratory tract. At higher concentration of Cl_2 one suffers from skin burns, redness of eyes, blurred vision and lung damage. At a concentration of about 1000 ppmv it becomes lethal.

(vii) Effects of Ozone (O_3)

Inhalation of ozone above its normal concentration causes pulmonary inflammatory response. Exposure to ozone at a concentration of 1.5 to 2 ppmv irritates eyes, throat and lung. Continuous or intermittent exposure to ozone may cause chronic bronchitic, bronchiolitic and fibrotic changes of lungs. Ozone is a potential mutagan as it degenerates chromosome in lymphocytes. Its threshold limit value is 0–1 ppmv.

Other photochemical oxidants present in polluted air, such as peroxyacetyle nitrate (PAN), peroxybenzoly nitrate cause effects similar to those of ozone.

Threshold Limit Value (TLV)

The Industrial Threshold Limit Value set by the American Conference of Governmental Industrial Hygienists (ACGIH) refer to indoor air-borne concentration of substances and represent the conditions under which it is believed that nearly all healthy adult workers may be exposed eight hours a day, five days per week without adverse effects.

Effects of Suspended Solid Particles (SSP)

Air-borne particles enter the respiratory system and get deposited in the different regions of the respiratory system depending upon their size, shape and density. The large (5 µm and more) and denser particles are deposited in the nasal region and are removed by mucous discharges. Finer and lighter particles penetrate deeper into the system. Particles about 2 µm in size and finer enter into the lungs. Finer particles having larger external and internal surface areas (per unit mass) adsorb gaseous pollutants present in air and carry them deep inside the lungs. Particles with adsorbed pollutants cause more harm. The particles themselves may be toxic.

The effects of some air-borne gaseous pollutants on human beings and their TLV are summarized in Table 2.4.

Table 2.4 : TLV and Biological Effects of Some Common Gaseous Pollutants

Pollutants	TLV in ppmv		Biological Effects
	TWA	STEL	
Carbon monoxide (CO)	50	400	O_2 transportation by haemoglobin is affected. Cardio-vascular system is affected. May cause death.
Hydrogen sulphide (H_2S)	10	15	Irritates eyes and the entire respiratory tract.
Chlorine (Cl_2)	1	3	Irritates eyes, skin and the respiratory tract. Damages lungs. At high concentration causes death.
Ammonia (NH_3)	25	35	Irritates skin, respiratory tract, mucous membranes and eyes. At high concentration causes serious edema, asphyxia and finally death.
Nitrogen oxides :			
NO	25	—	Less toxic than NO_2.
NO_2	5	—	Irritates eyes, throat and lungs. At high concentration causes pulmonary edema and finally death.
Ozone (O_3)	0.1	0.3	Irritates eyes, throat and lungs. Causes pulmonary congestion, asthma, edema.
Sulphur dioxide (SO_2)	2	5	Irritates conjunctiva, upper respiratory tract and throat. At high concentration causes death.

TWA : Time Weighted Average concentration for 8 hours workday and 5 days workweek.

STEL : Short Term Exposure Limit : 15 minute time weighted average which should not exceed any time during a workday.

2.5.5 Effects on Land and Water Bodies

Particulate matter emitted from industrial units settle on land, buildings and other structures which give them a grimy look. Such deposits on land may interfere with soil fertility. Acid gases, such as CO_2, NO_x, SO_2 react in the atmosphere and are deposited on land and water bodies either in the form of acid rain by combining with rain water or as dry salt particles. Such acid deposition on land would adversely affect land fertility and vegetation growth. Plant nutrients and micro-nutrients present in soil would be leached away by acid rain as a result of which the affected land would not be able to support growth of various types of plants. Because of poor vegetation cover, rain water and wind will carry away the top soil layer and finally may turn the area arid.

Acid deposition on water bodies in general would affect the growth of aquatic plants and fish. However, fresh water bodies, which constitute only a very small fraction of the total hydrosphere, would be seriously affected by acid rain and salt deposits. Industrial units and human settlements located near the fresh water bodies would get affected once the water bodies would get affected due to acid rain.

2.5.6 Effects on Materials

Air-borne gaseous pollutants and particles affect buildings and other structures, equipment and machinery.

Gaseous pollutants may directly attack building materials, metals and non-metals by reacting irreversibly. In the case of metals the mechanism of attack may be electro chemical in nature. The extent of damage would depend on the temperature of the environment and the presence of moisture. Even in those cases where the surfaces are not directly attacked chemically but are covered by particle, they get damaged during the process of cleaning. The surfaces also get corroded by acid rain.

Particulate matter damages surfaces of equipment and machinery by abrasion and by getting lodged in between the moving parts. Particulate matter and gaseous pollutants may affect sensitive components of instruments and equipment either by getting deposited or by reacting chemically.

B. Stratospheric Effects

In the stratosphere very little emission of pollutants occurs directly. The only direct sources of emission are supersonic air-crafts and rockets. The exhaust from such sources may contain CO, CO_2 NO_x, SO_2, H_2O and hydrocarbons depending on the fuel used. Some pollutants also reach the stratosphere directly due to volcanic eruption. Other than these, some gaseous pollutants, which escape, complete chemical transformation in the troposphere, diffuse into the stratosphere. These are mainly NOx, chlorofluorocarbons and some hydrocarbons.

The above-mentioned pollutants react with the ozone molecules present in the ozone layer (of the stratosphere) and undergo oxidation. Absorption of UV solar radiation by the ozone molecules and the oxidation reactions (of Pollutants) cause a little warming of the stratosphere. This results in a slight positive (vertical) temperature gradient in the stratosphere.

In the ozone layer ozone molecules are produced by photochemical reactions as a result of absorption of solar UV radiation. Some of the ozone molecules get destroyed due to reactions with the pollutants present. As the concentration of the pollutants is increasing in the stratosphere the rate of destruction of ozone molecules is becoming more than its rate of production. This process is causing depletion of ozone molecules in the ozone layer.

The pollutants, which have been identified as the major agents responsible for depletion of ozone, are the chlorofluorocarbons (CFC). CFC is used as refrigerants in refrigerators and air-conditioners. Those are also used as aerosol spray, solvents, cleaning agents, foam-blowing agents, etc. The other ozone depleting substances (ODS) are methyl chloroform, carbon tetrachloride, methyl bromide and halons.

The CFC molecules, which find their way to the atmosphere, do not react chemically with oxygen in the troporsphere but diffuse to the stratosphere where UV radiation dissociates them and produces chlorine atoms. The atoms act as a catalyst in the conversion of ozone into oxygen. As a result of this process the concentration of ozone molecules in the ozone layer is getting depleted.

The ozone layer plays a very important role in protecting living beings on the earth by absorbing high-energy solar UV radiation (220-330 nm). Progressive depletion of the ozone layer would result in more infiltration of UV radiation, which would cause more harm to the living beings including man.

Human health gets affected as a result of overexposure to UV radiation as it causes skin cancer, cataracts and immune system suppression. UV radiation also damages plants, marine ecosystem and synthetic as well as natural polymers.

Scientists, politicians and even common people, over the world, are concerned about the progressive depletion of the ozone layer. At some places (for example, at the south pole) the ozone layer has become very thin, which is referred to as 'ozone hole'.

To forestall further reduction of the ozone layer and also to enhance its regeneration an International Agreement (Montreal Protocol) was signed in 1987 at Montreal. It was agreed that CFC production would be halved by 1995 and completely phased out by 2000. The Protocol was substantially amended in 1990 and 1992. The developed countries agreed to phase out CFC with HCFC (hydrochlorofluorocarbon) by 2000. HCFC mostly undergoes chemical transformation in the troposphere and the lower stratosphere and hence would not affect the ozone layer too much. It has been envisaged to phase out HCFC with HFC (hydrofluorocarbon) which is more ozone-friendly having zero ozone depletion potential. The United Nation Environmental Programme (UNEP) has proposed that HCFC production should be stopped by 2005.

2.6 Atmospheric Chemistry

From natural and man-made sources gaseous and particulate matters are emitted mainly into the troposphere.

The larger and heavier particulate matters settle down quickly after emission due to gravitational force. The finer and lighter particles remain suspended for a longer period. Some of these particles settle down while the others, particularly, the hygroscopic ones act as cloud forming nuclei and are precipitated along with rain.

The gaseous pollutants emitted into the troposphere mostly undergo chemical transformation due to oxidation reactions (either thermally or photo-chemically) and the transformed substances return back to the earth's surface either as dry particle or along with rain. The substances which reach the ground as dry particles are referred to as 'dry depositions', whereas the substances which come down with rain or snow are termed as 'wet depositions'. When rain water contains dissolved acids it is referred to as acid rain. Normally rain contains some dissolved carbon dioxide (CO_2) and has a pH level of about 5.6. When rain contains other dissolved acids and salts the pH may be around four. In very polluted atmospheric conditions rain water pH may be as low as three. The sinks of some common primary and secondary gaseous pollutants are listed in Table 2.5.

2.6.1 Tropospheric Reactions

Solar radiation initiates dissociation of some gas molecules present in the troposphere and thereby produces some free radicals. These free radicals then carry on chain reactions with nitrogen oxides, carbon monoxide, hydrocarbons and sulphurous compounds. Carbon bearing compounds are oxidized to CO_2 H_2O, aldehydes, acids, esters, etc. NO_x is oxidized to nitrogen dioxide to nitric acid, and sulphur compounds to sulphur trioxide to sulphuric acid. The acids produced may combine with ammonia and air-borne alkaline particles to form salts.

The probable intermediate steps through which some of the air-borne gaseous pollutants may undergo chemical transformation and the end products produced are listed hereunder.

Table 2.5 : Primary and Secondary Sinks of Some Common Gaseous Pollutants

Pollutant	Sinks
Ammonia (NH_3)	Wet precipitation, absorption and chemical reaction with soil, water bodies and vegetation
Carbon dioxide (CO_2)	Photosynthesis, absorption in water bodies.
Carbon monoxide (CO)	Tropospheric and stratospheric chemical reaction, soil microbial reaction.
Hydrocarbons (C_xH_y)	Tropospheric chemical and photochemical reactions producing particulates and smog. Soil microbial reaction, vegetation up-take, stratospheric chemical and photochemical reactions.
Hydrogen sulphide (H_2S)	Chemical reaction with structural materials and paints, oxidation to sulphur dioxide.
Sulphur dioxide (SO_2)	Chemical and photochemical reactions, dry and wet precipitation, vegetation up-take, absorption in water bodies.
Nitrogen Oxides (NO_x)	Chemical and photochemical reactions, dry and wet precipitation, soil chemical and microbial reactions, vegetation up-take, absorption in water bodies.
Chlorine (Cl_2)	Photochemical reaction in troposphere and stratosphere, precipitation, vegetation up-take, absorption in water bodies.
Ozone (O_3)	Chemical reaction with vegetation, soil and water bodies.

I. Sulphur Compounds

$$SO_2 + O_3 \longrightarrow SO_3 + O_2$$
$$2\,SO_2 + O_2 \longrightarrow 2\,SO_3$$
$$SO_2 + H_2O \longrightarrow H_2SO_3$$
$$2\,H_2SO_3 + O_2 \longrightarrow 2\,H_2SO_4$$
$$SO_3 + H_2O \longrightarrow H_2SO_4$$
$$O_3 + h\nu \longrightarrow O_2 + O^{\cdot}$$
$$O^{\cdot} + H_2O \longrightarrow 2\,OH^{\cdot}$$
$$OH^{\cdot} + SO_2 \longrightarrow HOSO_2^{\cdot}$$
$$HOSO_2^{\cdot} + O_2 \longrightarrow HO_2^{\cdot} + SO_3$$
$$H_2SO_4 + 2\,NH_3 \longrightarrow (NH_4)_2SO_4$$
$$H_2SO_4 + CaCO_3 \longrightarrow CaSO_4 + H_2O + CO_2$$
$$H_2S + O_3 \longrightarrow SO_2 + H_2O$$

H_2S + Paints & other substances (metals) → Sulphides

II. Nitrogen Compounds

$$NO_2 + h\nu \longrightarrow NO + O^{\cdot}$$
$$O^{\cdot} + O_2 + X \longrightarrow O_3 + X$$ (X may be some molecules, which absorb energy)
$$O_3 + NO \longrightarrow NO_2 + O_2$$

$$O_3 + NO_2 \longrightarrow NO_3^{\cdot} + O_2$$
$$O_3 + h\nu \longrightarrow O^{\cdot} + O_2$$
$$O^{\cdot} + H_2O \longrightarrow 2\ OH^{\cdot}$$
$$CO + OH^{\cdot} + O_2 \longrightarrow CO_2 + HO_2^{\cdot}$$
$$HO_2^{\cdot} + NO \longrightarrow NO_2 + OH^{\cdot}$$
$$OH^{\cdot} + NO_2 \longrightarrow HNO_3$$
$$RCH + OH^{\cdot} + O_2 \longrightarrow RCO_2^{\cdot} + H_2O$$
$$RCO_2^{\cdot} + NO \longrightarrow NO_2 + RCO^{\cdot}$$
$$2\ NO + O_2 \longrightarrow 2\ NO_2$$
$$NO_2 + NO_3^{\cdot} \longrightarrow N_2O_5$$
$$N_2O_5 + H_2O \longrightarrow 2HNO_3$$
$$HNO_3 + h\nu \longrightarrow OH^{\cdot} + NO_2$$

III. Alkanes

$$O_3 + h\nu \longrightarrow O_2 + O^{\cdot}$$
$$O^{\cdot} + H_2O \longrightarrow 2\ OH^{\cdot}$$
$$C_nH_{2n+2} + OH^{\cdot} \longrightarrow C_nH^{\cdot}_{2n+1} + H_2O$$
$$CO^{\cdot} + OH^{\cdot} \longrightarrow CO_2 + H^{\cdot}$$
$$H^{\cdot} + O_2 + X \longrightarrow HO_2^{\cdot} + X$$

(X may be some molecules, which absorb energy)

$$C_n H^{\cdot}_{2n+1} + O_2 + X \longrightarrow C_n H_{2n+1}\ O_2^{\cdot} + X$$
$$C_n H_{2n+1}\ O_2^{\cdot} + NO \longrightarrow C_n H_{2n+1}\ O^{\cdot} + NO_2$$
$$C_n H_{2n+1}\ O^{\cdot} + O_2 \longrightarrow C_n H_{2n}\ O^{\cdot} + HO_2^{\cdot}$$
$$HO_2^{\cdot} + HO_2^{\cdot} \longrightarrow H_2O_2 + O_2$$

IV. Alkenes

$$C_n H_{2n} + OH^{\cdot} \longrightarrow HO\ C_n H_{2n}^{\cdot}$$
$$HO\ C_n H_{2n}^{\cdot} + O_2 \longrightarrow HO\ C_n H_{2n}\ O_2^{\cdot}$$
$$HO\ C_n H_{2n} O_2^{\cdot} + NO \longrightarrow HO\ C_n H_{2n}\ O^{\cdot} + NO_2$$
$$R + O_3 \longrightarrow R'CHO + R''CHO_2^{\cdot}$$
$$R'CHO + O_2 + h\nu \longrightarrow R'CO^{\cdot} + HO_2^{\cdot}$$
$$R'CO^{\cdot} + O_2 \longrightarrow R'-\overset{\overset{\displaystyle O}{\|}}{C}-O-O^{\cdot}$$
$$R'-\overset{\overset{\displaystyle O}{\|}}{C}-O-O^{\cdot} + R'CHO \longrightarrow R'-\overset{\overset{\displaystyle O}{\|}}{C}-OOH + R'CO^{\cdot}$$
$$R''CHO_2^{\cdot} + NO \longrightarrow R''CHO + NO_2$$

$$R''CHO_2^{\cdot} + NO_2 \longrightarrow NO_3^{\cdot} + R''CHO$$
$$R''CHO_2^{\cdot} + SO_2 \longrightarrow SO_3 + R''CHO$$
$$R''CHO_2^{\cdot} + H_2O \longrightarrow R''COOH + H_2O$$

R is an alkene molecule

Polluted urban atmosphere contains NO_x, hydrocarbons and other pollutants. The NO_x molecules absorb solar radiation and produce oxidants take O_3, $O^{\cdot}$, $OH^{\cdot}$. These oxidants oxidize the hydrocarbons to aldehydes, peroxides and pernitrates. Nox are oxidized to nitric acid. Sulphur compunds are oxidzed to sulphuric acid. Under favourable temperature and humid conditions the secondary pollutants produce smog.

2.6.2 Stratospheric Reactions

Only high altitude aircrafts and rockets discharge their exhaust into the stratosphere directly. These exhausts may contain NO_x, hydrocarbons, CO, CO_2 and H_2O. Some pollutants, which have not completely reacted in the troposphere and CFC, which is less reactive under tropospheric conditions, diffuse into the stratosphere from the troposphere. All of these undergo chemical transformation by reacting with ozone (O_3) and some free radicals produced photochemically in the stratosphere. Some of the probable reactions through which transformations take place and the end products produced are listed hereunder.

I. Free Radical Formation

$$O_2 \xrightarrow{UV} O^{\cdot} + O^{\cdot} \text{ (UV shield)}$$
$$O^{\cdot} + O_2 + X \longrightarrow O_3 + X$$

(X may be some molecules, which absorb energy)

$$O_3 \xrightarrow{UV} O_2 + O^{\cdot} \text{ (UV shield)}$$
$$O_3 + O^{\cdot} \longrightarrow 2\,O_2$$
$$O^{\cdot} + H_2O \longrightarrow 2\,OH^{\cdot}$$
$$OH^{\cdot} + O_3 \longrightarrow HO_2^{\cdot} + O_2$$
$$O^{\cdot} + HO_2^{\cdot} \longrightarrow OH^{\cdot} + O_2$$

II. Hydrocarbons

$$O^{\cdot} + CH_4 \longrightarrow CH_3 + OH^{\cdot}$$

(CH_4 a typical hydrocarbon)

$$O_3 + CH_4 \longrightarrow OH^{\cdot} + CH_3 + O_2$$
$$CH_3 + O_2 + X \longrightarrow CH_3O_2^{\cdot} + X$$

(X may be some molecules, which absorb energy)

$$CH_3O_2^{\cdot} + NO \longrightarrow CH_3O^{\cdot} + NO_2$$
$$CH_3O^{\cdot} + O_2 \longrightarrow CH_2O + HO_2^{\cdot}$$
$$CH_4 + O_3 \longrightarrow CO + 2\,H_2O$$
$$CO + OH^{\cdot} \longrightarrow CO_2 + H^{\cdot}$$

III. Nitrogen Oxides

$$O^{\cdot} + NO_2 \longrightarrow NO + O_2$$
$$NO + O_3 \longrightarrow NO_2 + O_2$$
$$N_2O \xrightarrow{UV} N_2 + O^{\cdot}$$

$$O^{\cdot} + N_2O \longrightarrow 2\ NO$$
$$OH^{\cdot} + NO_2 \longrightarrow H\ NO_3$$

IV. Chlorofluorocarbons (CFCs)

$$CFC + O^{\cdot} \longrightarrow ClO^{\cdot} + Cl^{\cdot} + R$$
(May be Cl or F)

$$ClO^{\cdot} + O^{\cdot} \longrightarrow Cl^{\cdot} + O_2$$
$$Cl^{\cdot} + O_3 \longrightarrow ClO^{\cdot} + O_2$$
$$Cl^{\cdot} + CH_4 \longrightarrow HCl + CH_3$$
$$ClO^{\cdot} + NO_2 \longrightarrow ClO\ NO_2$$
$$OH^{\cdot} + Cl^{\cdot} \longrightarrow HO\ Cl$$
$$OH^{\cdot} + HCl \longrightarrow 2\ H_2O + Cl^{\cdot}$$

The transformed products diffuse back to the troposphere from where they are precipitated to the earth's surfaces.

2.7 Material Balance and Mass Conservation in the Troposphere

As a result of the natural processes as well as due to human activity materials undergo phase changes and chemical transformation. However, in spite of such changes the average composition of the troposphere has not changed much over the years. This indicates that there is a balance between the emissions into the troposphere and the recycle from it.

For material balance the entire biosphere, which is made up of land, ocean and atmosphere is to be considered as a single unit. Instead of taking into account the whole of the atmosphere it would be sufficient to take into account the troposphere only as very little material escapes the troposphere.

The cyclic processes, which are instrumental in conservation of water, oxygen, nitrogen, carbon and sulphur, are qualitatively depicted through Figs. 2.4 to 2.8.

2.7.1 The Hydrological Cycle

Figure 2.4 shows a simplified version of the hydrological cycle. Water evaporates from land and water surfaces into the atmosphere. Some water vapour is emitted because of transpiration. Combustion of fossil fuels, agricultural residues, forest residues and volcanic eruptions also cause emission of water vapour into the atmosphere. The total amount of emission from the above mentioned sources is relatively small compared to that due to evaporation from land and water bodies.

In the atmosphere water vapour condenses to form cloud and finally precipitates as rain and snow. Some of the precipitates get stored in ponds, lakes, etc. and some run off to rivers and finally to the oceans. The remaining portion percolates the ground. A part of this water is utilized by vegetation for their metabolic processes and the remaining portion finally ends up as ground water.

Human beings utilize surface as well as ground water for domestic, agricultural and industrial purposes. Most of it is returned back to nature with impurity level higher than what was present initially at the source.

2.7.2 The Oxygen Cycle

The two essential life-sustaining materials are oxygen and water. Most of the water taken in by the living beings is returned back to nature as water. But the oxygen taken in by them is converted to CO_2 and exhaled, Moreover, oxygen used for industrial processes is converted to oxides, such as H_2O, CO_2, CO, NO_x, SO_2 and other compounds containing oxygen. Natural processes, like crustal oxidation and bacterial action also produce oxides. The only process by which molecular oxygen is

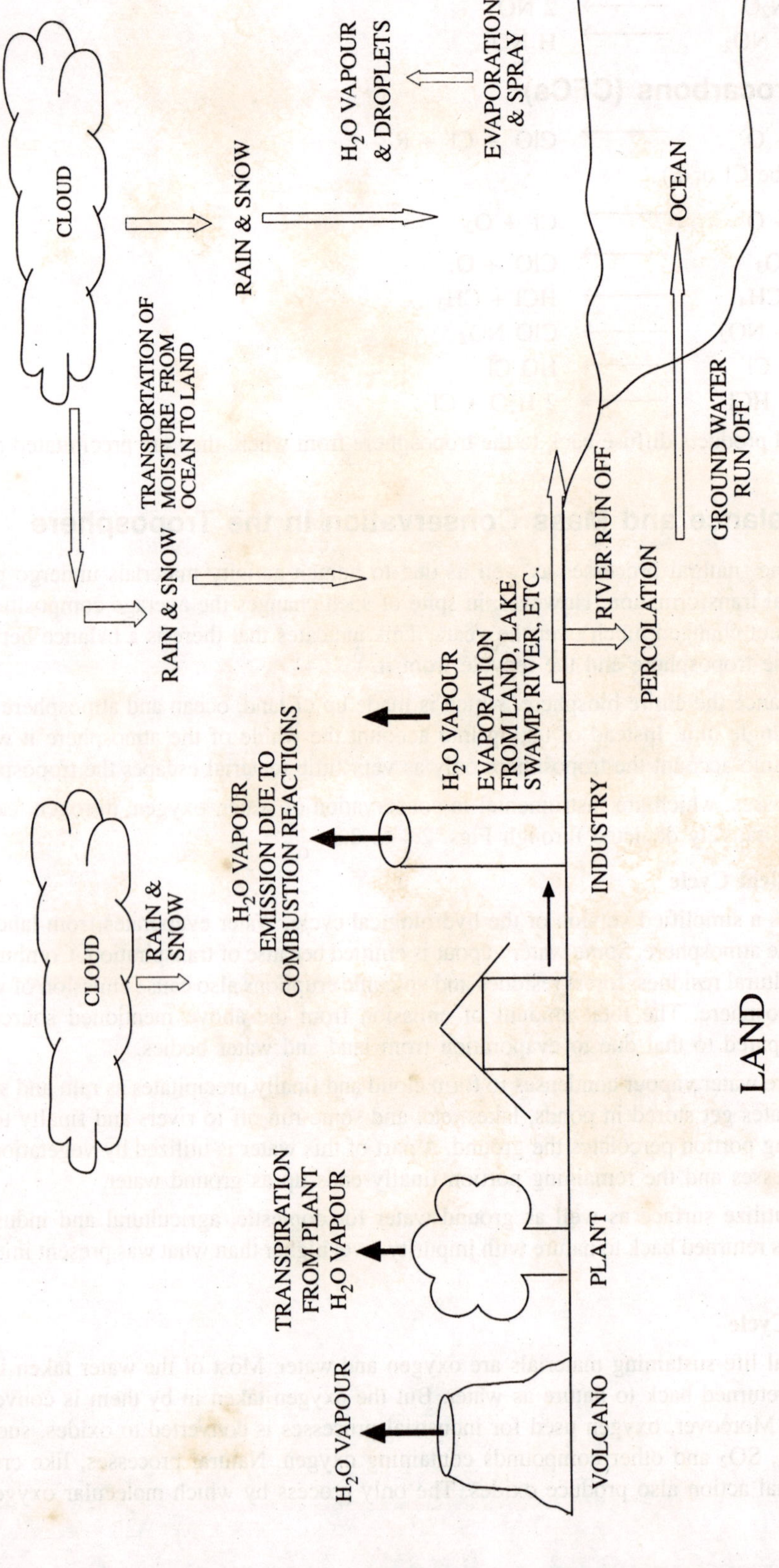

Fig. 2.4 : The Hydrological Cycle.

regenerated is the Photosynthesis process. During photosynthesis vegetations take up CO_2 and water and release oxygen according to the reaction :

$$CO_2 + H_2O \xrightarrow{h\nu} HCHO + O_2 \qquad (2.2)$$

A simplified version of the oxygen cycle is shown in Fig. 2.5.

2.7.3 The Nitrogen Cycle

Nitrogen is one of the basic ingredients (aminoacids) of all living beings. The only form in which nitrogen can be assimilated by living beings is ammonia and its compounds. Atmospheric molecular nitrogen is converted to ammonia and other nitrogenous compounds by various agencies. These are then assimilated by vegetation and microorganisms and converted to proteins. Herbivores and carnivores cannot synthesize proteins. Herbivores get proteins from plants and carnivores get them from herbivores.

Bacterial decomposition of dead vegetation and animals converts proteins to ammonia, a part of which is taken up by vegetation for protein synthesis. Of the remaining portion a part escapes to the atmosphere and the rest is leached away. Some bacteria convert nitrates to nitrites to nitrogen.

Industrial operations, particularly combustion processes produce nitrogen oxides (NOx) which are finally converted to nitric acid (HNO_3) as a result of tropospheric reactions. Nitric acid thus produced is precipitated as nitrates or acid rain.

Atmospheric nitrogen through industrial processes is converted to ammonia, which is then converted to nitrogenous fertilizers.

In a simplified way the nitrogen cycle is depicted in Fig. 2.6

2.7.4 The Carbon Cycle

Varous compounds of carbon are emitted into the atmosphere. The major portion is emitted as CO_2 and CO. The other carbon compounds emitted are hydrocarbons and various natural and synthetic organic compounds including halogenated compounds.

CO is oxidized to CO_2 in the atmosphere. A large fraction of the emitted CO_2 as well as that produced as a result of atmospheric oxidation of the emitted carbon compounds take part in the photosynthesis reaction. Another part is precipitated as CO_2 dissolved in rain water. The remaining portion accumulates in the atmosphere. The rate of accumulation of CO_2 is increasing since the beginning of the 'Industrial Revolution'. The concentration of CO_2 in the atmosphere has increased during the last one hundred years from about 290 ppm to about 320 ppm. The recent rate of increase is approximately 0.7 ppm/year. It is apprehended that, the 'greenhouse effect' resulting from progressive build-up of CO_2 in the atmosphere would cause global warming.

Hydrocarbons and other organic compounds emitted during industrial operations and natural processes are oxidized to aldehydes, acids and various other oxygenated compounds. These are subsequently wet precipitated. However, the rate of transformation of the organic compounds in the troposphere being slow, their tropospheric concentrations are on the rise. Like CO_2 these compounds also cause 'greenhouse effect'. In Fig. 2.7 a simplified version of the carbon cycle is depicted.

2.7.5 The Sulphur Cycle

The sulphur compounds released to the atmosphere are SO_2, SO_3, mercaptans, sulphuric acid and sulphates. Sulphur in H_2S and that in mercaptans is oxidized to SO_2. SO_2 is further oxidized to SO_3, which is finally converted to H_2SO_4. Some of the H_2SO_4 combine with air-borne alkaline particles and form sulphates. Free sulphuric acid and sulphates are precipitated on land and water bodies. Such deposits lower the pH of the receiving bodies. Acid deposits on land may interfere with vegetation growth. Acquatic life may also get affected at low pH.

H_2SO_4 and sulphates, which infiltrate the soil, are partly converted to SO_2 and H_2S due to bacterial action. These gases find their way to the atmosphere. The remaining sulfates are leached away and finally end up in surface and ground water. The sulphur cycle is shown in Fig. 2.8.

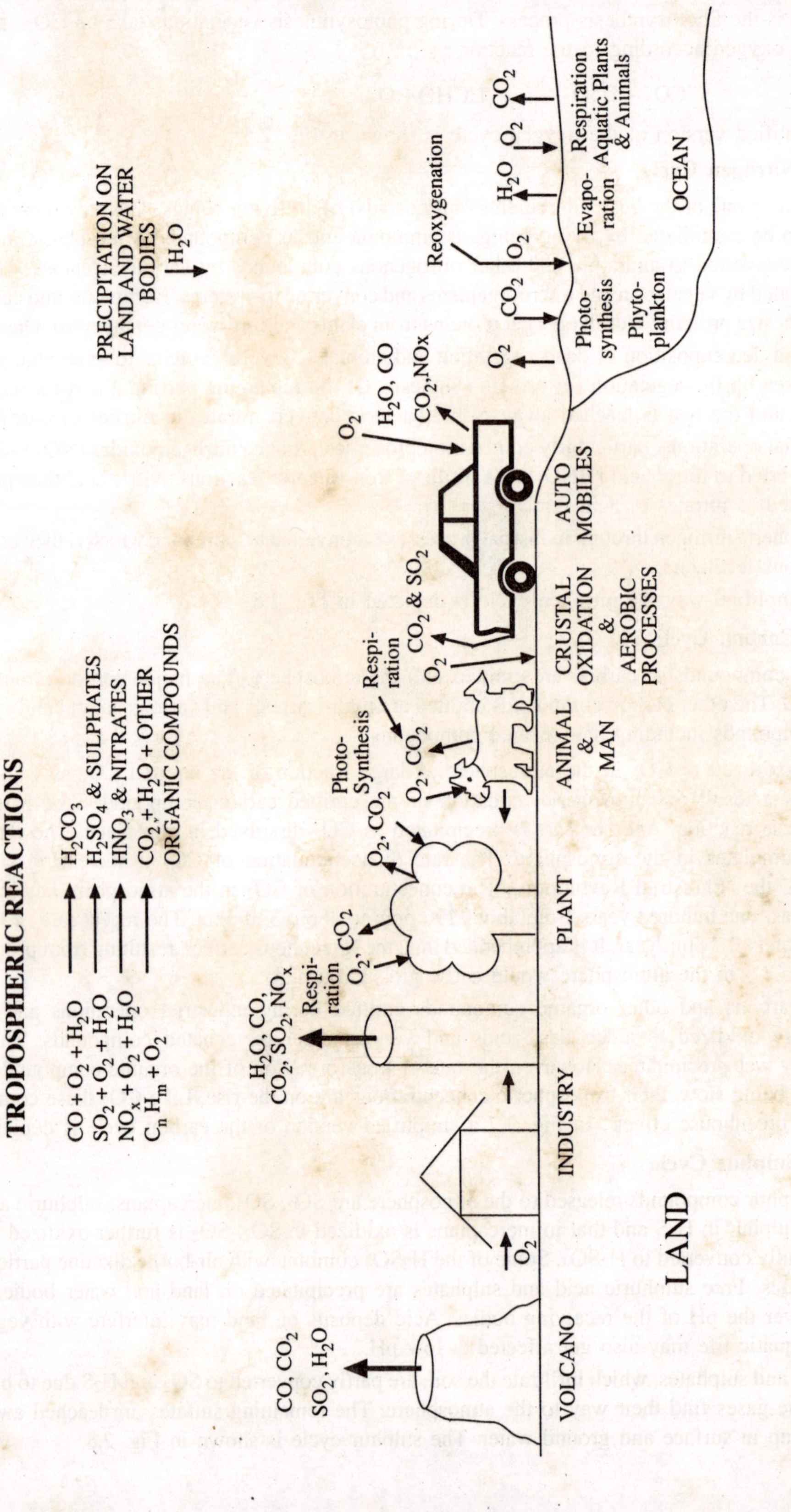

Fig. 2.5 : The Oxygen Cycle.

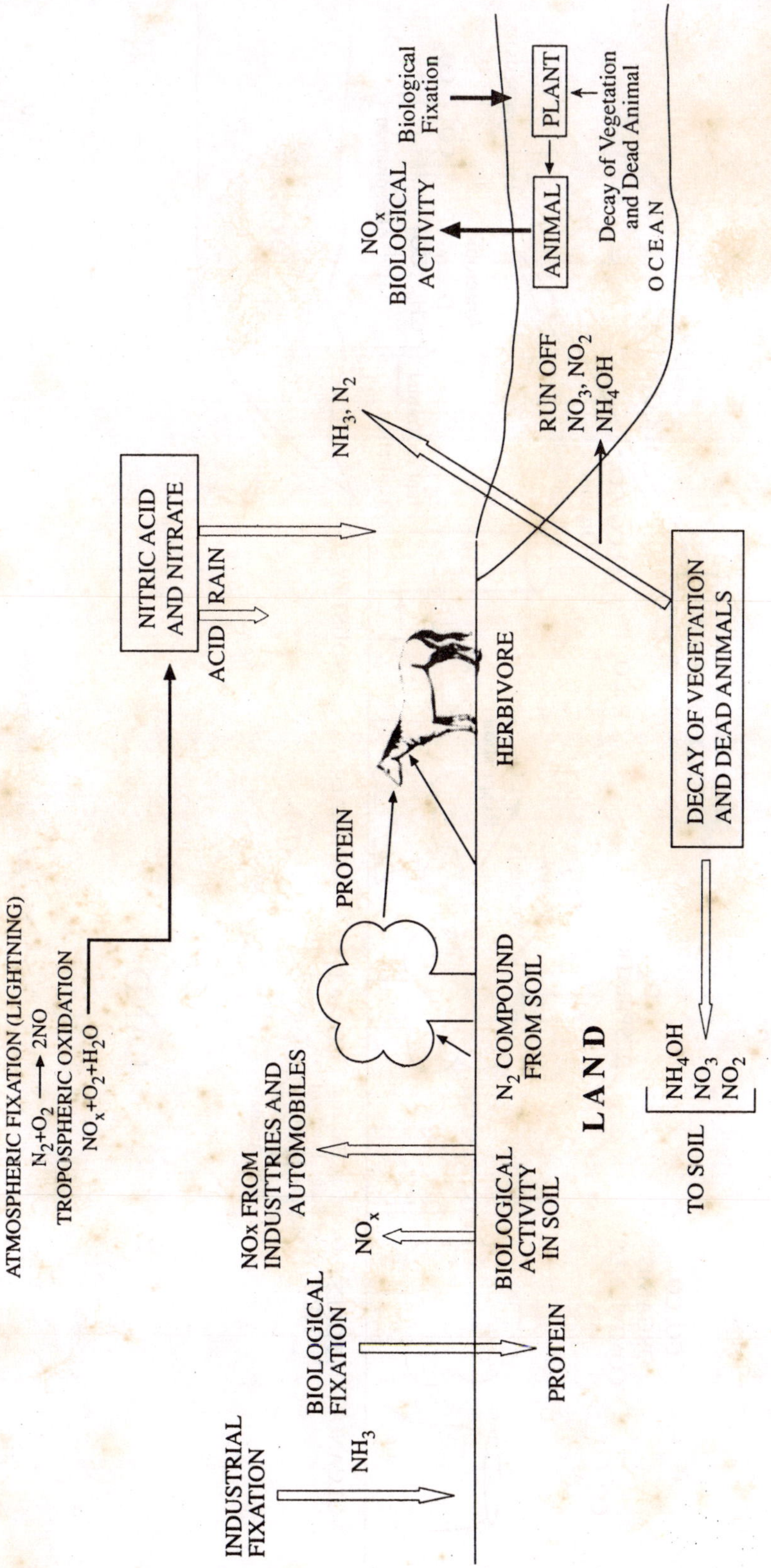

Fig. 2.6 : The Nitrogen Cycle.

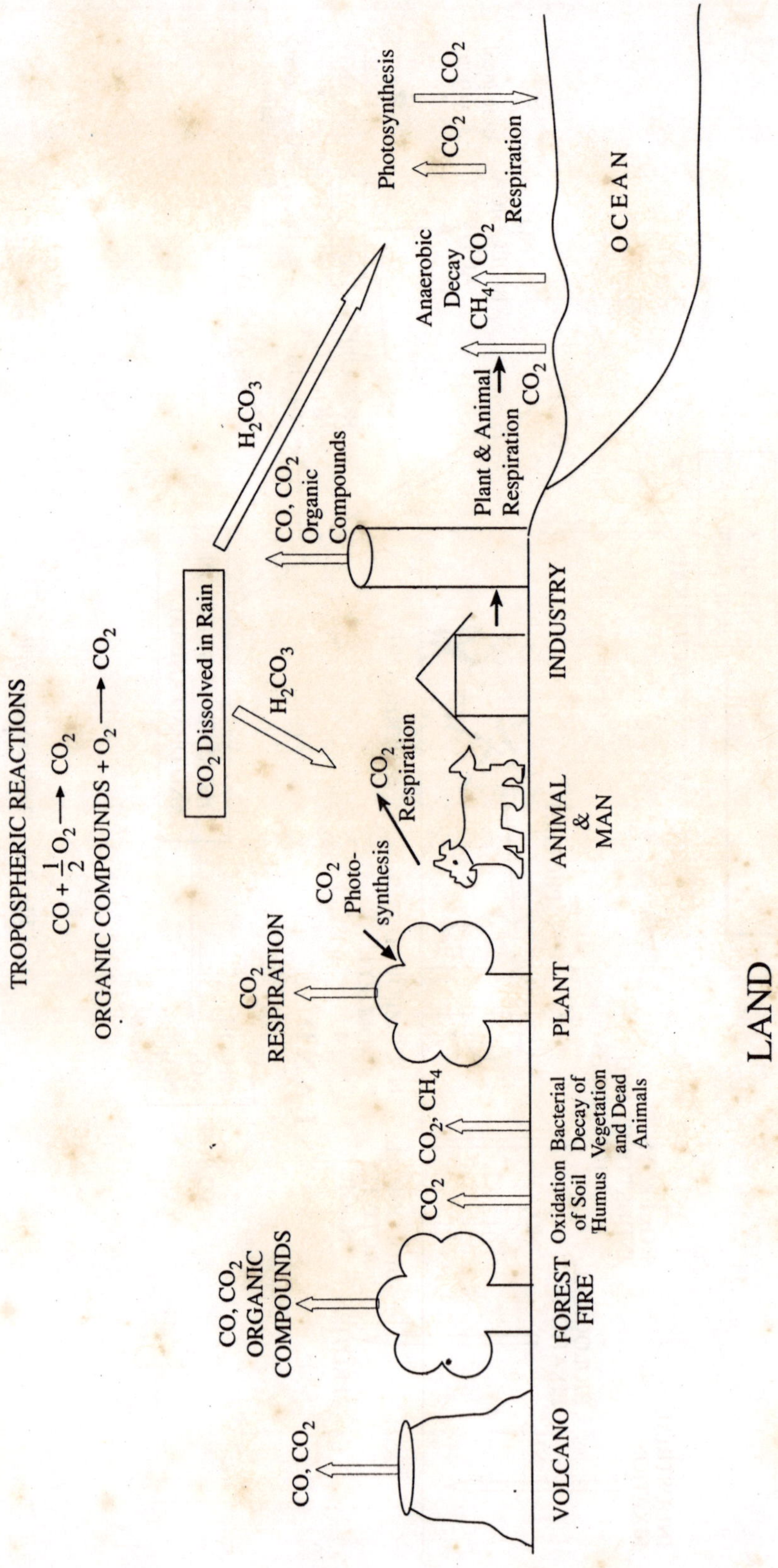

Fig. 2.7 : The Carbon Cycle.

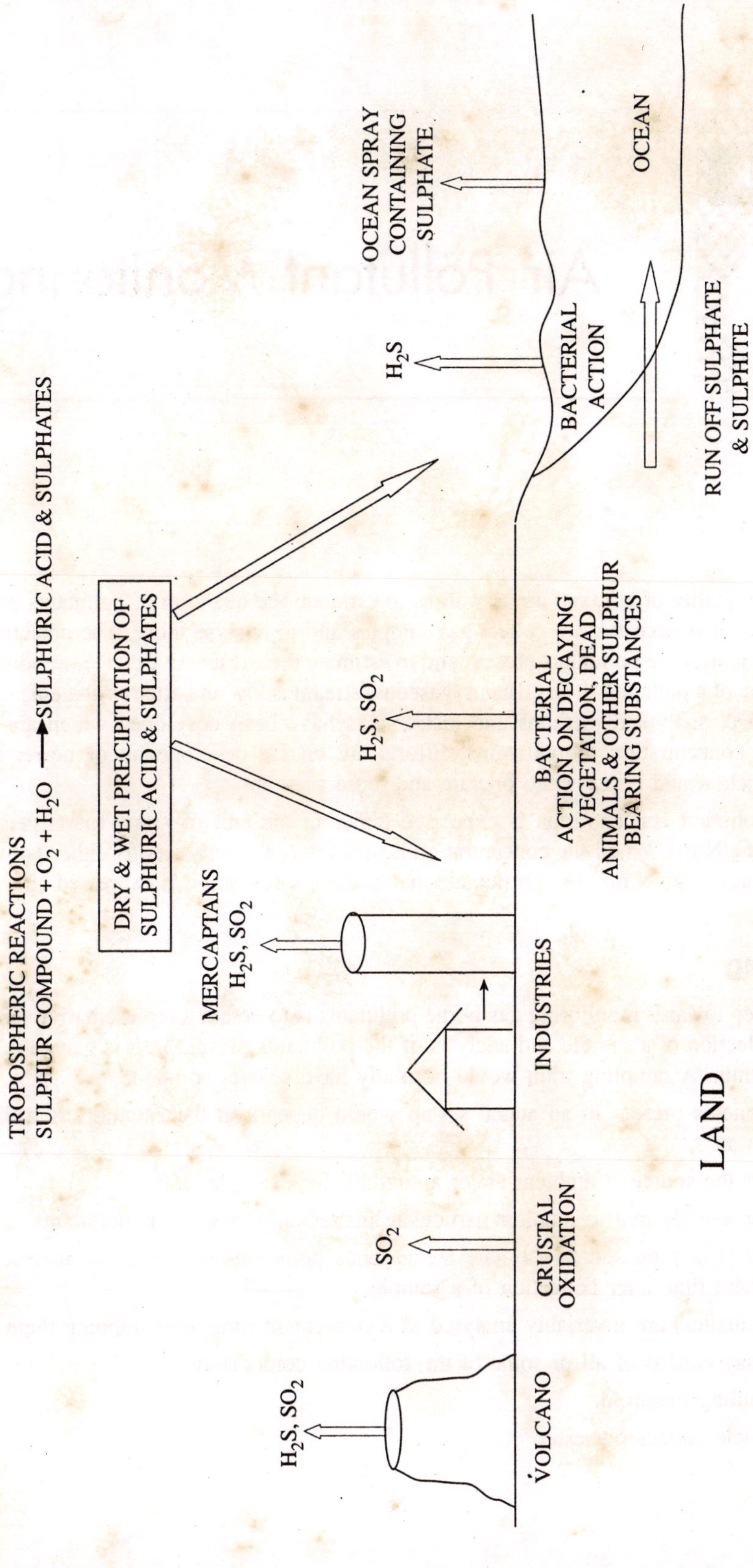

Fig. 2.8 : The Sulphur Cycle.

CHAPTER 3

Air Pollutant Monitoring

To ascertain the quality of ambient air as well as to estimate the quantum of pollutants emitted from different sources, it is necessary to collect gas samples and to analyse those. The objectives of such analysis are to identify the pollutants present and to estimate their respective concentrations. Normally the concentration of a pollutant in an effluent (gaseous) stream is low and after its abatement it becomes still lower. Hence, analytical methods and instruments have been developed which are capable of measuring low concentration of pollutants. Efforts are on for development of newer techniques/ instruments which would be easier to operate and more accurate.

Gaseous pollutant concentration is expressed either in the unit of ppmv (parts per million by volume) or in mg/N m^3. When the concentration is still lower the unit used is either ppbv (parts per billion by volume) or µg/N m^3. For particulate matter the concentration is expressed either in mg/m^3 or in µg/m^3.

3.1 Sampling

The first step towards monitoring gas-borne pollutants is to obtain a representative sample. A set-up used for collection of a sample and analysis of the pollutants present in it is generally referred to as a sampling train. A sampling train would normally have several components.

The components present in an actual set-up would depend on the situation as well as on the objectives, such as

1. whether the source is ambient air or a conduit, for example, a stack;
2. whether it is desired to monitor particulate matter only or gaseous pollutants;
3. whether it is proposed to estimate the gaseous pollutants in situ or to analyse them at a convenient time after collection of a sample.

Particulate matters are invariably analysed at a convenient time after trapping them.

A set-up may consist of all or some of the following components :

(i) a sampling manifold,

(ii) a particle collector/arrester,

(iii) a heater/cooler/condenser,

(iv) a suction pump (adjustable volume type),

(v) a flow-meter,

(vi) on-line gaseous pollutant monitoring instruments or bubblers or a sample collector.

The following figure (3.1) shows schematically some alternative arrangements of sample trains.

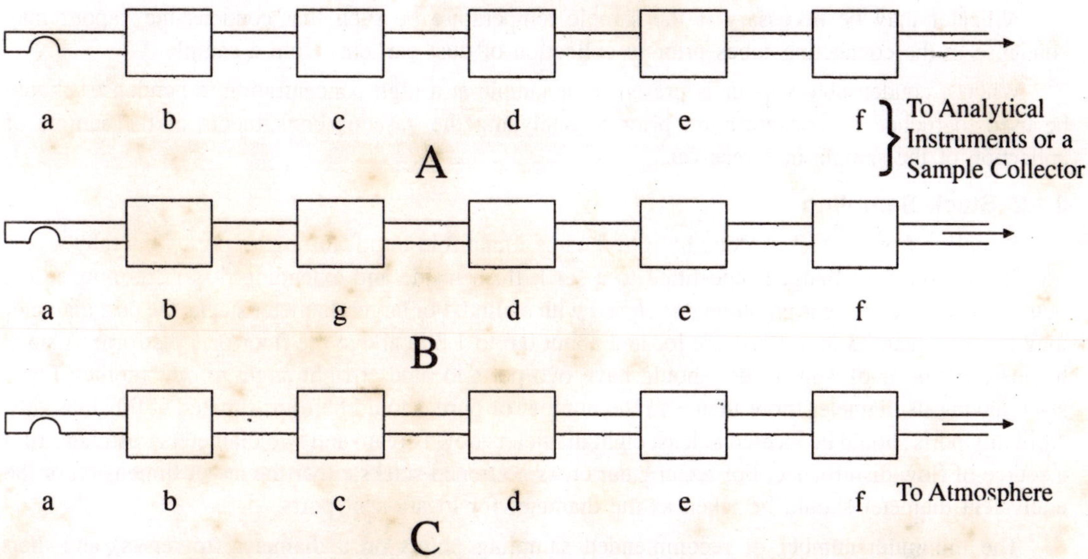

Fig. 3.1 : A Schematic Diagram of a Sample Train.

(a) Manifold, (b) Cooler/Heater, (c) Particle collector, (d) Condenser, (e) Pump,
(f) Flowmeter, (g) Filter.

A. A Train for Particulate and Gaseous Pollutant Monitoring.

B. A Train for Gaseous Pollutant Monitoring only.

C. A Train for Particulate Monitoring only.

While collecting a gaseous sample it should be kept in mind that an effluent stream flow rate and its composition may change with time and at a given time those may depend on the location of the sampling point. Because of these, standard procedures have been recommended for sampling so that the sample collected is a time averaged one. When on-line analyzers are used the sample is an instantaneous one.

3.1.1 Sampling Train

A manifold should be a part of the sampling train when sampling is to be done from a stack or a source other than the ambient atmosphere. It should be made of a non-reactive and non-adsorptive material, such as Teflon or glass or some heat and corrosion resistant alloy. It should be as short as possible and it should not be twisted, as otherwise there may be accumulation of particles inside it. To prevent thermal damage to the manifold it may be cooled but care should be taken so that the sample temperature does not drop below its dew point.

A dust collector is used when analysis of suspended particulate matter (SPM) is desired. Otherwise, a dust arrester is to be used.

A mechanical pump or a suitable device is used to aspirate a sample.

A flowmeter is used to measure the total volume of the sample passing through a sample collector train.

A cooler may be required as a part of a sampling train, if the gas temperature be such that the components of the train may get thermally damaged during sampling.

A heater may be necessary if the sample temperature be such that condensable vapour may condense in the connecting tubes prior to collection of dust particles from a sample.

When a condensable vapour is present in a sample at a high concentration, a condenser should be used to reduce its concentration prior to analyzing the gaseous constituents of the sample or collection of the sample in a receiver.

3.1.2 Stack Sampling

Sampling from a stack is done by introducing a manifold into it through a port. Generally a port is a 75 mm standard flanged pipe fitted to a stack flush inside and extending 50 to 200 mm on the outside. When sampling is not done it is closed with a blind. For larger diameter stacks the port diameter may be more than 75 mm. Ports are located about 0.6 to 1.8 m above the floor or a platform. A stack having a diameter of 3 m or less should have two ports located at right angle to one another. For a stack having its diameter more than 3 m the number of ports should be four, situated at 90° intervals. Normally ports should be located at least eight diameters downstream and two diameters upstream from a source of flow disturbance. For rectangular cross-sectioned stacks either the larger dimension or the equivalent diameter should be taken as the diameter for location of ports.

The minimum number of recommended sampling points on a diameter (traverses) and their locations depend on the position of a sampling port in respect to the upstream and downstream flow disturbance sources. Prior to sampling, the manifold mouth should be perfectly aligned with the flow direction in the stack and directed upstream.

For complete analysis of a sample from a stack, an isokinetic sampling train consisting of a nozzle, a heater wrapped probe and a heated filter holder followed by some impinger absorbers connected in series and immersed in an ice bath should be used. The absorption train should be followed by a gas drying tube (containing silica gel), a pump (variable stroke diaphragm pump), a dry gas meter and a calibrated orifice meter. After fitting the train to a stack the pump is switched on and the flow rate is adjusted so as to obtain a sample under isokinetic condition. When samples are to be analysed at regular intervals an online analyzer unit may be used instead of an impinger absorber train.

3.1.3 Ambient Air Sampling

For sampling ambient air the basic unit normally used is known as a 'high volume sampler', particularly when it is desired to analyse the particulate matter. The major components of such a unit are : (a) filter, (b) a blower and (c) a flowmeter. When it is desired to estimate the gaseous pollutants also either on–line instruments or a sample collector or a train of bubblers are used in tandem with the components already mentioned.

3.2 Particulate Monitoring

The purpose of particulate monitoring may be to estimate particulate mass concentration, particle size distribution and particle chemical composition.

When it is desired to estimate particle mass concentration only a suitable filter may be used. The filter medium may be made of cellulose fibre/polymeric fibre/glass fibre/synthetic membrane. The choice will depend on the gas temperature. The mass of arrested particles on a filter is estimated from the difference in the filter weight before and after filtration. The filter should be oven–dried before weighing in order to avoid any error creeping in because of absorption of moisture or any other vapour, during or prior to filtration.

A filter would not be a suitable device when it comes to estimation of the particle size distribution and/or chemical analysis of the particles, as quantitative recovery of the arrested particles from a filter is next to impossible. For ascertaining the size distribution and chemical analysis of gas-borne particulate matter one uses an impinger or a series of impingers. The particles collected in the impinger (s) along with condensed vapour, if any, are recovered quantitatively and anlyzed after drying.

For particulate monitoring from a stack sampling should be done under isokinetic condition, that is, the gas velocity through the sampling manifold should be the same as that through the stack at the sampling point. If sampling is done under super-isokinetic condition, then the collected particles would have a larger proportion of finer and lighter particles than the actual. Whereas when sampled under sub-isokinetic condition the collected particles would contain more of the larger and heavier particles. Since in practice it is difficult to maintain strictly isokinetic condition, the deviation from isokinetic condition should not be more than ±10%.

To maintain isokinetic sampling condition it is necessary to measure the stack gas velocity at the sampling point. The velocity is measured with a type–S (Stauscheibe or reverse type) pitot tube–manometer assembly. Figure 3.2 shows such an assembly.

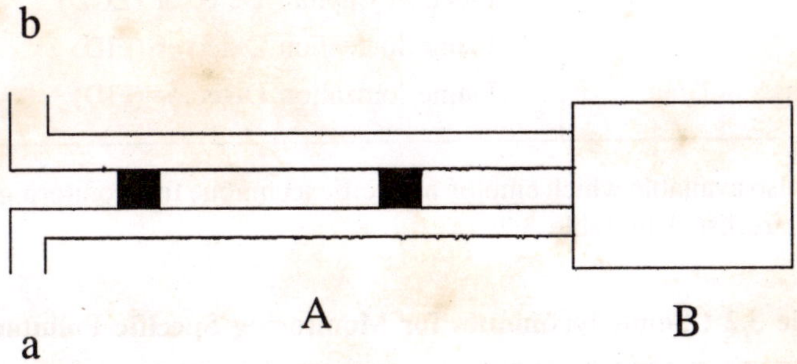

A. Pitot Tube
   (a) Tube opening facing upstream,
   (b) Tube opening facing downstream.

B. Differential Pressure Measuring / Gas Velocity Displaying Device.

Fig. 3.2 : Stauscheibe / Reverse Type Pitot Tube Assembly.

3.3 Gaseous Pollutants Monitoring

Gaseous pollutants may be monitored either in situ or at a convenient time after collection of a sample. Before analyzing a sample it must be freed from particulate matter and condensable vapour. In situ analysis is preferred as it yields data quickly. However, when a sampling point is located at a remote location or when data are not required immediately, a sample may be collected and the concentration of the pollutants in the sample may be estimated at a convenient time.

3.3.1 In Situ Analysis

When it is required to monitor a sample as soon as it is collected in situ analysis is carried out with the help of analytical instrument/ instruments placed in-line with a sampling train. Such a se-tup may be used for continuous emission monitoring (CEM). Very often this calls for providing a suitable housing for the instruments, as those are sensitive to dust, humidity and temperature. For online analysis of a gas a measured volume of it (free from dust) is introduced into an instrument (unit), which would measure, display or record the concentration of one or more constituents in the sample.

3.3.1.1 Instrumental Methods

Instruments (CEM analyzers) are available for monitoring gaseous pollutants like SO_2, NO, NO_2, O_3, CO and hydrocarbons. These instruments employ diverse techniques and may be used for analysis of stack gas as well as ambient air. Of the different techniques, the gas chromatography (GC) is a versatile one as it may be used for estimation of several pollutants, such as SO_2, NO_x, CO and hydrocarbons. The vital component of a gas chromatography is its detector, which identifies and senses the concentration of the different constituents of a sample. A detector may be constituent specific. In Table 3.1 some pollutant specific detectors are listed.

Table 3.1 : Some Pollutant Specific Gas Chromatograph Detectors

Pollutant	Detector Type
SO_2	Flame Photometric Detector (FPD)
NO_x	Electron Capture Detector (ECD)
CO	Flame lonization Detector (FID)
Hydrocarbons	Flame lonization Detector (FID)

Instruments are also available which employ a specific technique for monitoring a specific pollutant only. Some of these are listed in Table 3.2.

Table 3.2 : Some Techniques for Monitoring Specific Pollutants

Pollutant	Technique
CO	Non-dispersive Infrared Photometry (NDIR)
O_3	Chemiluminescence, Coulometry.
NO, NO_2	Chemiluminescence,
SO_2	Conductometry, Coulometry, NDIR, Spectrometry, Electrochemical Method.

The basic principles of the above mentioned techniques are briefly discussed hereunder.

Gas Chromatography

The basic components of a Gas Chromatography are :

(i) a packed column (a coiled tube) containing some granular particles (sometimes impregnated with a liquid). The column serves as an absorbing/adsorbing bed,

(ii) a column housing with temperature control,

(iii) suitable arrangements for introducing a gas sample and a carrier gas at the column base (inlet), and

(iv) a detector located immediately after the column.

The procedure for analysis is to inject a pre-determined volume of a gas sample at the base of the column. The column contains a pre-selected adsorbent, which would depend on the constituents present in the sample to be analyzed. The constituents get adsorbed on the adsorbent bed and get desorbed by a stream of pre-selected carrier gas flowing through the column. Partitioning of the sample constituents between the bed and the carrier gas occurs repeatedly as the constituents are carried towards the column exit by the carrier gas. Each constituent will travel at its own speed through the column and finally come out of the column and reach the detector in the form of a band. The time interval between two bands and the width of each band depend on the partitioning coefficient ratio of the constituents under the given system parameters. The detector gives out a signal indicating the time of emergence of a band.

The signal prolongs as long as a specific constituent continues to come out of the column. The magnitude of the signal would depend on the concentration of the constituent in the carrier gas, which in turn would depend on its concentration in the sample. The data are recorded as a plot of time vs. the specific constituents concentration in the carrier gas. Based on the area under the plot, the concentration of the specific constituent in the sample is estimated. Nowadays microprocessor based gas chromatographs are available, which produce printout listing the specific constituents present and their concentration in a sample analyzed.

Non-Dispersive Infrared Photometry (NDIR)

The principle involved in this technique is preferential absorption of infrared radiation by a constituent, for example, carbon monoxide (CO) present in a gas sample. A unit would have the following components :

(i) an infrared source,

(ii) a chopper,

(iii) a sample cell (flow type)

(iv) an infrared detector, and

(v) a reference cell (filled with a non-infrared absorbing gas).

A 'Non-Dispersive Infrared' unit works as detailed below :

The chopper would intermittently expose the sample cell and the reference cell to infrared radiation. The incident radiation would pass through the reference cell virtually unabsorbed and would reach the detector. The intensity of radiation transmitted through the sample cell would get reduced due to absorption by CO present in the sample flowing through the cell. The difference between the amounts of energy reaching the detector via the reference cell and that via the sample cell would be proportional to the CO concentration in the sample. Some constituents, such as water vapour present in a sample interferes with the quantitative estimation of CO.

Chemiluminescence Technique

This technique is based on the fact that when a pollutant is reacted with a specific reactant (in large excess) the product molecules formed would be at a higher state of excitation. As the product molecules revert from the higher state of excitation to their normal (ground) state, energy is released in the form of light. The intensity of the emitted light would be directly proportional to the concentration of the pollutant present in a sample. The emitted light intensity is normally measured with the help of a photo-multiplier.

For estimation of ozone (O_3) concentration in a sample the reactant used is ethylene. In the case of NO the reactant should be O_3. For estimation of NO_2 it is at first quantitatively reduced to NO and then estimated as NO.

Conductometric Technique

The basic idea behind this technique is the fact that when a specific pollutant is absorbed in a suitable liquid, the electrical conductivity of the resulting solution would be different from that of the absorbent. The change in conductivity would be proportional to the concentration of the pollutant present in a sample.

The liquid (absorbent) should be so chosen that it would absorb only one of the pollutants present in a sample. Generally, distilled water or an aqueous solution is used as an absorbent.

Coulometric Technique

Coulometric analysis is carried out by reacting a specific pollutant present in a gaseous sample with an aqueous solution of KI or KBr in an electrolytic cell whereby iodine or bromine is liberated. The liberated halide is reduced at the cathode of the cell. The current through the coulometer would be proportional to the amount of the liberated halide, which in turn would be proportional to the concentration of the specific pollutant present in the sample.

This method is not specific to ozone because it measures the total oxidants present in a sample.

Spectrometric Technique

This technique is somewhat similar to the NDIR. Light (IR/UV) from a source is filtered to screen out light of all wavelengths except a narrow band which is absorbed by a specific pollutant present in a gaseous sample. Such rays of the selected wavelength band are allowed to pass through a cell, through which a filtered, condensable free gas sample would be flowing. The intensity of the transmitted radiation relative to that of the unattenuated beam would be proportional to the concentration of the pollutant present in the sample.

Electrochemical Technique

An electrochemical analyzer may consist of a semi-permeable membrane, an electrolyte film, a sensing electrode and a reference electrode immersed in the electrolyte. A gas stream containing the pollutant whose concentration is to be estimated is passed over the semi-permeable membrane. The pollutant may migrate selectively across the membrane and generate a signal (voltage) in the electrolyte film.

The signal (voltage) would be picked up by the sensing electrode. The voltage difference between the sensing electrode and the reference electrode would be proportional to the pollutant concentration in the sample.

3.3.1.2 Chemical Methods

There are two chemical methods, namely (1) Qucik method and (2) Classical method.

Quick Method

The quick method yields information within a short time. It does not require a skilled operator. For each pollutant a specific detector is used. The concentrations of some pollutants may range from low to rather high. For such a pollutant a detector having the appropriate range has to be chosen depending on the situation.

A set-up for quick analysis consists of a sealed glass tube (detector) filled with a pollutant specific reagent adsorbed on some inert granules or the reagent itself in granular form and a hand-operated positive displacement pump. The tube is fitted with plugs at each end, which act as filters. These also hold the granular particles as a packed bed. A direct reading scale (generally in ppmv unit) is printed on the outside surface of the tube along its length. The marking starts immediately after the leading end filter plug. The method is suitable for monitoring the pollutants present in ambient air.

The operating procedure of such a unit is to break the sealed ends of a detector tube (specific for a specific pollutant) and attach the same to a pump in such a way that a gas sample is drawn through the leading end of the tube. By operating the pump a known volume of a sample (as specified by the detector manufacturer) is to be aspirated through the tube. Instantaneous reaction between the reagent and the pollutant would take place resulting in a sharp change in colour of the granular bed in the tube. The length of the stained portion of the granular bed would depend on the concentration of the pollutant present in a sample, which can be read from the printed scale on the tube. A tube can be used only once. Selector tubes are available for monitoring common inorganic gaseous pollutants as well as a wide variety of organic pollutants.

Classical Method

The classical method is also referred to as wet chemistry method. This method is relatively time consuming and its accuracy depends on the skill of an analyst. In this method a known volume of a dust-free gas sample is allowed to flow at a moderate rate through a series of bubblers, each containing a solvent with or without some dissolved reagents. Each bubbler would trap only a specific pollutant depending on the solvent/ reagent present. The bubblers are to be properly sequenced. Once a sample has been allowed to flow through the train of bubblers those are to be detached and their contents are to be quantitatively analysed for estimating the trapped pollutants.

3.4 Sample Collection and Analysis at Convenience

It is sometimes preferred to collect a gas sample and subsequently analyze the same in a laboratory at a convenient time. In order to carry out analysis in this way it is necessary to preserve a sample as it is or to segregate each constituent (pollutant) quantitatively and then preserve them. To achieve this goal any one of the following steps may be adopted :

(i) Collection of a Sample in an Evacuated Receiver

A dust-free gas sample is collected either in an evacuated rigid metallic container or in a flexible bag made of a polymer film. The material of construction of the container should be so chosen that the pullutants would not interact physically or chemically with the container during storage and thereby cause a change in the composition of the sample collected. A sample should be cooled to room temperature and freed from solid particles and condensable vapour before collection in a container. The container filled with a sample should then be transported to a laboratory for analysis. In the laboratory the sample may be withdrawn from the container either by squeezing the polymer bag or by means of a pump from the rigid container. Analysis of the retrieved sample may be carried out either with the help of suitable instruments or by suitable chemical methods.

(ii) Collection in a Medium

Liquid or solid collection medium may be used for retaining quantitatively the pollutants present in a gas sample either as it is or in a segregated form for their subsequent estimation.

(a) Liquid Medium

When a liquid medium is used the unit is referred to as a 'bubbler system'. The system may have several bubblers in series, each containing a liquid in which a specific pollutant will be either physically absorbed or chemically reacted. Through each bubbler a known volume of the sample is bubbled and subsequently the quantity of the trapped pollutant is estimated by a suitable chemical analytical method. In Table 3.3 the chemical composition of bubbler liquids and the anlytical methods employed for estimation of some common pollutants are listed.

Table 3.3 : Bubbler Liquid Composition and Analytical Approaches used for estimation of some Common Gaseous Pollutants

Pollutant	Bubbler liquid composition	Analytical approach
Ammonia (NH_3)	0.1 N Sulphuric Acid.	Colorimetry, Nessler Reagent
Carbon dioxide (CO_2)	0.1 N Barium hydroxide.	Titration with oxalic acid.
Hydrogen Sulphide (H_2S)	5% Cadmium sulphide solution	Iodometric titration.
Nitrogen dioxide	Saltzman reagent	Colorimetry.
Ozone (O_3)	1% Potassium iodide in 1 N potassium hydroxide.	Colorimetric estimation of the liberated iodine.
Sulphur dioxide (SO_2)	Sodium tetrachloromercurate.	Colour developed by adding bleached pararosaniline and formaldehyde.

(b) Solid Medium

This method of collection is based on the fact that when a dust and condensable vapour-free gas sample is passed over a bed of adsorbent, such as activated carbon/activated silica gel, the pollutants present in the sample get adsorbed quantitatively.

The procedure adopted for collection and preservation of the pollutants in a gas sample is to pass a known volume of a pollutant bearing gas through a container containing an adsorbent bed whereby the pollutants are retained on the adsorbent granules and most of the carrier gas flows out. After collection the container is sealed and taken to a laboratory for analysis.

The very first step towards analysis of the adsorbed constituents is to desorb them quantitatively by heating the container while a stream of inert gas flows throught the container at a moderate rate. The desorbed constituents are carried into a measuring system by the inert gas stream. An alternative procedure for quantitative recovery of the adsorbed constituents is to extract those with a known volume of a liquid (a solvent). Subsequently the concentrations of the constituents (Pollutants) present in the liquid extract are estimated either chemically or with the help of suitable instruments.

Based on the discussion so far it may be concluded that the methods used for gaseous pollutant monitoring may be classified into two groups : (i) the instrumental methods and (ii) the chemical methods. The merits and demerits of these methods are listed in Table 3.4.

Table 3.4 : Merits and Demerits of Instrumental and Chemical Methods for Analysis of Gaseous Pollutants

	Instrumental Methods	Chemical Methods
Merits	* Analysis takes a short time * Accuracy of measurement would depend on the instrument used and not on the operator's skill.	Standard samples are not essential for calibration. Setups are relatively cheap.
Demerits	* Standard samples are often required for instrument calibration. * Trained operators are required. * Instruments are costly.	Analysis generally takes a longer time. Accuracy of measurement would depend on the skill of the analyst.

CHAPTER 4

Gas-borne Pollutant Abatement Methods

To abate air pollution from a process plant it is necessary to install a pollution control system made up of one or more devices as an integral part of the process plant. The system should be capable of removing the pollutants (particulates as well as gaseous) from the gaseous stream or streams being discharged from a process plant. After removal of the pollutants the gaseous stream/streams are vented to the atmosphere normally through a vertical conduit which is known as a **stack** or **chimney**. A stack is also an integral part of an abatement system. The installed system should be capable of bringing down the concentration of each pollutant to such a level that its concentration at the ground level would not exceed the legally stipulated limits under any circumstances.

Before planning and designing an abatement system one must know the specific pollutants present in a gaseous stream, their respective concentration, the process parameters which influence their generation and the characteristics of the carrier gas. The basic information about an effluent gaseous stream, which must be known before selecting and designing the different devices (equipment) making up an abatement system are listed in Table 4.1.

Once the information listed in Table 4.1 about an effluent stream are available it would be possible to chalk out one or more schemes for pollution abatement depending on whether it is desirable/ economical to recover one or more of the constituents present in an effluent stream.

It must be emphasised here that the aim of the system design should not be to reduce the pollutants' concentration to zero level but to such an extent that on disposal of the treated stream through a stack the ground level concentration of each pollutant (including the particulates) would not be more than its stipulated legal limit.

Table 4.1 : Basic Information Required for Designing a Gaseous Pollution Abatement System

Information required	Pertaining to
1. Flow rate 2. Constituents 3. Pressure 4. Temperature 5. Humidity (with respect to moisture or any other vapour present) 6. Inflammability 7. Toxicity	**Carrier Gas**
1. Constituents 2. Size range 3. Mass distribution 4. Hygroscopicity 5. Reactivity 6. Abrasiveness 7. Corrosiveness 8. Electrical conductivity 9. Toxicity	**Particulate Matter**
1. Constituents 2. Toxicity 3. Reactivity 4. Odorous Component 5. Inflammability 6. Corrosiveness 7. Normal concentration of each constituent 8. Expected concentration of each constituent during an accident/upset condition.	**Gaseous Pollutants**

4.1 Pollutant Classification and Treatment Methods

Pollutants, emitted from an industrial unit along with a gaseous effluent stream, may be classified in different ways depending upon the criterion used for classification. Based on the physical criterion the pollutants may be classified as :

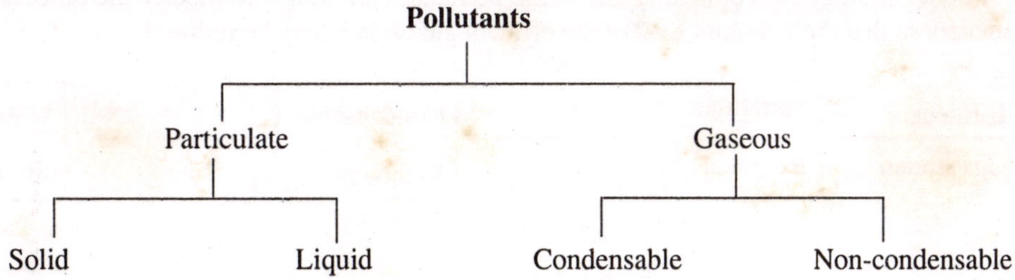

From chemical point of view the classification would be :

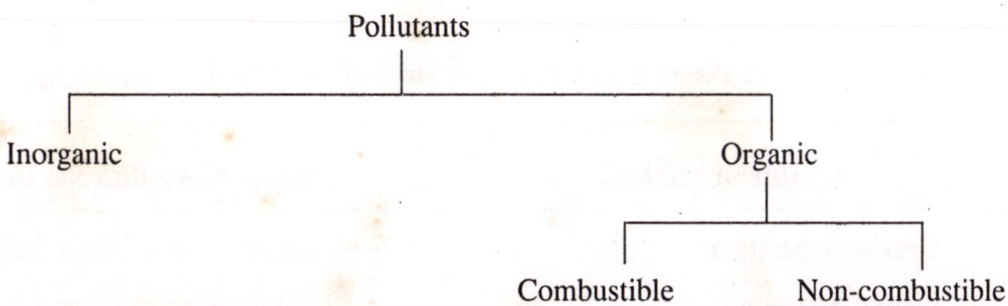

The organic pollutants may also be classified as biodegradable and non-biodegradable.

The techniques/methods which are used for removal of gas-borne pollutants may be classified into three groups, namely, physical, chemical and biological. These methods are listed in Table 4.2.

The different treatment methods and their areas of application are listed in Table 4.3. The treatment methods, which may be used, for removal of a specific type of pollutant are listed in Table 4.4.

Table 4.2 : Classification of Gas-borne Pollutant Treatment Methods

Physical Method	Chemical Method	Biological Method
Gravity Separation	Gas Phase Reaction	Aerobic Reaction
Inertial Separation	Gas—Solid Reaction	
Centrifugal Separation	Gas—Liquid Reaction	
Filtration		
Electrostatic Separation		
Scrubbing		
Absorption		
Adsorption		
Condensation		

It is not possible to develop a generalized flow sheet outlining the sequence of treatments for abatement of the different pollutants present in a gaseous effluent stream as the type/types of pollutants present in a waste gas stream would depend on its source. The treatment scheme shown below (Fig. 4.1) may be suitably modified depending on the situation.

A better strategy for combating gas-borne pollutant emission is to modify the process itself or its parameters so that the pollutant load of the effluent gas stream may be reduced.

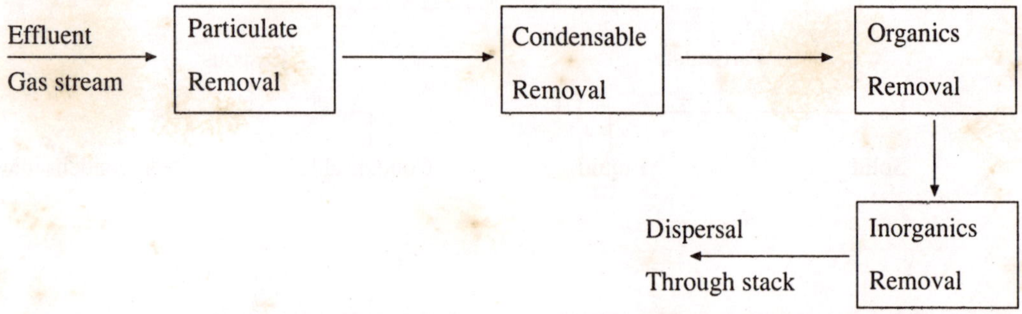

Fig. 4.1 : General Treatment Sequence of a Waste Gas Stream.

Table 4.3 : Waste Gas Treatment Methods and Their Areas of Application

Treatment Method	Areas of Application (to remove)
Gravity Separation	Solid particles and liquid droplets
Inertial Separation	Solid particles and liquid droplets
Centrifugal Separation	Solid particles and liquid droplets
Filtration.	Solid particles and liquid droplets
Electrostatic Separation	Solid particles
Scrubbing	Solid particles, liquid droplets and some inorganic & organic gaseous pollutants
Condensation	Vapours.
Absorption	Vapours and Gases
Adsorption	Vapours and Gases
Gas Phase Oxidation (Combustion)	Volatile Organic Compounds (VOCs)
Gas Solid Reaction	Inorganic (Gaseous) Compounds
Gas Liquid Reaction	Inorganic (Gaseous) Compounds
Aerobic (Biological) Reaction	Biodegradable Organics

Table 4.4 : Different Treatment Methods for Removal of a Specific Type of Gas-borne Pollutant

Pollutant Type	Treatment Methods
Solid Particulate Matter	Gravity Separation, Inertial Separation, Centrifugal Separation, Filtration, Electrostatic Separation, Scrubbing.
Liquid Particulate Matter (droplets)	Gravity Separation, Inertial Separation, Centrifugal Separation, Filtration.
Vapour	Condensation, Absorption, Adsorption.
Volatile Organic Compounds (VOCs)	Combustion, Condensation, Absorption, Adsorption, Aerobic (Biological) Oxidation.
Inorganic (Gaseous) Compound	Gas—Solid Reaction, Gas—Liquid Reaction, Absorption

The working principles of the equipment, which are used for abatement of the different types of gas-borne pollutants, their design approach and other related information are presented in the subsequent sections of this chapter.

4.2. Particulate Abatement Devices

Gas-borne solid particle from process industries may be removed by installing any one or a combination of the devices listed under Table 4.4. The mechanisms by which those devices bring about separation of the particulate matter are different. These devices have some limitations in terms of the particle size and physical characteristics like particle density, carrier gas temperature, pressure, etc. The devices are listed hereunder.

1. Gravity settler,
2. Inertial separator,
3. Centrifugal separator,
4. Filters,
5. Electrostatic separator, and
6. Scrubber.

The devices belonging to the first five types are referred to as **dry collectors** and the devices belonging to the sixth type are referred to as **wet collectors**. In the dry collectors the waste-gas temperature must not be allowed to drop below its dew point so that the separated particles may remain free flowing. In wet collectors the influent dust laden gas stream is brought in contact with a liquid stream, generally water, whereby the particulates agglomerate and form a slurry. The slurry thus produced has to be further treated before finally recovering or discarding the solid particles.

4.2.1 Gravity Settler

When a dust laden gas stream flows through a chamber, the dust particles experience the following forces in the vertical direction : (i) a gravitational force acting downward, (ii) a buoyant force acting upward, and (iii) a drag force in the direction opposite to the direction of motion of the particles. As a result the particles attain a net downward velocity, which under steady state condition is termed as the terminal velocity, U_t. The particles also experience a velocity in the horizontal direction, which would be the same as that of the carrier gas (assuming no slip at the gas—particle interface).

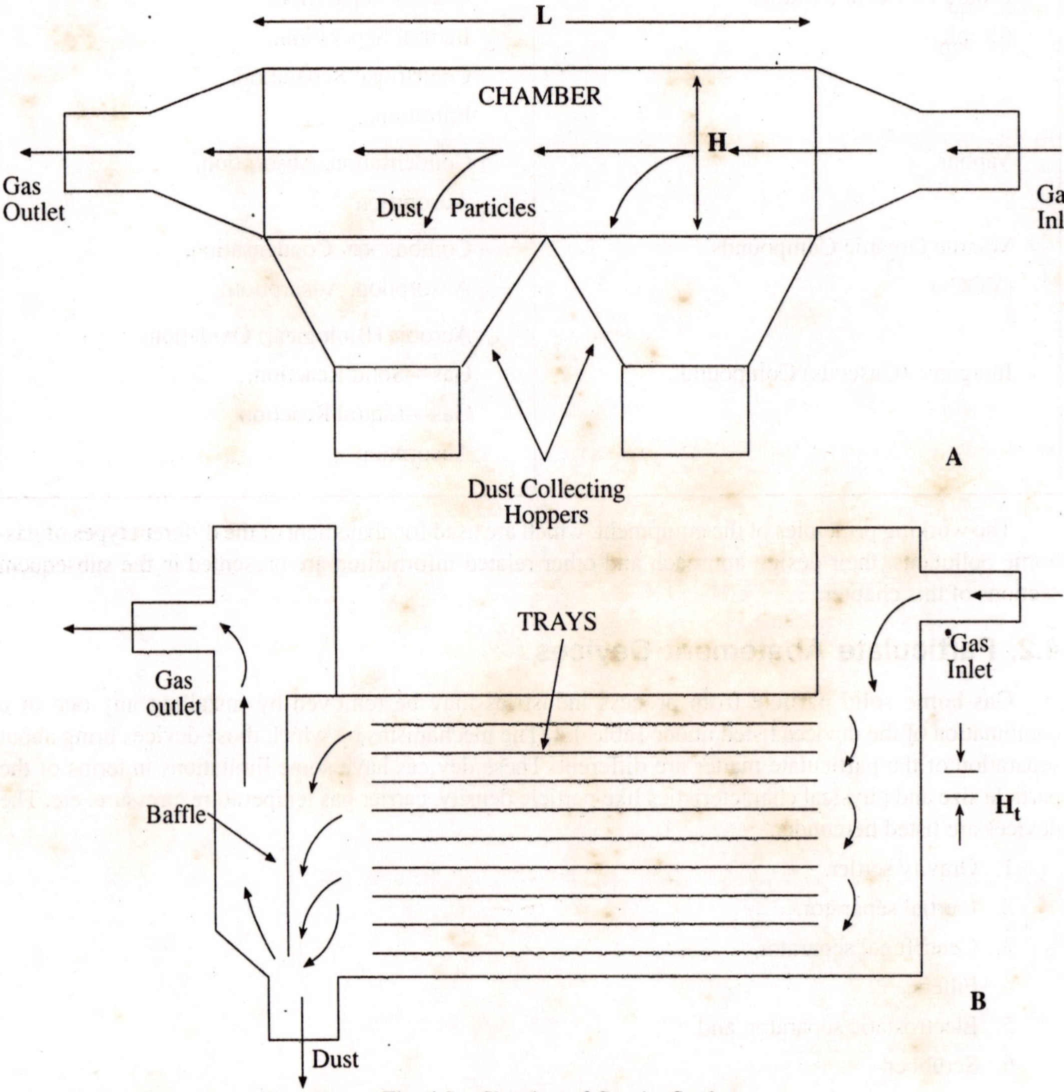

Fig. 4.2 : Sketches of Gravity Settlers.
A. Single Chamber Gravity Settler.
B. Multi-tray Gravity Settler.

The dust particles, which are retained in the chamber, get separated from the carrier gas stream and the rest are carried away. Such a chamber is termed as a gravity settler. The degree of dust removal from a gas stream in a gravity settler depends on the following factors :

(i) Gas velocity in the chamber,

(ii) Particle size distribution,

(iii) The terminal velocities of the particles, which in turn depend on the particle sizes, particle densities, gas (carrier) velocity and gas density.

(iv) The Chamber length.

and (v) The Chamber height.

Gravity settlers are of two types : (i) single chamber (without any tray inside) and (2) multi-tray chamber (also known as Howard settler). Figure 4.2 shows sketches of gravity settlers.

Construction-wise a single chamber is the cheapest. The dust particles retained are collected in a hopper/hoppers at the base from where the particles are removed from time to time. A multi-tray chamber would be costlier and would have several slightly inclined trays having an uniform gap in between the trays. The trays are provided with a suitable mechanical device so that the accumulated dust layers on the trays may be removed without any interruption of the flow process.

The settlers may be made of any metal, which would be capable of withstanding the gas temperature, the corrosive environment and abrasion of particles. There are no pressure and temperature limitations so far as the entering gas is concerned. It may be necessary to insulate a settler in order to prevent cooling of the influent gas below its dew point and consequent vapour condensation.

In a single chamber settler particles larger than 40 μm may be removed efficiently whereas a properly designed multi-tray chamber can remove particles as small as 10 μm.

One of the major advantages of a gravity settler is its low-pressure drop. The overall pressure drop can be calculated by adding the pressure drops due to (i) entrance expansion, (ii) frictional loss in the chamber itself and (iii) exit contraction.

$$\Delta P = \rho_g \frac{U^2}{2}\left[k_i + \frac{f\,L}{R_H} + k_e\right], \tag{4.1}$$

where, ΔP = pressure drop,

U = gas velocity in the chamber,

ρ_g = gas density,

f = friction factor,

k_i = inlet resistance factor = $\left(\frac{WH}{A_1} - 1\right)^2$,

k_e = outlet resistance factor = $0.45\left(1 - \frac{A_o}{WH}\right)$,

R_H = hydraulic radius = $\frac{WH}{2(W+H)}$,

A_i, A_o = cross sectional area of the inlet and the outlet ducts respectively,

H = chamber height,

L = chamber length,

and W = chamber width.

GRAVITY SETTLER DESIGN APPROACH

For designing a gravity settler the following information are required in consistent units :

1. Volumetric gas flow rate,
2. Dust particle size and mass distribution analysis (dpi vs. m_{dpi}),
3. Average particle density, ρ_p,
4. Gas Density and viscosity, ρ_g, μ_g, and
5. The desired removal efficiency (η_{dpi}) of the target particle size.

It has been mentioned earlier that a particle having a diameter dpi attains a terminal velocity $U_{t,\,dpi}$ as a result of the forces (already listed) acting on it. The expression for $U_{t,\,dpi}$ works out to be

$$U_{t,dpi} = \left[\frac{4g\ dpi(\rho_p - \rho_g)}{3\ C_D \rho_g}\right]^{1/2} \tag{4.2}$$

where C_D = drag coefficient,

$$\left.\begin{aligned} &= 24\ Re_p^{-1.0}\ for\ \ Re_p < 2 \\ &= 18.5\ Re_p^{-0.6}\ for\ \ 2 < Re_p < 500 \\ &= 0.44 \qquad\quad for\ \ Re_p > 500 \end{aligned}\right] \tag{4.3}$$

$$Re_p = (dpi\ U_{t,dpi}, \rho_g)/\mu_g$$

If the particles be fine, such that, $dpi \le \lambda_m$

where λ_m = mean free path of the gas molecules

$$= \frac{3\ \mu_g}{\rho_g \left(\frac{8g\ RT}{M_g}\right)^{1/2} \times \pi} \tag{4.4}$$

Mg = molecular weight of the carrier gas.

The actual terminal velocity of such particles would be

$$U_{t,\,dpi}\ actual = U_{t,\,dpi}\ \ calculated \times K_m, \tag{4.5}$$

where K_m = Cunningham factor

$$= 1 + \frac{\lambda_m}{dpi}\left[1.644 + 0.552\ e^{\frac{-0.656\ dpi}{\lambda_m}}\right] \tag{4.6}$$

The particles, which normally one would be interested in removing in a gravity settler would not be too fine, hence $U_{t,\,dpi}$ of such particles may be calculated by using the Eq. (4.7), which is obtained by assuming $C_D = \frac{24}{Re_p}$ and substituting the same in Eq. (4.2)

$$U_{t,\ dpi} = \frac{g\ dpi^2\left(\rho_p - \rho_g\right)}{18\ \mu_g}. \tag{4.7}$$

It should be mentioned here that for design purpose it is assumed that the particles would attain their respective terminal velocities immediately after entering a settling chamber.

The size of a gravity settler may be arrived at through the following steps :

Step I : Evaluate the $U_{t,\ dpi}$ for all particle sizes using the Eqs. (4.2) to (4.6) or Eq. (4.7) depending upon the *dp*.

Step II : Select a suitable linear gas velocity *U* through the proposed settler. As a general rule *U* ranges between 0.3–3 m/s. Usually it is taken as 0.3 to 0.6 m/s.

Step III : Decide the settler length *L*. It is decided based on either the space available for installation of the settler or to meet the allowable pressure drop across the settler or to satisfy both.

Step IV : Evaluate the residence time in the chamber, τ,

where $\tau = L/U$

Step V : Estimate the settler height *H*. The equations/relations to be used for estimating *H* depends on whether the proposed settler is a single chamber settler or a multi-tray settler and whether the flow inside the settler is laminar or turbulent.

Step VI : The width *W* of the chamber is to be estimated using the relation $W = Q/HU$, obtained by balancing volumetric flow rate.

where Q = volumetric flow rate of the carrier gas.

(A) A Single Chamber Settler, Laminar Flow ($Re = \left(\frac{4\ R_H\ U\ \rho_g}{\mu_g}\right) < 2100$) Condition :

The settler height, *H*, is estimated based on the desired removal efficiency of the target particle size, *dpi*, using the relation,

$$H = \frac{\left(U_{t,\ dpi}\right)\tau}{\eta_{dpi}}. \tag{4.8}$$

For the particles having sizes other than *dpi* the removal efficiency is calculated using the relation.

$$\eta_{dp} = h_{dp}/H \tag{4.9}$$

where $h_{dp} = (U_{t,\ dp})\ \tau$.

Using the information obtained so far the overall efficiency of the settler is estimated with the help of the relation.

$$\eta_{overall} = \Sigma m_{dp} \times \eta_{dp} / \Sigma m_{dp} \tag{4.10}$$

It should be noted that η_{dp} may have a maximum value of 1.0.

In case the calculated value of $\eta_{overall}$ does not meet the desired performance of the settler, the Eqs. (4.8) to (4.10) are to be reworked based on a new (assumed) *dpi* or a new (assumed) η_{dpi} or a new set of *dpi* and η_{dpi} till the desired performance criterion is satisfied.

(B) Single Chamber Settler, Turbulent Flow Condition

The settler height *H* is estimated based on the target particle size *dpi* and assuming a separation efficiency $\eta_{dpi} = 1$ using the relation,

$$H = U_{t,\ dpi} \times \tau \tag{4.11}$$

For each of the other particles having diameter $dp \neq dpi$the settling height h_{dp} is calculated using Eq. (4. 12).

$$h_{dp} = U_{t,dp} \times \tau \tag{4.12}$$

Next the removal efficiencies of each of the different particle sizes having $dp < dpi$ are calculated using the Eq. (4.13)

$$\eta_{dp} = 1 - e^{\frac{-(U_{t,\ dp})\tau}{H}} = 1 - e^{\frac{-h_{dp}}{H}} \tag{4.13}$$

The separation efficiency of the particles having $dp > dpi$ is taken as 1.0. The total removal efficiency of all the particles is finally evaluated using Eq. (4.10).

In case the calculated overall performance based on Eq. (4.10) does not match the desired performance the Eqs. (4.10), (4.11), (4,12) and (4.13) are reworked choosing a different target particle size *dpi* till the desired performance is met.

(C) Multi-tray Settler Design

In the case of a multi-tray settler the distance between two consecutive trays H_t, is of importance. It is generally of the order of 30 cm. The number of trays in a chamber, *N*, is estimated using the relation,

$$N = (H/H_t). \tag{4.14}$$

Rearranging Eq. (4.14) the chamber height may be expressed as

$$H = NH_t. \tag{4.15}$$

It is evident that for estimation of *H*, H_t and *N* are to be preselected.

Once H_t is fixed the overall performance of a multi-tray settler has to be estimated using the appropriate Eqs. (4.2) to (4.13) depending on whether the flow is likely to be laminar or turbulent. The relation to be used for estimation of *W* would be

$$W = \frac{Q}{NH_tU}$$

If the performance of the proposed settler is found to be unsatisfactory the problem should be reworked assuming a new *N*.

The minimum sized particle which would be removed to a desired extent in a specified settler may be expressed as

$$dpi = \left[-\frac{18\mu_g Q\ ln(1-\eta_{dpi})}{NWL\ g\ (\rho_p - \rho_g)} \right]^{0.5}. \tag{4.16}$$

where g = acceleration due to gravity.

It should be pointed out here that the actual efficiency of a settler will be less than the calculated one using Eq. (4.10), because of the following reasons :

(i) re-entrainment of the settled particles,

(ii) particles do not attain their terminal velocities soon after entering a settler, and

(iii) non-spherical shape of the particles.

Example 4.1

It is proposed to install a gravity settler for complete removal of dust particles having 40 μm diameter from a carrier gas. The other pertinent information are :

Carrier gas flow rate = 21, 600 m^3/hr at 50°C and pressure slightly above 1 atm,

Particle density (ρ_p) = 2.5 g/cm^3.

The physical properties of the carrier gas may be taken as that of air at the operating condition.

Find : (a) suitable dimensions of a single chamber settler assuming laminar flow in the chamber,

(b) the removal efficiency of the same settler if the flow in the chamber be turbulent,

(c) if the same settler be fitted with trays approximately 30 cm apart what minimum sized particles may be removed with 100 percent efficiency?

Solution :

(a) Single chamber settler assumptions :

(i) flow inside the settler would be laminar,

(ii) Settling particle Reynolds number (Re_p) would be less than 2,

(iii) carrier gas velocity through the settler, U = 0.4 m/s.

Carrier gas density (ρ_g) at 50°C and 1 atm.

$$\rho_g = \frac{Molecular\ \ weight\ \ of\ \ air}{Molal\ \ volume\ \ of\ \ air\ \ at\ \ 50°C\ \&\ 1atm.}$$

$$\rho_g = \frac{28.84}{22.4 \times 323/273} = 1.088\ \ g/l = 1.088\ \ kg/m^3$$

Carrier gas viscosity (μ) at 50°C and 1 atm (from literature)

μ_g = 0.019 centipoise = 1.9 × 10^{-5} kg/m s.

The free settling velocity ($U_{t,\ dpi}$) is calculated using Eq. (4.2) and (4.3)

$$U_{t,\ dpi} = \left[\frac{4\ g\ dpi\left(\rho_p - \rho_g\right)}{3\ C_D \times \rho_g}\right]^{1/2}$$

and $C_D = 24 / Re_p$ for $Re_p < 2$

$Re_p = (dpi \times U_{t,\ dpi}\ \rho_g)/\mu_g$

The resulting expression for $U_{t,\ dpi,}$ according Eq. (4.7) is

$$U_{t,\ dpi} = \frac{g\ dpi^2\left(\rho_p - \rho_g\right)}{18\ \mu_g}$$

$$= \frac{9.81 \times \left(40 \times 10^{-6}\right)^2 (2500 - 1.088)}{18 \times 1.9 \times 10^{-5}} = 0.1147\ \ m/s.$$

To check $Re_p < 2$

$$Re_p = \frac{40\times10^{-6}\times0.1147\times1.088}{1.9\times10^{-5}} = 0.263 \text{ which is less than 2.}$$

The dimensions of a settler may be estimated using the following relations if the flow in the settler be laminar.

L (settler length) $= U\tau$
H (settler height) $= \eta_{dpi}\, U_{t,\,dpi}\, \tau$
W (settler width) $= Q/HU$

where Q = carrier gas volumetric flow rate,
U = carrier gas velocity through the settlers,
η_{dpi} = removal efficiency of particles having diameter dpi,
and τ = residence time in the settler.

The numerical values of L, H and W of a settler depend on the values of Q, U, $U_{t,\,dpi}$, η_{dpi} and τ.

For this example the values of Q, U, dpi and η_{dpi} are

dpi = 40 μm
Q = 21, 600 m^3/hr = 6 m^3/s
U = 0.4 m/s
$U_{t,\,dpi}$ = 0.1147 m/s
and η_{dpi} = 1.0 (complete removal of 40 μm particles).

Since τ is not specified, several values of τ are assumed and the corresponding values of L, H, and W are calculated as listed below :

τ, s	L, m	H, m	W, m
10	4	1.147	13.08
15	6	1.72	8.72
20	8	2.29	6.55

The dimensions of a suitable settler would depend on the space available for its installation.

Let the proposed settler dimensions be

$L = 8$ m, $H = 2.29$ m and $W = 6.55$ m corresponding to $\tau = 20$ s

Now it has to be checked whether the flow inside the settler would be laminar or turbulent by calculating Reynolds number,

$$Re = DU\rho_g/\mu_g$$

For a non-circular duct, $D = De = 4\,R_H = 4\left[\frac{WH}{2(W+H)}\right]$

$$= 3.39 \text{ m.}$$

$$Re = \frac{3.39\times0.4\times1.088}{1.9\times10^{-5}} = 77{,}649.$$

Hence the flow inside the settler would be turbulent.

(b) Since the flow inside the settler would be turbulent its efficiency should be estimated using Eq. (4.13)

$$\eta_{dpi} = 1 - e^{\frac{-U_{t,\,dpi} \times \tau}{H}}$$

$$= 1 - e^{\frac{-0.1147 \times 20}{2.29}} = 0.632 = 63.2\%.$$

(c) If the proposed settler be fitted with trays approximately 30 cm apart, the number of trays inside the settler would be

$$N = \frac{H}{H_t} = \frac{2.29}{0.3} = 7.33 \approx 8.$$

This would result in a tray spacing, $H_t = 2.29/8 = 0.28$ m

The linear velocity of gas in the settler would be

$$U = \frac{Q}{NWH_t} = \frac{6}{8 \times 6.55 \times 0.28} = 0.41m.$$

$$And \ \text{Re} = \frac{De \ U \ \rho_g}{\mu_g}$$

$$= \frac{4(WH_t) \times 0.41 \times 1.088}{2(W + H_{t)}) \times 1.9 \times 10^{-5}} = 11680.$$

Therefore, the flow would be turbulent.

As the flow inside the multi-tray settler would be turbulent, the minimum sized particles which would be completely removed may be calculated using Eq. (4.16)

$$dpi = \left[\frac{-18\mu_g Q \ In(1 - \eta_{dpi})}{NWLg(\rho_p - \rho_g)}\right]^{0.5}.$$

Complete removal means $\eta_{dpi} = 1$, However substitution of $\eta_{dpi} = 1$ in the above equation would result in an indeterminate *dpi*. Hence η_{dpi} is taken as 0.999 and and *dpi* calculated using Eq. (4.16),

$$dpi = \left[\frac{-18 \times 1.9 \times 10^{-5} \times 6 \times In(1 - 0.999)}{8 \times 6.55 \times 8 \times 9.81(2500 - 1.088)}\right]^{0.5}$$

$= 37.1$ μm.

4.2.2 Inertial Separator

Suspended solid particles carried by a gas stream attain almost the same velocity as the gas stream itself. As a result the momentum and hence the inertia (of motion) of the larger and denser particles are more compared to those of the lighter and finer particles. When such a gas stream changes its direction of flow inside an equipment, the direction of flow of the particles having higher inertia continue to follow the old (previous) direction and finally come to rest after impinging on some surface. The lighter and finer particles get carried away by the gas stream itself as the drag force overcomes the inertia. Such an equipment is termed as an **'inertial separator'**. The dust removal efficiency of an inertial separator can be improved only by reducing the drag force on the particles. This can be achieved by lowering the gas velocity in the separation zone.

Inertial separators are of different types. Figure 4.3 shows sketches of some types of inertial separators.

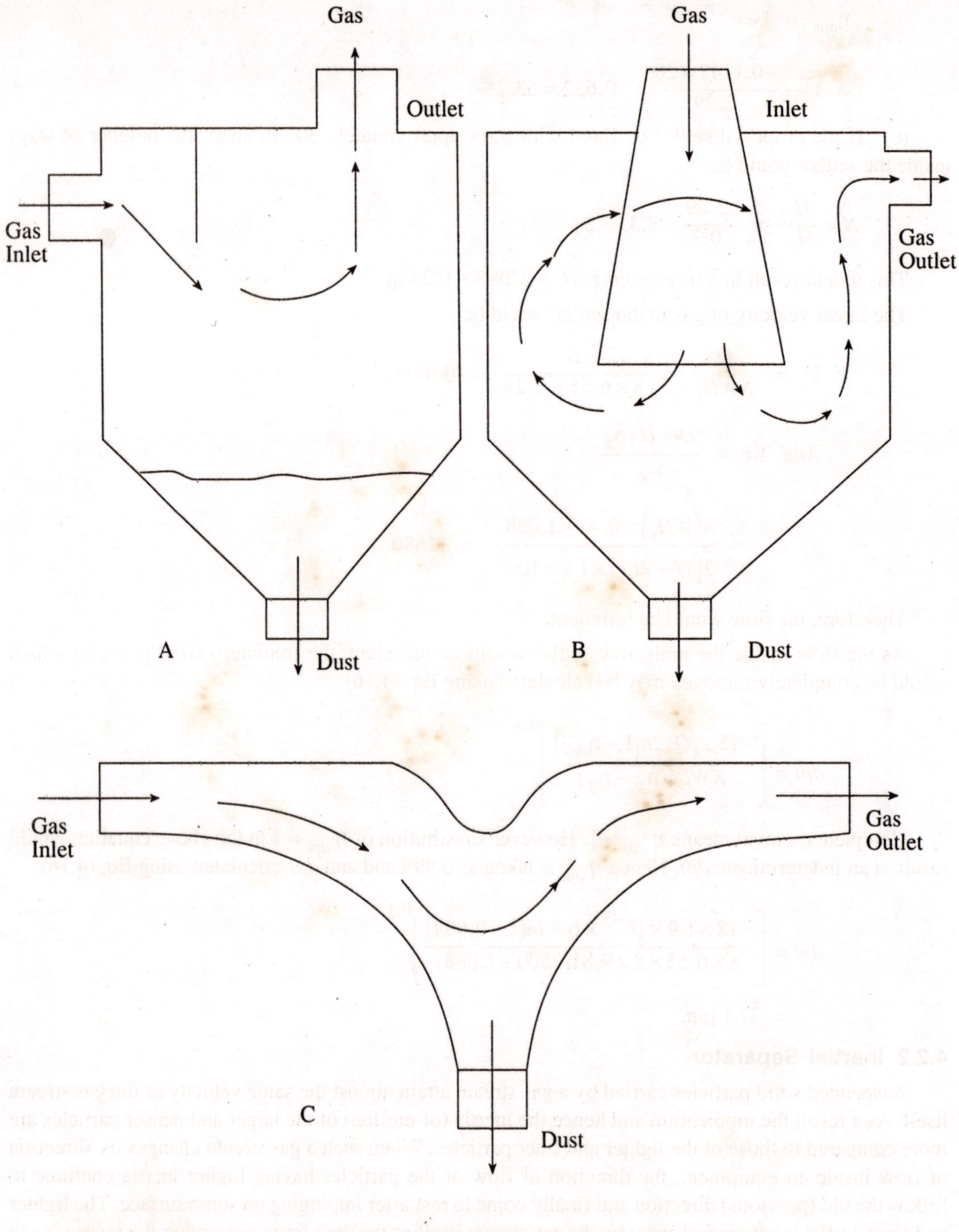

Fig. 4.3 : Sketches of Some Types of Inertial Separators.

A. Baffle Type, B. Downward Entry Type, C. Rounded Trap Type.

The entering gas velocity in an inertial separator may be around 10 m/s and that in the separator is normally about 1 m/s. The size of an inertial separator is ususally smaller than that of a gravity settler having similar capacity and efficiency, but the pressure drop would be higher.

For an inertial separator there is no pressure and temperature limitation.

4.2.3 Centrifugal Separator

A centrifugal separator is commonly known as a cyclone separator. It is an inertial type of separator, however, the force which brings about separation, is centrifugal. Its upper part is cylindrical, whereas the lower portion is an inverted truncated cone. Dust laden gas enters the cylinder near the top either through a side opening or axially through the top with a tangential velocity. The clean gas comes out at the top through a central circular outlet. The separated solid particles are discharged through a central outlet at the bottom.

In the case of a side entry cyclone the inlet to the cyclone is placed tangentially and hence the entering gas acquires a tangential velocity. The axial entry cyclones are fitted with vanes so as to impart a tangential velocity to the entering gas.

The dust laden gas after entering a cyclone moves downwards as a descending outer vortex because of its tangential velocity, reaches almost the cone apex and then it reverses its direction, moving upwards as an ascending inner vortex. Finally the gas leaves the cyclone through a centrally located outlet at the top.

The larger and heavier dust particles while moving downwards along with the spirally moving gas stream experience a centrifugal force, as a result of which they migrate towards the wall. Finally they slide down towards the bottom outlet, which is generally fitted with a rotary valve.

The finer and lighter particles are carried away by the outgoing gas stream.

The centrifugal force acting on a particle of mass m may be expressed as:

$$F = m \times a \tag{4.17}$$

where a = acceleration = $U_{\tan}^2 / R$,

U_{tan} = tangential velocity,

R = cyclone radius,

$m = \dfrac{\pi dp^3 \rho_p}{6}$ (assuming the particle to be spherical),

dp = particle diameter,

ρ_p = particle density.

Hence,
$$F = \frac{\pi}{6}\, dp^3 \rho_p \, \frac{U_{\tan}^2}{R} \tag{4.18}$$

From Eq. (4.18) it is evident that for a particle having a diameter d_p and density ρ_p the centrifugal force acting on it is directly proportional to $U_{\tan}$ and inversely proportional to R. Hence, its removal efficiency in a cyclone would increase with the increase in $U_{\tan}$ and decrease with the increase in R.

Cyclones having diameters 1 m or more can handle higher gas flow rates but are less efficient in removing particles finer than 30 μm. Pressure drop across such a cyclone may be about 2.5-15 cm of water. Cyclones having a diameter 30 cm or less are referred to as high efficiency cyclones. Their gas handling capacity is less but they are quite efficient in removing particles as small as 10 μm. Pressure drop across a small cyclone is usually about 10 cm to 30 cm of water. Because of their low gas handling capacity several cyclones are often operated parallely and are placed in a single housing. Such an assembly is referred to as a multi-cyclone.

Figure 4.4 shows a sketch of a standard cyclone. The dimensions of the different portions of such a cyclone are expressed as ratios to its diameter. These ratios differ somewhat depending on the cyclone type. Cyclones are classified as high efficiency, medium efficiency and conventional cyclone. In Table 4.5 the relative dimensions of above named types of cyclones are listed.

Table 4.5 : Relative Dimensions of the Different Portions of Standard Cyclones

Portion Fig. 4.4	Proportion Relative to Diameter		D_c
	High Efficiency	Medium Efficiency	Conventional
B_c	0.2	0.375	0.25
D_c	1	1	1
D_e	0.5	0.75	0.5
H_c	0.5	0.75	0.5
J_c	—	—	0.25
L_c	1.5	1.5	2.0
S_c	0.5	0.875	0.625
Z_c	2.5	2.5	2.0

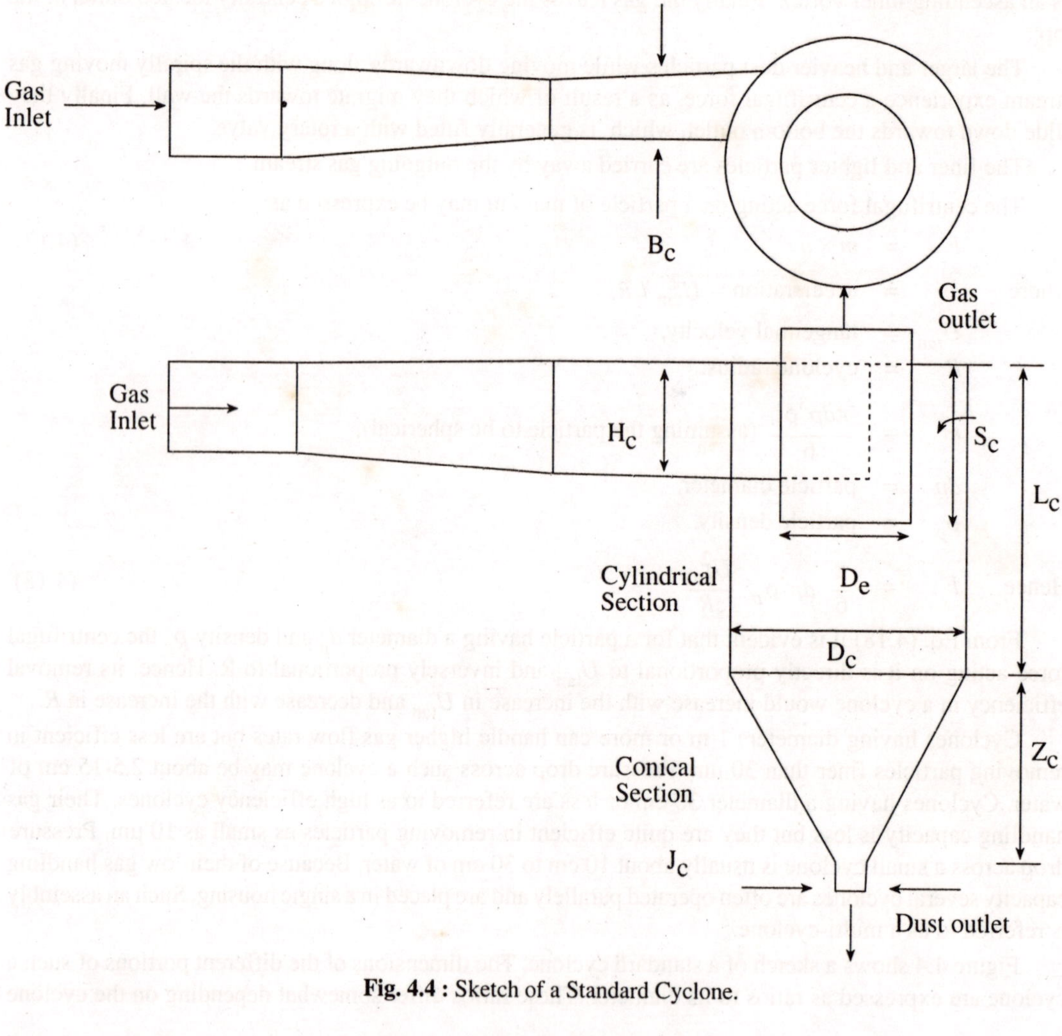

Fig. 4.4 : Sketch of a Standard Cyclone.

The advantages of a cyclone separator are its simplicity in construction and lower cost. As there are no moving parts in a cyclone its maintenance cost is low. It requires less floor space. A properly designed cyclone may be operated at a pressure as high as 500 atm and temperature as high as 1000°C.

Design Approach of a Cyclone Separator

In order to design a cyclone the size analysis of the dust particles present in an influent gas stream should be available. The particle cut size d_{50} must also be known. d_{50} stands for the particle diameter, 50% (by mass) of which needs to be removed from a dust laden gas stream.

Once these information are known a cyclone diameter D_c is assumed, d_{50} corresponding to that D_c is calculated using the procedure given hereunder. If the calculated d_{50} does not match the desired d_{50} a new D_c is assumed and the calculation is repeated.

After establishing the D_c, the removal efficiencies of the dust particles having diameters other than d_{50} are estimated using a plot as shown in Fig. 4.5.

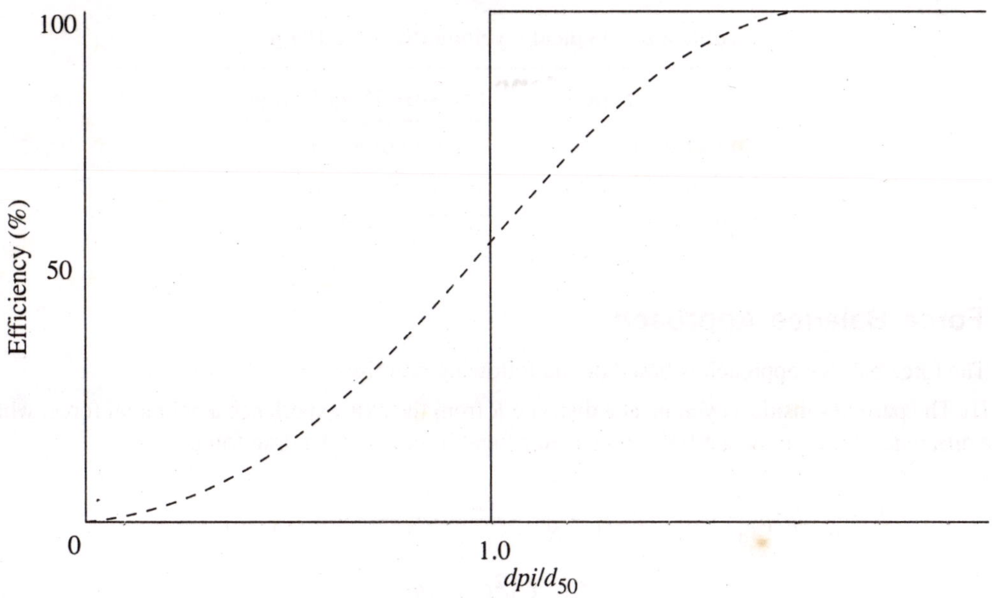

Fig. 4.5 : Cyclone Efficiency vs. dpi/d_{50}.

The overall efficiency of the proposed cyclone is then calculated using the relation given in Eq. (4.10)

$$\eta_{overall} = \Sigma m_{dpi}.\eta_{dpi} / \Sigma m_{dpi}.$$

There are two approaches in designing a cyclone separator :

(1) Lapple's approach and (2) Force balance approach.

1. Lapple's Approach

This approach is based on the following expression for d_{50}

$$d_{50} = \left[\frac{9\ \mu_g\ B_c}{2\pi\ N_e U_I(\rho_p - \rho_g)}\right]^{1/2} \tag{4.19}$$

where N_e = effective number of turns in the descending outer vortex which generally

ranges between 1 and 10 $\approx \dfrac{\left[L_c+(Z_c/2)\right]}{H_c}$

U_I = entering gas velocity which ranges between 6 to 24 m/s

Usually it is taken as 16 m/s.

The corresponding expression for pressure drop across a cyclone is

$$\Delta P = \frac{13\ \rho_g U_I^2 H_c B_c}{2\ D_e^2} \tag{4.20}$$

The pressue drop depends on the cyclone type. Some typical data are listed in Table 4.6.

Table 4.6 : Typical Cyclone Pressure Drop

Cyclone Type	Pressure Drop Range
Low efficiency	5-10 cm of water
Medium efficiency	10-15 cm of water
High efficiency	20-25 cm of water

2. Force Balance Approach

The force balance approach is based on the following premises :

(i) The particles inside a cyclone at a distance R from the axis experience a net radial force, which is the difference between the net field force (centrifugal force), and the drag force.

$$F = \frac{\pi}{6}\ dp^3\rho_p\left[1-(\rho_g/\rho_p)\right]\ \frac{U_{\tan}^2}{R} - \frac{C_D\ U_R^2\ \rho_g \pi dp^2}{8}$$

$$= \frac{\pi}{6}\ dp^3\ \rho_p\ \frac{U_{\tan}^2}{R} - \frac{C_D\ U_R{}^2 \rho_g \pi\ dp^2}{8},\ (\text{since}\ \rho_g << \rho_p) \tag{4.21}$$

assuming the particles to be spherical,

where U_{tan} = tangential velocity,

U_R = radial velocity,

C_D = drag coefficient,

= $24/Re_p$, for $Re_p < 2$

(ii) Particles having a diameter d_{50} will be subjected to a net force zero at

$R = R_o = De/2$

(R_o = radius of exit core. It is approximately half of that of the gas outlet duct).

Hence at $R = R_o$, the Eq. (4.21) simplifies to

$$U_{R_o}^2 = \frac{U^2{}_{\tan,\ R_o}}{R_o} \times \frac{4}{3}\ \frac{\rho_p}{\rho_g}\ \frac{d_{50}}{C_D}, \tag{4.22}$$

$$\text{where } C_D = \frac{\dfrac{24}{d_{50}\, U_{R_o}\, \rho_g}}{\mu_g}.$$

Rearrangement of Eq. (4.22) yields,

$$d_{50} = \left[\frac{18\mu_g R_o\, U_{R_o}}{\rho_p\, U^2_{\tan,\, R_o}}\right]^{1/2}. \tag{4.23}$$

(iii) $U_{\tan,R} = \dfrac{Constant}{R^{0.5}}$ *for* $\dfrac{D_e}{2} \leq R \leq \dfrac{D_c}{2}$

$$\text{Hence, } U_{\tan,R_o} = U_{\tan,\, R_1} \times \left(R_1 / R_o\right)^{1/2} \tag{4.24}$$

where $R_1 = \left(D_C - B_C\right)/2.$

$$\text{(iv)} \quad U_{R_o} = \frac{Q}{2\,\pi\, R_o\left[L_C + Z_C - S_C\right]} \tag{4.25}$$

where Q = Volumetric gas flow rate.

(v) An expression for $U_{tan,}\, R_1$ is obtained by balancing the moments of forces of the fluid at the inlet and outlet and the wall shear force about the cyclone axis.

$$\frac{U_{\tan,\, R_1}}{U_I} = \frac{\left[\left(R_o / R_1\right) + 4fs\,\left(A_S / A_1\right)\right]^{1/2} - \left(R_o / R_1\right)^{1/2}}{2\; fs\left(A_s / A_1\right)} \tag{4.26}$$

where fs is analogous to the friction factor = 1/200

A_1 is the inlet duct cross-sectional area $= B_c H_c$

A_s is cyclone surface area exposed to the

Spinning gas $\approx \pi\, \left(D_C L_C + D_C Z_C + D_e S_c\right)$

The design procedure is to select a d_{50} and assume a cyclone diameter D_c. The cyclone diameter D_c should be so chosen that $U_I = Q/B_C\, H_C$ is within the operating inlet velocity range (6—24 m/s, usually 16 m/s).

Next d_{50} is calculated utilizing Eqs. (4.25), (4.24), (4.23) and (4.22). In case the calculated d_{50} does not match the pre-selected d_{50}, the steps are repeated with another assumed cyclone diameter. The process is repeated till a cyclone diameter is found which results in a d_{50} close to the pre-selected d_{50}.

Pressure drop across such a cyclone may be calculated using the relation.

$$\Delta P = \rho_g \left(U^2_{\tan,R_o} - U^2_{\tan,R_1} + U_0^{\,2} + U_I^{\,2} / 2\right) \tag{4.27}$$

where U_0 = Cyclone exit velocity = $\dfrac{Q}{\dfrac{\pi}{4}\, D_e^2}$

It should be pointed out here that the actual separation efficiency would be less than that calculated using Eq. (4.10) because of the following effects :

1. bouncing back of particles from the wall into the inner vortex,
2. particles being picked up from the cone apex by hopper flow, and
3. re-entrainment of particles because of eddies.

Example 4.2

A conventional cyclone separator is to be designed for removing 50 percent of particles having a diameter 5 μm and density 2.5 g/cm^3 from a gas (air) stream flowing at a rate of 7200 m^3/hour at 30°C.

Solution :

From literature the viscosity of air at 30°C is found to be 0.018 centipoise.

0.018 centipoise = 1.8×10^{-4} g/cms = 1.8×10^{-5} kg/m s.

A preliminary estimate of a cyclone diameter (D_C) to meet the above mentioned duty is obtained using the Lapple's approach, Eq. (4.19) assuming

$U_I = 16 m/s$ *and* $\rho_p >> \rho_{g\,(air)}$

Given data :

$\rho_p = 2.5$ g/cm^3 = 2500 kg/m^3

$d_{50} = 5$ μm = 5×10^{-6}m

Q = volumetric gas flow rate

= 7200 m^3/hr = 2 m^3/s .

From Eq. (4.19)

$$d_{50} = \left[\frac{9\ \mu_g\ B_c}{2\ \pi\ N_e\ U_I(\rho_p - \rho_g)}\right]^{1/2}$$

where $N_e = \dfrac{[L_C + (Z_C/2)]}{H_C}$.

For a conventional cyclone $H_C = 0.5\ D_C,\ L_C = 2\ D_C,\ Z_C = 2\ D_C$ *and* $B_C = 0.25\ D_C$

Hence $N_e = (1/0.5\ D_C)\ [2\ D_C + (2\ D_C/2)] = 6$

Rearrangement of Eq. (4.19) enables one to estimate B_c and subsequently D_c.

$$B_C = 0.25 D_C = \frac{d_{50}^{\ 2} \times 2\pi\ N_e\ U_I\ \rho_p}{9\ \mu_g}$$

$$= \frac{(5 \times 10^{-6})^2 \times 2\pi \times 6 \times 16 \times 2500}{9 \times 1.8 \times 10^{-5}} = 0.2327\,\text{m}.$$

Hence the estimated cyclone diameter,

$D_C = 4 \times B_C = 4 \times 0.2327 = 0.93$ m.

Following the force balance approach a cyclone diameter, D_c, is assumed and d_{50} is calculated with the help of Eq. (4.23).

$$d_{50} = \left(\frac{18\mu_g R_o U_{R_o}}{\rho_p U^2_{\tan,\ R_o}} \right)^{1/2}$$

First trial : Assumed $D_c = 0.9\ m.$

$$R_O = \frac{D_e}{2} = \frac{D_c}{4} = 0.225\ m$$

From Eq. (4.25),

$$U_{R_o} = \frac{Q}{2\ \pi\ R_o\ [L_C + Z_C - S_C]}$$

$L_C = 2D_C = 1.8$ m,
$Z_C = 2D_C = 1.8$ m,
$S_C = 0.625\ D_C = 0.5625$ m

$$U_{R_o} = \frac{2}{2\pi \times 0.225(1.8 + 1.8 - 0.5625)}$$

$= 0.466$ m/s.

From Eq. (4.24)

$$U_{\tan, R_o} = U_{\tan, R_1} \times (R_1 / R_o)^{1/2},$$

where $R_1 = \dfrac{D_C - B_C}{2} = \dfrac{D_C - (D_C/4)}{2} = \dfrac{D_C(1-0.25)}{2}$

$= 0.3375$ m.

From Eq. (4.26),

$$\frac{U_{\tan,\ R_1}}{U_I} = \frac{[(R_o/R_1) + 4 fs\ (A_s/A_1)]^{1/2} - (R_o/R_1)^{1/2}}{2\ fs(As/A_1)}$$

$$U_I = \frac{Q}{B_C\ H_C} = \frac{Q}{D_C/4 \times D_C/2} = 19.753\ m/s$$

$fs = 1/200$

$$A_1 = B_C H_C = D_C^2/8 = 0.10125\ m^2$$

$$A_s = \pi\ (D_C L_C + D_C Z_C + D_e S_C) = 10.974 m^2$$

$$U_{\tan, R_1} = \frac{19.753 \left\{ \left(\frac{0.225}{0.3375} + \frac{4 \times 10.974}{200 \times 0.10125} \right)^{1/2} - \left(\frac{0.225}{0.3375} \right)^{1/2} \right\}}{\frac{2 \times 10.974}{200 \times 0.10125}}$$

$= 15.803$ m/s.

$$U_{\tan,R_o} = U_{\tan,R_1} \times \left(\frac{R_1}{R_o}\right)^{1/2}$$

$$= 15.803 \times \left(\frac{0.3375}{0.225}\right)^{1/2}$$

$$= 19.3543.$$

From Eq. (4.23),

$$d_{50} = \left(\frac{18\mu_g Ro\ U_{RO}}{\rho_p\ U^2_{\tan,\ RO}}\right)^{1/2}$$

$$= \left(\frac{18 \times 1.8 \times 0^{-5} \times 0.225 \times 0.46}{2500 \times 19.3543^2}\right)^{1/2}$$

$$= 6.02\ \mu m > 5\ \mu m.$$

Second trial :

Assumed $D_C = 0.8$ m.

$R_o = D_C/4 = 0.2$ m

$$U_{R_o} = \frac{Q}{2\ \pi R_o[L_C + Z_C - S_C]} = 0.5894\ m/s$$

$$U_I = \frac{Q}{B_C H_C} = 25\ m/s$$

$$R_1 = \frac{D_C - B_C}{2} = 0.3\ m$$

$$A_1 = B_C\ H_C = 0.08\ m^2$$

$$A_s = \pi\left(4\ D_c^2 + 0.3125\ D_c^2\right) = 8.671\ m^2$$

$$\frac{U_{\tan,\ R_1}}{U_I} = \frac{\left[(R_o / R_1) + 4 fs(A_s / A_1)\right]^{1/2} - (R_o / R_1)^{1/2}}{2\ fs\ (A_s / A_1)} = 20\ m/s.$$

$$U_{\tan,R_o} = U_{\tan,R_1} \times (R_1 / R_o)^{1/2} = 24.495.$$

$$d_{50} = \left(\frac{18\ \mu_g R_o U_{R_o}}{\rho_p U^2_{\tan,R_o}}\right)^{1/2} = 5.05\ \mu m \approx 5.0\ \mu m.$$

The calculated Cyclone diameter is 0.8 m.

4.2.4 Filters

Unlike the other types of separation devices discussed earlier filtration operation is carried out in a semi-batch mode. During the first part of the operation dust particles from a dust laden gas stream are arrested in the device itself and a relatively clean (dust free) gas stream flows out. The component in a filter, which actually arrests the dust particles is referred to as a filter medium. As the amount of accumulated dust particles on the filter medium increases the resistance to gas flow increases. It results in an increase in the pressure difference across the filter with time. Finally, a stage is reached when the pressue difference equals a pre-set value. At this point the gas inflow is stopped and the next stage of the operation, that is removal of the accumulated dust particles (cleaning) is started. After a substantial quantity of the accumulated dust has been removed the filtration operation (inflow of dust laden gas) is resumed.

Filters are classified according to the type of filter medium used. The media used are :

1. aggregate medium (gravel) and
2. fibrous medium (paper, fibrous mat, felt, woven fabrics, etc.).

4.2.4.1 Gravel Filter

Aggregate filter medium is used for high temperature and other special applications. A typical filter installation consists of several filter modules arranged parallely. A module is shown in Fig. 4.6.

One of the most appealing aspects of a gravel filter is its capacity to withstand high temperature. Gravels found in natural formation is used. Its selection depends on the influent gas temperature. Quartz gravels can withstand an operating temperature close to 800 °C. However, the actual operating temperature limitation of a gravel filter depends on the structural material used for its construction. The moving parts of a gravel filter are a back flash valve and a raking mechanism. Since these are operated intermittently, the wear on these parts are low. The bottom of the filter acts as a cyclone separator. During the cleaning operation air or some other gas is allowed to flow in the opposite direction and the raking mechanism is switched on. The dislodged dust particles get collected in the hopper below. The accumulated dust particles are removed from the hopper from time to time. The pressure drop across a gravel filter may range between 12–40 cm of water.

4.2.4.2 Fabric Filter

Some fibrous media, such as paper and fibrous mat are difficult to clean and reuse and hence those are usually disposed off after use. These are not suitable for industrial gas cleaning.

Fibrous media, like, woven and felt cloths are extensively used for recovery of valuable materials from industrial waste gases as well as to check air pollution.

A fabric filter also known as a **bag filter** uses tubes (made of cloth) open at one end and closed at the other as the filtering medium. Several tubes are suspended vertically in a housing from a wire frame with the open ends located at the bottom. Dust laden gas enters a housing near its bottom and moves up the tubes through their open ends. The clean gas flows out through the cylindrical surfaces of the tubes while the dust particles are retained inside. A suitable mechanism is incorporated in the housing for removal (cleaning operation) of the accumulated dust particles from time to time. Cleaning operation may be carried out online or off-line.

Pre-treatment

The fabrics used cannot withstand high temperature. Hence it is necessary to cool the incoming gas so as to bring down its temperature below the recommended maximum operating temperature of the fabric chosen. It should be borne in mind that the entering gas should be within 30 °-60 °C above its dew point as otherwise condensation may occur on the bag surfaces. Condensation would result in clinging of moist solid particles to the filter media , which would hinder the cleaning operation.

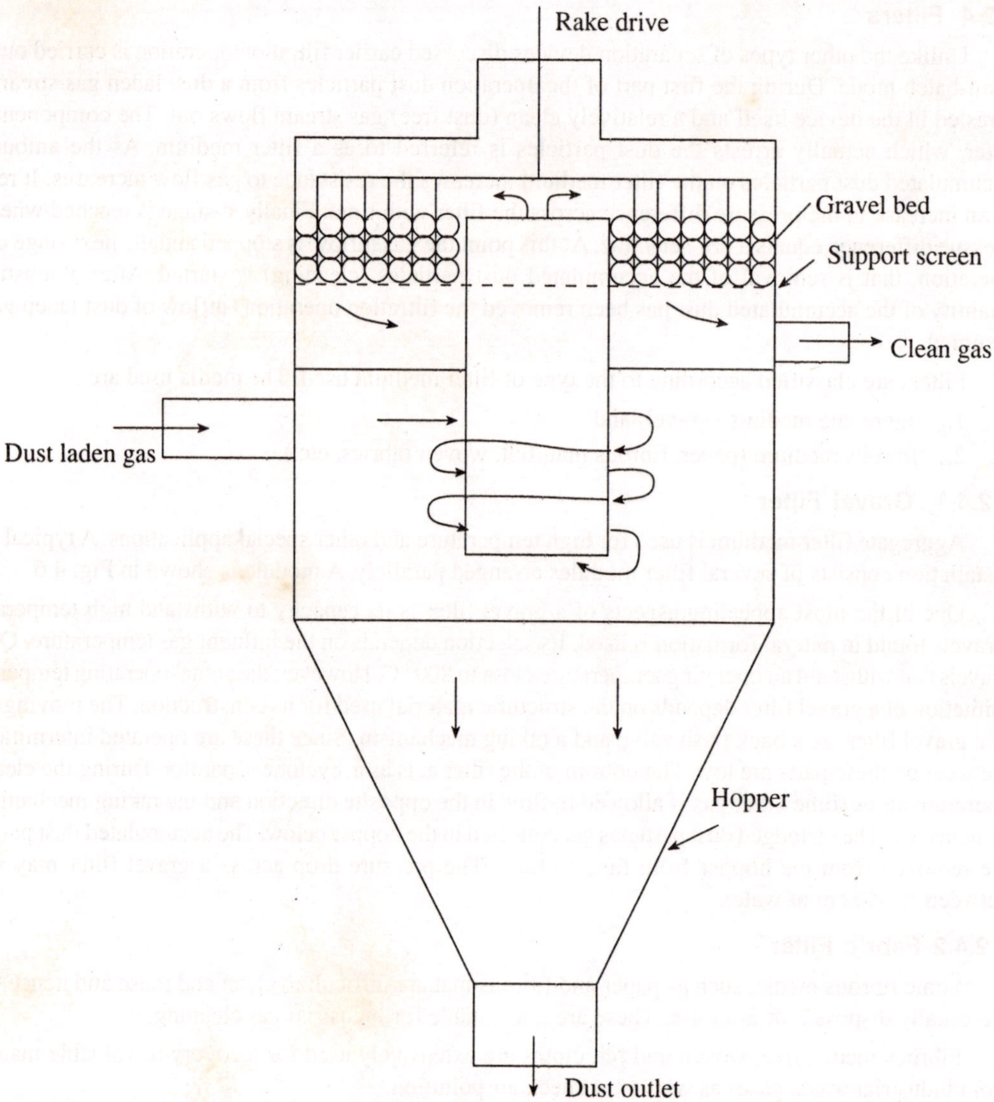

Fig. 4.6 : Schematic Diagram of a Gravel Filter.

To reduce the load on a fabric filter it would be better to preclean the entering gas using a gravity settler/cylone separator so as to remove particles larger than 20-30 μm when appreciable amounts of those are present.

Fabric Filtration Mechanism

Particulate matter from a carrier gas is removed by fabrics by sieving, direct impaction, interception owing to Van der Waal's force, Brownian diffusion and electrostatic attraction. Electrostatic charge generation may be due to friction between gas and fabrics and between the particles and fabrics.

Woven cloths are made by weaving yarns. When new, the gaps between the yarns are fairly large and some of the particles penetrate the pores easily. Some particles are arrested on the cloth. As filtration continues more and more dust particles accumulate on the cloth and thereby form a 'filter cake'. The cake now acts as the filter medium and it is more effective than the cloth itself.

Felt cloth is made by pushing barbed needles through two or more layers of woven cloth and thereby combining them and then roughing up the surface layer. The inside layer gives strength and dimensional stability, while the randomly oriented fine fabrics on the surface provide high collection efficiency for small particles.

Fabric Materials

Filter bags are made from cotton, wool, acrylics, nylon, nomex, polyester, polypropylene, teflon and fiber glass. Of the nine fabrics named the first two are natural and the rest are synthetic. While selecting a fabric for a specific situation the following factors should be taken into consideration : operating temperature, carrier gas acidity/ alkalinity, abrasiveness of the particles, air-to-cloth ratio and finally its cost. The characteristics of the above named fabrics are listed in Table 4.7.

Table 4.7 : Characteristics of Filter Fabrics

	Temperatures °C		Resistance to					
Fabric	**Max. Surge**	**Opera-ting**	**Abra-sion**	**Acid Mineral**	**Acid Org.**	**Alkali**	**Fluo-ride**	**Solvent**
Cotton	105	80	G	P	G	G	P	E
Wool	120	95	G	F	F	P/F	—	G
Polyamide (Nylon 6 & 66)	120	95	E	P	F	V.G.	—	E
Aromatic Polyamide (Nomex)	50	40	E	F	G	V.G.	G	E
Polyester (Dacron)	160	135	E	G	G	G	P/F	E
Polyolefin (Polypropylene)	90	90	E	E	E	E	P	G
Polyfluoro-carbon (Teflon)	260	65	F	E	E	E	P/F	E
Acrylic (Orlon)	125	115	G	G	G	F	—	E
Fiber glass	290	260	F	V.G.	E	P	P	E

Note: E—Excellent, F—Fair, G—Good, P—Poor,
V.G.—Very Good.

Filter Cleaning

Periodic cleaning of filter bags is essential to maintain the desired gas flow rate. Cleaning can be achieved either by flexing a bag and thereby breaking up and dislodging the dust layers or by reversed air flow through bags or by a combination of both. Mechanical shaking of bags by flexing them is quite effective in dust removal unless the particles are too deeply imbedded in the fabrics. However, mechanical shaking results in more fabric wear. Woven fabrics can endure such treatment. Fragile fabrics, such as fiber glass and felt cloth should not be subjected to mechanical shaking. Air cleaning can be brought about in several ways, such as, reverse air flow, pulse jet and blow-ring.

Reverse flow cleaning is carried out by taking off-stream a module. High volume low-pressure air is allowed to flow counter-current to the normal flow direction. Because of reverse flow flexing of bags takes place and dust layers are dislodged. Sonic generators are sometimes used to augment the cleaning operation. As this process does not cause much strain to the fabric it may be conveniently used for fragile fabrics also.

In pulse jet cleaning a stream of high pressue (upto about 9 kg/cm^2) air jet is introduced into a bag at its top for a short duration (about 0.1 sec or less). As the jet expands the bag experiences a shock and shaking. The resulting cleaning is quite good. Pulse-jet cleaning may be used for cleaning all types of fabrics other than cotton and fiber glass. The process may be used online or offline. A pulse-jet cleaner does not have any moving parts.

A blow-ring type cleaner uses a jet of air issuing through a series of orifices on the inside of a hollow metal ring, which closely encircles a bag. The ring is moved up and down the outside of a bag by a motorized chain and sprocket arrangement. Air from a blower is directed to the ring through a flexible hose. The air jet impinges on a small portion of a bag and pushes that portion inward. The filter cake is broken and dislodged. Since during this type of cleaning operation the remaining portions of the bag may continue to operate normally it may be carried out online. Any type of fabric, woven, felted or fragile may be cleaned using this technique, as those are not strained much. This type of cleaning arrangement is not used for large installations because of its high cost and complicated machinery.

The System

A bag house is generally made of several modules, each module being an independent unit. In each module several bags are housed properly supported. The bag diameter may range between 7 to 30 cm. Generally it is about 15 cm. The height of a bag may range between 0.75 m to 8 m.

Dust laden gas enters a module through an inlet duct. The inlet ducts of the different modules are connected to a common manifold. Very often baffles and diffusers are provided in a manifold for proper distribution of the dust-laden gas. During filtration gas may flow from inside to outside of a bag or the other way. The clean gas may be discharged into the atmosphere directly from a module or ducted to another common manifold for further treatment.

Each module is provided with a suitable bag-cleaning gadget, mechanical or pneumatic as discussed earlier. Each module would have a hopper to receive the dust dislodged during cleaning operation. Each hopper in turn is fitted with a dust-discharging device, such as a double trapping valve or a rotary air lock.

Even non-flammable dusts may be explosive and hence each module is provided with a protection device/ devices, such as explosion-proof electrical fittings, explosion vent (explosion door/hinged panel), and sprinklers to take care of an emergency situation. Access doors are provided for replacement of defective bags and other maintenance work. Figure 4.7 shows a schematic diagram of bag filter module.

Sizing a Bag Filter

To estimate the total (net) cloth area required the following basic information are required :

Gas flow rate, in m^3/min;

Gas moisture content, in % R. H;

Gas temperature, in °C;

Particle load, in g/m^3 of carrier gas,

Particle size distribution, in µm;

SO_2 content (if any), in ppm;

Particle (solid) density, in g/cm^3;

Gas Acidity/Alkalinity.

Based on the above mentioned information one has to select a suitable fabric and its type, i.e., woven/felted. Consistent with the selected fabric and its type, a cleaning method is also to be selected. Next the filtration rate expressed as air-to-cloth ratio (A/C) is ascertained utilizing the data given in Table 4.8. The air-to-cloth ratio depends on the composition of the dust particles, cleaning method to be employed as well as whether woven/felted fabric has been chosen.

Table 4.8 : Air-To-Cloth Ratio, A/C, $\frac{m^3 gas}{min} \times \frac{1}{m^2}$

Cleaning Method	Shaker	Pulse Jet	Reverse Air
A/C	0.5-1.2	1.5-4.5	0.3-0.66

Air-to-Cloth ratio should be chosen based on manufacturers guideline. Normally a lower value is assumed for the woven cloth and a higher value for the felt cloth.

The gross cloth area is estimated as :

$$A_{gross} = F \times A_{net}. \tag{4.28}$$

Where, $A_{net} = Q/_{A/C}$

A/C Air-To-Cloth Ratio, in $\frac{m^3 gas}{min\ m^2}$

Q gas flow rate, in m^3 gas/min and F factor ranging between 1.04 to 2.

1.04 for a very large value of A_{net} and 2 for a small value of A_{net}.

Bag House Efficiency and Pressure Drop

Bag house efficiency depends on the dust particle size, particle loading, the fabric used and the cleaning method employed. A properly designed unit may have an efficiency of 99% or more for particle size larger than 1 µm. The pressure drop is normally of the order of 7.5 to 15 cm of water.

4.2.5 Electrostatic Precipitator (ESP)

Of the different types of dry particle separators electrostatic precipitators are the most efficient. The process basically consists of passing a dust laden gas through a conduit in which a high voltage d.c. field is maintained. The dust particles get charged and are deposited on the grounded (electrically) surface of the conduit while the clean gas flows out of the conduit. The conduit may be horizontal (made up of two parallel plates facing each other and closed at the top) or vertical (a pipe). Horizontal type ESP is more common. Exactly midway between the two plates several metal pieces (wires strips) are kept suspended. These serve as the discharge electrodes and the plates as the collectors. In the case of a vertical pipe a wire suspended vertically along the centre line serves as the discharge electrode and the inner surface of the pipe acts as the collector. The collected dust particles are dislodged periodically by rapping, vibrating or washing the collector surfaces.

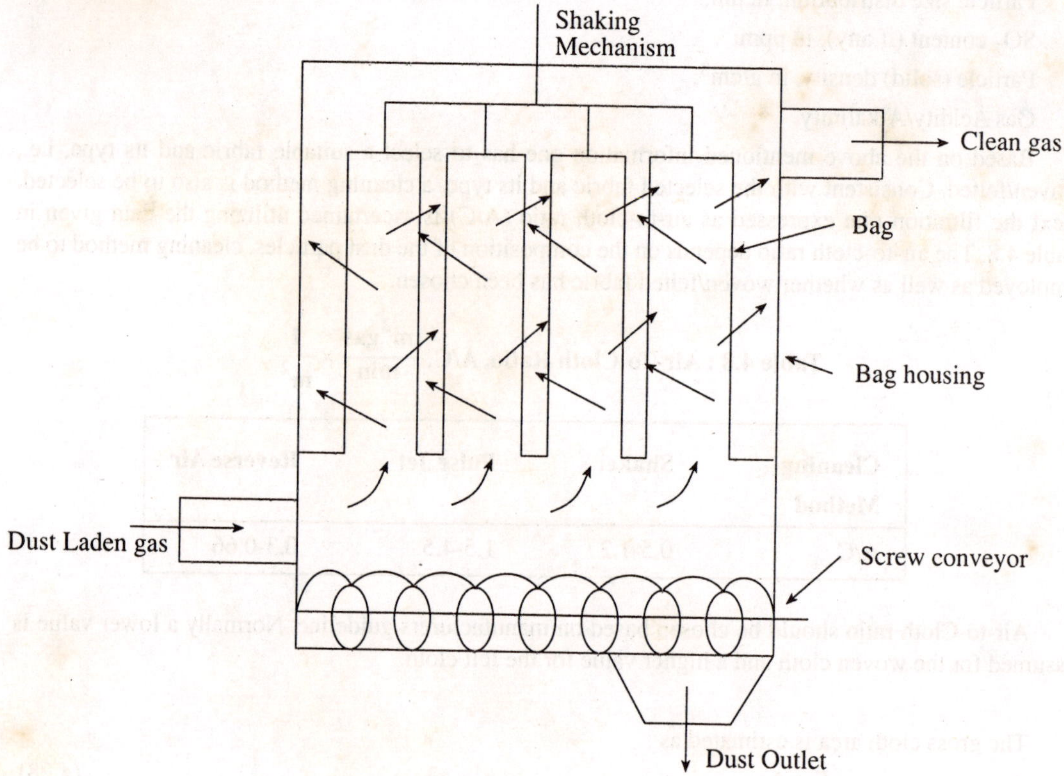

Fig. 4.7 : Schematic Diagram of a Bag Filter.

The dislodged dust particles are finally collected in a hopper placed below the conduit and those are removed periodically with the help of a suitable mechanical device. In the case of a horizontal ESP dust laden gas flows horizontally in between the plates from one end to the other whereas in a vertical ESP the gas flows vertically upward.

For dry collection dust build-up on the collector is allowed up to about 6 mm or more and then strongly rapped so that dust is dislodged as large clumps, which would not be re-entrained. Weaker and frequent rapping would produce flakes of dislodged dust, which may be easily re-entrained. Wet collectioin of dust can be achieved either by spraying water intermittently or continuously on the collector or by means of a weir arrangement. The discharge electrodes must also be cleaned by rapping those at intervals.

Field Strength and Electrodes

A field strength of about 3 to 6 kV/cm (d.c.) is normally employed with the help of transformers coupled with silicon rectifiers and automatic voltage regulators. Because of the high field strength corona discharges take place, which produce high velocity electrons. A negative corona (corona on a negative wire) is more effective as it is more stable and efficient. For efficient operation an optimum sparking rate is 50-100 sparks per minute. Pulsed energisation of an ESP at intervals of millionth or micro seconds improves collection efficiency and reduces power consumption.

In some designs the discharge electrode diameter is about 3 mm, in others it is large. Irregular shaped discharge electrodes having pointed protrusions develop high intensity local field and initiate corona discharge. Square, triangular and barbed wires are sometimes used as discharge electrodes. Some manufacturers use metal strips instead of wires. Collector plates may have fins/baffles to prevent re-entrainment of the dislodged dust particles and to give them mechanical strength.

Particle Registivity and ESP Housing

Particles having low electrical registivity (10^4-10^7 ohm-cm) tend to lose their charge easily, drop off the plate and become re-entrained. Particles having high resistivity (10^{11}-10^{13} ohm-cm) tend to adhere to the collector plate and insulate it. Dust laden gas containing high resistivity dust may be conditioned by adding NH_3, SO_2, steam etc. to the gas stream.

The operating pressue of an ESP may range between slight vacuum to about 10 atm pressure and temperature as high as 600 °C.

An ESP is housed in a gas-tight housing made of steel or concrete. However, if necessary, from corrosion point of view the housing may be lined with lead or plastic. When water cleaning of the collector is done, mist and some soluble gases are also removed along with the dust particles.

In a specific situation a combination of the alternatives listed below may be chosen for construction/ operation of an ESP :

(i) dry/wet precipitation,

(ii) horizontal /vertical gas flow,

(iii) single/segmented plate type,

and (iv) operation under pressure/vacuum,

ESP Mechanism

Due to high voltage difference between the central discharge electrode and the ground collector, corona discharge takes place. During corona discharge electrons are emitted and they accelerate to high velocities. Such electrons on impact with gas molecules like, O_2, ionize them and release electrons which continue the process of gas ionization. The gaseous ions then charge the suspended dust particles in their neighbourhood either by collision (bombardment) or by diffusion. Particles larger than 1 μm are generally charged by collision, whereas finer particles are charged by diffusion. The charged particles then migrate to the ground collector and give up their charges. Some re-entrainment of particles may occur in the case of dry collectors. In the case of wet collectors re-entrainment is virtually absent.

The field strength is so maintained that there is limited sparking frequency. During sparking there is an instantaneous voltage drop resulting in collapse of the electrostatic field and consequent stoppage of dust collection. Excessive sparking means loss of input power in the spark current.

In an ESP a particle is subjected to the gravitational force, a drag force and an electrical field force. The field force would attract the particle towards the collector whereas the drag force would oppose its motion towards the collector. The resultant force would cause the particle to migrate towards the collector at some velocity, which is termed as the 'drift velocity'. The magnitude of the drift velocity of a particle depends on factors, such as, mode of particle charging, particles size, gas velocity, field strength, and particle resistivity, etc.

The drift velocity of a particle charged by bombardment may be calculated using the relation

$$U_{p,\ dp} = 3.694 \times 10^{-6} \frac{E^2 P\ dp}{\mu} \ . \tag{4.29}$$

However, if charging takes place by diffusion, the drift velocity may be approximated as

$$U_{p,\ dp} = 3.097 \times 10^{-4} K_m E / \mu \tag{4.30}$$

where, $U_{p,\,dp}$ = drift velocity of particles having a diameter dp, in m/s.
E = field strength, in kV/cm; $P = 3\varepsilon/(\varepsilon+2)$
ε = dielectric constant of the system; dp = particle diameter, in micron;
μ = gas viscosity in centipoise; Km = Cunningham factor.

Typical drift velocity data of some specific particles are listed in Table 4.9.

Table 4.9 : Typical Drift Velocity of Some Specific Particles

Particles	Drift Velocity, cm/s
Pulverized Coal Fly Ash	10-13
Cement Dust (Wet Process)	10-11
Cement Dust (Dry Process)	6-7
Blast Furnace Dust	6-14
Open Hearth Furnace Dust	4-6
Catalyst Dust	7
Cupola Dust	3-4
Sulphuric Acid Mist	5-7

It is to be pointed out here that for design purpose ESP manufacturers use their field experience instead of relying on the drift velocity data calculated based on Eqs. (4.29) and (4.30).

Pre-treatment

To reduce the dust load on an ESP the influent gas stream may be pre-treated in a gravity settler or a centrifugal separator (cyclone). In the case of dry ESP the influent gas should be at a temperature, say 25°-50°C above its dew point, hence, if required, the gas should be pre-heated.

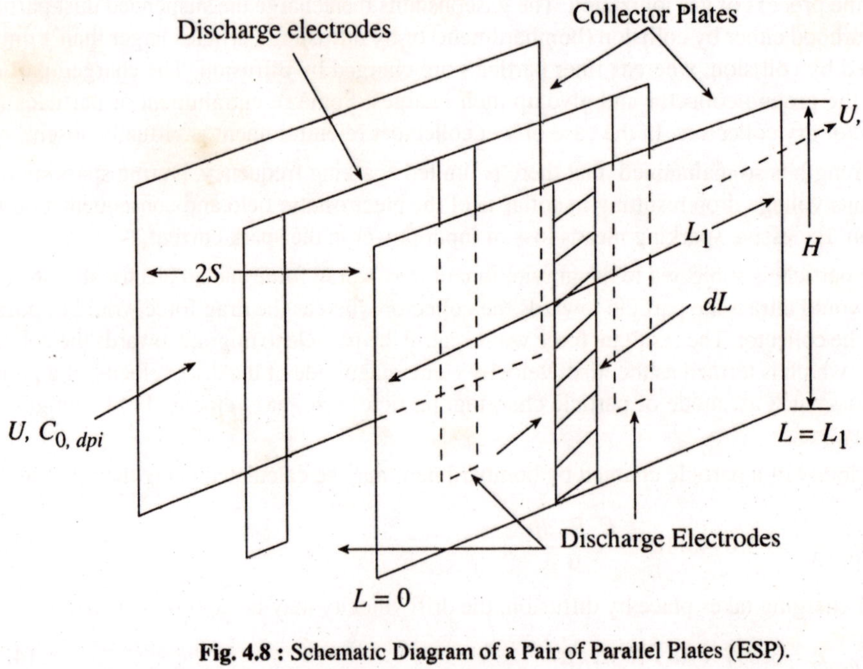

Fig. 4.8 : Schematic Diagram of a Pair of Parallel Plates (ESP).

ESP Collection Efficiency

A schematic diagram of a parallel plate set-up is shown in Fig. 4.8.

A dust laden carrier gas carrying suspended particles of different sizes flows between two parallel plates at a linear velocity *U* horizontally. The particles after entering the channel get charged and move towards the collector plates at their respective drift velocities.

Let us analyse the progressive changes in concentration of the particles (having a diameter *dpi*) as the carrier gas moves from the entrace end to the exit end. A material balance across an elemental length *dL* yields the Eq. (4.31)

$$\frac{dC}{C} = \frac{U_{p,\,dpi} \times 2HdL}{U \times 2\ SH} \tag{4.31}$$

Integration of Eq. (4.31) between $L = 0$ and $L = L_l$ results in

$$\ln \frac{C_{1,\,dpi}}{C_{0,\,dpi}} = \frac{U_{p,\,dpi} \times 2\ HL_1}{U \times 2\ SH} = \frac{U_{p,\,dpi} \times A}{q} \tag{4.32}$$

where H = Height of a plate,

L_l = Length of a plate,

$2\,S$ = Plate spacing,

$U_{p,\,dpi}$ = Drift velocity of particles having a diameter *dpi*

U = Horizontal gas velocity thorough the ESP,

A = Collector surface area of two plates = $2\,L_1\,H$

q = Volumetric gas flow rate through a channel between two plates = Q/n,

n = Number of Channels,

Q = Total volumetric gas flow rate.

An expression for the collection (removal) efficiency of such an unit for particles having a diameter *dpi* may be obtained by rearranging Eq. (4.32).

$$\frac{C_{0,dpi} - C_{1,\,dpi}}{C_{0,\,dpi}} = \eta_{dpi} = 1 - e^{\frac{-U_{p,\,dpi}A}{q}} = 1 - e^{\frac{-U_{p,\,dpi}\,L_1}{US}} \tag{4.33}$$

Though Eq. (4.33) is derived for a pair of parallel plates it is also valid for a tubular collector.

It has been reported that the experimental collection efficiency data fits Eq. (4.34) better than the theoretically derived Eq. (4.33).

$$\eta_{dpi,\ \text{expt}} = 1 - e\left(\frac{-U_{p,\,dpi}\ A}{q}\right)^m, \tag{4.34}$$

where the numerical value of m ranges between 0.4 to 0.7. The value of m may be approximated as 0.5

If it is desired to remove all the particles of a specific size dpi from a dust laden gas stream, then minimum length of a parallel plate collector (L_{dpi}) should be equal to $SU/U_{p,\,dpi}$ so that the particles which are at the mid-plane between the plates at the entrance would be able to reach the plates before the carrier gas sweeps them away out of the channel.

Under this condition those particles having drift velocities greater than $U_{p,\,dpi}$ would also be completely removed but those having lower drift velocities would be partially removed.

It is to be noted here that the particles take some time to get charged and acquire their drift velocities after entering a channel. The charging time 't_c' is about 0.3 sec. Hence the required minimum collector length for 100% removal of particles having a diameter *dpi* is

$$L_{dpi,}(100\%) = \frac{SU}{U_{p,dpi}} + U \times t_c . \tag{4.35}$$

ESP Design Approach

For estimating the dimensions of an ESP (*L, H, S*, and the number of parallel channels, *n*) the basic information required are particle size and mass distribution data, total volumetric gas-flow rate and the desired overall removal efficiency. Based on these an ESP may be sized through the following steps :

Step I : A specific particle size *dpi* is chosen whose complete removal is desired.

Step II : Influent gas velocity *(U)*, plate spacing (2*S*), plate height *(H)* and field strength *(E)* are assumed.

Step III : The drift velocities of the dust particles are estimated using Eqs. (4.29) and (4.30).

Step IV : L_{dpi} is calculated using Eqs. (4.33) and (4.35), whichever is larger should be accepted.

Step V : The removal efficiencies of the dust particles having a diameter other than *dpi* are estimated using Eq. (4.34).

Step VI : The overall collection efficiency of the proposed ESP is estimated using Eq. (4.10).

$$\eta_{overall} = \Sigma m_{dpi.} \times \eta_{dpi} / \Sigma m_{dpi}$$

If the estimated overall efficiency does not match the desired efficiency, then some of the parameters listed in step II are changed and the steps III, IV, V and VI are reworked till the estimated overall removal efficiency matches the desired one.

The ratio of the effective length to the effective height of an ESP is referred to as the Aspect Ratio (A.R.). It generally ranges between 0.5 to 2. For 99.5 $^+$% removal efficiency the A.R. should be greater than 2.

The number of parallel channels in a module is estimated using the relation,

$$n = Q/q, \tag{4.36}$$

where Q is the total volumetric gas-flow rate.

ESP Performance

An ESP is used to remove particles ranging in size from 300 μm to 1μm and the overall removal efficiency may be as high as 99.9%. Since the efficiency is a logarthmic function of the collector area, the area required for 99 % collection is about twice that required for 90% collection. The efficiency may be more than 99% for particles larger than 2 μm. The pressure loss is less than 2.5 cm of water. Power consumption is about 75-750 kW per 10,000 Nm^3/min gas-flow rate.

The actual performance of an ESP may be poorer than the calculated one because of re-entrainment, improper electrical setting, badly adjusted rapper, excessive dust build-up, channelling of gas, high electrical resistivity, low SO_2 content of the carrier gas. Sectionalized units have higher efficiency.

Normally an ESP operates in the particle resistivity range of 10^4–10^{12} ohm-cm. For resistivity less than 10^4 the particles lose their charge easily and hence are not collected. For resistivity more than 5×10^{10} particles are held rigidly to the collector. Strong rapping required for dislodging such particles results in re-entrainment.

Advantages and Disadvantages of an ESP

Advantages

1. Low pressure drop (draft loss),
2. Can handle gas at high temperature and pressure,
3. High collection efficiency even for small particles < 0.1 μm,
4. Variation of gas-flow rate and dust loading do not affect the efficiency much,
5. Can be operated both in dry and wet conditions,
6. Can handle corrosive gases,
7. Maintenance cost is low as there are fewer moving parts,
8. Low operating cost compared to other high efficiency dust removal systems.

Disadvantages

1. Initial cost is high,
2. More space is required,
3. It is not suitable for combustible dust and or gases,
4. Actual removal efficiency may be low if not operated properly,
5. Conditioning agents may be required for resistive particles.

In Table 4.10 the normal range of variation of the parameters of plate type commercial ESPs are listed.

Table 4.10 : Normal Range of Variation of Parameter Values of Plate Type Commercial ESPs

Parameter	Range of Variation
Plate height	3.5-9 m
Plate length	1.8-9 m
Plate spacing	20-30 cm
Drift velocity	3-20 cm/s
Gas velocity	0.6-3 m/s
Field voltage	30-100 kV
Field strength	2.8-6 kV/cm
Corona current	0.03-3 mA/m of charging electrode
Pressure drop	0.25-1.2 cm water gauge
Power consumption	75-750 kW per 10,000 Nm^3/min
Max. operating temperature	550°C
Collection efficiency	90-99.5%

Example 4.3

Design a suitable parallel plate electrostatic precipitator (ESP) for 99.5 percent removal of particles having a diameter 20 μm from a carrier gas (air) flowing at the rate of 30,000 m^3/hour at 30 °C.

Following data may be used for design purpose :

Particle drift velocity ($U_{p,\, dpi}$) = 0.1 m/s

Plate spacing ($2S$) = 20 cm

Length to height ratio (L/H) = 1 : 1.5

Gas Velocity(U) = 1 m/s

Solution :

Since $U_{p,\ dpi}$ is given it is not necessary to calculate the same using either Eq. (4.29) or Eq. (4.30). From Eq. (4. 33).

$$\eta_{dpi} = 1 - e\left(\frac{-U_{p,dpi}\ A}{q}\right) = 1 - e\left(\frac{-U_{p,dpi}\ L_1}{US}\right),$$

where A = Collector surface area per channel = $2\ L_1 H$

and q = Volumetric gas flow through each channel = 2 SHU.

Substituting the data given in Eq. (4.33)

$$0.995 = 1 - e\left(\frac{-0.1 \times 2L_1H}{0.2 \times H \times 1}\right) = 1 - e^{-L_1}.$$

Rearrangement of the above yields

e^{-L_1} = 1-0.995 = 0.005

L_1 = –In 0.005

Hence, L_1 = 5.298 = 5.3 m.

From Eq. (4.35),

$$L_{dpi}, 100\% = \frac{SU}{U_{p,\ dpi}} + U \times t_c$$

$$= \frac{0.1 \times 1}{0.1} + 1 \times 0.3$$

$$= 1 + 0.3 = 1.3\text{m}.$$

Therefore, the length is taken as 5.3m.

L/H is given as 1/1.5

Therefore, $H = 1.5\ L = 7.95$ m.

The required number of channels n is estimated using Eq. (4.36).

$$n = \frac{Q}{q} = \frac{Q}{2\ SHU}$$

$$n = \frac{30{,}000 m^3 / hour}{0.20 \times 7.95 \times 1 \times 3600}$$

$$= 5.24 \approx 6.$$

4.2.6 Scrubbers

Scrubbers are widely used in industries for removal of dust particles, suspended liquid droplets and also for absorption of gaseous pollutants from effluent gas streams.

In a scrubber a gas stream is brought in contact with a liquid stream (generally water) either in the form of a spray or a pool as a result of which the suspended particles are collected in the liquid stream and thereby form a slurry. The treated gas saturated with water vapour and containing some water droplets comes out of the scrubber. The slurry often needs further treatment before its final disposal. In dry cleaners discussed earlier one does not encounter this problem.

In a scrubber the mechanism of collection of larger particles ($dp > 0.3$ μm) is predominantly interception and impingement, leading to agglomeration of particles. The finer particles ($dp < 0.3$μm) are mainly collected due to diffusion. If a gas stream cools down below its dew point coming in contact with the scrubbing liquid then the process of dust collection gets boosted.

One finds such a wide variety of industrial scrubbers that it becomes very difficult to classify them properly. All conceivable means of contacting gas and liquid streams have been and are being employed. A classification based on scrubber internals and scrubber liquid flow pattern is given in Table 4.11.

Table 4.11 : Scrubber Classification

Scrubber Type	Scrubber Internals	Gas-liquid flow pattern
1. Plate Column	(i) Sieve plate,	Countercurrent
	(ii) Bubble cap,	
	(iii) Baffle plate	
2. Packed Bed	(i) Fixed bed	Countercurrent/
	(ii) Floating bed	*Cocurrent*
3. Fiber Bed	(i) Rotating hollow cylinder partially dipping in a water trough	Liquid flowing in and out of the trough
	(ii) Fiber plate	Spray
4. Spray Contactors	**A. Vertical Devices :**	
	(i) Spray chamber	Countercurrrent/Cocurrent.
	(ii) Ejector venturi	*Cocurrent*
	(iii) Annular orifice	*Cocurrent*
	(iv) Rod banks	*Cocurrent*
	(v) Venturi with a cyclone separator	*Cocurrent*
	B. Horizontal Devices :	
	(i) Baffle/Packing	*Cocurrent*
	(ii) Packing	Crosscurrent
	(iii) Venturi with cyclone separator	*Cocurrent*
	C. Centrifugal devices :	
	(i) Central spray	Crosscurrent
	(ii) Wall spray	Crosscurrent
	(iii) Spray near gas entry point	*Cocurrent*
5. Mechanically Aided Contractors	(i) Motor driven fan, liquid sprayed at the gas inlet.	*Cocurrent*
	(ii) Atomized liquid	*Cocurrent*

Scrubbers are also classified as 'low energy' and 'high energy' type as listed below :

Low Energy Type

Scrubber : Spray, Packed bed, Impingement plate.
Pressure drop, ΔP : 2.5-15 cm of water guage.
Water-flow rate : 400-800 lit/1000 m^3 of gas.
Collection efficiency : 90-95% for particles above 5-10 μm.

High Energy Type

Scrubber : Venturi.
Pressure drop, ΔP : As high as 175 cm of water guage.
Water-flow rate : 400-1400 lit/1000 m^3 of gas.
Collection efficiency : 99% for particles even finer than 2 μm.

Some of the scrubbers listed in Table 4.11 are described hereunder. Their performance and other relevant data are tabulated in Table 4.12.

4.2.6.1 Plate Columns

Sieve Plate

In sieve plate columns the flow is countercurrent. The scrubbing liquid enters at the top and flows down. The gas enters near the bottom and flows up. Water flows over plates forming a pool about 2.5 cm deep on each plate. The dust-laden gas enters a plate through its perforations and bubbles through the liquid pool on it. The mechanism of dust collection is interception and impingement. The pressure drop across such a column depends on the number of plates employed and the depth of liquid on each plate. The collection efficiency depends on the number of plates in a column, perforation diameter and gas velocity. It may be 90% or more for particle size 5 μm and larger

Bubble Cap and Baffle Plate Column

These scrubbers are vertical towers with one or more perforated plates mounted horizontally inside like the sieve plate columns. The difference lies in the fact that at a short distance above each perforation on a plate a cap or a baffle is placed submerged in the liquid pool on the plate. Because of impingement on the obstruction and subsequent change in direction of the flowing gas the collection efficiency is higher than that of a sieve plate column. The efficiency increases as the hole diameter decreases. Decrease of gas velocity also increases the efficiency. The efficiency decreases with the decrease in the particle size. Because of improper removal of the collected particles from plates scaling and plugging of the perforations may take place.

4.2.6.2 Packed Scrubbers

A packed bed scrubber is also a vertical tower in which the dirty gas generally enters at the bottom and flows up through a bed of packings resting on a packing support. The scrubbing liquid is introduced at the top and is distributed throughout the cross section of the tower. As the gas flows up through the tortuous channels in between the packings it comes in contact with wet packing surfaces where the particles are arrested due to inertial interception and impingement.

Packed scrubbers are of two types : fixed bed type and floating bed type.

A fixed bed may be either countercurrent or cocurrent type. In a cocurrent type both gas and liquid enter at the top. In a fixed bed the packings are heavy and they rest on a packing support. Fixed beds are susceptible to choking at high dust load and low voidage.

In floating type packed beds plastic balls made of polyethylene, polypropylene or other thermo plastic materials are generally used as they are resistant to corrosion and lighter than water. The packings are confined between two perforated horizontal plates. The distance between the plates is normally about 0.5 m. A floating type bed is countercurrent type. The gas enters at the bottom at a velocity of about 2 to 4 m/s. At low velocities the packings form a fixed bed on the lower support plate, while at high gas velocities the packings form a fixed bed below the restraining upper plate. At an intermediate velocity the packing would be floating and in turbulent motion.

For treatment of gases containing corrosive constituents FRP (glass fiber reinforced plastic) may be used for construction of such columns instead of rubber or plastic lined steel or such other materials.

Collection efficiency increases as smaller packings are used since they provide more surface area per unit packed volume. Use of smaller size packing would result in higher-pressure drop.

4.2.6.3 Fiber Bed

A bed made of knitted plastic, fiber glass, metal wire or meshed fiber is used as a filter. Such a bed has a void percentage around 97-99%. The bed is kept wet and it is flushed with the scrubbing liquid. This helps in collecting particles and removing the collected particles in the form of a slurry. Collection of particles due to impaction improves as fiber diameter decrease and gas velocity increases, whereas collection by diffusion increases as gas velocity decreases. The wire/fiber diameter should be small for efficient operation but must be able to provide sufficient mechanical strength so as to support its weight along with those of the collected particles and retained liquid.

4.2.6.4 Spray Contactors

In these scrubbers a dust-laden gas is brought into contact with atomized liquid droplets. Atomization may be achieved by forcing the scrubbing liquid through nozzles or it may be induced by allowing the gas to flow at a high velocity (60-120 m/s) through a venturi or an orifice type device. The liquid droplets collect the soild particles by inertial impaction and impingement. The removal efficiency is dependent on the particle size, liquid drop size, gas velocity and liquid to gas ratio. The dust laden droplets are separated from the gas by using gravity settlers or packed beds or cyclone type devices.

In spray scrubbers, where liquid droplets are removed by gravity settling the cut size is around 2 μm and the optimum droplet diameters for fine particle collection is 100 to 500 μm. For cut size around 0.7 μm high velocity sprays are more efficient. The liquid to gas ratio in spray scrubbers is in the range of 4000-14000 lit/1000 Nm^3.

Centrifugal Scrubber can recover particles smaller than those recovered by spray scrubbers. The cut diameter is between 2 to 3 μm. The collection efficiency is 97% or more for particles > 1 μm.

Venturi Scrubber

Venturi Scrubbers are high efficiency wet scrubbers where particles even finer than 2 μm are effectively removed. These are as efficient as ESPs and fabric filters. Initial cost of a venturi scrubber is less than that of an ESP or a bag house, however the operating cost is high. If the particles to be removed are sticky/flammable/corrosive, a venturi scrubber is a better choice over an ESP or a bag house.

A venturi scrubber is basically a convergent-divergent duct with a throat where the cross section is the minimum. It may have a cylindrical or rectangular cross section. The gas enters the convergent section and the scrubbing liquid may be introduced either at the entrance of the convergent section or at the throat in the form of a spray. When the gas and liquid droplets pass through the throat at a high velocity the particles are collected in the liquid droplets due to interception, impingement and diffusion. The collection efficiency increases as the throat length is increased with consequent increase in pressure drop. The optimum ratio of throat length to diameter is 3 : 1. The particle laden liquid droplets as they come out of the divergent sections are separated from the gas in a cyclone or a mist eliminator. When the influent gas is hot, the scrubbing liquid is introduced at the section where the convergent section starts, but when the gas temperature is not high or it is almost saturated with moisture the liquid is introduced at the throat. The gas velocity at the throat ranges between 50-180 m/s at which it is most efficient. When the gas flow rate is high a rectangular venturi is used. The liquid to gas ratio normally ranges between 900-1400 lit/1000m^3. A liquid flow rate of 400 lit/1000 m^3 is insufficient to cover the throat. The collection efficiency does not improve much beyond a liquid flow rate of 1400 lit/1000 m^3. The converging angle is generally 25°– 28° and the diverging angle is 6°– 7°.

The pressure drop ΔP, across a venturi scrubber may be calculated using the relation,

$$\Delta P = 1 \times 10^{-5} V^2 L \tag{4.37}$$

where, ΔP is in cm of water gauge,

V = gas velocity at the throat, in m/s, and L = liquid flow rate in lit/1000 m^3. At a liquid rate of 650 lit/1000 m^3 the ΔP calculated using Eq. (4.37) is quite accurate, but at a liquid rate of 1600 lit/1000 m^3 the calculated ΔP is higher than the actual.

Impingement and Entrainment Scrubbers

In such scrubbers the gas to be scrubbed is passed through a trap partly or completely filled with water. The suspended particles are arrested by inertial impaction. The treated gas entrains some water droplets, which also help in removing some of the suspended particles.

Mechanically Aided Scrubbers

This type of scrubbers use a motor driven device to bring about intimate contact between a dirty gas and liquid droplets. The motor driven device is often a fan, which moves the gas. The scrubbing liquid is introduced as a spray at the hub of the fan. The finer droplets move with the gas. The larger droplets hit the fan blades and wash the deposited particles. While leaving the blades at their tips the liquid gets atomized. The dust-laden droplets are separated from the gas with the help of a suitable device. For producing liquid droplets (spray) the rotor may be partially submerged or water may be injected between the rotor and stator. Such devices may experience high erosion,abrasion and Corrosion

In Table 4.12 the performance and other related information about some types of scrubbers are listed.

Table 4.12 : Performance and Pertinent Data of Scrubbers

Pertinent Data \ Scrubber Type	Gravity Spray	Cyclone/ Central Spray	Plate Column	Packed Bed	Venturi Scrubber	Mechanically Induced Spray
Pressure drop ΔP, cm water guage	1.5-5	2.5-35	2.5-20	4-8 per m of bed height	14-170	1.5-10
Liquid rate lit/1000 m^3	650-2600	650-1600	400-650	1000-2600	600-2000	550-650
Collection efficiency for 5 μm particles	80%	87%	97%	99%	99%	99%

It is to be noted here that a scrubbed gas stream would invariably contain liquid droplets and its temperature would not be much higher than that of the influent scrubbing liquid. Hence the treated gas stream has to be freed from liquid droplets and mists and then reheated before purging the same to the atmosphere through a stack.

4.3 Removal of Liquid Droplets and Mists

The mechanisms by which suspended liquid droplets and mists may be removed are similar to those for solid particle removal. Removal of suspended liquid droplets is somewhat easier than that of solid particles. Liquid droplets coalesces easily on interception and drain off. Unlike solid particles, liquid droplets once separated are not re-entrained easily. Some of the devices, which are used, for removal of solid particles may also be used for removal of suspended liquid droplets.

The following types of devices are commonly employed for removal of gas-borne liquid droplets :

(a) Packed beds,
(b) Cyclones,
(c) Baffle system,
(d) ESP,
(e) Filter.

Packed beds and cyclones do not need any scrubbing liquid for arresting liquid droplets. Draining of collected liquid from an ESP collector surface occurs due to gravity and does not require any hammering.

A special type of filter media is a pad made of knitted wire or fibrous mesh occupying the entire cross section of a vertical tower. It is very often used for filtering liquid droplets and mists. Such pads made of 0.3 to 1.5 mm diameter wire or fibre has high void volume and causes low pressure drop even at high gas velocities. These devices are termed as 'mist eliminators' or 'demisters'. Very fine wires or

Figure 4.9 Shows Sketches of Some Types of Scrubbers :

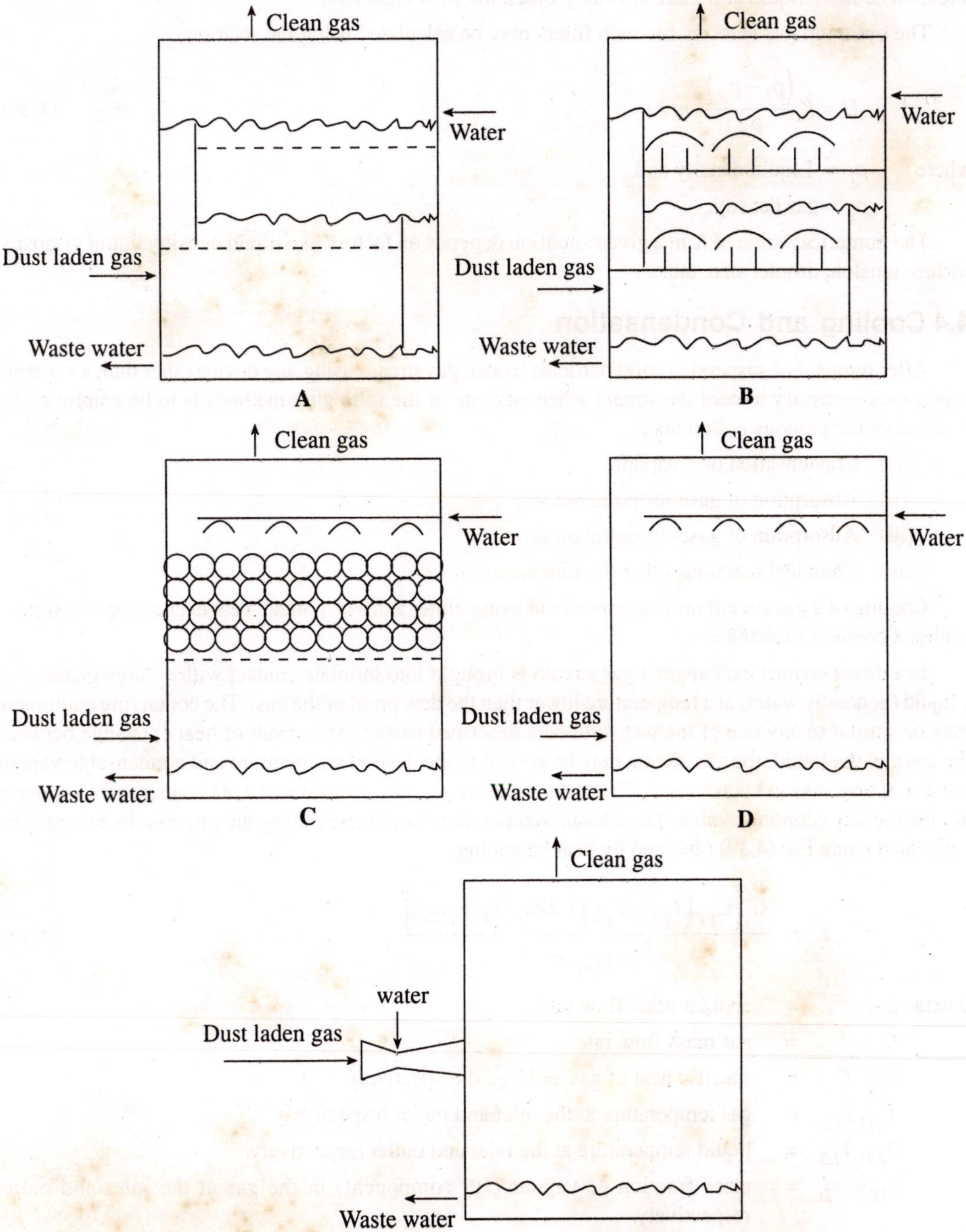

Fig. 4.9 : Schematic Representation of Some Types of Wet Scrubbers.

A. Sieve Plate Column,
B. Bubble Cap Column,
C. Packed Bed Tower,
D. Spray Chamber,
E. Venturi Scrubber.

fibres are not used for fabricating the pads and the pads are not densely packed as that would cause retention of more liquid and thereby finally block the flow channels.

The optimum gas velocity for such filters may be calculated using the relation

$$U = K\frac{(\rho_l - \rho_g)}{\rho_g} \quad m/s \tag{4.38}$$

where ρ_l = Liquid density and

ρ_g = gas density.

The numerical value of K in a given situation depends on factors like liquid density, liquid viscosity, surface tension, droplet size, etc.

4.4 Cooling and Condensation

After removal of suspended solid particles from a gas stream using any device other than a scrubber it becomes necessary to cool the stream when any one of the following methods is to be employed for removal of the gaseous pollutants :

(i) Condensation of a vapour,

(ii) Absorption of gaseous pollutant (s),

(iii) Adsorption of gaseous pollutant (s),

(iv) Chemical reactions other than incineration.

Cooling of a gas stream may be carried out using either a direct contact heat exchanger or a surface (indirect contact) exchanger.

In a direct contact exchanger a gas stream is brought into intimate contact with a large quantity of a liquid (generally water) at a temperature lower than the dew point of the gas.. The contacting equipment may be similar to any one of the wet scrubbers described earlier. As a result of heat exchange between the gas and the liquid, the gas stream may be cooled to the desired temperature and condensable vapour present, if any, may get condensed. This type of exchanger may be used when the condensable vapour is not having any economic value. The coolant temperature would rise during the process. Its rate may be calculated using Eq. (4.39) obtained by heat balancing.

$$L = \frac{G\left[C_{pg}\left(T_{g1} - T_{g2}\right) + \Sigma\lambda_i\ (y_{1i} - y_{2i})\right]}{C_{pl}\ (T_{L2} - T_{L1})} \tag{4.39}$$

where L = coolant mass flow rate,

G = gas mass flow rate,

C_{pg}, C_{pl} = specific heat of gas and liquid respectively,

T_{g1}, T_{g2} = gas temperature at the inlet and outlet respectively,

T_{L1}, T_{L2} = liquid temperature at the inlet and outlet respectively,

$y_{1i} - y_{2i}$ = mass fraction of vapour (ith component) in the gas at the inlet and outlet respectively,

and λi = latent heat of condensation of the ith component.

If the gas is not cooled below its dew point then the gas would pick up some vapour (of the coolant) during the process. In such a situation the coolant rate may be calculated using Eq. (4.39a).

$$L = \frac{G\left[C_{pg}\left(T_{g1} - T_{g2}\right) - \lambda_{L,\,T_{g2}}\left(y_{2L} - y_{1L}\right)\right]}{C_{p1}\left(T_{L2} - T_{L1}\right)} \tag{4.39a}$$

where y_{1L}, y_{2L} = mass fraction of coolant vapour in the gas at the inlet and outlet respectively,

$\lambda_{L,\,T_{g2}}$ = latent heat of vaporization of the coolant at T_{g2}.

Indirect contact (surface) exchangers are generally shell and tube type. The tubes may be with or without fins. Of the two fluids (hot gas and coolant) one would flow through the tubes and the other would flow outside the tubes. The coolant may be either air or some other fluid depending upon whether the exchanger will act as a cooler or a cooler-cum-condenser. In Table 4.13 some guidelines for coolant selection and its inlet temperature are given.

Indirect Contact Exchanger Design Approach

The basic design equation for a shell and tube heat exchanger is

$$q = U_h\ A_h\ \Delta tm = LC_{pl}\left(T_{L2} - T_{LI}\right)$$

$$= G\left[C_{pg}\left(T_{g1} - T_{g2}\right) + \Sigma\lambda_i\ \left(y_{1i} - y_{2i}\right)\right]. \tag{4.40}$$

Eq. [4.40] is applicable when cooling is accompanied by condensation of vapour. When there is no condensation the term $\Sigma\lambda i\ (y_{1i} - y_{2i})$ will be equal to zero. The symbols L, C_{p1}, T_{L1} and T_{L2} refer to the coolant stream flow rate, specific heat of liquid, inlet and outlet temperatures.

Where q = rate of heat transfer,

U_h = overall heat transfer coefficient,

A_h = Heat transfer area,

and Δtm = mean temperature difference, a function of T_{L1}, T_{L2}, T_{g1} and T_{g2}.

The actual expression for evaluation of Δtm depends on the flow arrangement of the fluids in an exchanger.

Figure 4.10 shows a sketch of a shell and tube type cooler-condenser.

Table 4.13 : Indirect Contact Exchanger Coolant Selection Guidelines

Gas outlet Temperature T_{g2}, °C	Coolant	Coolant inlet Temperature T_{L1}, °C
$T_{g2} > 25$ °C	Air/Water	$T_{L1} = (T_{g2} - 8$°C)
25 °C > T_{g2} > 10°C	Chilled Water	,, ,,
10 °C > T_{g2} > –30 °C	Chilled brine solution, ($CaCl_2$ solution), Ethylene glycol.	,, ,,
–30 °C > T_{g2} > –65 °C	Refrigerant.	,, ,,

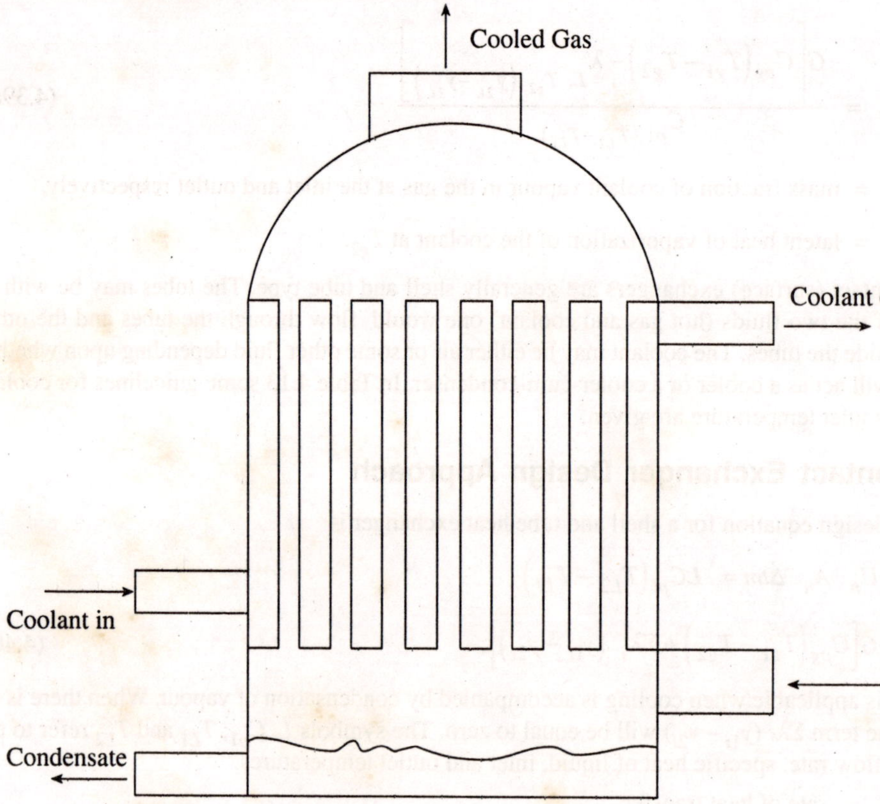

Fig. 4.10 : Shell and Tube Cooler-Condenser.

The overall heat transfer co-efficient, U_h, can be evaluated by combining the individual co-efficient using Eq. (4.41).

$$\frac{1}{U_h} = \frac{1}{h_g} + \frac{x}{k_m} + \frac{1}{h_l} + \frac{1}{h_d} \tag{4.41}$$

Where h_g = gas side coefficient,

k_m = metal thermal conductivity,

x = tube-wall thickness,

h_l = coolant side coefficient,

and $1/h_d$ = resistance due to dirt-layers deposited on tube surfaces (inside and outside)

Typical values of the above named parameters are listed in Table 4.14.

Table 4.14 : Typical Values of Individual Heat Transfer Coefficient

Individual Coefficient	Numerical Value Range
h_g Gas side :	$\frac{\text{K cal}}{\text{hr m}^2\ °C}$
(a) Only Cooling	50–250
(b) Vapour condensation	
(i) water vapour	5000–50000
(ii) organic vapour	1000–2000
k_m/x Tube wall	9000–30000
h_l Coolant (water) side	1000–4000
h_d Scale deposits	500–10000

For evaluation of U_h in a specific situation the individual coefficient should be estimated using information and correlations available in standard books on Heat Transfer.

4.5 Absorption of Gaseous Pollutants

When a waste gas containing some gaseous pollutants is brought into direct contact with a liquid, some of the pollutants may get transferred to the liquid. This transfer process may occur either due to solubilization of the pollutants in the liquid or due to chemical reactions of the pollutants with the liquid or with some chemical (s) present in the liquid. The transfer process without any chemical reaction is termed as *physical absorption* and that with chemical reaction(s) is termed as *absorption accompanied by chemical reaction*.

In the (physical) absorption process the solute (gaseous pollutant) is termed as *absorbate* and the solvent (liquid) as the *absorbent*. The gas carrying the absorbate is referred to as the *carrier gas*. This process is a reversible one, that is, under certain circumstances transfer of solute occurs from the gas phase to the liquid phase and under some other situations transfer takes place in the opposite direction. The other process, namely, absorption accompanied by chemical reaction is an irreversible one, that is, transfer occurs from the gas phase only.

The physical absorption process takes place through the following steps :

1. The solute (gaseous) molecules migrate from the bulk of the gas phase to the gas-liquid phase boundary (interface) by molecular and/or eddy diffusion;
2. Transfer of absorbate molecules across the interface;
3. Transfer of absorbate molecules into the bulk of the absorbent by molecular and/or eddy diffusion.

In the case of an absorption accompanied by chemical reaction process the first two steps are similar to those of a physical absorption process. However, during the third step the absorbate molecules react with the reactant present in the absorbent and form new compound(s).

4.5.1 Absorption Theory

Transfer of a chemical species between a gas phase and a liquid phase takes place because of a potential difference of the species between the phases. This potential difference is referred to as the *chemical potential gradient.* When the chemical potential of a species becomes same in the two phases in contact with one another they are said to be in equilibrium. Under this condition, no net transfer of the species takes place between the phases. When the phases are not in equilibrium with respect to a species, then its transfer occurs from the phase in which its chemical potential is higher to the other phase in which its potential is lower.

The chemical potential of a species in a particular phase is related but not equal to its concentration in that phase. When two phases, in contact with each other, reach equilibrium with respect to a species, its concentration in the respective phases would be related to one another. Such a relation is termed as *equilibrium relation*. The equilibrium relation of a chemical species in a gas-liquid system may be expressed as

$$p_A = H_A . X_A \tag{4.42}$$

Where, p_A = partial pressure of the species A in the gas phase,

X_A = mole fraction of the species A in the liquid phase,

and H_A = Henry's law constant, the numerical value of which is temperature dependent and may also be concentration (X_A) dependent. The numerical value of H_A depends on the solute—solvent system. Generally it increases with increase in temperature.

An alternative expression of the equilibrium relation is

$$Y_A = m_A . X_A \tag{4.43}$$

where, Y_A = moles of species A per mole of the carrier gas,

X_A = moles of species A per mole of solute free solvent,

m_A = proportionality constant, which like H_A is temperature and concentration dependent.

The rate of mass transfer of a species from one phase (gas) to another phase (liquid) per unit of interfacial area is expressed as

$$\begin{aligned} N_A &= k_{YA}(Y_g - Y_i) &&= k_{XA}(X_i - X_l) \\ &= k_{YA}(Y_{g2} - mX_i) &&= k_{XA}\{(Y_i/m) - X_l\} \\ &= K_{YA}(Y_g - Y^*) &&= K_{XA}(X^* - X_l) \end{aligned} \tag{4.44}$$

where N_A = moles of solute A transferred from the gas phase to the liquid phase per unit interfacial area per unit time,

k_{YA}, k_{XA} = individual gas/liquid phase mass transfer coefficient respectively,

K_{YA}, K_{XA} = overall gas/liquid phase mass transfer coefficient respectively,

Y^* = equilibrium gas phase concentration corresponding to the bulk liquid phase concentration X_l,

X^* = equilibrium liquid phase concentration corresponding to the bulk gas phase concentration Y_g,

X_i, X_l = solute concentration at the interface and bulk liquid phase respectively.

Y_i, Y_g = solute concentration at the interface and bulk gas phase respectively.

The individual and the overall transfer coefficients are related. Equations (4.45) and (4.46) show their relation.

$$\frac{1}{K_Y} = \frac{1}{k_Y} + \frac{m}{k_x} \tag{4.45}$$

and
$$\frac{1}{K_x} = \frac{1}{mk_Y} + \frac{1}{k_x} \tag{4.46}$$

The individual mass transfer coefficient k_x and k_Y may be calculated using empirical equations generally expressed as

$$\text{Sh} = \alpha\,(Re)^m.\,(\text{Sc})^n \tag{4.47}$$

where Sh = Sherwood number, $k_l l/D_{AB}$

Re = Reynolds number, $lU\rho/\mu$

Sc = Schmidt number, $\mu/\rho D_{AB}$

l = characteristic dimension of the absorber internals

U = linear fluid velocity in the absorber,

D_{AB} = molecular diffusivity of species A in a mixture of species A and B;

μ = fluid viscosity,

ρ = fluid density.

α, m and n are constants whose numerical values depend on the absorber internals. The relevant information about these may be found in books on Mass Transfer.

4.5.2 Absorption Equipment

The purpose of an absorption equipment is to bring a gas stream and a liquid stream into intimate contact with one another so that a solute (a gaseous pollutant) may get easily transferred from the gas phase to the liquid phase. It should be noted here that by this process a pollutant is merely transferred from a gas phase to a liquid phase only and it is not converted into an innocuous substance. If it is desired to recover the solute because of its economic value, then it is to be desorbed subsequently from the solution.

The equipment which may be used to carry out an absorption process are : a packed tower, plate tower, spray chamber and venturi scrubber. Of these the most often used equipment is a packed tower, which is quite efficient and relatively less costly. It is a cylindrical vertical column with packings inside it. The packings may be made of plastic or metal or ceramics, which provide larger surface area per unit packed volume for gas-liquid contact. Packings of different geometries and sizes are available. The criteria for choosing a packing geometry and size are large surface area, high bed void fraction and lower cost. Higher bed void fraction offers less resistance to gas and liquid flow. The other internals of a packed bed are a liquid distributor, redistributor(s), a packing support and a gas distributor. Normally in a packed tower the liquid flows down over the packing surface in the form of films and the gas flows up through the void space past the liquid films.

Plate towers are of three different types: sieve plate, bubble cap plate and valve tray. A plate tower is a cylindrical vessel with several horizontal plates stacked one above another, spaced at some distance from one another. The absorbent (liquid) entering at the top of a tower flows across each plate and cascades down, while forming a pool on each plate. The gas containing a solute/solutes (pollutants) enters at the bottom of the tower and flows up. It enters each plate through small holes and bubbles through the liquid pool on it. Transfer of the solute from the gas phase to the liquid phase takes place when the gas bubbles through the pool. In the case of sieve plates the holes (through which gas flows) are small and those are not covered. In the case of bubble cap trays and valve trays the holes are of larger diameter (than those of sieve plates) and are partially covered. The plate towers are quite efficient but they are more expensive than the packed towers.

Spray chambers may be with or without packings. The liquid is introduced at the top in the form of a spray and it flows down, whereas the gas flow may be horizontal or vertical. These are generally less efficient than the packed/plate towers.

In venturi scrubbers both gas and liquid are introduced at the converging end of a venturi and they flow cocurrently. In some equipment the liquid is introduced at the throat. As the liquid breaks up into small droplets it provides large contact area for mass transfer. Its efficiency as an absorber is low.

When it is planned to use either a packed tower or a plate tower the gas stream should be pre-treated to remove particulate matter as otherwise the particles may accumulate in the tower and thereby clog it. However, when a spray chamber (without packing) or a venturi scrubber is used as an absorber, pre-cleaning of the gas is not essential

4.5.3 Packed Tower Design Approach

Since packed absorption columns are more often used for absorbing gaseous pollutants from gas streams the design approach of such a column is outlined hereunder.

Prior to absorption in a packed column an influent gas stream should undergo the following pre-treatments :

Cooling of the influent gas streams would reduce its volumetric flow rate and increase the solubility of the pollutant (s) in the solvent selected. As a result the the size of the absorber will be smaller and the quanity of solvent required will be less. During absorption each of the pollutants present in a gas stream would be removed to some extent *or other* depending on its solubility in the selected solvent. A solvent is primarily selected for removing a specific pollutant and an absorber is designed so as to achieve the desired degree of removal of that specific pollutant.

While selecting a suitable solvent the factors/parameters to be considered are :

1. high solubility of the targeted absorbate,
2. low vapour pressure of the solvent at the operating temperature,
3. low price,
4. low/nil toxicity, and
5. whether the solvent is to be recovered and reused.

The data and information required for designing an absorber are :

(i) maximum (expected) flow rate of the carrier gas, G mole/hr;
(ii) temperature and pressure of the influent gas stream;
(iii) concentration of the targeted pollutant in the influent and its desired degree of removal;
(iv) solubility data/equilibrium relation;
and (v) the type of packing, its size and other characteristics.

Once these information are available one would be able to calculate the following using appropriate equations and thereby design a suitable absorber.

(i) required solvent flow rate, *L* mole/hr,
(ii) column diameter *D*,
(iii) column height *Z*,
(iv) pressure drop across the packed bed.

4.5.3.1 Required Solvent Rate

The minimum solvent rate (L_{min}) may be calculated assuming that the solvent leaving the absorber would become saturated with respect to the solute concentration in the influent gas stream. Figure 4.11 shows a schematic diagram of a packed absorber.

An expression for L_{min} is obtained by rearranging the solute balance equation across an absorber,

$$L_{\min} = \frac{G(Y_1 - Y_2)}{X_1^* - X_2} \tag{4.48}$$

where $X_1^* = Y_1/m$

X_1, X_2 = solute concentration in the solvent at the outlet and inlet respectively, in mole ratio unit,

Y_1, Y_2 = gas phase solute concentration at the inlet and outlet respectively, in mole ratio unit.

In practice X_2 and Y_1 would be known. Y_2 would be related to Y_1 through its desired degree of removal, i.e., the removal efficiency,

$Y_2 = Y_1\,(1-\eta_r)$, η_r = removal efficiency,

Evaluation of L_{min} using Eq. (4.48) would be proper if the equilibrium relation were linear, i.e., $Y = mX$ and m independent of X. In most cases the solute (pollutant) concentration in the gas phase would be low and hence m would be independent of X.

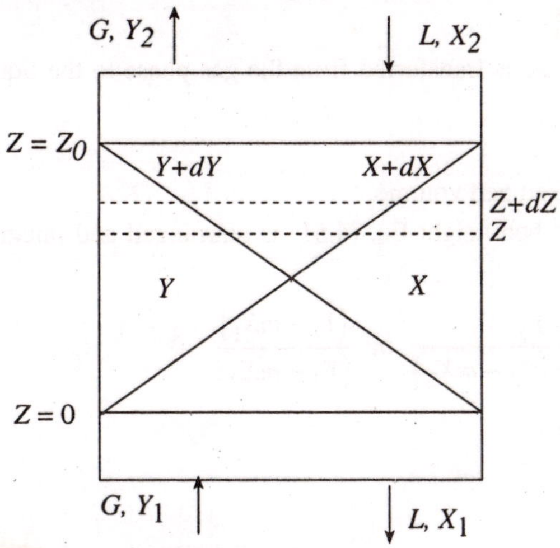

Fig. 4.11 : Schematic Diagram of A Packed Bed Absorber.

The actual solvent rate is normally taken as

L_{actual} = 1.25 to 2.0 times the L_{min}.

It should be pointed out here that an absorber is never designed taking $L_{actual} = L_{min}$ as it would result in a very high value of Z_0.

As L_{actual} is increased the calculated column height would decrease, but the column cross section would increase. The L_{actual} should be finally decided from the total cost (initial cost plus operating cost) point of view. Another factor which should be taken into consideration for estimation of L_{actual} is the minimum liquid rate required for wetting the packings in the column.

4.5.3.2 Column Diameter

At a given gas and liquid flow rates if the column diameter is reduced, the liquid hold up (the mass of liquid in the column at any instant) in the column would increase. This would result in a decrease in available void space for gas flow through the column. Consequently the gas velocity (linear) would increase and the the gas side pressure drop across the bed would also increase. Higher gas side pressure drop hinders liquid flow. If the column diameter be further reduced, the column would get filled up with liquid. This condition is referred to as *flooding*. The gas mass velocity at this condition is termed as *flooding velocity*. The operating gas velocity is taken as 60 to 75% of the flooding velocity. Based on actual operating gas velocity the column cross-sectional area is calculated using Eq. (4.49).

$$A_{col} = \frac{\pi}{4} D^2 = \frac{G \times M_g}{G_n \times f}, \quad (4.49)$$

where A_{col} = column cross-sectional area,

G_n = superficial gas mass velocity at flooding,

f = fraction of the flooding velocity corresponding to which a column cross section is estimated = 0.6 to 0.75,

and M_g = gas (mixture) molecular weight.

G_n depends on the gas and liquid physical properties such as ρ_g, ρ_L, μ_L, packing characteristics and the liquid to gas mass flow rate ratio. It may be estimated with the help of plots available in standard books on Mass Transfer.

4.5.3.3 Column Height

Steady state solute balance equation across an elemental packed height (Fig. 4.11) of a column may be written as

$$G\,dY = L\,dX. \tag{4.50}$$

Taking into account the fact that the solute is transferred from the gas phase to the liquid phase, (4.50) may be rewritten as

$$-GdY = K_Y\,(Y-mX)\,a\,A_{col}\,dX \tag{4.51}$$

where a = packing surface area per unit packed bed volume.

To obtain an expression for the packedd bed height Eq. (4.51) is rearranged and integrated. The resulting equation is

$$Z_0 = \frac{G}{K_Y\,a\,A_{col}} \times \frac{Y_1 - Y_2}{(Y_1 - mX_1)-(Y_2 - mX_2)}\; ln\, \frac{(Y_1 - mX_1)}{(Y_2 - mX_2)} \tag{4.52}$$

This equation is generally represented as

$$Z_0 = H_{OG} \times N_{OG}$$

where $H_{OG} = \dfrac{G}{K_Y a\, A_{col}}$

= height equivalent to a transfer unit,

and $N_{OG} = \dfrac{Y_1 - Y_2}{(Y_1 - mX_1)-(Y_2 - mX_2)}\; ln\, \dfrac{(Y_1 - mX_1)}{(Y_2 - mX_2)}$

= number of transfer units.

Z_0 thus calculated stands for the height of the packed section of an absorber, which is necessary to reduce the pollutant concentration in the gas phase from Y_1 to Y_2.

The actual height of a column would be more than Z_0 in order to provide space for a demister and a liquid distributor at the top, liquid redistributor(s) in between the packed sections, a gas distributor, a packing support and a liquid seal at the bottom.

4.5.3.4 Pressure Drop Across A Packed Tower

In order to estimate the pressure drop across a packed section of a column one finds out ΔP/Z (pressure drop per unit packed bed height) based on the already decided operating parameters, the physical properties of the gas-liquid system and the packing characteristics utilizing information available in books on Mass Transfer. Using this information the pressue droip across a packed bed is estimated with the help of Eq. (4.53),

$$\Delta P_{bed} = Z_0\,(\Delta P/Z) \tag{4.53}$$

The actual pressure drop across a tower would be higher than that estimated using Eq. (4.53) because of the tower internals mentioned earlier other than the packings.

4.6 Adsorption of Gaseous Pollutants

When a fluid containing some dispersed substances is brought in contact with some specially treated/prepared solid particles, the molecules of the dispersed substances may be retained on the surfaces of the solid particles. This phenomenon is temed as *adsorption*. The solid material is referred to as an *adsorbent* and the substance retained on an adsorbent is termed as *adsorbate*. Adsorption is not only an effective method for removal of pollutants from gaseous streams, but also for abatement of water-borne pollutants. In this section adsorption of gaseous pollutants would be discussed.

The phenomenon of adsorption has been investigated experimentally and various theories have been proposed to explain the observations. But a theory, which may explain most of the observations, is yet to be developed.

It is presumed that an interaction between the adsorbate molecules and the active sites on the adsorbent surface cause retention of an adsorbate on an adsorbent. The interactive force, which brings about adsorption, has been theorized as either physical or chemical in nature. When an adsorbate is held due to physical attractive force the process is referred to as *physical adsorption*. The quantity of heat evolved during this process is almost the same as the latent heat of condensation of the adsorbate. The attractive force, which brings about physical adsorption is weak in nature, hence the adsorbed molecules may be removed (desorbed) from the solid particles either by raising the system temperature or by reducing the partial pressure of the adsorbate (by evacuation or by passing an inert gas) or by the combined effect of the two. The desorption process is an endothermic one.

In some cases an adsorbate is retained on an adsorbent surface because of chemical bonding between the two. It does not mean that a new chemical compound is formed, but the force of adhesion is rather strong. Such a process is termed as *chemisorption*. It is characterized by the evolution of relatively a large quantity of heat, which is similar in magnitude to that of an exothermic chemical reaction. Chemisorption is almost an irreversible process. During removal of a chemisorbed substance the adsorbate molecules often undergo chemical changes.

Since both chemisorption and physical adsorption occur on the adsorbent surface, a good adsorbent should have a large specific surface area (surface area per unit mass). The specific surface area increases with the decrease in particle size and increase in porosity of the adsorbent particles. To be a good adsorbent the solid particles should not only have high specific area but also possess proper interactive force / active sites with respect to the specific adsorbate.

The mass of adsorbate retained per unit mass of an adsorbent would be related to the adsorbate concentration in the fluid at equilibrium at a given temperature. Based on Langmuir's analysis of the phenomenon the equilibrium relation may be expressed as

$$X^*_i = mY_i^{1/n} \tag{4.54}$$

where X^*_i = mass of adsorbate i retained per unit mass of an adsorbent, and Y_i = mass of adsorbate i present in a unit mass of the fluid (carrier gas) at equilibrium.

m and n are specific constants for a specific adsorbate-adsorbent system. They are temperature dependent.

For $n \leq 1$, the adsorption process is considered to be favourable and for $n > 1$ it is unfavourable. For a specific adsorbate—adsorbent system the numerical values of m and n depend on the manufacturing process of the adsorbent. Those are evaluated experimentally.

Once an adsorbent has attained equilibrium with respect to an adsorbate, it would not be able to adsorb the adsorbate any further. The adsorbent has to be either discarded or regenerated for reuse. For regeneration of an adsorbent and or recovery of the adsorbate, generally the spent adsorbent is heated while a stream of an inert gas is passed over it. In the case of a physical adsorption process, steam or air at a moderate temperature (100 °C or more) is normally used. The desorbed substance may be collected (if valuable) or further treated before disposal. However, for regeneration of an adsorbent from a chemisorption process air at high temperature is passed over the spent adsorbent whereby the adsorbed substance gets oxidized and removed.

Commercially used adsorbents are activated carbon, silica, silica gel, molecular sieves (alumina silicates), alumina and some other metal oxides. The most commonly used adsorbent is granular activated carbon (GAC).

Commonly used adsorbers are fixed bed type, which are operated in cycles. A fixed bed adsorber consists of a housing containing a bed of granular absorbent particles. As a fluid stream carrying a pollutant (adsorbate) flows through the bed the pollutant gets adsorbed. Gradually the adsorbent particles become saturated. Once the pollutant in the treated stream reaches a pre-determined level as stipulated in the pollution control standards, the adsorption process is discontinued and the bed is regenerated. After regeneration of the bed, it is put on stream again.

An adsorber system may have several configurations. The simplest one would be a two-bed system in which when one bed is being regenerated the other one would be online. A bettter arrangement would be a three-bed system in which two beds are operated in series while the third one would be regenerated. In such a set-up the second bed acts as the polishing bed. When the volumetric flow rate of a fluid stream to be treated is rather large, then several units may be operated parallely.

Other than fixed bed, fluidized bed and moving bed adsorbers are also used. They are operated without any interruption for regeneration. From these beds partially spent adsorbent particles are removed, regenerated outside the beds and returned continuously. In such units the adsorbent particles undergo attrition due to inter-particle abrasion, as well as due to wall abrasion. Flow of solid particles in these adsorbers mayt not be smooth. However, the hold-up of adsorbent would be much less compared to that in a fixed bed system having the same capacity. Since regeneration is done outside the adsorber it may be carried out under drastic conditions, if necessary.

4.6.1 Fixed Bed Adsorber Design Approach

When a fluid stream containing an adsorbate enters a fixed bed adsorber, most of the adsorption takes place at the feed end to start with. Gradually the adsorbent particles present near the feed end becomes staurated with adsorbate and the effective adsorption zone (Z_a) shifts towards the exit end. That portion of an adsorber where most of adsorption takes place is referred to as the *effective adsorption zone*. Figure 4.12 shows progressives saturation of an adsorbent bed in an adsorber during the process. It also shows that the effective adsorption zone (Z_a) finally reaches the exit end.

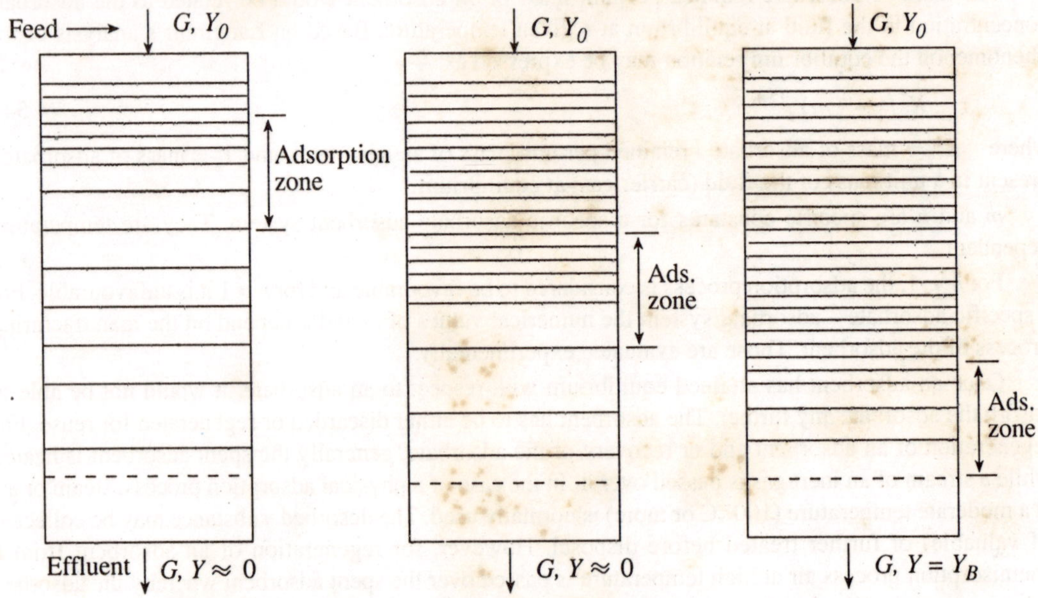

Fig. 4.12 : Schematic Diagram Showing Progressive Saturation of an Adsorbent Bed.

Figure 4.13 shows that the adsorbate concentration (Y) in the treated stream increases as the operation progresses and finally at time $\theta = \theta_B$ the concentration becomes Y_B. If the adsorbate be a pollutant, then Y_B would stand for its maximum permissible emission concentration from environmental pollution point of view. The time θ_B is referred to as the *break through time*. Continuation of the adsorption process beyond θ_B would result in further increase in pollutant concentration beyond Y_B in the treated effluent stream. At $\theta = \theta_B$ the operation is to be discontinued and the bed is to be regenerated.

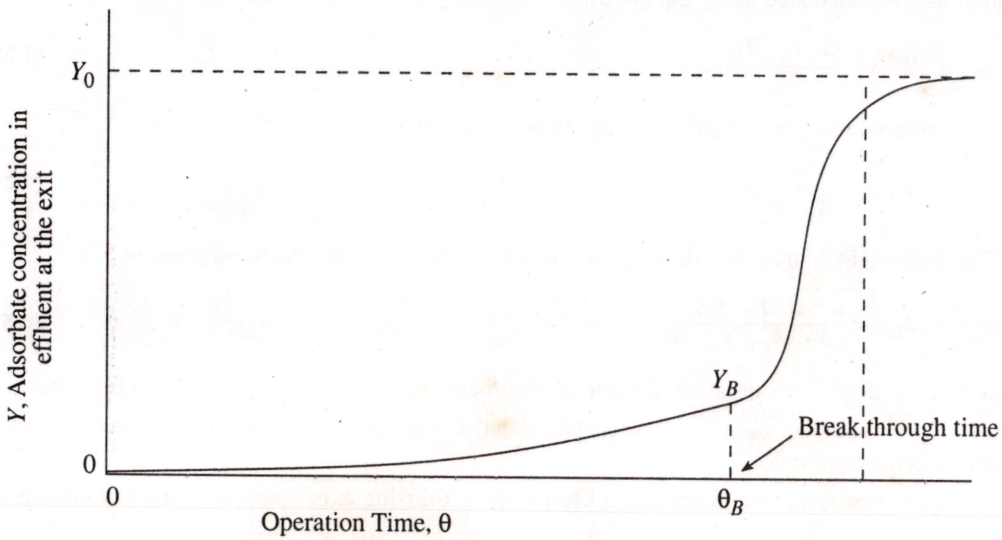

Fig. 4.13 : Adsorbate Concentration at Adsorber exit vs. Time.

In designing a fixed bed adsorber for abatement of gasborne pollutant one has to estimate its cross–sectional area and its packed height so as to have a pre-selected 'break through time' θ_B. The following information would be required for design purpose :

1. flow rate of the influent stream, G;
2. pollutant concentration in the influent, Y_0;
3. the maximum permissible pollutant concentration in the treated effluent, Y_B;
4. pre-selected 'break through time' θ_B, and
5. characteristics of the selected adsorbent.

The column cross-sectional area of an adsorber may be estimated using the following expression :

$$A_{col} = \frac{\text{Volumetric flow rate of the influent gas}}{\text{Superficial linear gas velocity in the column}}.$$

Normally for commercial units the superficial gas velocity employed is in the range of 6 to 24 m/min. If operated at a higher velocity the pressure drop across the bed would be higher and consequently the operating (energy) cost would be more. For estimating the column inlet and outlet pipe diameter the gas velocity is selected in the range of 600–900 m/min.

For estimation of the packed bed height, L_0, one assumes a θ_B. Based on this and the characteristics of the selected adsorbent the packed bed height L_0 may be calculated using either a thumb rule approach or an analytic approach.

For finding the packed bed height using a thumb rule approach the information required are : (i) the 'adsorption capacity' (X_c) of the selected adsorbent and (ii) the bulk density (ρ_b) of the adsorbent. The adsorption capacity X_c is defined as the mass of adsorbate which a unit mass of an adsorbent may adsorb while treating an influent gas stream having a pollutant concentration Y_0 and thereby reduce the pollutant concentration to its permissible limiting value Y_B in the treated gas. X_c and ρ_b may either be obtained from an adsorbent manufacturer/supplier or estimated experimentally in a laboratory. Laboratory based data would be more reliable for design purpose. Once these data are available the total mass of adsorbent required may be calculated using Eq. (4.55),

$$W = \frac{G\ Y_0\ \theta_B}{X_c}. \tag{4.55}$$

The corresponding bed height (L_0) may be obtained utilizing Eq. (4.56)

$$L_0 = \frac{W}{A_{col}\ \rho_b}. \tag{4.56}$$

The bed height L_0 may be calculated according the analytical approach using Eq. (4.57)

$$L_0 = \frac{G\ Y_0\ \theta_B}{X_s\ A_{col}\ \rho_b\ \ \Phi} \tag{4.57}$$

where Φ = degree of saturation of the total adsorbent bed at time θ_B, expressed as a fraction,

and X_s = pollutant concentration on adsorbent in equilibrium with gas phase concentration Y_0 expressed as a weight ratio.

X_x may be estimated either using Eq. (4.54) or utilizing experimentally obtained equilibrium data.

It should be noted here that at time θ_B from the start of the process, the major portion of the bed (except the adsorption zone Z_a near the exit end of the column) would be saturated. The Zone Z_a would be partially saturated. Hence Φ may be expressed as

$$\Phi = \frac{L_0 - (1-f)Z_a}{L_0} \tag{4.58}$$

where f = degree of saturation of the adsorption Zone Z_a.

$$f = \int_0^{Z_a} \frac{X\ dZ}{X_s\ Z_a} = \int_0^1 \frac{X}{X_s}\ d\left[\frac{Z}{Z_a}\right] \tag{4.59}$$

It is now apparent that in order to find L_0 one has to estimate f and Z_a at first.

The gas phase material balance equation of an adsorbate across an elemental bed height dZ in the adsorption zone Z_a over a time interval $d\theta$ may be written as

$$-G\ dY\ d\theta = K_Y\ A_{col} \cdot a\ (Y - Y^*)\ dZ\ d\theta + A_{col}\ \varepsilon\rho_g\ (\partial Y / \partial\theta)\ d\theta\ dZ \tag{4.60}$$

Adsorbate transfer from the gas phase	Adsorbate transferred to adsorbent	Accumulation of adsorbate in the void space

where ε = void fraction and a = surface area per unit packed volume.

The last term on the right hand side of Eq. (4.60), being small compared to the other terms, may be neglected and the equation may be rewritten as

$$\int_0^{Z_a} dZ = -\int_{Y_o}^{Y_B} \frac{G\,dY}{K_Y A_{col} a} \frac{1}{\left(Y - Y^*\right)} = \int_{Y_B}^{Y_o} \frac{G}{K_Y A_{col} a} \frac{dY}{\left(Y - Y^*\right)}. \tag{4.61}$$

The integrated form of Eq. (4.61) may be written as

$$Z_a = \frac{G}{K_Y A_{col} a} \int_{Y_B}^{Y_0} \frac{dY}{\left(Y - Y^*\right)} = H_{OG} . N_{OG}, \tag{4.62}$$

where $H_{OG} = \dfrac{G}{K_y A_{col} a}$,

$$N_{OG} = \int_{Y_B}^{Y_o} \frac{dY}{Y - Y^*}$$

and Y^* = equilibrium gas phase pollutant concentration corresponding to the adsorbed pollutant concentration X on adsorbent surface.

N_{OG} which is equal to $\displaystyle\int_{Y_B}^{Y_0} \frac{dY}{Y - Y^*}$,

may be evaluated numerically or graphically taking help of a plot similar to the Fig. 4.14. However, a problem arises as corresponding to $Y = Y_0$, $Y^* = Y_0$ and hence N_{OG} would be infinite. To circumvent this difficulty N_{OG} is approximated as

$$N_{OG} = \int_{Y_B}^{Y_o} \frac{dY}{\left(Y - Y^*\right)} \approx \int_{Y_B}^{Y_e} \frac{dY}{\left(Y - Y^*\right)} \tag{4.63}$$

where Ye is assigned a numerical value slightly less than Y_0

To estimate H_{OG} it is necessary to know the numerical values of K_Y and a. In the absence of such information one may have an estimate of H_{OG} with the help of Fig. 4.15 for which the information required are ε and d_p,

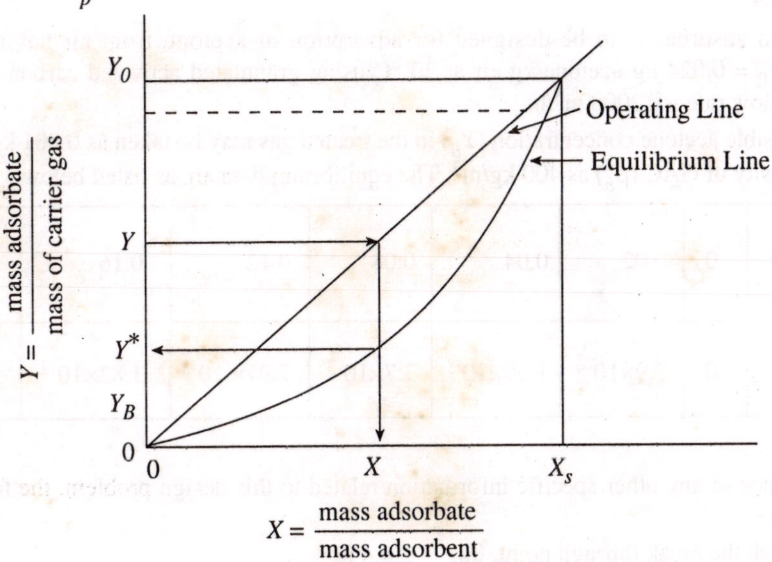

Fig. 4.14 : Typical Equilibrium Curve and Operating Line of a Fixed Bed Adsorber.

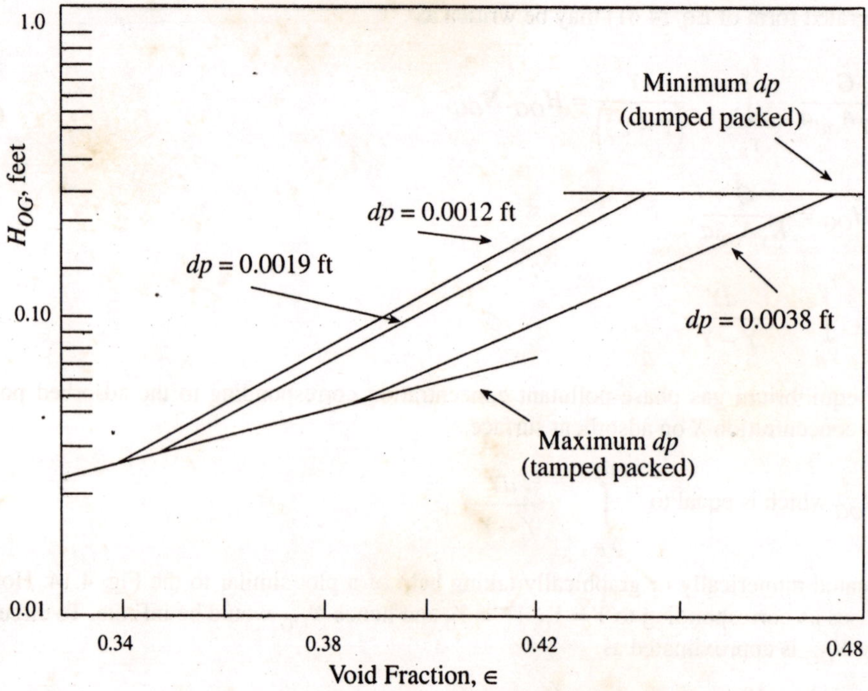

Fig. 4.15 : H_{OG} for Fixed Bed Adsorption (Johnston).

where $\in$ = bed void fraction,

and d_p = average adsorbent particle diameter

After evaluation of Z_a using Eq. (4.62), f is to be calculated numerically using Eq. (4.59). Finally Φ and L_0 are evaluated using Eq. (4.58) and Eq. (4.57) respectively.

Example 4.4

A fixed bed adsorber is to be designed for adsorption of acetone from air having an initial concentration, Y_0 = 0.024 kg acetone/kg air at 30 °C using granulated activated carbon (GAC). The volumetric gas flow rate is 12000 m^3/hr.

The permissible acetone concentration (Y_B) in the treated gas may be taken as 0.001 kg acetone/kg air and bulk density of GAC (ρ_b) as 400 kg/m^3. The equilibrium data are as listed below.

$X, \frac{g_{acetone}}{g_{carbon}}$	0	0.02	0.04	0.08	0.12	0.16	0.20
$Y, \frac{g_{acetone}}{g_{air}}$	0	7.9×10^{-4}	1.59×10^{-3}	3.7×10^{-3}	7.97×10^{-3}	1.82×10^{-2}	3.22×10^{-2}

Solution :

In the absence of any other specific information related to this design problem, the following are assumed :

Time to reach the break through point, θ_B = 4 hr

Superficial gas velocity in the adsorber = 0.25 m/s

H_{OG} = 0.03 m

Using the assumed values of θ_B, the superficial velocity and H_{OG} and information specified in the problem, the packed adsorber height L_o is estimated with the help of the thumb rule approach utilizing the following equations/relations :

$$A_{col} = \frac{\text{Volumetric gas flow rate}}{\text{Superficial gas (linear) velocity}}$$

$$W = \frac{G\ Y_0 \theta_B}{X_c}$$

and $$L_0 \quad \frac{W}{A_{col}\ \rho_b}$$

Finally accepting the adsorber packed height L_0 as calculated using Eq. (4.56), θ_B is recalculated following the analytical approach.

$$\theta_B = \frac{L_0\ X_s A_{col}\ \rho_b\ \Phi}{G\ Y_0}$$

$$\Phi = \frac{L_0 - (1-f)\ Z_a}{L_0}$$

$$Z_a = H_{OG}\ N_{OG}$$

$$N_{OG} = \int_{Y_B}^{Y_0} \frac{dY}{(Y - Y^*)} \approx \int_{Y_B}^{Y_e} \frac{dY}{(Y - Y^*)}$$

$$\approx \sum_{Y_B}^{Y_e} \frac{\Delta Y}{(Y - Y^*)_{av}}.$$

Y_e is taken as 0.0235.

$$Z / Z_a = \frac{H_{OG} \int_{Y_B}^{Y} \frac{dY}{Y - Y^*}}{H_{OG} \int_{Y_B}^{Y_e} \frac{dY}{Y - Y^*}}.$$

$$\text{And } f = \int_0^1 = \frac{X}{X_s}\ d\left(\frac{Z}{Z_a}\right)$$

$$= \sum_0^1 \left(\frac{X}{X_s}\right)_{av} \Delta\left(\frac{Z}{Z_a}\right).$$

Plotting of the supplied equilibrium data and drawing of an appropriate operating line resulted in a figure similar to that of Fig. 4.14. From that figure the value of X_S is found to be 0.177. For estimation

N_{OG} and f by numerical integration the required values of Y, X, and Y^* are read from the figure and the calculated values of

$$\frac{1}{Y-Y^*},\ \Sigma\frac{\Delta Y}{\left(Y-Y^*\right)_{av}},\frac{X}{X_s},\ \frac{Z}{Z_a}\ \ and\ \ \Sigma\left(\frac{X}{X_s}\right)_{av}\Delta\left(\frac{Z}{Z_a}\right)$$

are listed hereunder.

The thumb rule approach yields the following information :

$$A_{col} = \frac{12000\ m^3/hr}{0.25\ m/s\times 3600} = 13.33\ m^2$$

From Eq. (4.55),

$$W = \frac{G\ Y_0\ \theta_B}{X_c}$$

In the absence of specific data X_c is taken as equal to X_s,

where G = mass flow rate of the carrier gas (air)

$$= \text{total mass flow rate} \times \frac{1}{1+0.024}$$

$$= \frac{total\ \ volumetric\ \ flow\ \ rate}{22.4}\times\frac{273}{273+30}\times M_{influent}$$

$$M_{influent} = \text{molecular weight of the influent gas} = \frac{1+0.024}{\frac{1}{28.84}+\frac{0.024}{58}} = 29.18\ .$$

Therefore G = 13,754.3 kg/hr

$$W = \frac{13,754.3\ \times\ 0.024\ \times 4}{0.177} = 7460\ \ \text{kg of}\ \ GAC.$$

From Eq. (4.56),

$$L_0 = \frac{W}{A_{col}\ \rho_b} = \frac{7460}{13.33\ \times\ 400}$$

$$= 1.399 \approx 1.4\ \text{m}.$$

Y	X	Y^*	$\frac{1}{Y-Y^*}$	$\Sigma\frac{\Delta Y}{(Y-Y^*)_{av}}$	$\frac{Z}{Za}$	$\frac{X}{X_s}$	$\Sigma\left(\frac{X}{X_s}\right)_{av}\Delta\left(\frac{Z}{Z_a}\right)$
Y_B = 0.001	0.007	3×10^{-4}	1428.3	0	0	0.0359	0
0.002	0.014	5×10^{-4}	666.7	1.0475	0.2079	0.0791	0.01195
0.004	0.0275	1.0×10^{-3}	333.3	2.0475	0.4064	0.1554	0.03522
0.006	0.041	1.6×10^{-3}	227.3	2.608	0.5177	0.2316	0.05676
0.012	0.081	3.8×10^{-3}	121.95	3.656	0.7257	0.4576	0.12843
0.014	0.095	4.8×10^{-3}	108.7	3.887	0.7715	0.5367	0.1512
0.016	0.108	6.3×10^{-3}	103.09	4.099	0.8135	0.6102	0.17528
0.018	0.121	8.1×10^{-3}	101.01	4.303	0.8541	0.6836	0.20154
0.020	0.135	11.3×10^{-3}	114.93	4.519	0.8969	0.7627	0.23249
Y_e = 0.0235	0.159	18×10^{-3}	181.81	5.038	1	0.8983	0.31811

From Eq. (4.63)

$N_{OG} = 5.038$

From Eq. (4.62),

$Z_a = H_{OG}\, N_{OG} = 0.03 \times 5.038 = 0.151.$

From Eq. (4.59),

$$f = \sum_{0}^{1} \left(\frac{X}{X_s}\right)_{av} \Delta\left(\frac{Z}{Z_a}\right) = 0.31811.$$

$$\Phi = \frac{L_0 - (1-f)\; Z_a}{L_0} = \frac{1.4 - (1 - 0.31811) \times 0.151}{1.4}$$

$= 0.926.$

From the rearranged Eq. (4.57).

$$\theta_B = \frac{L_0\; X_s\; A_{col}\, \rho_b\; \Phi}{G\; Y_0} = \frac{1.4 \times 0.177 \times 13.33 \times 400 \times 0.926}{13{,}754.3 \times 0.024}$$

$= 3.706 \approx 3.71$

The proposed adsorber would have

Column cross-section, A_{col}	$= 13.33\ m^2$
Packed granular bed height, L_0	$= 1.4$ m
Mass of $GAC = A_{col} \times L_0 \times \rho_b$	$= 13.33 \times 1.4 \times 400$
	$= 7{,}465$ kg.

Time to reach the break through point,

$\theta_B = 3.71$ hr.

4.7 Chemical Treatment of Gaseous Pollutants

Chemical treatment of gaseous pollutants is a better option as it very often converts pollutants into some innocuous substances. However, chemical treatment methods may involve higher operating cost compared to that of the physical treatment methods because of the cost of chemicals used.

The chemical treatment methods may be classified into two groups, namely, (1) the methods for treatment of inorganic pollutants and (2) the methods for treatment of organic pollutants, which are generally referred to as VOCs (Volatile organic Compounds).

The methods for inorganic pollutant treatment are pollutant specific, that is , for each specific pollutant a specific chemical is to be used and specific reaction conditions are to be maintained. The methods for treatment of some common gaseous inorganic pollutants are discussed in Chapter 5.

For treatment of VOCs the methods employed are combustion reaction based. These methods are classified as (i) thermal incineration, (ii) catalytic incineration and (iii) bio-oxidation. Prior to subjecting a gas stream containing VOCs to a combustion process it should be pre-treated for removal of particulates and condensables. Under this Section the chemical treatment methods for VOC abatement are outlined. Further information on this topic is included in Chater 5.

4.7.1 Thermal Incineration

Of the three methods used for oxidation of VOCs, thermal incineration takes place at about 650 °C or higher temperature, whereas the others are carried out at a lower temperature.

For incineration, i.e., combustion of two ingredients, namely, a combustible substance and oxygen are required. The VOCs present in a waste gas stream constitute the combustible component and oxygen from air serves as the other constituent. The main products of a combustion process are CO_2, H_2O. Some amount of NO_x and SO_x are also produced. Some organic compounds may also be present in the product stream if the process be incomplete.

To achieve complete combustion, that is, for complete oxidation of VOCs (pollutants) it is necessary to provide excess air (oxygen) over that required stoichiometrically because of imperfect mixing of the ingredients before and during combustion. For the process to be self-sustaining the mixture should neither be too lean nor too rich with respect to the combustible components. The limiting compositions are referred to as the *lower* and *upper explosive limits*. Between these limits combustion takes place upon ignition but may explode if the process is not properly controlled. The numerical values of the lower and upper explosive limits of a mixture depend on the species of combustibles present in the mixture. However, care should be taken that the oxygen content in the mixture should never be less than 15%.

The degree of completion of a combustion reaction depends on the temperature, residence time and turbulence in the combustion zone. Lower degree of completion would mean presence of unburnt organic compounds (pllutants) in the treated effluent. The rate of reaction increases with the increase in temperature. Hence at a higher temperature the residence time (in combustion chamber) required for complete combustion would be shorter. In other words, at a higher temperature a smaller chamber would do the job. However, to maintain a higher temperature auxiliary fuel may be needed, if the combustible constituents present in the mixture do not have enough calorific value. The calorific value of a mixture depends on the concentration of the combustible species present in the mixture.

While designing a thermal incinerator one may encounter any one of the following three types of situations :

Type-I

The gas to be treated would have sufficient calorific value and hence no auxiliary fuel would be required, but air (oxygen) has to be supplied. Such a situation implies that the mixture would have a composition above the upper explosive limit.

Type-II

The gas may neither require any auxiliary fuel nor any air, that is, its composition would be in between the lower and upper explosive limits. Such a gas should be handled carefully as otherwise the flame may strike back, i.e., propagate back from the combustion chamber to its source.

Type-III

The gas may not have sufficiently high calorific value so as to maintain the desired temperature in the combustion chamber. This implies that the mixture composition would be below its lower explosive limit. For combustion of such a gas an auxiliary fuel would be required to sustain the combustion process.

It has been mentioned earlier that Type I gas mixture would have a relatively high calorific value, hence it may be gainfully utilized as a fuel. It may be incinerated in a boiler furnace or a process heater or a properly designed combustion chamber with an arrangement for supplying adequate quantity of air. The basic equipment needed for combustion of a Type I gas mixture is a low NO_x burner.

However, if there be no scope for utilization of the heat produced during incineration the gas mixture may be flared, that is, the combustion process is carried out in open atmosphere where atmospheric turbulence provides oxygen for combustion as well as promotes mixing. The device is referred to as a *flare stack*. It is a stack/ chimney at the base of which the gas is introduced. The gas flows up the stack and as it is about to emerge it meets a pilot flame. The pilot flame is maintained with a pre-mixed fuel gas-air mixture. It is used to ignite the gas mixture as well as to anchor the resulting flame. The combustion products including those resulting from incomplete combustion are directly discharged into the atmosphere. The combustion products may include HC (hydrocarbons), CO, and some stable intermediate products, such as NO_x, SO_2, HCl and carbon particles besides CO_2 and H_2O. The combustion efficiency may be improved by pre-mixing the gas to be incinerated with air and/or by injecting steam near the flame, which would promote turbulence. The heat generated during combustion is wasted.

The major consideration for a flare site selection and its stack height estimation should be safety for the plant operating personnel and equipment around the flare from its radiative heat intensity. A flare should be located in a place with sufficient free space around it, so that a man may be able to run to safety from the flare heat, if necessary.

For estimation of flare stack height one should consider the maximum radiative heat intensity to which the process equipment (particularly petroleum crude and petroleum fraction storage tanks) around the stack may be subjected to. The diameter of a stack is to be calculated based on the anticipated maximum volumetric flow rate of the gas mixture and its flame velocity. The other data required for calculation of stack height and diameter are ambient temperature, the average calorific value of the VOC mixture, its average molecular weight, density and flame emissivity and the average wind velocity at the stack height.

Figure 4.16 shows a schematic representation of a flare stack.

It should be pointed out here that flares might be used only for high volume concentrated waste gas streams.

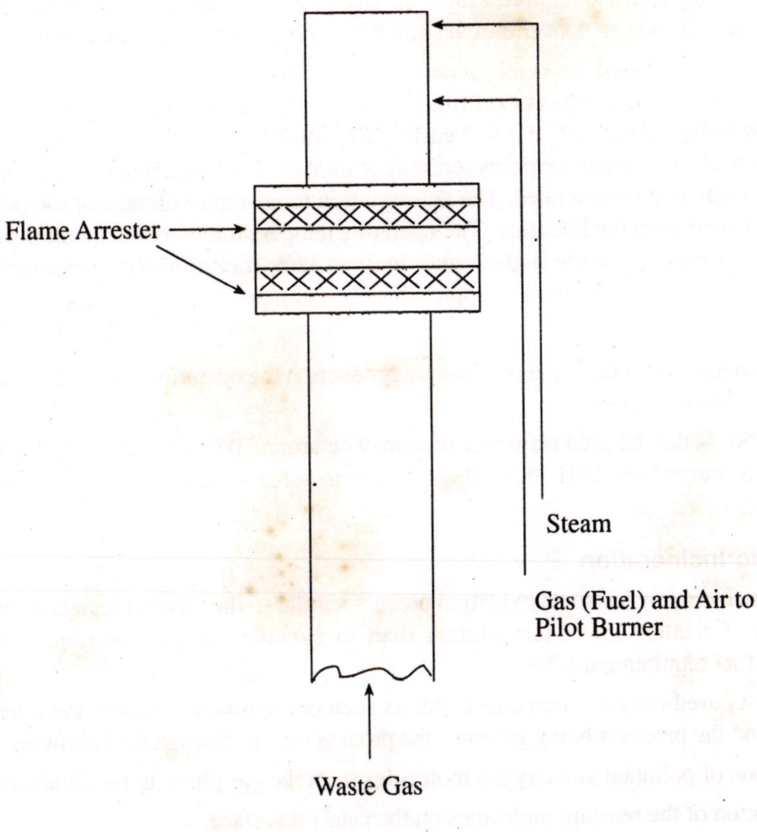

Fig. 4.16 : Schematic Representation of a Flare Stack.

The Type II gas mixture should be handled carefully as those are explosive mixtures. Such a mixture should be diluted with air or an inert gas so as to bring down the mixture composition below its lower explosive limit prior to incineration. For incineration of the diluted mixture some amount of an auxiliary fuel may be needed. It may appear paradoxical that a combustible mixture is diluted and then incinerated with the aid of some supplementary fuel. However, from safety point of view it becomes imperative. If the diluted mixture is burnt in a boiler furnace or a process heater no auxiliary fuel would be needed.

If it is planned to burn the original gas mixture without dilution in a combustor the following precautions must be taken :

(a) For compression of the mixture prior to feeding into an incinerator a steam-jet ejector should be used. Mechanical devices should not be used as frictional heat may cause explosion.

(b) To prevent striking back of the flame from an incinerator one must take the measures listed hereunder.

  (i) In the gas pipeline (leading to the incinerator) flame arresters, such as screens, perforated plates should be fitted.

  (ii) The selected pipe diameter should be such that the gas velocity through the pipe would be higher than the theoretical flame velocity of the mixture.

  (iii) The gas mixture must pass through a seal pot.

Handling and incineration of Type III gas mixtures pose no problem from safety point of view. For the desired degree of destruction of the combustible (pollutant) present in such a gas mixture it is to be injected into a combustion chamber fired with an auxiliary fuel and maintained at the required temperature. Proper turbulence and oxygen concentration should be maintained in the incinerator.

An incinerator to be used for combustion of a Type III gas mixture may be a box or a cylindrical chamber at one end of which a gas or oil fired burner is located. The gas mixture to be incinerated is introduced close to the burner so that it will easily mix with the combustion products and thereby attain the required temperature. Turbulence promoters may be used to bring about quick mixing of the combustion products and the gas to be incinerated. The auto-ignition temperature of each of the pollutants present should be ascertained from the literature. The operating temperature of the incinerator should be at least a few hundred degrees above the highest auto-ignition temperature of the components present. The incinerator chamber volume (V) may be approximately estimated using the relation,

$$V = t \times Q,$$

where Q = volumetric flow rate of the combustion products at the operating temperature, and t = required residence time in the incinerator.

At about 750 °C the required residence time may be around 0.01 sec. Around 650 °C the residence time has to be increased from 0.01 sec to about 0.1 sec to achieve the same degree of destruction of the pollutants.

4.7.2 Catalytic Incineration

Catalytic incineration is also an oxidation process similar to the thermal incineration. However, the process occurs at a much lower temperature than that of thermal incineration. Consequently the supplementary fuel requirement is less.

The catalysts used are solid particles either as such or supported on some inert ceramic material. The reactants and the products being gaseous, the process occurs through the following steps :

1. diffusion of pollutant and oxygen molecules from the gas phase to the catalyst surface,
2. adsorption of the reactant molecules on the catalyst surface,
3. reaction of the adsorbed molecules,
4. desorption of the product molecules from the catalyst surface, and finally,
5. diffusion of the product molecules to the bulk of the gas phase.

Two types of catalysts are normally used :

(i) noble metal, such as platinum, palladium alone or in combination, supported on nickel alloy or alumina or ceramic,

(ii) base metals or metal oxides, such as aluminium, chromium, cobalt, copper, iron, manganese, vanadium, zinc supported or unsupported.

The second type of catalyst is cheaper and is easy to prepare.

Metallic supports are generally in the form of a ribbon on which the catalyst is deposited. The ribbons are then crimped and formed into a mat.

Ceramic supports may be either in the form of pellets or a honeycomb structure.

The catalyst is sometimes admixed with a substance known as a promoter, which increases the catalyst activity by modifying the catalyst crystal structure and size.

The desired properties of a catalyst are (i) high activity at lower temperature, (ii) structural stability, (iii) resistance to attrition and (iv) low pressure drop across the catalyst bed.

The catalyst activity very often decreases with use. This may happen because of (1) chemical reaction between catalyst particle and some substances, such as bismuth, arsenic, antimony, zinc, lead, tin, mercury, phosphorous, halogens, etc. even when these are present in trace amounts in waste gases, (2) adsorption of some chemicals (chemisorptions) on catalyst surface and (3) physical coating of the catalyst surface with tarry matter. Catalyst also suffers loss in activity as a result of aging. This may be due to change in the crystal structure of metal (catalyst) because of erosion, vaporization and attrition. Normally catalyst life is 3 to 5 years.

A catalytic incinerator may consist of the following components/sections :

(1) a pre-heating sections (2) a burner,
(3) a mixing chamber, (4) a catalyst bed,
(5) a blower.

A schematic diagram of a catalytic incinerator is shown in Fig. 4.17.

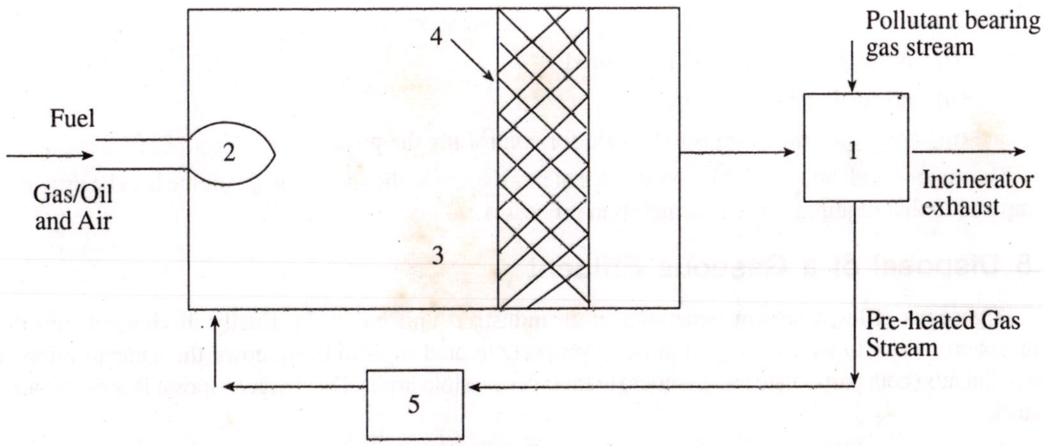

1. Pre-heater, 2. Burner Flame, 3. Mixing Chamber,
4. Catalyst Bed, 5. Blower.

Fig. 4.17 : Schematic Diagram of a Catalytic Incinerator.

A catalytic incinerator works in the way described below.

An incoming pollutant bearing gas stream may be pre-heated prior to feeding the same into the mixing chamber. In the mixing chamber the gas stream gets mixed with the hot flue gas from the burner so that the mixture may attain the temperature at which catalytic oxidation would take place. The purpose of the burner would be to produce the heat required to maintain the mixing chamber and the catalyst bed at the desired temperature. The fuel may be either a gas or an oil. The catalyst bed is arranged in such a fashion that the influent stream admixed with hot flue gas has to pass through the bed and no portion may bypass the bed. It should be so fitted to the combustion chamber that the same may be easily taken out for reactivating or replacement. It may be necessary to install a blower so as to overcome the pressure losses at different sections of the incinerator assembly.

Complete destruction of the pollutants present in a waste gas stream is difficult to achieve in an incinerator and it may not be necessary. 98-99 percent destruction may bring down the pollutant concentration to the permissible emission limit. Most of the VOCs on complete combustion produce CO_2 and H_2O. Some carbon monoxide may also be produced due to incomplete combustion. Some VOCs on incineration may produce pollutants like SO_2, SO_3, halogens and halogenated compounds, such as Cl_2, HCl.It may be necessary to treat the incinerator exhanust stream (in order to remove the above named pollutants) before its final disposal.

4.7.3 Bio-oxidation

Bio-oxidation of a pollutant bearing gas stream may be carried out when

(i) the pollutants present are biodegradable,

(ii) the stream does not contain any pollutant toxic to aerobic bacteria, and

(iii) the volumetric flow rate of the stream is not high.

This process is similar to the combustion process in the sense that the main products of oxidation would be CO_2 and H_2O. However, the process takes place at ambient temperature and heat evolved is dissipated easily. It is carried out by passing a pollutant bearing gas stream admixed with an adequate quantity of air through a bed of porous soil pre-seeded with the right species of aerobic microbes. The microbes use the VOCs for their metabolic activity. Oxygen required for this purpse is taken from air. The bed size should be such that there would be sufficient contact time for attaining the desired extent of pollutant destruction.

The major advantages of this process over the incineration processes are :

(i) no supplementary fuel is required,

(ii) no costly process equipment is needed,

and (iii) very little attention is to be paid for controlling the process.

The major disadvantage of this process is that more space in the form of bed volume is to be provided compared to that required for the incineration processes.

4.8 Disposal of a Gaseous Effluent

A gaseous effluent stream generated in an industrial unit has to be finally discharged into the atmosphere,. Prior to its discharge it must be properly treated so as to bring down the concentration of the pollutants (both particulate and gaseous) to their permissible limits. Discharge/disposal is done through a stack.

A stack or a chimney is a vertical cylindrical or rectangular conduit. When a gaseous stream is discharged through a stack the pollutants present in the stream get dispersed into the atmosphere. A stack cannot abate the pollutants present, but it releases the pollutant at a suitable height so that when the pollutants diffuse back to the earth's surface their concentration would be below the permissible limit of each pollutant even under the most unfavorable weather condition.

As a gas stream issues out of a stack it flows upward to some height due to its kinetic energy and buoyancy before it is swept away in a horizontal direction by wind. The pollutants present in the gas stream (after emerging from the stack) get dispersed both in the horizontal and vertical directions because of molecular and eddy diffusion. Effluence of a gas stream from stack and the profile of the resulting plume under ideal condition are sketched in Fig. 4.18.

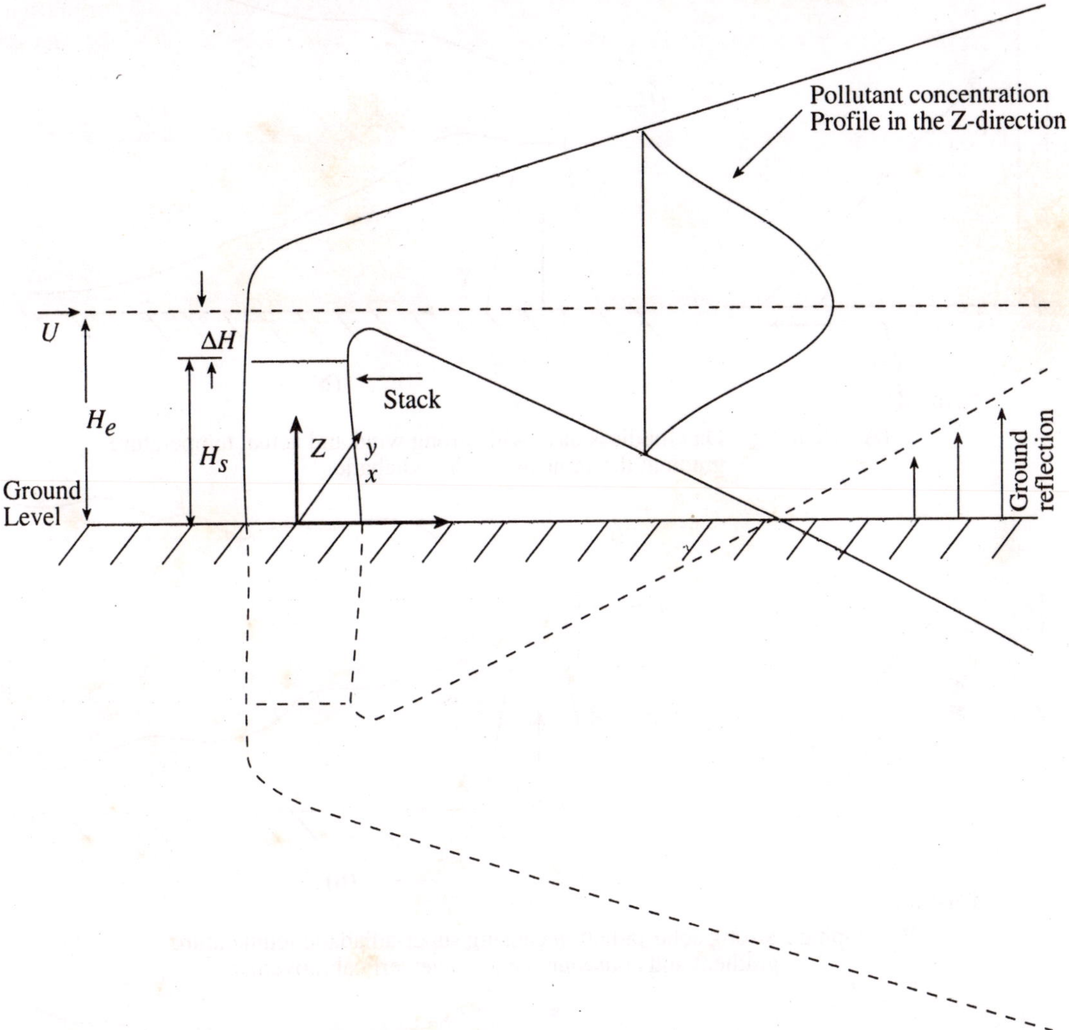

Fig. 4.18 : Plume Profile Development under Ideal Condition with Ground Reflection.

4.8.1 Actual Plume Profile

The actual plume profile downwind depends on the temperature gradient in the troposphere, the wind velocity and the topography in the immediate neighbourhood of a stack. The tropospheric temperature gradient depends on the incoming solar radiation intensity during the day and the degree of cloud cover at night.

Dispersion of the pollutants in a plume depends on vertical air movement resulting from the tropospheric temperature gradient and also on the prevalent wind speed. Based on the above mentioned factors the atmospheric condition has been classified into different stability classes. In Table 4.15 the Pasquill-Gifford stability designations are listed.

Figures 4.19A-G show the different types of plume profile corresponding to various atmospheric stability conditions.

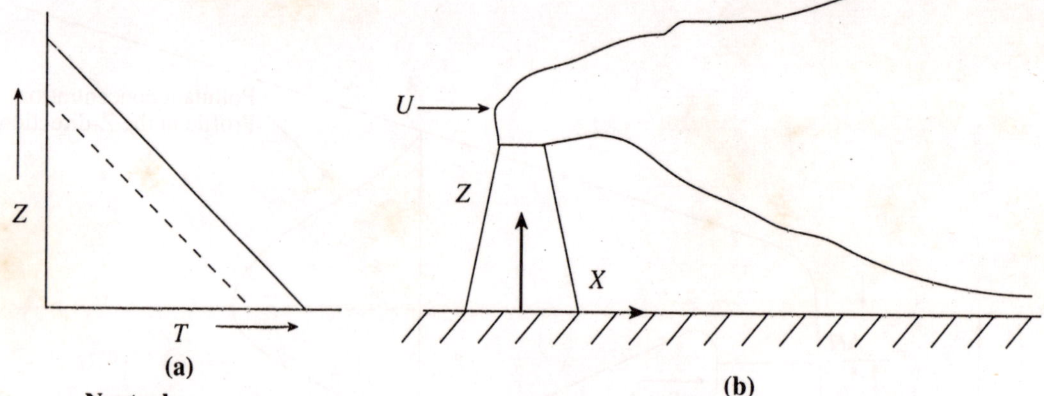

Neutral

(A) Conning : On cloudless days with strong wind and actual temperature gradient the same as the dry adiabatic.

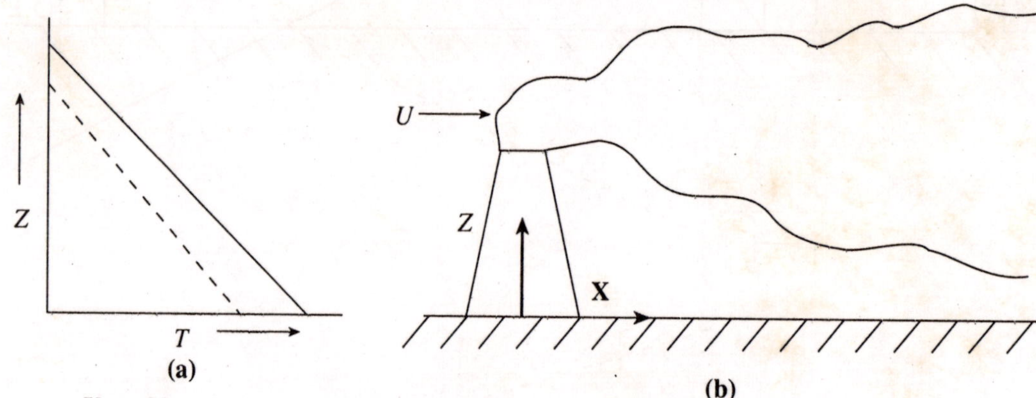

Unstable

(B) Looping : Strong solar radiation causing super-adiabatic temperature gradient and consequent excessive vertical movement.

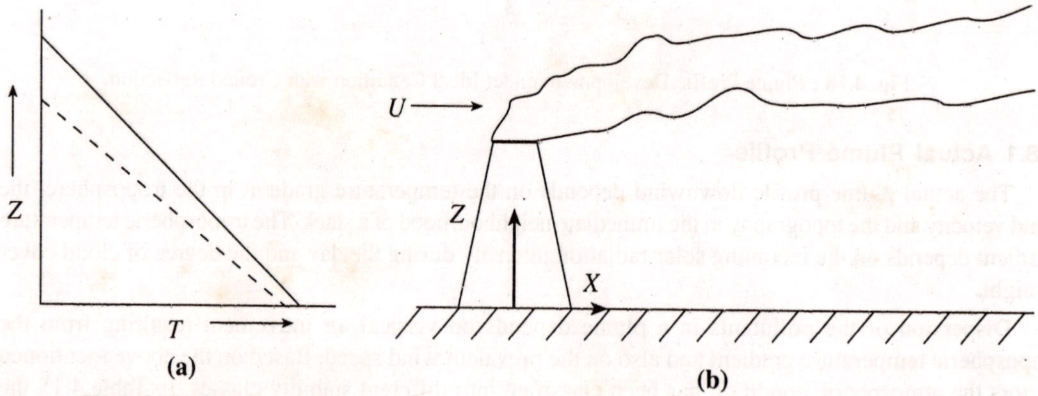

Slightly Stable

(C) Spiralling : Strong solar radiation causing sub-adiabatic temperature gradient, moderate wind.

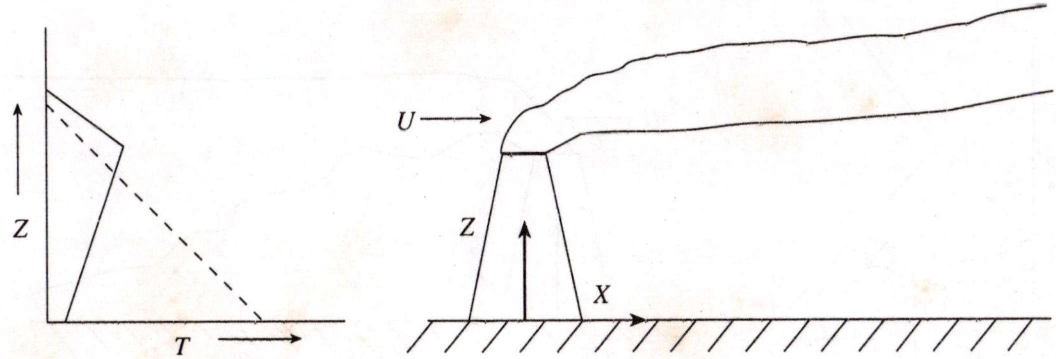

(a) (b)

Surface Inversion

(D) Fanning : Inversion up to the stack height, consequently vertical movement suppressed below the stack.

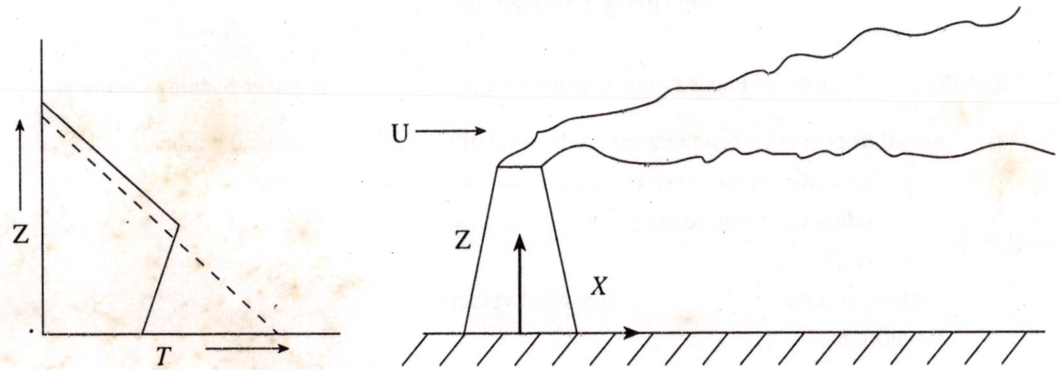

(a) (b)

Inversion below stack level

(E) Lofting : Inversion not reaching the stack level. Vertical movement towards the ground suppressed but it continues above the stack.

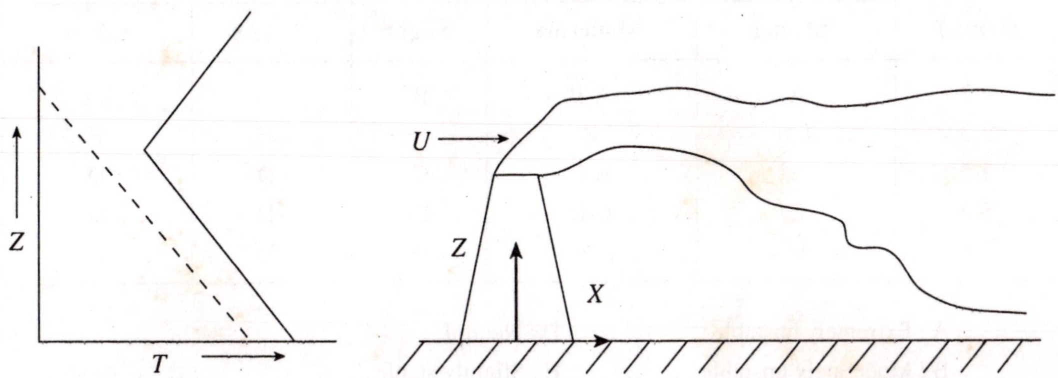

(a) (b)

Inversion above stack level and adiabatic below

(F) Trapping : Vertical movement suppressed above the stack level but continuous below.

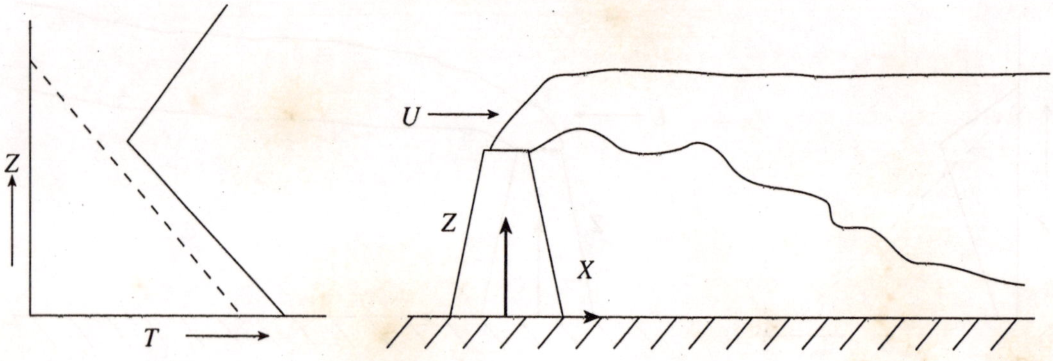

(a)

(b)

Inversion above stack level and super-adiabatic below.

(G) Fumigating : Vertical movement suppressed above the stack level but strong movement below.

Fig. 4.19 : A-G Sketches of Plume Profile Corresponding to Various Atmospheric Stability Conditions.

(a) Actual tropospheric temperature gradient relative to the dry adiabatic gradient.

Adiabatic temperature gradient, — — — —

Actual temperature gradient. ————

(b) Plume profile

T = temperature. U = wind velocity

Z = altitude.

Table 4.15 : Qualitative Atmospheric Stability Designations

Wind Velocity (U m/s)	Day Incoming Solar Radiation			Night Cloudiness	
	Strong	Moderate	Slight	≥ 4 / 8	≤ 3 / 8
< 2	A	A-B	B	—	—
2-3	A-B	B	C	E	F
3-5	B	B-C	C	D	D
5-6	C	C-D	D	D	D
> 6	C	D	D	D	D

A : Extremely unstable

B : Moderately unstable

C : Slightly unstable

D : Neutral

E : Slightly stable

F : Moderately stable.

4.8.2 Stack Design Approach

It has been mentioned in Section 4.8 that a stack is used for discharging a waste gas stream at a suitable height from the ground. Once discharged, the constituents (including the pollutants, if any) of the waste gas get dispersed. Some portions of those diffuse back to the earth's surface.

To design a stack one has to find its height H_s, such that the concentration of the pollutants, which have diffused back to the ground level, should not be more than their respective permissible limits even under the worst atmospheric conditions. It is also necessary to estimate the cross-sectional area of a stack so that the pressure at the base of the stack would be sufficient to overcome the resistance to flow of the gas stream through the stack.

4.8.2.1 Stack Height Estimation

Stack height may either be estimated using some empirical relations or using a semi-empirical approach. The empirical relations do not take into consideration the weather condition, whereas the semi-empirical approach takes into account the plume rise, wind velocity and weather condition. It goes without saying that the second approach gives a better estimate of the stack height.

4.8.2.2 Empirical Approach

The empirical equations listed below may be used for estimation of stack height :

A. Stack height for thermal power stations

(i) a boiler having less than 200 MW capacity :

$$H_s = 14Q^{0.3} \tag{4.64a}$$

(ii) a boiler having more than 200 MW capacity :

$$H_s = 220 \text{ m} \tag{4.64b}$$

(iii) a boiler having 500 MW or more capacity :

$$H_s = 275 \text{ m} \tag{4.64c}$$

B. Stack height of plants other than power plants

(i) $$H_s^* = 30 \text{ m} \tag{4.64d}$$

(ii) $$H_s = 14Q^{0.3} \tag{4.64e}$$

(iii) $$H_s = 74\ Q_1^{0.27} \tag{4.64f}$$

where H_s = stack height in m

Q = SO_2 emission rate in kg/hr

and Q_1 = particulate emission rate in tonnes/hr.

*If the calculated H_s using Eq. (4.64e) or (4.64f) be more than 30 m, then the calculated stack height should be accepted.

4.8.2.3 Semi-empirical Approach

In this approach the stack height is estimated through the following steps :

Step-I

A stack height, H_s, is assumed, The assumed height may be the one calculated using the empirical approach outlined in Section 4.8.2.2.

Step-II

Plume rise, ΔH, is calculated using a suitable semi-empirical equation. A few of the equations reported in the literature are enumerated in Section 4.8.2.5. These equations are based on the conjecture that plume rise is influenced by two factors namely,

(i) momentum of the issuing stream from the stack, and (ii) the buoyancy of the stream resulting from the difference in density of stack gas and that of the ambinet air at the physical stack height. The correlations proposed by the different authors are based on the data available to them. Some authors have taken into consideration the weather stability criterion while developing their correlations.

Step-III

The effective stack height H_e is taken as

$$H_e = H_s + \Delta H \tag{4.65}$$

Step-IV

Using Eq. (4.67) and the estimated H_e, the maximum concentration of each of the different pollutants (present in the effluent gas stream) at the ground level is estimated corresponding to the different atmospheric stability designations. If those are within their respective permissible limits, then the assumed H_s is accepted as the actual stack height. If not, then based on a higher value of H_s than the earlier assumed one based on the Steps II, III and IV are repeated till an acceptable H_s is found which satisfies the criterion specified in Step IV.

4.8.2.4 Pollutant Concentration Profile in a Plume

An equation expressing the pollutant concentration profile in a plume resulting from a continuous point source under steady state condition has been developed on the basis of the following assumptions

(i) $C_{x,y,z} \propto 1/U$

(ii) $C_{x,y,z} \propto Q$

and (iii) the concentration profile at any downwind location (x,y,z) follows the Gaussian normalized probability distribution curve in the Y-and Z-directions.

Based on the above mentioned assumptions the derived equation representing the concentration profile is

$$C_{x,y,z} = \frac{Q}{2\pi\sigma_y\sigma_z U} \; e^{-1/2\left(\frac{y}{\sigma_y}\right)^2}\left\{e^{-1/2\left(\frac{Z-H_e}{\sigma_z}\right)^2} + e^{-1/2\left(\frac{Z+H_e}{\sigma_z}\right)^2}\right\} \tag{4.66}$$

where $C_{x,y,z}$ = concentration of a pollutant at a location having coordinates x,y & z,

Q = mass of the specific pollutant emitted per unit time,

U = wind velocity at height H_e,

σ_y = standard deviation of the dispersion coefficient in the y-direction,

and σ_z = standard deviation of the dispersion coefficient in the z-direction.

The numerical values of σ_y and σ_z depend on the weather condition, wind velocity and the distance of a location from the stack base in the horizontal downwind direction, i.e., the X-coordinate.

The term, $e^{-1/2\left(\frac{Z+H_e}{\sigma_z}\right)^2}$

in Eq. (4.66) represents increased pollutation concentration because of ground reflection.

The concentration of any pollutant at any X would be the maximum at the plume centreline corresponding to $y = 0$ and $Z = H_e$ under 'neutral condition'. The expression for the ground level concentration of any pollutant under the plume centreline would be

$$C_{x,0,0} = \frac{Q}{\pi\sigma_y\sigma_z U} \quad e^{-1/2}\left(\frac{H_e}{\sigma_z}\right)^2. \tag{4.67}$$

If σ_y and σ_z be related to the downwind distance X as

$$\left.\begin{aligned} \sigma_y &= a_y \; X^b \\ \sigma_z &= a_z \; X^b \end{aligned}\right\} \tag{4.68}$$

and

that is, their ratio be independent of X, then the maximum ground level concentration of any specific pollutant may be expressed as

$$C_{X_{\max}\,0,0} = \frac{2Q}{\left(\pi\; H_e^{\,2}\; U\right)e}\;\frac{\sigma_z}{\sigma_y}. \tag{4.69}$$

where $X_{\max}$ is the distance from the stack base in the downwind direction at which the pollutant concentration would be the maximum at the ground level.

It follows that at that very location, i.e., at $X_{\max}$

$$\sigma_{z,\,X_{\max}} = \frac{H_e}{\sqrt{2}} \tag{4.70}$$

Plots of the empirically estimated values of σ_y and σ_z corresponding to the different qualitative stability designations as parameters are shown in Fig 4.20 A and 4.20 B respectively.

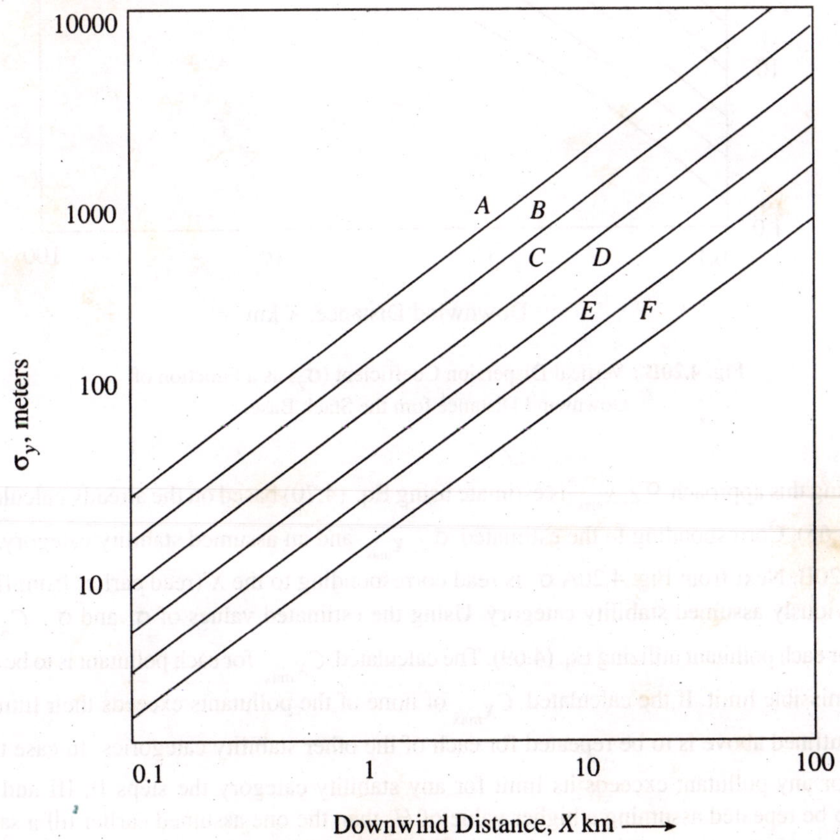

Fig. 4.20A : Horizontal Dispersion Coefficient (σ_y) as a Function of Downwind Distance from the Stack Base.

Pasquill-Gifford Stability Designations :

A : Extremely unstable

B : Moderately unstable

C : Slightly unstable

D : Neutral

E : Slightly stable

F : Moderately stable.

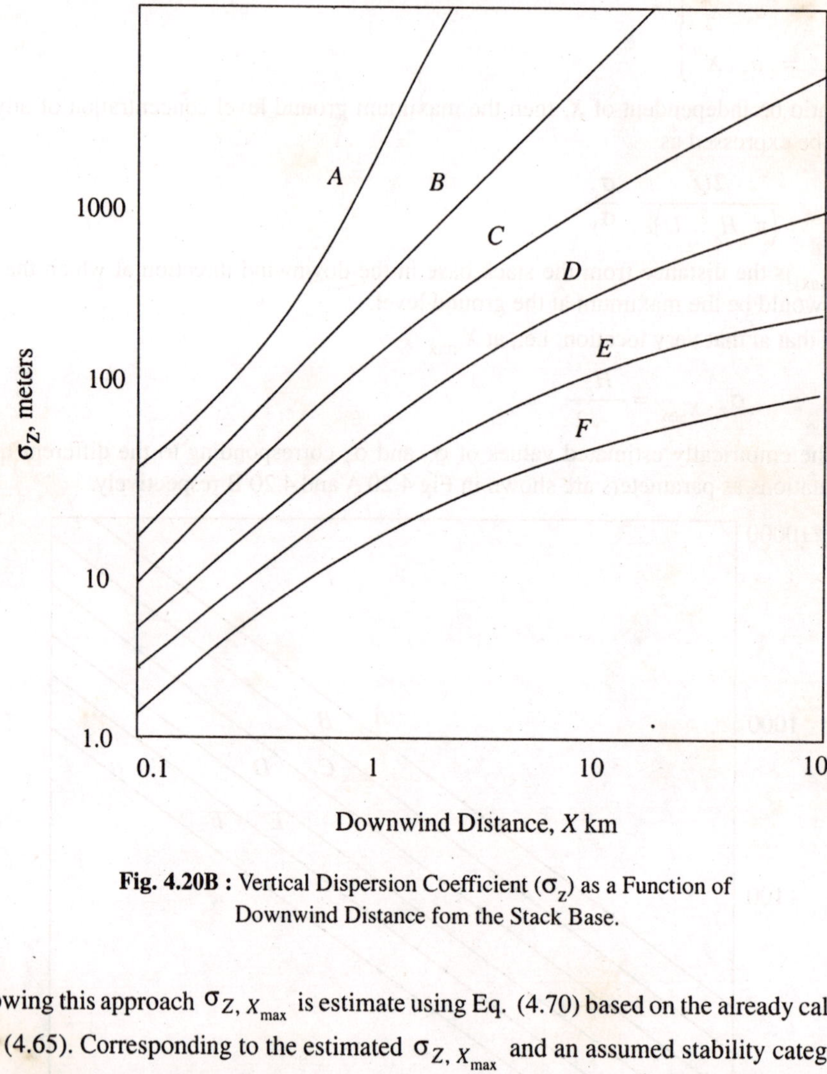

Fig. 4.20B : Vertical Dispersion Coefficient (σ_z) as a Function of Downwind Distance fom the Stack Base.

Following this approach $\sigma_{Z,\,X_{max}}$ is estimate using Eq. (4.70) based on the already calculated value of H_e Eq. (4.65). Corresponding to the estimated $\sigma_{Z,\,X_{max}}$ and an assumed stability category, X is read from Fig. 4.20B. Next from Fig. 4.20A σ_y is read corresponding to the X (read earlier from fig. 4.20B) and the previously assumed stability category. Using the estimated values of σ_y and σ_z, $C_{X_{max},0,0}$ is calculated for each pollutant utilizing Eq. (4.69). The calculated $C_{X_{max}}$ for each pollutant is to be compared with its permissible limit. If the calculated $C_{X_{max}}$ of none of the pollutants exceeds their limit then the procedure outlined above is to be repeated for each of the other stability categories. In case the $C_{X_{max}}$ calculated for any pollutant exceeds its limit for any stability category the steps II, III and IV listed earlier are to be repeated assuming a higher value of H_s than the one assumed earlier till a satisfactory solution is arrived at.

Referring to the Figs. 4.20A and 4.20B it should be pointed out that the correlation between σ_y and X may be reasonably well represented by the relation $\sigma_y = a_y X^b$, but that between σ_z and X does not match the correlation $\sigma_z = a_Z X^b$.

A better correlation would have the form

$$\left.\begin{aligned}\sigma_y &= a'_y x^m \\ \text{and} \quad \sigma_z &= a'_z x^n\end{aligned}\right\}. \tag{4.71}$$

The numerical values of a'_y, a'_z, m and n have been found to depend on the atmospheric stability designation. Various estimates of a'_y, a'_z, m and n have been reported in the literature. One such estimate is given in Table 4.16.

Table 4.16 : Numerical Values of Coefficients and Exponents related to Eq. (4.71)

Pasquill-Gifford Stability Designation	a'_y,	a'_z,	m	n
A	213	452	0.862	2.100
B	156	109	0.882	1.090
C	104	60.6	0.904	0.916
D	68	31.3	0.910	0.619
E	50.1	35.0	0.914	0.369
F	33.7	23.0	0.907	0.310

Combining Eqs. (4.67) and (4.71) one obtains

$$C_{X,0,0} = \frac{Q}{\pi a'_y a'_z X^{m+n} U} e^{-1/2} \left(\frac{H_e^2}{(a'_z)^2 X^{2n}} \right). \tag{4.72}$$

The corresponding expression for $C_{X_{\max},0,0}$ becomes

$$C_{X_{\max},0,0} = \frac{Q}{\pi a'_{y,} a'_z U} \left(\frac{n}{m+n} \frac{H_e^2}{a_z'^2} e \right)^{-\left(\frac{m+n}{2n}\right)}. \tag{4.73}$$

A better stack height estimation procedure would be to follow the steps listed under Section 4.8.2.3 in conjunction with Eq. (4.73) instead of using Eq. (4.69).

4.8.2.5 Plume Rise Correlations

Different investigators have attempted to correlate the plume rise (ΔH) with the pertinent variables. Some of those are listed hereunder.

1. Holland's equation is possibly the earliest one and it is a simple one.

$$\Delta H = \frac{U_s D_s}{U} \left(1.5 + 2.68 \times 10^{-2} P \frac{T_s - T_a}{T_s} D_s \right). \tag{4.74}$$

where ΔH = plume rise, (m)
U = wind velocity, (m/s)
U_s = stack gas velocity at stack exit, (m/s)
D_s = stack diameter at exit, (m)
P = stack gas pressure at exit, (kPa)
T_s = stack gas temperature at exit, (K)
T_a = ambient air temperature at physical stack height, (K)

As this equation does not take into account the atmospheric stability condition, Holland has suggested that the estimated ΔH should be multiplied by a factor of 1.1 to. 1.2 for unstable condition and by 0.8 to 0.9 for stable condition. Subsequent studies have shown that Holland's equation gives a rather conservative estimate of ΔH by a factor of 2 to 3.

2. Moses and Carson have proposed equations which are dependent on the stability criteria as given below :

$$\text{Unstable, } \Delta H = \frac{3.74}{U}\left(U_s D_s + 3.03\ Q_h^{1/2}\right), \text{ for } \frac{\partial\theta}{\partial z} < -0.22 \tag{4.75a}$$

$$\text{Neutral, } \Delta H = \frac{0.35}{U}\left(U_s D_s + 15.46\ Q_h^{1/2}\right), \text{ for } -0.22 \le \frac{\partial\theta}{\partial z} < 0.85 \tag{4.75b}$$

$$\text{and Stable, } \Delta H = \frac{1.04}{U}\left(-U_s D_s + 4.41\ Q_h^{1/2}\right), \text{ for } \frac{\partial\theta}{\partial z} \ge 0.85 \tag{4.75c}$$

where Q_h = heat emission rate, kcal/s
$\theta = (T_s - T_a), K$

and $\frac{\partial\theta}{\partial z}$ = lapse rate, $\frac{K}{100m}$.

3. ASME Task Group has recommended two equations. For unstable and neutral conditions the recommended equations is :

$$\Delta H = 7.4\ H_s^{2/3}\ \frac{F^{1/3}}{U} \tag{4.76a}$$

For stable condition the equation recommended is :

$$\Delta H = 2.9\left(\frac{F}{U \times S}\right)^{1/3} \tag{4.76b}$$

where $F = gU_s\left(\frac{D_s}{2}\right)^2\left(\frac{T_s - T_a}{T_s}\right)$.

g = acceleration due to gravity (m/s^2)
U = stack top wind velocity (m/s)
T_a = ambient temperature at stack height (K)
T_s = stack gas temperature at stack exit (K)
H_s = physical stack height (m)
U_s = stack gas velocity at exit (m/s)
D_s = stack diameter at exit (m)

$$S = \frac{g}{\theta_0}\frac{\partial\theta}{\partial z}$$

$\theta_0 = (T_s - T_a)$ at stack height (K)

$\frac{\partial\theta}{\partial z}$ = lapse rate, $\left(\frac{K}{m}\right)$

These equations are applicable at stack top wind velocity 7 m/s or more.

4.8.2.6 Estimation of Stack Cross-Sectional Area/Diameter and Stack Pressure Drop

The stack gas volumetric flow rate may be expressed as

$$\bar{Q}_1 = U_s A_s = U_s \frac{\pi}{4} (\bar{D}_s)^2 \tag{4.77}$$

where $\bar{Q}_1$ = average volumetric flow rate of stack gas (the volumetric flow rate at the stack base and that at the top would be different as the stack gas temperature would vary from the base to the top because of heat loss through the stack) (m^3/s).

$\bar{D}_s$ = average stack diameter, m.

Assuming a suitable stack gas velocity in the range of 10-15 m/s the stack cross-sectional area/diameter may be estimated using Eq. (4.77).

Once the stack gas velocity (U_s), stack diameter (D_s) and the stack height are known, the stack pressue drop/stack base pressure may be calculated utilizing a modified Bernouli (energy balance) equation as given below :

$$P_1 = P_a + g(\bar{\rho}_s - \rho_a) H_s + \frac{2 f U_s^2 \bar{\rho}_s H_s}{\bar{D}_s} \tag{4.78}$$

where P_1 = pressure at stack base, Pascal,

P_a = pressure at stack exit (which is the same as the ambient air pressure at that height), (Pascal).

$\bar{D}_s$ = average stack diameter, (m),

f = friction factor = $0.046\ R_e^{-0.2}$

g = acceleration due to gravity, (m/s^2),

H_s = stack height, (m),

U_s = stack gas velocity, (m/s),

ρ_a = ambient air density, (kg/m^3),

$\bar{\rho}_s \rho_s$ = average stack gas (including dust particles) density, (kg/m^3),

$$Re = \frac{\bar{D}_s U_s \bar{\rho}_s}{\mu_s}$$

μ_s = stack gas viscosity, kg/m.s.

Example 4.5

A stack is to be designed for a coal fired furnace in which 500 T of coal having 2% sulphur, 20% ash and the rest carbon is to be burnt.

The following information/data may be used for design purpose :

Excess air to be used	=	15%
Stack gas exit temperature	=	430 K
Ambient air temperature	=	298 K
Stack gas velocity	=	10 m/s

Wind Velocity	=	4 m/s
Maximum permissible ground level SO_2 concentration (Industrial area)	=	80 μg/m^3

Solution :

Basis 500 T coal burnt per day.

Coal constituent and quantity	Combustion gaseous product (assuming complete combustion)	Theoretical Oxygen required
Carbon 0.78 × 500 T = 390 T	CO_2 = 32,500 kg mole	32,500 kg mole
Sulfur 0.02 × 500 T =10 T	SO_2 = 312.5 kg mole	312.5 kg mole
Ash 0.2 × 500 T = 100 T		

Total theoretical oxygen required = 32,812.5 kg mole.

Actual O_2 to be supplied = 1.15 × theoretical = 37,734.375 kg mole

Nitrogen in air ($N_2 : O_2$ = 79 : 21) = 141,953.125 kg mole

Flue gas constituent		**kg mole/day**
CO_2	—	32,500.0
SO_2	—	312.5
O_2	—	4,921.875
N_2	—	141,953.125
Total flue gas	—	179,687.5 kg mole/day which is equivalent to

$$\frac{179,689.5 \times 22.4 \times 430}{273 \times 24} = 264,155.983 \text{ m}^3/\text{hr} \quad \text{at 430 K and 1 atm pressure}$$

$$\text{Stack cross-sectional area } \left(\pi/4\ \overline{D_s}^2\right) = \frac{\textit{Flue gas volumetric flow rate}}{\textit{Stack gas velocity}}$$

$$= \frac{264,155.983}{10 \times 3600} = 7.3377\ m^2$$

Stack diameter, $\overline{D_s}$ = 3.06 m.

Stack Height (H_s) Estimation

(i) A preliminary estimate of the stack height is obtained based on the empirical approach Eq. (4.64e)

$H_s = 14\ Q^{0.3}$, Q = SO_2 emission in kg per hour.

SO_2 emission per day 312.5 kg mol = 833.33 kg/hr

From Eq. (4.64e)

H_s = 105.29 m = 105 m.

(ii) A preliminary estimate of the effective stack height H_e is obtained using Eq. (4.65)

$H_e = H_s + \Delta H$

Plume rise (ΔH) is calculated using Holland's equation, Eq. (4.74).

$$\Delta H = \frac{U_s D_s}{U}\left(1.5 + 2.68 \times 10^{-2} P \frac{T_s - T_a}{T_s} D_s\right)$$

$$\Delta H = \frac{10 \times 3.06}{4}\left(1.5 + 2.68 \times 10^{-2} \times 101.3 \frac{430 - 298}{430} \times 3.06\right)$$

$$= 30.98 \text{ m} \approx 31 \text{ m}.$$

From Eq. (4.65)

$H_e = H_s + \Delta H = 105 + 31 = 136$ m.

(iii) The ground level maximum concentration of SO_2 is to be calculated using Eq. (4.73)

$$C_{x_{max},0,0} = \frac{Q}{\pi a'_y a'_z U}\left\{\frac{n}{m+n}\left(\frac{H_e}{a'_z}\right)^2 e\right\}^{-\left(\frac{m+n}{2n}\right)}$$

where Q = SO_2 emission in g/s

$$= \frac{833.33 \times 1000}{3600} = 231.48 \text{ g/s}.$$

H_e = 136 m.

a'_y, a'_z, m and n are to be read from Table 4.16 corresponding to a Pasquill-Gifford stability designation which is likely to result in the maximum value of SO_2 concentration at the ground level. Scanning the Tables 4.15 and 4.16 corresponding to wind velocity U = 4 m/s it appears that Pasquill-Gifford stability designation D would result in maximum SO_2 concentration. The values of a'_y, a'_z, m and n read from Table 4.16 are

$a'_y = 68$, $a'_z = 31.3$, $m = 0.910$ and $n = 0.619$.

$$\text{Hence, } C_{x_{max},0,0} = \frac{231.48}{\pi \times 68 \times 31.3 \times 4}\left\{\frac{0.619}{0.91 + 0.619}\left(\frac{136}{31.3}\right)^2 e\right\}^{-\frac{0.91+0.619}{2\times 0.619}}$$

$$= 204.2 \ \mu\text{g/m}^3$$

204.2 μg/m^3 is higher than the permissible limit 80 μg/m^3,

$C_{x_{max},0,0}$, is recalculated corresponding to higher assumed values of H_e as listed below :

Assumed H_e	**Calculated** $C_{x_{max},0,0}$
155 m	147.8 μg/m^3 > 80 μg/m^3
175 m	109.6 μg/m^3 > 80 μg/m^3
190 m	89.4 μg/m^3 > 80 μg/m^3
200 m	78.78 μg/m^3 ≈ 80 μg/m^3

Therefore, the stack height which would result in a ground level SO_2 concentration close to 80 μg/m^3 is

$H_s = H_e - \Delta H = 200 - 31 = 169$ m.

Stack diameter, $D_s = 3.06$ m.

4.8.3 Plume Dust Deposition

Dust particles, which are emitted through a stack, get dispersed like the gaseous pollutants. But the particles being larger in size and denser than the stack gas/ air, start settling immediately after emission because of gravitational force. The particles finally attain their respective terminal velocities. The terminal velocity of a particle having a diameter *dpi* may be expressed as

$$U_{t,\ dpi} = \left(\frac{4g\ d_{pi}\left(\rho_p - \rho_a\right)}{3\ \rho_a C_D} \right)^{1/2}, \qquad (4.79)$$

where $U_{t,\ dpi}$ = terminal velocity of particles having a diameter dpi and density ρ_p, m/s

g = acceleration due to gravity, m/(s^2)

dpi = particle diameter (m)

ρ_a = ambient air density kg/(m^3)

ρ_p = particle density kg/(m^3)

C_D = drag co-efficient

Assuming the dust particles to be spherical C_D may be evaluated using any one of the following relations depending on the particle Reynolds number;

$$\text{Re}_{p.\ dpi} = \frac{d_{pi} U_{t,\ dpi}\ \rho_a}{\mu_a}$$

$$\left.\begin{aligned} C_D &= 24\,\text{Re}_{p,dpi}^{-1.0}, && \text{for Re}_{p,dpi} < 2 \\ C_D &= 18.5\,\text{Re}_{p,dpi}^{-0.6}, && \text{for Re}_{p,dpi} < 500 \\ C_D &= 0.44, && \text{for Re}_{p,dpi} > 500 \end{aligned}\right\} \qquad (4.80)$$

The dust particles finally settle on the ground. Relatively larger particles get deposited along the plume axis while the finer particles are deposited all around. Since the wind direction and its speed change from time to time, the plume orientation changes consequently. Hence the time average dust deposition rate is estimated at different locations as a function of *X*, the downwind distance from the stack base. According to Bosanquet et al. the deposition rate at a point P at a distance *X* from the stack base may be expressed as

$$W_{dpi} = 10^6\ b\frac{Q_{dpi}\ F}{H_e^2}, \qquad (4.81)$$

where W_{dpi} = deposition rate of particles having a diameter *dpi* and density ρ_p, tons per sq. mile per annum.

Q_{dpi} = emission rate of particles having a diameter *dpi* and density ρ_p (g/s)

b = the fraction of time the wind is in a 45 deg. sector (from the stack) enclosing point P

F = a function of $U_{t,\,dpi}/U$ and X/H_e (as shown in Fig. 4.21)

H_e = equivalent stack height.

The rate of dust deposition at the point P in the axial plane of plume may be calculated using Eq. (4.82)

$$W_{dpi} = 4.43\times10^{6}\ \frac{Q_{dpi}}{H_e^{\,2}}\ .F \qquad (4.82)$$

The total deposition rate of all the particles having different sizes may be estimated by summing up the rates of the individual particles as shown below :

$$W_{\text{total}} = \Sigma_{dpi}\ W_{dpi} \qquad (4.83)$$

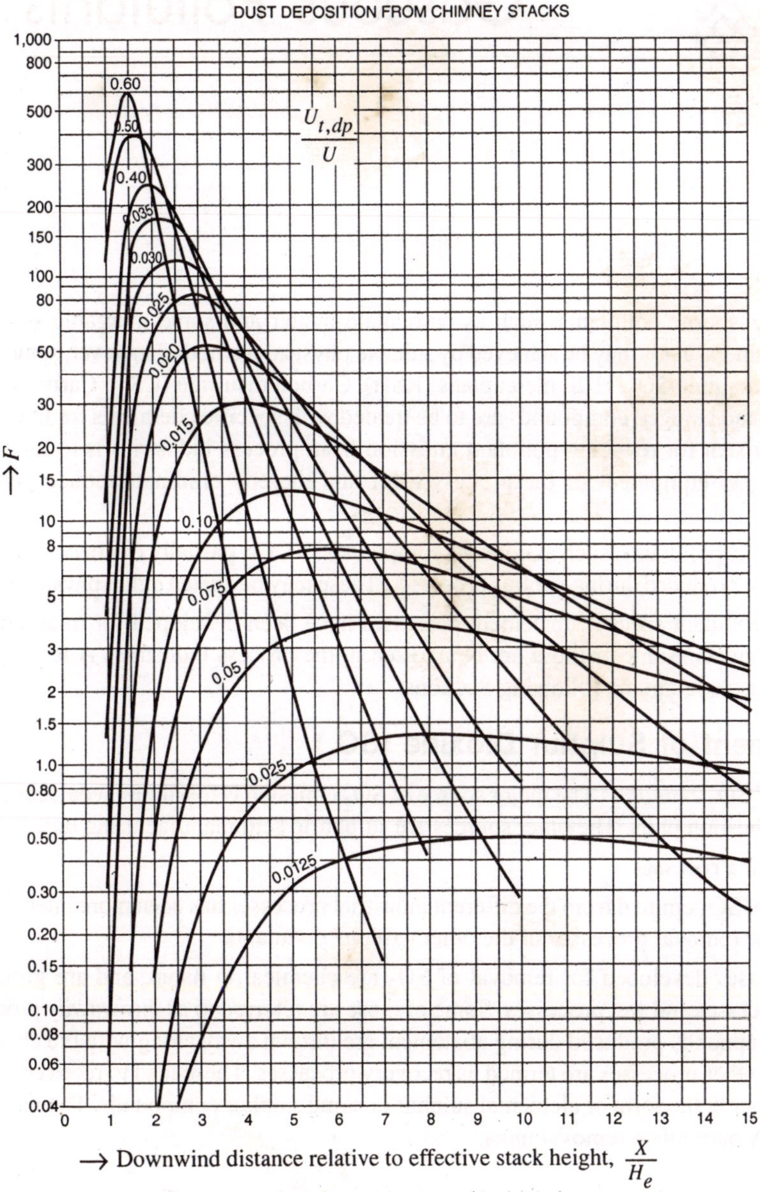

Fig. 4.21 : Dust Deposition Factor F (Bosanquet et al.).

CHAPTER 5

Abatement of Some Specific Gaseous Pollutants

Abatement of gasborne pollutants, such as particulate matter and some inorganic substances e.g., as ammonia and mineral acids may be achieved by suitable physical methods. However, some other inorganic pollutants, for example SO_2, H_2S, mercaptans (RSH), Carbon disulfide (CS_2), Carbonyl sulfide (COS) NO_x, halogens and halogen compounds are to be treated with specific chemicals for thier abatement. An alternative approach for reducing pollutant emission from process industries is to modify the process conditions/process equipment or the process itself and thereby eliminate/reduce generation of the pollutants.

Some organic pollutants, such as odorous compounds, VOCs, partially oxidized organic compounds including CO are produced during various processes. These may be abated either physically or chemically.

Different pollutant specific abatement processes have been developed for treatment of the above mentioned pollutants. Some of those are being used in the process industries. A few of the abatement processes are discussed in the following Sections.

5.1 Abatement of Sulphur Dioxide (SO_2)

Sources of SO_2 *emission* : The major source of SO_2 emission is fossil fuel (coal, coke and petroleum fractions) combustion units. The other sources are sulphuric acid manufacturing units, smelters, etc.

Abatement Processes

Removal of SO_2 emitted from the different industrial processes has been more intensively researched compared to the removal processes of the other gaseous pollutants.

The processes developed for removal of SO_2 are chemical in nature and are grouped under two heads : dry processes and wet processes. Some of those are referred to as throwaway processes in which the sulphur compounds produced during abatement are thrown away along with the chemicals used for treatment. The other processes are termed as recovery processes. These lead to recovery of sulphur from a waste gas either in the form of elemental sulphur or some sulphur compounds. The recovery processes are preceded by particulate removal units.

5.1.1 Dry Processes

In these processes SO_2 bearing waste gases are treated with chemicals in the absence of water.

5.1.1.1 Dry Throwaway Process—Limestone/Dolomite Process

In this process lime stone or dolomite powder is injected into a combustion chamber in which the particles and the flue gas flow countercurrently. At high furnace temperature the calcium/magnesium carbonate decomposes to oxide which in turn reacts with SO_2 present in the flue gas to form sulphite and sulphate. The overall reations may be expressed as

$$2\,CaCO_3 + 2\,SO_2 + {}^1/_2\,O_2 \rightarrow CaSO_3 + CaSO_4 + 2\,CO_2 \quad (5.1)$$

$$2\,MgCO_3 + 2\,SO_2 + {}^1/_2\,O_2 \rightarrow MgSO_3 + MgSO_4 + 2\,CO_2 \quad (5.2)$$

The sulphite and sulphate produced along with the unreacted CaO/MgO are removed from the furnace, and are discarded.

Due to insufficient contact between CaO/MgO and the flue gas in most instances the SO_2 removal efficiency is low inspite of the fact that carbonate is added in large excess than the stoichiometric proportion.

Some typical performance data are :

Dolomite Process

Optimum particle size : 10-15 μm

Optimum dolomite addition : 2.5 times the stoichiometric amount.

Removal efficiency :

70% with 250 ppm SO_2
85% with 130 ppm SO_2

Limestone Process

Optimum limestone addition : 10% of the coal fired

Removal efficiency : 40–80% with 550–890 ppm SO_2

Higher removal efficiency may be achieved when limestone/dolomite is used in a fluidized bed coal combustor.

Though the limestone/dolomite based dry process is less efficient than the lime/limestone slurry wet process, it has the following advantages :

(i) flue gas can be treated at an elevated temperature,
(ii) no complex treatment unit is required.

This dry process has an edge over the dry recovery processes as those suffer from excessive loss of absorbent due to attrition and high investment cost because of the complexities of the regeneration units.

5.1.1.2 Dry Recovery Processes

A. Metal Oxide Process

(i) *Activated Manganese Oxide Process*

This process was developed by the Mitsubishi Heavy Industries. It consists of the following steps :

Step-I

Hydrated manganese oxide is brought in contact with a SO_2 bearing flue gas concurrently as a result of which manganese sulphate is produced.

$$Mn_2\,O_3 + 2\,SO_2 + {}^1/_2\,O_2 \rightarrow 2\,Mn\,SO_4 \quad (5.3)$$

Step-II

Manganese sulphate thus produced is reacted in a separate vessel with aqueous ammonia and air whereby ammonium sulphate is produced and manganese oxide is precipitated.

$$2\,MnSO_4 + 4\,NH_4OH + {}^1/_2\,O_2 \rightarrow 2\,(NH_4)_2SO_4 + Mn_2O_3 + 2\,H_2O \quad (5.4)$$

Step-III

The slurry produced is filtered. Manganese oxide is dried and recycled. Ammonium sulphate solution is concentrated and the resulting ammonium sulphate crystals are marketed.

SO_2 removal efficiency of this process may be around 90%.

(ii) *Copper Oxide Process*

In this process alumina supported copper oxide pellets react with SO_2 and O_2 present in a flue gas to produce $CuSO_4$ at about 400 °C

$$CuO + SO_2 + {}^1/_2\,O_2 \rightarrow CuSO_4 \quad (5.5)$$

Subsequently CuSO4 is reduced with hydrogen or methane around 400 °C, the reaction being

$$CuSO_4 + 2\,H_2 \rightarrow Cu + SO_2 + 2H_2O \quad (5.6)$$

Use of methane may lead to coke deposition and consequent plugging of the bed.

In the next step copper is oxidized with air and the reactor is put on-line.

SO_2 produced may be converted to sulphuric acid or elemental sulphur.

Since the process operates in a cycle at least two reactors are needed.

The process appears to be promising. However, it requires expensive reactors and a large supply of a reducing gas (H_2/CH_4).

(iii) *Alkalized Alumina Process*

This process is carried out by contacting countercurrently aluminium sodium oxide pellets of about 1.60 mm diameter with SO_2 bearing flue gas at about 330 °C which results in formation of alumino–sodium sulphate.

$$Na_2O.\,Al_2O_3 + SO_2 + {}^1/_2O_2 \rightarrow Na_2SO_4\,Al_2O_3 \quad (5.7)$$

The alumino–sodium sulphate pellets are then reduced in another tower countercurrently with H_2 and CO at about 650 °C to regenerate aluminium sodium oxide and to produce H_2S. H_2S thus produced is then treated for sulphur recovery.

This process may have a SO_2 removal efficiency of about 90%. However, the major problem encountered in this process is attrition of the pellets resulting in its loss. This loss adversely affects the economics of the process. It is yet to find commercial application.

B. Activated Carbon Processes

(i) *Reinluft Process*

This process is carried out in two stages. In the first stage a flue gas containing SO_2 is adsorbed on a moving bed of activated carbon particles at about 150–200 °C. The adsorber is operated countercurrently. Activated carbon particles used in this process is produced by vacuum carbonization of peat or similar material. The key to the economic potential of this process lies in availability of a low cost adsorbent.

During the adsorption process the following reaction takes place on the adsorbent surface :

$$SO_2 + {}^1/_2O_2 + H_2O \xrightarrow[\text{carbon}]{\text{Activated}} H_2SO_4 \quad (5.8)$$

In the second stage the carbon particles loaded with sulphuric acid coming out of the adsorber are treated for recovery of H_2SO_4 as such or as SO_2. The regenerated carbon particles are recycled back to the adsorber.

There are two alternative processes for recovery of sulphur bearing compounds from the loaded carbon particles :

(a) Wash the carbon particles with water. This results in the production of dilute sulphuric acid solution. The wet carbon particles are dried and recycled back. The drawback of this process is the difficulties encountered in storage, transport and marketing of the dilute sulphuric acid solution.

(b) Heat the sulphuric acid loaded carbon particles to about 380–450 °C. On heating SO_2, CO_2, CO and H_2O are produced and the carbon particles get reactivated. The gas produced contains about 10–15% SO_2 which may be uitilized to produce sulphuric acid. The regenerated carbon particles are recycled to the adsorber.

The removal efficiency of the Reinluft process is about 90%.

(ii) *Westvaco Process*

The Westvaco Process employs activated carbon particles in a moving bed. The intermediate product formed during the process is sulphuric acid but finally sulphur is recovered as elemental sulphur.

The process is carried out through the following steps.

Step-I

SO_2, O_2 and moisture present in a flue gas combine on activated carbon particles to produce sulphuric acid.

$$SO_2 + {}^1/_2\, O_2 + H_2O \xrightarrow[\text{carbon}]{\text{Activated}} H_2\,SO_4 \tag{5.9}$$

Step-II

Adsorbed sulphuric acid is reacted with H_2S to produce elemental sulphur on the carbon particles' surfaces.

$$H_2SO_4 + 3\,H_2S \rightarrow 4\,S + 4\,H_2O \tag{5.10}$$

Step-III

The carbon particles containing elemental sulphure particles is heated to produce sulphur vapour, which is condensed and collected as molten sulphur.

Step-IV

The residual sulphur present on the carbon particles is converted to H_2S by reacting with hydrogen (H_2) and thereby reactivating the carbon particles. H_2S generated is used in the Step II and the carbon particles are reused.

This process has been operated on a pilot scale. The reported SO_2 removal efficiency is 90%. It has been claimed that 99% removal efficiency may be achieved by using a deeper carbon bed.

The drawbacks of the process are :

(i) the size of the vessel required for housing carbon particles is large and the pressure drop across the bed is high;

(ii) the amount of hydrogen needed for removal of residual sulphur (Step IV) is much higher than the stoichiometric amount.

C. Molten Carbonate Process

Atomics International Molten Carbonate Process employs an eutectic melt containing 32% Li_2CO_3, 33% Na_2CO_3 and 35% K_2CO_3 by weight to absorb SO_2 from a waste gas at about 450 °C. SO_2 removal efficiency of this process has been found to be about 99% from an influent gas having 0.1 to 3% SO_2.

The reactions may be expressed as under :

$$SO_2 + M_2CO_3 \rightarrow M_2SO_3 + CO_2 \quad (5.11)$$

$$SO_2 + {}^1/_2\, O_2 + M_2CO_3 \rightarrow M_2SO_4 + CO_2 \quad (5.12)$$

The loaded melt is then reduced with a mixture of H_2 and CO whereby a gas stream containing H_2S, CO_2 and H_2O is produced along with regenerated carbonates. The regeneration process is carried out at about 525 °C.

An alternative process is to reduce the sulphite—sulphate melt to sulphide with carbon and air at around 750 °C. The sulfide-carbonate melt is further reacted with steam and CO_2 at about 450 °C which results in the formatioin of H_2S and carbonate melt.

H_2S produced may be used either for production of sulphuric acid or for production of elemental sulphur.

Although operation of a complete integrated unit employing this process is yet to be undertaken, the process is of interest because of the unique technology involved. This process may be used for sulphur recovery from dust-free stack gas.

5.1.2 Wet Processes

These processes are carried out by scrubbing SO_2 bearing waste gases either with an aqueous slurry or with an aqueous solution.

5.1.2.1 Wet Throwaway Processes

A. Lime/Limestone Based Processes

(i) *Conventional Processes*

In this process a flue gas stream freed from particulate matter is scrubbed with an aqueous suspension of powdered lime/limestone having 5-10% solid by weight. The SO_2 removal efficiency of this process is about 80 to 95%.

Even though limestone is much cheaper than lime, for some applications lime is preferred because of its higher reactivity.

The scrubbed gas is reheated before discharging the same into the atmosphere through a stack. The spent suspension from the scrubber bottom is fed into a recirculation tank from where a part of it is fed back to the scrubber with make-up water and freshly added lime/limmestone powder. The remaining portion is discharged into a settling pond. The settled sludge from the pond is discarded and the supernatant liquid is recirculated to the scrubber along with the aqueous suspension.

In the scrubber mainly bisulphite and bisulphate are produced. These undergo further reactions in the recirculation/delay tank. The reactions taking place in the scrubber are :

$$2CaCO_3 + 4\, SO_2 + O_2 + 2\, H_2O \rightarrow Ca\,(HSO_3)_2 + Ca\,(HSO_4)_2 + 2\, CO_2 \quad (5.13)$$

$$2\, Ca\,(OH)_2 + 4\, SO_2 + O_2 \rightarrow Ca\,(HSO_3)_2 + Ca\,(HSO_4)_2 \quad (5.14)$$

In the recirculation/delay tank the reactions occurring may be summarized as below :

$$CaCO_3 + Ca\,(HSO_3)_2 \rightarrow 2\, Ca\, SO_3 + H_2O + CO_2 \quad (5.15)$$

$$CaCO_3 + Ca\,(HSO_4)_2 \rightarrow 2\, Ca\, SO_4 + H_2O + CO_2 \quad (5.16)$$

$$Ca\,(OH)_2 + Ca\,(HSO_3)_2 \rightarrow 2\, Ca\, SO_3 + 2H_2O \quad (5.17)$$

$$Ca\,(OH)_2 + Ca\,(HSO4)_2 \rightarrow 2\, Ca\, SO_4 + 2\, H_2O \quad (5.18)$$

Chemical grade limestone containing 95% or more $CaCO_3$ is most suitable for this process. Dolomite being relatively inert is not suitable for this process. For the limestone-based process the L/G mass ratio must exceed 65 but for the lime-based process the L/G mass ratio around 35 has been found to be adequate. For 90% SO_2 removal lime to SO_2 ratio required is about 1.05-1.15 times the stoichiometric proportion because of its higher reactivity whereas for limestone the required ratio is around 1.25 to 1.6.

Limestone is cheaper compared to lime, but a limestone based scrubber size would be larger than that for a lime based scrubber because of higher L/G ratio for the former.

For a large installation the limestone process would be economical, whereas for a small installation the lime process would be more economical

Operating a scrubber at a low pH (pH not less than 5) promotes formation of hard calcium sulphate scales (in the scrubbers and recirculation systems), whereas operation at a higher pH (influent scrubber pH exceeding 8) promotes formation of soft calcium sulphite particles. The optimum pH for a limestone system is between 5.8 and 6. For a lime system slightly acidic pH is most suitable. Reaction between lime and CO_2 in flue gas causes precipitation of $CaCO_3$ above pH 6.7, which results in a higher lime consumption. Hence the pH for a lime system should not be allowed to exceed 6.7.

The residence time in a recirculation tank is about 10 minutes for a limestone system and the same is about 5 minutes for a lime system.

The approximate sludge composition of a limestone system and that for a lime system are listed in Table 5.1.

Table 5.1 : Approximate Sludge Composition of Limestone and Lime System

Component	Sludge Composition in percent by Weight	
	Limestone System	Lime System
$CaCO_3$	33	5
$CaSO_3$, 2 H_2O	58	73
$CaSO_4$, 2 H_2O	9	11
Ca $(OH)_2$	—	11

(ii) *Chiyoda Thoroughbred 121 Process*

Limestone slurry is used as absorbent in this process. However, it differs from the conventional limestone process in three respects, namely (1) the absorbent pH. (2) the reactor design and (3) introduction of air into the bottom part of reactor. Air is used for oxidation of SO_2 to SO_3.

The pH maintained in this process is around 4 to 5; as a result the sulphite formed is oxidized to sulphate.

The process is carried out in a special type single reactor called jet bubbling reactor. Since the process produces gypsum as the final product, there is no need for liquid recycle.

Trouble free smooth operation and SO_2 removal efficiency in the range of 97-99% with flue gas SO_2 concentration ranging from 1000-2000 ppm have been reported. High limestone utilization and high gypsum content of the sludge have been observed.

The overall reaction may be summarized as under :

$$CaCO_3 + SO_2 + {}^1/_2\, O_2 + 2\, H_2O \rightarrow Ca\, SO_4 .\, 2H_2O + CO_2 \tag{5.19}$$

(iii) *Double Alkali Proces*

In this process a flue gas is treated with a solution of sodium sulphite, which absorbs SO_2. The major reaction may be expressed as below :

$$Na_2\, SO_3 + SO_2 + H_2O \rightarrow 2\, Na\, H\, SO_3 \tag{5.20}$$

The other chemicals present in the spent solution may be sodium sulphite, sodium sulphate and sodium carbonate. A portion of the spent liquor is recycled to the absorber. The other portion is treated with lime or limestone powder. The reaction products are insoluble calcium sulphite and sulphate, soluble sodium sulphite (and hydroxide). The precipitate is thickened in a settler. The sludge is filtered and the cake is washed. The clear liquor from the settling and filtration operations along with make-up sodium carbonate is returned to the absorber.

Two independent cost studies have indicated that the cost of installing and operating a double alkali system is less than that of a limestone slurry scrubbing system for treatment of a relatively high sulphur-fuel flue gas.

(iv) *Dilute Acid Process*

This process is an alternative to the double alkali process. In this process SO_2 is absorbed in a dilute sulphuric acid (2–3% H_2SO_4) solution with iron as catalyst. The reactions occurring are :

$$2\,SO_2 + O_2 + 2\,H_2O \rightarrow 2\,H_2SO_4 \tag{5.21}$$

$$2\,Fe\,SO_4 + SO_2 + O_2 \rightarrow Fe_2\,(SO_4)_3 \tag{5.22}$$

$$Fe_2\,(SO_4)_3 + SO_2 + 2\,H_2O \rightarrow 2\,Fe\,SO_4 + 2\,H_2\,SO_4 \tag{5.23}$$

Sulphuric acid thus produced is reacted with limestone to precipitate gypsum.

SO_2 removal efficiency of this process has been reported to be about 90%.

B. Alkali Metal Based Process

This is also a throw away process in which neither lime nor limestone is used directly or indirectly. It is suitable for treatment of a relatively small flue gas stream containing SO_2. Alkali used for scrubbing is sodium hydroxide or carbonate.

In this process a flue gas stream is first cooled by passing it through a venturi scrubber. Next the cleaned, cooled gas is scrubbed with an alkali solution in a single sieve tray column. Finally the treated gas is reheated by adding hot air and discharged into the atmosphere through a stack.

The venturi scrubber is fed with a recycled solution whereas the sieve tray column is fed with a fresh alkali solution.

The advantage of this process is low capital cost. However, the total operating cost on account of the chemical cost and the cost for spent liquor disposal outweighs the low capital cost.

The reported SO_2 removal efficiency of this process is about 85%

5.1.2.2 Wet Recovery Processes

A. Metal Oxide/Hydroxide Processes

(i) *Magnesium Oxide Process*

This process is carried out in three steps.

Step-I

In the first step a pre-cleaned SO_2 bearing gas stream is scrubbed with an aqueous magnesia suspension. The resulting reactions are :

$$MgO + 2\,SO_2 + H_2O \rightarrow Mg\,(HSO_3)_2 \tag{5.24}$$

$$Mg\,(HSO_3)_2 + MgO \rightarrow 2\,Mg\,SO_3 + H_2O \tag{5.25}$$

$$2\,Mg\,SO_3 + O_2 \rightarrow 2\,Mg\,SO_4 \tag{5.26}$$

Step-II

In this step a portion of the magnesium sulphite-sulphate slurry along with the unreacted magnesia is recycled to the scrubber mixed with make-up magnesia and water. The other portion of the slurry is filtered and the cake is dried.

Step-III

In the third step the dried cake is mixed with coke and calcined in a kiln at about 850-900 °C. During calcination the following reactions take place :

$$Mg(HSO_3)_2 \rightarrow MgO + 2\,SO_2 + H_2O \quad (5.27)$$

$$Mg\,SO_3 \rightarrow MgO + SO_2 \quad (5.28)$$

$$Mg\,SO_4 + C + {}^1/_2\,O_2 \rightarrow MgO + SO_2 + CO_2 \quad (5.29)$$

The regenerated MgO is recycled to the scrubber and the SO_2 produced is utilized for sulphuric acid production.

The SO_2 removal efficiency of PECO's Craumby Unit 1 plant has been reported to be 96-98%.

(ii) *Mitsubishi Manganese Oxyhydroxide Process*

This process is carried out by scrubbing a pre-cleaned waste gas containing SO_2 with a three percent manganese oxy-hydroxide slurry whereby manganese sulphite and sulphate are produced as shown below.

$$Mn(OH)_2 + SO_2 \rightarrow MnSO_3 + H_2O \quad (5.30)$$

$$Mn(OH)_2 + SO_2 + 1/_2\,O_2 \rightarrow MnSO_4 + H_2O \quad (5.31)$$

The slurry from the scrubber outlet is reacted with ammonia and oxygen which results in the formation of an ammonium sulphate solution and regenerated Mn $(OH)_2$ particles. The suspension is filtered to separate Mn $(OH)_2$, which is recycled to the scrubber. The ammonium sulphate solution is concentrated to crystallize $(NH_4)_2\,SO_4$, which is marketed.

$$Mn\,SO_3 + 2\,NH_4OH + {}^1/_2\,O_2 \rightarrow Mn(OH)_2 + (NH_4)_2\,SO_4 \quad (5.32)$$

$$Mn\,SO_4 + 2\,NH_4OH \rightarrow Mn(OH)_2 + (NH_4)_2\,SO_4 \quad (5.33)$$

The SO_2 removal efficieency of this process may be around 97%.

B. Activated Carbon (Lurgi Sulphacid) Process

The Lurgi Sulphacid process is carried out by passing a waste gas containing about 0.1 to 1.5 percent SO_2 through a bed of activated carbon. The carbon bed catalyses oxidation of SO_2 to SO_3, which reacts with water sprayed on the bed. A dilute sulphuric acid solution having a concentration of 10-15% H_2SO_4 is produced. The dilute acid is concentrated to about 60-70% by utilizing the heat of the incoming gas (190-210 °C) thereby cooling the gas to 40-50 °C prior to its entry into the carbon bed. The gas coming out of the carbon bed is re-heated before stack disposal.

The SO_2 removal efficiency of this process is about 95%.

C. Citrate Process

This process is based on the fact that solubility of SO_2 in water is low but it increases considerably when water is buffered with sodium citrate. The basic reaction taking place during the process is :

$$SO_2 + H_2O \rightarrow H_2SO_3 \quad (5.34)$$

During absorption of SO_2 in citrate buffered solution some SO_2 may get oxidized to SO_3 which in turn is converted to H_2SO_4. To suppress the oxidation reaction thiosulphate is aded to the scrubbing solution.

The sulphurous acid (H_2SO_3) solution produced is then reacted with H_2S, which results in the formation of elemental sulphur. The elemental sulphur is separated from the solution by floatation. The solution is recycled to the scrubber.

This process was developed by the Salt Lake City Metallurgy Research Centre of the U.S. Bureau of Mines for recovery of SO_2 from smelter gases. Subsequently pilot plant scale trials were conducted on coal fired boiler stack gas. The results of the trials on both smelter and boiler stack gas have been found to be promising. The sulphur removal efficiency has been reported to be 95-97%.

D. Sulphidine Process

Sulphidine process uses a mixture of xylidine and water having an approximate ratio of 1 : 1 as the scrubbing liquid. Xylidine and water are immiscible but when some SO_2 reacts with xylidine the system becomes miscible.

The process is carried out in a set of two absorbers operating countercurrently in series. Dust-free SO_2 bearing gas is introduced at the bottom of the first absorber at the top of which the liquid stream leaving the second absorber is fed. The gas leaving the first absorber is introduced at the bottom of the second absorber, which is scrubbed with a recovered xylidine-water mixture.

The scrubbed gas leaving the second absorber is further scrubbed with dilute sulphuric acid for recovery of xylidine vapour before finally venting the treated gas.

The liquor leaving the first absorber is thermally stripped indirectly for recovery of SO_2. The gas from the stripper containing xylidine and water vapour besides SO_2 is passed through a cooler-condenser for condensation of xylidine and water. The gas (mainly SO_2) is next water scrubbed for further recovery of xylidine vapour.

The liquid stream emerging from the thermal stripper is cooled and mixed with (1) the liquid from the cooler-condenser, (2) the liquid from the water-wash column, and (3) the liquid from the dilute sulphuric acid scrubber. A part of the water layer of this mixture is discarded so as to have a xylidine-water mixture having a ratio of 1 : 1 in the remaining stream. This stream is fed back into the second absorber as absorbent.

From time to time an aqueous soda ash solution is added to the recycle stream so that xylidine sulphate present in the stream is converted to xylidine.

This process is not economical when the SO_2 content of a waste gas is low because of loss of xylidine.

E. Dimethylaniline (ASARCO) Process

ASARCO Process is a better one than the Sulphidine process in the sense that it can treat a waste gas having SO_2 content 3.5% or more.

A SO_2 bearing waste gas is first scrubbed with dimethylaniline and then with a soda ash solution to remove the traces of SO_2 from the treated gas. Finally, the exhaust gas is scrubbed with dilute sulphuric acid to remove dimethylaniline before purging it through a stack.

SO_2 rich dimethylaniline is steam stripped for recovery of SO_2. The resulting steam-SO_2 mixture is scrubbed with sulphuric acid in order to obtain dry SO_2. The recovered SO_2 may either be liquefied or converted to sulphuric acid. Up to 99% SO_2 recovery has been reported.

Regenerated dimethylaniline is recycled to the scrubber.

The advantages of this process over the Sulphidine process are low reagent loss, low steam consumption and less labour requirement.

F. Ammonia (COMINCO) Process

This process is carried out in two stages. In the first stage SO_2 is removed from waste gases from roaster plants by scrubbing with aqueous ammonia solution whereby ammonium bisulphite is produced:

$$NH_4OH + SO_2 \rightarrow NH_4(HSO_3) \tag{5.35}$$

In the second stage the bisulphite solution is treated with sulphuric acid. The resulting mixture is air stripped. The air stripped solution contains ammonium sulphate whereas the gas stream contains SO_2, air and moisture.

$$2NH_4 (HSO_3) + H_2SO_4 \rightarrow (NH_4)_2 SO_4 + 2 H_2 SO_3 \tag{5.36}$$

$$(NH_4)_2 SO_4 + 2H_2 SO_3 + air \rightarrow (NH_4)_2 SO_4 + 2 SO_2 + 2 H_2O + air \tag{5.37}$$

The ammonium sulphate solution is concentrated to produce ammonium sulphate crystals. SO_2-air gas mixture after drying is used to produce sulphuric acid.

SO_2 removal efficiency has been observed to vary from 85-97%. The major factors on which the removal efficiency depends are :

(i) height of the packed bed,

(ii) operating tempetature, and

(iii) liquid to gas (L/G) mass ratio in the absorber.

G. Sodium Sulphite (Wellman-Lord) Process

Originally this process was based on potassium sulphite-bisulphite cycle. However, currently less expensive sodium salts are being used.

In this process a waste gas stream containing SO_2 is scrubbed with a sodium sulphite solution, which results in the formation of sodium bisulphite. The reaction may be summed up as

$$Na_2 SO_3 + SO_2 + H_2O \rightarrow 2 NaHSO_3 \tag{5.38}$$

The bisulphite solution thus formed is concentrated in a forced circulation evaporator under vacuum. The concentrated solution is then subjected to steam-stripping at a higher temperature. which causes decomposition of bisulphite to sulphite. Sodium sulphite thus produced crystallizes from the solution. The reaction may be expressed as :

$$2 NaHSO_3 \rightarrow Na_2SO_3 + SO_2 + H_2O \tag{5.39}$$

Na_2SO_3 crystals are separated, dissolved and the solution is returned to the absorber. Moist SO_2 gas is dried and fed to a sulphuric acid plant.

The average removal efficiency of SO_2 has been observed to around 91%.

H. Sodium Hydroxide Process

Scrubbing of a flue gas containing SO_2 with sodium hydroxide solution results in the formation of bisulphite and sulphite.

$$2 Na OH + CO_2 \rightarrow Na_2 CO_3 + H_2O \tag{5.40}$$

$$Na_2 CO_3 + SO_2 \rightarrow Na_2 SO_3 + CO_2 \tag{5.41}$$

$$Na_2 SO_3 + SO_2 + H_2O \rightarrow 2Na (HSO_3) \tag{5.42}$$

$$Na OH + SO_2 \rightarrow NaH SO_3 \tag{5.43}$$

The sodium sulphite-bisulphite solution is then treated with zinc oxide (ZnO) dust whereby $ZnSO_3$ is precipitated and NaOH solution is regenerated. NaOH solution is recycled to the absorber.

The precipitated $Zn SO_3$ is roasted after drying.

$$Zn SO_3 \rightarrow ZnO + SO_2 \tag{5.44}$$

ZnO is reused and SO_2 is fed to a sulphuric acid plant.

I. Biological Process

This process has been developed jointly by Monsanto Enviro-Chem System and UOP system for treatment of FCC exhaust gas containing N_2, O_2, H_2O, CO_2, CO, SO_x and NO_x along with some catalyst dust particles. SO_x concentration range was 250-2300 ppm and that of NO_x about 200 ppm in the gas.

The process consists of scrubbing the exhaust gas in a reverse-jet wet scrubber with $NaHCO_3$ solution. The major reaction taking place during scrubbing is

$$Na\,HCO_3 + SO_2 \rightarrow Na\,HSO_3 + CO_2 \tag{5.45}$$

Some sodium bisulphite may get oxidized to $Na_2\,SO_4$ due to the presence of oxygen in the gas being treated.

The gas-liquid mixture containing some solid particles separates into two streams in an adjoining vessel. The gas exits at the top of the vessel and the liquid flows into a sump. The liquid from the sump after filtration is mainly recycled to the scrubber while a portion is fed to an anaerobic bio-reactor

In the bioreactor the sulphite and sulphate are reduced either to sodium bisulphide with a limited supply of a suitable reducing agent or to H_2S when a larger amount of the reducing agent is used. The reducing agent may be a low-purity hydrogen gas or ethanol or methanol. Ethanol or methanol may be used as the carbon source for the micro-organisms.

In the anaerobic reactor the reactions taking place are :

(I) with a limited supply of a reducing agent—

$$NaHSO_3 + 3\,H_2 \rightarrow NaHS + 3\,H_2O \tag{5.46}$$

$$Na_2\,SO_4 + 4\,H_2 + CO_2 \rightarrow NaHS + NaHCO_3 + 3\,H_2O \tag{5.47}$$

(II) with a larger supply of a reducing agent—

$$NaHSO_3 + 3\,H_2 + CO_2 \rightarrow NaHCO_3 + H_2S + 2\,H_2O \tag{5.48}$$

$$Na_2SO_4 + 4\,H_2 + 2\,CO_2 \rightarrow 2\,Na\,HCO_3 + H_2S + 2\,H_2O \tag{5.49}$$

When H_2S mixed with CO_2 is produced, the gas is led to an amine absorber or some other sulphur recovery unit. The liquid containing $NaHCO_3$ from the anaerobic reactor outlet is recycled to the absorber.

However, if NaHS be present in the anaerobic reactor effluent, it is fed to an aerobic reactor for regeneration of $NaHCO_3$ and production of elemental sulphur according to the reaction :

$$NaHS + {}^1/_2\,O_2 + CO_2 \rightarrow NaHCO_3 + S \tag{5.50}$$

The slurry containing elemental sulphur is filtered and the filtrate containing $Na\,HCO_3$ is recycled to the scrubber.

The overall sulphur removal efficiency of the entire process may be as high as 98%.

5.2 Abatement of Hydrogen Sulphide (H_2S)

Sources : The sources of H_2S are natural gas, refinery gas, coal gas, waste gases from Kraft pulp liquor evaporators, and smelters. These gases may contain mercaptans, carbon disulphide (CS_2), carbonyl sulphide (COS), etc. besides H_2S.

There are several processes for abatement of H_2S from a waste gas, but only a few of these are discussed under this Section. These processes may be either dry type or wet type.

5.2.1 Dry Process

The dry process for removal of H_2S from a waste gas is carried out by reacting H_2S with activated ferric oxide. The reaction product is ferric sulphide.

$$Fe_2\,O_3 + 3\,H_2S \rightarrow Fe_2\,S_3 + 3\,H_2O \tag{5.51}$$

The process may be conducted either in a fixed bed reactor or a fluidized bed reactor.

A. Fixed Bed Process

The process is carried out in two stages. During the first stage H_2S laden gas is passed at ambient temperature through a bed containing reactive ferric oxide (α and γ forms) mixed with some fibrous or granular materials moistened with about 40% water. When a substantial portion of the ferric oxide has been converted to sulphide the waste gas flow is shut off and the second stage of operation is started. During this stage air at ambient temperature is passed through the bed, which results in regeneration of ferric oxide and liberation of elemental sulphur according to the reaction below :

$$2\,Fe_2\,S_3 + 3\,O_2 \rightarrow 2\,Fe_2\,O_3 + 6\,S \tag{5.52}$$

The liberated elemental sulphur may be recovered by solvent extraction.

For smooth operation of this process at least two beds are required, so that when in one bed the abatement reaction is taking place, the other bed is regenerated.

B. Fluidized Bed Process

In this set–up two circulating fluidized beds are required. In the first bed H_2S reacts with fluidized granules of activated ferric oxide at aboutt 340-360 °C. From this bed the granules containing ferric sulphide and unreacted ferric oxide flow into the second bed where the sulphide particles are roasted at about 800 °C to regenerate ferric oxide and to recover S as SO_2. The ferric oxide particles are returned back to the first bed and SO_2 is sent to an acid plant.

5.2.2 Wet Processes

There are many wet processes for removal of H_2S from a waste gas. Some of these processes are outlined hereunder.

A. Girbotol Proces

This process consists of absorption of H_2S in an amine solution and then stripping the dissolved H_2S with steam. The amine to be used in a particular situation depends on whether the waste gas contains COS and/or CO_2 besides H_2S.

A 15-20% mono-ethanol amine aqueous solution may be used if the gas to be scrubbed does not contain COS, as COS forms diethanol urea which is heat stable.

Since mono-ethanol amine has high vapour pressure, the H_2S regenerated by indirect steam heating of the impregnated solution has to be scrubbed for recovery of the entrained amine. Scrubbing may be done with water, but if H_2S is to be recovered as a dry gas, then either diethylene glycol or triethylene glycol should be used as the scrubbing liquid instead of a mono-ethanol amine solution. Since mono-ethanol amine also absorbs CO_2, it is not a suitable absorbent in the presence of CO_2.

Diethanol amine is a better absorbent than mono-ethanol amine as its vapour pressure is less than that of mono-ethanol amine. Diethanol amine may be used even when COS is present along with H_2S, as COS does not form diethanol urea. If a waste gas to be scrubbed contains both H_2S and CO_2, a 30% aqueous solution of triethanol amine or methyl-diethanol amine should be used for selective absorption of H_2S

B. Potassium Phosphate Process

When CO_2 is present along with H_2S a 40% aqueous solution of potassium phosphate may be used as an absorbent. This solution absorbs H_2S preferentially. From the impregnated solution H_2S is stripped with live steam.

C. Sodium Carbonate Process

When H_2S is not accompanied by CO_2 a 3 to 3.5% aqueous of $Na_2\,CO_3$ may be used as an absorbent. During absorption sodium hydrogen sulphide and sodium bicarbonate are formed :

$$Na_2CO_3 + H_2S \rightarrow NaHCO_3 + NaHS \quad (5.53)$$

For regeneration of carbonate and recovery of H_2S the spent solution is to be steam stripped under vacuum.

An alternate method for regeneration of the spent solution is to oxidize it with oxygen in the presence of about 0.5 percent ferric oxide in suspension whereby Na_2CO_3 is regenerated and elemental sulphur is precipitated.

$$NaHCO_3 + NaHS + {}^1/_2\,O_2 \xrightarrow{Fe_2O_3} Na_2CO_3 + S + H_2O \quad (5.54)$$

An alternate process (when CO_2 is present along with H_2S) is to use ammonium carbonate solution for absorption instead of sodium carbonate solution. For regeneration of the spent solution oxidation is carried out with oxygen in the presence of Fe_2O_3.

Another alternate process (Thylox process) uses sodium thioarsenate solution as the absorbent. In this processs for the oxidation-regeneration reaction no catalyst is required. The reactions may be represented as under :

Absorption Reaction

$$Na_4As_2S_5O_2 + H_2S \rightarrow Na_4As_2S_6O + H_2O \quad (5.55)$$

Regeneration Reaction

$$Na_4As_2S_6O + {}^1/_2\,O_2 \rightarrow Na_4As_2S_5O_2 + S \quad (5.56)$$

D. Stretford Process

Stretford process is a H_2S selective process. It can reduce the residual H_2S content in a treated gas to a very low level. The operating temperature is relatively low, about 40 °C.

The absorbent used in this process for H_2S removal is an aqueous alkaline liquor containing sodium carbonate, bicarbonate, vanadate and sodium salt of anthraquinone disulphonic acid (ADA) having a pH in the range of 8.5 to 9.5.

The gas to be treated is scrubbed countercurrently with the solution in an absorber where practically most of the H_2S is removed. The residual H_2S content may be less than 1 ppm.

From the absorber the solution flows into an oxidizer (reaction tank) where regeneration of absorbent and formation of elemental sulphur take place due to intimate mixing with air.

Elemental sulphur produced in the oxidizer is separated by floatation and is removed as a froth having about 10% solid by weight. The regenerated solution after removal of sulphur is pumped back to the absorber.

E. LO-CAT Process

This process is claimed to be the most suitable one for removal of H_2S when it is present in ppm level in an exhaust gas stream. It has been developed to eliminate odour problem due to the presence of H_2S. This is a liquid phase reduction-oxidation process which results in conversion of H_2S to elemental sulphur.

The scrubbing liquid is a dilute aqueous organic-chelated iron solution. The iron oxidizes H_2S while itself gets reduced. The spent solution from the scrubber is then oxidized with air whereby the absorbent is regenerated for reuse and elemental sulphur is produced.

This process is H_2S specific. It does not remove other sulphur bearing compounds such as COS, CS_2, mercaptans. It can reduce H_2S to a very low level in the treated gas. It is superior to the other oxidation-reduction processes because of its higher catalytic activity and non-toxicity.

Of the different H_2S abatement processes available now this one has been found to be quite economical particularly for treatment of a large gas stream having low H_2S content.

F. Cataban Process

The catalytic agent used in this process is an aqueous solution containing 2-4% chelated ferric iron. The chelate may be used over a wide range of pH 1.0 to 11.0 and a temperature range from below ambient to about 130 °C as it is stable over the above mentioned range.

During the process ferric ion oxidizes H_2S to elemental sulphur and gets itself reduced to ferrous ion. Simultaneously air oxidation of ferrous ions to ferric ions takes place. The reactions may be represented as :

$$2\,Fe^{3+} + H_2S \rightarrow 2\,Fe^{2+} + S + 2\,H^+ \quad (5.57)$$

$$2\,Fe^{2+} + {}^1/_2\,O_2 + H_2O \rightarrow 2\,Fe^{3+} + 2\,OH^- \quad (5.58)$$

This process may be used particularly for abatement of H_2S at a low concentration if the objective is not to recover sulphur. When the influent gas stream contains oxygen, no aeration would be required for oxidation of ferrous ions.

G. Giammarco-Vetrocoke Process

A solution of potassium carbonate containing potassium arsenite is used for absorption of H_2S in the Giammarco-Vetrocoke Proceess. It is used for removal of H_2S from coke-oven gas, synthesis gas as well as natural gas. The H_2S content of the treated gas may be as low as 1 ppm even in the presence of CO_2 at a high concentration and operating temperature close to 150 °C.

For regeneration of the spent liquor it is oxidized with O_2 (air). Elemental sulphur is produced as the final product.

The chemical reactions taking place during the absorption-regeneration process may be summerised as follows :

$$KH_2\,As\,O_3 + 3\,H_2S \rightarrow KH_2\,As\,S_3 + 3\,H_2O \quad (5.59)$$

$$KH_2\,As\,S_3 + 3\,KH_2\,As\,O_4 \rightarrow 3\,KH_2\,As\,O_3S + KH_2\,As\,O_3 \quad (5.60)$$

$$3\,KH_2\,As\,O_3S \rightarrow 3\,KH_2\,As\,O_3 + 3\,S \quad (5.61)$$

$$3\,KH_2\,As\,O_3 + 1\tfrac{1}{2}\,O_2 \rightarrow 3\,KH_2\,As\,O_4 \quad (5.62)$$

The actual reaction mechanism and steps are complex and the overall reaction may be expressed as

$$3\,H_2S + 1\tfrac{1}{2}\,O_2 \rightarrow 3\,S + 3\,H_2O \quad (5.63)$$

The role of carbonate is to maintain proper pH.

5.3 Abatement of Nitrogenous Compounds

The nitrogenous gaseous compounds which are produced during industrial operations and emitted to the atmosphere can be classified into two groups :

(i) basic compounds and

(ii) acidic compounds/oxides.

The abatement method, which may be employed in a particular situation, would depend on the chemical nature of the compounds to be abated. The various methods are outlined hereunder.

5.3.1 Abatement of Basic Compounds

Sources : Some industrial operations and manufacturing processes cause emission of basic nitrogenous compounds, such as ammonia, amine, pyridine, etc. The major sources are ammonia synthesis and nitrogen fertilizer industries, coal carbonization units, amine production units and processes using amines.

Abatement Process

The above named compounds are basic in nature and are highly reactive. These may be easily abated from a waste gas by scrubbing with water or with a dilute sulphuric acid solution.

5:3.2 Abatement of Acidic Compounds/Oxides

Sources :·Nitrous acid (HNO_2) and nitric acid (HNO_3) get emitted from nitric acid manufacturing/ concentrating units and nitration units. Along with these acid vapours, oxides of nitrogen (commonly referred to as NO_x) are invariably emitted.

The major sources of NO_x emission are mobile as well as stationary combustors used for combustioin of fossil fuels and their derivatives. The other sources of NO_x emission are nitric acid pickling and anodizing operations.

The stable oxides of nitrogen are nitric oxide (NO), nitrogen dioxide (NO_2), nitrogen sesquioxide (N_2O_3), nitrogen tetraoxide (N_2O_A), and nitrogen pentoxide (N_2O_5). These are toxic and corrosive gases. In the troposphere they form nitrous and nitric acid and also take part in photochemical reactions.

Abatement Processes : Acid Vapour Removal

Abatement of nitrous/ nitric acid vapours from a waste gas stream may be carried out by scrubbing with water or with an alkali solution. The choice of an absorbent would depend on whether it would be a recovery process or a throw away process.

Abatement Processes : NO_x Removal

A. Absorption in Water

Removal of NO_x by absorption in water is rather futile. NO_2 reacts with water to produce HNO_2 and HNO_3. HNO_2 in turn produces NO. NO as such is not soluble in water or alkali solution. NO reacts with O_2 (in air) and produces NO_2. This process is slow. The reactions occurring during absorption are :

$$2\,NO_2 + H_2O \longrightarrow HNO_2 + HNO_3 \tag{5.64}$$

$$3\,HNO_2 \longrightarrow 2\,NO + HNO_3 + H_2O \tag{5.65}$$

$$2\,NO + O_2 \longrightarrow 2\,NO_2 \tag{5.66}$$

The removal efficiency of NO_x by absorption in water is rather low, about 30-50%.

B. Absorption in Alkali Solution

Abatement of NO_x from waste gases by scrubbing with aqueous solutions of various alkaline substances, such as sodium hydroxide, sodium carbonate, calcium hydroxide, ammonium carbonate, bicarbonate, sulphite and bisulphite have been tried. Alkali scrubbing may result in a removal efficiency of about 90%. However, removal of NO_x from a flue gas by alkali scrubbing is not economical due to the presence of CO_2 in flue gas. CO_2 would react with alkali, hence chemical consumption would be high..

C. Catalytic Decomposition of NO_x

Catalysts, such as platinum, platinum-rhodium alloys, copper oxide on silica gel and various other oxides have been tried for decomposition of NO_x. None has been found to be satisfactory, particularly for decomposition of NO.

D. Catalytic Reduction of NO_x

Reduction of NO_2 to NO has been found to be easier using fuels like natural gas, coke-oven gas, CO, H_2, kerosene vapour, etc., with platinum or palladium catalysts. These catalysts are costly. Moreover, the fuel consumption is high and the process becomes uneconomic when NO_x removal is attempted from a wastegas (such as a flue gas) containing a relatively large proportion of oxygen, as all of oxygen would react with the fuel used before reduction of NO starts.

E. Salective Catalytic Reduction of NOx (SCR)

Catalytic reduction of NOx with ammonia has been found to be quite effective even for the treatment of flue gases. The catalyst used is Vanadia (V_2O_5) on Titania (TiO_2) base. Vanadia promotes oxidation of SO_2 (present in a flue gas) to SO_3, which combines with ammonia resulting in higher ammonia requirement. When Tungsten oxide is used as a constituent of a catalyst, it reduces oxygen concentration on catalyst surface and thereby inhibits the SO_2 oxidation. SO_2 oxidation is favourable above 370°C. The SRC process may be conveniently carried out above 315 °C around which ammonia activity (for NOx reduction) is high and formation of ammonium salt (sulphate) is retarded. For this process either anhydrous ammonia or aqueous ammonia (containing 20 to 30% NH_3) may be used. NO_x removal efficiency may be as high as 95%. The reactions (listed hereunder) during SCR are very efficient, with a reagent stoichiometry of approximately 1.0 (moles of NH_3 per mole NO_x reduced).

$$4\,NO + 4\,NH_3 + O_2 \xrightarrow{\text{Catalyst}} 4\,N_2 + 6\,H_2O + \text{heat} \tag{5.67}$$

$$2\,NO_2 + 4\,NH_3 + O_2 \xrightarrow{\text{Catalyst}} 3\,N_2 + 6\,H_2O + \text{heat} \tag{5.68}$$

Ammonia slip (escape of unreacted ammonia) value may range from 2 to 10 ppm.

F. Non-Catalytic NO_x Reduction

NO_x reduction can be achieved without any catalyst by injecting ammonia or urea into areas of a furnace where the flue gas temperature ranges from 830-1200 °C. The NO_x removal efficiency may be in the range of 70-80% under optimum conditions (adequate reaction time, good mixing of reagent—flue gas and lower temperature). Injection area temperature in excess of approximately 930 °C results in the production of N_2 from reagent decomposition and at a temperature higher than 1200 °C the reagents get oxidized to NO_x.

Ammonia slip may be around 10-50 ppm. Some undesirable reactions like oxidation of NH_3 to NO and NO_2 and formation of $(NH_4)_2\,SO_4$ would also take place.

G. Biological Method for NO_x Removal

This method developed by Monsanto Enviro-Chem. System and UOP System is carried out in two steps. In the first step a NO_x bearing gas is scrubbed with an aqueous iron chelate [Fe (EDTA)] solution. NO_2 dissolves in water and NO forms a water-soluble nitrosyl complex with iron chelate.

$$NO + Fe\,(EDTA) \rightarrow Fe\,(EDTA)\,NO \tag{5.69}$$

In the second step the solution containing dissolved NO_2 and nitrosyl complex of iron EDTA is treated anaerobically with ethanol as the reducing agent. The overall reactions are :

$$6NO_2 + 2\,C_2H_5\,OH \rightarrow 3\,N_2 + 4\,CO_2 + 6\,H_2O \tag{5.70}$$

$$6\,Fe\,(EDTA)\,NO + C_2H_5\,OH \rightarrow 3\,N_2 + 2\,CO_2 + 3\,H_2O + 6\,Fe\,(EDTA) \tag{5.71}$$

A NO_x removal efficiency of more than 80% has been reported.

H. Control of NO_x Production

It is well known that the combustion processes are the major source of NO_x emission. Hence considerable attention has been paid to develop startegies whereby NO_x production during fossil fuel combustion may be controlled. Less production of NO_x means less NO_x to be abated and hence more economical.

It has been ascertained that during combustion of fossil fuels NO_x is produced in two ways :

(i) production NO_x due to oxidation of N_2 in air at high temperature (referred to as 'thermal NO_x') in the combustion zone,

(ii) production of NO_x due to oxidation of nitrogenous compounds present in the fuels (referred to as 'fuel NO_x')

The NO_x present in flue gases has been found to contain 90-95% nitric oxide (NO) and the rest being nitrogen dioxide (NO_2).

For control of NO_x emission from stationary combustors a two-stage approach is now being followed.

In the first stage the objective is to reduce formation of NO_x without sacrificing the combustion efficiency. This is achieved by employing some or all of the following steps :

(a) Using low NO_x burners it is possible to reduce NO_x formation by 10-60%. Low NO_x burners are available for new as well as retrofit applications. The basic principle of low NO_x burners is to control and balance the air-to-fuel ratio in the combustion zones so that the high-temperature zones are not oxygen rich.

(b) Using air staging a fuel rich, i.e., lean oxygen combustion zone is created whereby NO_x formations is reduced. Above this zone an oxygen rich zone is maintained so as to complete combustion of CO and VOCs.

(c) Fuel staging is done with a view to reduce the temperature of the combustion zones. At the bottom part of a furnace about 70-80% of the total heat load is realized with less excess air. In the zone above the remaining heat load is realized with air-to-fuel ratio control and finally in the topmost zone the combustion reactions are completed by supplying adequate quantity of air and providing sufficient space.

(d) Operational modifications, such as flue gas recirculation to the combustion zone, reduction of air reheat, injection of steam or water into the combustion zone reduce NO_x formation by lowering the combustion zone temperature.

In the second stage of NO_x emission control strategy the flue gas containing NOx is subjected to the 'Selective Catalytic Reduction (SCR)' process as discussed earler (Sec. 5.3.2.E.)

For controlling NO_x emission from automobiles catalytic converters are being used now a days.

5.4 Abatement of Fluorine and Fluorides

Sources : Compounds of fluorine (F_2), such as HF (hydrogen fluoride), SiF_4 (silicon tetrafluoride), H_2SiF_6 (fluosilicic acid), etc., are produced and emitted when phosphate rock is treated with acid and also during production of aluminium and cryolite. The other sources of emission of fluorine and fluorine compounds are units producing fluorine based inorganic and organic compounds.

Abatement Processes

Fluorine compounds in general are highly soluble in water and hence those are removed from waste gases by scrubbing with water in spray towers or packed towers or venturi scrubbers. Cocurrent or countercurrent operations may be carried out. Removal efficiency is often more than 95%.

Elemental fluorine is not readily soluble in water. However, it can be scrubbed easily with 5-10% caustic solution, which results in the formation of NaF. Caustic soda concentration used for scrubbing should not be below 2% as at lower concentration of NaOH, F_2O is produced, which is highly poisonous. The spent liquor containing sodium fluoride is then treated with lime (CaO) whereby caustic soda is regenerated and CaF_2 being insoluble in water is precipitated. The regenerated caustic soda solution is returned to the scrubber.

5.5 Abatement of Chlorine and Chloride

Sources : Chlorine (Cl_2), hydrogen chloride (HCl) and chlorides are emitted from caustic-chlorine plants. Smelting operations and processes employing chlorine gas and hydrochloric acid also cause emission of chlorine and chlorine compounds.

Abatement Processes

Elemental chlorine is more soluble in water than fluorine. It is removed from a waste gas stream by scrubbing with water or lime suspension. Unlike CaF_2, $CaCl_2$ is highly soluble in water and hence remains in solution.

Hydrogen chloride and other inorganic chlorine compounds are highly soluble in water. Those are easily removed by scrubbing with water.

5.6 Abatement of Carbon Monoxide

Sources : Carbon monoxide (CO) is emitted as a result of incomplete combustion of fossil fuels, agricultural residues, etc. Emission of CO is invariably associated with emission of hydrocarbons, aldehydes, etc. A large portion of the total CO emission takes place from internal combustion engines.

Abatement Processes

From a waste gas CO and associated organic compounds may be removed by catalytic oxidation whereby those are converted to CO_2 and H_2O.

Modern day automobiles are fitted with catalytic converters immediately after an engine. The process occurs in two stages. In the first stage NO_x reacts catalytically with CO and hydrocarbons (HC) and thereby produces CO_2 , H_2O and N_2. In the the second stage, the remaining amounts of CO and HC react with air catalytically and produce CO_2 and H_2O. Finely divided platinum on ceramic base is used as catalyst for both stages. The catalyst being susceptible to lead poisoning, lead-free petrol (gasoline) must be used in the automobiles fitted with after converters.

5.7 Abatement of VOCs (Volatile Organic Compounds)

Sources : The major sources of VOC emission are the fossil fuel combustion units (both stationary and mobile), furnaces, distillation columns, crackers, reformers located in petroleum refineries and petrochemical manufacturing units. The other sources are the organic chemical industries. Emissions from these sources along with some carrier gasses are collected and treated before their final discharge to the atmosphere.

Other than the above mentioned sources VOC emission also takes place from flare stacks, petroleum crude and product storage and handling units. Regulation of emissions from such sources and their abatement methods are discussed in Section 5.8.

VOC Abatement Processes

Several processes are available for abatement of VOCs from a waste gas stream. For selecting a suitable process in a given situation one should take into consideration the following factors : volumetric flow rate of the stream, its VOC concentration and the market value of the VOC (s), if recovered. The available processes may be grouped into two groups, namely physical methods and combustion-based methods.

5.7.1 The Physical Methods

The physical methods are condensation, absorption and adsorption. These methods may be used either singly or in a series when it is intended to recover the VOCs because of their market value.

5.7.1.1 Condensation

This process consists of cooling directly or indirectly an influent gas stream containing VOCs below its dew point. This results in condensation of some of the VOCs. The treated gas stream would still have residual VOCs. The concentration of the residual VOCs would depend on the coolant inlet temperature.

Condensers are located upstream of absorbers/adsorbers/incinerators. The purpose of using a condenser may be either to recover valuable organics or to reduce the VOC load on the downstream unit(s). It goes without saying that a condenser may be used only when the concentration of the VOC in a waste gas stream is relatively high. The removal efficiency may be about 50-90% depending on the initial VOC concentration and coolant inlet temperature.

5.7.1.2 Absorption

For removal of VOCs from a gas stream generally it is scrubbed with a high boiling organic liquid (an oil). Scrubbing is done either in a packed tower or a sieve plate tower or a spray chamber. The process (absorption) may be carried out either cocurrently or countercurrently. Common practice is to scrub countercurrently.

During this process the VOCs get dissolved in the absorbent (solvent). The treated gas stream may be further processed or discharged to the atmosphere depending on its residual VOC content. The residual concentration depends on the initial VOC concentration in the influent gas stream, VOC solubility in the solvent (which is temperature dependent) and the gas to solvent mass ratio.

From the VOC-laden solvent VOC is recovered by stripping with steam and the VOC-free solvent is returned to the absorber. A properly designed absorber may have a VOC removal efficiency of 90% or more. VOC-steam mixture is cooled and condensed.

This process is not normally economical if the VOC concentration in an influent gas stream is less than 200-300 ppm.

5.7.1.3 Adsorption

When a gas stream containing VOCs is passed through a bed of adsorbent particles, say activated granular carbon particles, the VOC molecules are retained on the outer surfaces as well as on the surfaces of the micro and macro-pores of the particles. Actually adsorption occurs on some specific spots (active sites) of the adsorbent particles. When most of the active sites of majority of the particles are occupied by the VOC molecules the rate of adsorption becomes slow and the process is discontinued. The bed is then regenerated, that is, the adsorbed substances are removed by passing a stream of hot gas or steam. The desorbed substances may be recovered by condensation. The bed is reused for adsorption operation. If the adsorbed molecules are strongly held on the particle surfaces, regeneration is done by air-oxidation at a higher temperature whereby the adsorbed molecules are converted to CO_2 and H_2O. Some portions of the carbon (adsorbent) particles also get oxidized to CO_2

The adsorption capacity of an adsorbent depends on the molecular weight of adsorbate (VOC), the type and concentration of VOCs, and the carrier gas temperature, pressure and humidity. The capacity increases with the decrease of temperature and increase of pressure. The capacity is adversely affected as the relative humidity (RH) exceeds 50% as water molecules are preferentially adsorbed. An adsorbent would have a higher capacity for adsorption of halogenated and aromatic hydrocarbons than that for oxygenated compounds such as alcohols, ketones and aldehydes. Of the different commercially available adsorbent granular activated coconut shell charcoal has been found to be ideal for VOC adsorption.

VOC removal efficiency in an adsorption system may be around 95%. However, it depends on the operating temperature and pressure, adsorption and regeneration cycle duration, the type and concentration of the VOC molecules present in a gas stream.

Theoretically there is no upper limit to the VOC inlet concentration; however, in practice 10,000 ppm of VOC is taken as the upper limit. For handling a gas stream having a higher VOC concentration either a larger bed or a shorter cycle has to be used and the process may not be economical. Adsorption of VOC from a gas stream having low (VOC) concentration (say, less than 10 ppm) would pose a problem, as recovery of VOC from the desorbed stream would be difficult because of its low VOC content.

Adsorption is not commonly employed for treatment of streams containing highly volatile compounds, high boiling compounds, polymerizable compounds and gas streams carrying liquid and solid particles.

5.7.2 Combustion Based Processes

The combustion (oxidation) processes may be either non-catalytic or catalytic. The non-catalytic processes may be carried out in the following ways :

(i) Direct incineration,

(ii) Recuperative oxidation,

(iii) Regenerative oxidation,

(iv) Flares, and

(v) Oxidation in existing boilers and process heaters.

In general, combustion based processes have a high VOC removal efficiency, say, about 98%. The combustion products are CO_2 and H_2O. NO_x and SO_2 may also be produced during combustion.

5.7.2.1 Non-Catalytic Combustion Processes

These processes are generally operated at a higher temperature, 800-1100 °C. The VOC destruction efficiency depends on the residence time, turbulence, mixing and availability of oxygen in the combustion zone. Supplementary fuel may or may not be required depending on the calorific value of a VOC-laden gas.

(i) **Direct Incineration**

Direct incineration is carried out in a refractory lined combustor fitted with a supplementary fuel-fed burner. The supplementary fuel requirement in a given situation would depend on the calorific value of the VOC-laden gas.

(ii) **Recuperative Oxidation**

In recuperative oxidation units, the incoming VOC bearing gas is pre-heated by exchanging heat indirectly with the outgoing flue-gas before the incoming gas is fed into a combustor. The heat recovery from flue gas may be between 40-70%, as a result the supplementary fuel requirement would be less.

(iii) **Regenerative Oxidation**

A regenerative oxidation unit has a combustion chamber and two packed beds containing beads of ceramics or other materials. When an incoming VOC containing stream passes through a hot bed it gets heated while the bed cools. The stream next enters the combustion chamber and undergoes combustion reactions. The flue gas from the combustor would flow through the second bed and heat the packing while getting cooled itself. The packed beds are operated in a cyclic way, that is, the process flow is reversed at regular intervals. The heat recovery in such a unit is very high, consequently either no fuel or a relatively small quanity of a supplementary fuel would be required. These units are not suitable for all types of VOC laden gases.

(iv) **Flares**

Flares are basically used as a safety device to burn waste gases produced during process upsets without utilizing any supplementary fuel. It is suitable for high flow rate waste gas having a calorific value more than 2600 kcal/Nm^3. Heat cannot be recovered from the resulting combustion products and complete combustion of VOCs cannot be ensured.

(v) **Oxidation in Existing Boilers and Process Heaters**

Existing boilers or process heaters can be used to incinerate VOC-laden gas streams. The advantages are no capital expenditure and no supplementary fuel requirement. Such units would not be able to take care of large variations in waste gas flow rate and its calorific value. In these types of equipment incineration of waste gases, which are likely to produce corrosive compounds, should be avoided. The performance of such equipment would be affected if the waste gas calorific value be less than 1300 kcal/Nm^3.

5.7.2.2 Catalytic Combustion Process

Catalytic oxidation of VOC-laden waste gases may be carried out at a lower temperature, say, 400-500 °C using a lesser amount of supplementary fuel. The influent (waste gas) is normally pre-heated to about 260-480 °C prior to feeding the same into a catalyst chamber. The VOC destruction efficiency may be in the range of 95-98% depending on VOC composition and concentration, catalyst type and characteristics, operating temperature, oxygen concentration and space velocity. Presence of liquid and solid particles and polymerized compounds affect the destruction efficiency.

Oxides of platinum, copper or chromium are generally used as catalyst. These get poisoned by lead, arsenic, mercury, sulphur and halogen. At high VOC concentration the catalyst bed temperature may rise to 550-600 °C or more whereby the catalyst may get deactivated.

5.8 VOC Emission from Other Sources

Sources : VOC emission also occurs from sources other than those listed under Section 5.7. These sources are the various equipment, such as, storage tanks, pumps, compressors, pipeline fittings, safety devices, drains, waste water treatment facilities, manual sampling points, sumps, etc., installed in petroleum refineries, petrochemical and organic chemical manufacturing units including pharmaceutical production units, and any other units using organic chemicals. These sources are scattered in a plant and emissions from them are often discontinuous. Such emissions are referred to as fugitive emission. These cannot be collected and treated. Hence common practice is to control/ prevent emission from these sources as far as possible. Another source of fugitive emission is the flare stacks.

5.8.1 Fugitive Emissions

(i) Emissions occur from storage tanks, tankers and trucks due to evaporation of volatile organic liquids during filling and discharging. Increase of ambient temperature also causes emission from such tanks.

Emission from fixed roof storage tanks may be reduced to some extent by replacing those by internal/ external floating roof tanks. The alternative methods for reducing/controlling emission from fixed roof tanks are vapour scrubbing, and vapour (carbon) adsorption. Vapour balancing may also be resorted to. Vapour balancing may be achieved by connecting the vapour space of a discharging tank to that of the corresponding filling tank by means of a pipeline. The emitted vapour from the different fugitive sources may be collected and fed into an incinerator. However, it may not be practically feasible.

Emission also takes place from internal and external floating roof tanks. Emission from such sources may be reduced by providing primary and secondary seals.

Emission from tanks may also take place due to evaporation during ambient temperature rise.

(ii) Emission of organic liquid and vapour takes place from different types of devices and pipeline fittings, which are used in process industries. Such devices and fittings are valves, relief valves, safety valves, pumps, compressors, rupture discs, sampling points, sumps, water treatment plants etc.

It is next to impossible to trap, collect and treat emissions from these sources. The best way to control such fugitive emissions is to install leakproof devices and fittings and have better housekeeping.

Double mechanical seals effectively reduce emission from rotating equipment. Seal-less pumps, such as magnetically coupled pumps, canned pumps, diaphragm pumps check fugititive emissions. Non-rising stem valves and valves having stem packing are effective in reducing emissions. Discharge from pressure relief valves and rupture discs may be captured in an enclosed space and then treated.

5.8.2 Flare Stack Emission

Flares are used to destroy (burn) VOCs emitted from sources on which there is no rigid control. However, a flare itself may cause emission due to incomplete combustion. Emission from a flare may contain carbon monoxide, some intermediate combustion products, NO_x, SO_2 and carbon particles. Proper fuel-air ratio is to be maintained to promote better combustion. Excess of primary air to a flare reduces soot and smoke formation. Steam injection to a flare could eliminate soot formation.

5.9 Abatement of Odorous Compounds

Sources : Odorous compounds are produced during various chemical processes. The common odoriferous compounds are : hydrochloric acid, sulphur dioxide, formaldehyde (pungent odour), hydrogen sulphide (rotton egg odour), phosphine (decaying fish odour), chlorine (suffocating ordour), methyl mercaptan (decayed cabbage odour), chlorophenol and phenol (medicinal odour). Even when a relatively small amount of any odorous compound is present in an environment its odour is perceptible.

Abatement Processes

An abatement process to be used in a given situation would depend on (i) the source, (ii) the specific chemical present and (iii) its concentration. The abatement process may be anyone or a combination of the following methods :

Prevention, Circumvention and Treatment.

Prevention

If an odorous compound finds its way-out through a leak in a process equipment (gland) or pipeline, or pipe fittings or pumps or compressors, etc., the best way to stop such leaks is to practise good house-keeping and preventive maintenance.

Circumvention

The way to handle emission of odorous compounds depends on whether the emission is continuous/regular or accidental. Continuous/regular emissions are to be collected and led to a suitable treatment unit. Accidental emissions may be either dispersed by blowing air or spraying some pleasant smelling chemicals to the odour source till the source is eliminated.

Treatment

The method to be employed for treatment of continuous/regular emission of an odorous substance would depend on the chemical nature of the substance and its concentration. Anyone of the following methods may be used for treatment : absorption, adsorption, incineration.

CHAPTER 6

Water Pollution

Water is one of the major inputs for the different types of human activities, namely agricultural, domestic, recreation and industrial activities. Water of proper quality is not only essential for survival and well being of man but also equally essential for all types of living beings.

Although about 70% of the earth surface is covered with water, most of it, about 98% is salt water and the remaining 2% is fresh water. About 70% of the fresh water is permanently frozen as arctic ice and glaciers. Of the remaining 30% fresh water, only about one per cent is accessible to man from sources such as lakes, rivers, man-made reservoirs and shallow underground aquifers. The rest are tied up as soil moisture and in deep underground aquifers.

The above named fresh water sources get depleted when water is withdrawn from them for sustaining human activities; however, they get replenished as a result of wet and dry precipitation. All of the precipitated water is not available for human activities because a large fraction run off, a fraction evaporates, and a fraction percolates through the earth's surface. It is to be pointed out here that although man uses mainly fresh water for his activities but for some purposes he uses slightly saline (brackish) water.

The total quantity of water needed in a particular country or a region depends on its extent of industrialization and its agricultural activities. The quality of water required depends on the specific purpose for which it is to be used.

The quantity of water available in a particular region depends on precipitation of water in the form of rain and snow as well as on the river or rivers passing through that region. The availability also depends on large water body/bodies, like lakes and reservoirs located in the region. Table 6.1 shows water consumption pattern and availability in India.

Table 6.1 : Annual Water Consumption Pattern and Availability in India (km^3)

Activity	Consumption		
	1985	**2000**	**2025**
Irrigation	470	630	770
Domestic	16.7	24.2	40
Industries	10	30	120
Power Generation	4.3	5.8	15
Miscellaneous	39	60	105
Total	540	760	1050

Availability :

Total Rainfall	4,000 km^3
Utilizable	1,050 km^3
(i) Surface	700 km^3
(ii) Ground water	350 km^3

(*Source* : *Journal of Indian Water Works Association, 23, p. 141—151, 1991.*)

Table 6.2 shows water consumption rates of some specific Indian Industries.

Table 6.2 : Water Consumption Rate of Some Specific Indian Industries

Sl. No.	Name of the Industry	Water Consumption
1.	**Oil Refineries** : (a) having once through cooling water system. (b) having re-circulation cooling water system.	Max : 27589 cu. m/1000 tonnes Crude processed. Medium : 23521 cu. m/1000 tonnes Crude processed. Min : 18020 cu.m/1000 tonnes Crude processed. Max : 5652 cu.m/1000 tonnes Crude processed. Medium : 1760 cu.m/1000 tonnes Crude processed. Min : 1350 cu.m/1000 tonnes Crude processed.
2.	**Small Pulp and Paper Industry** : (a) Agricultural residue based (b) Using waste paper	 200-350 cu.m/tonne of paper made 100-150 cu.m/tonne of paper made

Contd.

Table 6.2 (Contd.)

Sl. No.	Name of the Industry	Water Consumption
3.	**Fermentation Industry**	8.5 litre/kg of grain processed.
4.	**Brewery Industry**	1.45 litre/L of beer.
5.	**Sugar Industry with 1250 tonnes/ day crushing capacity**	1300-2600 cu.m/day
6.	**Pesticide Industry :**	
	(a) BHC	17.6-43.3 cu.m/tonne
	(b) DDT	41.5-170 cu.m/tonne
	(c) DDVP	30.5 cu.m/tonne
	(d) Butachlor	8.07 cu.m/tonne
	(e) Monocrotophos	0.5-120 cu.m/tonne
	(f) Malathion	18.5-50 cu.m/tonne
	(g) Dimethoate	2-30 cu.m/tonne
	(h) Endosulfan	9.07 cu.m/tonne
7.	**Thermal Power Plants for once through cooling system :**	
	(a) 30 MW capacity	Min : 80 cu.m/day Max : 90 cu.m/day
	(b) 110 MW capacity	Min : 125 cu.m/day Max : 175 cu.m/day
8.	**Jute Processing Industry**	Water : 676.5 litres per tonne product Steam : 399.3 litres per tonne product
9.	**Slaughter house, meat and sea-food Industry.**	
	(a) Frozen meat : Large	0.35-1.5 cu.m/tonne
	Medium	0.25-1.3 cu.m/tonne
	Small	0.40-2.0 cu.m/tonne
	(b) Processed meat	5-35 cu.m/tonne
	(c) Frozen shrimp : Large	1.8-7.3 cu.m/tonne
	Medium	1.2-17.5 cu.m/tonne
	Small	2.3-5.5 cu.m/tonne
	(d) Cephalopods	2.3-4.7 cu.m/tonne
	(e) Squids/Cuttlefish	2.4-6.5 cu.m/tonne
	(f) Fresh Fishes	1.8-3.6 cu.m/tonne

Source : Comprehensive Industry Document Series, CPCB, Govt. of India, N. Delhi.

Water withdrawn from a fresh water source will invariably contain some impurities (constituents other than water). For some purposes water withdrawn may be used as such (untreated). For some other purposes water withdrawn from a source has to be treated for removal of some specific impurities or all of the impurities. For example, for irrigation purpose untreated water is used, but for domestic (including recreational) and industrial (including power generation) purposes treated water is required. For thermal power plants, boiler feed water should be freed from dissolved substances and micro-organisms. For some specific purpose the treated water must be free from pyrogen.

Of the total amount of water withdrawn from a freshwater source for a specific purpose, only a small fraction is used up and the rest is discarded. The portion discarded is referred to as waste water. Waste water generated during a process is either returned to the original source or to some other water body. The quality of waste water is always inferior to that of the source. Therefore, unregulated and untreated discharge of waste water from a process into a fresh water source would lower its quality and may render it unfit for further use not only by human beings but also for other living beings.

Large water bodies (fresh/brackish/ salt water), through natural processes, are capable of withstanding and assimilating some types of impurities entering into them along with waste water streams, provided the concentration of the impurities are low. However, if relatively large quantities of degradable impurities and/or impurities which do not undergo natural decay find their way into some water bodies, those may become polluted and hazardous in the long run. Once a water body becomes too contaminated, pre-treatment of its water may become uneconomic even for its use for irrigation purpose let alone for domestic/industrial purpose. Such apprehension is not a hypothetical one or a pessimistic projection but is based on real life experience in different parts of the developing and developed countries. Quite a few rivers and lakes and innumerable number of smaller water bodies the world over have become too contaminated to support life. Some of these have been and are being rejuvenated at a great expenditure.

It has now been accepted by all concerned that in order to avoid irreparable degradation of water bodies it is essential that each and every waste water stream should be properly treated prior to its discharge so as to keep the levels of the impurities in the receiving water bodies within specified limits.

To avoid building up of impurities in water bodies the ideal solution would be to recycle and reuse waste water streams if necessary after some treatment without any discharge. The idea of zero discharge of waste water is very welcome from pollution control point of view; however, its implementation may be cost prohibitive. With judicial planning and at some cost it is feasible to recycle and reuse some liquid effluent streams.

6.1 Water Pollutants, Their Sources and Effects

Water from natural sources invariably contains some ingredients, which are referred to as impurities. An impurity is referred to as a pollutant if it adversely alters the water quality and renders it unsuitable for its intended use. It should be pointed out here that water from a particular source may be unfit for an intended use if the concentration level of some pollutant (s) be high.

6.1.1 Pollutant Classification

The pollutants present in a sample of water may be classified in various ways, such as,

(i) suspended or dissolved,

(ii) inorganic or organic,

(iii) biodegradable or non-biodegradable,

(iv) viable or non-viable, etc.

Such a general classification of the pollutants present in a water sample is of very little help in ascertaining the quality of the sample. Hence some specific attributes as listed below have been identified which when specified express the quality of a sample of water. Standard methods for quantitative estimation of those attributes have been developed. Some of these methods are discussed in Chapter 7. The attributes are :

Colour,
Oil and grease,
Suspended solids,
Biodegradable dissolved organic matter,
Non-biodegradable dissolved organic matter,
Dissolved inorganic substances,
pH
Odour,
Plant nutrients,
Toxic materials,
Pathogenic and non-pathogenic organisms,
Radioactive matter.
Heat (temperature), etc.

Though quantitative estimates of all the items listed above depict the quality of a water sample, but very often it is sufficient to estimate quantitatively only a few of the attributes depending on the source of a sample and its intended use.

6.1.2 Sources of Water Pollutants

The sources of pollutant bearing waste water are : (a) storm and run-off water; (b) domestic, institutional and municipal effluents, and (c) industrial effluents.

Rain and snow absorb pollutants present in air. Rainwater while running off leaches some of the pollutants present in soil. The leachate may contain the products of putrefaction of decaying vegetables and animal carcasses, and chemicals such as fertilizers, insecticides, herbicides, etc. It is not possible to treat storm and run-off water, and thereby check pollution from this source. However pollution may be controlled from this source to some extent by using biodegradable agricultural chemicals.

Domestic, institutional and municipal waste water may contain biodegradable and non-biodegradable organic matter and some dissolved inorganic substances. Waste water from these sources should be treated to the required extent prior to its discharge into water bodies and thereby control emission of water-borne pollutants.

The major source of water-borne pollutants is the industrial effluents. They would contain biodegradable and non-biodegradable organic substances and inorganic substances. They may also contain some toxic substances. Not only process effluents and effluents from utility services carry pollutants but storm and wash water carry spilled chemicals. To control pollution from this source it is essential to pre-treat these effluent streams prior to their final discharge or reuse.

6.1.3 Effects of Water-borne Pollutants

Pollutants present in an effluent stream affect an ecosystem directly and may affect human beings directly or indirectly. Hence it is essential to ascertain in which way or ways a pollutant present in an effluent stream may degrade an ecosystem into which it finds its way. Its maximum concentration, which the receiving ecosystem can withstand without causing much harm to the associated flora and fauna should also be established.

The effects normally observed may be grouped as : (i) physical effects, (ii) chemical effects, (iii) biological effects, and (iv) radioactive effects. These are discussed in the next page.

(i) Physical Effects

Pollutants, such as colouring matter, suspended particles, free fats, oils, greases and heat (hot effluent) affect an ecosystem physically. They bring about changes in the following ways :

(a) Colouring matter and suspended particles when present in water cause turbidity and decrease penetration of light in a water body. Less light penetration hinders photosynthetic activity of aquatic plant. This in turn affects other aquatic flora and fauna.

(b) Free fats, oils and greases when in a water body they form a film on its surface. Such a film reduces re-oxygenation of the water body, which results in lower dissolved oxygen concentration. This in turn affects metabolic activities of aquatic flora and fauna. Very low dissolved oxygen concentration would lead to decay of aquatic flora and fauna. Moreover, aquatic living beings including micro-organisms die when they get smeared with oily substances.

(c) Hot water from a process plant when discharged into a water body its temperature would increase. This rise in temperature would reduce the dissolved oxygen concentration in the water body, as the solubility of oxygen in water is inversely proportional to temperature. Lowering of oxygen concentration in water would adversely affect the metabolic activities of the aquatic plants, fishes and micro-organisms.

(d) Dissolved inorganic salts render water 'hard' and make it unsuitable for agricultural, municipal and industrial uses.

(ii) Chemical Effects

Some pollutants affect an ecosystem by interfering with the environment or by directly affecting the flora or fauna present in the ecosystem. The chemical effects may be classified as (a) oxidation effect, (b) chemical nutrient effect, (c) physiological effect and (d) toxic effect.

(a) **Oxidation Effect :** Some inorganic and organic pollutants when present in water react with the dissolved oxygen (DO) in water biochemically (in the presence of microbes) or chemically and thereby reduce the DO concentration.

(b) **Chemical Nutrient Effect :** When an effluent stream containing pollutants like nitrogen and phosphorous compounds in relatively larger quantities is discharged into a water body then the surface of the water body may get covered with a thick layer of algae. Such profuse growth of algae is termed as *algal bloom.* Due to algal bloom reoxygenation of the water body and light penetration into it would get reduced. Because of insufficient light penetration, photosynthesis of other aquatic plants would suffer. Lower DO content of water may cause anaerobic biodegradation of the algae and other aquatic plants. This would result in production of foul smelling gases. Such a situation is referred to as eutrophic condition.

(c) **Physiological Effect :** An effluent stream containing nitrates when discharged into a water body and if water from that body is used as drinking water, it would cause serious health problems, particularly in infants. The nitrates get reduced to nitrites due to bacterial action in the intestine. Nitrite combines with hemoglobin to form a complex, which reduces the oxygen carrying capacity of blood. Nitrite may get further reduced to amines and nitrosoamine as a result of further bacterial action. Amines and nitrosoamines may cause gastric cancer.

(d) **Toxic Effect :** Some inorganic and organic chemicals are toxic to living beings in general, while some may be toxic to some specific species. Some of these chemicals do not accumulate in the system of a living being and hence when present in water at a low concentration they may not be harmful. However, some toxic chemicals go on accumulating in the system of a living being. As and when their concentration builds up, the toxic effects are manifested. Sometimes the primary host (the first species which accumulates the toxic substance) is not affected but some other higher species (in the food chain hierarchy) may get affected.

(iii) Biological Effects

Effluents from some industrial units and institutions may contain pathogens (disease causing bacteria, virus, etc.) in relatively large numbers. Such an effluent when discharged into a water body may affect its aquatic flora and fauna. The health of the people who may use contaminated water is very likely to be affected.

(iv) Radio Active Effects

Effluents containing radioactive substances when discharged into water bodies may cause mutation of the associated flora and fauna. The radio active substances may accumulate in the flora and fauna of the ecosystems and subsequently cause mutation of the higher species through the food chain.

6.2 Tolerance Limits of Pollutants in Treated Effluent

It is apparent from the discussion so far that for the well-being of all living beings it is essential that liquid effluents from each and every source should be properly treated prior to their final discharge or reuse. Total removal of all the pollutants from a waste water stream would be cost prohibitive, hence it is desirable that an effluent should be treated to such an extent that the treated effluent would not damage the ecosystem of the receiving water body. With this end in view each country has laid down the tolerance limits of the pollutants in treated effluents based on the following considerations :

(i) the information available about polluting effects of the different pollutants,

(ii) the techno-economic aspects of the different treatment processes,

(iii) usage of a treated effluent as such or the quality and usage of the receiving body into which final discharge of the treated effluent is intended

Appendix IIIA shows the general standards for discharge of effluents in India. In Appendix IIIB the maximum permissible limits of discharge from some specific industries in India are listed.

In Tables 6.3 the drinking water quality according to the WHO standard is listed. In IS 10500 : 1991 the Indian Standard for drinking water has been laid down.

Table 6.3 : WHO Guideline Values for Chemicals that are of Health Significance in Drinking Water

Chemical	Guideline Values (mg/litre)	Remarks
Acrylamide	0.0005[b]	
Alachlor	0.02[b]	
Aldicarb	0.01	Applies to aldicarb sulfoxide and Aldicarb sulfone.
Aldrin and dieldrin	0.00003	For combined aldrin plus dieldrin.
Antimony	0.02	
Arsenic	0.01 (P)	
Atrazine	0.002	
Barium	0.7	
Benzene	0.01[b]	
Benzo [a] pyrene	0.0007[b]	
Boron	0.5 (T)	
Bromate	0.01[b] (A,T)	
Bromodichloromethane	0.06[b]	
Bromoform	0.1	
Cadmium	0.003	

Contd.

Table 6.3 (Contd.)

Chemical	Guideline Values (mg/litre)	Remarks
Carbofuran	0.007	
Carbon tetrachloride	0.004	
Chloral hydrate (trichloroacetaldehyde)	0.01 (P)	
Chlorate	0.7 (D)	
Chlordane	0.0002	
Chlorine	5 (C)	For effective disinfection, there should be a residual concentration of free chlorine of $\geq$ 0.5 mg/litre after at least 30 min contact time at pH < 8.0.
Chlorite	0.7 (D)	
Chloroform	0.2	
Chlorotoluron	0.03	
Chlorpyrifos	0.03	
Chromium	0.05 (P)	For total chromium.
Copper	2	Staining of laundry and sanitary ware may occur below guideline value.
Cyanazine	0.0006	
Cyanide	0.07	
Cyanogen chloride	0.07	For cyanide as total cyanogenic compound.
2, 4-D (2, 4-dichloro-phenoxy acetic acid)		Applies to free acid.
2, 4-DB	0.09	
DDT and metabolites	0.001	
Di (2-ethylhexyl) phthalate	0.008	
Dibromoacetonitrile	0.07	
Dibromochloromethane	0.1	
1,2-Dibromo-3-chloropropane	0.001[b]	
1,2-Dibromoethane	0.0004[b] (P)	
Dichloroacetate	0.05 (T,D)	
Dichloroacetonitrile	0.02 (P)	
Dichlorobenzene, 1, 2	1(C)	
Dichlorobenzene, 1, 4-	0.3 (C)	
Dichloroethane, 1, 2-	0.03[b]	
Dichloroethene, 1, 1-	0.03	
Dichloroethene, 1, 2-	0.05	
Dichloromethane	0.02	

Contd.

Table 6.3 (Contd.)

Chemical	Guideline Values (mg/litre)	Remarks
1,2-Dichloropropane (1,2- DP)	0.04 (P)	
1,3-Dichloropropene	0.02[b]	
Dichloroprop	0.1	
Dimethoate	0.006	
(EDTA)	0.6	Applies to the free acid.
Endrin	0.0006	
Epichlorohydrin	0.0004 (P)	
Ethylbenzene	0.3 ©	
Fenoprop	0.009	
Fluoride	1.5	Volume of water consumbed and intake from other sources should be considered when setting national standards.
Formaldehyde	0.9	
Hexachlorobutadiene	0.0006	
Isoproturon	0.009	
Lead	0.01	
Lindane	0.002	
Manganese	0.4©	
MCPA	0.002	
Mecoprop	0.01	
Mercury	0.001	For total mercurry (inorganic plus organic).
Methoxychlor	0.02	
Metolachlor	0.01	
Microcystin—LR	0.001 (P)	For total microcystin–LR (Free plus cell-bound).
Molinate	0.006	
Molybdenum	0.07	
Monochloramine	3	
Monochloroacetate	0.02	
Nickel	0.02 (P)	
Nitrate (as NO_3^-)	50	Short-term exposure.
Nitrilotriacetic acid (NTA)	0.2	
Nitrite (as NO_2^-)	3	Short-term exposure.
	0.02 (P)	Long-term exposure.
Pendimethalin	0.02	
Pentachlorophenol	0.009[b] (P)	
Pyriproxyfen	0.3	
Selenium	0.01	
Simazine	0.002	

Contd.

Table 6.3 (Contd.)

Chemical	Guideline Values (mg/litre)	Remarks
Styrene	0.02 (C)	
2,4,5-T	0.009	
Terbuthylazine	0.007	
Tetrachloroethene	0.04	
Toluene	0.7 (C)	
Trichloroacetate	0.2	
Trichloroethene	0.07 (P)	
Trichlorophenol, 2, 4, 6-	0.2[b] (C)	
Trifluralin	0.02	
Trihalomethane		The sum of the ratio of the concentration of each to its respective guideline value should not exceed 1.
Uranium	0.015 (P,T)	Only chemical aspects of uranium addressed.
Vinyl chloride	0.0003[b]	
Xylene	0.5 (C)	

[a] P = provisional guideline value, as there is evidence of a hazard, but the available information on health effects is limited; T = provisional guideline value because calculated guideline value is below the level that can be achieved through practical treatment methods, source protction, etc; A = provisional guideline value because calculated guideline value is below the achievable quantification level; D = provisional guideline value because disinfection is likely to result in the guideline value being exceeded; C = concentrations of the substance at or below the health-based guideline value may affect the appearance, taste or odour of the water, leading to consumer complaints.

[b] For substances that are considered to be carcinogenic, the guideline value is the concentration in drinking water associated with an upper-bound excess lifetime cancer risk of 10^{-5} (one additional cancer per 100000 of the population ingesting drinking water containing the substance at the guideline value for 70 years). Concentrations associated with upper-bound.estimated excess lifetime cancer risks of 10^{-4} and 10^{-6} can be calculated by multiplying and dividing, respectively, the guideline value by 10.

Source : WHO Guidelines for drinking water quality, third edition, Volume 1, Recommendations.

CHAPTER 7

Water Pollution Monitoring

Quantitative analysis of samples collected from untreated/treated liquid effluent streams or water bodies are carried out as a routine. The information thus obtained help one to ascertain

(a) the quality of the untreated/treated effluent streams/water bodies,

(b) whether any treatment is required for improving the quality of the sources from which samples have been taken,

(c) the performance of an existing treatment facility, if any.

Based on the above mentioned observations it would be possible to decide whether—

(i) a treatment facility needs to be designed and installed in order to achieve the desired quality of the treated water;

(ii) the operating parameters/conditions of the process/existing waste water treatment units need to be changed;

(iii) the existing waste water treatment facility need any modification.

The tests normally carried out with a collected water sample reveal quantitative information about the common categories of pollutants present in the sample. However, if it is apprehended that some toxic ions or some toxic chemicals may be present in the sample, then those are to be identified and their respective concentrations are to be estimated.

Accuracy of the information obtained about the quality of a source from which a sample has been collected, depends on the analytical methods employed, the skill of the analyst and above all whether the sample collected is a representative one or not.

7.1 Sampling

A source from which a sample is to be collected may not be a homogeneous one and its quality may not be time invariant. If a source be a flowing stream and its flow rate be time dependent, then the quality of the sample collected from such a source would be time dependent. While collecting a sample from a source one should bear in mind the above mentioned factors and employ a proper sampling technique in order to obtain a representative sample from the source.

Two basic sampling techniques normally used are :

(a) **Grab sampling :**

It is carried out by collecting a sample at a specific pre-determined instant.

(b) **Composite sampling :**

It is achieved by collecting several grab samples and mixing those judiciously so as to obtain an average sample.

Analysis of a grab sample from a source would represent the quality of the source at the time of sampling only. A grab sample collected at the right time may yield information about the peak pollutant load of a waste water stream. Such information are essential for adjusting the process parameters of an effluent treatment plant (ETP) so as to operate the same properly.

Collection of a grab sample from a homogenous source (an effluent stream or a water body) poses no problem. But when a source is a non-homogeneous one, a grab sample should be collected carefully. From such a source a sample should neither be collected from the surface nor from the bottom but from a point about two–third of the way from the surface.

To obtain a time-averaged and flow-averaged composite sample, several grab samples should be collected from an effluent stream at pre-planned time intervals over a period of 24 hours. The collected samples should be mixed in proportion to the flow rates at the respective intervals. Analysis of such a composite sample would yield information about the daily average concentration of the pollutants present in an effluent stream.

7.2 Sample Preservation

The ideal thing to do is to analyse a sample at the earliest after collection. But for various reasons it is not often possible. In such situations the samples should be stored at 3 to 4 °C. During storage chemical changes may occur in the samples and as a result the pollutants' concentration may change. To prevent such changes it may be necessary to add chemicals (preservatives), which would arrest chemical changes of pollutants during storage. A preservative is a pollutant specific chemical and hence it is not to be added to the entire sample but to that portion set aside for estimation of concentration of a specific pollutant.

7.3 Analysis

In general, the concentration of pollutants even in a highly polluted effluent/ water body is low when expressed in terms of mass per unit volume. Hence, for their estimation special techniques and instruments are used.

The concentration of pollutants being low generally those are expressed in the unit of mg/L (weight of a pollutant in mg per litre of a waste water sample) or ppm (weight of a pollutant per million parts of a waste water sample by weight). In the case of waste water having a low solute content the numerical value of the pollutant concentration will be the same independent of whether it is expressed in mg/L or ppm. If a pollutánt concentration be very low it is expressed either in µg/L or ppb.

Broadly speaking the analytical methods used for analysis of waste water samples may be classified into the following three groups :

(a) Classical methods,

(b) Colourimetric methods, and

(c) Newer Instrumental methods,

The classical methods are those, which are developed initially for estimation of pollutant concentration. These methods are less costly in terms of laboratory equipment, instruments and chemicals, but are analyst-skill dependent. These tests in general are more time consuming.

The colourimetric methods are quick but may require sophisticated instruments and special chemicals. These methods do not require that much of skill.

The newer instrumental methods are very quick but specific instruments/ accessories may be required for each specific pollutant.

The procedures for estimation of the different types of pollutants as well as those for each specific pollutant have been detailed in standard reference books* and publications. The basic procedures for estimation of some of the common pollutant attributes are outlined in the next Section.

7.4 Process Outlines for Estimation of Some Common Pollutant Attributes

7.4.1 Total Residue

The total residue of a waste water sample is estimated by evaporating and drying a known volume of the sample in an oven as collected/received, that is, along with the associated suspended solids, if any, in a weighed dry crucible at 103-105 °C. The increase in weight of the crucible represents the total residue of the sample and it is expressed in mg/L unit.

7.4.2 Dissolved Residue

When the process outlined under the Section 7.4.1 is carried with a known volume a filtered waste water sample the increase in weight of the crucible would represent the amount of dissolved solids present in the sample. It is also expressed in mg/L unit

7.4.3 Fixed Solids and Volatile Solids

The crucible containing the total residue is to be ignited in a a furnace at about 500 °C. As a result the organics present in the residue would get burnt and the inorganics may get converted to their oxides. The crucible with its contents is to be cooled to room temperature and then a few millilitres of ammonium carbonate solution is to be added to the crucible to moisten the residue. Finally, the crucible with its contents is to be dried in an oven at 103-105 °C. The weight of the residue would represent the fixed solids, which is expressed in the unit mg/L. The difference between the Total Residue and the Fixed Solids would represent the Volatile Solids (VS) in the waste water sample.

7.4.4 Suspended Solids (S.S.)

To estimate the suspended solid content of a waste water sample, a known volume of the sample is filtered through a 2 mm thick acid-alkali washed asbestos layer in a Gooch crucible. The crucible along with the retained solids is dried in an oven at 103-105 °C and weighed. The increment of weight over the initial dry weight of the crucible with asbestos mat would be the weight of the Suspended Solids collected. It is expressed in the unit of mg/L.

7.4.5 Fixed Suspended Solids

The Gooch crucible containing dried suspended solid (Ref. Sec. 7.4.4) is to be subjected to the same procedure as outlined under Section 7.4.3. The weight of the final residue would represent the Fixed Suspended Solids of the sample.

---

* Standard Methods for the Examination of Water and Waste water. Prepared by the American Public Health Association, American Water Works Association, Water Pollution Control Federation, Pub : American Public Health Association.

7.4.6 Turbidity

The turbidity of a water sample is expressed in terms of Jackson Candle Unit (JCU). A candle turbidity meter is calibrated using either water from a natural source or a specifically prepared Kaolin suspension in water.

The basis of turbidity measurement is the fact that fine solid particles suspended in a liquid interfere with transmission of incident light by absorption and scattering. The degree of interference depends on the concentration, size and colour of the particles as well as on the colour of the liquid, Hence, turbidity test of a liquid sample does not reveal a precise estimate of the amount of fine suspended particles present in the sample. However, it gives an indirect measure of the amount of fine suspended solid particles present in a sample.

The classical method for turbidity measurement consists of pouring a sample of turbid water in a long flat-bottom standard glass tube under which a standard lighted candle is placed. Further pouring of the sample is continued till the profile of the flame is just obliterated. The height of the sample in a tube is inversely related to its turbidity.

In order to estimate the turbidity of a sample its height in a glass tube is found out as outlined above. In the similar fashion the height of a sample of known turbidity is found out. From these data the turbidity of the sample is calculated.

The present practice is not to use the classical method but to use either a photometer (based on the light absorption principle) or a nephelometer (based on the light scattering principle). When a nephelometer is used the turbidity of a sample is expressed in NTU (naphelometric turbidity unit).

7.4.7 Colour

The basis of colour measurement is comparison of the colour of a sample of water with that of standard water samples coloured with potassium chloroplatinate and cobaltous chloride (mixed in different proportions). The sample to be tested has to be centrifuged for removal of suspended particles (including coloids) prior to its colour testing. The classical method is to take a suspended solid-free water sample in a Nessler tube and compare its colour with the colour of standard samples in Nessler tubes. The present practice is to use photoelectric colourimeters.

7.4.8 Odour

A proper instrument for identification and quantitative estimation of odour of a wastewater sample is yet to be developed. The testing is entirely dependent on the olfactory senses of a tester. The ordor of a wastewater sample is at first identified as that of a known natural odour and then it is quantified as a threshold odour number.

The threshold odour number of a sample is the dilution ratio at which the odour is barely detectable by sniffing. Dilution is to be carried out with odour free water. Sniffing may be done either at 20 °C (cold odour quality) or at 58–60 °C (hot odour quality).

7.4.9 Conductivity

The specific electrical conductivity of a water sample is expressed in terms of micro–mho/cm or µS cm^{-1}. It depends on the concentration of the dissolved ionized substances present in a water sample and the temperature at which measurement is done. The specific conductance increases with increase in ionic concentration and temperature. The conductivity is sometimes expressed in mg/L of total dissolved solids (TDS).

The electrical conductivity of a sample in micro-mho/cm or µS cm^{-1} at 25 °C when multiplied by a specific factor gives a rough estimate of the dissolved inorganic present in the sample in the unit of mg/L. The factor is around 0.55 for a sample containing an appreciable concentration of free acid/alkali and it is around 0.70 to 0.75 when a sample is appreciably saline.

The instrument normally used for conductivity measurement is either a parallel plate conductivity cell along with a Wheatstone-bridge unit or a multi–electrode potentiometric sensor. For conductivity measurement a suspended-solid-free sample is to be used.

7.4.10 Hardness

Hardness of water is a measure of its capacity for precipitating soap. Soap is precipitated mainly by Ca and Mg ions commonly present in water. Other polyvalent metal ions such as Al, Fe, Mn, Sr, Zn also cause hardness. Hardness causes fouling of heat exchanges.

To evaluate the hardness of a water sample it is necessary to estimate the concentration of each of the above mentioned ions in the sample. The hardness of a water sample is reported as $CaCO_3$ equivalent (mg/L, $CaCO_3$). It is calculated by multiplying the concentration of each polyvalent cation (in mg/L) by a specific factor and adding up those products. A less accurate method is to estimate the concentrations of Ca and Mg ions only by EDTA titration and calculate the hardness based on those information.

7.4.11 Alkalinity

The alkalinity of a water sample reflects its capacity to neutralize a strong acid to a designated pH. It is estimated by titrating a measured volume of a water sample with a standard solution of sulfuric acid or hydrochloric acid to a pre-selected end point (pH). Titration may be carried out either by using an indicator (bromocresol green–methyl red) or with the help of a Potentiometric Titrator.

7.4.12 pH

The pH of a water sample is a measure of its acidity or alkalinity. Quantitatively,

$$pH = \log_{10} \frac{1}{[H^+]},$$

where $[H^+]$ stands for hydrogen ion concentration expressed in g–ion/litre of the sample.

The ionic product of water is represented by $Kw = [H^+] \times [OH^-]$. Its numerical value is 10^{-14}

If the hydrogen ion $[H^+]$ concentration in a water sample is more than that of hydroxyl ion $[OH^-]$ then the sample is referred to as acidic. When they ($[H^+]$ and $[OH^-]$) are equal, that is, each has a concentration of 10^{-7} g–ion/L the sample is termed as neutral. However, if hydroxyl ion concentration in a sample be more than that of hydrogen ion, then it is referred to as alkaline. The pH of an acidic water sample may range between 0 to 7 and that of an alkaline sample between 7 to 14.

The pH of a sample of water may be estimated approximately by using some organic chemical solutions (referred to as indicators) which change colour at some specific hydrogen/hydroxyl ion concentration. To measure pH-accurately now a days a pH-meter is used which consists of a pH probe and a millivolt-meter. A pH-probe is an assembly of a hydrogen ion permeable sheathed glass electrode and a reference electrode. The difference in emf between the glass electrode and the reference electrode depends on the hydrogen ion concentration of a sample of water into which the probe is dipped, and its temperature. The millivolt-meter specially built for a specific probe is fitted with a temperature compensating element. The meter is graduated in terms of millivolt as well as pH.

7.4.13 Temperature

Temperature of a water sample may be measured with the help of a liquid-in-glass thermometer or a thermocouple or a resistance thermometer. For measuring temperature of a flowing stream or a water body a thermocouple is normally used. The measured temperature is normally reported in °C.

7.4.14 Oils, Fats and Greases

Oils, fats and greases may be present in free form or in the form of an emulsion in wastewater. These are insoluble in water but soluble in various organic solvents. For estimation of these in a water sample, they are extracted from a known volume of the sample with a light petroleum fraction (termed as petroleum ether) having a boiling point range of 40 to 60 °C. From the extract most of the petroleum ether is to be distilled off leaving behind a small portion of the solvent along with the extracted oils, fats and greases. Finally, the last traces of the solvent are to be evaporated on a water bath in a current of warm air. The weight of the residue left is the weight of oils, fats and greases present in the sample. It is expressed in mg/L unit.

7.4.15 Dissolved Oxygen

The solubility of oxygen in water is low. The saturation concentration of oxygen in water depends on water temperature and the superincumbent oxygen pressure. Table 7.1 shows the solubility of oxygen from air (at 1 atm pressure) in freshwater at different temperatures.

Table 7.1 : Oxygen Solubility in Freshwater from Atmospheric Air

(At 760 mm Hg pressure)

Temperature °C	0	5	10	15	20	25	30	35
Oxygen Concentration, mg/L	14.6	12.8	11.3	10.2	9.2	8.4	7.6	7.1

Since aquatic flora and fauna, including the water-borne micro-organisms, meet their oxygen need from the dissolved oxygen its estimation is essential for judging the quality of a water body/stream. The classical method for estimation of dissolved oxygen (DO) is known as the *Winkler's method*.

The Winkler's method is carried out through the following three steps :

Step-I

A known volume of a sample to be tested is mixed with solutions of manganous sulphate ($MnSO_4$) and alkaline potassium iodide (NaOH and KI). As a result the following reactions take place :

$$Mn\,SO_4 + 2\,NaOH \rightarrow Mn\,(OH)_2 + Na_2\,SO_4$$

$$2\,Mn\,(OH)_2 + O_2\,(\text{dissolved}) \rightarrow 2\,Mn\,O_2\,(\text{ppt}) + 2\,H_2O$$

Step-II

The mixture is then acidified with sulphuric acid whereby iodine is liberated according to the reaction.

$$Mn\,O_2 + 2\,KI + 2\,H_2\,SO_4 \rightarrow Mn\,SO_4 + K_2\,SO_4 + I_2 + 2\,H_2O$$

Step-III

Finally, the liberated iodine is estimated quantitatively by titration with a standard sodium thiosulfate solution in the presence of starch as the indicator according to the reaction below :

$$I_2 + 2\,Na_2\,S_2O_3 \rightarrow 2\,Na\,I + Na_2\,S_4O_6$$

Since all of the above mentioned reactions occur quantitatively, it is possible to estimate the concentration of dissolved oxygen in the sample from the volume and concentration of thiosulphate solution used to titrate the liberated iodine. Dissolved oxygen is expressed in the unit mg of O_2 per litre of a sample.

A suitably modified Winkler's method is used when interfering chemicals, such as nitrate, nitrogen, ferrous and ferric salts, etc., are present in a sample.

Estimation of dissolved oxygen by Winkler's method needs a skilled hand. It is not a convenient method for estimation of DO in a field.

The current practice is to use an electrical device consisting of a DO probe and a micro-ammeter. A DO probe consists of two electrodes insulated from one another and the assembly is covered with an oxygen permeable membrane. When such a probe is dipped in a sample of water the dissolved oxygen permeates through the membrane and a galvanic cell is set up as a result of which a current flows through the ammeter connecting the two electrodes. The magnitude of the current depends on the rate of oxygen permeation, which in turn depends on the dissolved oxygen concentration in the sample. This method is very quick. It may be used in a laboratory as well as in the field. Moreover, no skill is needed to use such an instrument.

7.4.16 Biochemical Oxygen Demand (BOD)

Dissolved and suspended organic substances present in a water body/stream may act as food for the micro–organisms present in it. (Micro organisms are present everywhere unless special care is taken to exclude them from a specific area). The process of assimilation of dissolved/and or suspended organic substances by aerobic organisms occurs through a series of reactions which are referred to as biochemical pathways. In some of these reactions the dissolved oxygen in water would take part, as a result of which the dissolved oxygen concentration in water would decrease. The rate of oxygen depletion in a water body/stream would depend on the following factors :

1. the species of organisms present and their population,
2. the nature and concentrations of the organic substances present,
3. the temperature, and
4. the concentration of dissolved oxygen.

The total depletion of DO would depend on the elapsed time since the beginning of the process as well as on the factors already mentioned.

It should be noted here that the extent of DO depletion in a water sample during an aerobic microbial process is not the true index of the total organic substances present in the sample, but it represents the extent to which biodegradation of the organic substances has been brought about by the microbes present. Since DO depletion is dependent on the duration of the process and the factors listed earlier, a standard procedure has been developed to carry out a test so as to obtain some information about the biodegradable organic substances present in a sample. This attribute is referred to as $BOD_{5,20\,°C}$. Basically $BOD_{5,20\,°C}$ represents mg of oxygen used up by microbes while metabolizing the organic substances in a one litre sample under aerobic conditions at 20 °C over a period of five days

The basic approach for $BOD_{5,20\,°C}$ estimation is to dilute a measured volume of a sample with a sufficient volume of inoculated, air-saturated distilled water pre-mixed with some microbial nutrients. A standard BOD bottle of 300 ml capacity is filled with the mixture and stoppered so as to exclude any entrapped air and to prevent any ingress of air. The bottle is incubated at 20 °C for 5 days. Another BOD bottle is filled with inoculated air-saturated distilled water pre-mixed with microbial nutrients and incubated at 20 °C for 5 days. DO of the mixtures are determined before and after incubation. Based on these data BOD of the sample is calculated as follows :

$$BOD_{5,\,20°C}\ \text{mg/L} = \frac{(A-C)-\left[(B-D)\ \{(V-\vartheta)/V\}\right]}{\vartheta/V}$$

Where A = initial DO of the sample mixed with inoculated dilution water,

B = initial DO of inoculated dilution water only,

C = DO of the sample mixed with inoculated dilution water after incubation for 5 days,

D = DO of inoculated dilution water only after incubation for 5 days,

ϑ = volume in litre of the sample added to BOD bottle,

and V = volume in litre of BOD bottle.

The biochemical oxidation process is not completed in 5 days time but goes on for several days. Hence BOD_5 is not a measure of the total oxygen required for complete biochemical oxidation of the biodegradable organic substances present in a water sample. The total biochemical oxygen demand is termed as BOD ultimate (BOD_{ult}).

Usually it is assumed that the oxygen uptake process during BOD estimation obeys a first order rate equation. Based on this assumption the BOD_{ult} may be related to the BOD data for a shorter period by the following equation ;

$$BOD_t = BOD_{ult}\,(1-e^{-kt}) \tag{7.1}$$

where k = a first order rate constant,

and t = incubation period in days.

Since Eq. (7.1) has two unknowns, namely, BOD_{ult} and k, for estimation of those one needs to find out experimentally BOD at time t_1 and t_2.

Eq. (7.1) may be valid if the organic substances present in a water sample are predominantly carbonaceous and a negligible fraction is proteinaceous. Figure 7.1 shows how BOD of a sample changes with time (incubation period) when a relatively large amount of protein is present along with the carbonaceous materials in a water sample.

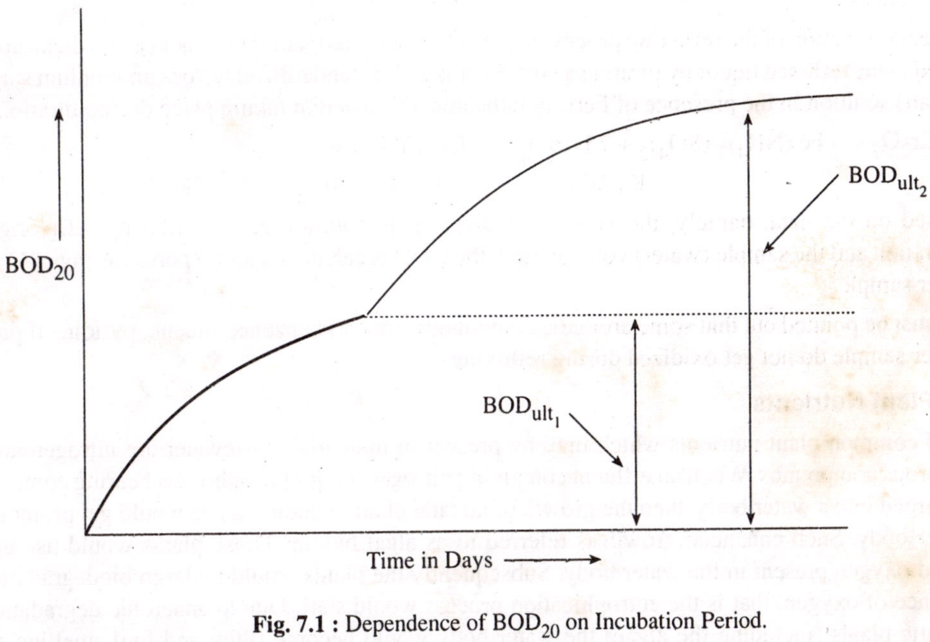

Fig. 7.1 : Dependence of BOD_{20} on Incubation Period.

$BOD_{ult_1} = BOD_{ult}$ for mainly carbonaceous materials,

$BOD_{ult_2} = BOD_{ult}$ for both carbonaceous and proteinaceous materials,

The major drawback of the BOD estimation method outlined above is that one has to wait for 5 days in order to evaluate BOD_5 of a sample. Hence this method is not a suitable one for process monitoring.

Because of this drawback some instruments have been developed with the help of which one can estimate the BOD of a sample of water within a short period, say, one and a half to two hours.

7.4.17 Chemical Oxygen Demand (COD)

It has been pointed out earlier that it takes 5 days to complete a BOD test. Moreover, this test reveals incomplete information about the total amount of organic substances present in a water sample because of the following reasons :

1. during this test only a portion of the dissolved biodegradable organic substances gets oxidized and a relatively small portion of the suspended biodigradable organic substanced gets oxididised.
2. none of the non-biodegradable organic substances are oxidized, and
3. none of the inorganic substances gets oxidized.

To overcome these shortcomings of the $BOD_{5,\,20°C}$ test, a test has been developed whereby all of the oxidizable organic substances both biodegradable and non-biodegradable as well as oxidizable inorganic substances are oxidized with a chemical oxidizing reagent in a shorter period of time. It is referred to as Chemical Oxygen Demand (COD) test.

The test is carried out by refluxing a measured volume of a water sample with a measured volume of a potassium dichromate ($K_2Cr_2O_7$) solution of known concentration and a proportionate amount of concentrated sulphuric acid solution. During refluxing all of the oxidizable substances are oxidized to their respective oxides. The reactions may be expressed as :

$$\begin{matrix}\text{Oxidizable}\\ \text{Substances}\end{matrix} + K_2Cr_2O_7 + H_2SO_4 \rightarrow K_2SO_4 + Cr_2\,(SO_4)_3 + \text{Oxides}$$

After completion of the refluxing process the excess (unreacted) amount of potassium dichromate is estimated in the refluxed liquor by titrating a portion of it with a standardized ferrous ammonium sulphate (Mohr salt) solution in the presence of Ferroin indicator. The reaction taking place during titration is

$$K_2Cr_2O_7 + 6\,Fe\,(NH_4)_2\,(SO_4)_2 + 7\,H_2SO_4 \rightarrow Cr_2\,(SO_4)_3 + K_2\,SO_4 + 3\,Fe_2\,(SO_4)_3 + 6\,(NH_4)_2\,SO_4 + 7H_2O$$

Based on the data, namely, the volume of dichromate solution reacted (during refluxing), its concentration and the sample (water) volume used, the COD is calculated and reported as mg of O_2/L of the water sample.

It must be pointed out that some aromatic compounds, such as benzene, toluene, pyridine if present in a water sample do not get oxidized during refluxing.

7.4.18 Plant Nutrients

The common plant nutrients which may by present in industrial wastewater are nitrogenous and phosphorous compounds. When an effluent containing nitrogen and/or phosphorous bearing compounds is discharged into a water body, then the growth of aquatic plant including algae would get promoted in the water body. Such enhanced growth is referred to as algal bloom. Those plants would use up the dissolved oxygen present in the water body. Subsequently the plants would undergo biodegradation in the absence of oxygen, that is the eutrophication process would start. Due to anaerobic degradation of the aquatic plants (including the algae) the water body would become filthy and foul smelling gases would be emitted. Hence estimation of the plant nutrients present in a wastewater stream needs to be carried out to enable one to devise a suitable treatment scheme.

7.4.18.1 Nitrogen Estimation

Nitrogen may be present in a wastewater stream in the form of free ammonia, ammonical salts, amino acids, etc. These nitrogenous compounds may be estimated by the Kjeldahl methods. However, this method cannot be used to estimate nitrogen, when it is present as nitrite, nitrate, azide, nitro, nitroso and oximates in a water sample.

The basic principle of the Kjeldahl method is to heat a sample containing nitrogenous compounds with sulphuric acid, potassium sulphate and mercuric sulphate catalyst. During this process the nitrogenous compounds present in the sample are converted to ammonium bisulphate. The mixture is made alkaline by adding caustic soda and distilled. An aqueous ammonical solution distills over which is collected. The ammonium hydroxide present in the distillate is then colourimetrically estimated. Nitrogen estimated in this way is expressed (as N) in mg/L unit.

The reagents used for the colourimetric method are aqueous solutions of mercuric iodide and sodium hydroxide.

7.4.18.2 Phosphorous Estimation

Phosphorous may be present in a waste water sample as inorganic phosphates, such as pyro, meta tripoly and orthophosphate as well as organo-phosphorous compounds. Total phosphorous estimation is carried out by converting all of the phosphorous compounds present to orthophosphate by boiling a sample of water with potassium persulphate and sulphuric acid. Orthophosphate so produced is then estimated colourimetrically

The colourimetric method consists of addition of acidified ammonium molybdate and amino-napthol–sulfonic acid solutions or ammonium molybdate and stannous chloride solutions to a dilute orthophosphate solution. It gives rise to an intense blue colour.

The phosphorous content of a sample is expressed (as P) in mg/L unit.

7.4.19 Bacteriological Assessment

Wastewater may contain pathogenic (disease causing) as well as non-pathogenic organisms. From public health point of view the presence of pathogens in an effluent would be alarming as those would contaminate the water body/bodies into which the effluent is discharged. Hence, care should be taken so that contaminated effluents do not find their way into water bodies without prior disinfection.

To guard against such possibilities it is necessary to ascertain whether an effluent contains any pathogen or not. It is a difficult task, as there is no general test for detection of the different species of pathogens. To overcome this difficulty the practice is to try to detect coliform bacteria (Bact. Coli.) which are almost invariably present along with other pathogens. Coliform are easily detectable. They survive over a long period of time. Coliform like other water-borne pathogens reside in the digestive tracts of warm– blooded animals and hence the presence of coliform in a sample of waste water is an evidence of recent excretal contamination of the waste water stream. Presence of colifom in a sample would mean that other pathogens may also be present.

The presence or absence of coliform in a water sample may be ascertained by conducting the following tests :

(A) Presumptive test, (B) Confirmed test, and (C) Completed test.

The tests are carried out by inoculating lactose or lauryl tryptose broth fermentation tubes with portions of a sample and incubating those for 24-48 hours at 35 ± 0.5 °C. Production of gas during incubation would indicate that coliform are present in the sample.

7.4.20 Bioassay

The objective of carrying out a bioassay test is to ascertain whether an effluent stream of waste water is toxic and if so, to what extent.

An effluent may contain inorganic and/or organic toxic substances. For each of the substances, which are established toxicants, the threshold limits have been ascertained. Hence, if it be known which specific toxic substance or substances are present in an effluent stream, then one may analytically estimate their respective concentrations and decide about the toxicity of the stream.

However, identification of the toxic substances present in a sample and estimation of their concentrations are tedious. Moreover, toxicity of a sample is not an additive property. Sometimes the effect of the toxicants is synergistic and sometimes it is antagonistic. Hence, it is necessary to ascertain the toxicity of a waste water sample by bioassay.

The specific information one may obtain by carrying out a bioassay test is whether an effluent when discharged into a water body would adversely affect its aquatic flora and fauna, particularly the fish species present.

The test is carried out in a laboratory aquarium to ascertain which minimum dilution of an effluent stream would make it non-toxic to fish. For laboratory test the dilution water used may be either from a natural source or prepared in the laboratory by adding some chemicals to distilled water. A control test is also carried out using the dilution water alone. The species of fish to be used for a test should be carefully chosen and they should be acclimated to the test condition prior to carrying out a laboratory trial.

CHAPTER 8

Water-borne Pollutant Classification, Treatment Techniques and Control Strategy

The pollutants present in a liquid effluent stream may be broadly classified according to their physical and chemical nature as shown below :

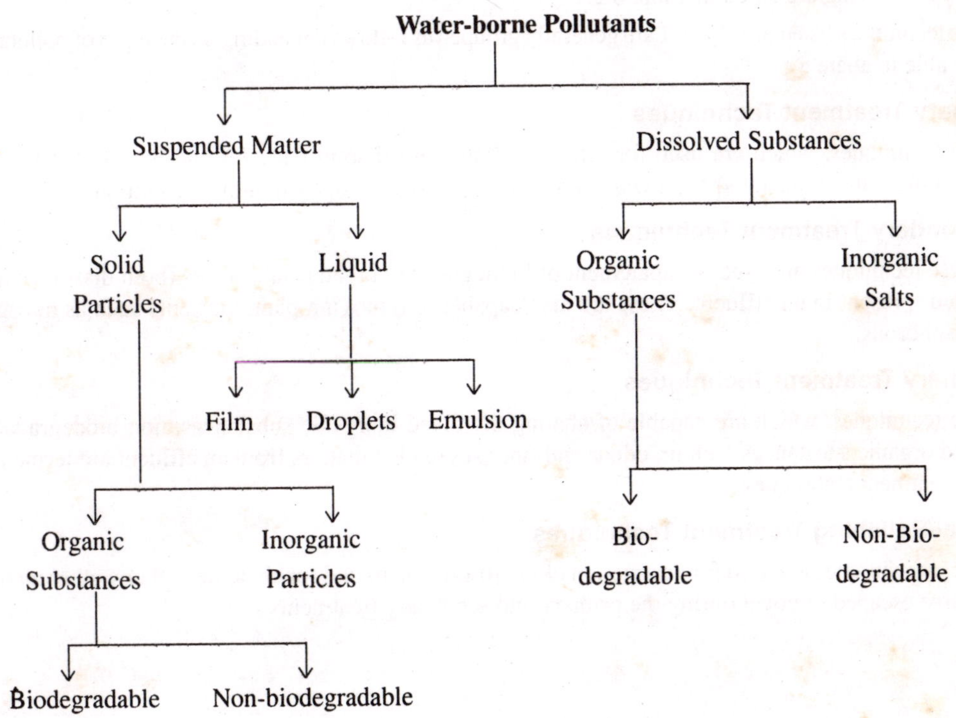

Fig. 8.1 : Water-borne Pollutant Classification.

8.1 Treatment Techniques

Over the years several techniques have been developed for removal of pollutants from waste water. Some of these may be used for removal of several pollutants, whereas, some may be used for removal of some specific pollutants only. These techniques may be classified into the following three groups depending on their causative factors as shown in Table 8.1.

Table 8.1 : Classification of the Waste Water Treatment Techniques Based on their Causative Factors

Physical	Chemical	Biological
Screening	pH Regulation	Aerobic Treatment
Gravity separation	Precipitation	Anaerobic Treatment
Dissolved Air Flotation	Oxidation	
Filtration	Reduction	
Membrane based processes	Resin-based process	
Adsorption	Disinfection	
Desorption		
Coagulation and flocculation		
De-emulsification		
Sterilization		

The purpose for which the above mentioned techniques may be used, and the pollutants they are capable of removing are listed in Table 8.2.

The techniques listed in Table 8.1 are generally grouped as follows depending on the types of pollutants they are able to abate :

I. Primary Treatment Techniques

The techniques, which are used for removal of suspended solid particles and immiscible liquids (films, droplets and emulsions) from waste water are termed as primary treatment techniques.

II. Secondary Treatment Techniques

These techniques are used for abatement of biodegradable organic substances (both dissolved and suspended) present in an effluent. These are also capable of removing plant nutrients such as nitrogen and phosphorous.

III. Tertiary Treatment Techniques

The techniques, which are capable of abating dissolved inorganic substances, non-biodegradable dissolved organic substances, colour, odour and finer suspended matters from an effluent are termed as tertiary treatment techniques.

IV. Final/Polishing Treatment Techniques

These techniques are used for destruction of micro-organisms and for abatement of any other matter, which have escaped removal during the primary and secondary treatments.

Table 8.2 : Treatment Techniques, Basic Purpose and Consequent Pollutant Removal

I. Physical Techniques

Technique	Basic Purpose	Pollutant Removed
Screening	Large particulate removal.	Light and heavy particles of inorganic and organic substances.
Gravity Separation	Heavy particles, free oil and grease removal.	Finer suspended particles, oil, grease and BOD.
Dissolved Air Floatation	Both heavy and light particles, free oil and grease removal.	Finer suspended particles, free oil, grease and BOD.
Filtration	Both heavy and light particles removal.	Suspended solid particles (organic as well as inorganic) and BOD.
Adsorption	VOCs dissolved/suspended (non particulate) non-biodegradable organic substances, colour and odour removal.	Recalcitrant organic substances, recoverable organic compounds, colour and odour.
Desorption	Removal of ammonia, VOCs.	Free ammonia, VOCs.
Membrane Separation	Dissolved inorganic and organic substances removal.	Dissolved inorganic and organic substances and BOD.
Coagulation and Flocculation	Colloidal particles removal.	Turbidity (due to suspended fine solid particles) and BOD.
De-emulsification	Dispersed phase separation.	Turbidity (due to suspended fine liquid droplets) and BOD.
Sterilization	Complete destruction of micro-organisms.	Micro-organisms.

II. Chemical Techniques

Technique	Basic Purpose	Pollutant Removed
pH Regulation	Neutralization, pH adjustment.	Adjustment of H^+/OH^- concentration, precipitation of heavy metal ions.
Precipitation	Dissolved inorganic substance removal.	Some inorganic cations and anions.
Oxidation and Reduction	Specific dissolved substances removal.	Specific toxic substances and some recalcitrant organic compounds.
Resin-Based Processes	Removal of some dissolved inorganic and organic substances.	Dissolved ionized substances, and some non-biodegradable organic substances.
Disinfection	Destruction of micro-organisms.	Destruction of pathogenic micro-organisms.

III. Biological Techniques

Aerobic Treatment	Biodegradable dissolved and suspended organic substances.	Biodegradable organic substances, BOD, some nitrogenous and phosphorous compounds.
Anaerobic Treatment	Biodegradable dissolved and suspended organic substances.	Biodegradable organic substances, BOD, some nitrogenous and phosphorous compounds.

Scanning of Table 8.2 reveals that for abatement of a specific type of pollutant more than one technique is available. For selection of a suitable technique in a given situation one should take into account (i) the initial concentration of the targeted type of pollutant, (ii) the quantity of waste water to be treated, and (iii) the treatment cost.

In Table 8.3 the different techniques, which may be used for abatement of some specific types of pollutants, are listed.

Table 8.3 : Techniques Useful for Removal of Specific Pollutants

Pollutant	Techniques for Removal
Suspended Particulate Matter (SPM)	Screening, Gravity separation, Centrifugal separation, Filtration, Dissolved Air Floatation, Coagulation and Flocculation, Sedimentation.
Fats, Oils and Grease (FOG) (free and emulsified)	Gravity separation, Centrifugal separation, Dissolved Air Floatation, Coagulation and Flocculation, De-emulsification.
Dissolved Biodegradable organic Substances (BOD & COD)	Aerobic treatment, Anaerobic treatment, Membrane separation, Adsorption, Oxidation.
Dissolved Non-biodegradable Organic Substances	Adsorption, Oxidation, Membrane separation.
VOCs	Adsorption, Desorption.
Dissolved Inorganic Salts	Precipitation, Oxidation, Reduction, Reverse osmosis, Electrodialysis, Evaporation, Ion exchange.
Dissolved Gases	Stripping, Heating & Stripping.
Acidity and Alkalinity	Neutralization
Plant Nutrients	Aerobic-anaerobic treatment, Precipitation.
Organic Sludge	Biological treatment, Incineration, Wet oxidation, Thickening, Filtration, Soil conditioning.
Micro-organisms	Disinfections, Sterilization.

8.2 Control Strategy

The techniques, which may be used for treating a liquid effluent stream from an industrial unit, would depend on the types of pollutants present in the effluent and their respective concentrations. The overall scheme would depend on whether the treated water would be reused within the unit itself or outside its boundary or it is to be disposed off. If it is proposed to dispose off the treated effluent, one should examine carefully the feasibility of the following alternative disposal methods : pounding, discharge into a water body/public sewer system, land irrigation, and bore hole injection.

Before chalking out a strategy for handling and treatment of an effluent stream one needs to decide on the following two pre-treatment steps :

1. Whether the effluent streams from the different sections of a plant are to be segregated and treated separately or those may be combined together, that is, equalized and then treated. Equalization would enable one to feed waste water to the downstream treatment units at a more or less uniform rate having a time averaged pollutant concentration.
2. Whether neutralization, that is, pH regulation of an effluent stream is necessary prior to its further treatment.

After arriving at appropriate decisions with respect to the above mentioned steps one should explore the different alternative schemes for treatment of the effluent stream. While exploring the alternatives one must bear in mind that in general waste water treatment processes do not yield any revenue. Hence the scheme finally chosen should be such that it would produce a treated effluent having the desired quality but the overall treatment cost (fixed cost plus operating cost) would be the minimum. The proposed scheme may be broadly represented as shown in Fig. 8.2. It should be pointed out here that the actual scheme finally selected may have all of the sections shown in Fig. 8.2 or only some of them depending on the pollutants initially present in the stream to be treated and the quality of the treated effluent desired.

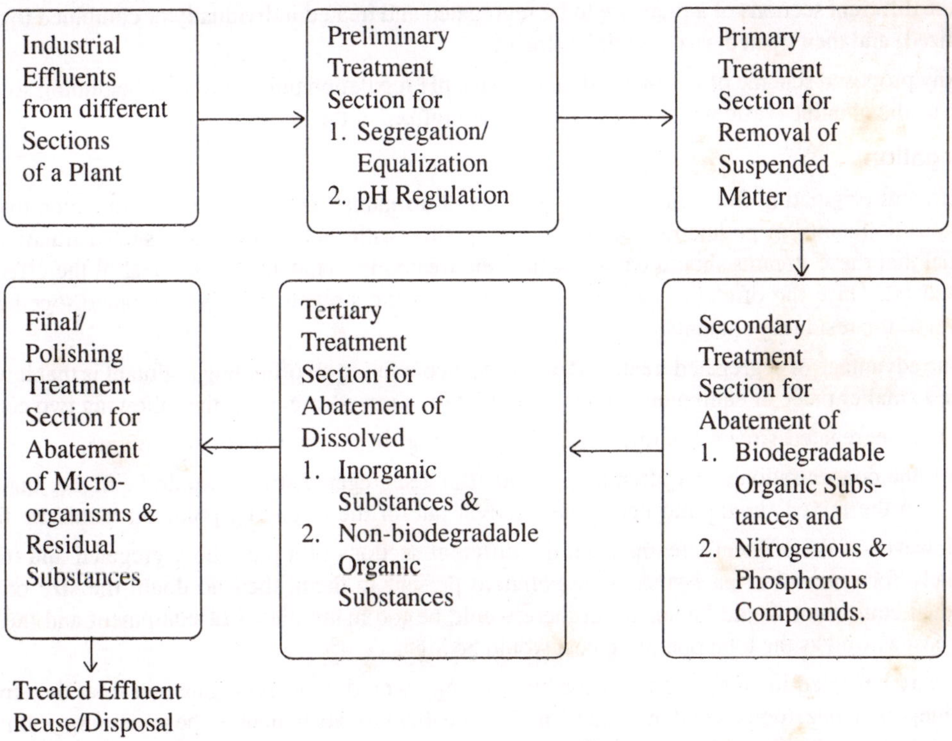

Fig. 8.2 : A Broad Scheme for Treatment of an Industrial Plant Effluent.

CHAPTER 9

Water-borne Pollutant Abatement Methods

For proper treatment of a waste water stream from an industrial plant a judicious combination of the techniques listed in Chapter 8 is to be employed so as to keep the overall treatment cost the minimum and at the same time bring down the concentration of the pollutants to the regulation limit.

Before chalking out a scheme of treatment it has to be decided whether the effluent streams originating from the different sections of a plant are to be segregated and treated individually or combined together (equalized) and then treated as a combined stream.

Any proposed scheme of treatment should have a pH regulation unit at the very beginning so that a highly acidic/alkaline waste water stream may be neutralized at the outset.

Segregation

Effluent originating from one or more sections of an industrial plant may contain some toxic or hazardous pollutants, or pollutants which are incompatible with each other. Under such a situation it is essential that these streams should be segregated and treated individually for removal of the offending pollutant (s). Once the offending pollutants are removed the streams may be combined together for removal of the residual pollutants.

The advantage of segregated treatment of a stream containing an offending pollutant is that it would require a smaller piece of equipment compared to that for a mixed stream on the following two counts :

(i) a segregated stream volume would be a fraction of the mixed stream volume,

(ii) the concentration of an offending pollutant in a segregated stream would be higher than that in the mixed stream and hence the removal rate of the offending pollutant would be faster.

However, if the effluent streams from the different sections of a plant be segregated and treated separately for removal of each and every pollutant present in them, then no doubt the size of each individual equipment would be small but there would be too many pieces of equipment and the total initial cost as well as the total operating cost would be high.

It may be stated in conclusion that the best strategy would be to segregate and treat the streams containing toxic/hazardous pollutants and then combine them for abatement of the remaining pollutants. Such a scheme would be more economical.

Equalization

Equalization means mixing the effluent streams from the different sections of a plant in a reservoir called an *equalization tanks* or *basin*. From the basin the mixed waste water is withdrawn at a predetermined rate for feeding the downstream treatment units.

Very often the waste water streams emanating from the different sections of a plant have fluctuating flow rates and varying concentration of the pollutants present. Hence equalization is necessary in order to feed the downstream treatment units at a more or less uniform hydraulic load (flow rate) and at an average pollutant load (concentration).

The basis for design of the treatment units is normally the average load. However, due to process upsets/disturbances sometimes the actual load may be more than the estimated average one. Such an excess load is referred to as a *shock load*. In practice the treatment units are overdesigned so that their performance would not suffer because of occasional shock loads.

An equalization basin should be sized so that at no point of time the basin would either go dry or overflow. To estimate the size of such a basin the data required are the combined instantaneous inflow rates over a period of 24 hours. Based on these data the cumulative inflow at different instances is calculated. The constant hourly outflow rate is estimated by dividing the total cumulative flow for a day by 24. Based on these data the differences between the cumulative inflow and cumulative outflow at various instances are calculated. The required minimum volume of a basin is then determined by adding the maximum positive and negative differences. The following example demonstrates the procedure. In practice the basin volume should be at least 10-20% more than the calculated minimum volume in order to take care of the occasional 'shock loads'.

Example 9.1: Equalization Tank

Based on the following instantaneous waste water flow rate data from an industrial unit calculate the size of an equalization unit.

Time of day	6 a.m.	8 a.m.	10 a.m.	12 p.m.	3 p.m.	6 p.m.
Inflow rate m^3/hr	29.5	27.2	45.4	45.42	34.1	43.15

Time of day	9 p.m.	11 p.m.	1 a.m.	3 a.m.	6 a.m.
Inflow rate m^3/hr	25.0	68.2	47.7	34.1	29.5

Solution : Based on the data supplied Table : Ex. 9.1 is prepared.

Table : Ex. 9.1

Time of day	Inflow rate m^3/hr	Cumulative inflow, m^3	Cumulative outflow, m^3	Cumulative inflow–Cumulative outflow, m^3
6 a.m.	29.5	0	0	0
8 a.m.	27.2	56.7	78.65	–21.95

Contd.

Table : Ex. 9.1 (Contd.)

Time of day	Inflow rate m^3/hr	Cumulative inflow, m^3	Cumulative outflow, m^3	Cumulative inflow–Cumulative outflow, m^3
10 a.m.	45.4	129.3	157.3	–28.0
12 noon	45.42	220.12	235.95	–15.83
3 p.m.	34.1	339.4	353.925	–14.525
6 p.m.	43.15	455.275	471.9	–16.625
9 p.m.	25.0	557.5	589.875	–32.375
11 p.m.	68.2	650.7	668.525	–17.825
1 a.m.	47.7	766.6	747.175	+19.425
3 a.m.	34.1	848.4	825.825	+22.575
6 a.m.	29.5	943.8	943.8	0

The third column (cumulative inflow) corresponding to 8 a.m. and 10 a.m. are calculated as follows :

$$\text{At 8 a.m. cumulative inflow} = \frac{29.5 + 27.2}{2} \times 2 = 56.7 \text{ m}^3 \text{ and}$$

$$\text{At 10 a.m. cumulative inflow} = 56.7 + \frac{(27.2 + 45.4)}{2} \times 2 = 129.3 \text{ m}^3.$$

The fourth column (cumulative outflow) is calculated by multipying the hourly outflow rate by the time difference between a time of the day and the base time (in this example 6 a.m.) Hence, corresponding to 8 a.m. the cumulative outflow is

$$\frac{943.8}{24} \times 2 = 78.65 \text{ m}^3, \text{ and at 10 a.m. cumulative outflow } \frac{943.8}{24} \times 4 = 157.3 \text{ m}^3$$

Table : Ex. 9.1 shows that the maximum negative difference and positive difference between the cumulative inflow and the cumulative outflow are -32.375 m^3 and $+22.575$ m^3 respectively.

Hence the minimum volume of the equalization basin should be 32.375 m^3 + 22.575 m^3 = 54.95 m^3.

To take care of shock hydraulic overload, the actual basin volume may be taken as 20% more than the calculated minimum volume,

$54.95 \text{ m}^3 \times 1.2 = 65.94 \text{ m}^3 \approx 66 \text{ m}^3$.

An equalization basin should be preceded by screening and grit removal units so as to prevent deposition and accumulation of solids in the basin. It may be either an earthen basin with its edges protected with concrete blocks/gravels or a concrete tank. A square plan is better. A basin may have mechanical agitators and /or aeration units in order to prevent sedimentation of fine particles. Aeration may help in reduction of BOD to some extent. Facilities should be provided for removal of accumulated solids and grease. Figure 9.1 shows a schematic sketch of an equalization basin.

In order to dampen the flow and pollutant load variations the following alternative arrangements are sometimes provided in the overall plan. However, these may be adopted for individual treatment units and not for the system (ETP) as a whole.

(1) Recirculate a portion of the treated effluent from a unit along with its influent. This is very often practiced for adjusting the influent BOD level of an aerobic trickling filter.

(2) Split the influent into or more fractions and introduce those progressively into a treatment unit. In a step aerated activated sludge unit this approach is used.

(3) Use two or more units in series through which a waste water stream is passed as in the case of an adsorption/ion exchange process. Such an arrangement enables one to isolate and regenerate the lead unit once it gets almost saturated and put a regenerated unit on –stream.

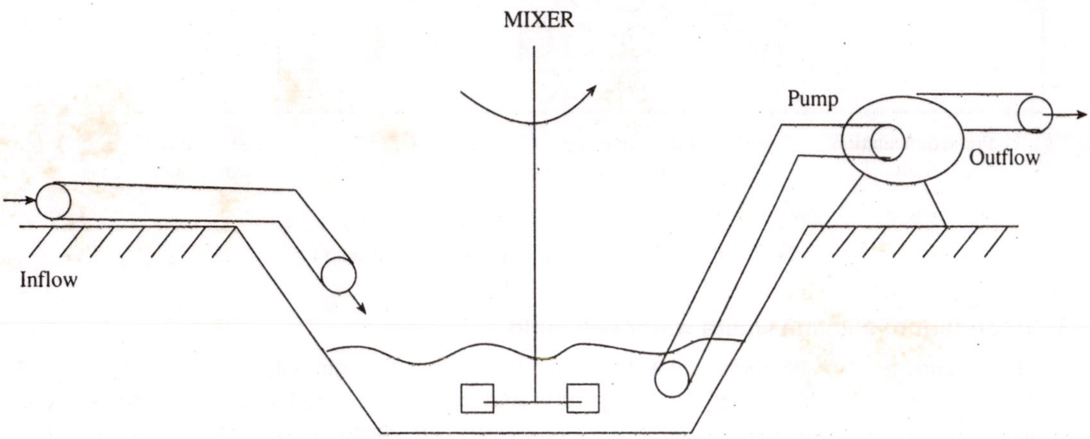

Fig. 9.1 : Schematic Sketch of an Equalization Basin.

pH Regulation

Regulation of waste water pH is required for various treatment processes. At the initial stage the pH of a waste water stream should be close to 7 so that cheaper materials of construction may be used for the primary treatment units. For the secondary treatment units the pH should be in the range of 6.5 to 8.5. For precipitation reactions and oxidation–reduction processes it may be necessary to maintain either an acidic or an alkaline pH.

Neutralization/pH regulation may be carried out through any one of the following steps depending upon the situation :

1. Mixing acidic and alkaline stream

The cheapest method for pH regulation would be mixing an acidic waste water stream with an alkaline one, if those are discharged from the same plant or some neighbouring plants. If such mixing does not yield the desired pH of the mixture, then an acid or an alkali may be added to supplement the process.

2. Treatment of acidic waste water with alkali

An acidic waste water stream may be treated with any one of the following chemicals :

Limestone ($CaCO_3$), Lime (CaO), Soda ash (Na_2CO_3), Caustic soda ($NaOH$).

The first two may be added in the form of lumps or powder or an aqueous suspension, whereas the last two are added as aqueous solutions. Costwise limestone is the cheapest and caustic soda is the costliest. Close pH regulation is easier with Na_2CO_3/NaOH solutiion. Treatment with limestone/lime would not only result in pH regulation but may also reduce BOD/COD and TDS as the reaction products may be insoluble. As the reaction products settle they may trap some of the suspended particles. Neutralization with Na_2CO_3/NaOH would increase the TDS as the reaction products would be soluble in water. Figure 9.2 shows a sketch of a limestone neutralizer.

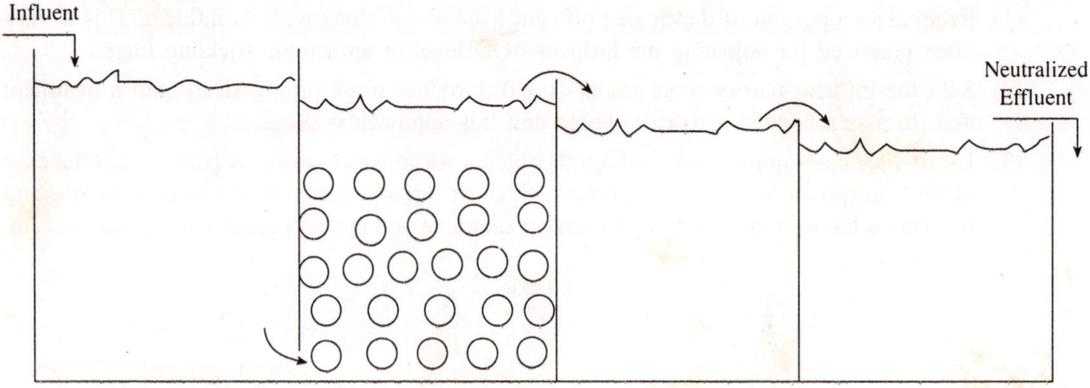

Fig. 9.2 : Sketch of a Limestone Neutralizer.

3. Treatment of alkaline waste water with acid

For treatment of an alkaline waste water stream the chemicals commonly used are carbon dioxide (CO_2 in flue gas), hydrochloric acid (HCl), sulphuric acid (H_2SO_4). pH regulation is easier with aqueous HCl/H2SO_4. From chemical cost point of view flue-gas is the cheapest. However, while selecting a chemical one should take into account the cost of equipment for storage, handling and dispensing of the chemical selected.

Since waste water treatment does not earn any revenue, the unit cost of chemicals to be used for pH regulation should be low. However, when the amount of chemical required is small, relatively costly chemical may be used.

It should be mentioned here that during some processes, such as secondary treatment (both aerobic and anaerobic), precipitation, oxidation and reduction it may be necessary to monitor and regulate the pH of the liquid mass being treated.

9.1 Primary Treatment

After pH regulation and equalization a waste water stream is subjected to primary treatment. The objective of primary treatment is to remove the suspended matters from waste water. Selection of a technique/techniques to be employed for removal of suspended matters from a waste water stream depends on whether the particles are solid or liquid. Technique selection would also depend on solid particle density and size. Removal of solid particles is essential as those are likely to accumulate in pipelines, pumps and subsequent treatment units and thereby disrupt the effluent treatment plant (ETP) operation. Removal of suspended liquid (oils, fats and greases) from waste water needs to be carried out as those may adversely affect the performance of the secondary and tertiary treatment units.

Larger solid particles (15 mm or more) are removed by screening. Coarse (0.1 mm or larger) and denser particles are arrested in a grit chamber or a hydrocyclone. Denser particles finer than 0.1 mm (but not colloids) may be settled in a thickener or removed by the dissolved air floatation (DAF) or induced air floatation technique. In fact, complete removal of fine particles both heavier and lighter can be achieved by filtration only. However, filtration operation for removal of fine particles in generally employed only as a part of the final (polishing) treatment and not as a part of the primary treatment.

For removal of suspended solid particles operations are carried out in the following sequence :

1. Screening,
2. Grit removal (Grit chamber–95% removal if 0.2 mm or larger; Hydrocyclone—95% removal of 0.1 mm or larger),
3. Thickening/sedimentation,
4. DAF/induced air floatation,
5. Colloid removal.

9.1.1 Screening

Screening should be done at the very entrance of a waste water treatment facility. The purpose is to remove large particles both lighter and heavier than water in order to protect the down stream treatment units from clogging.

The objectionable materials which need to be removed are rags, pieces of rubber and plastics, component/broken parts of machineries and other sundry materials. The screens used are metallic and they have uniform rectangular or circular openings. These may consist of parallel bars or rods, gratings, perforated plates, wire mesh, etc. The screenings are removed either manually or mechanically and may finally be disposed of either as landfill material or by incinerating.

Screens are classified as coarse, medium or fine depending on the size of the apertures. Coarse screens have 75-150 mm openings, medium ones have 20-50 mm and fine screens have less than 20 mm openings.

Screens are generally of two types :

1. a rack composed of parallel bars or rods placed at an angle with the horizontal plane.
2. a moving screen, either a horizontal rotary drum or a vertical rotating disk made of perforated plate or wire mesh.

A rack is constructed by placing bars or rods parallely at an angle with the horizontal plane so as to cover the entire width of a waste water flow channel. The bars or rods are welded to a frame having a horizontal platform at its top. The platform may have perforations so that the racking stored temporarily on it may drain. An alternate arrangement is to place a cart on the platform for collection and removal of the racking.

The bars are usefully 10 to 15 mm wide at the upstream side and taper slightly towards the downstream side. The clearance between the bars and the angle of a rack with the horizontal plane depend on whether it is to be manually or mechanically cleaned. The commonly used features of a rack are given in Table 9.1.

Table 9.1 : Rack Clearance and Angle

Type of Rack	Clearance between bars	Angle with the horizontal plane
Manually cleaned	25-50 mm	30° to 45°
Mechanically cleaned	15-75 mm	45° to 80°

The cleaning frequency depends on the rate of accumulation of suspended waste water borne solids. Manual cleaning is achieved by sweeping a rake manually upward periodically, whereas mechanical cleaning is done with the help of an upward travelling rake. A mechanical rake may be operated either continuously at a slow speed or intermittently.

The linear velocity of waste water in the approach channel should not be less than 0.3 m/s in order to avoid deposition of sediments in the channel. The velocity through the screens should normally be 0.6 m/s to 1.2 m/s.

The head loss through a bar screen is normally between 0.08 to 0.15 m. It should not be more than 0.3 m. Other than bar screens, rotary drum and disk screens made of stainless steel or nonferrous perforated sheets or wire mesh are also used. The openings of such screens generally range between 0.2 mm to 3 mm.

Rotary drum screens are placed horizontally with the upstream end open and the downstream end closed. It is placed in a channel covering its entire width and normally it is kept half-submerged. Through the open end of the drum waste water enters and the filtrate flows out through the peripheral openings. The drum rotates at a slow speed (4 to 7 rpm). As the drum rotates the collected solids are raised up above the water level and finally those are backwashed into a trough or a conveyor located within the drum near about the highest point of the drum.

A vertical circular disk made of a screen rotates on a horizontal shaft about half submerged covering the entire cross section of an open channel. Waste water flows through the screen openings and the suspended solid particles are retained on its surface. As the screen carrying the solid particles rises above the liquid level those are backwashed into a trough.

Comminution

An alternative to screening operation is comminution. It eliminates the problems associated with the collection, removal, storage and handling of screenings. Comminuting devices known as comminutors intercept the large suspended solid particles and cut up those by shredding and grinding into small pieces without removing them from water. The shredded and ground particles pass through the comminutor. Those are finally separated from waste water in a grit chamber or a primary settling tank.

9.1.2 Grit Removal

Grits are granular inorganic solid particles heavier than water. Removal of such particles from waste water are necessary to achieve the following objectives :

1. to prevent wear and tear of mechanical components of downstream treatment equipment, such as pumps, agitators, etc., due to abrasion,
2. to avoid clogging of pipelines, and
3. to prevent accumulation in the secondary treatment units which would otherwise require frequent cleaning

The inorganic solid particles being heavier than water get separated from a flowing stream due to gravity. A chamber in which such separation is carried out is referred to as a *Grit Chamber*. The Chamber is so designed that very little of the suspended organic particles, which are generally lighter than water would settle in it.

Alternatively grits may be removed from a wastewater stream in a hydrocyclone

A grit chamber is basically an open channel at the discharge (outlet) end of which a weir or such other obstruction is placed so as to maintain a constant liquid velocity in the channel irrespective of the liquid depth in it. Generally a grit chamber is designed for removal of about 95% of the solid particles of 0.2 mm size. The liquid velocity maintained in a grit chamber is in the range of 0.15 m/s to 0.30 m/s. Most often the velocity is around 0.3 m/s. The solid particles, which settle on the channel bed, are removed either manually or mechanically.

A grit chamber may be either of rectangular or parabolic (trapezoidal) cross section. The flow control device used at the outlet end of a grit chamber of rectangular cross section may be either a proportional type weir or a sutro type weir or a parshall flume.

Both proportional weir and sutro weir have a weir and an orifice as shown in Figs. 9.3A and 9.3B.

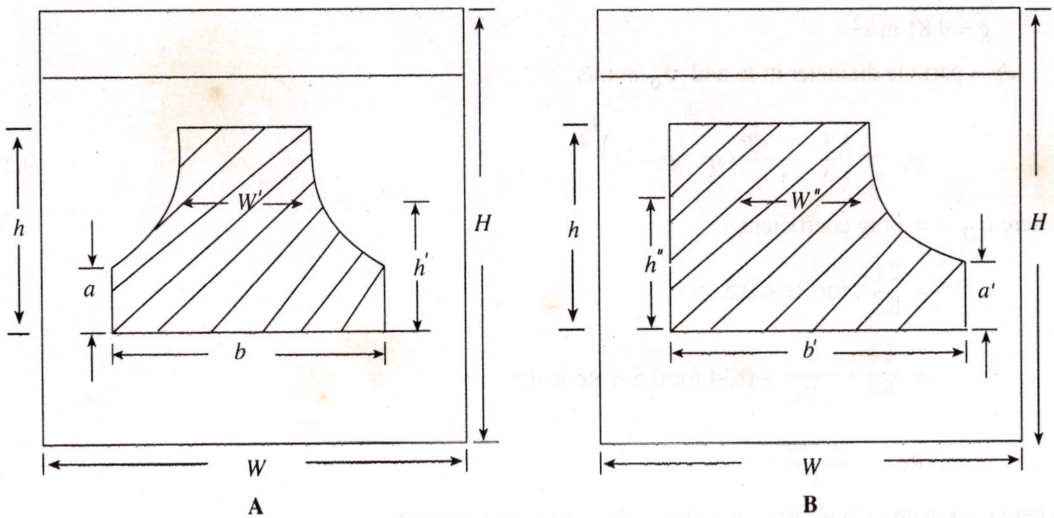

Fig. 9.3A : Proportional Weir. **9.3B :** Sutro Weir.

The lower edge of a proportional weir is straight and horizontal. It is located at a height of 15 to 30 cm above the channel bed. The sides of the orifice are curved. The sutro weir is a type of proportional weir. One side of its orifice is straight and vertical whereas the other side is curved.

9.1.2.1 Rectangular Cross-Section Grit Chamber Design Approach

In a grit chamber discrete particles of relatively coarser sizes settle under the influence of gravity while the flowing waste water tries to carry these towards the outlet end of the chamber. The dimensions of the chamber should be such that most of the particles of a pre-selected size would settle on the chamber floor before being dragged out of the channel. Normally it is designed for total removal of particles having size 0.2 mm or larger from a waste water stream.

The flow control device and the chamber cross section should be designed in such away that liquid velocity through the chamber would be uniform irrespective of the waste water volumetric flow rate at a given instant of time.

Rectangular Chamber Sizing and Weir Design

The dimensions of a rectangular grit chamber and the weir may be estimated through the following steps :

Step-I

Select the smallest particle size, which needs to be retained in the chamber. Ascertain its density. In the absence of the specific information the following may be assumed :

$dp = 0.2$ mm, and $sp.\ gr. = 2.65$

Step-II

Calculate the scouring velocity ϑ_o and the free settling velocity of the selected particle using Eqs. (9.1) and (9.2) respectively

$$\vartheta_o = \left(\frac{8c}{f}\ g(sp.gr.-1)dp\right)^{1/2}, \tag{9.1}$$

where $c = 0.03$ for granular sandy particles and 0.06 for sticky particles,

$f = 0.03$

$g = 9.81$ m/s^2

dp = particle diameter in m and ϑ_o in m/s

$$\upsilon_s = \left(\frac{4}{3}\ \frac{g\ dp}{C_D}(sp.\ gr - 1)\right)^{1/2} \tag{9.2}$$

where C_D = drag coefficient

$$= \frac{24}{\text{Re}}, \text{ for Re} < 0.5$$

$$= \frac{24}{\text{Re}} + \frac{3}{\sqrt{\text{Re}}} + 0.34 \text{ for } 0.5 < \text{Re} < 10^4$$

$$\text{Re} = \frac{\upsilon_s\ dp}{\nu}$$

where ν = kinematic viscosity of water at the operating temperature.

When sufficient information are not available for estimation of υ_o and υ_s, those are taken as 0.3 m/s.

Step-III

The cross-sectional area of the chamber is estimated as

$$A = \frac{Q}{\upsilon_o} \tag{9.3}$$

where Q = maximum volumetric flow rate of the waste water stream in m^3/s.

Step-IV

The liquid depth h in the channel corresponding to the flow rate Q is estimated assuming a suitable chamber width W using Eq. (9.4),

$$h = \frac{A}{W}. \tag{9.4}$$

Actual chamber depth H is taken as

$H = h$ + free board height + depth of accumulated grit/depth of mechanical conveyor.

The free board height is taken as 0.3 to 0.6 m and the conveyor depth as 0.15 to 0.3 m.

Step-V

The theoretical ratio of chamber length L to the liquid depth h must be the same as that of υ_o to υ_s for complete removal of the pre-selected particles of size dp.

$$\frac{L_{theo}}{h} = \frac{\upsilon_o}{\upsilon_s} \text{ or } L_{theo} = \frac{\upsilon_o}{\upsilon_s}\ h. \tag{9.5}$$

The actual length of the chamber should be taken as

L_{actual} = 1.5 to 2 times the calculated theoretical length L_{theo}.

Such dimensions of a grit chamber should result in a detention time of about 30 to 60 seconds.

Step-VI Weir Design

A. Proportional Weir

For a symmetrical (proportional) weir the dimensions (Fig. 9.3.A) to be calculated are h, W', a and b. h for a proportional weir is calculated using Eq. (9.4).

The flow rate through such a weir is given by the following equation :

$$Q = 0.61b\,(2ag)^{1/2}\left(h-\frac{a}{3}\right) \tag{9.6}$$

The dimension of a ranges between 25 to 50 mm. Normally it is taken as 37 mm.

b is estimated using Eq. (9.6) after assuming a suitable value of a. The profile of the curved edges of the weir (orifice) is obtained using Eq. (9.7) as shown below.

$$\frac{W'}{b} = 1-\frac{2}{\pi}\tan^{-1}\left(\frac{h'}{a}-1\right). \tag{9.7}$$

B. Sutro Weir

A sutro weir is an asymmetric proportional weir (Fig. 9.3B). Its design procedure is similar to that for a proportional weir. The following equations are to be used for calculation of the weir dimensions, a', b', w'' and h. h is taken as the same as that calculated using Eq. (9.4). The dimension of a' may be taken as 37 mm. b' is estimated using Eq. (9.8) given below.

$$Q = 0.61\, b'\,(2a'g)^{1/2}\left(h-\frac{a'}{3}\right). \tag{9.8}$$

The curved edge profile of the weir is estimated using Eq. (9.9) as given here under.

$$\frac{w''}{b'} = 1-\frac{2}{\pi}\tan^{-1}\left(\frac{h''}{a'}-1\right)^{1/2} \tag{9.9}$$

9.1.2.2 Trapezoidal Cross-Section Grit Chamber Design Approach

A grit chamber fitted with a fixed width type weir should theoretically have a parabolic cross-section so as to maintain a constant forward velocity in the chamber irrespective of the liquid depth in it. The head loss at the control section of such a chamber is much less compared to that for a rectangular cross section chamber. However since it is difficult to construct a chamber having a parabolic cross-section, the actual cross-sectional profile is approximated by a trapezoid.

The dimensions of such a grit chamber and those of the control weir may be estimated using the following procedure :

Step-I

The scouring velocity υ_0 and the free settling velocity υ_s of the smallest sized particles, which are to be retained in the grit chamber, are to be calculated using Eqs. (9.1) and (9.2) respectively.

Step-II

Using the calculated value of υ_0 the cross-sectional area of the chamber is estimated with the help of Eq. (9.3).

Step-III

In this type of grit chamber the width is a function of the liquid level above the grit storage space/ space for a mechanical conveyor. The maximum width, W_{max}, of the chamber is assumed. Based on this assumed W_{max} and the specified maximum waste water flow rate, the liquid depth in the proposed chamber is to be calculated using Eq. (9.10)

$$h = \frac{3}{2} \frac{Q_{max}}{W_{max} \times \upsilon_o} \tag{9.10}$$

The actual chamber depth H is to be taken as

$H = h$ + free board height + depth of accumulated grit/depth of mechanical conveyor.

The width of the chamber at its base depends on the width of the conveyor to be used. It may be taken as 0.6 m in the absence of any specific information.

Based on the assumed $W_{max,}$ the base width and the calculated h, the dimensions of a trapezium approximating a parabola are ascertained as shown in Fig. 9.4.

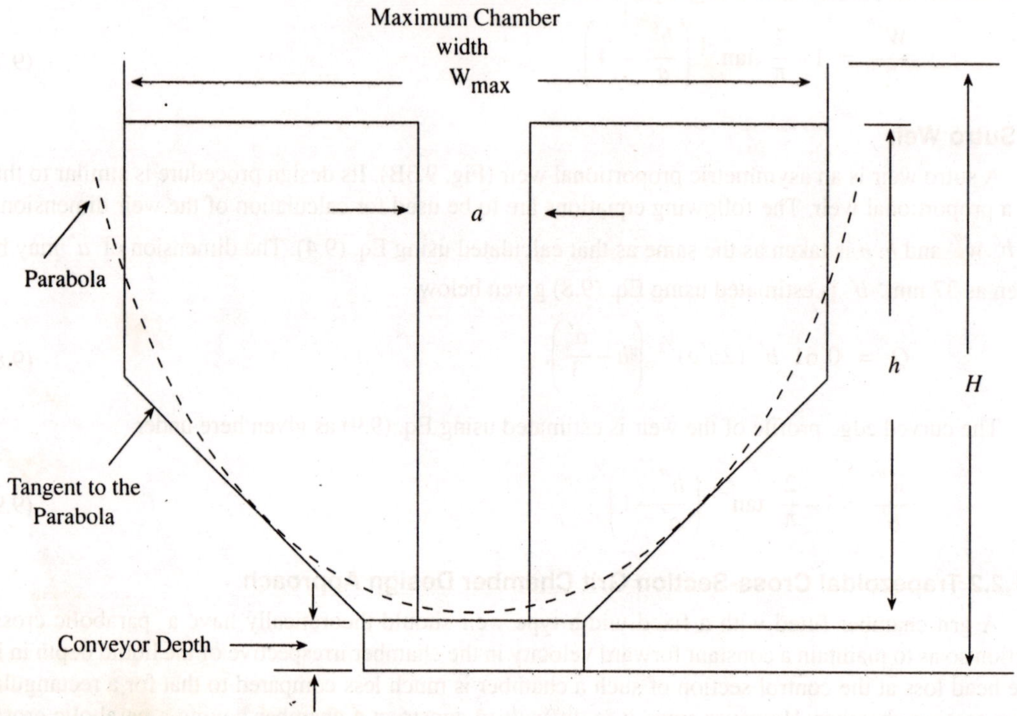

Fig. 9.4 : Trapezoidal Grit Chamber.

Step-IV

The length of a trapexoidal grit chamber is calculated in the same way as that for a chamber of rectangular cross section i.e. using Eq. (9.5) :

$$L_{theo} = \frac{\upsilon_o}{\upsilon_s} h$$

and L_{actual} = 1.5 to 2 times the $L_{theo.}$

Step-V

The control section for a trapezoidal grit chamber is a vertical rectangular opening having a constant width a. The width a is calculated using the energy balance equation between an upstream point and the critical point (control section).

$$h+\frac{\upsilon_o^2}{2g} = d_c + \frac{\upsilon_c^2}{2g} + 0.1\ \frac{\upsilon_c^2}{2g} \tag{9.11}$$

where d_c and υ_c are the depth and the liquid velocity at the critical points respectively.

The last term on the right hand of Eq. (9.11) stands for the head loss at the weir. At the critical point

$$d_c = \frac{2\upsilon_c^2}{2g} \tag{9.12}$$

h and υo being known, υ_c is calculated using Eq. (9.13) which is obtained by combining Eqs (9.11) and (9.12) and rearranging the combined equation

$$\upsilon_c = \left\{\frac{2g}{3.1}\left(h+\frac{\upsilon_o^2}{2g}\right)\right\}^{1/2}. \tag{9.13}$$

The width a of the weir is to be estimated by balancing the volumetric flow rate across the control section.

$$a = \frac{Q_{\max}}{d_c \times \upsilon_c}. \tag{9.14}$$

Example 9.2 : Grit Chamber

A grit chamber is to be designed for handling waste water at a rate of 1035 m^3/hr. The following information are available

Average ambient temperature = 26 °C,

Sp. gr. of grit particles to be separated = 2.60

Diameter of the smallest grit particles (sandy) to be removed = 0.25 mm.

Solution :

Rectangular grit chamber fitted with a proportional weir.

Dimensions of a Rectangular Chamber

The following equations and relations are to be used for finding the dimensions of a rectangular chamber.

υ_o = scouring velocity

$$= \left(\frac{8c}{f}\ g(sp.gr.-1)\ dp\right)^{1/2}$$

c = 0.03 (for granular particles)

f = 0.03

g = 9.81 m/s^2

dp = 0.25 mm = 2.5×10^{-4} m

υ_s = free settling velocity

$$\upsilon_s = \left(\frac{4}{3}\ \frac{g\ dp}{C_D}\ (sp.gr.-1)\right)^{1/2}$$

$$C_D = \frac{24}{\text{Re}} \;, \; for \;\; \text{Re} = \frac{\upsilon_s \; dp}{\nu} < 0.5$$

$$= \frac{24}{\text{Re}} + \frac{3}{\sqrt{\text{Re}}} + 0.34 \;\; for \;\; \text{Re} > 0.5$$

Chamber cross-sectional area

$$A = \frac{Q}{\upsilon_o}$$

Liquid depth in the chamber

$$h = \frac{A}{W}$$

W = chamber width

H = chamber depth
= h + free board (0.3 to 0.6 m)
+ accumulated grit depth/mechanical conveyor depth
(0.15 to 0.3 m)

Chamber length (theoretical)

$$L_{theo} = \frac{\upsilon_o}{\upsilon_s} h$$

L_{actual} = 1.5 to 2 times L_{theo}.

$$\upsilon_o = \left(\frac{8c}{f} \; g \; (sp.gr.-1) \times dp\right)^{1/2} = \left(\frac{8 \times 0.03}{0.03} \times 9.81(2.6-1) \times 2.5 \times 10^{-4}\right)^{1/2}$$

= 0.177 m/s.

$$\upsilon_s = \left(\frac{4}{3} \; \frac{g \; dp}{C_D} \; (sp. \; gr. - 1)\right)^{1/2}.$$

1st Trial : Let Re $\approx$ 0.5.

$$C_D = \frac{24}{\text{Re}} = \frac{24}{0.5} = 48.$$

Therefore,

$$\upsilon_s = \left(\frac{4}{3} \times \frac{9.81 \times 2.5 \times 10^{-4}}{48} (2.6-1)\right)^{1/2}$$

= 0.01 m/s

$$\text{Re} = \frac{\upsilon_s \; dp}{\nu}$$

At 26 °C, ρ = density of water = 0.9968 g/cm^3

μ = water viscosity = 0.8737 centipoise

$$\nu = \mu / \rho = \frac{0.8737 \times 10^{-2}}{0.9986} \frac{cm^2}{s} = 0.8749 \times 10^{-6} \frac{m^2}{s}$$

$$Re = \frac{\upsilon_s \, dp}{\nu} = \frac{0.01 \times 2.5 \times 10^{-4}}{0.8749 \times 10^{-6}} = 2.8575.$$

2nd Trial : Assume Re = 3.

$$C_D = \frac{24}{Re} + \frac{3}{\sqrt{Re}} + 0.34, \text{ since } Re > 0.5$$

$$= \frac{24}{3} + \frac{3}{\sqrt{3}} + 0.34,$$

$$= 8 + 1.73 + 0.34 = 10.07.$$

$$\upsilon_s = \left(\frac{4}{3} \times \frac{9.81 \times 2.5 \times 10^{-4}}{10.07} (2.6 - 1) \right)^{1/2}$$

$$= 2.28 \times 10^{-2} \text{ m/s}.$$

$$Re = \frac{2.28 \times 10^{-2} \times 2.5 \times 10^{-4}}{0.8749 \times 10^{-6}} = 6.5$$

$$C_D = 5.19$$

Corresponding $\upsilon_s = 0.0317$ m/s

Further repeated trials lead finally to $\upsilon_s = 0.039$ m/s.

Chamber Cross-Sectional Area

$$A = \frac{Q}{\upsilon_o}$$

$$Q = 1035 \, m^3/hr = 0.2875 \, m^3/s$$

$$\upsilon_o = 0.177 \, m/s$$

$$A = \frac{0.2875}{0.177} = 1.624 \, m^2$$

Liquid Depth in the Chamber

$$h = \frac{A}{W}$$

W = chamber width = 1.5 m (assumed)

$$h = \frac{1.624}{1.5} = 1.083 \, m \approx 1.1 \, m.$$

Actual Chamber Depth

H = h + free board + conveyor depth

= (1.1 + 0.3 + 0.2) m = 1.6 m.

Chamber Length

$$L_{theo} = \frac{\upsilon_o}{\upsilon_s} h = \frac{0.177}{0.039} \times 1.1 = 4.99\ m$$

$$\approx 5\ m.$$

$$L_{actual} = 1.5 \times L_{theo.} = 7.5\ m.$$

Proportional Weir Design

$$Q = 0.61\ b\ \sqrt{2\ ag}\left(h - \frac{a}{3}\right)$$

$$Q = 0.2875\ \text{m}^3/\text{s}$$

$$h = 1.1\text{m},$$

a ranges between 25 to 50 mm.

Assumed a = 50 mm = 0.05 m.

$$b = \frac{Q}{0.61\ \sqrt{2 \times 0.05 \times 9.81}\ (1.1 - \frac{0.05}{3})}$$

$$= \frac{0.2875}{0.6545} = 0.439 \approx 0.44\text{m}$$

The profile of the curved edges of the weir is calculated using Eq. (9.7).

$$W' = b\left(1 - \frac{2}{\pi}\ \tan^{-1}\left(\frac{h'}{a} - 1\right)^{1/2}\right)$$

$$b = 0.44\ \text{m},\ a = 0.05\ \text{m}.$$

The calculated values of w' corresponding to the several assumed values of h' are listed below :

h', m	0.05	0.10	0.15	0.20	0.30	0.40	0.50	0.60	0.70	0.80	1.00	1.10
w', m	0.44	0.22	0.172	0.147	0.118	0.101	0.090	0.082	0.076	0.071	0.063	0.060

Trapezoidal Grit Chamber

Flow rate, Q = 1035 m^3/hr = 0.2875 m^3/s

υ_o = 0.177 m/s

Liquid depth in the chamber is to be calculated using Eq. (9.10) :

$$h = \frac{3}{2}\ \frac{Q_{max}}{W_{max}\ \upsilon_o}.$$

The chamber width is assumed to be 1.75 m.

$$Hence,\ h = \frac{3}{2} \times \frac{0.2875}{1.75 \times 0.177} = 1.392\ m \approx 1.4\ m.$$

Chamber depth, $H = h$ + free board + conveyor depth

$= (1.4 + 0.3 + 0.2)$ m = 1.9 m.

Theoretical length of the chamber,

$$L_{theo} = \frac{\upsilon_o}{\upsilon_s} h = \frac{0.177}{0.039} \times 1.4 = 6.35\,m.$$

Actual lengh $L_{actual} = 1.5\, L_{theo} = 9.53 \approx 9.5$ m.

Weir width a is calculated using the following equations :

$$d_c = \frac{2\upsilon_c^2}{2g}$$

$$\upsilon_c = \left[\frac{2\ g}{3.1}\left(h + \frac{\upsilon_o^{\ 2}}{2g}\right)\right]^{1/2}.$$

$$\text{And } a = \frac{Q_{max}}{d_c \times \upsilon_c}$$

$$\upsilon_c = \left[\frac{2\times 9.81}{3.1}\left(1.4 + \frac{0.177^2}{2\times 9.81}\right)\right]^{1/2}$$

= 2.978 m/s

$$a = \frac{Q}{d_c \times \upsilon_c} = \frac{Q}{\dfrac{2\upsilon_c^2}{2g} \times \upsilon_c}$$

$$= \frac{0.2875}{\dfrac{2\times 2.987^2}{2\times 9.81} \times 2.978} = 0.107 \text{ m.}$$

Trapezoidal Chamber Profile

The Chamber profile is calculated through the following steps

Step-I

The profile of a parabola is estimated satisfying the condition,

$$\text{Cross-sectional area} = \frac{Q}{\upsilon_o} = \frac{0.2875}{0.177} = 1.6243\,m^2,$$

corresponding to the liquid depth 1.4 m above the conveyor.

Let the equation of the parabola be $\left(\frac{W'}{2}\right)^2 = \alpha h'$,

where h' = liquid depth above the conveyor

and W' = width of the parabola corresponding to h'

Area of the section of the parabola corresponding to $h' = \text{h} = 1.4$ m

and $W' = W = 1.75$ m is

The area A of a parabola having height h and width W is expressed as

$$\frac{4}{3}\, h \times \frac{W}{2} \;=\; \frac{4}{3}\, h \times \sqrt{\alpha h} \;=\; 1.6243\, m^2$$

$$\text{or,}\quad \sqrt{\alpha} \;=\; \frac{3 \times 1.6243}{4 \times (1.4)^{1.5}} \;=\; 0.7354$$

Hence, the profile of the parabola would be

h', m	$\pm \frac{W'}{2} = \pm\sqrt{\alpha h'}, m$
0.1	0.233
0.2	0.329
0.4	0.465
0.5	0.520
0.6	0.570
0.8	0.658
1.0	0.735
1.2	0.806
1.4	0.870
1.7	0.959

Step-II

These data are plotted to a suitable scale and a smooth curve is drawn through the points as shown in Fig. Ex. 9.2 At h' = 0 a tangent is drawn to the parabola. On this line ± 0.3 m are marked which stands for the width of a conveyor. The conveyor width is taken as 0.6 m in the absence of any specific information about the conveyor width. Tangents are drawn to the parabola through the points 0, ± 0.3. Two vertical lines are drawn through the points 1.7, ± 0.875. These lines intersect the tangents drawn earlier at point B and E. The trapezoidal figure $ABCDEF$ represents the profile of the grit chamber.

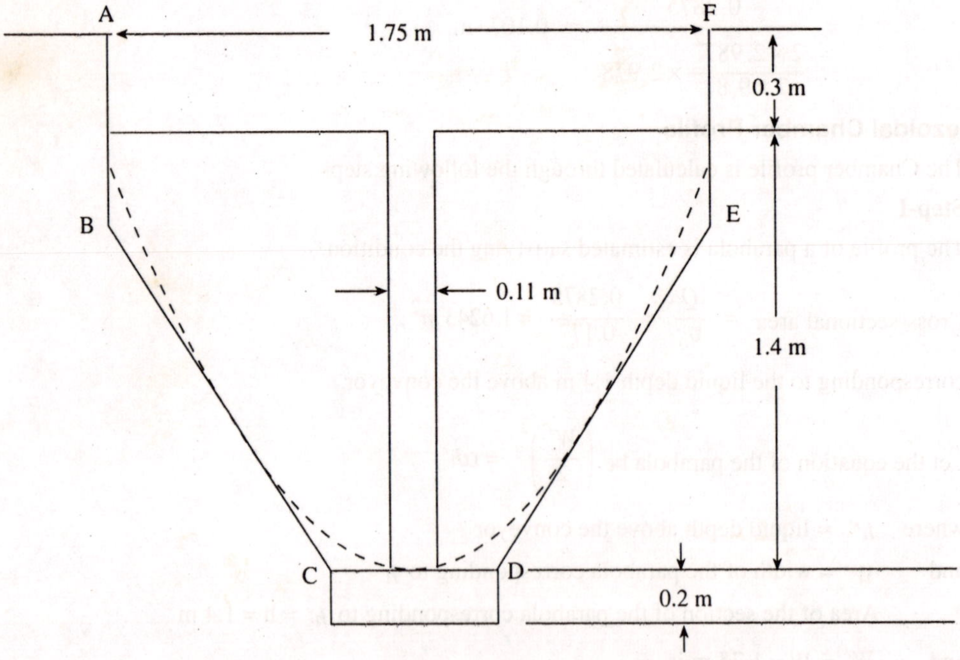

Fig. Ex. 9.2 : Trapezoidal Grit Chamber.

9.1.2.3 Hydrocyclone

In a grit chamber the solid particles settle on the floor due to gravitational force, whereas in a hydrocyclone separation of particles from the bulk of waste water takes place due to centrifugal force.

A hydrocyclone is somewhat similar in appearance to a conventional dust cyclone as shown in Fig. 9.5. Normally its diameter is much smaller compared to that of a dust cyclone.

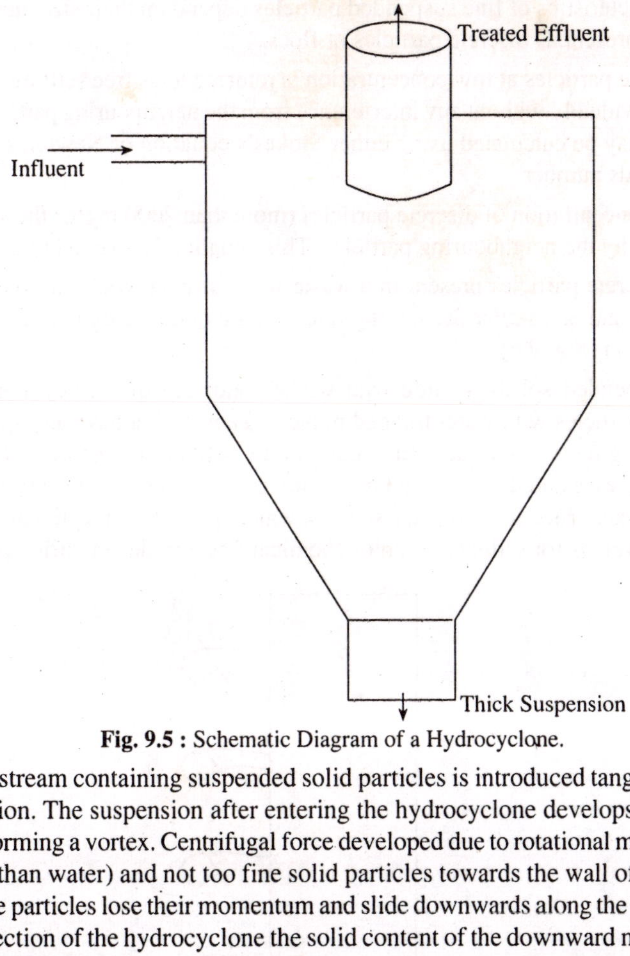

Fig. 9.5 : Schematic Diagram of a Hydrocyclone.

A waste water stream containing suspended solid particles is introduced tangentially near the top of the cylindrical portion. The suspension after entering the hydrocyclone develops rotational motion and spirals downward forming a vortex. Centrifugal force developed due to rotational motion of the suspension forces the heavier (than water) and not too fine solid particles towards the wall of the hydrocyclone. On reaching the wall the particles lose their momentum and slide downwards along the wall. As the suspension enters the conical section of the hydrocyclone the solid content of the downward moving slurry increases and water carrying finer as well as lighter particles moves upwards in the form of an inner vortex. Finally, a thicker slurry leaves the device at the apex of the cone, whereas a relatively cleaner stream containing the remaining particles leaves through a vented overflow opening located centrally at the top of the cylindrical section.

In a hydrocylone the pressure difference between the tangential inlet and the central outlet at the top is relatively (relative to that of grit chamber) high. Hence, either the influent (to a hydrocyclone) should be under pressure or a pump has to be installed for pumping the influent. The pressure at the inlet should be at least 0.5 kg/cm^2 higher than that at the outlet.

9.2 Thickening/Sedimentation

Thickening is also a gravity separation process like the grit removal process. This operation is also referred to as sedimentation. It is used for removal of fine discrete particles as well as flocs (clusters of very fine particles) heavier than water as a part of the primary treatment scheme. It is also used for removal of suspended particles (sludge) after secondary treatment and for removal of precipitates produced during tertiary treatment. Particles finer than 0.2 mm are separated from waste water by thickening/sedimentation.

The objective of thickening/sedimentation is to split a suspension into a cleaner overflow and a bottom sediment/sludge having a solid content more than that in the influent.

The settling characteristics of fine suspended particles depend on their size, density, concentration, and whether they are present as discrete particles or flocs.

Settling of discrete particles at low concentration is referred to as free settling. During free settling the particles settle individually without any interference from the neighbouring particles. The free settling velocity of particles may be calculated using either Stokes's equation or Newton's equation depending on the particle Reynolds number

At higher solid concentration of discrete particles (more than 2000 mg/L) the settling of individual particles is influenced by the neighbouring particles. This situation is referred to as hindered settling.

Normally the discrete particles present in a waste water stream would not have uniform size and density; hence, for designing a settler the settling rate data are obtained experimentally by carrying out tests in a settling column (Fig. 9.6).

Most of the suspended solids in industrial waste water are of a flocculent nature. Flocs are agglomerates of fine particles with water trapped in them. They do not have any specific geometry and size, hence their settling rates cannot be estimated with the help of any theoretically derived equation. While settling they coalesce and their size and mass increase. As a result their settling velocity changes. This type of settling takes place in secondary settlers, which are used for sedimentation of aerobic and anaerobic sludges as well as for sedimentation of chemical flocs produced during precipitation.

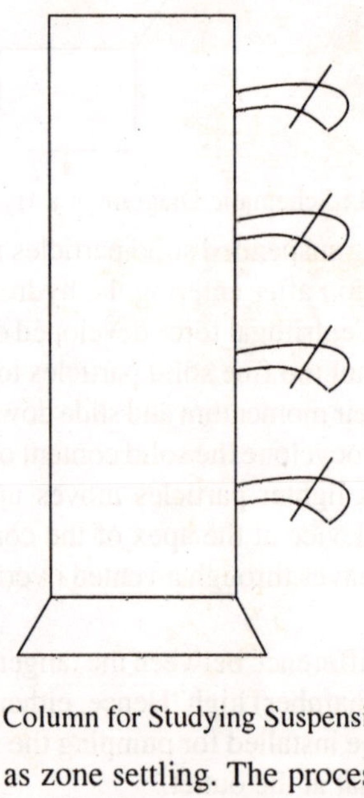

Fig. 9.6 : Sketch of a Settling Column for Studying Suspension Settling Characteristics.

The settling of flocs is referred to as zone settling. The process takes place through the following stages during a batch trial : (1) The flocs initially homogeneous start settling without coalescence retaining relatively fixed position with respect to each other. A distinct solid-liquid interface develops at the top. The flocs closer to the bottom of a settler rest on the floor and start coalescing. (2) The thickness of the top layer free from flocs and that of the bottom most coalesced layer increase. The homogeneous zone thickness decreases. A zone having a consistency intermediate between the homogeneous layer and the coalesced layer is formed in between the two. (3) As settling continues the homogeneous layer disappears altogether. (4) Compression of the coalesced sludge starts due to its weight. Some of the trapped water comes out of the coalesced layer in the form of small geysers as a result of which the sludge volume decreases further.

From the above description it is evident that during separation of flocculent suspensions, both clarification of the liquid overflow and thickening of the sludge underflow take place.

The settling characteristics of a flocculent suspension are to be experimentally evaluated for designing a settler by carrying out batch tests in a settling column (Fig. 9.6). The data to be collected would depend on the type of the settler to be designed.

For evaluation of the settling characteristics of discrete particles/flocs present in a wastewater sample, a transparent plastic column about 3 m high and 15 cm in diameter fitted with sampling taps at intervals of about 0.6 m may be used (Fig. 9.6). To carry out a test, a column should be filled with a wastewater sample. The height of liquid in the column should preferably be the same as that of the proposed settling equipment. The settling process should be allowed to proceed and data collected. The data to be obtained and the method of their analysis would depend on the nature of the suspended particles (discrete/floc), their concentration and the type of the settler to be designed.

The equipment used for carrying out separation of discrete fine particles/flocs is termed as a *thickener* or a *clarifier*, which may be either of rectangular cross section or circular cross section.

A rectangular thickener/classifier is basically a rectangular tank, at one end of which a wastewater stream is introduced. From the other end of the tank the effluence (relatively clean water) overflows. In such a tank, water flows horizontally from the influent end to the effluent end while the suspended solid particles experience a vertical downward velocity due to gravity.

The particles, which settle on the tank bottom, are scraped into sludge hopper located near the influent end. Scraping may be done either manually or mechanically. Sludge is removed from the sludge hopper either with the help of a pump or by utilizing hydrostatic head difference. The width of a mechanically scraped tank is limited by the width of the scraper mechanism to be employed. The sludge settled on the floor or a small capacity thickener is swept manually into a sludge hopper. The width of such a thickener is relatively smaller compared to that of a mechanically swept thickener.

Sometimes rectangular tanks are provided with inclined baffles near the top. Such units are termed as *tube* or *lamella settlers*. The tube size/lamella spacing is typically 25-50 mm. Those are arranged at an angle greater than 40° with the horizontal plane. Insertion of baffles improves sedimentation efficiency. Figure 9.7 shows a sketch of a typical rectangular tank.

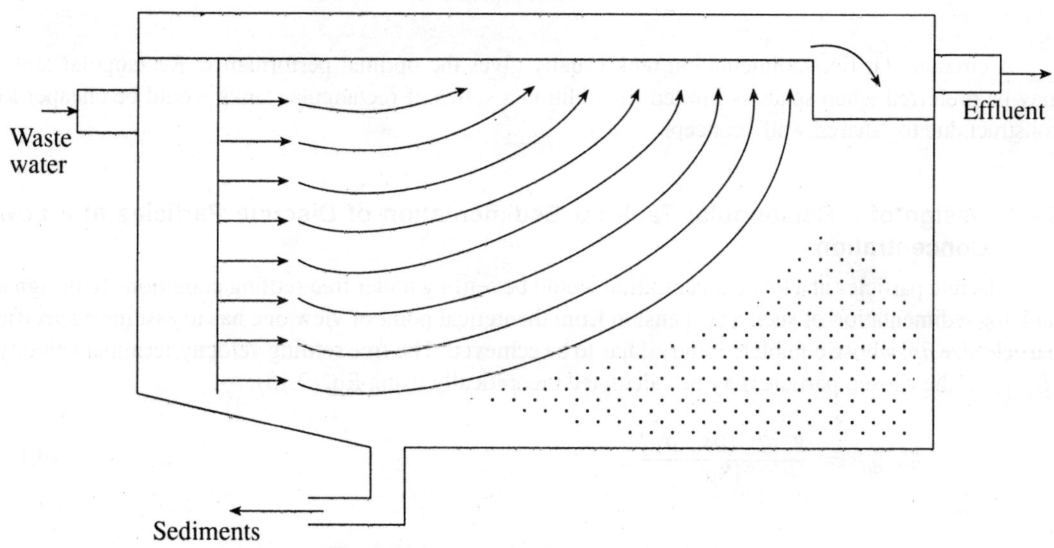

Fig. 9.7 : Rectangular Sedimentation Tank.

A circular sedimentation tank has cylindrical top mounted on an inverted truncated cone. A sludge hopper is located just below the cone. It is fitted with a centrally mounted scraper rotating at a low speed. Figure 9.8 shows a typical circular sedimentation tank

The influent is introduced at the centre near the top of a circular thickener. The liquid (water) after entering flows towards the periphery of the tank and overflows from there. The suspended particles settle due to gravity. The slow speed rotating scraper induces the sludge to settle and guides it to sludge hopper.

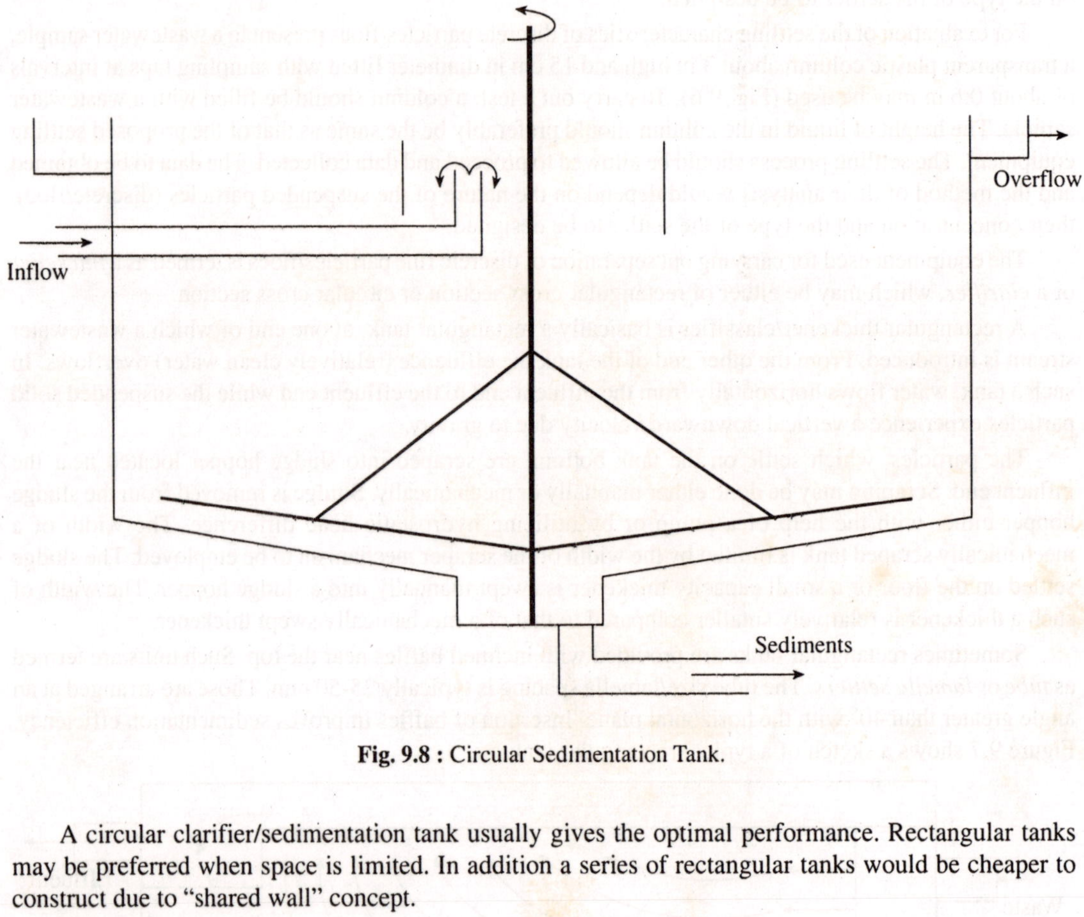

Fig. 9.8 : Circular Sedimentation Tank.

A circular clarifier/sedimentation tank usually gives the optimal performance. Rectangular tanks may be preferred when space is limited. In addition a series of rectangular tanks would be cheaper to construct due to "shared wall" concept.

9.2.1 Design of a Rectangular Tank for Sedimentation of Discrete Particles at a Low Concentration

Discrete particles at a low concentration would be settling under free settling condition. To design a tank for sedimentation of such a suspension from theoretical point of view one has to assume a specific particle size *dp*, whose complete removal has to be achieved. The free settling velocity/terminal velocity $(U_{t,\,dp})$ of the chosen particle may be calculated theoretically using Eq. (9.15).

$$U_{t,\,dp} = \frac{g\ dp^2(\rho s - \rho_L)}{18\mu}, \tag{9.15}$$

Where, g = acceleration due to gravity,

ρ_s = particle density,

ρ_L = liquid density,

and μ = liquid viscosity.

Utilizing the estimated $U_{t,\,dp}$ the residence time, τ, in the tank is evaluated with the help of Eq. (9.16)

$$\tau = \frac{H}{U_{t,\,dp}}, \tag{9.16}$$

where, H = height of the proposed tank.

Once τ is known the length L of the tank is calculated using the relation

$$L = \tau U \tag{9.17}$$

where U = liquid velocity in the tank in the forward direction.

Using this approach it would not be possible to estimate the total overall separation efficiency of the proposed tank or to design a tank having a desired overall separation efficiency. Hence, for designing a settling tank it is essential to obtain data by conducting experimental trials in a settling column. The data to be collected and their further processing should be done as outlined hereunder.

Batch Test Data

Time, min	0	t_1	t_2	t_3	....
C/C_0 at H_1	1	x_1	x_4	x_7	....
C/C_0 at H_2	1	x_2	x_5	x_8	....
C/C_0 at H_3	1	x_3	x_6	x_9	....

where C = suspension concentration at depth H from the top of the column.

C_0 = initial suspension concentration,

x_1, x_2 = suspension concentration at depth H_1, H_2 ... respectively at time t_1, t_2 ... relative to the initial concentration, C_0.

H_1, H_2 are measured from the free surface.

Based on the experimentally obtained data the settling velocities at various times and various depths are calculated and tabulated as shown below.

Time, min	0	t_1	t_2	t_3	....
υ, m/min at	H_1	H_1/t_1	H_1/t_2	H_1/t_3	....
υ, m/min at	H_2	H_2/t_1	H_2/t_2	H_2/t_3	....
υ, m/min at	H_3	H_3/t_1	H_3/t_2	H_3/t_3	....

where υ stands for the suspension settling velocity.

The data recorded in these two tables are combined and presented as $P = C/C_0$ vs. υ as shown hereunder.

υ, m/min	H_1/t_1	H_2/t_1	H_3/t_1	H_1/t_2	H_2/t_2	H_3/t_2	....
$P = C/C_0$	x_1	x_2	x_3	x_4	x_5	x_6	....

These are plotted with P as the ordinate and υ as the abscissa and through those points a smooth curve is drawn as shown in Fig. 9.9. P stands for the fraction of particles having a settling velocity less than υ.

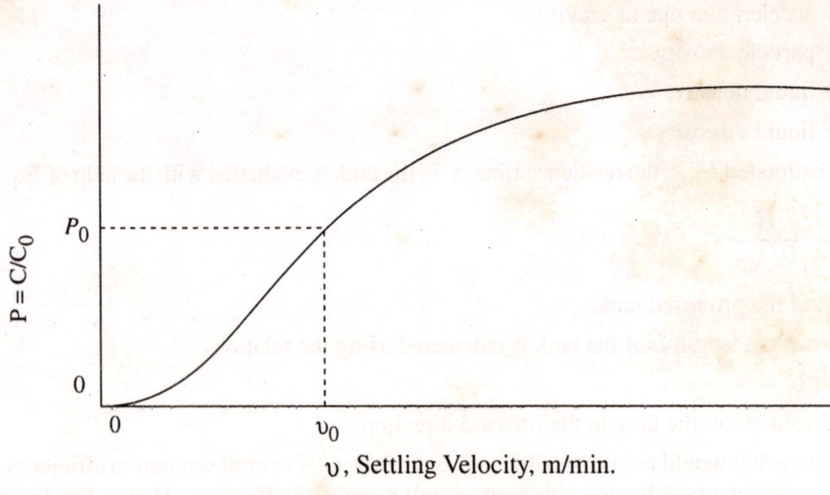

Fig. 9.9 : *P* vs. *υ* Plot.

Design Approach

Let υ_0 be any specific settling velocity. Particles having a settling velocity $\upsilon \geq \upsilon_0$ would be completely removed in a sedimentation tank and those would constitute $(1-P_0)$ fraction of the initial mass of particles present in a waste water stream. Particles (lighter and finer) having a settling velocity $\upsilon < \upsilon_0$ would be partially removed. The overall removal efficiency *R*, in such a situation may be expressed as

$$R = (1 - P_0) + \int_0^{P_0} \frac{\upsilon}{\upsilon_o} \, dP$$

$$= (1 - P_0) + \frac{1}{\upsilon_0} \int_0^{P_0} \upsilon \, dP \tag{9.18}$$

The second term on the right hand side of Eq. (9.18) is to be estimated by numerical/graphical integration.

The expression for *R* in (Eq. (9.18) is based on the assumption that the particles of various sizes and densities would be uniformly distributed over the entire depth of the proposed settling tank at the inlet end and their settling velocities in the tank (under flowing condition) would be the same as those in the settling column.

The dimension of the proposed tank may be calculated through the following steps :

Step-I

Assume a numerical value for υ_0 and corresponding to that *R* is calculated using the data obtained by carrying out trials in a settling column.

If the calculated value of *R* be not acceptable then Step I is iterated with a new assumed value of υ_0. This step is repeated till the value of *R* obtained is close to the desired value.

Step-II

Once an acceptable value of *R* is obtained the loading rate, i.e., the overflow rate is taken as υ_0 m^3/m^2 day.

Step-III

The horizontal cross-sectional area of an ideal tank having a overflow rate υ_0 is estimated as

$$A_{ideal} = \frac{Q}{\upsilon_0}, \ m^2,$$

where Q = volumetric flow rate of waste water in m^3/day.

Step-IV

·Actual tank cross-sectional area is calculated by multiplying A_{ideal} by 1.5,

$$A_{actual} = 1.5 \times A_{ideal}.$$

Step-V

The dimensions of the proposed tank are estimated using the following relations :

Tank height, $H_{tank} = H_0$ (column height) + free board height.

$$\text{Tank width, } W = \frac{Q}{H_0 \times \text{flow through velocity}}$$

$$\text{Tank length, } L = \frac{A_{actual}}{W}.$$

The other details are finalized following the normal practice as listed in Table 9.2.

9.2.2 Design of a Rectangular Tank for Sedimentation of Flocculant Particles at a Low Concentration

Flocs are agglomerate of several fine particles with trapped water in their structure. They settle with their structure intact, hence their settling rate is slower than that of discrete particles

The settling rate of a flocculant suspension is experimentally studied in a settling column (Fig. 9.6). The data are recorded and analysed as indicated below. It is to be noted here that the design approach of a rectangular settling tank for a flocculant suspension is different from that for a discrete particle settling tank.

Step-I

During batch sedimentation test in a column the per cent removal data (y) of the suspended particles at different depth at different time are recorded.

Time, min	t_1	t_2	t_3	t_4	....
Depth below free surface	Per cent Removal				
H'	y_{11}	y_{12}	y_{13}	y_{14}	....
H''	y_{21}	y_{22}	y_{23}	y_{24}	....
H'''	y_{31}	y_{32}	y_{33}	y_{34}	....
H_0	—	—	—	—	....

where H_0 is the depth of the proposed settling tank.

Step-II

These per cent removal data are plotted with depth as the ordinate and time as the abscissa. Through the data points isopercent removal lines are drawn either by interpolation or using judgement.

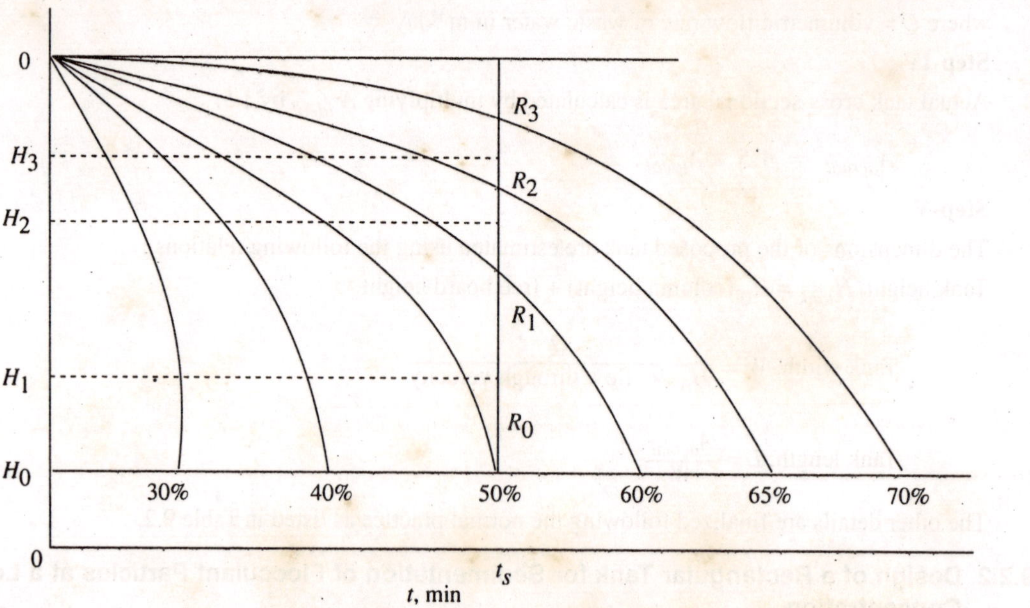

Fig. 9.10 : Isopercent Removal Plot.

Step-III

Using a plot such as Fig. 9.10 the total removal R, in an ideal horizontal flow sedimentation tank having a depth H_0 for a specific detention time t_s is estimated using the expression given below :

$$R = R_0 + \frac{H_1}{H_0}(R_1 - R_0) + \frac{H_2}{H_0}(R_2 - R_1) + \frac{H_3}{H_0}(R_3 - R_2) + \ldots \tag{9.19}$$

where R_0 is the percent removal at H_0 corresponding to the selected detention time t_s. $H_1, H_2, H_3 \ldots$ are the average depths between isopercent lines directly above t_s. R_1, R_2, R_3 --- are the isopercent removal figures directly above t_s as marked on the plot (Fig. 9.10).

Step-IV

The overflow rate from an ideal tank having a depth H_0 and a detention time t_s is expressed as

$$\frac{Q}{A} = \frac{H_0}{t_s}. \tag{9.20}$$

Step-V

For different ts, R and Q/A are calculated. These are plotted as shown in Fig. 9.11.

Step-VI

For designing an ideal sedimentation tank having a desired per cent removal R', the detention time t_0 and the overflow rate $(Q/A)_{ideal}$ are estimated using a plot similar to Fig. 9.11.

It should be noted here that the design parameters estimated for an ideal tank (as outlined above) are based on the data obtained in a test column under quiescent condition and without any overflow. In an actual tank these conditions would not prevail and hence the removal efficiency of an actual tank would be less than that of an ideal tank having the same design parameters.

The factors which will influence the removal efficiency of an actual tank are : (1) scouring, and (2) wind induced turbulence. Rectangular tanks fitted with inclined baffles have relatively higher efficiency as the above mentioned two factors are countered to some extent.

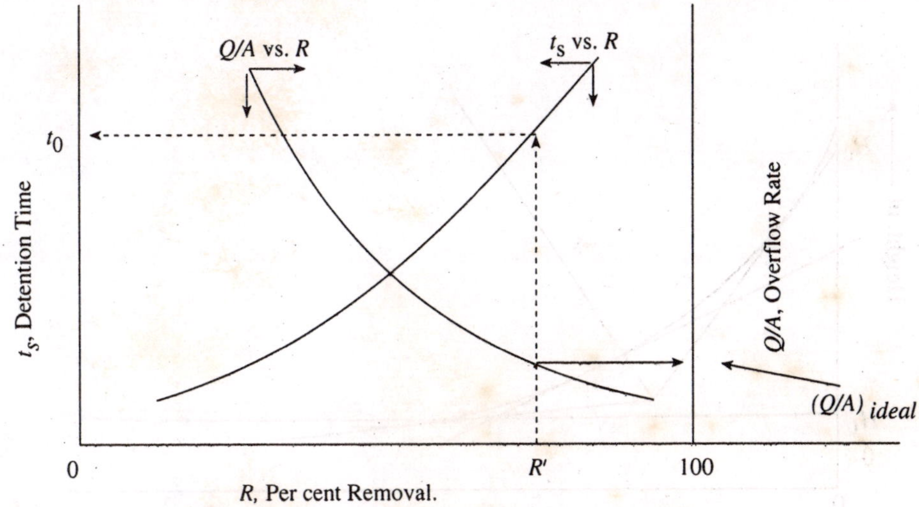

Fig. 9.11 : Detention Time and Overflow Rate vs. Percent Removal R.

The thumb rules used for actual design are :

Detention (Residence) time = 1.75 t_0

$$\text{Overflow rate} = \frac{(Q/A)_{ideal}}{1.5}$$

Tank depth, $H = (H_0)$ + depth for sludge holding + free board height.

$$\frac{L}{H} \approx 12/1, \quad \frac{L}{W} \approx \frac{4}{1}$$

Baffle location = 5 to 10% of L near the influent end,

Baffle height (depth) = 0.5 to 1 m.

9.2.3. Design of a Circular Sedimentation Tank

For designing a circular tank batch sedimentation trials are carried out in a transparent cylindrical column. The data collected for this purpose are different from those for a rectangular settling tank. The change in liquid-suspension interface height at different time is noted. The design approach is detailed below.

Step-I

During a batch sedimentation test the clear liquid-suspension interface heights at different time are recorded. The initial height of the suspension in the column should be the same as that of the proposed settler.

Interface height, m	H_0	H_1	H_2	H_3
Time, min	0	t_1	t_2	t_3

Step-II

These data are plotted with height as the ordinale and time as the abscissa. Through these data points a smooth curve is drawn as shown in Figures 9.12.

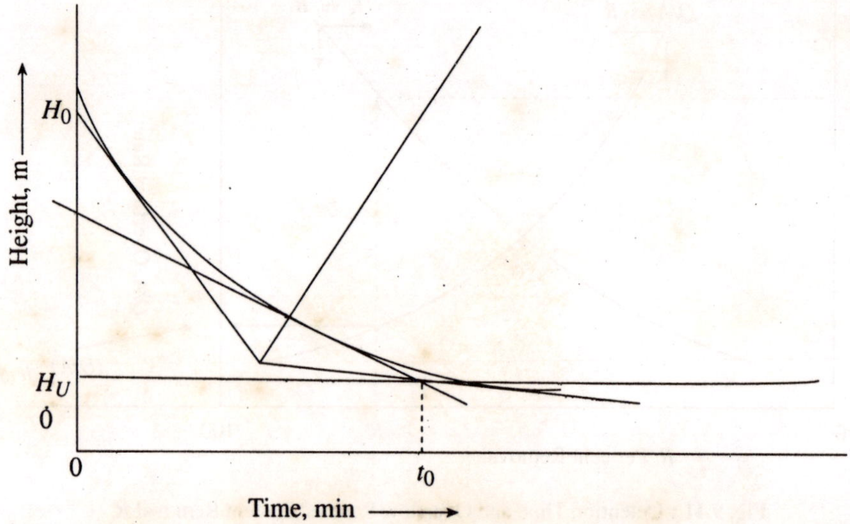

Fig. 9.12 : Settling Curve for a Low Concentration Suspension.

Step-III

Corresponding to the desired sludge under flow concentration C_U the sludge height H_U is calculated based on the material balance equation

$$H_U = \frac{H_0 \; C_0}{C_U} \tag{9.21}$$

where C_0 is the initial suspension concentration.

Step-IV

Next on the settling curve (Fig. 9.12) the following geometric constructions are carried out.

(a) H_U is located on Fig. 9.12 and a horizontal line is drawn through H_U.

(b) Tangents are drawn to the extremities of the settling curve. The angle formed by the tangents is bisected. At the point of intersection of the bisector and the settling curve a tangent is drawn. From the point of intersection of this tangent and the horizontal line through H_U a vertical line is drawn on the abscissa (time axis). The point of intersection on the time axis is designated as t_0. t_0 so obtained represents the time required for the suspension to attend the desired underflow sludge concentration C_U while settling in a circular sedimentation tank under flowing conditions.

Step-V

The surface loading of the proposed tank and the tank cross-sectional area are to be estimated using Eqs. (9.22) and (9.23) respectively.

$$\frac{Q}{A} = \frac{H_0}{t_0} \tag{9.22}$$

$$A = \frac{Q t_0}{H_0} \tag{9.23}$$

where Q = volumetric flow rate of waste water to be clarified.

Step-VI

The tank diameter is calculated using Eq. (9.24)

$$D = \{A / (\pi / 4)\}^{1/2} \quad (9.24)$$

Some typical parameters of rectangular and circular sedimentation tanks are listed in Table 9.2.

Table 9.2 : Typical Parameters of Rectangular and Circular Sedimentation Tanks

Parameter	Rectangular Tank	Circular Tank
Surface Loading	25–30 m^3/m^2 day	25–30 m^3/m^2 day
Side Wall Depth	3–5 m, generally 3.5 m	3–5m, generally 4.5 m
Free Board	0.5 m	0.4–0.5 m
Bottom Slope	1 in 100 to 1 in 150 at the inlet	1 in 8 to 1 in 12
Sludge withdrawal pipe dia.	Minimum 200 mm	Minimum 200 mm
Weir Loading	—	Not to exceed 300 m^3/m day
Detention Time	$1^1/_2$ to 2 hours	2 to $2^1/_2$ hours
Travelling speed of scraper	0.3—0.9 m/min	2 RPH
L or D	15–90 m, generally 30 m, max 100 m	4–60 m, Generally 30m, max 60 m
W	3–24 m, generally 6-10 m	
Entrance pipe/channel velocity	0.5 m/s	0.3 m/s
Baffle Depth	0.5–1 m	0.5–1.5 m
Average flow through velocity	Less than 0.6 m/min	

Example 9.3 : Circular Thickener

A circular thickener is to be designed based on the following settling characteristic data of a waste water stream having a suspended solid concentration 5000 mg/L.

Time, min	0	20	40	60	80	100	120	140	160
Interface height, m	2.5	1.56	0.97	0.75	0.63	0.53	0.44	0.39	0.36

The thickener has to handle the waste water stream at the rate of $0.12\ m^3/s$. It is desired that the solid content of the underflow should be 25000 mg/L.

Solution :

The problem is solved graphically through the following steps :

1. The settling characteristic data are plotted as in Fig. Ex. 9.3 and a smooth curve is drawn through the data points.
2. Tangents are drawn to the extremities of the settling curve, which interesect and form an angle *A*.
3. The angle *A* is bisected.
4. The bisector intersects the settling curve at a point *B*.
5. A tangent is drawn to the settling curve at the point *B*.
6. Corresponding to the desired sludge underflow concentration C_U = 25,000 mg/L, the sludge height H_U is calculated using Eq. (9.21)

$$H_U = \frac{H_0 C_0}{C_U} = \frac{2.5 \times 5000}{25000} = 0.5\ m$$

7. $H_U = 0.5\ m$ is located on the Fig. Ex. 9.3 and a line is drawn parallel to the *X*-axis through H_U.
8. The tangent drawn at the point *B* intersects the line through H_U at a point *C*.
9. From the point *C* a vertical line is drawn which meets the *X*-axis at to = 77 min.
10. The surface loading of the proposed tank and its cross-sectional area are estimated using Eqs. (9.21), (9.22) and (9.23) respectively.

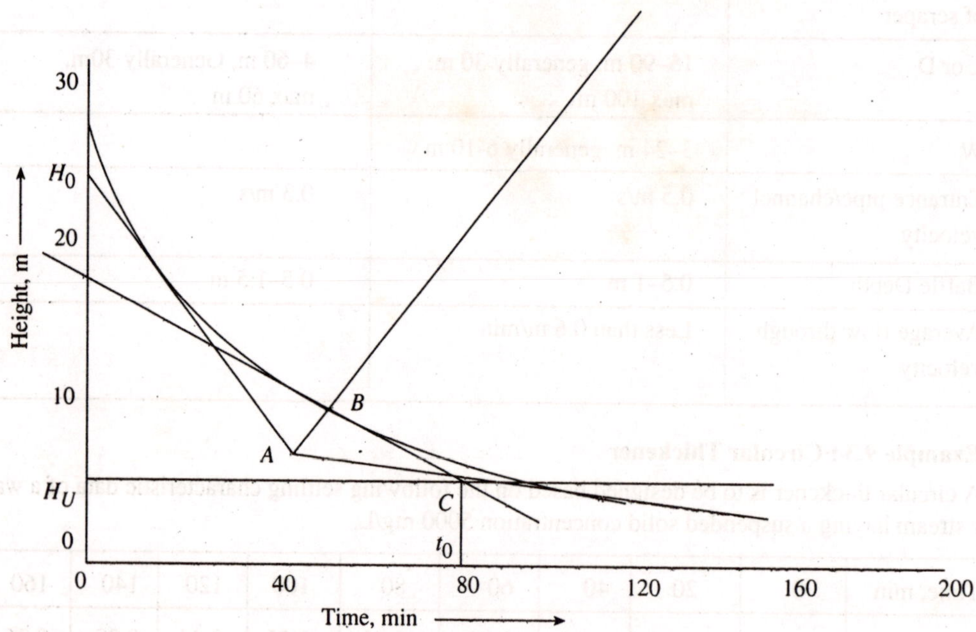

Fig. Ex. 9.3 : Circular Thickener.

Surface loading,

$$\frac{Q}{A} = \frac{H_0}{t_0} = \frac{2.5\ m}{77\ \text{min}} = 46.75\ \frac{m^3}{m^2\ \text{day}}$$

Settler cross-sectional area,

$$A = \frac{Q\ t_0}{H_0} = \frac{0.12 \times 60 \times 77}{2.5} = 221.76\ m^2$$

Diameter, $D = 16.8$ m.

9.3 Air Floatation

For removal of finer solid particles from a waste water stream air floatation process may be used as an alternative to the sedimentation process. Air floatation process is capable of separating/removing not only finer solid particles (both denser and lighter than water) but also droplets of oil, fat and grease. Finer and less denser solid particles have low terminal velocity; hence their sedimentation would require longer detention time. Even then the removal efficiency may not be high. Removal of such particles can be achieved more efficiently by the air floatation process.

Air floatation process is carried out in two stages. In the first stage either air is dispersed in waste water or dissolved in it. When air is dispersed in waste water as fine bubbles, the process is termed as induced air floatation (IAF), whereas when air is dissolved in waste water the process is termed as dissolved air floatation (DAF). Dissolution of air in waste water may be carried out either at atmospheric pressure or at an elevated pressure. In the second stage the air waste water mixture is fed into a tank referred to as a floatation tank. In this tank the suspended particles with attached air bubbles float up as their effective density becomes less than that of water. They form a scum layer at the air-water interface. The scum layer is removed by surface skimmer. The larger and heavier particles settle on the floatation tank floor and are removed as sludge. A relatively clear effluent is withdrawn from a suitable location below the scum layer.

9.3.1 Induced Air Floatation (IAF) Process

Induced air floatation process is somewhat similar to the froth floatation process used for ore beneficiation. In this process air is dispersed in waste water in the form of fine bubbles by any one of the following techniques : (1) diffusion of air through a porous medium submerged in a tank containing waste water, (2) rotation of a straight vaned rotor suspended in waste water, (3) mixing of air and a waste water stream with the help of an eductor or a nozzle.

In industrial IAF units the devices used are either rotors or venturi eductors or nozzles. A venturi eductor/nozzle is a simpler device than a rotor. Gas dispersion is better when a venturi eductor or a nozzle is used than that when a rotor is used.

Air dispersion, floatation and scum removal are carried out in a floatation cell. An IAF system consists of several (normally four) floatation cells operating in series. As waste water flows from cell to cell progressively more and more suspended matters are removed.

9.3.2 Dissolved Air Floatation (DAF) Process

It has been mentioned earlier that air may be dissolved in waste water either at atmospheric pressure or at an elevated pressure. When air is dissolved at atmospheric pressure the second stage of operation, that is, the floatation operation is carried out under vaccum in a closed chamber. Hence, the process is referred to as vaccum floatation. However, when air is dissolved in a waste water stream at an elevated pressure the second stage of operation is carried out in a tank open to atmosphere. Such a process is termed as Dissolved Air Floatation (DAF). For large scale operation more often this (DAF) process is used.

9.3.2.1 Vacuum Floatation

In this process air is dissolved in a waste water stream at atmospheric pressure in an absorber. The aerated waste water stream is then allowed to flow through a pressure reducing valve into an enclosed cylindrical floatatiom tank maintained under vaccum. The tank is fitted with a suitable scum removing mechanism.

In the floatation tank the dissolved air gets released as tiny air bubbles, which get attached to the suspended particles. The suspended particles with the attached air bubbles float up and form a scum layer at the air-water interface. The scum removing mechanism sweeps the scum to the tank periphery and discharges the same into a sump, which is also maintained under vacuum. From the sump sludge is pumped out. The treated water is removed from the floatation tank with the help of another pump.

9.3.2.2 Dissolved Air Floatation (DAF)

This process differs from the vacuum floatation process in two respects, namely, (i) air dissolution is carried out under pressure and not atmospheric pressure (as in the case of vaccum floatation) and (ii) the floatation operation is carried out in an open tank and not in an enclosed tank under vacuum.

The flow arrangement in the air dissolution section depends on the flow rate of the waste water stream as well as on the suspended particle concentration in it. The details of the floatation section are independent of the above mentioned factors.

The alternative arrangements of the air dissolution section are (i) low pressure full flow pressurization unit, (ii) high pressure partial flow pressurization unit, and (iii) high pressure recycle flow pressurization unit. These arrangements are described hereunder.

(i) Low Pressure Full Pressurization Unit

Such an unit is used when a waste water stream flow rate is not high and the suspended solid particle concentration in it is low. The air dissolution unit is operated at a pressure of 3 to 4 atm. Figure 9.13 shows a sketch of such an unit.

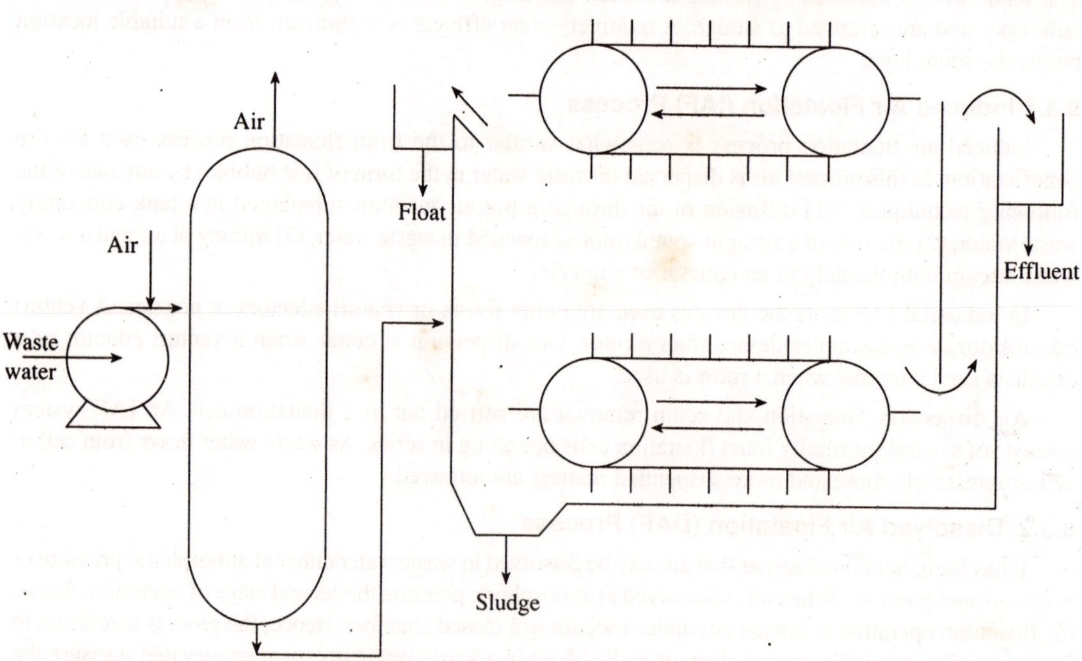

Fig. 9.13 : Dissolved Air Floatation—Full Flow Unit.

(ii) High Pressure Partial Flow Pressurization Unit

A partial flow pressurization unit is used when the waste water flow rate is high and its suspended solid concentration is low. In this arrangement a portion of a waste water stream is pressurized and mixed with air at about 5 to 6 atm. The pressurized mixture of wastewater and air is subsequently depressurized and mixed with the remaining portion of the waste water stream. A sketch of such a. unit is shown in Fig. 9.14. This arrangement is used in order to avoid having a larger pressurization unit being operated at a pressure of 3 to 4 atm.

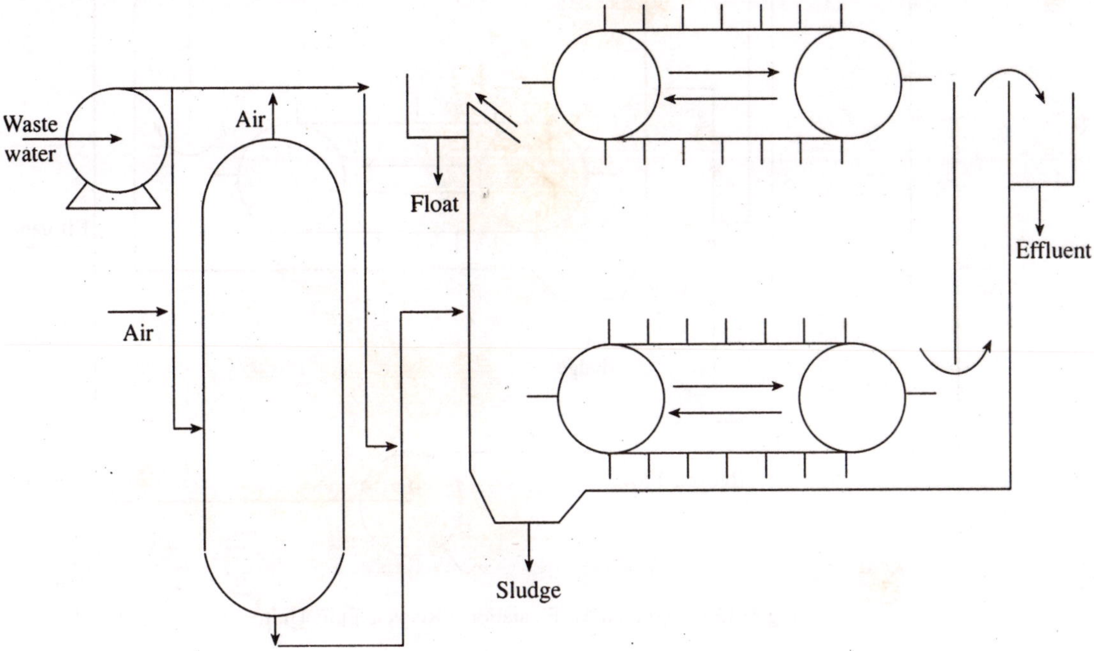

Fig. 9.14 : Dissolved Air Floatation—Partial Flow Unit.

(iii) High Pressure Recycle Flow Pressurization Unit

Recycle flow arrangement is used when a waste water stream contains too much of suspended solid particles. In this process air is dissolved in a portion of the recycled (treated) effluent from a floatation tank. Pressurization and air dissolution is carried out at 5 to 6 atm. This mixture is then mixed with the incoming waste water stream and finally fed into a floatation tank after depressurzation. This arrangement helps to avoid accumulation of solid particles in the air dissolution tank. Figure 9.15 shows a sketch of recycle flow pressurization unit.

9.3.3 Floatation Unit Design Approach

9.3.3.1 Absorber Design

It has been mentioned in Section 9.3.2.2 that a Dissolved Air Floatation Unit is made up of an air absorber and a floatation tank. The unit would have some accessories besides the above mentioned two items.

The purpose of an absorber is to dissolve air in waste water containing suspended solids or in recycled treated water. This process is carried out under pressure. Since air does not react with water the dissolution process is a physical one. In an absorber (a column with some internals) air and water are

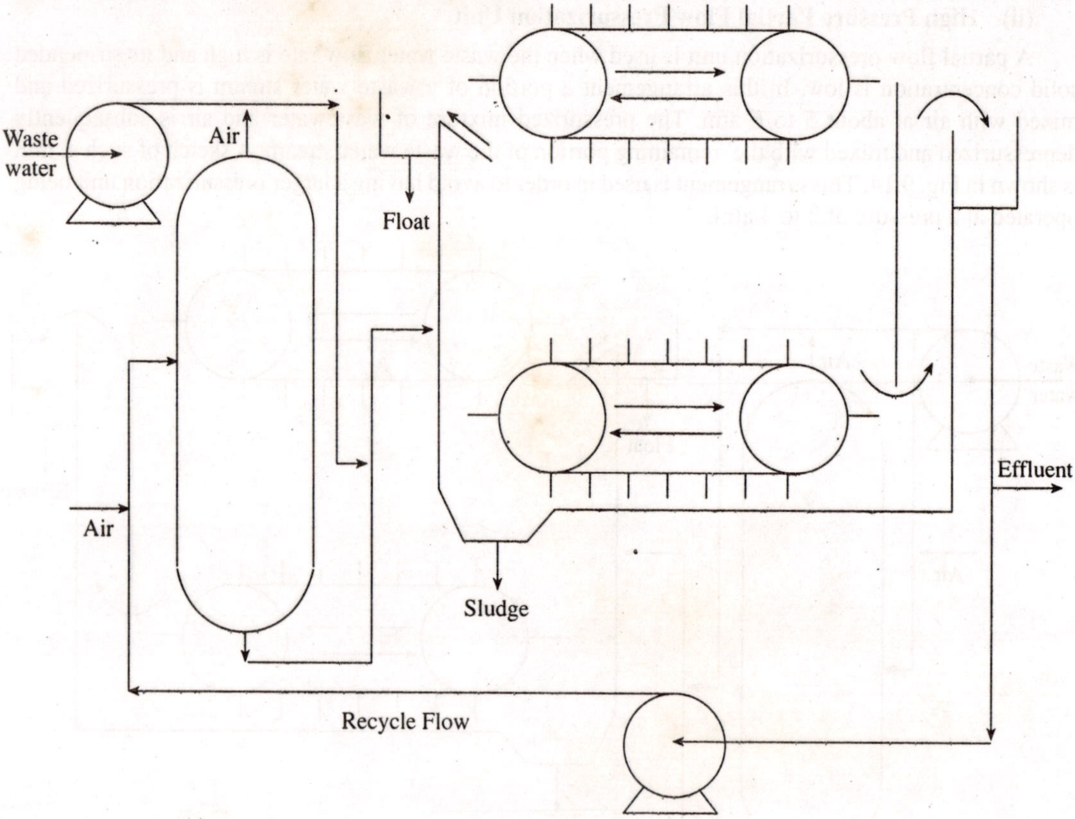

Fig. 9.15 : Dissolved Air Floatation—Recycle Flow Unit.

brought into intimate contact with each other. The column internals should be such that accumulation of solid particles inside it would be negligible.

Since solubility of air in water is low, the equilibrium line would be a linear one. There would be no resistance to mass transfer in the gas phase. The absorber dimensions may be estimated following the approach outlined in section 4.5.3.

The quantity of air which would get dissolved in an absorber may be estimated using the following equations :

(i) Full Flow Pressurization

$$\frac{\text{Dissolved Air}}{\text{Suspended Solids}} = \frac{F\ C_s\ f\ P}{FX} \tag{9.25}$$

(ii) Partial/Recycled Flow Pressurization

$$\frac{\text{Dissolved Air}}{\text{Suspended Solids}} = \frac{R\ C_s\ f\ P}{FX} \tag{9.26}$$

where C_s = Solubility of air in water at 1 atm pressure and at the operating temperature..

f = Fraction saturation in an absorbers, it depends on the size of the absorber and its internals. It may be as high as 0.8 to 0.9.

F = waste water inflow rate to the absorbers.

P = absorber operating pressure in atm.

R = partial/recycle inflow rate to the absorber.

X = suspended solid concentration in the waste water stream.

The detention time in an absorber may be about 0.5 to 3 min.

9.3.3.2 Floatation Tank Design

Waste water containing dissolved air after depressurization would enter a floatation tank. On depressurization the concentration of the residual dissolved air would be C_s. The quantity of released air would be $F.C_s (f P-1)$ or $R\ C_s (fP-1)$ depending on the full flow pressurization or partial/recycle flow pressurization absorption process. The released air in the form of tiny bubbles would get attached to the suspended solid particles and liquid droplets. These would then rise upwards and reach the air-water interface.

The basic information required for sizing a floatation tank is the rise rate of the float expressed in cm/min unit. This information is to be obtained by carrying out experimental trials.

The detention time τ in a floatation tank may be estimated using the relation

$$\tau = \frac{H_0}{Rise\ \ rate} \tag{9.27}$$

where H_0 = Liquid depth in the tank $\approx$ 1.5 – 3 m.

The detention time in a floatation tank may be 20—60 minutes. The actual tank depth H would be $H = H_0$ + free board height.

The horizontal cross–sectional area of the floatation tank may be calculated using Eq. (9.28).

$$A = \frac{F\tau}{H_0} \tag{9.28}$$

The width W of the tank would depend on the width of the sludge removal mechanism.

Comparison of IAF and DAF Systems

An IAF system requires smaller space and lower capital cost than a DAF system. A DAF system requires less power than that required for an IAF system. In a DAF system addition of a chemical coagulant is more effective as flotation takes place in a quiescent condition. Whereas in an IAF system floc formation and its growth get impaired due to its high turbulence, consequently addition of chemical coagulants becomes less effective.

9.4 Filtration

Filtration is another method, which is used for separation of solid particles from a suspension. This method is capable of removing particles of any size and density. However, it cannot separate colloidal particles from a suspension.

During filtration liquid flows through the interstices of a filter medium while the suspended particles are retained on the medium. The particles are arrested by a combination of mechanisms, such as inertia, impaction, interception and adsorption. Particles finer than the interstices may pass through along with the liquid (filtrate) while the retained particles form a layer on the filter medium. The deposited layer acts as an additional filter media and prevents some of the finer particles from passing through along with the filtrate. As the operation continues more and more particles accumulate on the filter medium and the resistance to liquid flow increases. This results in a decrease in the filtration rate if the operation is carried out at a constant pressure. When the rate becomes rather low the operation is stopped and the accumulated particles are removed physically (by backwashing) and then the filtration operation is restarted. Backwashing produces a by-product containing a concentrated suspension which is normally returned to a settler/sedimentation tank.

The rate of filtration in general is much slower than that of screening, grit removal and sedimentation. Because of this limitation it is not used for waste water treatment as such. However, it is used to remove (i) residual biological floc after settling, (ii) residual precipitates (after sedimentation) of metal hydroxides, phosphate, etc., and (iii) as a pretreatment prior to operations like activated carbon adsorption, ion exchange process, membrane separation, etc.

The equipment normally used for filtration are of two types : (1) granular bed and (2) rotary filter.

9.4.1 Granular Bed Filters

A granular bed may be either monomedium or dual media or multimedia type. The media used commercially as anthracite coke, sand, garnet, diatomaceous earth, charcoal, activated carbon, synthetic resin, etc.

Flow through a filter bed may be either downflow or upflow, downflow being more common. Filter beds are classified as shallow, conventional and deep depending upon the bed depth. Typical bed depths are :

Bed Type	Bed Depth
Shallow bed	25–50 cm
Conventional bed	50–95 cm
Deep bed	180–210 cm

In shallow and deep beds monomedium is used. Coarser granules (2–4 mm) are used in deep beds, whereas in shallow and conventional beds relatively finer granules (0.2–2 mm) are used. The extent of particle removal depends on the media size as well as on the particle size. The granules size should be so chosen that it would provide higher removal efficiency than the desired one.

Fine granules are normally used in propriety type filters having automatic backwashing facility or pulsatory flow arrangement. Such units require frequent backwashing during plant upset condition or treatment of high solid containing waste water. Coarse media filters are characterized by longer filter runs. These can withstand plant upset conditions.

In downflow dual/multimedia units coarser granules form the upper layer (s) and finer granules are placed below. Such an arrangement makes it possible to carry on the filtration operation for a longer period. It also facilitates backwashing. These are generally used for tertiary treatment,

A granular filter is normally a vertical cyclindrical vessel made of concrete or steel. At the bottom of the vessel a grid is placed. Figure 9.16 shows a sketch of a typical granular filter. On the grid a layer of gravel is laid. The gravel layer acts as the support for the filter bed. In downflow unit an influent distributor is placed above the bed and an effluent collector is located below the grid. Arrangements are provided for introduction of backwash water and its removal. A portion of the filtrate is used for backwashing. An arrangement for air scouring of the filter bed is sometimes incorporated. Air scouring facilitates removal of solid particles lodged in between the granules.

The decision about the type bed and the type of media to be used in a given situation depends on the suspended solid loading as well as on the size and physical nature of the particles present in an influent stream.

Granular medium filtration is in general a semi-continuous or a cyclic operation. To avoid interruption of the process at least two beds are used so that when one is backwashed the other would be in operation. Generally, backwashing period is shorter than the filtration run period. The time in service in between two successive cleaning is termed as the *run length*. In downflow filters most often flow occurs through the bed due to gravity. However, to enhance the filtration rate sometimes the process is carried out under pressure.

Modified granular beds have been developed which operate virtually continuously.

The filtration rate in a downflow granular bed may be enhanced by maintaining a higher fluid head/pressure above the bed. Too high a rate would cause penetration of the solid particles beyond the coarse medium and accumulation of the particles on the finer medium. Too low a filtration rate would result in accumulation of the solid particles on the top surface of the coarse medium only. The effluent quality depends to some extent on the filtration rate. Addition of coagulants prior to filtration improves the effluent quality.

Too much of solid accumulation in a bed would require larger volume of backwash water. Backwashing may be facilitated in either of two ways : (1) surface agitation during washing and (2) air scouring during washing.

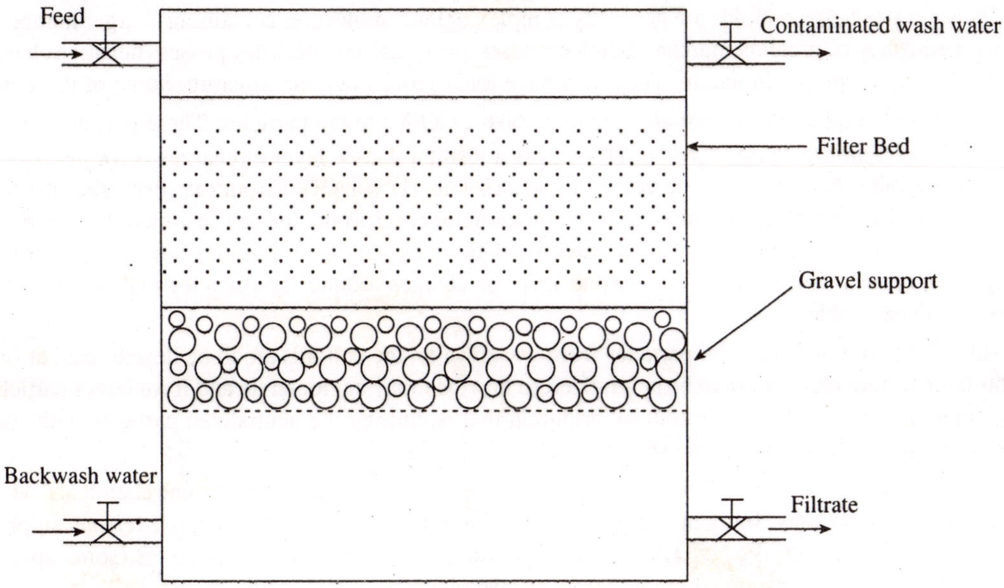

Fig. 9.16 : Granular Filter Bed.

9.4.2 Rotary Filters

Different types of rotary filters are commercially available. Unlike granular filters, rotary filters are generally operated continuously without any interruption for removal of the retained solid particles

The rotary filters are known by various names, such as rotary drum filter, rotary screen, micro-strainer, etc. A rotary filter is often a hollow cylinder, one circular end of which is open and the other is closed. The periphery (cylindrical surface) is covered with a screen. The screen may be made of stainless steel or a fabric. The screen openings may be coarse (6 mm or more). Fine screens would have openings less than 6 mm, whereas micro-screen openings may range from 20–70 μm. These are mounted with their axis horizontal and are placed in a pool of water to be filtered. They are partly submerged and rotated at a low speed (say, about 4 r.p.m.) The filtrate may pass through the screen from outside to inside or the other way. The particles are retained on the screen surface. As the cylinder rotates the retained particles emerge out of the water pool. When the retained particles reach a suitable position, they are removed from the screen surface with a spray of water or a scraper. In most filters filtrations occurs because of hydrostatic head difference between the inside and outside of a filter, but in the case of drum filters filtration takes place due to pressure gradient.

The particle removal efficiency (of fine particles) of a rotary filter may be less than that of a granular bed. The efficiency may be increased by reducing the rotational speed and by incomplete removal of the accumulated particles. The particles adhering to the screens augment screening operation. However, these steps would result in a reduction of the filtration capacity.

9.5. Coagulation and Flocculation

Very fine particles, particularly, the colloids (10–1000 A) cannot be separated from a waste water stream by any one of the processes/operations discussed earlier. These particles cannot be separated by sedimentation as their settling velocity is too low. They pass through a filter bed being smaller than the filter medium pore dimensions. On the other hand, colloids being charged particles, they repel each other and thereby they keep themselves in suspension.

Waste water-borne colloids are generally complex organic molecules containing a larger number of atoms. These may be proteins. starches, hemicelluloses, polypeptides, etc. They possess negative charges and are mostly lyophillic in nature. They may have ionic groups in their structure. Some of these may ionize in water and thereby impart charges (e.g. NH_2^+, COO^-) to the particles. These particles in turn attract ions of opposite charge (OH^- or H^+) and as a result a double layer of charges is formed around them. Some other particles have an ability to adsorb ions (H^+ or OH^-) from the dispersing medium (water). The character of the adsorbed ions on the particles controls the manner in which these particles would behave in an electric field. Such particles with adsorbed charges attract ions of the opposite charge and form a double-layer. The double layer of charges around the particles makes a colloidal suspension very stable.

In order to remove colloidal particles from waste water, the colloids are to be destabilized at first, that is their surface charges are to be neutralized so that they may agglomerate and form larger particles. Agglomeration may be brought about by bridging, that is, uniting the neutralized particles with some other substances having thread-like structure.

Charge neutralization of colloidal particles may be carried out by addition of some chemicals, which are termed as coagulants. Inorganic salts, such as aluminium sulphate [$Al_2(SO_4)_3$], ferrous sulphate [Fe SO_4], ferric sulphate [Fe_2 (SO_4) $_3$], ferric chloride [Fe Cl_3] and poly-electrolytes (some specific types of organic polymers) are commonly used as coagulants.

Inorganic Coagulants

Aqueous solutions of inorganic coagulants (salts) under suitable pH conditions produce metal hydroxide (gel-like) precipitates which acquire positive charge. These are capable of neutralizing the charges of the colloidal particles. The hydroxides acquire higher charges than the metal ions and they are more effective coagulants.

The neutralized colloidal particles coalesce and form agglomerates. These are then trapped by the settling flocs of hydroxide precipitates.

The metal ions (Al^{3+}, Fe^{2+}, Fe^{3+}) react with water alkalinity and phosphate ions present in waste water, if any. They also cause precipitation of some of the heavy metals present in waste water. The effective pH range of these coagulants are :

Ion	Effective pH range	Dosage range
Al^{3+}	5.5-8.5	5–20 mg/L as Al
Fe^{2+}	8-10	—
Fe^{3+}	Above 4	20–100 mg/L as $FeCl_3$

Studies have indicated that aluminum sulphate is a more effective coagulant for treatment of waste water containing carbonaceous compounds whereas iron sulphates are more effective in coagulating proteinaceous colloidal particles.

Aqueous solutions of the inorganic coagulating agents (inorganic salts) are acidic and hence they are corrosive. A 1% solution of $FeCl_3$ has a pH around 2. The dissolution tanks, pipelines, pumps and other auxiliaries used for storage and handling of these solutions are to be made of corrosion resistant materials.

Polyelectrolytes

Some synthetic water soluble organic polymers carry ionic charges along their polymer chains. These are termed as polyelectrolytes. Those carrying positive charges are called cationic and those carrying negative charges are called anionic. There are some polymers, which do not carry any electric charges. These are called non-ionic. All these polymers at low concentration produce flocs of these polylectrolytes. The cationic type is in general more effective in destabilizing colloids.

The mechanisms by which the ionic type polyelectrolytes bring about removal of colloids are (1) by adsorbing colloid particles at the charged sites of the polymer chains, (2) by cross-linking of the polymer chains to form bridges between the colloidal particles, and (3) by trapping the colloidal particles in three dimensional flocs. The non-ionic type polyelectrolytes cannot neutralize colloid charges. They remove colloidal particles by forming bridges and trapping. The non-ionic polyelctrolytes are used as coagulation and flocculation aids.

An aqueous solution of a polyelectrolyte is almost neutral in pH and hence no corrosion resistant material of construction is required for the accessories used for storage, transport and dosing of such a solution. The dosage required may be about 0.1 to 2 mg/L of waste water. A stock solution containing about 0.1 to 2% of a polyelectrolyte is generally used for dosing.

Polyelectrolyte sludge is relatively denser than the metal hydroxide sludge and it dewaters easily. However, polyectolytes are costlier than the inorganic coagulants. The inorganic coagulants produce larger quantities of sludge than the polyelectrolytes.

Coagulant Aids

Certain insoluble inorganic particulate materials, such as activated carbon, activated silica, bentonite powder, limestone powder, etc. when added along with inorganic coagulants or polyelectrolytes help floc formation. These particles act as floc nuclei. As they have density the flocs produced settle quickly and dewater easily.

Jar Test

An appropriate dosage of a coagulant (inorganic salt/polyelectrolyte) is ascertained by conducting jar tests. For carrying out jar tests equal volume of waste water samples are taken in several jars made of glass or plastic. To these jars different amounts of a coagulant (in the form of a concentrated solution) is added. While dosing a jar its contents are vigorously mixed. Then stirring is continued slowly for about 30 minutes to promote floc formation. Finally, the flocs are allowed to settle for about 60 minutes.

The minimum (coagulant) dose, which gives satisfactory clarification, is accepted as the appropriate dose of that coagulant. Similar tests are conducted with other coagulants.

In some situations a combination of an inorganic coagulant and a polyelectrolyte produces quick settling flocs and clearer treated effluent. Only by conducting jar tests selection and dosage of the right coagulant and/or polyectrolyte can be decided.

Coagulation and Flocculation Set-up

The following pieces of equipment are required for carrying out coagulation and flocculation processes :

1. A storage vessel for a coagulant/polyelectrolyte.
2. A feeder and auxiliaries for feeding a coagulant/polyelectrolyte into a dissolution tank.
3. A dissolution tank for preparation of a concentrated stock solution.
4. A holding tank for storing a stock solution.
5. A dosing pump and auxiliaries for addition of the stock solution into a mixer.
6. An in-line mixing device or vessel fitted with a suitable mechanical agitator for quick dispersion of the dosed solution in the incoming waste water stream.

During dosing very rapid and thorough mixing is essential as otherwise there will be local reactions and hence more of the coagulant/ polyelectrolyte will be required in order to achieve the desired degree of clarification

7. A flocculation chamber provided with slow moving paddles, which promote formation and growth of flocs.

Stationary arms located between paddles break up liquid rotation and thereby promote floc growth. The parameters normally maintained in a flocculation chamber are :

Detention time	= 20-60 min
Paddle tip speed	= 0.3–1 m/s

8. A settling/floatation chamber for separation of flocs from the treated water.

Coagulation and flocculation techniques may be used not only for removal of colloids but also for removal of very fine particles. Fine particles get trapped in the flocs and are removed.

It should be mentioned here that this method would not be economical for suspended particle removal if the particle concentration were less than 50 mg/L. If the suspended particle concentration be high (>2000 mg/L) then settling of flocs is hindered due to excessive inter-particle contact.

9.6 Removal of Oils and Greases

Waste water may contain not only suspended solid particles but also semi-solid and liquid particles/ droplets of fats, oils and greases. These may enter waste water as waste products from processes and a or spent lubricants from process equipment. Of these, fats and greases may be in solid or semi-solid state at ambient temperature. Oils if present would be in liquid state. They are lighter than water and, in general, insoluble in water. Other than these sometimes insoluble/slightly soluble organic compounds (liquid) may also be present in waste water.

In waste water oils and greases are present in dispersed state. Depending on their degree of dispersion they are referred to either as free or as emulsion. When the particle sizes are larger or when present in the form of a film on water surface the state is termed as a free state. But when those are present in the form of finely dispersed particles, say, in the range of 0.1 to more than 1 μm in diameter, the state is termed as an emulsion.

9.6.1 Removal of Free Oils and Greases

The processes for separation and removal of free oil, fat and grease from waste water are based on the fact that those are lighter than water. When a pool of waste water containing these substances is left relatively undisturbed they rise to the free surface and float. Dissolved air floatation operation or induced air floatation operation or injection of finely dispersed air in a pool of waste water increases the rate of rise of the dispersed particles and thereby enhances the separation process. Once they reach the free air-water surface they form a layer, which is skimmed off and removed.

For treatment of a low flow rate waste water stream containing free oils and greases a 'grease trap' is used. Figure 9.17 shows a sketch of a 'grease trap'. The floating layer of oil and grease, which accumulates at the top of the chamber, is removed manually from time to time.

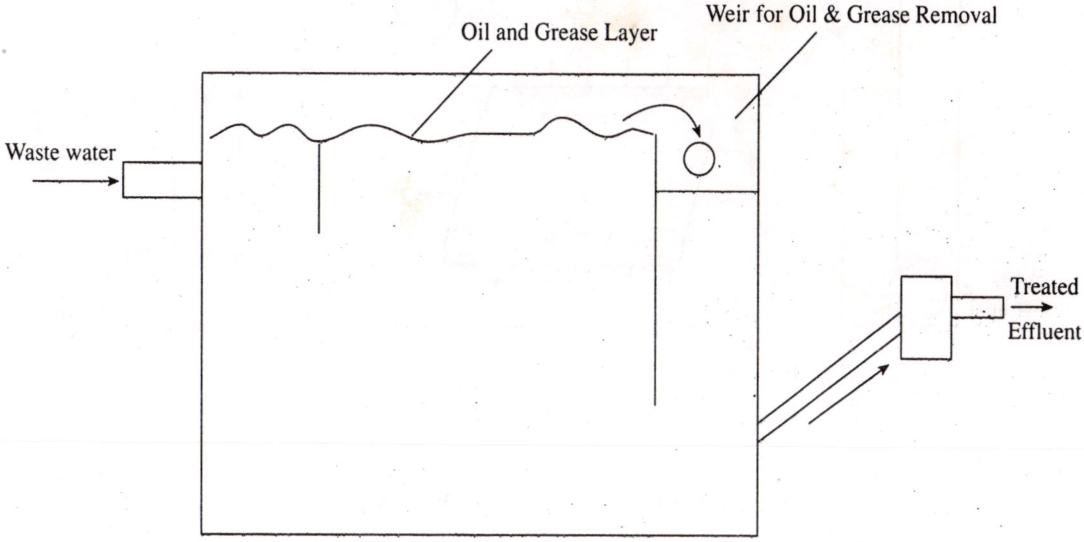

Fig. 9.17 : Grease Trap.

For treatment of a high flow rate waste water stream the size of the (separation) chamber would be large. The floating oil and grease layer has to be removed continuously using a suitable mechanical device. Moreover, the settle sludge, if any, has also to be removed from the chamber. In such a chamber sometimes air is introduced as fine bubbles to aid the floatation process. Figure 9.18 shows a sketch of an American Petroleum Institute (API) separator, which may be used when the floating layer contains only oil. The skimmer in an API separator is a rotating pipe having rectangular longitudinal slots. It scoops the floating oil layer and thereby removes it. A belt-skimmer may be used for removal of floating oil as well as grease.

An API separator is capable of separating oil droplets larger than 0.15 mm. However, when a relatively large amount of finer oil droplets, say, 0.06 mm in diameter, are present in a wastewater stream an API separator fitted with inclined parallel plates or corrugated plates may be used.

Such a separator may produce a treated effluent having oil content of 10 mg/L corresponding to an influent oil content around 1%. However, if the influent oil content were more than 1%, the separation efficiency may decrease due to shearing and re-entrainment of the collected oil droplets. This problem may be partly overcome by using a cross-flow arrangements.

9.6.2 Removal of Emulsified Oil

Waste water originating from process industries sometimes contains finely dispersed oils and greases. When the dispersed partice size range from 0.1 to more than 1 μm in diameter, they do not coalesce and rise to the free surface readily. Such dispersions are known as emulsions. These are stable, that is, they remain dispersed.

The stability of such dispersions may be due to the smaller particle size and the molecular structure of the dispersed phase and/or due to the presence of some chemicals (termed as emulsifiers) on the surfaces of the dispersed droplets. These chemicals get adsorbed as a film on the dispersed droplet surfaces and thereby prevent their coalescence.

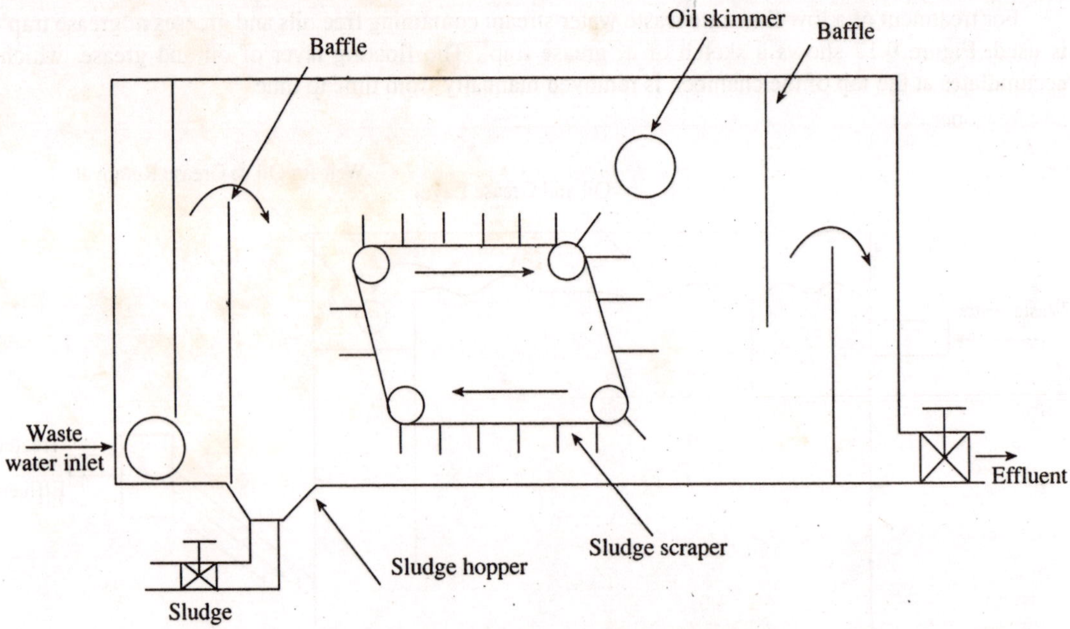

Fig. 9.18 : API Gravity Oil—Water Separator.

In the absence of an emulsifier an oil-in-water emulsion may cream on standing, that is, the dispersed particles (oil droplets) may concentrate at the free surface (air–water interface) without coalescing.

The first step in removing oil droplets present as an emulsion in waste water is to de-emulsify, i.e., break up the emulsion whereby the fine droplets would coalesce and form larger drops. One de-emulsification is completed the larger oil droplets are separated in an API separator.

De-emulsification, i.e., breaking up of an emulsion can be achieved by any one of the following processes or a combination of some of them.

1. Physical Processes :
   (a) Coalescence by agitation,
   (b) Coalescence by heating,
   (c) Coalescence by centrifuging.
2. Electrical Processes.
3. Chemical Processes.

1. Physical Processes

Agitation : Gentle agitation brings the dispersed droplets present in a wastewater stream closer to each other and thereby induces them to coalesce. Such coalescence breaks the emulsion. The free larger oil drops then rises upwards and forms a layer at the air-water interface.

Heating : On heating an oil-water emulsion the viscosity of the continuous phase (water) decreases. This lowering of viscosity results in thinning of the water layers separating the oil droplets from each other. Consequently, the droplets come closer to each other and coalesce. During heating of an emulsion gentle stirring helps the process of coalescence.

Centrifuging : When an emulsion is centrifuged at a high speed, the lighter phase (oil droplets) moves towards the centre while the denser phase (water) goes towards the periphery. The oil droplets coalesce resulting in breaking of emulsion. However, a high speed centrifuge being a costly piece of equipment is used only when the objective is to recover the emulsified oil.

2. Electrical Processes

In this process a high voltage D.C. field is applied to an oil-in-water emulsion. For the process to be successful the continuous phase (water phase) should be electrically conductive. Since the initial investment and the operating cost of an electrical process unit are high it is not used for de-emulsification of waste water.

3. Chemical Processes

De-emulsification of an oil-in-water emulsion may be done chemically either by addition of an electrolyte or by adding a chemical (de-emulsifier) which would react with the emulsifying agent present.

Addition of electrolytes containing bivalent or trivalent actions (positively charged ions) or polyelectrolytes (polymers) breaks an emulsion and causes the droplets to coalesce. It should be pointed out here that use of polyvalent cationic salts, such as iron or aluminium salts would result in generation of large quantities of sludge.

When an emulsifier is present in an emulsion, de-emulsification can be done by adding a chemical which would react with the emulsifier, thereby making the same ineffective. If the chemical nature of the emulsifier present and its concentration be known then it would be easier to select a suitable de-emulsifier (chemical) and to decide its dose. When an unknown emulsifier is present, the chemical to be added for counter-acting the emulsifier and its dose have to be decided by conducting laboratory trials.

The process to be used and the conditions to be maintained for emulsion breaking in a given situation are established by carrying out trials in a laboratory. At a low concentration of oil (say, up to 1%) physical methods may work, but at a higher concentration chemical treatment may be necessary.

9.7 Secondary Treatment

After primary treatment, that is, removal of suspended matter, particularly the inorganic particulate matter, oils and greases from a wastewater stream, it may be subjected to secondary treatment provided soluble and/or suspended organic substances are present in the stream.

The secondary treatment is also known as biological treatment. It is capable of abating biodegradable dissolved and/or suspended organic substances. By secondary treatment it is also possible to remove dissolved nitrogenous and phosphorous compounds from a waste water stream.

Organic substances which undergo degradation in the presence of micro-organisms (microbes, which are omnipresent) are termed as biodegradable substances. Micro-organisms produce enzymes (complex proteinaceous substances) which act as catalysts for biodegradation processes. These processes occur through a series of reactions, which are referred to as biochemical pathways. The reactions may take place in the presence of dissolved oxygen. These are referred to as aerobic reactions (processes). Some reactions take place in the total absence of oxygen. Those are termed anaerobic/obligate anaerobic processes. The reactions occurring under aerobic condition would be different from those under anaerobic condition. There are some microbes, which are capable of carrying out biological reactions both under aerobic as well as anerobic conditions. These microbes are referred to as facultative microbes and the processes are termed as facultative ones.

For biological treatment of waste water containing organic substances (dissolved and/or suspended) a host of microbes are used and the conditions maintained may be either aerobic or anaerobic. For better understanding of these processes it is necessary to get familiar with the basic characteristics of the different types of microbes, which are briefly discussed hereunder.

9.8 Fundamentals of Microbes

Prior to the invention of microscope, living beings were classified into two groups, namely, plants and animals. Plants are immotile, whereas the animals are motile. After the invention of microscope microbes/micro-organisms became visible. They have the basic characteristics of living beings, that is, they are capable of reproducing themselves, but structurally they are different from the macro-plants and animals. The microscopic living beings are termed as protists.

The protists have relatively simple structure. They may be unicellular or multicellular. Even in the multi-cellular ones, the cells are not internally different and those are not organized as tissues. Macro-plants and animals have tissues, which perform different functions. Protist classifications is given in Table 9.3.

Table 9.3 : Classification of Protists

Protists	Prokaryotes	Bacteria, Blue-green algae
	Eukaryotes	Algae, Fungi, Protozoa

Figures 9.19A and 9.19B show typical structures of prokaryote and eukaryote cells.

Besides the protists there are some sub-microscopic viable particles known as viruses. These are visible only under electron microscope. Their size ranges between 0.02-0.08 μm. Basically they are either a DNA or an RNA surrounded by a shell of protein. They are incapable of reproducing on their own. They infect host cells and induce them to replicate themselves and thereby produce more viruses.

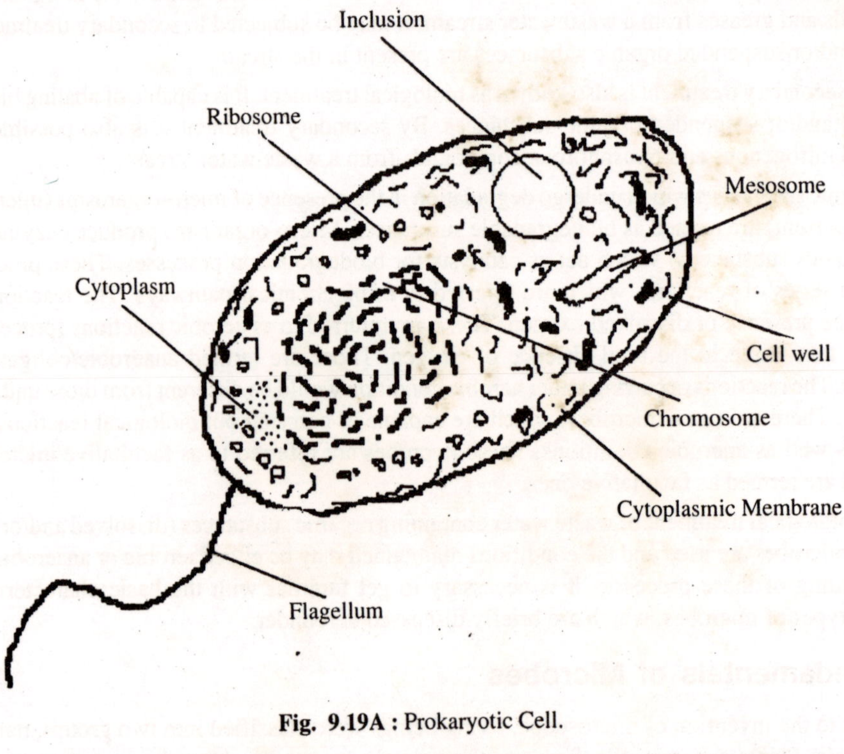

Fig. 9.19A : Prokaryotic Cell.

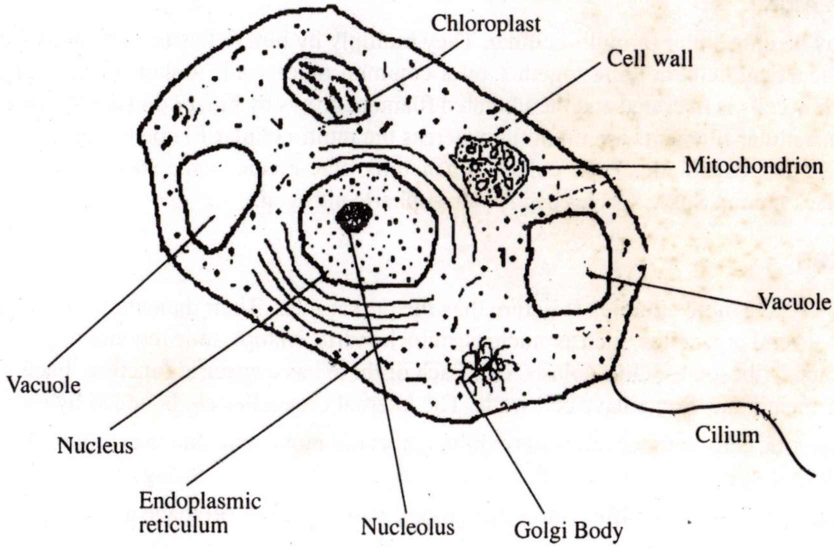

Fig. 9.19B : Eukaryotic Cell.

Prokaryotes

Prokaryotes are unicellular and usually are smaller than 5 μm in diameter. They have very simple structure and are bounded by a membrane. Most of them have rigid cell walls. Inside a cell there is a nucleus and cytoplasm. The nucleus is not separated from cytoplasm by a membrane. The enzymes which take part in respiration and photosynthetic reactions are located in the cell membrane or in its folding. Prokaryotes are not phagotropic, i.e., they cannot intake food. They secrete extra-cellular hydrolytic enzymes, which hydrolyze suspended organic particles and dissolve large organic molecules into smaller ones. They hydrolyze smaller molecules then enter the cells by various mechanisms. The prokaryotes normally move with the help of flagella, which are helical fibril protruding through the cell membrane, Basically, there are two groups of prokaryotes, namely, bacterial and blue-green algae.

Bacteria

Bacteria are unicellular. Their size ranges between 0.2 to 2 μm. They are classified into three groups : myxobacteria, spirochetes and eubacteria. Depending on their shape they are termed as cocci (spherical), bacilli (rod like), and spirilla (spirals).

Myxobacteria are rod shaped, having thin delicate walls. They move by gliding action. They obtain their food by splitting (lyzing) other organisms, such as bacteria, fungi, algae, etc.

Spirochetes are helicoidal in shape, having delicate flexible walls. Their are relatively long compared to their width. They live in mud and water and are anaerobic. Some are parasitic.

Eubacteria

Bacteria, other than the myxobacteria and spirochetes, are grouped as eubacteria. Their shapes may be rod like to spherical or spiral. Some of them have flagella and are motile, while the others are immotile. They have been sub-classified according to their metabolic and energetic characteristics. In general, they are unicellular, but some form aggregates, while some others are filamentous.

Blue-Green Algae

They may be unicellular or multi-cellular. They multiply by binary fission. The multi-cellulars are filaments of identical cells holding together by a common outer wall. A short portion of a filament containing a few cells is liberated and the liberated filament grows by binary division of the cells in one plane, The unicellular filaments are immotile whereas the multi-cellular filaments can glide. The blue-green algae are photosynthetic. Their colour is generally blue-green. Some species have red, purple, brown and black colour. Some species can fix atmospheric nitrogen.

Eukaryotes

Eukaryotes have more complex structure than the prokaryotes. Their diameter is more than 20 μm. Each cell has several organelles, such as nucleus, mitochondria, endoplasmic reticulum, golgi apparatus, vacuole, lysomes, ribosomes, chloroplasts, etc. Each of these has a specific function. Each cells has an outer cellular membrane. Some have cell walls. The internal organelles are bounded by membranes.

The eukaryotic cells without cell walls exhibit amoeboid movement due to cytoplasmic movement, called cytoplasmic streaming. Those with cell walls move with the help of flagella.

Eukaryotes have been classified into three groups, namely algae, protozoe and fungi.

Eukaryotic Algae

These may be unicellular or multi-cellular. In multi-cellular ones the cells are not different from one another. They are phtosynthetic, Some have cell walls and hence they are osmotrophic. Those without cell walls ingest smaller organisms phagotrophically. They can grow in inorganic media. These are not of importance in waste water treatment. However, they symbiotically help bacteria as they produce oxygen during phtosynthesis. Proliferation of algae in the presence of inorganic nutrients cause problem during filtration as the run period decreases. There are six major groups of eukaryotic algae. most of them have flagella, the exception being the red algae. They differ from the others in their chloroplast pigment colour, cell wall composition and reserve food composition.

Protozoa

These are unicellular, non-photosynthetic and motile. Some are parasitic and the other are phagotrophic. The majorities are aerobic and a few are anaerobic. The phagotrophic ones ingest smaller organism and organic matter. The group suctoria preys on the protozoa. They help in bio-flocculation.

The protozoa have been grouped into five major groups : Mastigophora, Sarcodina, Sporozoa, Ciliate and Suctoria.

Mastigophora have flagella. Generally they are parasitic. Some are pathogenic, some are not.

Sarcodina—The main mode of movement of this group is amoeboid type movement with the help of pseudopods. Some have flagella. Some are phagocitic, while some are parasitic. Amoeba which cause amoebic dysentery in humans belong to this group.

Sporozoa are osmotropic parasites. Some are immotile, while the others move by gliding action. They have no role in waste water treatment. They are pathogenic.

Ciliate—This group is important in waste water treatment. They are phagotropic. They have short hair like projections (Cilia). With the help of Cilia they move and capture food. There are two sub-groups, one free swimming type and the other stalked type.

Suctoria—They possess Cilia at the early stage of their life cycle. Later on they develop tentacles. With the help of the tentacles they prey on other protozoa.

Fungi

Fungi are mostly multinucleate and have a structure known as mycelium. Majority of them are aerobic, while some are anaerobic. They live on all types of organic matter, even on bacterially degraded organic residues. The major groups are : Phycomycetes, Ascomycetes, Basidiomycetes and Fungi—Imperfecti. Yeasts are unicellular fungi. Fungi reproduce either by budding or by binary fission. They have some industrial applications.

In general fungi are of no use in waste water treatment.

Other than the protists some small heterotrophic multi-cellular aerobic animals known as Rotifiers may be present in aerobic waste water treatment units. They have two sets of rotating Cilia on their heads. Those are used for motility as well as for capturing food.

9.8.1 Microbial Interaction in Waste Water Treatment

For waste water treatment almost always a microbial community having various species of organisms finds its way into a treatment unit. These organisms may enter a treatment unit from the surrounding environment as well as along with the waste water itself. Very often a portion of the biomass (microbes) produced during waste water treatment is recycled to the treatment unit. For abatement of a specified pollutant sometimes some specific organisms are added.

Waste water invariably would contain various chemicals (pollutants) and for their abatement the presence of diverse types of microbes is helpful and sometimes essential. These organisms interact with one another during the process.

The population of individual species of microbes may undergo change with the qualitative and quantitative variation of the characteristics of a waste water stream entering a treatment unit, but the system may have an overall stability if a broad spectrum of microbes were present in the system. However, if restricted community, that is, some selected species be used in a particulate situation, the system may get upset easily due to shock changes in flow/characteristics of the waste water stream being treated.

The interactions amongst the various species of microbes present in a wastewater treatment system may be of the following types : neutral, benevolent and antagonistic

Neutral Interaction

When the species present in an ecosystem do not use the same substrate (food) their environmental requirement is different and they do not utilize the metabolic products and by-products of one another then there interaction is said to be neutral. In a community of micro-organisms in any ecosystem such an interaction is very rare.

Benevolent Interaction

In an ecosystem sometimes one organism helps another organism in its metabolic activity or in maintaining ones environmental requirement and they do not harm each other. Such an interaction between the organisms is referred to as benevolent interaction.

There are two types of benevolent interactions, namely, Commensalism and Mutualism.

Sometimes the metabolic products or by-products of one organism is used by another organism. Such interaction between two species is termed as commensalism interaction. Examples of such interactions are : (1) glucose or a growth factor produced by one organism being utilized by other organisms (2) phenol (toxic to some organisms) consumed by one organism in an ecosystem so that the other organisms present in the system may not get harmed.

When the organisms present in an ecosystem help each other then the interaction is termed as *mutualism*. An example is the interaction between algae and bacteria in an aerobic treatment unit. Algae during photosynthesis produce O_2, which helps aerobic bacteria in their metabolic activity. Bacteria producing CO_2 during respiration help algae in photosynthesis.

Antagonistic Interaction

Sometimes one type of organism competes with another of the same resource or one type prevents growth of another or there is a predator–prey relationship between two types of organisms. In such situations the interaction amongst the species said to be antagonistic. Some examples of antagonistic type of interactions are : (1) facultative and obligate aerobic bacteria vying for dissolved oxygen, (2) algae producing O_2 during photosynthesis and thereby preventing growth of obligate anaerobe, and (3) protozoa preying upon bacteria.

9.8.2 Microbe Physiology

Microbial cells contain about 80 per cent water. The remaining portion is made up of C, O_2, H_2, N_2, P and S. Metals like Na, K, Ca, Mg, Fe are also present in microbial cells. The C, O_2, H_2 and N_2 constituents of a cell are often approximated (on ash-free basis) by the formula $C_5H_7O_2N$. For synthesis (reproduction) of new microbes other than H_2 and O_2 (which may be obtained from water) the major elements required are C and N_2. A relatively small amounts of P and S are required and very small quantities of the above listed metals are also needed. The microbes obtain the various constituents for their reproduction from their environment (ecosystem). The microbes also need energy for their movement as well as to carry out their metabolic (catabolic and anabolic) activities. The sources of the above named constituents required for reproduction of microbes in a waste water treatment system are :

N_2 Source :

For synthesis of proteins and nucleic acids nitrogen bearing compounds are to be added to a wastewater treatment unit if those are not present as a constituent of the pollutants present.

O_2 Source :

Autotrophes use CO_2 and H_2O as the sources of O_2. Heterotrophes use oxygen bearing organic compounds and H_2O.

C Source :

Autotrophes use CO_2 as the carbon source whereas heterotrophes use organic compounds as the source of carbon.

S Source :

Sulphur required for protein synthesis is obtained from sulphur bearing compounds normally present in waste water.

P Source :

Phosphorous required for synthesis of nucleic acids and phospho–lipids are obtained from inorganic phosphates and organo–phosphorous compounds normally present in waste water.

For energy transfer for movement as well as for metabolic activity organo-phosphorous compounds ATP (Adenosine triphosphate), ADP (Adenosine diphosphate) and AMP (Adenosine monophosphate) are required. These are synthesized by the microbes utilizing phosphorous (inorganic/organic) present in waste water.

The classification of microbes based on their metabolic and energetic characteristics are as listed in Table 9.4.

Table 9.4 : Classification of Microbes

Groups	Carbon Source	Energy Source	Example
Photo-autotrophes	CO_2	Sunlight	Algae and photo-synthetic bacteria
Chemo-autotrophes	CO_2	Oxidation of inorganic compounds.	Bacteria
Photo-heterotrophes	Organic compounds	Sunlight	Purple non-sulphur Bacteria
Chemo-heterotrophes	Organic compounds	Oxidation of organic compounds	Bacteria, Protozoa, Fungi

From Table 9.4 it is evident that the chemo-heterotrophes are most useful for the treatment of waste water containing organic substances. The photo-autotrophes are of some use as they enrich waste water with dissolved oxygen, which is produced during photosynthesis.

The following criteria are used for classification of chemo-heterotrophes.

1. the process by which they meet their energy need,
2. the temperature range in which they are more active.

The chemo-heterotrophes which use dissolved O_2 to oxidize organic compounds to produce energy are called *aerobes*. Those which produce energy by decomposing organic compounds (fermentation processes) in the absence of dissolved O_2 are called *anaerobes*. There is a third group, which behaves aerobically in the presence of dissolved oxygen and anaerobically in the absence of dissolved oxygen. This group is called *facultative microbes*.

Classification of chemo-heterotrophes according to the temperature range in which they are more active is given in Table 9.5.

Table 9.5 : Classification of Chemo-heterotrophes based on their Optimum Temperature Range

Sub-group	Optimum Temperature Range, °C
Psychrophilic (Cryophilic)	12-18
Mesophilic	25-40
Thermophilic	55-65

The metabolic and energetic reactions, which are carried out by the chemo-heterotrophes are grouped as Catabolic route, Amphibolic route, Anaplerotic route and Anabolic route. Through these steps the organisms obtain their energy and synthesize compounds such as nucleic acids, proteins, polysaccharides, lipids, etc. and finally produce new microbial cells. The specific activities carried out along the above mentioned routes are summarized hereunder.

Catabolic Route

Generally catabolic activities are carried out in two stages. In the first stage the suspended organic matter present in waste water are solubilized and the larger dissolved organic molecules are hydrolyzed (splitted) into smaller molecules. Extra-cellular enzymes take part in these reactions. The relatively small amount of energy liberated during this step is not available to the cells (microbes) as the reactions occur outside the cells.

During the second stage of the catabolic processes the smaller organic molecules already produced diffuse inside the cells. There further splitting of the diffused molecules as well as some oxidation reactions take place. The energy liberated during this step is available to the cells.

Amphibolic Route

The starting materials for these reactions are the materials (molecules) produced during the second stage of the catabolic process. As a result of the amphibolic reactions some intermediate compounds are produced for biosynthesis and some oxidation reactions also take place.

During an aerobic process the final products of oxidation reaction are CO_2 and H_2O. The products of oxidation during an anaerobic process are CO_2 and some other organic molecules (not components for biosynthesis). These are referred to as *fermentation products.*

Anaplerotic Route

The intermediates produced during the amphibolic process are not enough to meet the total demand for the biosynthesis processes. Hence some more intermediates are produced by this route.

Anabolic Route

During this process the intermediates produced by the amphibolic route and the anaplerotic route are subsequently polymerized and finally the different components of the cells are produced. Ultimately it leads to the production of new cells.

It should be mentioned here that all of the activities (chemical reactions) occurring inside a cell are enzyme (complex proteinacious compounds) catalyzed.

9.8.3 Enzymatic Kinetics

All chemical reactions taking place inside the cells of micro–organisms (intracellular) or immediately-outside the cells (extra-cellular) are enzyme catalyzed. Enzymes are reaction specific, that is , each enzyme is capable of carrying out a specific reaction utilizing a specific substrate (reactant). Like inorganic catalysts, enzymes may get poisoned (inhibited) by some chemicals. Enzymes also get affected at higher temperature and adverse pH condition, which may be due to some structural changes occurring in them.

The kinetics of enzymatic reactions have been studied by several scientists. They have developed rate equations based on their proposed models. Some of these are discussed hereunder. The basic equation is referred to as Michaelis–Menten equation.

Enzymatic reactions in the absence of any inhibitor are assumed to occur through two steps. In the first step, a substrate (reactant) molecule *(S)* combines with an enzyme molecule *(E)* to form an enzyme-substrate complex (ES). This reaction is considered to be a reversible one. In the second step, the complex (ES) undergoes an irreversible reaction whereby the enzyme molecule is liberated and one or more products are formed. The overall process may be represented as

$$E + s \underset{k_{-1}}{\overset{k_1}{\rightleftharpoons}} ES \xrightarrow{k_2} E + P$$

For modelling the enzyme-substrate complex formation reaction two hypothesis have been proposed. According to one hypothesis this reaction attains equilibrium instantaneously. According to the other this reaction reaches a 'pseudo–steady–state' condition instantaneously, that is, the rate of formation of the *ES* complex becomes the same as the rate of disappearance of the complex by the reverse reaction. The final equation developed for the rate of disappearance of substrate/the rate of product formation is identical irrespective of which the above mentioned hypothesis are accepted.

$$-r_s = r_p = V = \frac{V_m[S]}{K_m + [S]} \tag{9.29}$$

where $-r_s = -\frac{d[S]}{dt}$ = rate of disappearance of substrate,

$r_p = \frac{d[P]}{dt}$ = rate of formation of product

$[S]$ = substrate concentration

$[P]$ = product concentration

K_m, V_m = Michaelis–Menten kinetic constants

$$K_m = \frac{k_1 - 1 + k_2}{k_1}$$

V = rate of reaction = velocity of reaction.

Eq. (9.29) is known as the Michaelis–Menen equation. To evaluate the kinetic constants (K_m and V_m) for a specific reaction, the substrate concentration, $[S]$ vs. time, t data are experimentally obtained. The data so obtained may be plotted in various ways (as shown in Figures 9.20A, B, C & D) for estimation of K_m and V_m. The Figures 9.20A, B, C & D are based on the modified forms of Michaelis–Menten equation.

Inhibition Reactions

Enzymatic reactions may get inhibited (retarded) in various ways. The inhibitors may be some chemicals (I) other than the substrate, the substrate itself (at high concentration) and the product (at high concentration). The inhibition reactions have been variously termed as 'Competitive Inhibition', *'Uncompetitive Inhibition', 'Non-competitive Inhibition', 'Substrate Inhibition' and 'Product Inhibition'.*

Symbolic representation of the different types of inhibition reactions and their respective rate expressions are as follows :

Competitive Inhibition :

$$E + S \leftrightarrow ES, ES \rightarrow E + P, E + I \leftrightarrow EI$$

$$r_p = \frac{V_m[S]}{K_m\left(1 + \frac{[I]}{K_1}\right) + [S]}, \tag{9.30}$$

where $[I]$ = inhibitor concentration,

K_1 = equilibrium constant for the *EI* dissociation reaction.

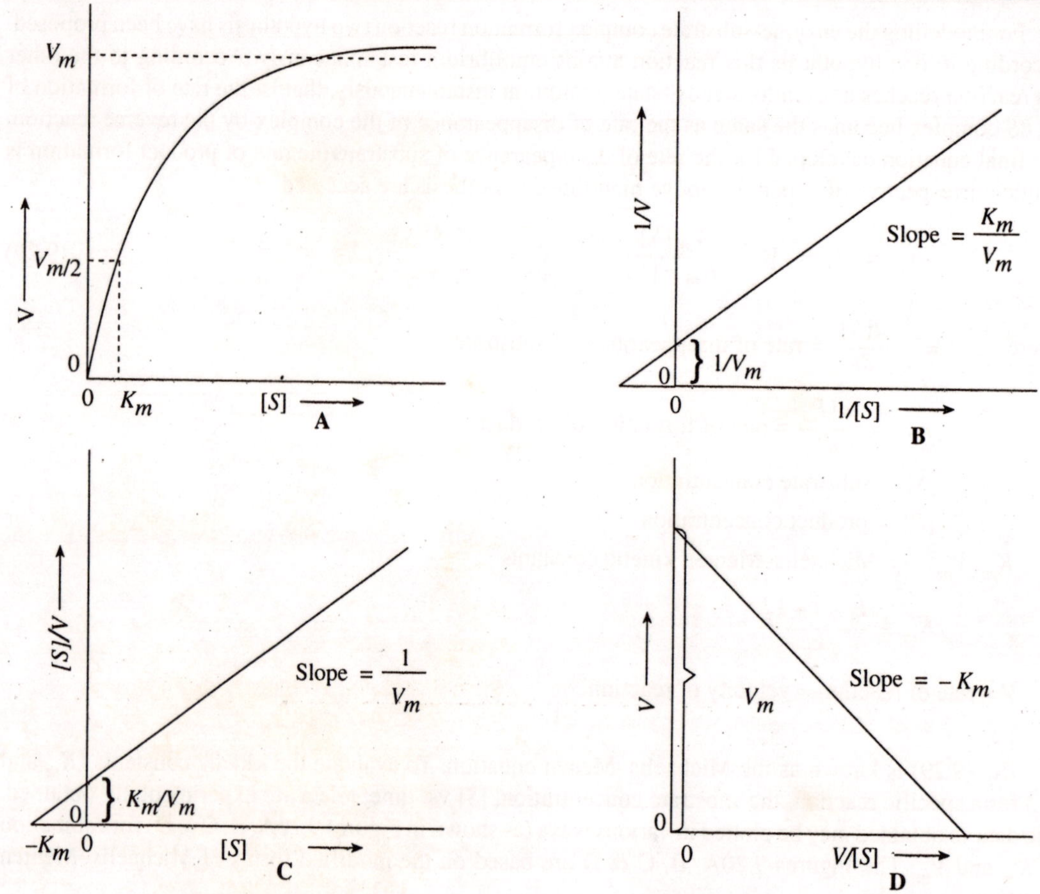

Fig. 9.20 : Plots for evaluation of kinetic parameters K_m and V_m

A : Michaelis-Menten Plot, **C** : Hanes Plot,
B : Lineweaver-Burk Plot, **D** : Hofstee Plot.

Uncompetitive Inhibition :

$$E + S \leftrightarrow ES, ES + I \leftrightarrow IES, ES \leftrightarrow E + P,$$

$$r_p = \frac{V_m\ [S]}{K_m + [S]\ (1 + \frac{[I]}{K_I})} \tag{9.31}$$

where K_1 = equilibrium constant for the *IES* dissociation reaction.

Non-Competitive Inhibition :

$$E + S \leftrightarrow ES, E + I \leftrightarrow EI, ES + I \leftrightarrow IES, ES \rightarrow E + P,$$

$$r_p = \frac{V_m\ [S]}{K_m + [S]\left(1 + \frac{[I]}{K_I}\right)} \tag{9.32}$$

Substrate Inhibition :

$$E + S \leftrightarrow ES, ES + S \leftrightarrow SES, ES \leftrightarrow E + P,$$

$$r_p = \frac{V_m\ [S]}{K_m + [S] + \dfrac{[S]^2}{K'_m}} \tag{9.33}$$

where K'_m = equilibrium constant for the *SES* dissociation reaction.

Product Inhibition :

$$E + S \leftrightarrow ES, ES + P \leftrightarrow PES, ES \leftrightarrow E + P,$$

$$r_p = \frac{V_m\ [S]}{K_m + [S]\left(1 + \dfrac{[P]}{K_p}\right)}, \tag{9.34}$$

where K_p = Equilibrium constant for the *PES* dissociation reaction.

It should be pointed out here that the above mentioned models and rate equations are based on the premise that inhibition occurs due to non-availability of some enzyme molecules for the enzyme-substrate complex formation reaction because of some secondary reactions.

9.8.4 Microbial Growth Process

Microbes need carbon, oxygen, hydrogen, nitrogen and some other elements for synthesis of cell components, which finally leads to the reproduction of new cells, The organisms need energy for carrying out the synthesis reactions and for the maintenance of activities other than for reproduction. Maintenance energy need means energy required for carrying out cell functions, such as *motility, osmoregulation, phagocytosis, cytoplasmic streaming*, etc. Maintenance energy also includes energy needed for synthesizing some cell components, which are required for replacement of the broken down components. Some cell components break down as their free energies are higher compared to those of the original building blocks from which they are synthesized.

When a specially prepared mixture of organic substances (referred to as a medium) is inoculated (as happens in a batch operation) with some species of organism, then the microbe population in that mixture passes through a typical growth process as shown in Fig. 9.21. The organic substance present in a medium, which acts as the carbon source for the microbes, is termed as the substrate.

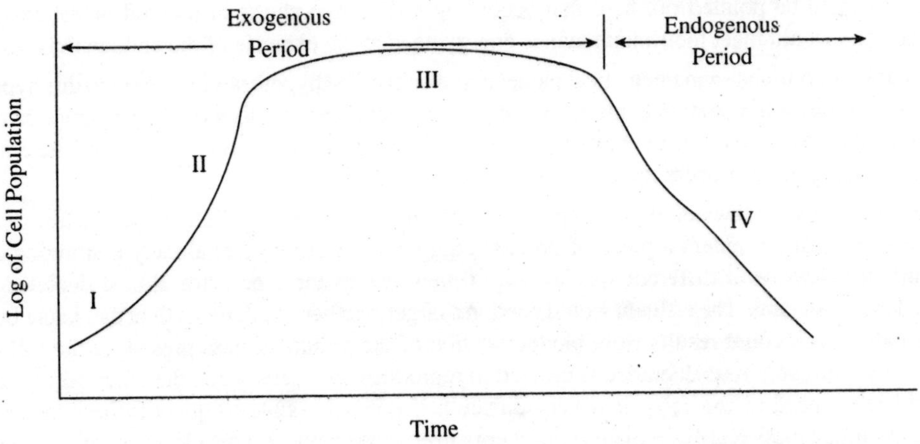

Fig. 9.21 : Typical Growth Process of Organisms during a Batch Operation.

It should be pointed out here that the total population of microbes present in an ecosystem at any instant of time is made up of two groups, namely, 'viable organisms' and 'dead organisms'. Viable organisms are those, which are capable of reproducing whereas the 'dead' ones are living but incapable of reproduction. They utilize energy for carrying out all types of activities except reproduction.

Figure 9.21 shows that the rate of microbe population growth during a batch operation passes through different phases. These are normally referred to as Phases I, II, III and IV.

Phase I is termed as the 'lag phase'. During this phase the population (of viable cells) increases slowly as the organisms take time to get acclimatized with its environment.

Phase II is known as the 'log phase' as during this period the population increases exponentially utilizing the substrate available in the medium.

Phase III is known as the 'stationary phase'. During this period the population of the viable cells remains almost static due to non–availability of sufficient substrate. The rate of production of new cells during this period is virtually the same as the rate of conversion of viable cells to dead cells. During this phase the available substrate is mainly utilized to meet the maintenance energy demand of the cells.

Phase IV is termed as the 'decay phase'. No substrate is available during this period. The cells metabolize their stored food to meet their maintenance energy need. Progressively some of the cells undergo lysis, that is, disintegrate and thereby furnish organic substances to the remaining cell to meet their maintenance energy need. Lysis results in decrease in cell population, which is referred to as cell 'decay'

During the Phases I to III the substrate available in a medium meets the growth and or maintenance energy need of the organisms. This period is termed as the exogenous period. During the phase IV, in the absence of any substrate, the cells metabolize their stored food as well as the substances liberated as a result of lysis of some cells. This period is referred to as the endogenous period.

It has been mentioned earlier that chemo-heterotrophes play the major role in biological treatment of waste water. They utilize the substrate (pollutants) present in waste water to meet their material (for biosynthesis) and energy need. Two alternative hypothesis have been postulated to explain how microbes achieve this.

According to one hypothesis cells synthesize their organelles and endogenous (food) reserve utilizing the substrate. Sequentially a part of the endogenous reserve is degraded to meet the maintenance energy need of the cells.

According to the other hypothesis substrate is utilized to meet the synthesis requirement as well as to meet the maintenance energy need concurrently. Conceptually and logically this hypothesis is more realistic. It should be pointed out here that according to this hypothesis at the end of the exogenous period the cells would meet their maintenance energy need at the expense of the endogenous reserve.

It is easier to formulate a mathematical model based on the first hypothesis even though this hypothesis is not a logical one. A mathematical model based on the second hypothesis would be a complicated one, as it must contain terms to represent both the exogenous and the endogenous processes and the criteria as to when the endogenous process term would gain importance.

In a continuous wastewater treatment process an influent containing pollutants (with a low or almost nil microbe population) enters a piece of process equipment (a bioreactor) already containing a large population of microbes of different species. An effluent leaves the bioreactor almost depleted of the biodegradable pollutants. The effluent would contain a larger number of microbes than that in the influent. This increase in cell count results from biodegradation of the pollutant mass present in the influent. A portion of the pollutant mass degraded is utilized to reproduce new cells while the other portion goes to meet the energy need of the cells. It is very difficult, if not impossible to quantify how much of the degraded pollutant mass is utilized to meet the energy need of the cells. But development of a quantitative correlation of the cell mass growth rate the pollutant mass depletion rate is very much possible.

F rom wastewater treatment point of view one would be interested in developing an expression for the overall rate of depletion of pollutant mass in an influent stream so that the same may be used for designing a suitable process equipment.

9.8.5 Cell Growth Kinetics

Cells multiply by binary fission of viable cells. Hence the rate of cell (mass) growth (in the absence of predators, cell death and cell decay) during a batch operation would depend on the concentration of the viable cells in a bioreactor at any instant of time. It may be expressed as—.

$$\frac{d[X_V]}{dt} = r_{G}, X_V = \mu[X_V] \tag{9.35}$$

where, r_G, X_V = rate of production of viable cells (mass) per unit volume of a bioreactor,

$[X_V]$ = concentration of viable cells (mass) at any instant,

and μ = specific growth rate constant.

The numerical value of μ for a specific microbe-substrate combination depends on the substrate concentration, micro-nutrient concentration, pH, temperatture, etc., in a bioreactor.

Investigators, based on their experimental trials at controlled pH, temperature and micro-nutrient concentration have obtained a general correlation for μ as a function of substrate concentration *[S]* as shown in Eq. (9.36)

$$\mu = \frac{\mu_m [S]}{K_s + [S]}. \tag{9.36}$$

The numerical values of μ_m and K_s have been found to depend on pH, temperature and micro-nutrient concentration for any specific microbe-substrate system.

Equation (9.36) is known as Monod equation. It is similar in form to that of Michaelis—Menten equation for enzymatic reaction [Eq. (9.29)].

Combination of Eqs. (9.35) and (9.36), results in Eq. (9.37)

$$r_{G,X_V} = \frac{\mu_m [S] [X_V]}{K_s + [S]} \tag{9.37}$$

It should be pointed out here that in a waste water treatment unit a mixed population of microbes and a variety of pollutants (chemicals) would be present. For such an unit μ_m and K_s cannot be compiled by combining data from literature for specific microbe–substrate systems. For each individual situation μ_m and K_s have to be experimentally evaluated.

During biological treatment of wastewater the microbes present utilize the carbon sources (substrate, i.e., biodegradable organic compounds) for reproduction as well as to meet maintenance energy needs. Under aerobic condition the energy generation steps would produce CO_2 and H_2O as the end products, whereas under anaerobic conditions the reaction products would be mainly CO_2 and CH_4.

Since substrates are utilized for cell mass growth as well as to produce energy, the mass rate of cell growth would be less than that of the substrate utilization. The relation between the two is normally expressed as

$$-\frac{d[S]}{dt} = -r_s = \frac{r_{G,X_V}}{y}, \tag{9.38}$$

where y is termed as the yield, that is, the mass of viable cells produced per unit mass of substrate utilized.

Since a waste water stream invariably contains a number of organic compounds (pollutants) it is customary to express the substrate concentration, $[S]$, either in terms of BOD or COD in mg O_2/L unit and not in terms of the concentrations of the individual pollutants present.

The yield, y, would have a maximum value if the maintenance energy need be nil. Under such a situation y is represented by the symbol y_g. Even if the maintenance energy were nil y_g would have a value less than one as the biosynthesis (growth) process needs energy. The numerical value of y has been found to depend on the substrate used, its concentration, the species of organism used and the environmental factors such as temperature, pH, etc.

Experimental studies have revealed that the numerical value of y is about 0.5 when waste water is treated aerobically. But under anaerobic treatment conditions the value of y has been found to be around 0.1

On combining Eqs. (9.35) and (9.38) one obtains Eq. (9.39),

$$-r_s = \frac{r_{G,X_V}}{y} = \frac{\mu\,[X_V]}{y} = q\,[X_V]$$

$$= \frac{\mu_m [S]\,[X_V]}{y\,\{K_s + [S]\}} = \frac{q_m\,[S]}{K_s + [S]}, \tag{9.39}$$

where $q = \dfrac{\mu}{y}$ and $q_m = \dfrac{\mu_m}{y}$.

It is to be noted that during a biological process several viable cells become 'dead' and some undergo lysis (decay). Hence the net rate of growth of viable cells may be expressed as—

$$\frac{d[X_V]}{dt} = \mu\,[X_V] - b_V\,[X_V] - \gamma_V\,[X_V] \tag{9.40}$$

where $b_V\,[X_V]$ = rate of lysis of viable cells., and

$\gamma_V\,[X_V]$ = rate of generation of 'dead' cells.

The net rate of growth of 'dead' cells may be expressed as

$$\frac{d\,[X_d]}{dt} = \gamma_V\,[X_V] - b_d\,[X_d] \tag{9.41}$$

where $[X_d]$ = concentration of 'dead' cells, and

$b_d\,[X_d]$ = rate of lysis of 'dead' cells.

It has been mentioned earlier that microbes present in any system are of two types, namely 'viable' and 'dead'. The concentration of the total cell population (mass) at any given instant would be the sum of the concentration of each type at that instant,

$$[X] = [X_V] + [X_d] \tag{9.42}$$

where, $[X]$ = concentration of total cell mass.

An expression for the rate of change of the total cell mass during an exogenous process may be obtained by combining Eqs. (9.40), (9.41) and (9.42)

$$\frac{d\,[X]}{dt} = \frac{d\,[X_V]}{dt} + \frac{d\,[X_d]}{dt}$$

$$= \mu[X_V] - b_v[X_V] - b_d[X_d] \tag{9.43}$$

Biochemical reactions are basically chemical reactions catalyzed by (extra/intracellular) enzymes. Therefore, the specific rate constants, e.g., μ, b and γ are temperature dependent. Their numerical values increase with increase in temperature. Their temperature dependence may be represented by the Arrhenius type relation,

$$k = k_0 \; e^{-E/RT} . \tag{9.44}$$

However, often the relation is expressed empirically as

$$k = k_0 \; \theta^{(t-t_0)} \tag{9.45}$$

where k_0 corresponds to some base temperature t_0 expressed in °C and k corresponds to the operating temperature t °C. The numerical value of θ has been found to range between 1.03 to 1.1 Generally it is taken as 1.08.

The numerical values of the experimentally evaluated kinetic parameters, μ_m, K_s, γ and b depend on the substrate-organism combination, as well as nutrient concentration, pH and temperature maintained during a particular investigation. It has been observed that for an easily degradable substrate the numerical value of μ_m is high, whereas, that for a substrate which is difficult to degrade the value of μ_m is low. The numerical value of K_s is low in the case of an easily degradable substrate and high for a substrate which is difficult to degrade.

Some typical values of the kinetic parameters for mixed culture aerobic wastewater treatment processes are listed in Table 9.6

Table 9.6 : Typical Value of Mixed Culture Kinetic Parameters for Aerobic Waste Water Treatment Around 20 °C

Parameter	Range of Values
μ_m	0.2–0.5 hr^{-1}
K_m	60–300 mg BOD_5/L
γ	0.002–0.005 hr^{-1}
b*	0.001–0.004 hr^{-1}

*Generally, it is assumed that $b_V = b_d$.

It has been found that the viable cell mass growth rate for both aerobic processes and anaerobic processes follows the Eq. (9.37). Experimental data show that for anaerobic processes μ_m is lower and K_s is higher compared to those listed for aerobic processes in Table 9.6.

9.9 Aerobic Treatment of Waste Water

Waste water from industrial processes may contain both biodegradable and non-biodegradable organic substances. Organic substances may be present in the dissolved state and/or in the form of a suspension. Aerobic treatment processes are suitable mainly for abatement of dissolved biodegradable organics. These processes can also degrade finely dispersed organics to some extent.

The aerobic organisms utilize to biodegradable organics partly for their growth and partly to obtain energy through oxidative reactions using dissolved molecular oxygen. The products of the oxidative reactions are mainly CO_2 and H_2O. Some other compounds are also produced when the organic compounds being oxidized contain elements like nitrogen, sulphur and phosphorous. Nitrogen in nitrogenous compounds is converted to amines, ammonia, and finally oxidized to nitrite and nitrate. Sulphur in sulphur bearing compounds is converted to sulphite and sulphate. Phosphorous in organo-phosphorous compounds is oxidized to phosphates. During aerobic treatment of waste water a large portion of the pollutants abated are utilized by the organisms to produce new cells.

Waste water originating from an industrial unit would invariably contain several biodegradable substances. To abate them several species of microbes are needed. During start-up of a treatment unit the microbes present/added take some time to get acclimatized with their environment. An aerobic treatment process may take sometimes a few weeks to get stabilized, that is, to reach a pseudodynamic equilibrium state.

Hence aerobic treatment of industrial waste water is carried out in a continuous mode even when a basic industrial process generating effluent is a batch or a periodic one. Aerobic units normally used for treatment of industrial waste water are of various types, namely, aerobic lagoon, completely mixed aerated lagoon, activated sludge unit, trickling filter and rotating biological contractor. Their variation lies in the methods of bringing the pollutants (present in wastewater), microbes and oxygen (air) in intimate contact. The basic features of these units are listed in Table 9.7.

Table 9.7 : Basic Features of Aerobic Treatment Units

Units	Aeration Mode	Physical State of Organisms	Special Features
Aerobic Lagoon	Molecular diffusion of Atmospheric oxygen	In suspension due to gas evolution	There may be algal growth. No control over the organism population.
Completely Mixed Aerated Lagoon	Forced aeration	In suspension due to aeration and agitation	No control over the organism populations.
Activated Sludge Unit	Forced aeration	In suspension due to aeration and agitation	Organism population controlled by sludge recycle.
Trickling Filter	Flow of air due to natural draft.	Immobilized on packing surfaces	Gravity flow of waste-water over immobilized cells on packings.
Rotating Biological Contactor	Forced convection	Immobilized organisms over rotating disc surface	Discs with immobilized cells partially dipped in waste water rotating at a low speed.

Description, performance and design approach of the different aerobic units are detailed in the subsequent Sections.

9.9.1 Aerobic Lagoon

An aerobic lagoon is a shallow basin having a depth of about 30 to 60 cm. It is made shallow so that even near its bottom aerobic condition may prevail. The sides of the basin are protected by rip-rap so as to prevent their erosion by wind-generated ripples on the surface. A waste water stream (influent) enters a lagoon through pipes of open channels and flows lengthwise. The treated water (effluent from the lagoon) flows out through pipes, the inlet ends of which are covered with screens in order to prevent egress of algae and other suspended solid particles. Very often algae grow on the surfaces of such lagoons. The algae may remove some of the heavy metal ions, which may enter a lagoon dissolved in the influent. Algae produce oxygen during photo-synthesis which helps in re-oxygenation of lagoon water.

The reactions and changes taking place in an aerobic lagoon may be represented schematically as shown in Fig. 9.22.

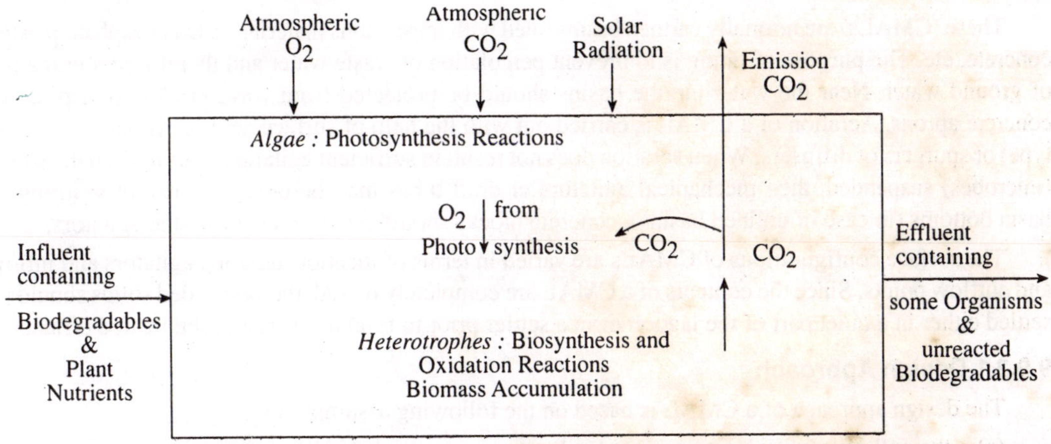

Fig. 9.22 : Schematic Representation of Aerobic Lagoon Reactions.

Aerobic organisms need dissolved oxygen for the oxidative reactions. The major source of oxygen is the atmosphere. Oxygen from the atmosphere gets dissolved in lagoon water due to molecular diffusion.

The treatment process is furthered by the following factors :

(a) large air-water interfacial area,

(b) turbulence at the air-water interface,

(c) lower ambient temperature.

Solubility of oxygen in water is higher at a lower temperature, but lower temperature would cause slowing down of the biochemical reactions.

The size of an aerobic lagoon for a specific situation and the operating parameters may be ascertained using the data listed in Table 9.8.

Table 9.8 : Design and Performance Parameters of Aerobic Lagoons

Depth	=	0.3 to 0.6 m.
Length : Width	=	3 : 1
Loading Rate	=	100-200 kg BOD/hectare per day
Nutrient Ratio :		
BOD : N : P : K	=	100 : 5 : 1 : 1
Detention Time	=	2 to 6 hours
BOD in Influent	=	less than 200 mg/L
BOD Removal Efficiency	=	80 – 90%
Bacterial Cell Production	=	0.5 kg/kg BOD removed.

Aerobic lagoons can stand flow and load fluctuations only to some extent. Their major shortcomings are lack of control on re-oxygenation and microbe population. Moreover, as there is very little agitations in a lagoon most of the microbes collect close to the floor of a basin. Some of the organisms settle on the basin floor.

9.9.2 Completely Mixed Aerated Lagoon

A completely mixed aerated lagoon (CMAL) differs from a conventional (shallow) aerobic lagoon in two respects, namely, (1) air (oxygen) is supplied with the help of mechanical devices, and (2) agitators are often installed to keep the microbes suspended. These features provide better contact between the microbes and the pollutants (substrate) and also to maintain a higher concentration of dissolved oxygen. Since re-oxygenation of lagoon water does not depend on molecular diffusion of atmospheric oxygen a CMAL is invariably made much deeper than a conventional aerobic lagoon.

These (CMALs) are normally earthen basins lined with impervious materials, such as asphalt, plastic, concrete, etc. The purpose of lining is to prevent percolation of waste water and thereby contamination of ground water. Near the waterline the basins should be protected from wave erosion by rip-rap or concrete aprons. Aeration of a CMAL is carried out with the help of surface aerators (floating or fixed type) or spurgers or diffusers. When aeration does not result in sufficient agitation so as to keep the solids (microbes) suspended, then mechanical agitators or draft tubes may be used. To prevent scouring of basin bottoms (in case of unlined basins), concrete blocks should be placed beneath the agitators.

The surface configurations of CMALs are varied in terms of location aerators, agitators and inflow and outflow points. Since the contents of a CMAL are completely mixed, the suspended solids should be settled either in a quiet part of the lagoon or in a settler prior to final discharge of the treated effluent.

9.9.2.1 Design Approach

The design approach of a CMAL is based on the following assumptions :

(a) the pollutants are present in dissolved state (no suspended solid present),

(b) the basin contents are completely mixed,

(c) no sludge recycle,

(d) microbe concentration in an influent stream is negligible,

(e) steady state operating condition prevails.

An idealized CMAL basin is shown schematically in Fig. 9.23

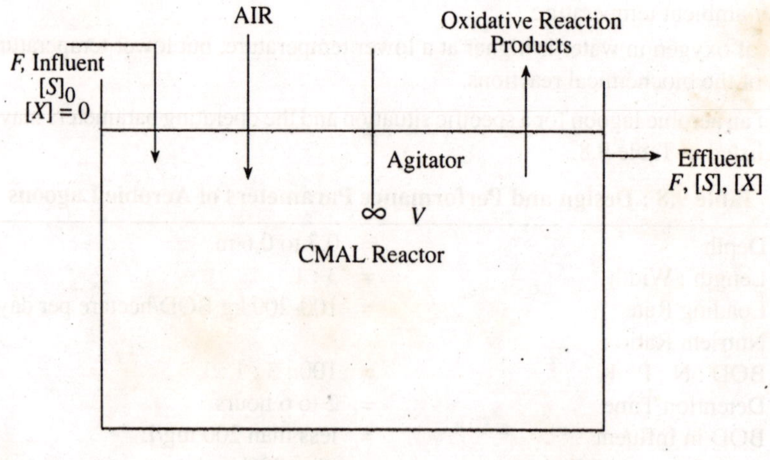

Fig. 9.23 : Schematic Sketch of a CMAL.

F = waste water inflow rate, L/Hr,
$[S]_0$ = pollutant concentration in influent, mg BOD/L,
$[S]$ = pollutant concentration in effluent, mg BOD/L,
V = reactor volume, L
$[X]$ = $[X_V] + [X_d]$
$[X_V]$ = viable cell concentration, mg/L
$[X_d]$ = dead cell concentration, mg/L

Viable cell balance around a reactor yields Eq. (9.46)

$$F \times 0 - F\,[X_V] + \mu\,[X_V]\;V - \gamma\,[X_V]\;V - b\,[X_V]\;V = 0. \tag{9.46}$$

Inflow Rate, Outflow Rate, Growth Rate, Death Rate, Decay Rate

Simplification of Eq. (9.46) results in

$$\mu = \frac{1}{\tau} + \gamma + b. \tag{9.47}$$

where $\tau = V/F$ = detention time/space time/residence time/hydraulic retention time (HRT).

According to the Monod equation, Eq. (9.36).

$$\mu = \frac{\mu_m[S]}{K_s + [S]}.$$

Combining Eqs. (9.36) and (9.47) and rearranging the resulting equation one obtains Eq. (9.48)

$$[S] = \frac{K_s\left[(1/\tau) + \gamma + b\right]}{\mu_m - \left[(1/\tau) + \gamma + b\right]}. \tag{9.48}$$

From Eq. (9.48) it appears that for a specific value of τ the pollutant concentration $[S]$ in an effluent is independent of $[S]_0$, that is, the influent pollutant concentration. But it should be noted here that the kinetic parameters μ_m, K_s, γ and b depend on $[S]_0$, hence $[S]$ indirectly depends on $[S]_0$. Therefore before proceeding with the design calculations of a CMAL it would be necessary to estimate experimentally the kinetic parameter using the influent to be treated under the desired environmental condition.

Eq. (9.48) is rearranged to obtain suitable equations for evaluation of residence time τ and reactor volume V as shown hereunder.

$$\tau = \frac{V}{F} = \frac{K_s + [S]}{[S]\;(\mu_m - \gamma - b) - K_s(\gamma + b)} \tag{9.49}$$

$$\text{and} \quad V = \frac{F\{K_s + [S]\}}{[S]\;(\mu_m - \gamma - b) - K_s\;(\gamma + b)}. \tag{9.50}$$

Examination of Eq. (9.48) reveals that the pollutant concentration $[S]$ in a CMAL effluent would be minimum for a specific set of kinetic parameters and a large value of τ, that is,

$$\frac{1}{\tau} \approx 0.$$

The resulting expression for $[S]_{min}$ is

$$[S]_{\min} = \frac{K_s\ (\gamma + b)}{\mu_m\ - (\gamma + b)} \tag{9.51}$$

This implies that if $[S]_{\min} > [S]_{desired}$ then it would not be possible to achieve the $[S]_{desired}$ by using a single CMAL. In such a situation one should envisage installing two or more CMALs operating in series and design those.

When $[S]$ is replaced by $[S]_0$ in Eq. (9.49), the modified expression of τ is represented by the symbol $\tau_{\min}$ as shown below

$$\tau_{\min} = \frac{K_S + [S]_0}{[S]_0\ (\mu_m - \gamma - b) - K_S\ (\gamma + b)} \tag{9.52}$$

Equation (9.52) signifies that if a reactor is operated at $\tau_{\min}$ the pollutant concentration at the reactor outlet would be the same as that at its inlet. In other words, under this condition there would be no abatement of the pollutants in a CMAL. If a reactor is operated at the space time $\tau_{\min}$, gradually all the microbes present in a CMAL would be washed out of the unit and hence the biological (pollutant abatement) process would come to its end.

In actual practice there is always some flow fluctuation of the influent. To take care of such flow fluctuations and to safeguard against a CMAL slipping into the 'washout' state, the thumb rule used for estimation of a CMAL volume is to assume $\tau_{actual} \geq 10\tau_{\min}$.

It is essential that the biomass (organisms) produced in a CMAL be separated from the treated effluent by settling prior to its final discharge. To achieve this the practice is to have a actual $\tau_{actual} \geq 5$ days. This would enable the organisms produced to form flocs, which would settle easily.

CMAL design equations for treatment of waste water containing dissolved and suspended organics as well as inert solids have also been formulated and reported in literature.

9.9.2.2 CMAL Oxygen Demand

For aerobic treatment of biodegradable pollutants it is essential that an adequate amount of oxygen should be supplied to a CMAL. With this end in view the theoretical oxygen demand needs to be estimated.

The following derivation of an expression for the theoretical oxygen demand is based on the assumptions listed below :

1. The influent contains only soluble biodegradable pollutants.
2. About 50% of the pollutants abated in a CMAL is converted to new organisms and the remaining portion is oxidized to meet energy need.
3. The pollutant (substrate) concentrations is expressed in terms of mg BOD/L.
4. The influent does not contain any organism.

BOD balance around a CMAL leads to Eq. (9.53)

$$F\,[S]_0 - F\,[S] \quad - F\beta\,[X] \quad = RO_2 \tag{9.53}$$

Inflow BOD	Outflow BOD	BOD equivalent to microbe produced.	Theoretical oxygen demand

where β = BOD equivalent per unit mass of organisms, mg BOD/mg of cell.

$[X]$ = concentration of organisms present in the treated effluent, mg/L,

RO_2 = Oxygen utilization rate under steady state condition, mg/hr.

Since $[X] = [X_V] + [X_d]$, to obtain an expression for $[X]$, it is necessary to derive suitable expression for $[X_V]$ and $[X_d]$ in terms of the BOD removal rate in CMAL. Such expressions may be derived by writing mass balance equations for viable and dead cells across a CMAL.

The rate of viable cell growth per unit CMAL volume may be expressed as in Eq. (9.54)

$$r_{G,X_V} = \mu[X_V] = \frac{yF\{[S]_0 - [S]\}}{V} = \frac{y\,\{[S]_0 - [S]\}}{\tau} \tag{9.54}$$

Rearrangement of Eq. (9.54) and combination of the same with Eq. (9.47) leads to an expression for $[X_V]$.

$$[X_V] = \frac{y\,\{[S]_0 - [S]\}}{\tau\,\mu} = \frac{y\,\{[S]_0 - [S]\}}{1 + \gamma\tau + b\tau} \tag{9.55}$$

Mass balance of dead cells around of CMAL results in the following equation :

$$F \times 0 - F\,[X_d] + \gamma[X_V]\,V - b\,[X_d]\,V = 0 \tag{9.56}$$

Inflow Outflow Generation Decay

Combining Eqs. (9.55) and (9.56) and rearranging the same, one obtains an expression for $[X_d]$ as,

$$[X_d] = \frac{\gamma\tau\,[X_v]}{1 + b\tau} = \frac{\gamma\tau\;y\;\{[S]_0 - [S]\}}{(1 + b\tau)\;(1 + \gamma\tau + b\tau)}. \tag{9.57}$$

The following expression for $[X]$ is obtained by combining Eqs. (9.55) and (9.57)

$$[X] = [X_v] + [X_d] = \frac{y\{[S]_0 - [S]\}}{1 + b\tau}. \tag{9.58}$$

Finally an expression for RO_2 (the theoretical oxygen demand) for a CMAL treating an influent containing only dissolve biodegradables is obtained by substituting Eq. (9.58) in (9.53) and rearranging the same.

$$RO_2 = \frac{F\{[S]_0 - [S]\}\;(1 + b\tau - \beta y)}{1 + b\tau}. \tag{9.59}$$

Since during operation of a CMAL there may be shock flow changes as well as organic load changes, provision for oxygen (air) supply should be made so that the actual oxygen transfer rate is about 40-50 percent more than the theoretically estimated oxygen demand.

It must be pointed out here that oxygen is transferred to the waste water pool in a CMAL by dispersing atmospheric air with the help of a suitable device. The extent of oxygen transferred to water from that supplied air depends on the efficiency of the aeration system as well as on the pool temperature.

The design and performance parameters of aerated lagoons are listed in Table 9.9.

Table 9.9 : Design and Performance Parameters of Completely Mixed Aerated Lagoons (CMAL)

Depth	2 to 6 m.
Space Time	5 days or more. When an influent contains both dissolved and suspended organics it may be 10 days or more.
Influent BOD	Soluble BOD 200 – 500 mg/L. However, a CMAL may be used even when BOD > 500 mg/L. .
BOD Removal Efficiency	60–90%
Power Requirement	0.01-0.012 kW/m^3
Organic Loading	About 0.08 kg BOD/M^3 day
Oxygen Requirement	0.7 to 1.4 times the BOD removed.

The merits of aerated lagoons over aerobic lagoons are :

1. Because of forced aeration dissolved oxygen concentration in a CMAL is higher than that in an aerobic lagoon and the microbes are well suspended. As a result the reaction rate (BOD removal rate) in such a lagoon is higher than that in an aerobic lagoon.
2. As a CMAL is much deeper than an aerobic lagoon less land (area) is required for teatment of a specific influent steam.
3. Higher flow rate of waste water and high strength waste water may be treated in these lagoons.
4. These are more resistant to organic and pH shock loads because of good mixing and longer residence time.
5. Because of forced aeration these act as cooling ponds. Hence, relatively hot wastewater streams may be treated in such lagoons.

The major drawbacks of these lagoons are :

1. There is no control over the microbe population (MLSS) in these lagoons.
2. If there be any large shock (flow) overloading of a CMAL, the BOD removal efficiency will decrease due to decrease in the residence time.
3. During winter because of cooling due to forced aeration the lagoon temperature would drop and hence BOD removal efficiency will decrease.

Example 9.4 : Completely Mixed Aerated Lagoon (CMAL)

A completely mixed aerated lagoon (CMAL) is to be designed for treating a waste water stream. Based on the wastewater characteristics and other data given below calculate

(i) reactor volume,

(ii) reactor surface area (assume a suitable lagoon depth, say, 3 m), and

(iii) air supply rate (assume oxygen transfer efficiency to be 20%)

Influent (suspended solid-free) rate = 150 m^3/hr,

influent BOD = 1200 mg/L,

Desired BOD removal = 75%

μ_m = 0.2 hr^{-1}, K_m = 100 mg BOD/L,

b = 0.002 hr^{-1}, γ = 0.001 hr^{-1}, y = 0.5

β = 1.25 mg BOD/mg cell.

Solution :

τ and τ_{min} are calculated using Eq. (9.49) and Eq. (9.52) respectively.

$$\tau = \frac{V}{F} = \frac{K_s + [S]}{[S]\ (\mu_m - \gamma - b) - K_s\ (\gamma + b)}$$

$$= \frac{100 + 0.25 \times 1200}{(0.25 \times 1200)\ (0.2 - 0.001 - 0.002) - 100\ (0.001 + 0.002)}$$

$$= \frac{400}{58.8} = 6.8 \text{ hr}.$$

$$\tau_{min} = \frac{K_s + [S]_0}{[S]_0(\mu_m - y - b) - K_s(\gamma + b)}$$

$$= \frac{100 + 1200}{1200(0.2 - 0.001 - 0.002) - 100(0.001 + 0.002)}$$

$$= \frac{1300}{236.1} = 5.5 \text{ hr}.$$

It is recommended that τ_{actual} should be equal to or more than 10 times τ_{min}.

Hence, $\tau_{actual} = 10 \times 5.5 = 55$ hrs

Since $\tau = \frac{V}{F}$

Lagoon volume, $V = \tau \times F = 55 \times 150 = 8250$ m^3

Assuming lagoon depth = 3 m.

Lagoon surface area, $A = \frac{V}{\text{Depth}} = \frac{8250 \text{ m}^3}{3 \text{ m}} = 2750 \text{ m}^2$

The theoretical oxygen required is calculated utilizing Eq. (9.59)

$$RO_2 = \frac{F\{[S]_0 - [S]\}\ (1 + b\tau - \beta y)}{1 + b\tau}$$

$$= \frac{150 \times 10^3\ (1200 - 0.25 \times 1200)\ (1 + 0.002 \times 55 - 1.25 \times 0.5)}{1 + 0.002 \times 55}$$

$$= \frac{65,475,000}{1.11} = 58,986,486 \text{ mg / hr}$$

$$= 58.986 \text{ kg / hr}$$

The recommended oxygen delivery rate is 1.4—1.5 times the theoretical one.

Oxygen transfer efficiency is given as 20 %

Hence oxygen to be supplied = $1.4 \times 58.986 / 0.2$

= 412.9 kg/hr.

Therefore, air supply rate should be

$$\frac{412.9}{0.21} = 1966 \ \text{kg/hr}.$$

9.9.3 Activated Sludge Unit

An activated sludge unit is somewhat similar to a a CMAL in construction. However, the treated effluent from an activated sludge unit containing suspended microbes as flocs is settled in a settler prior to its discharge. A part of the settled sludge is recycled to the reactor while the remaining portion is either disposed off as such or treated in an anaerobic unit. The process is schematically shown in Fig. 9.24. Since the sludge contains microbes, by varying the recycle stream flow rate, it is possible to regulate the microbe population in the reactor.

Activated sludge reactors are generally rectangular tanks made of concrete. However some are made of steel. Sometimes earthen basins are used. When air is used for reoxygenation open tanks are used, but when high purity oxygen is used for meeting the oxygen demand the reactors are closed tanks.

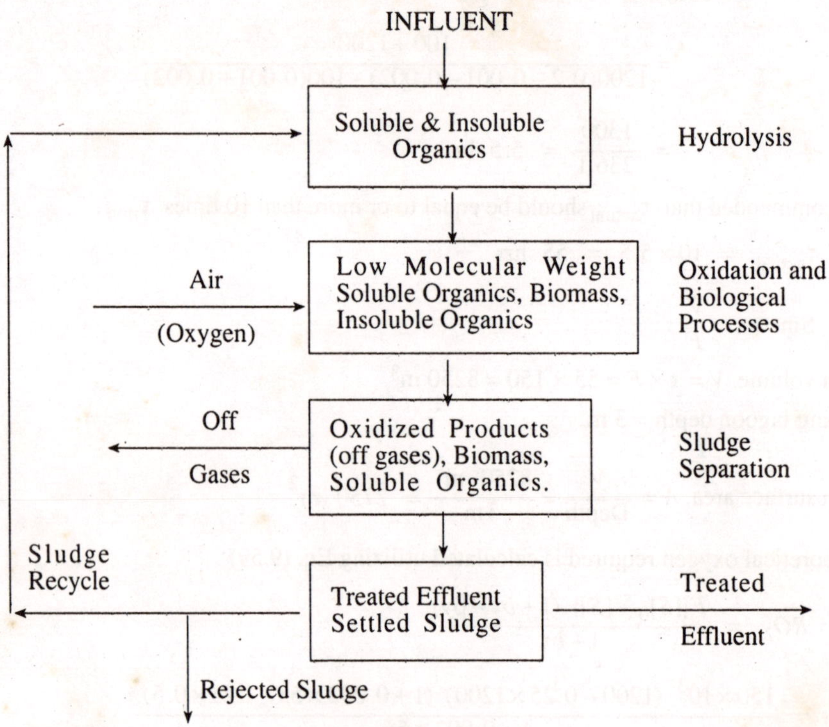

Fig. 9.24 : Schematic Representation of Activated Sludge Process.

The aeration device used in an activated sludge unit may be either a diffused aeration equipment or a turbine aeration equipment or a surface aerator. Manufacturers designate their equipment in terms of oxygen transfer capacity, expressed as kilogram oxygen transferred per kilowatt-hour of energy consumed (kg O_2/kWh).

Diffused aeration (submerged) units are of two types : (1) units producing fine bubbles, and (2) units producing coarse bubbles. For production of fine bubbles the diffusers are made of porous ceramic plates/domes/tubes or finely perforated metallic tubes/perforated pipes covered with a porous synthetic membrane. Filtered air is to be used in these devices in order to avoid plugging of the pores. Fine bubble diffusers have high oxygen transfer efficiency. Coarse bubble units are basically spargers having bigger holes. For these filtered air is not required.

Turbine aeration equipment are also submerged type. Such a device disperses compressed air fed through a ring sparger located beneath turbine blades. Rotating turbine blades shear the bubbles and circulate them.

A surface aerator may be either a draft tube type or a surface impeller type. These devices spray a large volume of liquid over the surface of a tank. The sprayed liquid drops, droplets and exposed turbulent liquid surface in contact with the atmospheric air get reoxygenated.

If the chosen aeration device does not keep the microbes suspended, then mechanical agitators are used. The effluent from an activated sludge unit is fed into a settler for separation of suspended biomass (microbes). The overflow from a well designed settler would be almost free from suspended solid particles.

Sometimes the influent to a reactor may contain only dissolved pollutants. Under such circumstances the suspended solids present in the reactor effluent would be microbe flocs. These solids are referred to as *Mixed Liquor Suspended Solids* (MLSS). The MLSS concentration in an activated sludge reactor would depend on the sludge recycle rate from the settler (F_r) and the solid content $[x]_r$ of the recycled sludge as well as on the biomass synthesized in the reactor itself. It should be pointed out here that if an influent contains suspended solids (both suspended organics and inert), then the solid particles present in the reactor would be made up of microbe flocs, unreacted solid organics and inert solids.

Several variations of activated sludge units (reactors) have been developed. These are classified based on the distribution patterns of the influent, the recycled sludge and location of aerators in a reactor. Some of these are briefly described hereunder and their sketches are shown in Fig. 9.25.

Conventional (Uniform Aeration) Activated Sludge Unit

In such a unit the entire quantity of the influent stream and the recycle sludge are introduced at the front (feed) end of the reactor. Aerators are uniformly distributed along the length of the reactor. The treated effluent flows out from the rear end of the reactor. In units of this type the oxygen demand is highest at the feed end (where the pollutant concentration is the highest) and lowest at the discharge end. Consequently progressively less and less oxygen is utilized lengthwise. This results in a loss of energy spent for aeration.

Tapered Aeration Activated Sludge Unit

As in a conventional unit, the influent and the recycle sludge are introduced at the front end of a tapered aeration unit. However, the aeration rate is lowered progressively from the feed end to the discharge end taking into consideration the reduction of oxygen demand lengthwise. In this way the energy loss due to escape of unutilized oxygen is reduced.

Step Feed Activated Sludge Unit

In step feed units the recycle sludge is introduced at the front end of a reactor, whereas the influent stream is distributed uniformly along the length of the reactor in steps. Because of stepwise distribution of influent the oxygen demand would be almost uniform along the length. Hence, in such units uniform aeration rate is maintained lengthwise.

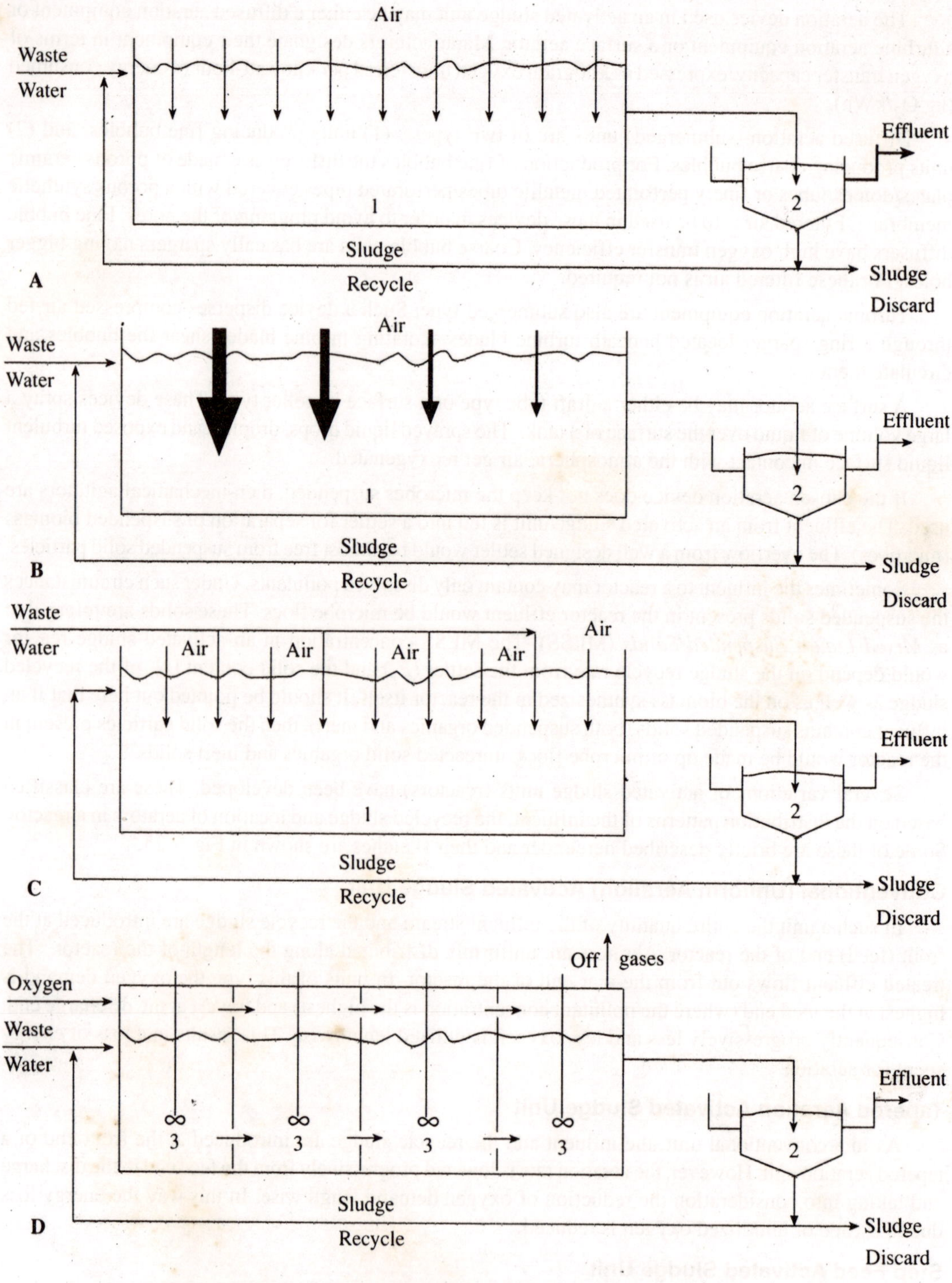

Fig. 9.25 : Different Types of Activated Sludge Units.

A. Conventional Unit, **B.** Tapered Aeration Unit,
C. Step Feed Unit, **D.** Pure Oxygen Unit.
1. Aeration Basin. **2.** Settler. **3.** Multistage Unit.

High Purity Oxygen Activated Sludge Unit

In the activated sludge units discussed earlier, atmospheric air is supplied as the source of oxygen. As air contains approximately twenty-one mole percent oxygen, the DO concentration would be low and hence the rate of oxidative reactions would be slow.

The total energy spent for aeration of the reactors would not be useful, as a large portion of it would go towards handling nitrogen accompanying the oxygen. Of course the nitrogen accompanying oxygen would keep the reactor contents agaitated while bubbling through the liquid pool. This helps in keeping the biomass suspended and increasing the oxygen transfer rate from the gas bubbles to the liquid pool.

In order to enhance the rate of oxidative reactions sometimes high purity oxygen is used in an activated sludge unit instead of air. The top of such a unit is kept gas-tight in order to prevent escape of oxygen. The gas finally leaving the reactor would contain mainly CO_2, water vapour, some O_2, some nitrogen and some partially oxidized organic compounds. As oxygen used is of high purity the DO concentration in the reactor liquor would be high. Consequently, the reaction rate would be high. As a result a smaller reactor would be required to achieve a desired degree of BOD reduction compared to that of a conventional aerated activated sludge unit. However, for operating a high purity oxygen unit an on site air-separator must be available for supplying high purity oxygen to the unit.

This process is carried out in a closed-top tank having several stages connected in series. The influent, recycle sludge and oxygen are fed to the first stage wherefrom the liquor containing suspended microbes and gas (oxygen) flow cocurrently to the subsequent stages. Each stage of the reactor is fitted with an agitator in order to keep the microbes suspended and a suitable device, such as a blower and a sparger for dispersion of oxygen in the liquor. From the last stage the off gas and the effluent along with microbe flocs are purged. The off gas is vented to the atmosphere and the effluent is fed to a settler. From the settler a portion of the sludge is recycled.

The influent to a high purity oxygen unit should be screened in order to avoid ingress of suspended solid particles.

The total cost of such a unit would include the cost of an air—separator.

Oxidation Ditch Activated Sludge Unit

An oxidation ditch is either a ring or an oval shaped channel. A sketch of an oxidation ditch is shown in Fig. 9.26. In such a channel circulation of the channel contents, aeration and mixing are achieved by

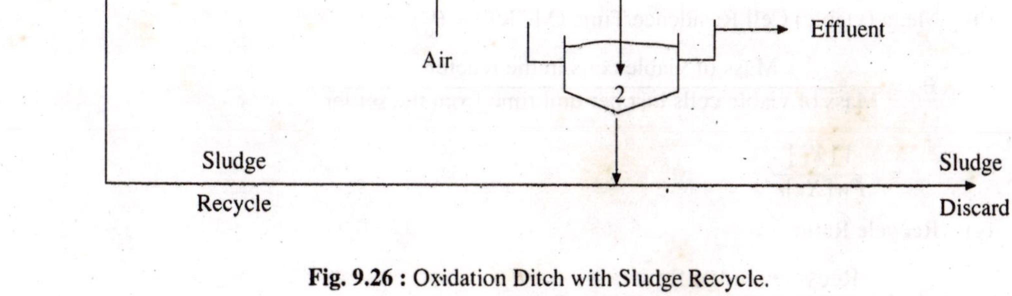

Fig. 9.26 : Oxidation Ditch with Sludge Recycle.

1. Oxidation Ditch **2.** Settler

using surface aerators. Screened influent and recycled sludge get diluted on entering the ditch. Flow in the channel is plug—flow type.

Figure 9.27 shows schematically an activated sludge unit.

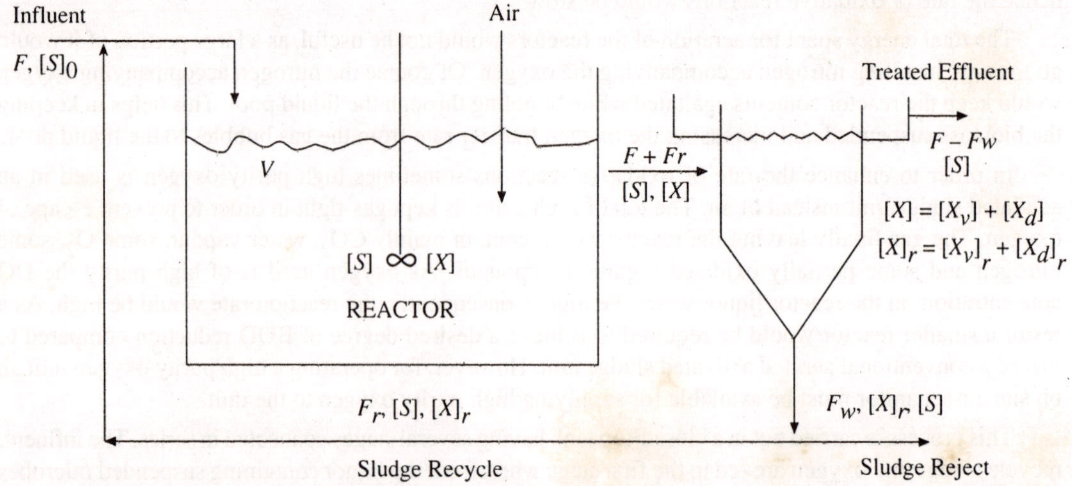

Fig. 9.27 : A Schematic Diagram of An Activated Sludge Unit.

F = waste water inflow rate, L/hr,

F_r = sludge recycle flow rate, L/hr,

F_w = rejected sludge flow rate, L/hr,

$[S]_o$ = substrate concentration in inflow, mg BOD/L,

$[S]$ = substrate concentration in treated effluent, mg BOD/L,

V = reactor volume, L,

$[X]$ = total cell concentration, mg/L,

$[X]_r$ = total cell concentration in recycle, mg/L,

$[X_d]$ = dead cell concentration, mg/L,

$[X_d]_r$ = dead cell concentration in recycle, mg/L,

$[X_v]$ = viable cell concentration, mg/L,

$[X_v]_r$ = viable cell concentration in recycle, mg/L.

The following parameters and factors are of importance in designing and operation of activated sludge units :

(a) Viable cell concentration in the reactor = $[X_v]$,

(b) Mean (viable) Cell Residence Time (MCRT) = θ_c

$$\theta_c = \frac{\text{Mass of viable cells in the reactor}}{\text{Mass of viable cells lost per unit time from the settler}}$$

$$= \frac{V[X_v]}{Fw[Xv]r},$$

(c) Recycle Ratio,

$$\alpha = \frac{\text{Recycle sludge flow rate}}{\text{Influent flow rate}} = \frac{F_r}{F},$$

(d) Space time, τ

$$\tau = \frac{\text{Reactor volume}}{\text{Influent flow rate}} = \frac{V}{F},$$

(e) Solid Residence Time, SRT

$$\text{SRT} = \frac{\text{Mass of solid in the reactor}}{\text{Mass of solid discarded per unit time}}$$

(f) $\frac{\overline{F}}{M}$ (Food to microbe) ratio

$$\frac{\overline{F}}{M} = \frac{\text{Mass of food (substrate) in the influent}}{\text{Mass of cells in the reactor}} = \frac{F[S]_0}{V(X)}$$

(g) Mixed Liquor Suspended Solids (MLSS)

MLSS = concentration of suspended solids in the reactor.

= [X],when the influent is free from suspended biomass, organics and inert solids.

9.9.3.1 Activated Sludge Unit Design Approach

The approach is based on the following assumptions / premise :

(a) the influent contains only soluble substrate;

(b) microbial concentration in the influent is negligible;

(c) steady state operation;

(d) the reactor contents are completely mixed and adequate supply of oxygen is provided;

(e) the settler overflow has negligible concentration of microbes; and

(f) no reaction takes place in the settler.

The symbols used in the following derivations are the same as those listed under Fig. 9.27.

Viable cell balance around a reactor leads to Eq. (9.60).

$$F_r[X_v]_r - (F+F_r)\ [X_v] + \mu[X_v]V - b[X_v]V - \gamma[X_v]V \doteq 0 \tag{9.60}$$

Inflow Outflow Net generation

Incorporation of $\alpha = \frac{F_r}{F}$ and $\tau = \frac{V}{F}$ in Eq. (9.60) and rearrangement of the same yields Eq. (9.61)

$$\mu = \frac{1}{\tau}\left\{(1+\alpha) - \alpha\ \frac{[X_v]_r}{[X_v]}\right\} + \gamma + b = \frac{G}{\tau} + \gamma + b \tag{9.61}$$

(9.58)

where, $G = 1 + \alpha - \alpha\ \frac{[X_v]_r}{[X_v]}$.

Viable cell balance around the settler succeeding the reactor results in Eq. (9.62)

$$(F+F_r)\ [X_v] - F_w[X_v]_r\ - F_r[X_v]_r - (F - F_w)\times 0 = 0 \tag{9.62}$$

Inflow Discard Recycle to reactor Outflow

Replacement of F_r by αF in Eq. (9.62) and rearrangement of the same leads to Eq. (9.63)

$$1+\alpha-\alpha\ \frac{[X_v]_r}{[X_v]}=\frac{F_w[X_v]_r}{F[X_v]}=G. \tag{9.63}$$

Modification of Eq. (9.63) yields Eq. (9.64).

$$G\ =\ \frac{F_w[X_v]_r}{F[X_v]}=\frac{V[X_v]}{F[X_v]}\Big/\frac{V[X_v]}{F_w[X_v]_r}$$

$$=\frac{\tau}{\theta_c}=\ 1+\alpha-\alpha\ \frac{[X_v]_r}{[X_v]}, \tag{9.64}$$

where θ_c = stands for MCRT as defined earlier.

Combining Eqs. (9.61) and (9.64) one obtains Eq. (9.65)

$$\mu=\frac{1}{\theta_c}+\gamma+b. \tag{9.65}$$

Rearrangement and further simplification of Eq. (9.64) yields Eq. (9.66)

$$\frac{F_w}{F}\ =\ \frac{\tau\alpha}{\theta_c(1+\alpha)-\tau}. \tag{9.66}$$

F_w/F represents the fraction of inflow discarded as sludge.

Combination of Eqs. (9.36) and (9.65) and rearrangement of the same results in the following expression for the substrate concentration [S] in the reactor effluent :

$$[S]\ =\ \frac{K_s\ \{(1/\theta_c)+\gamma+b\}}{\mu_m-\{(1/\theta_c)+\gamma+b\}}. \tag{9.67}$$

Rearrangement of Eq. (9.67) results in an expression for MCRT, i.e., θ_c.

$$\theta_c=\frac{K_s+[S]}{[S]\ (\mu_m-\gamma-b)-K_s\ (\gamma+b)}. \tag{9.68}$$

If θ_c be very large then the expression for [S] as in Eq. (9.67) reduces to

$$[S]=[S]_{\min}\ =\ \frac{K_s\ (\gamma+b)}{\mu_m-(\gamma+b)} \tag{9.69}$$

$[S]_{\min}$ stands for the minimum substrate concentration in an activated sludge unit effluent that can be achieved corresponding to a very large value of MCRT, (θ_c).

If [S] is replaced by $[S]_0$ in Eq. (9.68) the expression for θ_c becomes :

$$\theta_c\ =\ \theta_{c\min}=\frac{K_s+[S]_0}{[S]_0(\mu_m-\gamma-b)-K_s(\gamma+b)} \tag{9.70}$$

Eq. (9.70) implies that if an activated sludge unit is operated at $\theta_c = \theta_{c,\min}$, the substrate concentration at the reactor outlet will be the same as that at its inlet, that is, no pollutant abatement would take place. When an activated sludge unit is operated at $\theta_c \le \theta_{c,\min}$ 'wash out' would occur. Wash out in an activated sludge unit is not related to its space time, τ, so long as recycle takes place.

If τ be more than $\theta_{c,\min}$ and accidentally recycle stops, the reactor would get converted into a CMAL. Under such a situation 'wash out' would not occur.

In order to obtain a suitable expression for the space time, τ, and thereby to estimate the required reactor volume, V, it is necessary to formulate substrate and dead cell mass balance equations around a reactor as shown hereafter.

Substrate balance around a reactor yields Eq. (9.71) :

$$F[S]_0 + \alpha F[S] - (F+\alpha F)[S] + r_s V = 0 \tag{9.71}$$

In flow Outflow Conversion

where

$$-r_s = \frac{r_{G}, x_v}{y} = \frac{\mu[X_v]}{y} = \frac{(1/\theta_c + \gamma + b)\ [x_v]}{y}.$$

Re-arrangement of Eq. (9.71) yields the following expression for $[x_v]$,

$$[X_v] = \frac{y([S]_0 - [S]}{\mu(V/F)} = \frac{y([S]_0 - [S])}{(1/\theta_c + \gamma + b)\tau}. \tag{9.72}$$

Dead cell mass balance around a reactor would result in Eq. (9.73)

$$F \times 0 + \alpha\ F[x_d]_r - (F + \alpha F)\ [x_d] + \gamma[x_v]V - b[x_v]V = 0. \tag{9.73}$$

In flow Outflow Generation Decay

It is likely that the ratio $\frac{[x_d]r}{[x_d]}$ would be the same as the ratio of $\frac{[x_v]r}{[x_v]}$

Equation (9.73) is rearranged. In the rearranged equation the term,

$\frac{[x_d]r}{[x_d]}$ is replaced by. $\frac{[x_v]r}{[x_v]}$ The term $\frac{[x_v]r}{[x_v]}$ in the resulting equation is replaced by incorporating Eq. (9.64). Finally the following expression is obtained for $[x_d]$,

$$[x_d] = \frac{\gamma\tau[x_v]}{G + b\tau} = \frac{\gamma\tau[x_v]}{(1/\theta_c + b)\tau} = \frac{\gamma[x_v]}{1/\theta_c + b}. \tag{9.74}$$

Combination of Eq. (9.72) and (9.74) finally yields Eq. (9.75)

$$[x] = [x_v] + [x_d] = \frac{y([X]_0 - [S])}{(1/\theta_0 + b)\tau} \tag{9.75}$$

$$\text{Or, } [x]\tau = \frac{y([S]_o - [S]}{(1/\theta_c + b)} \tag{9.76}$$

In an activated sludge reactor if the influent does not contain any suspended solid, then the microbe mass concentration $[x]$ in it would be the same as its MLSS.

After evaluating $[x]\ \tau$ with the help of Eq. (9.76) a suitable value of $[x]$ is assumed and based on the same, τ is calculated. However, the calculated value of τ should not be less than $\theta_{c,\,min}$. Once τ is known the reactor volume is to be estimated using the relation

$$V = F\tau. \tag{9.77}$$

9.9.3.2 Activated Sludge Reactor Oxygen Demand Estimation

In an activated sludge unit oxygen is supplied to meet the quantity of oxygen required for carrying out the biochemical reactions. In order to obtain an expression for the quantity of oxygen required an oxygen balance equation has to be formulated around the reactor.

While formulating the equation it is assumed that the influent and the recycle stream do not contain any dissolved oxygen. The soluble substrate concentration and the cell mass concentration entering and leaving the reactor are expressed in terms of BOD.

The oxygen uptake in an activated sludge reactor goes to reduce the BOD of influent and the recycle stream. It has been assumed that the influent would contain only soluble substrate whereas the recycle would contain both soluble substrate and suspended microbes. The reactor effluent would contain both soluble substrate and microbes.

Hence the reactor oxygen demand would be equal to influent BOD plus recycle BOD minus effluent BOD.

$$\text{Oxygen Demand} = F\,[S]_0 + \alpha F\,\{[S]+\beta\,[X]_r\,\} - (F+\alpha F)\,\{[S] + \beta\,[X]\}, \tag{9.78}$$

where $[S]_0$ and $[S]$ are expressed in terms of mg BOD/L,

$[X]_r$ and $[X]$ are expressed in terms microbe mass per litre,

and β stands for BOD equivalent to a unit mass of microbes.

Replacing the term $\frac{[X]_r}{[X]}$ by $\frac{[Xv]_r}{[X_v]}$ in the expression for oxygen demand and combining the same with the Eqs. (9.64) and (9.75) the final expression for oxygen demand obtained is

$$\text{Oxygen demand} = \frac{F([S]_0 - [S])\;(1 + b\theta_c - \beta y)}{1 + b\theta_c}. \tag{9.79}$$

It is to be borne in mind that occasionally there may be an increase in the hydraulic load as well as the organic load of an activated sludge reactor. To take care of such situations the actual amount of oxygen to be made available to an activated sludge reactor should be 40–50 per cent more than that calculated with the help of Eq. (9.79)

Normally an activated sludge unit is designed so as to achieve a desired effluent BOD for a specified influent flow rate and BOD load. However, sometimes the objective may be to achieve a rather low effluent BOD. Such an unit is referred to as an Extended Aeration Unit. The operating parameters of such units are high MLSS, low F/M ratio and large hydraulic residence time. Sometimes the objective is to operate an activated sludge unit at a high throughput without paying proper attention to the effluent quality, these units are referred to as High Rate Units. These are operated at a low MLSS, high F/M ratio, shorter HRT and high loading.

In Table 9.10 the design and performance parameter ranges of the different types of activated sludge units are listed.

The basic advantage of an activated sludge unit over an aerated lagoon is its smaller reactor size for the same capacity and hence the energy requirement per unit volume of influent treated is less.

Activated sludge units require closer control on MLSS and oxygen supply. For proper operation of such units skilled manpower is required. These units are vulnerable to hydraulic , organic and toxic shock loads because of their smaller reactor size.

Table 9.10 : Design and Performance Parameter Ranges of Activated Sludge Units

Parameters	Conventional Unit	Extended Aeration Unit	High Rate Unit	High Purity Oxygen Unit
pH	6.5–9	6.5–9	6.5–9	6.5–9
MCRT, θ_c, days	3–15	20–30	< 3	3–15
τ, hour	3–15	≈ 24	≈ 0.5	1-3
MLSS, mg/L	1500–3000	5000–7000	500–1500	4000–8000
Recycle ratio, α	0.1–0.3	0.75–1.5	0.25–1	0.25–0.5
$\overline{F}/M$	0.2–0.5	< 0.1	0.5–1.5	0.5–1
BOD removal	70–95%	95–98%	50–75%	85–95%
Depth, m (a) with air diffuser	3–5			
(b) with surface aerator	1–3			
Width/Depth	1–2.2			
BOD loading kg BOD/day/1000 m^3	400–800		800–1600	1600–3200
Air required Nm^3/kg BOD removed	50–100		25–50	
DO mg/L	2			4–8

Example 9.5 : Completely Mixed Activated Sludge (CMAS) Unit

Calculate the following for a proposed completely mixed activated sludge (CMAS) unit for treatment of a waste water stream containing only soluble substrate :

(a) reactor volume, (b) recycle ratio,

(c) reactor oxygen demand (d) settler underflow rate.

The waste water characteristics and other data to be used for design purpose are

influent rate = 200 m^3/hr.

Influent BOD = 1000 mg/L,

Treated effluent BOD desired = 20 mg/L,

Reactor MLSS = 3000 mg/L,

Settler sludge (biomass) concentration = 10,000 mg/L

$\mu_m = 0.40$ hr^{-1} K_s = 120 mg BOD/L

$b = 0.004$ hr^{-1}, γ = 0.003 hr^{-1}

$y = 0.45$, β = 1.2 mg BOD/mg cell.

Solution :

The equations and relations listed hereunder are to be used for solving this example,

$$\theta_c = \frac{K_s + [S]}{[S]\ (\mu_m - \gamma - b) - K_s(\gamma + b)}$$

$$3 < \theta_c < 15$$

$$\theta_{c,\min} = \frac{K_s + [S]_0}{[S]_0(\mu_m - \gamma - b) - K_s\ (\gamma + b)}$$

$$[S] = \frac{K_s\{1/\theta_c) + \gamma + b\}}{\mu_m - \{(1/\theta_c) + \gamma + b\}}$$

$$[x]\tau = \frac{y([S]_0 - [S])}{(1/\theta_c + b)}$$

$$or,\ \tau = \frac{y([S]_0 - [S])}{[X]\ (1/\theta_c + b)}$$

$$\tau > \theta_{c,\min}$$

$$V = F\tau$$

$$\alpha = \frac{1 - (\tau/\theta_c)}{([X]_r/[X]) - 1}$$

$$\frac{F_w}{F} = \frac{\tau\ \alpha}{\theta_c(1+\alpha) - \tau}$$

$$\text{Reactor oxygen demand} = \frac{F([S]_0 - [S])(1 + b\theta_c - \beta y)}{1 + b\theta_c}$$

The data supplied along with the example are substituted in the listed equations for evaluation of V, α, oxygen demand and settler underflow (F_w).

$$\theta_c = \frac{120 + 20}{20(0.4 - 0.003 - 0.004) - 120(0.003 + 0.004)}$$

$$= 19.94 \text{ hr.}$$

Calculated θ_c being less than 3 days, it is taken as 4 days.

$$[S] = \frac{120(1/96 + 0.003 + 0.004)}{0.4 - (1/96 + 0.003 + 0.004)} = 5.46 \text{mg/L}.$$

$$\theta_{c,\ \min} = \frac{120 + 1000}{1000(0.4 - 0.003 - 0.004) - 120(0.003 + 0.004)}$$

$$= 2.856 \text{ hr.}$$

$$\tau = \frac{0.45(1000 - 5.46)}{3000(\frac{1}{96} + 0.004)} = 10.348 \text{ hr.}$$

Hence, $\tau > \theta_{c,\ \min}$

$$V = F\tau = 200 \times 10.348 = 2070 \text{ m}^3$$

$$\alpha = \frac{1-(\tau/\theta_c)}{([X]_r/[X])-1}$$

$$= \frac{1-(10.348/96)}{(10000/3000)-1} = 0.382$$

$$F_w = \frac{F\alpha\tau}{\theta_c(1+\alpha)-\tau}$$

$$= \frac{200 \times 0.382 \times 10.348}{96(1+0.782)-10.348} = 6.46 \ \text{m}^3/\text{hr}.$$

$$\text{Theoretical oxygen demand} = \frac{F([S]_0-[S])\ (1+b\theta_c-\beta y)}{1+b\theta_c}$$

$$= \frac{200 \times 10^3 (1000-5.46)\ (1+0.004 \times 96 - 1.2 \times 0.45)}{1+0.004 \times 96}$$

= 121,299,387 mg/hr

= 121.3 kg/hr.

To take care of the occasional overloads, the actual oxygen demand should be estimated as 1.4 to 1.5 times the theoretical oxygen demand.

9.9.4 Trickling Filter

A trickling filter is a packed bed in which aerobic microbes form slime layers over the packing surfaces. Hence it is a fixed film reactor. An influent waste water stream is fed at the top of the bed which trickles down the slime covered packing surfaces. Air flows up through the void spaces in between the packings due to a natural draft. Since it is a packed bed waste water containing only dissolved biodegradable organics can be treated in a trickling filter. The feed must be free from suspended organics and inorganics.

As waste water containing pollutants flows downwards over the packing surfaces covered with a mixed population of aerobic microbe in the presence of an upflowing air stream, degradation of dissolved organics takes place. During the process new microbes produced thickens the slime layers, which peel off time to time and flow down along with the liquid flowing down. The treated waste water mixed with slime emerging from the packed bed collects in an under-drain system. A portion of the treated effluent may be recycled to the trickling filter mixed with the influent and the rest is discharged. The collected sludge is removed from the under-drain system periodically.

Previously spherical stones were used as packings. Nowadays mainly plastic packings are being used.

Stone packing size ranges from 5 cm to 10 cm in diameter having an approximate specific surface area of 30 m^2/m^3 and a void fraction around 50%. Smaller packings provide larger specific surface area but lower void fraction. Because of lower void fraction these are susceptible to clogging. The containment structure of a stone packed trickling filter is made of either reinforced concrete or such other strong material. The height of a packed bed normally does not exceed 2 m. The bed cross section is circular. The influent (as such or mixed with recycle) is distributed (at the top) either with a one or a two arm distributor which rotate at a rate of one revolution in about 10 minutes. The motion is caused by the reaction of the influent flowing out. Because of this low speed of rotation the liquid dosing is intermittent. As a result flooding of the bed does not occur in spite of low void fraction.

Plastic media may be either formed packings or structured modular packings. The formed packings are dumped inside a filter, whereas structured packings are generally stacked. Modules of structured packings are made up of thin plastic corrugated sheets placed parallel to one another and held together. Plastic packings have large specific surface area (98–340 m^2/m^3) and void fraction 90% or more. Since plastic is much lighter than stone, the containment structure would be lighter. The packed bed height may be 6–10 m. Since the void fraction is high even at a high hydraulic loading the air flow would not get hampered. The cross-section of a plastic media filled trickling filter may be either circular or rectangular. A circular cross-section bed may have either a four-arm type rotary liquid distributor or a fixed nozzle type distributor. A rectangular cross-section bed should have a fixed nozzle type distributor.

9.9.4.1 Trickling Filter Design Approach

Figure 9.28 shows a schematic diagram of a trickling filter.

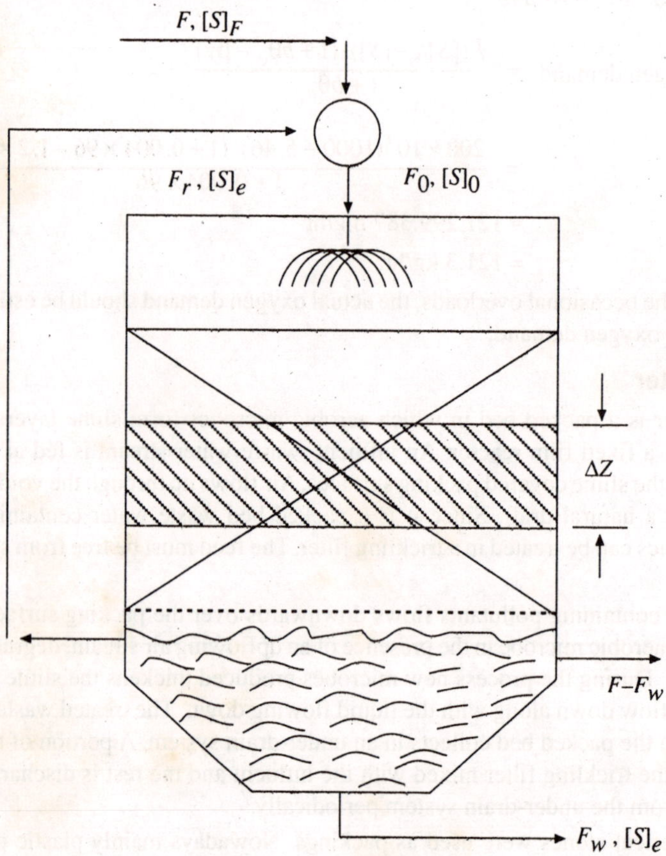

Fig. 9.28 : Diagram of a Trickling Filter.

F = influent flow rate, L/hr

F_r = recycle flow rate, L/hr

F_0 = $F + F_r = F + \alpha F$, L/hr

F_w = sludge flow rate, L/hr

L = packed height, m

$[S]_e$ = pollutant concentration in treated effluent, mg BOD/lit

$[S]_F$ = pollutant concentration in influent, mg BOD/lit

$[S]_0$ = pollutant concentration in mixed feed,

$$= \frac{F[S]_F + \alpha F[S]_e}{Fo} = \frac{[S]_F + \alpha[S]_e}{1+\alpha} \quad \frac{mg\ BOD}{L} \tag{9.80}$$

For designing a trickling filter an empirical equation, Eq. (9.81) correlating the pollutant concentration [S] with bed depth Z is used along with Eq. (9.82).

$$\frac{[S]}{[S]_0} = e^{-KZ} \tag{9.81}$$

$$\text{and} \quad K = K'\ [S]_0{}^m \left(\frac{F_0}{A}\right)^n \tag{9.82}$$

where A = cross-sectional area of a filter, m^2

$\frac{F_0}{A}$ Hydraulic loading expressed in $\frac{m^3}{m^2 day}$

K', m and n are empirical constants. Their numerical values depend on the type of packings used, the chemical nature of the pollutants present in a waste water stream, the initial concentration of the pollutants $[S]_0$ and the operating temperature. In a given situation the values of K', m and n should be obtained experimentally. Some typical values of K', m and n as reported in literature for plastic packings are :

K' = 75,100

m = – 0.40, –0.45

n = – 0.55, –0.65

Combining Eqs. (9.81) and (9.82) and noting that $[S] = [S]_e$ corresponding to $Z = L$ the final equation obtained is

$$\frac{[S]_e}{[S]_0} = e^{-K'[S]_0{}^m \left\{\frac{F(1+\alpha)}{A}\right\}^n .L} \tag{9.83}$$

Substitution of $[S]_0$ by $\frac{[S]_F + \alpha[S]_e}{1+\alpha}$ in Eq. (9.83) and rearrangement of the same yields Eq. [9.84]

$$L = \frac{In \dfrac{[S]_F + \alpha[S]_e}{[S]_e\ (1+\alpha)}}{K'\left\{\dfrac{[S]_F + \alpha[S]_e}{1+\alpha}\right\}^m \left\{\dfrac{F(1+\alpha)}{A}\right\}^n}. \tag{9.84}$$

In the absence of any recycle, that is, $\alpha = 0$, the Eq. (9.84) reduces to Eq. (9.85)

$$L = \frac{In \dfrac{[S]_F}{[S]_e}}{K'[S]_F^m \left(\dfrac{F}{A}\right)^n} \tag{9.85}$$

While estimating L utilizing either Eq. (9.84) or (9.85), the following are to be borne in mind :

1. The hydraulic loading, F_0/A or F/A can be varied over a limited range only. At a relatively low loading some portions of a filter bed may be dry and hence ineffective. At some high loading the bed may get flooded as a result of which it may become inoperative.

2. The upper limit of a packed bed height for stone packings is generally 2 m and that for plastic packings is 10 m.
3. The actual BOD removal efficiency may be less than the theoretical one because of channelling and / or excessive growth of slime layers.

In a given situation, that is, for specified values of $[S]_F$, $[S]_e$ and F the dimensions of a trickling filter may be estimated through the following steps :

(i) Select a packing medium and size and ascertain its characteristics, namely, specific surface area, void fraction and hydraulic loading limits.

(ii) Estimate of the numerical values of the empirical constants K', m and n either based on the published information or by experimental trials.

(iii) Assume a suitable value of the recycle ratio.

(iv) Calculate the packing height using Eq. (9.84) or (9.85) assuming a hydraulic loading within the range ascertained in step (1) above.

(v) Calculate the tower cross section area A as

$$A = \frac{F\ (1+\alpha)}{\text{Hydraulic loading}}\ .$$

(vi) Repeat steps (4) and (5) for some other assumed values of the hydraulic loading and the recycle ratio.

(vii) Finally the filter dimensions are optimized from the total cost (initial cost and operating cost) point of view.

The plus points of a trickling filter are its simple construction and operation. It may be used for treatment of specific pollutants with proper organisms. It can be used for nitrification. Removal of biomass from the effluent is easy. It is resistant to some extent to toxic pollutants, if present in waste water, because of short residence time. The organisms present on the surface of slime layers are only affected. However, prolonged exposure of the slime layers to toxic substances may affect the organisms seriously. It may be used as a roughing filter at a high hydraulic loading.

Trickling filters have the following limitations :

1. The empirical constants K', m and n being temperature dependent the performance gets affected due to changes in ambient temperature.
2. Its performance is susceptible to shock load.
3. It may take a long time to recover after an upset.
4. There may be vector and odour problems.
5. There is not much of control over the quality of the treated effluent.
6. As there is no control over the aeration rate, treatment of high BOD influent may lead to anaerobic condition at the top of a trickling filter.

The design and performance parameters of trickling filters are listed in Table 9.11.

Table 9.11 : Design and Performance Parameters of Trickling Filters

Parameter	Packing Type		
	Stone	Plastic	
		Formed	Structured module
Size, cm	2.5–12.5		61×61×122
Specific surface area, m^2/m^3	40–60	98–150	90–140
Void fraction, %	40–60	70–80	94–97
Bed depth, m	1–2.4	3–10	3–10
Recycle ratio	0-2	1–2	1–2
Hydraulic loading #	1–15		20–300
BOD removal efficiency, %	50–90	60–90	60–95

$\# \quad \dfrac{\text{m}^3 \text{of influent and recycle / day}}{\text{m}^2 \text{of bed cross section}}$

Example 9.6 : Trickling Filter

It is proposed to treat a waste water stream having a BOD concentration of 450 mg/L in a trickling filter so as to produce a treated effluent having 30 mg/L of BOD. The anticipated average flow rate is 65 m^3/hr. The plastic media to be used may have a minimum and maximum allowable hydraulic loading rate of 1.4 m^3/m^2 hr. and 10.8 m^3/m^2 hr. respectively. Experimental trials have revealed that the following kinetic parameter values may be used for design purpose :

$K' = 120$ (when $[S]$ is expressed in mg/L and F/A in m^3/m^2 day) and

$m = -0.4$

$n = -0.6$

Find suitable dimensions of a trickling filter assuming a hydraulic loading rate of 7.58 m^3/m^2 hr and (i) without any recycle, (ii) with a recycle ratio of 1.2.

Solution :

The length L of a trickling filter may be calculated using Eq. (9.84) :

$$L = \frac{In \dfrac{[S]_F + \alpha[S]_e}{[S]_e \ (1+\alpha)}}{K' \left(\dfrac{[S]_F + \alpha[S]_e}{1+\alpha}\right)^m \left(\dfrac{F(1+\alpha)}{A}\right)^n}$$

(i) To find L corresponding to zero recycle, Eq. (9.84) is simplified to Eq. (9.85).

$$L = \frac{In\dfrac{[S]_F}{[S]_e}}{K'[S]_F^m\left(\dfrac{F}{A}\right)^n}$$

$$= \frac{In\dfrac{450}{30}}{120(450)^{-0.4}(7.58\times 24)^{-0.6}}$$

$$= 5.898 \text{ m.}$$

Corresponding tower cross-sectional area :

$$A = \frac{F}{\text{Hydraulic loading rate}}$$

$$\frac{65\ m^3/hr}{7.58\ m^3/m^2\ hr} = 8.575\ m^2$$

Hence, tower diameter, D = 2.595 m

$$\approx 2.6\ m.$$

(ii) Corresponding to $\alpha = 1.2$

$$L = \frac{In\dfrac{[S]_F+\alpha[S]e}{[S]e\ (1+\alpha)}}{K'\left(\dfrac{[S]_F+\alpha[S]e}{1+\alpha}\right)^m\left(\dfrac{F(1+\alpha)}{A}\right)^n}$$

$$= \frac{In\dfrac{450+1.2\times 30}{30(1+1.2)}}{120\left(\dfrac{450+1.2\times 30}{1+1.2}\right)^{-0.4}\times(7.58\times 24)^{-0.6}}$$

$$= \frac{1.9965}{0.6103} = 3.27 \text{ m.}$$

Corresponding tower cross –sectional area :

$$A = \frac{F(1+\alpha)}{\text{Hydraulic loading rate}}$$

$$= \frac{65(1+1.2)\text{m}^3/\text{hr}}{7.58\text{m}^3/\text{m}^2\text{hr.}} = 18.865\ \text{m}^2$$

Hence, tower diameter, D = 3.849 m

$$\approx 3.85 \text{ m.}$$

9.9.5 Rotating Biological Contractor (RBC)

It is another type of fixed film aerobic reactor. In a trickling filter the microbe film coated packings are stationary, whereas in a rotating biological contactor (RBC) the surfaces coated with microbes rotate.

In an RBC some suspended microbes are also present. An RBC is made up of closely spaced circular disks mounted on a common horizontal shaft, which is placed in a tank containing waste water having dissolved biodegradable organics. The shaft is placed near or touching waste water–air-free surface in the tank. It rotates slowly at a constant speed thereby allowing any point on a disk to be alternately submerged into the waste water pool and exposed to air.

The tanks are made of concrete or steel and the disks are made of polystyrene or polyvinyl chloride or polyethylene. The disks are configured and corrugated as a result of which the available surface area and structural stability of the disks increase. The shaft carrying the disks may be rotated either mechanically or with the help of compressed air. In air driven units, cups (made of the same material as the disks) are attached to the perimeter of the disks. Air from a compressor is released into the submerged cups through air headers; the entrapped air in the submerged cups exerts a buoyant force on the assembly and causes the shaft to rotate.

In an RBC as waste water containing dissolved pollutants flows through, the slimy microbes covering the surfaces of the disks assimilate the pollutants. Rotations of disks impart a shear force to the microbe films covering the surfaces of the disks and thereby keep their thickness relatively constant. The acting shear force sloughs off some portions of the microbe films from the disk surfaces from time to time.

Due to rotation of the disks, portions of the disk surfaces carrying wet slime layers emerge from the liquid pool and come in contact with air, as a result of which the wet surfaces get reoxygenated. Some air gets entrapped from the atmosphere on the configurations and corrugations on exposed surfaces of the disks. As those portions get resubmerged oxygen transfer to the waste water pool takes place. The turbulence caused to the liquid pool due to rotation of the disks helps oxygen transfer to the liquid bulk. The rotation also helps to keep the sloughed organisms in suspension and thereby facilitate their participation in the biochemical reactions. The suspended organisms are ultimately carried away by the effluent leaving an RBC unit. The effluents from such units are clarified in a settler before final discharge.

The presence of a large amount of biomasses on the surfaces of the disks and those in suspension enables such units to withstand hydraulic and organic shock loads. This units are placed in series whereby short-circuiting is prevented. The flow may be either parallel to the shafts or perpendicular to them. The units (in series) are separated from one another by baffles. Parallel trains are installed so that some units may be isolated without disturbing the entire process. Figure 9.29 shows schematically some of the alternate arrangements of RBC units. Step feeding of the stages is also practised.

Overloading of the first stage may result in its low DO (dissolved oxygen) concentration. As a consequence its performance would be poor. To overcome such a situation the following steps may be taken :

1. reduction of organic loading to the first stage,
2. removal of the baffle between the first and the second stage,
3. step feeding of the assembly,
4. recycling a portion of the treated effluent from the last stage to the first stage,
5. supplying supplementary air to the first stage.

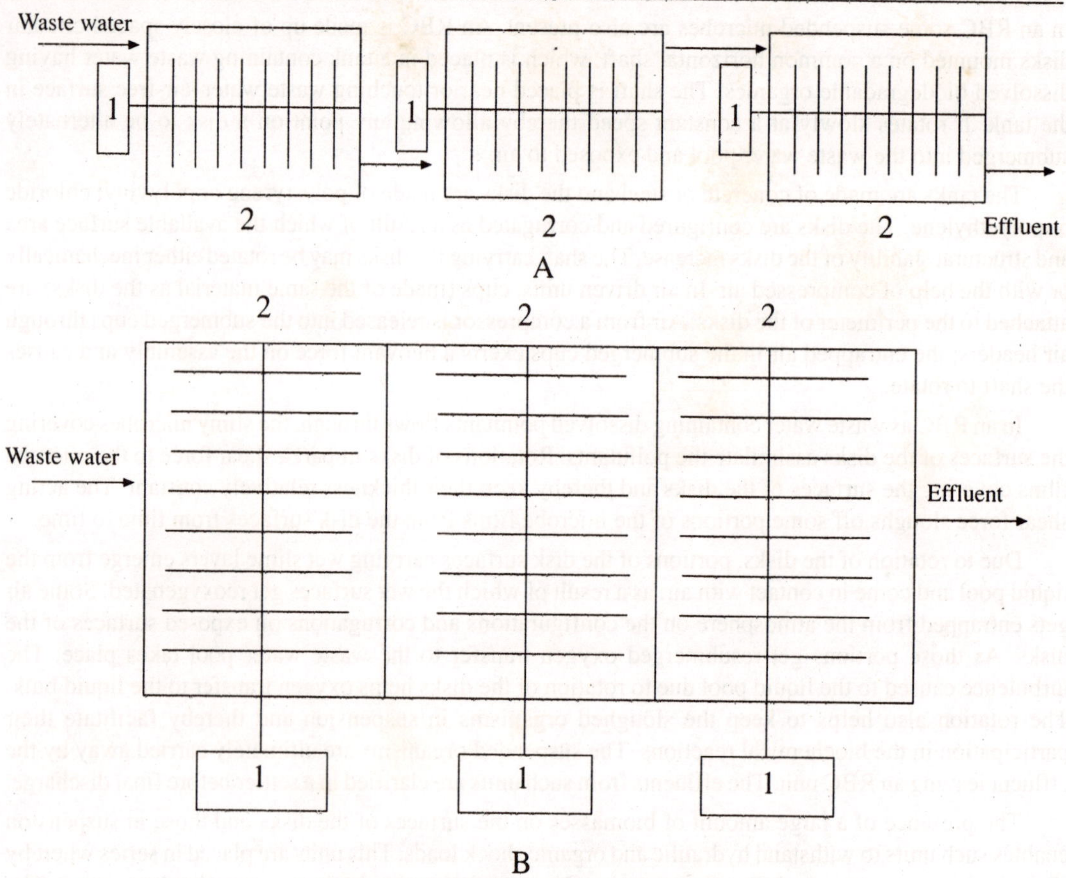

Fig. 9.29 : RBC Units Connected in Series.

A. Waste water Flow Parallel to the Shaft
B. Waste water Flow Perpendicular to the Shaft
1. Drive Motor
2. Disk Housing

9.9.5.1 RBC Design Approach

For designing a rotating biological contactor the factors to be considered are : (i) the influent characteristics, (ii) the desired effluent characteristics, (iii) organic loading, and (iv) number of stages to be installed.

In an RBC aerobic biodegradation of organic substrate (pollutants) takes place in various ways. When a portion of a disk surface emerges from the water pool in an RBC, a thin film of water covers the slime layers. The water film gets reoxygenated. Through the water film both oxygen and solute (pollutants) diffuse towards the slime surface where biochemical reactions take place. The rate of reaction depends on the rate of diffusion. As the disk rotates, the solute concentration in the exposed film decreases and the DO concentration increases. In the liquid pool, biochemical reactions occur on the submerged portion of the slime covered disk surface. The microbial growth sheared off from the surfaces of the disks due to rotation and kept in suspension also takes part in the biochemical reactions.

Scientists have tried to model the various stages of the complex process taking into account both external and internal mass transfer resistances as well as participation of both fixed film and suspended organisms in the biochemical reactions. Some of the equations developed are complicated and it is very difficult, if not impossible, to evaluate the associated constants using experimental data. Because of these drawbacks those equations are not useful from design point of view at present.

Based on the following simplifying assumptions a model of the RBC has been developed :

(i) Steady state condition prevails in an RBC. This implies that the rate of shearing off of organism from the disk surfaces is equal to the rate of their generation.

(ii) The turbulence in the reactor liquid pool is sufficient to keep the detached organisms in suspension.

(iii) The fixed and suspended organisms participate in substrate removal.

(iv) Oxygen and other nutrients are present in the liquid in excess so that the substrate concentration is the only growth limiting factor.

(v) The thickness of the liquid film is uniform over the aerated sector of the disk.

(vi) The external and internal mass transfer resistances are negligible.

(ii) The submerged and the aerated portions of the disk surfaces are exposed to the bulk substrate concentration.

(viii) The substrate concentration in the liquid pool of an RBC stage is uniform from the feed end to the discharge end and it is same as that of the treated effluent leaving the stage.

The above mentioned assumptions lead one to express the rate of biodegradation of the pollutants in an RBC by a Monod type relation :

$$-r_s = \frac{q[S]}{K_s + [S]}, \tag{9.86}$$

where $-r_s$ = rate of solute (pollutants) removal per unit disk surface area,

K_s & q = specific kinetic constants

and $[S]$ = solute concentration in an RBC stage.

Substrate balance around an RBC stage based on this model may be written as

$$F[S]_0 - F[S] = -r_s A = \frac{q[S]A}{K_s + [S]} \tag{9.87}$$

$$or, \ \frac{F}{A}([S]_0 - [S]) = \frac{q[S]}{K_s + [S]}, \tag{9.88}$$

where A = total disk surface area of an RBC stage in m^2

F = influent rate in L/hr

$[S]_0$ = influent solute concentration in mg BOD/L

and $[S]$ = effluent solute concentration in mg BOD/L.

Eq. (9.88) may be solved for a single stage RBC or for a multistage RBC either numerically (trial and error method) or graphically. The graphical method is shown in Fig. 9.30. The information required for solving Eq. (9.88) are the kinetic parameters q and K_s and either a disk surface area per stage or $[S]$ the desired solute concentration in the treated effluent.

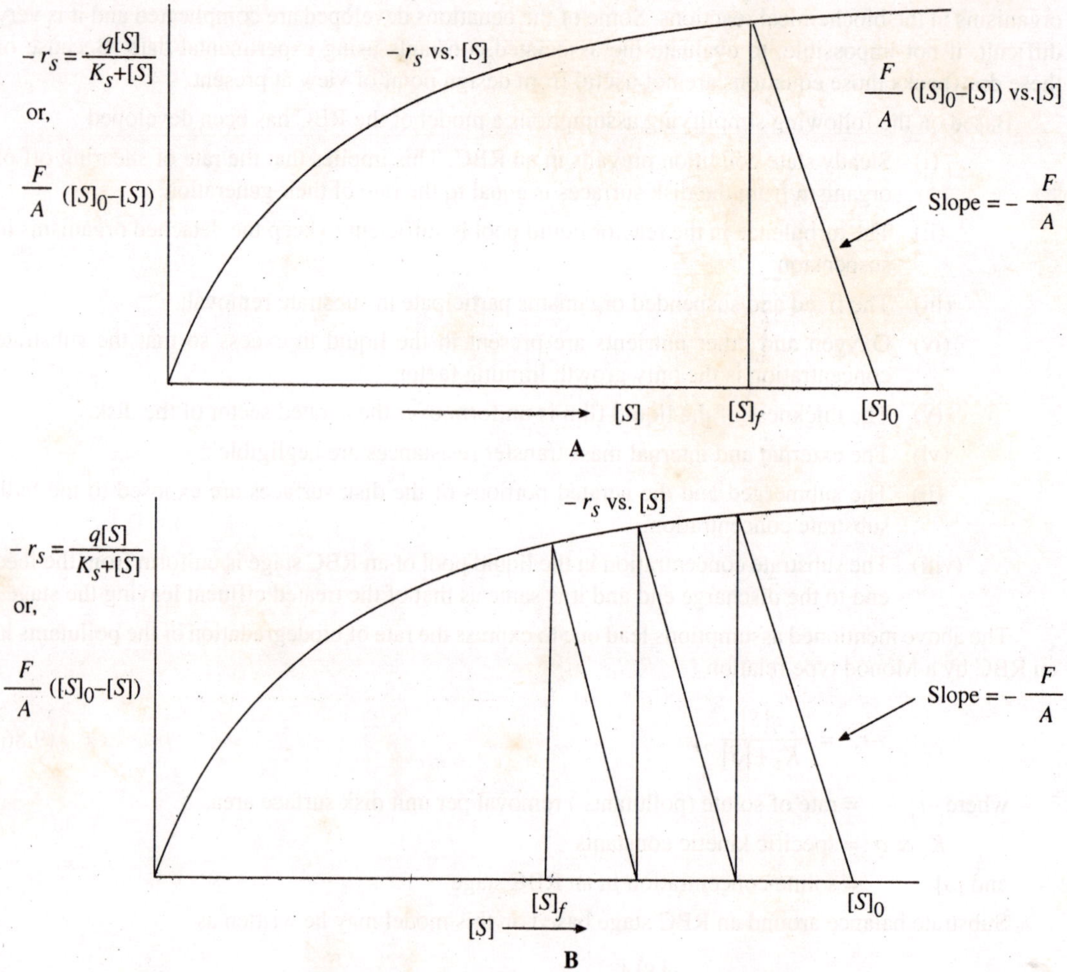

Fig. 9.30 : Graphical Approach for Solution of Eq. (9.88).

A. Single Stage RBC.

B. Multistage RBC, assuming F/A the same for all the stages.

Merits and Demerits

The major merits of an RBC are the following :

1. The slime layers on the disks of an RBC are totally wetted unlike those in a trickling filter.
2. By adjusting the rotational speed of an RBC it is possible to control to some extent the rate of re-oxygenation, the degree of turbulence and the slime film thickness, whereas those cannot be controlled in a trickling filter.
3. Very little oxidation of the suspended solid (sludge) would take place in an RBC as those would be larger in size compared to the suspended solids present in an activated sludge unit. This means that most of DO in an RBC would be available for biodegradation of the dissolved pollutants,
4. The energy required for rotating an RBC would be low, as the partly submerged disks would experience a buoyant force. An activated sludge unit of equivalent capacity may require more energy for agitation and supply of air (oxygen).

5. The settler size for removal of sludge from an RBC effluent would be smaller as the particles would be larger in size compared to those of an activated sludge unit.
6. Sludge recycle or recycle of treated effluent is not required.
7. Shock toxic load may not affect the slime film much and thereby affects its performance.

The demerits are :

1. Very little operational control of an installed RBC is possible other than changing its rotational speed. In this respect an activated sludge unit has more flexibility.
2. Virtually there is no control on the re-oxygenation process of a power driven RBC, of course in the case of a compressed air operated RBC the re-oxygenation process may be controlled to some extent.

Example 9.7 : Rotating Biological Contactor (RBC)

A waste water stream having a BOD concentration of 350 mg/L is to be treated in a three-stage RBC unit, each having the same surface area, that is, equal F/A ratio, so as to produce a treated effluent having 35 mg/L BOD. Find the disc surface area for each stage based on the following data :

Influent rate $= 7.5$ m^3/hr.

q $= 26900$ mg/m^2 day,

and K_s $= 125$ mg/L

Also list the additional information, which must be available for estimation of the volume of each tank.

Solution :

For estimation of disk surface area for each state Eq. (9.88) has to be modified as follows :

For the 1st stage $$-r_{s1} = \frac{q[S]_1}{K_s+[S]_1} = \frac{F}{A}\left([S]_0 - [S]_1\right) \tag{1}$$

For the 2nd stage $$-r_{s2} = \frac{q[S]_2}{K_s+[S]_2} = \frac{F}{A}\left([S]_1 - [S]_2\right) \tag{2}$$

For the 3rd stage $$-r_{s3} = \frac{q[S]_3}{K_s+[S]_3} = \frac{F}{A}\left([S]_2 - [S]_3\right) \tag{3}$$

where $[S]_0 = 350$ mg/L,

$q = 26900$ mg/m^2 day

$K_s = 125$ mg/L

$F = 7.5 \times 24$ m^3/day

$[S]_3 = 35$ mg/L.

The unknowns to be evaluated using these equations are $[S]_1$, $[S]_2$ and A (total wetted surface area, both the aerated and submerged) for each stage.

These equations, being non-linear, may be solved either numerically or graphically by the trial and error method.

For solving these equations graphically a table of $[S]$ vs. $\frac{q[S]}{K_s+[S]}$ is prepared as shown hereunder.

[S] mg/L	0	20	40	80	150	200	250	300	350
$\dfrac{q[S]}{K_s+[S]}$ $mg/m^2 day$	0	3,710	6,521	10,498	14,673	16,554	17,933	18,988	19,821

The tabulated data are plotted on a graph paper (Cartesian coordinate system) as shown in Fig. Ex. 9.7. Next a straight line having a negative slope (chosen intuitively) is drawn starting at $[S]_0 = 350$ mg/L, which interesects the curve $\dfrac{q[S]}{K_s+[S]}$ vs. S at a point *A*. From *A* a vertical line is drawn which meets the *X*-axis at $[S]_1$ a line is drawn having the previously chosen negative slope. This process is continued till a vertical line drawn results in a value of $[S]_1 = 35$ mg/L, the desired treated effluent BOD. Each line drawn with the chosen negative slope represents a stage. The number of such lines drawn stands for the number of stages required. In case the number of estimated stages be more or less than the number of specified stages (three in this problem) the process is to be repeated assuming a different value for the negative slope. Figure Ex. 9.7 shows that a chosen value of $F/A = 110$ L/m² day = 0.110 m³/m² day results in $[S]_3 = 38$ mg/L ≈ 35 mg/L corresponding to 3 stages.

$$\text{Hence, } A = \frac{F}{0.110} = 1631 \text{ m}^2.$$

To estimate the volume of each tank the additional information required are : disk diameter, degree of submergency of each disk, clearance between two adjacent disks and clearance between the disks and tank.

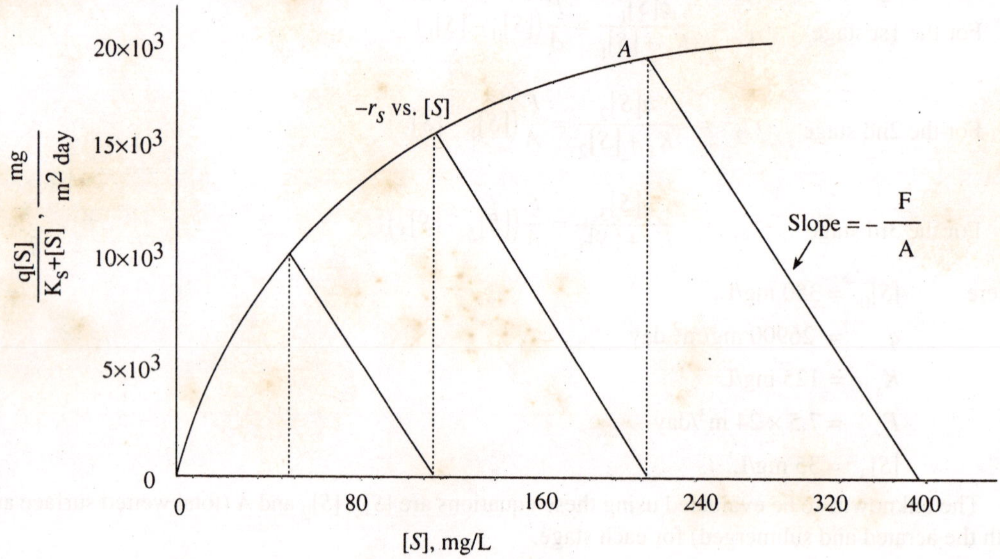

Fig. Ex. 9.7 : Multistage R.B.C.

9.10 Anaerobic Treatment of Waste water

Waste water containing biodegradable organics (dissolved and / or suspended) when subjected to anaerobic treatment, the organics undergo various biochemical reactions. The reactions are broadly classified as hydrolysis, acidogenesis and methanogenesis. The hydrolysis reactions are extra-cellular enzyme catalyzed. These reactions convert larger complex molecules (both soluble and insoluble) into simpler and smaller ones. The polysaccharides and proteins are converted to monomers. These products of hydrolysis act as substrates for a group of anaerobes, which convert them to organic acids. These groups of organisms are termed as acidogenes and the process is referred to as acidogenesis. The acidogenesis reactions are inter-cellular. During these reactions a small amount of hydrogen is also produced. The principal acids produced are acetic, propionic, butyric and a small quantity of valeric. The hydrolysis and acidogenesis reactions do not cause much reduction of BOD/COD. Higher acids (other than acetic acid) produced are converted into acetate and H_2 by acitogenic organisms. Another group of anaerobes called methanogenes convert acetic acid into methanc (CH_4) and carbon dioxide. These reactions are also intra-cellular. Some methanogenes combine H_2 and CO_2 and produce CH_4 and water (H_2O). The reactions involving methanogenes are referred to as methanogenesis.

Some methanogenic reactions are listed below :

Acetic acid $\quad CH_3\,COOH \rightarrow CH_4 + CO_2$

$\quad CH_3\,COO^- + H_2O \rightarrow CH_4 + HCO^-_3$

Hydrogen $\quad 4H_2 + HCO^-_3 \rightarrow CH_4 + 2H_2O + OH^-$

Figure 9.31 shows the entire anaerobic process schematically.

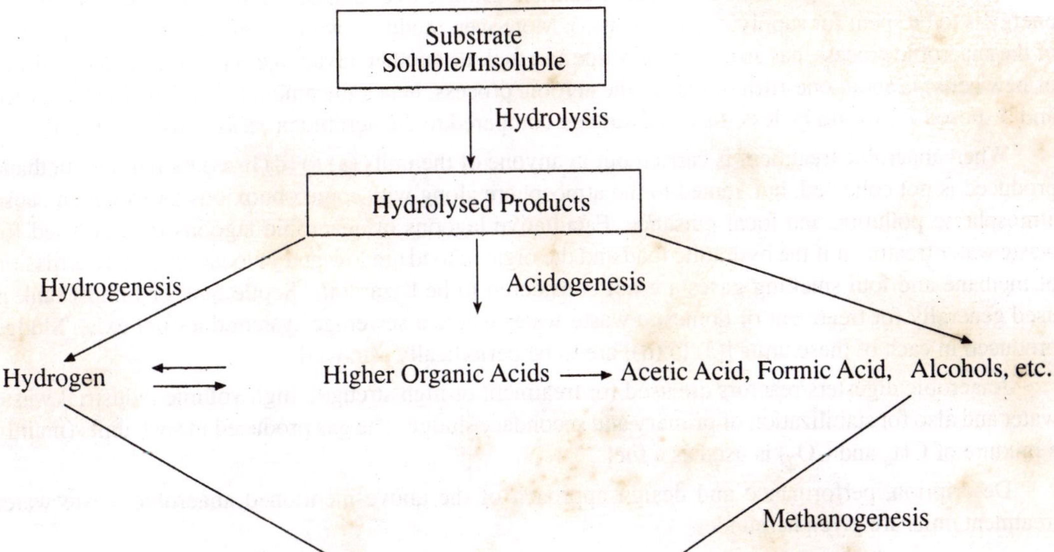

Fig. 9.31 : Representation of Waste Water Treatment—Anaerobic Process.

Some acidogenes are facultative while the others are obligate (strict) anaerobes. The acidogenes are not too sensitive to pH and inhibitors like heavy metals and sulfides. For the methanogenes the optimum pH ranges from 6.6 to 7.6. Below a pH of 6.2 the methanogenes become inactive (dormant). Some of the inorganic anaerobic process inhibitors are listed in Table 9.12.

Table 9.12 : Some Inorganic Anaerobic Process Inhibitors

Substance	Chemical Symbol	Substance	Chemical Symbol
Ammonium	NH_4^+	Nickel	Ni^{++}
Calcium	Ca^{++}	Potassium	K^+
Chromium	Cr^{6+}, Cr^{3+}	Sodium	Na^+
Copper	Cu^{++}	Sulfide	S^{--}
Magnesium	Mg^{++}	Zinc	Zn^{++}

9.10.1 For Anaerobic Treatment of Waste Water anyone of the following units may be used

(a) Facultative Lagoon,
(b) Anaerobic Lagoon,
(c) Septic Tank,
(d) Imhoff Tank,
(e) Anaerobic digester/reactor

The major advantage of the anaerobic treatment process over that of the aerobic process is that no energy is to be spent for supplying air (oxygen). Moreover, methane, which is produced as a by-product of the anaerobic process, has an economic value as a fuel. Its another advantage is that the yield (synthesis of new cells) is about one-fifth of that of the aerobic process, hence the amount of sludge to be handled and disposed off would be less. Its disadvantage compared to the aerobic process is its slower rate.

When anaerobic treatment is carried out in anyone of the units (a) to (d) listed earlier, the methane produced is not collected, but vented to the atmosphere along with some obnoxious gases which cause atmospheric pollution and local nuisance. Facultative lagoons or anaerobic lagoons may be used for waste water treatment if the hydraulic load and the organic load are low and in locations where emission of methane and foul smelling gases are not considered to be hazardous. Septic tank or Imhoff tank is used generally for treatment of domestic waste water where a sewerage system does not exist. Sludge produced in each of these units [(a) to (d)] are to be periodically removed.

Anaerobic digesters/reactors are used for treatment of high strength, high volume industrial waste water and also for stabilization of primary and secondary sludge. The gas produced in such units (mainly a mixture of CH_4 and CO_2) is used as a fuel.

Description, performance and design approach of the above mentioned anaerobic waste water treatment units are given hereunder.

9.10.2 Facultative Lagoon

The facultative process is not strictly anaerobic. This process is generally carried out in an earthen basin. The bottom of such a basin should be lined with an impervious layer of rubber/plastic/clay in order to prevent seepage of waste water. Alternatively the process may be carried out in a concrete tank. In a basin or tank stratification takes place. The top surface zone may be about 30–60 cm deep where aerobic reactions occur. In this zone re-oxygenation of waste water takes place due to molecular diffusion of atmospheric oxygen. There may be some algal growth on the free surface. The second layer (beneath the top layer) of the basin/tank is populated with facultative organisms.which act aerobically near the top of this layer and anaerobically towards the lower part of this layer. The bottom-most layer would not have any dissolved oxygen. In this layer only anaerobic reactions occur. Sludge (biomass) produced accumulates on floor of the basin/tank.

Influent waste water free from suspended matter is introduced close to the bottom and the treated effluent flows out through an outlet located at one of the sides of the tank close to the surface.

The gaseous products, such as CH_4, NH_3, H_2S and CO_2 formed in the anaerobic zone move upwards through the facultative and aerobic layers and finally escape to the atmosphere. While moving upward some of them may get oxidized. These gases cause atmospheric pollution and nuisance. Hence, facultative lagoons are not normally used for treatment of industrial waste water.

The design and performance parameters of a facultative lagoon are listed below :

Depth	:	1–2.5 m
Detention time	:	7–30 days
BOD loading	:	10–100 kg/ha*/day
Influent BOD	:	200–500 mg/L
BOD removal efficiency	:	70–80%

* 1 ha = 1 hectare = 10^4 m^2

9.10.3 Anaerobic Lagoon

Anaerobic lagoons are similar to the facultative lagoons in construction but are much deeper. During operation grease and some solid particles may float up to the surface and form a scum layer. This layer prevents re-oxygenation of the surface zone. Hence only a shallow layer close to the surface would contain facultative organisms, whereas the remaining portion of the lagoon would have anaerobes only. The zone close to the bottom would contain a sludge made up of unreacted solid particles (if any in the influent) and bacterial mass synthesized during the process.

Waste water having relatively high BOD and some suspended solids is introduced into the sludge layer, generally at the centre of a lagoon. As the liquid flows upward the dissolved and suspended organics undergo anaerobic degradation. The treated effluent with some suspended solid particles flows out through an outlet situated below the scum layer at one side of the lagoon. The gases produced as a result of the anaerobic reactions containing CH_4, CO_2, H_2S, NH_3, etc., escape to the atmosphere through some cracks in the scum layer. The surroundings of an anaerobic lagoon is more foul smelling than that around a facultative lagoon.

The design and performance parameters of an anaerobic lagoon are listed hereunder.

Depth	:	2.5–9 m
Length/width	:	2/1
Detention time	:	20–50 days
BOD loading	:	200–2200 kg/ha/day
Influent BOD	:	Over 500 mg/L
pH	:	6.6–7.6
BOD removal efficiency	:	50–80%

Bacterial cell production about 0.1 kg per kg of BOD removed.

9.10.4 Septic Tank

Septic tanks are almost similar to anaerobic digesters. These are unstirred and unheated. Unlike anaerobic lagoons these are completely enclosed. The tops of septic tanks are closed and fitted with covered access ports. These may be made of concrete/ polyethylene/fibreglass. The tanks must be structurally strong and water-tight. A septic tank may have a single chamber or two interconnected chambers. The influent inlet is fitted with a removable screen to prevent ingress of large particles. The line dips into the liquid pool inside the tank. The access ports are used for inspection, cleaning and venting the gaseous products (CH_4, CO_2, etc.). The suspended solids present in the influent settle at the bottom of the tank. The dissolved and the suspended biodegradables undergo anaerobic reactions. Grease and some solid particles float up and form a scum layer near the top of the tank, whereas the sludge accumulates at the bottom.

In a single-chamber unit the liquid outlet is located below the scum layer. The outlet is fitted with a siphon located just outside the tank, which prevents discharge of suspended solid particles and ingress of air. In a two-chamber unit the outflow from the first chamber containing a relatively small amount of suspended solids enters the second chamber. The entering solid particles along with the biomass produced in the second chamber settle to the bottom of the tank. This chamber is also provided with access ports and a liquid outlet fitted with a siphon. From a single-chamber unit as well as from a two-chamber unit the accumulated scum and the settled sludge are removed periodically. Figure 9.32 shows a sketch of a two-chamber septic tank.

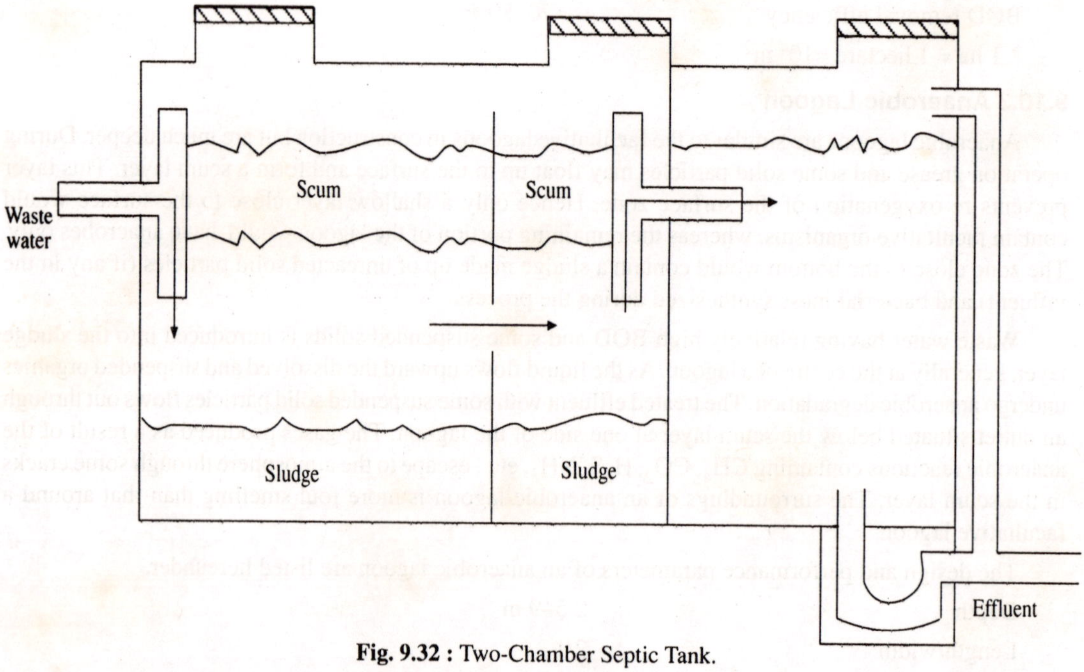

Fig. 9.32 : Two-Chamber Septic Tank.

The effluent coming out of a septic tank is finally disposed through a disposal field, which consists of a series of trenches filled with porous media. The solid particles, if any, are retained on the porous media, whereas the liquid infiltrates into the sub-soil. The liquid while residing in the trenches undergoes aerobic reactions to some extent.

It has been mentioned earlier that septic tanks are not normally used for treatment of industrial waste water.

9.10.5 Imhoff Tank

An Imhoff tank is a two-tier system. There are two chambers, one above the other. Both are open at the top. They are rectangular at the top and tapering towards the bottom. The upper tank acts as a sedimentation chamber, whereas the lower tank acts as an anaerobic digestion chamber. An overhanging lip located at the bottom of the upper chamber prevents gases and gas-buoyed particles produced in the lower chamber from entering the upper chamber. A sketch of an Imhoff tank is shown in Fig. 9.33.

Influent is introduced at one end of the upper chamber and the effluent from the same flows out through an opening located at the other end of this chamber. The waste water while flowing along the length of the upper chamber gets re-oxygenated as this chamber is open to the atmosphere at the top. In this chamber the dissolved substrates undergo aerobic reactions. The suspended solid particles, which enter the upper chamber along with the influent, settle through its bottom opening into the lower chamber. In the lower chamber the settled solids undergo anaerobic reactions. The gases produced in the lower chamber escape to the atmosphere through the gap between the upper and the lower chambers at the top. Some lighter solid particles and some gas-buoyed solid particles form a scum layer in the gap between the upper and the lower chambers at the top. The scum layer retards ingress of oxygen and thereby

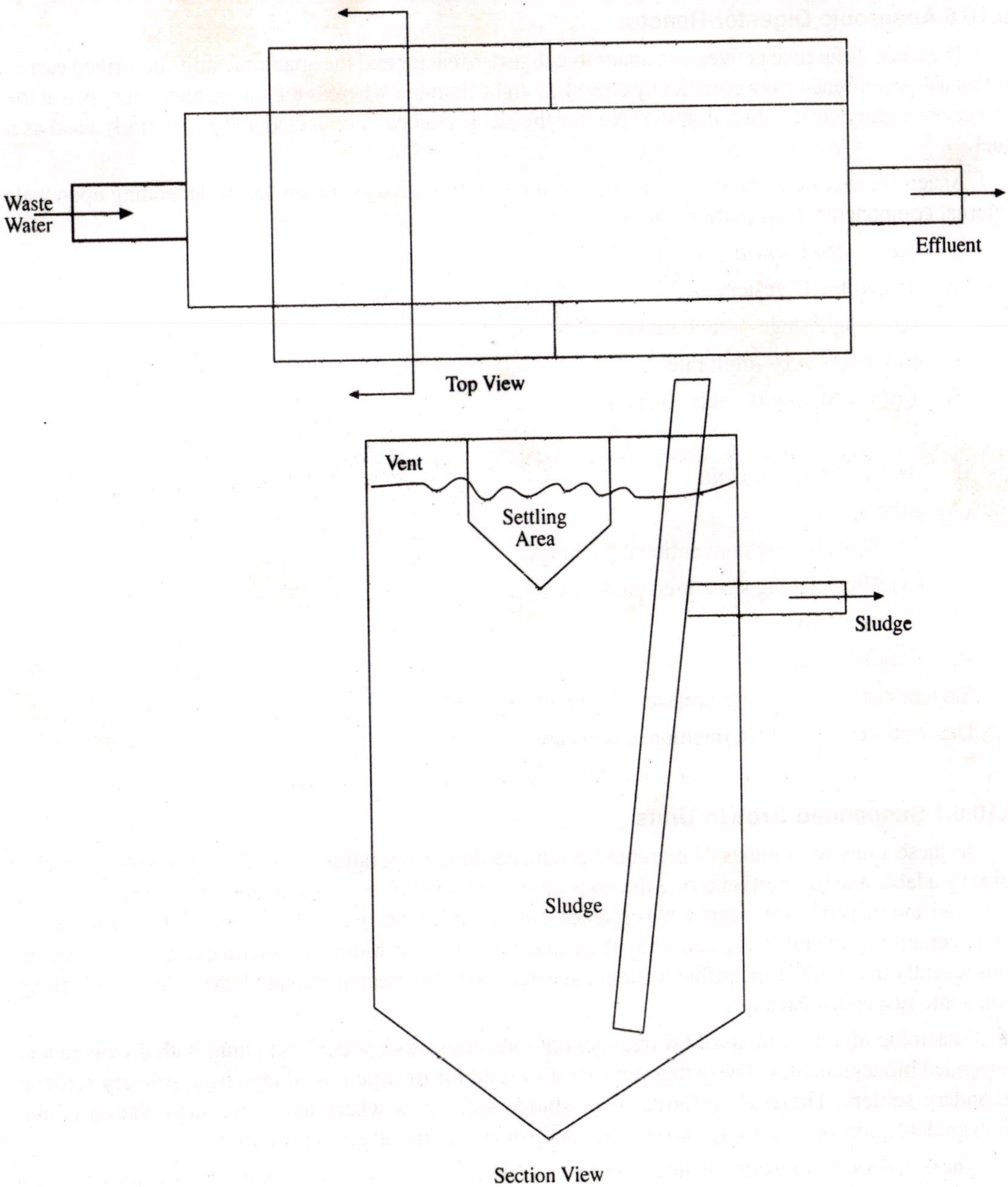

Fig. 9.33 : Imhoff Tank.

maintains almost anaerobic condition in the lower chamber. The accumulated sludge is removed from the lower chamber periodically through a sludge withdrawal pipe either mechanically or taking help of the hydraulic head difference.

The relatively clear liquid effluent from the upper chamber may be disposed of through a disposal field similar to that for a septic tank.

An Imhoff tank is not a suitable equipment for treatment of industrial waste water. It may be used instead of a septic tank when an influent contains a relatively larger amount of suspended solids.

9.10.6 Anaerobic Digester/Reactor

The basic difference between an anaerobic digester/reactor and the anaerobic units described earlier is that a digester/reactor is a completely closed air-tight chamber whereas the others are either open at the top or not tightly closed. In a digester/ reactor the gas produced is collected and is generally used as a fuel.

Anaerobic digesters/reactors are classified and sub-classified as shown below depending upon their internal components, flow pattern, etc.

I. *Suspended Growth Unit :*

(A) Anaerobic Digesters

  (i) Single stage—standard rate

  (ii) Two stage—high rate

(B) Upflow Sludge Blanket Reactor

II. *Attached Growth Units :*

(A) Filters

  (i) Units having conventional packings

  (ii) Units having structured packings

(B) Expanded Bed

(C) Fluidized Bed.

Sketches of some of these units are shown in Fig. 9.34.

Description of the above mentioned units are as follows :

9.10.6.1 Suspended Growth Units

In these units the biomass (microbes) produced during operation as well as any solid particles (biodegradable and/or inert) entering the units along with the influent would remain in suspension. The dissolved and suspended biodegradable organics undergo anaerobic reaction. As a result of these reactions a gas containing mainly CH_4 and CO_2 is produced and some biomass (microbes) are synthesized, consequently the BOD of the influent stream gets reduced. The treated effluent leaves such a unit along with some suspended particles.

Anaerobic digesters are used for treatment of industrial waste water containing both dissolved and suspended biodegradables. These digesters are also used for treatment of sludge from primary settlers/ secondary settlers. These are referred to as sludge stabilizers where anaerobic degradation of the biodegradable portion of a sludge takes place and some amount of gas is produced.

These digesters are made of steel or concrete. A digester has a conical bottom, a cylindrical body and a dome-shaped top. A gas (refereed to as biogas) produced due to anerobic reactions collects between the dome (roof) of the digester and the slurry surface from where it is transferred to a storage tank. The

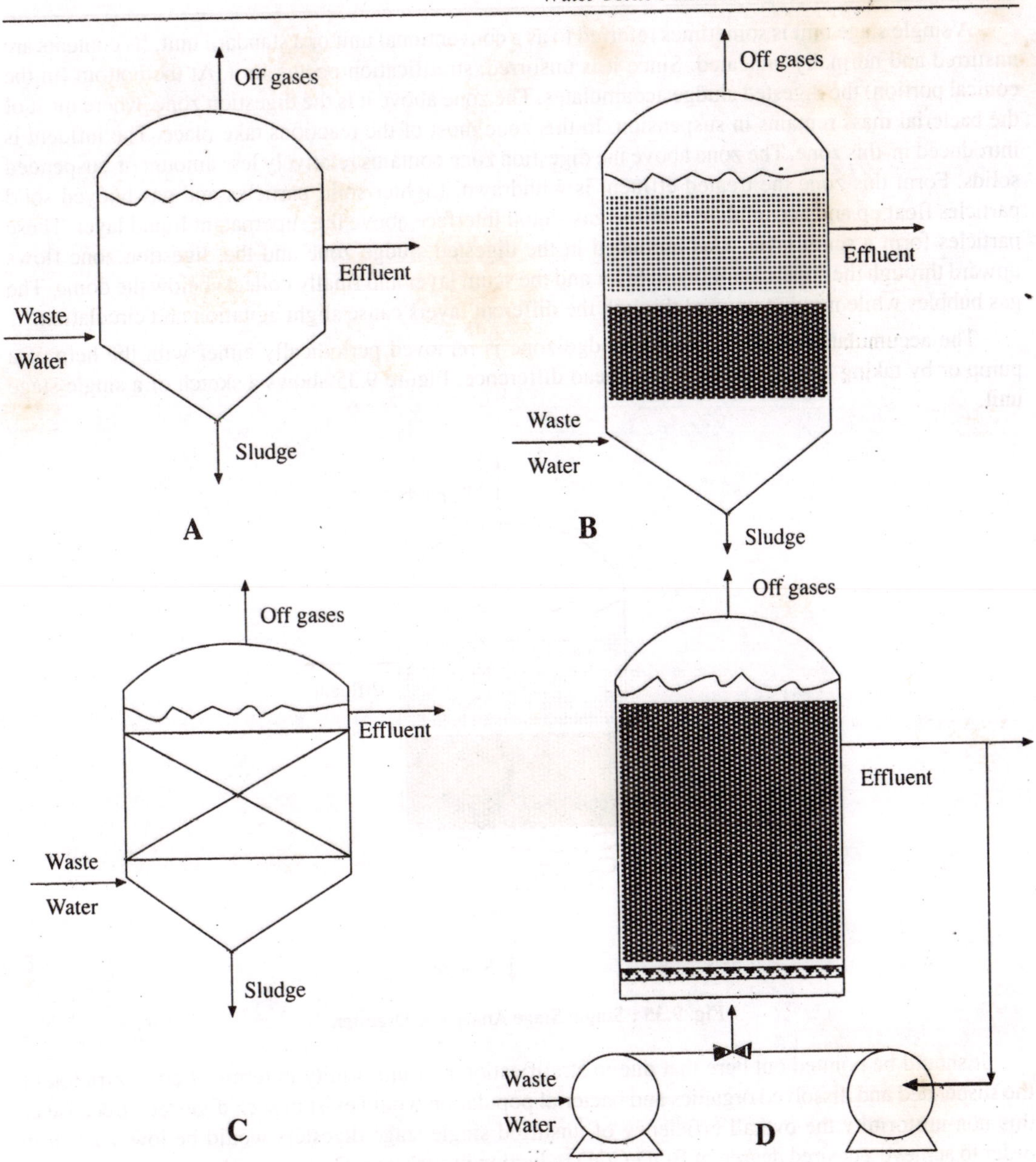

Fig. 9.34 : Different Types of Anaerobic Reactors.

A. Single Stage Anaerobic Digester,

B. Upflow Anaerobic Sludge Blanket Reactor,

C. Upflow Attached Growth Packed–Bed Anaerobic Reactor,

D. Upflow Expanded–Bed/Fluidized-Bed Anaerobic Reactor.

dome may either be an integral part of the digester, that is fixed to the digester body, or it may be floating. A floating dome slides up as more and more gas is produced and accumulates and slides down as the accumulated gas is withdrawn. The gap between a floating dome and a digester is made leak-proof in order to prevent leakage of the accumulated gas.

A single stage unit is sometimes referred to as a conventional unit or a standard unit. Its contents are unstirred and normally unheated. Since it is unstirred, stratification occurs in it. At the bottom (in the conical portion) the digested sludge accumulates. The zone above it is the digestion zone, where most of the bacterial mass remains in suspension. In this zone most of the reactions take place. The influent is introduced in this zone. The zone above the digestion zone contains relatively less amount of suspended solids. Form this zone the treated effluent is withdrawn. Lighter solid particles and gas-buoyed solid particles float up and accumulate near the gas-liquid interface above the supernatant liquid layer. These particles form a scum layer. Gas produced in the digested sludge zone and the digestion zone flows upward through the supernatant liquid layer and the scum layer and finally collects below the dome. The gas bubbles while moving upward through the different layers cause slight agitation and circulation.

The accumulated sludge from the sludge zone is removed periodically either with the help of a pump or by taking help of the hydraulic head difference. Figure 9.35 shows a sketch of a single stage unit.

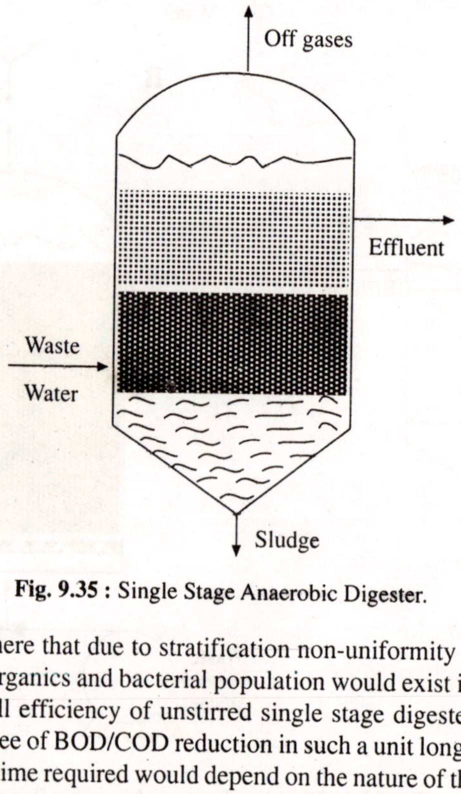

Fig. 9.35 : Single Stage Anaerobic Digester.

It should be pointed out here that due to stratification non-uniformity in terms of concentration of the suspended and dissolved organics and bacterial population would exist in such digesters. Because of this non-uniformity the overall efficiency of unstirred single stage digesters would be low. Hence, in order to achieve a desired degree of BOD/COD reduction in such a unit longer residence time (HRT) has to be provided. The residence time required would depend on the nature of the substrate to be treated and the operating temperature.

A two-stage unit is referred to as a high rate digester. It consists of two chambers connected in series. In the first chamber a waste water/sludge stream is introduced. The contents of the first chamber is thoroughly mixed and maintained at a temperature higher than the ambient temperature. Mixing is done either by gas circulation or by slurry recirculation or by mechanical agitation. A heating device (heat exchanger) may be located either outside the digester or inside it. The major reactions occurring in the first chamber would be hydrolysis and acidogenesis. To some extent methanogenesis would also take place. Because of higher temperature and well mixed digester contents, the reactions would proceed at a higher rate. From the first chamber slurry would overflow to the second chamber, which is generally unstirred. In the second chamber further reactions would take place. This chamber also acts as a settler.

Gas produced in the first chamber and that in the second chamber are fed into a storage vessel. The sludge settled in the first chamber is normally discarded, while that from the second chamber may either be totally discarded or partly recycled to the first chamber for maintaining a higher microbe concentration in it.

The chambers are similar in shape to that of a single stage unit. A sketch of a two stage unit is shown in Fig. 9.36.

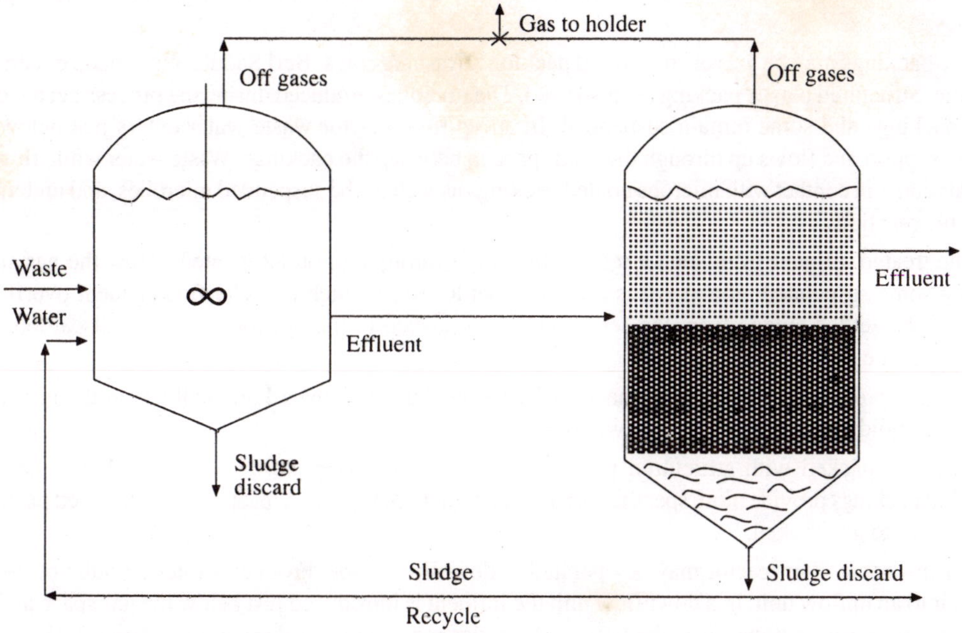

Fig. 9.36 : Two-Stage Anaerobic Digester with Sludge Recycle.

9.10.6.2 Up-flow Anaerobic Sludge Blanket Reactor

The other device belonging to the suspended growth type units is the Up-flow Anerobic Sludge Blanket (UASB) reactor. Such reactors are somewhat similar in construction to the single stage anaerobic digesters. However, these are suitable for treatment of waste water containing mainly dissolved biodegradable organics.

Influent is introduced close to the cone base of such a reactor, which flows upward through a sludge blanket. The sludge blanket is made up of bacterial mass produced as a result of the anaerobic reactions. The gas produced moves upward and may carry some solid particles. The solid particles form a layer at the liquid–gas interface. The gas collects under the dome and above the layer of solid particles. The treated effluent along with some suspended particles flows out into a settler through an outlet located close to the layer of the accumulated solid particles. Some sludge settles into the conical section of the reactor and is removed from time to time. The reactor sludge and the settler sludge are discarded.

9.10.6.3 Attached Growth Units

High strength waste water containing mainly dissolved biodegradable organics is best treated in attached growth type anaerobic units. In such units the microbes produced during the process get attached to the surfaces of reactor internals. The internals may be structured packings or conventional formed packings. Influents containing too much of suspended particles are likely to choke such reactors.

In some reactors granules are used instead of larger packings. The granules get coated with biomass and act as active sites for anaerobic reactions.

Classification of the attached growth reactors has been listed under Section 9.10.6, and those are described hereunder.

9.10.6.3.1 Anaerobic Filter Reactor

An anaerobic filter reactor is basically a packed bed. It is a cylindrical column fitted with a packing support near its bottom. Below the packing support the column has a conical section where sludge collects. The packing support may be either a perforated sheet or a grid having openings smaller than the packings.

The packings may be gravels or formed packings (Raschig rings, Berl Saddle, etc.) made of ceramic or plastic. Structured plastic packing are also used. The microbes produced during the process get attached to the packings and some remain suspended. In an up-flow reactor waste water enters just below the packing support and flows up through the void space in between the packings. Waste water while flowing upwards come in contact with microbe coated packings as well as the suspended microbes, and undergoes anaerobic reactions.

The treated effluent from such a reactor flows out through an outlet located below the gas space carrying some suspended biomass. It is fed into a settler from which the clarified effluent overflows. A part of the settled sludge from the settler may be recycled to the reactor the rest is discarded. The sludge from the reactor is discarded.

The gas produced as a result of anaerobic reactions bubbles upward and collects in the gas space above the liquid level from where it is withdrawn.

Reactors packed with structured packings are preferred over those packed randomly because structured packings provide more specific surface and higher void space. A reactor with structured packings is less likely to get choked.

An anaerobic filter reactor may be operated in downflow mode. From construction point of view it is similar to an upflow unit. In a downflow unit the influent is introduced just below the gas space and the treated effluent is withdrawn from the bottom. It carries more suspended material (biomass). Hence the effluent from such a reactor has to be settled in a properly designed settler prior to its final discharge.

9.10.6.3.2 Expanded Bed and Fluidized Bed Anaerobic Reactor

In these reactors coarse granular particles act as nucleus for biomass growth. These are similar to the anaerobic filters in construction. The particle support plate fitted to the column should have smaller openings so that the particles may not drop through them and at the same time the pressure drop across the support plate would not be excessive.

The influent is introduced in these reactors below the support plate and it flows upward through the particulate bed. Depending upon the superficial velocity of waste water flowing upward the particles may be resting on the support plate and in contact with one another or just touching each other or in suspension. When the particles are just touching each other the bed is said to be an expanded one. As the superficial velocity is further increased the particles become suspended and the bed is said to be fluidized.

Under expanded bed and fluidized bed conditions the total surfaces of the biomass covered particles get exposed to the flowing waste water stream and the dissolved organics experience more interaction with the biomass. Because of smaller particles size (compared to packed beds) the specific surface area is larger. Moreover, due to higher superficial velocity in expanded and fluidized beds the rate of pollutant transfer from the bulk of the liquid phase to the particle surfaces would be high. Consequently the rate of the anaerobic reactions would be faster. However, in order to maintain the required higher superficial velocity it is often necessary to recycle a part of the treated effluent along with the influent.

The gas produced during the process bubbles upward through the bed and accumulates in the gas space above the liquid level. The treated effluent containing some suspended biomass flows out through an outlet located below the gas–liquid interface. It is settled in a settler before its final discharge. Some biomass particles would pass through the support plate openings and collect in the conical bottom section of the column from where the collected particles are removed from time to time.

It may be mentioned here that expanded bed and fluidized bed reactors are yet to find wide industrial applications.

9.10.6.4 Anaerobic Digester Design Approach

A two stage anaerobic digester may be operated either with sludge recycle or without sludge recycle. Figure 9.36 shows a sketch of a two-stage digester with sludge recycle.

The first chamber of such a digester system is a well mixed digester and the second chamber acts only as a settler. The equations to be used for designing such a digester are the same as those used for designing a single stage (CSTR) activated aerobic sludge unit. The pertinent equations are listed hereunder.

$$\theta_c = \frac{K_s + [S]}{[S](\mu_m - \gamma - b) - K_s(\gamma + b)}$$

$$\theta_{c,\,\min} = \frac{K_s + [S]}{[S]_0(\mu_m - \gamma - b) - K_s(\gamma + b)}$$

$$[S] = \frac{K_s(1/\theta_c + \gamma + b)}{\mu_m - (1/\theta_c + \gamma + b)}$$

$$[x]_\tau = \frac{y\{[S]_0 - [S]\}}{1/\theta_C + b}$$

$$\tau = \frac{V}{F}$$

$$\alpha = \frac{F_r}{F} = \frac{1 - \dfrac{\tau}{\theta_c}}{\dfrac{[x_v]_r}{[x_v]} - 1} = \frac{1 - \dfrac{\tau}{\theta_c}}{\dfrac{[x]_r}{[x]} - 1}$$

and $$L = \frac{F[S]_0}{V} \tag{9.89}$$

where L = BOD loading per unit digester volume per day.

Methane production rate from such a unit may be calculated using Eq. (9.90)

Methane production rate, m^3/day at STP

$$= f\,F\,([S]_0 - [S])\,(1 - y\beta) \tag{9.90}$$

where f = 3.506×10^{-4}

F = Influent rate, m^3/day,

$[S]_0$ & $[S]$ = substrate concentration, mg BOD/L,

y = biomass yield under anaerobic condition, kg biomass kg BOD removed,

β = BOD equivalent to unit mass of dry biomass, mg BOD/mg dry biomass.

An anaerobic digester with sludge recycle may be designed through the following steps :

(i) The kinetic parameters, K_s, μ_m, γ, b, y and β for an anaerobic process should be obtained either experimentally or from the published literature. The numerical values of those depend on the pollutants (substrate) present in waste water/sludge and the microbes being used.

(ii) If the treated effluent substrate concentration $[S]$ be specified then θ_c (mean cell residence time) may be calculated using Eq. (9.68). If the calculated value of θ_c be less than 3 days or more than 15 days, then a suitable numerical value of θ_c should be assumed within the range 3 to 15 days. Corresponding to the assumed value of θ_c $[S]$ should be calculated using the same equation Eq. (9.68). The calculated value of $[S]$ should be an acceptable one.

(iii) Next a suitable value of $[x]$ (MLVSS) is assumed and τ (residence time) is calculated using Eq. (9.76). The estimated τ should not be less than $\theta_{c,min}$. In case it is less than $\theta_{c,min}$, a higher value of γ should be assumed and the corresponding value of $[X]$ should be estimated.

(iv) Based on the calculated value of τ, the digester volume V is to be estimated using Eq. (9.77).

(v) For estimation of the recycle ratio α using Eq. (9.64) one must know $[X]_r$, since the other factors, namely, τ and θ_c and $[x]$ are already evaluated. The value of $[X]_r$ the biomass concentration in the recycle sludge would depend on the settler design and performance.

(vi) Methane production per day from such a unit is estimated using the relation Eq. (9.90).

Figure 9.37 shows a sketch of a two stage anaerobic digester without recycle.

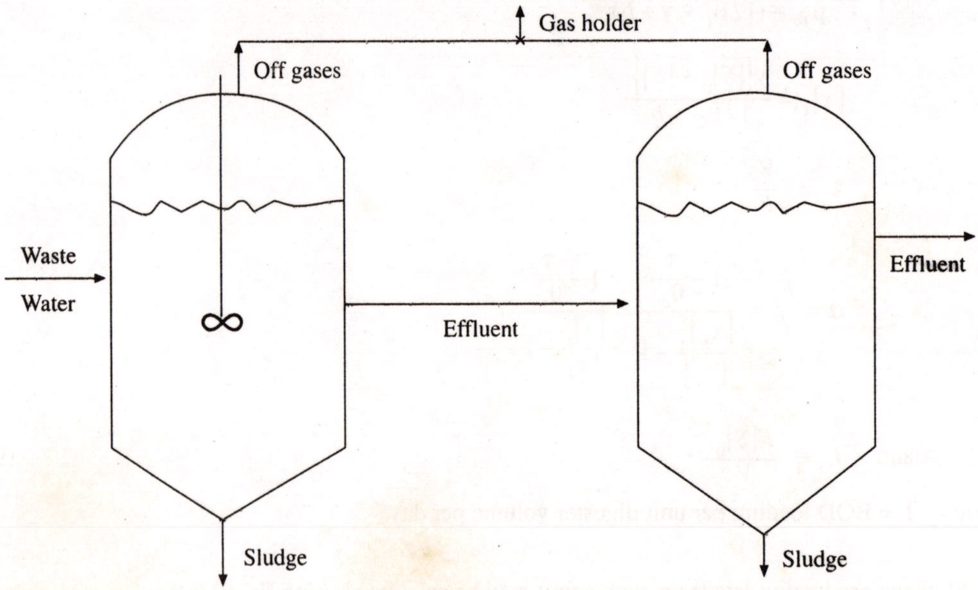

Fig. 9.37 : Two Stage Anaerobic Digester without Sludge Recycle.

The equations to be used for designing an anaerobic digester without recycle are similar to those used for designing a CMAL (completely mixed aerobic lagoon). The equations are listed below.

$$\tau_{actual} = \frac{K_s + [S]}{[S](\mu_m - \gamma - b) - K_s(\gamma + b)}$$

$$\tau_{min} = \frac{K_s + [S]_0}{[S]_0(\mu_m - \gamma - b) - K_s(\gamma + b)}$$

$$V = F\ \tau_{actual} \qquad (9.77)\ \text{modified}$$

τ_{actual} should be at least 10 times the τ_{min}.

Methane production from such an unit may be estimated using the relation Eq. (9.90).

Example 9.8 : Anaerobic Digester

A waste water stream having a soluble BOD of 20,000 mg/L and a flow rate of 15 m^3/hr is to be treated in a two-stage anaerobic digester with sludge recycle. Laboratory trials have indicated that an MCRT of 18 days would reduce the soluble BOD in the treated effluent to 3000 mg/L and result in a stable operation. The observed biomass production was 0.1 mg/mg of BOD removed. Asuming a recycle sludge biomass concentration 14,000 mg/L, loading rate of 5.6 kg BOD/m^3 day and $\beta = 1.25$ mg BOD/mg cell determine the following :

(a) Digester volume, (b) Cell concentration in the digester, (c) Recycle ratio, (d) Sludge waste rate, (e) Overflow rate from the settler and (f) Expected methane generation rate.

Solution :

The digester volume is estimated using the relation loading rate,

$$L = \frac{F[S]_0}{V}$$

$$\text{or } L = \frac{F[S]_0}{V} = \frac{15 \times 24 \dfrac{m^3}{day} \times 20000 \times 10^{-3} \dfrac{kg}{m^3}}{5.6 \dfrac{kg}{m^3 day}}$$

$$= 1285.7 \text{ m}^3$$

$$\left[1\ mg/L = 1\ g/m^3 = 1 \times 10^{-3}\ kg/m^3\right]$$

From Eq. (9.77)

$$\tau = \frac{V}{F} = \frac{1285.7\, m^3}{15 \times 24 \dfrac{m^3}{day}} = 3.57\ \ days.$$

As per Eq. (9.64)

$$\alpha = \frac{1 - \dfrac{\tau}{\theta_c}}{\dfrac{[X]_r}{[X]} - 1} = \frac{1 - \dfrac{3.57}{18}}{\dfrac{14000}{[X]} - 1}$$

Rearrangement and simplification of the above expression for $[X]$, the cell concentration in the digester is obtained.

$$[X] = \frac{14000\alpha}{\alpha + 0.8017}.$$

Cell mass balance around a digester results in the following equation :

$$\alpha F[X]_r + F\,([S]_0 - [S]) \times 0.1 = F\,(1 + \alpha)\,[X]$$

Substitution of the supplied data in the above equation and simplification of the same yields :

$15 \times 24 \times 14000\, \alpha + 15 \times 24 \times 17000 \times 0.1 = 15 \times 24\, (1 + \alpha)\, [X]$

Substituting, $[X] = \dfrac{14000\alpha}{\alpha + 0.8017}$ in the above and

solving the same it is found that,

$\alpha = 1.2664.$

The corresponding value of [X] is 8573 mg/L. For estimating the sludge waste rate, F_w, the relation used is

$$\theta_c = \frac{V[X]}{F_w[X]_r}$$, which on rearrangement yields

$$F_w = \frac{V[X]}{\theta[X]_r} = \frac{1285.7 \times 8573}{18 \times 14000} = 43.7\ m^3\ /\ day.$$

Overflow rate form the settler can be calculated by balancing volumetric flow around the entire system. The resulting equation is

$$F = F_w + Foverflow$$

or, $$F_{overflow} = F - F_w = 15 \times 24 - 43.7$$

$$= 316.3\ m^3/day$$

Expected methane production rate can be estimated using Eq. (9.90).

Methane production rate = $3.506 \times 10^{-4}\, F([S]_0 - [S])\, (1 - y\beta)$,

where F is in m^3/day.

$[S]_0$ and $[S]$ are in mg/L

y, biomass yield = 0.1, and $\beta = 1.25\ \dfrac{\text{mg BOD}}{\text{mg cell produced}}$

Methane production = $3.506 \times 10^{-4} \times 15 \times 24 \times (20,000–3000) \times 10^{-4}\, (1–0.1 \times 1.25)$

$= 1877.46\ m^3$/day at STP.

9.11. Tertiary Treatment

After proper primary and secondary treatments a waste water may still contain some or each of the following pollutants :

Suspended particles,

Dissolved organics, such as unreacted biodegradables, recalcitrant biodegradables,

Non-biodegradable organics,

Odoriferous and colouring matter,

Dissolved inorganics, and

Micro-organisms including pathogens.

The treatment methods used for abatement of the above mentioned pollutants are termed as *Tertiary Treatment Methods*. These methods and their effectiveness are listed in Table 9.13

Table 9.13 : Tertiary Treatment Methods and their Effectiveness

Treatment Methods	Capable of Removal
Filtration Air/Steam Stripping	Suspended solid particles Dissolved ammonia, volatile organic compounds (VOCs)
Adsorption	Dissolved organics including VOCs, colouring and odoriferous compounds.
Biological Processes	Nitrogenous and Phosphorous compounds.
Membrane separation process, such as, Micro filtration, Ultra filtration, Nanofiltration, Reverse Osmosis (RO).	Dissolved organics and inorganics.
Ion–exchange processes	Dissolved anions and cations.
Precipitation	Heavy metal ions and some other ionic substances.
Oxidation-Reduction	Organics and some inorganics.
Disinfection	Micro-organisms including virus.

From Table 9.13 it is apparent that for abatement of some types of the pollutants named earlier in this section more than one method is available. For abatement of such pollutants the choice of an appropriate method would depend on the initial concentrations of a specific pollutant, its permissible discharge limit and of course on the treatment cost.

The selection of a treatment scheme, that is, the treatment methods to be employed and their sequencing would depend on the pollutants present in a waste water stream, their concentration and whether the treated effluent is to be reused or disposed of.

The different treatment methods listed in Table 9.13 are briefly described hereunder.

9.11.1 Filtration

It is often necessary to employ filtration operation as a part of the tertiary treatment scheme for removal of very fine suspended particles from a waste water stream.

As a part of the primary treatment and after secondary treatment the majority of suspended particles are removed by sedimentation. Similarly after the precipitation process the precipitates are removed by sedimentation.

Sedimentation operation is capable of removing fine solid particles, however, very fine particles may still remain suspended. Such particles need to be removed from a waste water stream if the same is to be further treated by processes, such as, adsorption, ion exchange, membrane separation, disinfection, etc. Fine suspended particles interfere with the performance of the above mentioned processes. For removal of suspended particles after sedimentation generally a stream is subjected to filtration.

The equipment, which may be used for removal of fine and very fine suspended solid particles by filtration, are granular media filter, micro strainer, rotary drum filter, disk filter and membrane filter. Of these a granular media filter is the cheapest. These have been discussed in the earlier Sections. The criteria for selection of a filter type in a given situation are the concentration and size of the suspended particles, the stream flow rate and the degree of removal desired.

9.11.2 Air/Steam Stripping

Stripping operation is also referred to as desorption. In this operation dissolved solutes, such as gases and volatile liquids are transferred from a liquid phase to a gas/ vapour phase. The transferred solutes need further treatment for their recovery and/or disposal.

Steam stripping of waste water may be used if the solute (pollutant) concentration be relatively high. The other criterion for selection of the steam stripping operation is that the pollutants present should be highly volatile, that is, they should have low boiling point.

In this process live steam is brought in contact with waste water as a result of which the water temperature would increase and the pollutants would volatilize. A mixture of the solute vapour and steam is produced which is condensed. The condensate is to be further treated either for recovery of the solutes (if valuable) or for their destruction. A packed column may be used for this operation, at the top of which a pollutant bearing waste water is introduced. Steam is introduced at the base of such a column. This process would be viable if the recovered solutes are valuable.

If the pollutant concentration be low and they do not have any market value, then air may be used for stripping instead of steam. Air stripping may be applied for removal of pollutants, such as dissolved ammonia and/or volatile organic compounds. The equipment used for air stripping is a packed column operating countercurrently. The air stream leaving the column at its top would contain the pollutants and hence cannot be discharged to the atmosphere as such. The stream is to be treated by any one or a combination of the following processes : cooling (condensation), scrubbing, thermal/ catalytic oxidation, carbon adsorption. It should be pointed out here that if a waste water stream contaianing ammonium salts is to be air stripped; it is to be treated with lime at first so as to produce free ammonia.

Design Approach

In most cases of air-stripping operation the pollutant concentration in waste water would be low, hence the waste water may be considered to be a dilute solution. For such a solution the equilibrium relation (between a gas phase and the equilibrated liquid phase) is governed by Henry's law, which may be expressed as

$$y_e = m\, x_e \tag{9.91}$$

where m = equilibrium constant,

x_e = liquid phase solute concentration at equilibrium, expressed in mole fraction unit, and

y_e = gas phase solute concentration at equilibrium, expressed in mole fraction unit.

The numerical value of the equilibrium constant m depends upon the gas-solute-liquid system, its temperature and pressure. It is independent of the liquid phase solute concentration at low concentration.

Very often the molecular weight/average molecular weight of the pollutants present in waste water may not be known, hence the equilibrium relation has to be modified as

$$y' = m'\, x' \tag{9.92}$$

where x' and y' stand for pollutant concentration in the liquid phase and gas phase respectively and expressed in ppm, that is, mg/L unit.

Figure 9.38 shows a schematic diagram of a packed countercurrent air stripper.

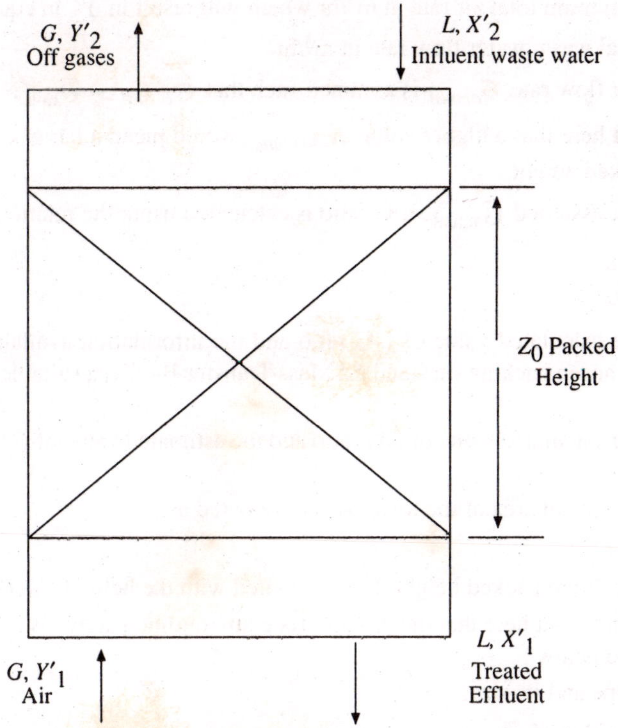

Fig. 9.38 : Countercurrent Packed Air–Stripping Column.

The packed height Z_0 of such a column may be estimated using Eq. (9.93).

$$Z_0 = \frac{L}{k_L a} \frac{In\left[\frac{x_2'}{x_1'}(1-A)+A\right]}{1-A} \tag{9.93}$$

where a = packing surface area per unit packed volume (its numerical value depends on the type and size of the packing to be used)

A = $L/m'G$,

G = air rate in $m^3/hr.m^2$

K_L = liquid phase mass transfer co-efficient in appropriate unit,

L = liquid rate in $m^3/hr.m^2$

m' = equilibrium constant, Eq. (9.92),

x' = liquid phase pollutant concentration in ppm unit.

The packed height Z_0, and the tower cross-sectional area may be calculated through the following steps :

1. A suitable type of packing and its size are chosen.
2. Minimum air flow rate is estimated using the relation :

$\overline{G}_{min}$ = Q/m' in m^3/hr,

= minimum total air rate in m^3/hr which will result in Y_2' in equilibrium with X_2'

Q = total waste water flow rate in m^3/hr.

3. An actual air flow rate G_{actual} is assumed such that $\overline{G}_{actual} > \overline{G}_{min.}$.

It should be noted here that a higher value of $\overline{G}_{actual}$ would mean a larger column cross-sectional area and a shorter packed height.

4. Based on the assumed $\overline{G}_{actual}$, L/G ratio is calculated using the relation

$$\frac{Q}{\overline{G}_{actual}} = \frac{L}{G}.$$

5. Utilizing the calculated value of *L/G* ratio and the information available about the flooding characteristics of the chosen packing (in standard Mass Transfer Books) a suitable numerical value of G is estimated.

6. Based on the calculated value of *L/G* ratio and the estimated value of *G* the numerical value of L is calculated.

7. The cross-sectional area of the tower A_c is evaluated as,

$$A_c = Q/L$$

8. Finally the column packed height Z_0 is estimated with the help of Eq. (9.93).

It needs to be pointed out here that the design procedure outlined above is based on two arbitrarily chosen factors as listed below :

1. a packing type and its size,
2. an assumed value of $\overline{G}_{actual}$.

Hence it is desirable to optimize the column size (cross-sectional area and packed height) by minimizing the total cost, that is, the sum of the initial cost and the operating cost (pumping cost).

9.11.3 Biological Processes

After secondary treatment, organics still left in a waste water stream may be mainly recalcitrant biodegradables and non-biode gradables. Other than those some organic nitrogenous and phosphorous compounds may also be present. These may be removed by biological treatment. These compounds are often referred to as plant nutrients as they promote growth of aquatic plants when a waste water stream containing these compounds is discharged into a water body.

Nitrogen and phosphorous compounds present in waste water may also be abated by methods other than biological methods. The non-biological treatment methods would be discussed in the next chapter. In the following Sections the biological methods are outlined.

9.11.3.1 Biological Treatment of Nitrogenous Compounds

Both inorganic and organic nitrogenous compounds present in waste water may be abated by biological methods. The treatment process is carried out in two consecutive steps, namely an aerobic step and an anaerobic step. These steps may be carried out during the secondary treatment itself. It should be mentioned here that for aerobic and anaerobic treatment of nitrogenous compounds specific organisms are needed and the steps must be carried out in separate reactors.

9.11.3.2 Nitrification Process

During aerobic treatment of waste water at first the complex carbonaceous and nitrogenous compounds are hydrolyzed to simpler molecules, which are subsequently oxidized. The nitrogenous compounds originally present in waste water and those added, if any, during secondary treatment as supplement are partly uitlized for synthesis of new cells and the remaining portions are converted to ammonium compounds. These compounds subsequently get oxidized to nitrite (NO_2^-) and nitrate (NO_3^-) in the presence of some specific organisms (Nitrosomonas and Nitrobacter bacteria). These bacteria are autotrophes. The reactions are trmed as nitrification reactions and they are slower than the carbonaceous oxidation reactions.

During nitrification not only oxidation (energy producing) reactions take place, but new microbial cells are also synthesized. The reactions may be summarized as under.

Oxidation Reactions :

$$NH_4^+ + \frac{3}{2} O_2 \xrightarrow{\text{Nitrosomonas}} NO_2^- + 2H^+ + H_2O$$

$$NO_2^- + \frac{1}{2} O_2 \xrightarrow{\text{Nitrobacter}} NO_3^-$$

Synthesis reactions :

$$4\,CO_2 + HCO_3^- + NH_4^+ + H_2O \rightarrow C_5H_7NO_2 + 5O_2$$

It should be pointed out here that the nitrification process does not convert the nitrogenous compounds to some innocuous substances but oxidizes a portion of them to nitrite and nitrate. The other portion is assimilated into biomass.

Nitrification process is sensitive to pH change and DO concentration. It is inhibited by a variety of organic and inorganic compounds. In the absence of inhibitors and at a DO concentration higher than 1 mg/L biochemical oxidation of carbonaceous and nitrogenous compounds occur simultaneously. This is referred to as a single-stage process. When organic inhibitors are present the carbonaceous compounds are oxidized at first and then nitrification is carried out in a second reactor.

Nitrification process may be conducted either in a suspended organism reactor, such as an activated sludge unit or in a fixed film reactor, like a trickling filter or a rotating biological contactor. A nitrification unit may be designed in the same way as that of an aerobic unit (as outlined in Sections 9.9.3.1, 9.9.4.1 and 9.9.5.1) using nitrification kinetic parameters. The numerical values of these parameters may be either estimated experimentally in a given situation or obtained from the published literature.

Nitrification rate data have been correlated using Monod's approach as given below :

$$-r_s = \frac{\mu_m\,[X][S]}{y\{K_s + [S]\}},$$

where r_s = ammonia–nitrogen substrate removal rate,
$[X]$ = microbe cell concentration,
$[S]$ = substrate concentration,
and y = biomass yield.

The rate of substrate removal has been found to be dependent on the temperature, pH and DO concentration.

The typical ranges of the design and performance parameters for the activated sludge type nitrification units are :

pH : 7.2 to 9.0
MLVSS : 1000 to 2500 mg/L
DO : > 2 mg/L
HRT : ≈ 2.5 hr.
MCRT : 5–10 days
Nitrification efficiency : > 90 %

9.11.3.3 Denitrification Process

Biological reduction of nitrite and nitrate in waste water is referred to as denitrification. During this process nitrite and nitrate mostly get reduced finally to molecular nitrogen and a portion gets incorporated into the synthesized biomass. Generally, methanol (CH_3OH) is added as a (carbon) supplement when sufficient organic carbon compounds are not present in an influent. The process is to be carried out in the absence of molecular oxygen (present as DO). In this sense the process is anaerobic. However, the pathways are some modifications of the aerobic ones, hence the process is sometimes referred to as anoxic process or anaerobic respiration process. The bacteria, which take part in this process, are facultative in nature. Various species, such as Achromobacter, Aerobacter, Alcaligenes, Bacillus, Flavobacterium, Micrococus, Proleus, Pseudomonas, etc. are often found to coexist in a denitrification unit.

It has already been mentioned that during denitrification a portion of the nitrite-nitrate nitrogen is incorporated into the biomass synthesized and the remaining portion takes part in the anaerobic respiration process. As a result the carbon compounds present in waste water get oxidized and nitrite—nitrate get reduced to molecular nitrogen and /or some oxides of nitrogen through various steps. The process may be represented as

$$NO_3^- \rightarrow NO_2^- \rightarrow NO \rightarrow N_2O \rightarrow N_2$$

It should be noted here that major portion of nitrate and nitrite undergoes the reduction reactions.

Denitrification reactions being reduction–oxidation reactions, for complete abatement of nitrite and nitrate at least the stoichiometric quantity of some oxidisable substances (organic matter) must be present. If sufficient quantity of oxidisable organic matter is not present in an influent, then methanol is added as a supplement. When organic matter initially present or supplemented is more than the stoichiometric amount the excess amount is biodegraded aerobically after the denitrification step.

From the foregoing discussion it is apparent that the denitrification process rate would depend on the concentration of both nitrite-nitrate nitrogen [N] and organic substrate [S]. The Monod type equation for this process is expressed as

$$\mu = \frac{\mu_m[N][S]}{(K_N+[N])\,(K_s+[S])}$$

Efforts have been made to evaluate the kinetic parameters of the dinitrification reactions, namely μ_m, *KN* and K_s experimentally. Design equations have been developed for suspended growth type reactors (CSTR) based on the above mentined kinetic parameters. Design equations for attached growth type reactors (packed bed) have also been developed. Some of these equations are listed in Table 9.14. It goes without saying that the kinetic parameters of the denitrification process are to be evaluated experimentally as those are substrate specific.

1. Suspended Growth Type Reactor (CSTR with recycle)

$$\theta_c = \frac{(K_s+[S])\,(K_N+[N])}{\mu_m[S][N]-b(K_s+[S])\,(K_N+[N])}$$

$$[X]\tau = \frac{Y([S]_0-[S])}{\frac{1}{\theta_c}+b}.$$

And $\tau = \frac{V}{F}$.

θ_c calculated using Eq. (9.59) based on an average load should be multiplied by a factor of safety in order to obtain the actual θ_c. The purpose of the factor of safety is to take care of the peak load/transient load and it is generally taken as 2 to 2.5.

2. Attache Growth Type Reactor (Packed Bed).

$$[N]^{0.5} = [N]_0^{0.5} - 0.5\ k_{\frac{1}{2}}\ a\tau \tag{9.94}$$

where $k_{\frac{1}{2}}$ = a kinetic parameter to be estimated experimentally,

a = area of packing surface per unit volume of packed bed,

τ = empty bed space time = LA_c/F,

L = packed bed height,

A_c = bed cross-sectional area,

F = influent volumetric flow rate.

$[N]_0$ & $[N]$ = nitrogen concentration in influent and effluent respectively.

The factors influencing the denitrification process are pH, temperature and dissolved oxygen (DO) concentration. The pH should range between 6.0 and 8.0. The denitrification rate decreases below pH and above 8.0. A pH around 7 is preferable. However, an initial (influent) pH lower than 7 do not pose any problem as during the process alkalinity is produced. In case a waste water tends to be more alkaline during treatment, its pH should be regulated so that it does not go beyond 8.0.

The denitrification rate increases with increase in temperature. Some investigators have observed that the rate levels off around 20 °C. This process being anaerobic in nature its rate becomes zero above a DO concentration of 1 mg/L

Equipment Selection

Denitrification may be carried out either in a suspended growth type reactor (CSTR) or in an attached growth type reactor. As dissolved oxygen inhibits the process there should be no ingress of air. The gases produced during the process, mainly N_2 and CO_2 should be vented.

The design and performance parameters of the above mentioned type reactors are listed in Table 9.14

Table 9.14 : Design and Performance Parameters of Denitrification Reactors

1. *Suspended Growth Type Reactors* :

pH	: around 7.0 (6.5–7.5)
MLVSS	: 1000–3000 mg/L
HRT	: 2.5 hr (approximately)
MCRT	: 1–5 days
Loading Rate	: 0.016 mgN/day/mg of MLVSS.
Surface Loading Rate	: 20 m^3/day/m^2 (approximately).
Removal Efficiency	: about 90%

Process Sequencing

Biological nitrogen removal processes are classified into two groups, namely 'single stage' or 'single sludge' and 'two-stage' or 'two-sludge'.

A 'single stage' process implies nitrification and denitrification steps being carried out consecutively without any sludge classifier/settler in between them. Several different variations of this type of treatment sequence are in vogue. An example of the 'single stage process' is the Bardenpho Process, which is shown schematically in Fig. 9.39.

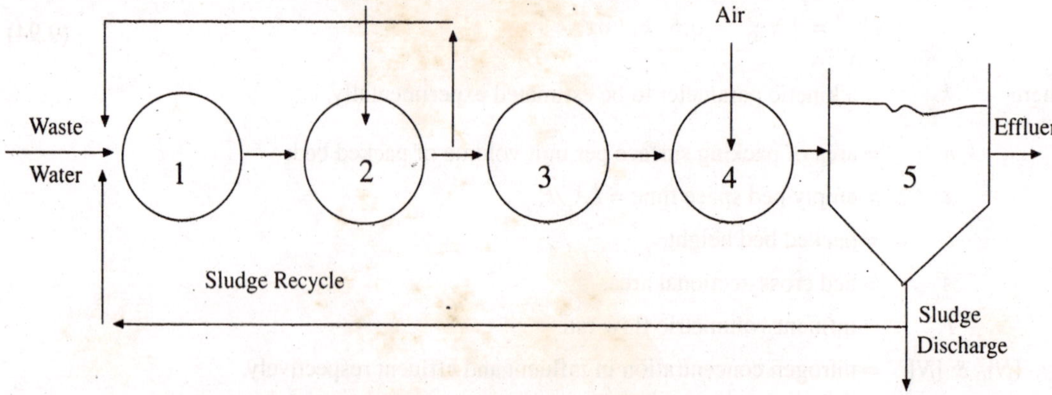

Fig. 9.39 : Single Stage Nitrification—Denitrification Process.

1. Anaerobic Denitrification Unit,
2. Aerobic nitrification Unit,
3. Anaerobic Denitrfication Unit,
4. Aerobic Unit for Removal of Residual BOD,
5. Clarifer.

The advantage of a 'single stage process' is that no supplementary carbon source (electron donor) is to be added. The carbonaceous compounds initially present in waste water act as the carbon source in the unit (1) and the biomass (cells) produced during the aerobic step (2) acts as the carbon source in the unit (3).

In a 'two-stage process' the first unit is an aerobic (nitrification) unit. It is followed by a clarifier/settler. The next unit is an anaerobic (denitrification) unit. It is followed by another clarifier/settler.

In such an arrangement it may be necessary to add methanol as a carbon source (electron donor) to the anaerobic unit. If methanol added is more than the stoichiometrical amount required for denitrification,

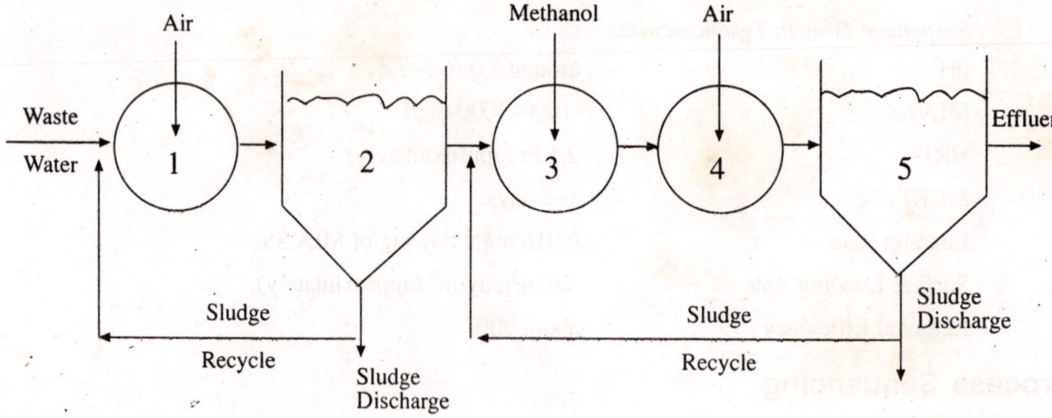

Fig. 9.40 : Two Stage Nitrification—Denitrification Process.

then an additional aerobic unit is to be provided in between the anerobic unit and the final clarifier in order to reduce the BOD level in the final effluent. In Fig. 9.40 a 'two-stage process' is shown schematically.

1. Aerobic Nitrification Unit,
2. Clarifier for Aerobic Sludge Separation,
3. Anaerobic Denitrification Unit,
4. Aerobic Unit for Removal of Residual Excess Methanol, if needed,
5. Clarifier for Final Sludge Removal.

It should be mentioned here that addition of methanol in excess (over the stoichiometric amount) is helpful for complete denitrification and to achieve a higher denitrification rate. It is to be pointed out that when methanol is added in large excess (say, about 3500 mg/L) it acts as a denitrification inhibitor. However, it is rarely necessary to add a large excess amount of methanol.

9.11.3.4. Biological Phosphorous Removal

Phosphorous compounds present in waste water may be removed either chemically or biologically. Chemical treatment means precipitation of phosphorous as aluminium phosphate/iron phosphate/calcium phosphate. Biological treatment results in incorporation of phosphorous into phosphorous accumulating cells. The advantages of the biological process over the chemical process are reduced chemical cost and less sludge production and disposal. Sometimes a combination of both of the processes is used.

The biological process is carried out in two stages. In the first stage an influent is treated anaerobically ($\tau \approx$ 0.5 to 1.0 hr) with phosphorous accumulating organisms. During this stage these organisms produce and store polyhydroxy butyrate (PHB) in the cells assimilating acetates and utilizing energy from transformation of ATP (adenosine triphosphate) to ADP (adenosine diphosphate). Consequently, orthophosphate is released. During the next aerobic stage (SRT $\approx$ 2 to 4 days) energy produced from oxidation of PHB enables the cells to pick up orthophosphate from waste water and convert and store those as polyphosphate. New cells produced during the aerobic stage also pick up phosphorous and store as polyphosphate.

Figure 9.41 shows the basic process schematically.

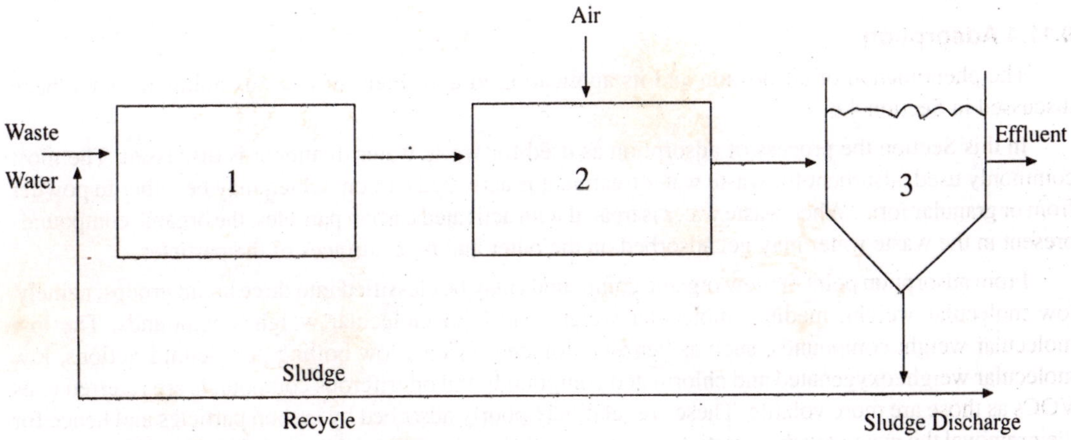

Fig. 9.41 : Biological Phosphorous Removal Basic Process.

1. Anaerobic Unit,
2. Aerobic Unit,
3. Clarifier.

Several Processes have been developed modifying the basic process for simultaneous removal of nitrogenous and phosphorous compounds biologically from waste water. A flow diagram of such a process is shown schematically in Fig. 9.42.

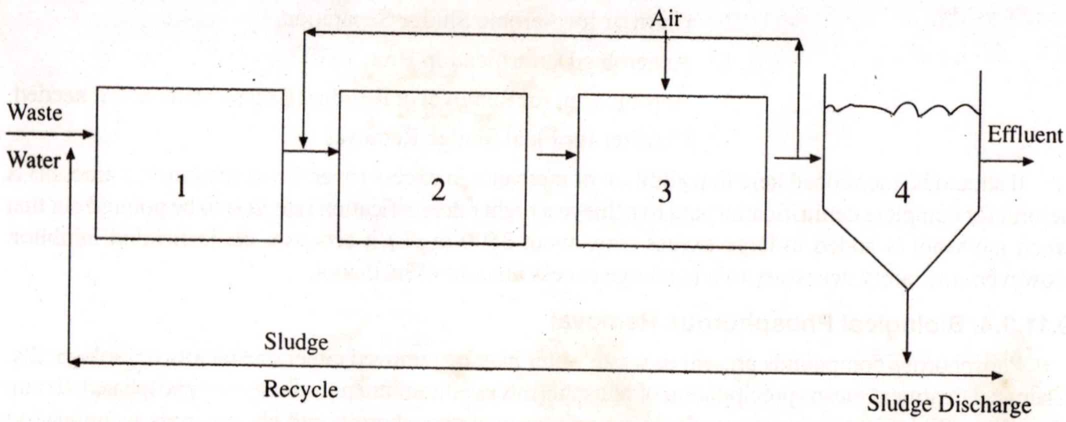

Fig. 9.42 : Biological Process for Simultaneous Removal of Phosphorous and Nitrogen.

1. Anaerobic Unit,
2. Anoxic Unit,
3. Aerobic Unit,
4. Clarifier.

When a waste water stream containing both nitrogenous and phosphorous compounds is subjected to aerobic treatment the nitrogenous compounds get oxidized to nitrite and nitrate. The nitrified liquor needs to be treated anoxically for denitrificatioin as otherwise the recycled aerobic sludge containing nitrite-nitrate would enter the anaerobic unit and would suppress the activity of the phosphorous accumulating organisms. This would result in a reduction of the phosphorous removal efficiency of the entire process.

9.11.4 Adsorption

The phenomenon of adsorption and its application in abatement of gaseous pollutants have been discussed in Section 4.6.

In this Section the process of adsorption as used for waste water treatment is discussed. The most commonly used adsorbent for waste water treatment is activated carbon, which may be either in powder from or granular form. When waste water is treated with activated carbon particles, the organic compounds present in the waste water may get adsorbed on the outer and pore surfaces of the particles.

From adsorption point of view organic compounds may be classified into three broad groups, namely, low molecular weight, medium molecular weight and high molecular weight compounds. The low molecular weight compounds, such as benzene, toluene, xylene, low boiling petroleum fractions, low molecular weight oxygenated and chlorinated compounds and odoriferous compounds are referred to as VOCs as those are more volatile. These are relatively poorly adsorbed by carbon particles and hence for their removal the mass of carbon particles needed would be more. The medium molecular weight organics are relatively less volatile and high molecular organics may be non-volatile. Oils, grease, polychlorinated hydrocarbons, chlorinated phenols, pesticides, herbicides, dyes, colouring matter belong to the high molecular weight hydrocarbons. These are strongly adsorbed by activated carbon particles and hence those can be easily removed from waste water by adsorption.

Activated carbon used for waste water treatment are produced by carbonization of coal, lignite, coconut shell and some agricultural residues. The carbonized products are further treated so as to improve their porosity and make them more active. Coal and lignite based activated carbons may be microporous (pores<20 A° diameter) type or macroporous (pores > 500 A° diameter) type. The microporous carbons would have a significant amount of mesopores (pores 20 – 500 A° diameter). Microporous carbons are good for adsorption of low molecular weight organics, whereas macroporous carbons are suitable for removal of medium to high molecular weight organics. Activated coconut shell carbons are mainly microporous (pore dimeter ≈ 10A°) and those are excellent for removal of low molecular weight organics.

When a waste water is contaminated with low as well as high molecular weight organics, the latter are preferentially adsorbed. As a result low molecular weight organics are poorly removed unless a relatively large amount of carbon is used.

From particle size point of view activated carbon is classified into two groups, classified, namely, powdered (fine) carbons and granulated carbons. Powdered carbons may have particle size ranging between 5–50 μm and have a large surface area per unit mass. A large portion of these particles is lost during regeneration . Hence, very often these particles are discarded after use. Granulated carbon particles size ranges between 0.1 to 2.5 mm. These are regenerated and reused.

The presence of inorganic salts in waste water may cause poor adsorption of organics due to precipitation of the sparingly soluble inorganics on the particle surfaces leading to pore blockage. Severe precipitation may lead to lumping of carbon particles, which would not only lower the adsorption capacity but may make the carbon particles unsuitable for regeneration. The potential of this menace may be ascertained by estimating the Langelier Index. A positive value of the Langelier Index would indicate the existence of such a problem. In such a situation it would be better to remove the inorganic salts prior to carrying out an adsorption operation.

When biomass and / or other particulate matters are present in a waste water stream those would get accumulated in an adsorber column. Build-up of such solid particles would give rise to higher pressure drop across a column. This would call for frequent backwashing which would reduce the carbon bed life. To overcome such a problem a filter should precede a carbon adsorber.

Before opting for installation of an adsorber it is necessary to check its feasibilituy. The objectives for assessing feasibility should be (1) to select a suitable type of activated carbon, and (2) to collect data for design purpose. Feasibility studies may be carried out using any one of the following approaches :

(a) to collect adsorption equilibrium data from different sources,
(b) to evaluate experimentally the adsorption isotherm for each specified carbon-waste water combination,
(c) to carry out small scale column trials,
(d) to carry out pilot scale trials.

The approaches (c) and / or (d) would yield more reliable information, whereas the approaches (a) or (b) would yield some preliminary information.

Of course prior to carrying out a feasibility study an analysis of the contaminants (pollutants) present in a waste water stream must be available.

9.11.4.1 Process Description

Treatment with Powdered Carbon

Waste water treatment with powdered carbon is carried out in a batch mode only, as the pressure drop across a column packed with such particles would be high. Generally, a stirred tank is used for such a process. The quantity of carbon required and the duration of a batch operation are estimated experimentally. After treatment the particles are removed from the treated effluent by filtration. As regeneration and reuse of the spent particles may not be economical those are disposed of suitably. This process may be used if powdered carbon be available at a low price, or if the quantity of waste water to be treated be rather small.

Treatment with Granular Carbon

For treatment of a waste water stream with granular activated carbon any one of the following types of equipment may be used : (i) a packed bed, (ii) an extended (expanded) bed and (iii) a moving bed. Through a packed bed waste water may flow either in the downward or in the upward direction. Through an extended bed the flow is in the upward direction. In a moving bed the flow is counter current, that is, waste water flows upwards and the carbon bed moves downwards. The bed housed in a vertical cylindrical column, which is fitted with a bed support near the bottom. A packed/an extended bed is operated in a semi-batch mode, that is, once the bed becomes saturated with the adsorbate it is taken off for carbon regeneration. In the case of a moving bed some of the spent particles are removed periodically from the bottom and some fresh/regenerated particles are added at the top. Such a bed is operated in a continuous mode. .

In a packed bed during adsorption there would be no attrition of the particles, as they would not move around. However, during backwashing (if an influent contains suspended solids) there may be some attrition and loss of fines.

In an extended bed or a moving bed attrition of particles would take place and hence there would be loss of fines.

An extended bed is operated at a higher upward velocity so as to keep the particles suspended. This increases the mass transfer rate, consequently the process becomes more efficient.

Waste water is normally treated in packed adsorption columns arranged either in series or in parallel. When the columns are arranged in series three columns are used. Two columns remain on line at any instant of time and a third column after regeneration treatment remains as a standby. The lead adsorber is operated till breakthrough occurs. During this period the second column acts as a polishing (back up) column. Once the first column reaches the breakthrough limit it is isolated for carbon regeneration and the second column is used as the lead column. The standby column is then connected in series and it acts as the polishing column. Such an arrangement does not require very frequent monitoring of the effluent from the lead column. When columns are operated parallely no back up column is required, however, very frequent monitoring of effluent from a column needs to be done in order to avoid its operation beyond the breakthrough limit.

9.11.4.2 Carbon Regeneration

Granulated carbon particles may be regenerated either by steam stripping in situ or by air oxidation after removing the particles from an exhausted column. Low and medium molecular weight adsorbates may be removed by steam stripping. During steam stripping a certain portion of the adsorbate may remain adsorbed. This remaining portion is referred to as the 'heel'. This residual adsorbate reduces the "working capacity" of a column. Reduction of 'heel' may be achieved either by prolonged steaming by using steam at a higher temperature. High molecular weight adsorbates are not amenable to steam stripping. Those are removed by air oxidation whereby the adsorbates get oxidized. During this process the surfaces of the carbon particles may undergo oxidation to some extent resulting in a loss of mass of the particles.

9.11.5 Membrane Separation Processes

A membrane separation process splits an influent steam into two streams, namely, a retentate/concentrate/reject stream and a permeate/lean stream. The permeate stream would contain very little of the solutes present in the influent, whereas the retentate would be a concentrated solution of the solutes. When a waste water stream is subjected to a suitable membrane separation process the pollutants present in it are neither destroyed nor converted to innocuous substances but those are concentrated in the retentate stream.

The heart of a membrane separation unit is a component, which is termed as a membrane. A membrane may be defined as a substance which when in contact with a fluid retains or captures preferentially some of the constituents present in the fluid and allows some other constituents to pass through the membrane or to remain undisturbed.

The state of aggregation of a membrane may be solid or liquid or gel. A solid membrane may be an inorganic film or a polymer film. A liquid membrane must be immiscible with the fluid form which some solutes are to be preferentially removed. Inorganic film, liquid and gel membranes have limited areas of application, whereas polymeric membranes have much wider fields of application.

A polymeric membrane may be either porous or non–porous. The driving force of the processes employing a polymeric membrane in most cases is pressure gradient. In a pressure driven separation process the membranes get fouled due to deposition of the retained constituents on their surfaces. They also get compacted because of the super-incumbent pressure. On account of these effects the permeation rate decreases with time.

It should be pointed out here that when a membrane separation process is used for treatment of a waste water stream the retentate would contain most of the pollutants and the same has to be further treated for abatement of the pollutants.

Membranes in general are costly and have short life. Moreover, the operating (power) cost is relatively high. Hence, normally membrane separation processes are not used for treatment of waste water streams unless the objective is to recover some valuable materials from a waste water stream or to recover the permeate for reuse.

Membrane separation processes have been classified as micro-filtration (MF), ultra-filtration (UF), nano-filtration (NF), reverse osmosis (OR), dialysis, electro-dialysis and gas separation. In Table 9.15 the characteristics, limitations and other salient features of these processes are listed.

Membrane Material

Various types of organic polymeric membranes are available commercially. Membranes made of cellulose acetate, aromatic polyamide, acryl–alkyl polyamide, polyvinyl alcohol, polycarbonate, polysulfone, polyacrylonitrile, polyethylene, polypropylene, polytetrafluoroethylene, etc. are available.

Selection of the membrane material in a given situation depends on the following factors :

1. the objective,
2. the constituents to be retained,
3. the other constituents present,
4. the influent pH,

and 5. the cost.

9.11.5.1 Process Description

Micro-filtration (MF) :

Micro-filtration membranes are porous. The pore size ranges between 0.02–2 μm. The retain particles (fine particles and colloids) as well as bacteria and other micro-organisms including some viruses. The permeate from such a process would contain dissolved inorganic and organic ions and molecules and viruses (smaller than 0.02 μm in linear dimension) and of course the carrier liquid (water). The process may be used for pre-treatment of waste water prior to nano-filtration or reverse osmosis. It is sometimes used as a part of a membrane bio-reactor (MBR) unit.

The mechanism of separation of this process is surface filtration/sieving. The particles larger than the pores are retained.

These membranes experience both internal as well as external fouling. Internal fouling occurs because of attachment of particles within the pores and adsorption/precipitation onto membrane surface. External fouling takes palace as a result of formation of a stagnant layer of particles carried to the membrane surfae by the permeating stream and retained by the membrane. The micro-filtration permeate flux is higher than those of ultra filtration, nano-filtration and reverse osmosis. It is a low pressure process.

Ultra-filtration (UF) :

This is also a low pressure process, however, in this case the pressure gradient is more than that for micro-filtration. UF membranes are porous like MF membranes. The pore size is smaller. These membranes allow water, dissolved inorganic and dissolved smaller organic molecules to pass through. In fact, in a specific situation the membrane (pore size) selection depends on the smallest molecular weight species to be retained. It is characterized by the 'molecular weight cut off' (MWCO) index. The rejection by a membrane does not depend on the MWCO alone but also on the structure (branching) of the solute molecules. Fouling and concentration polarization of UF membranes are more severe than those for MF membranes. The permeate flux and the pressure gradient depend on the membrane pore size.

Ultra filtration is generally used for production of high purity reuse water.

Nano-filtration (NF) :

Nano-filtration is known as 'loose RO'. It is capable of removing particles as small as 0.001 μm, such as high molecular weight organics, anions with higher charges (multivalent metal ions) and of course microbes including viruses. The permeate (water) is of good quality. It does not require much disinfections treatment. The pressure gradient for NF is less than that for RO but more than those for NF and UF.

Reverse Osmosis (RO) :

Of the different membrane separation processes used for treatment of contaminated water, reverse osmosis produces the best quality water. The membrances used for RO are referred to as an anisotropic (Asymmetric) non-porous membranes. Such a membrane has three layers : a dense surface skin, an intermediate layer and a porous base layer. The skin actually causes separation whereas the other two layers give mechanical support to the skin. The skin appears to be non-porous when examined under a scanning electron microscope. The skins of such membranes have scattered small defects (developed during production). Through these defects, leakage of influent (feed) along with the solutes takes place. Since the membranes are non-porous types a substantially large pressure difference needs to be maintained across the membranes.

Various models have been proposed to explain the reverse osmosis phenomenon. These are of two types : (a) non-porous solution model, and (b) porous transport model. Some other models have also been proposed. But none of these are able to account for all of the experimental observations.

The extent of rejection of inorganic (ionic) substances have been found to depend on the valency of ions. It increases with the increase in valency. The degree of rejection of organic molecules depends on their size, membrane (polymer) type and its structure.

RO membranes are also susceptible to fouling like MF and UF membranes. The permeate (water) flux rate in a RO process is much less compared to those in the MF and UF processes. Moreover, as a RO membrane is subjected to a higher operating pressure it gets compacted with time which results in progressive decrease in permeate flux.

An RO process should be preceded by processes like depth filtration/micro-filtration/ultra-filtration so as to reduce membrane fouling due to accumulation of particles and large molecules on membrane surface

Dialysis

The dialysis process is used to remove some specific solutes from an influent stream and not to split it into a retentate and a permeate stream as is done in the membrane separation processes discussed earlier. The membrane used is a homogeneous porous one. The pore size in a specific situation would depend on the solute molecule size, which one would like to remove from an influent.

During dialysis transport of solutes takes place across a membrane because of their concentration gradient and not due to pressure gradient. Solvent permeation across the membrane is prevented.

For carrying out a dialysis process an influent is made to flow over a membrane surface while another stream (the dialysate) flows over the other surface. The dialysate serves two purposes : (i) prevents bulk flow of the solvent across the membrane and (ii) it receives the solute (s) which migrate (diffuse) through the membrane. The dialysate composition should be such that it would have the same osmotic pressure as that of the influent. This would prevent bulk flow of the solvent across the membrane. The rate of diffusion of the solute molecule through the membrane would depend on its size and its concentration across the membrane.

This process is not used for treatment of waste water. A well known application of the dialysis process is blood purification.

Electrodialysis

Electrodialysis is somewhat similar to the dialysis process in the sense that it is not pressure driven. This process is carried out by maintaining a D.C. electric potential gradient across an assembly of membrane cells placed parallelly. It is capable of removing only ionic constituents from an influent stream.

An electrodialyser is made of several anion (+charged) and cation (–charged) semi-permeable membranes placed in alternate fashion so as to form channels in between two adjacent membranes. Two membranes enclosing a volume of an influent constitutes a cell. An assembly of such cells is placed between two electrodes (a cathode and an anode), which are connected to a D.C. source. The D.C voltage impressed upon a cell is not large enough to cause electrolytic dissociation but sufficient to carry on migration of ions through the membrances. The cation exchange membrances allow only the positively charged cations to pass through and migrate towards the cathode, while the anion exchange membranes permit the negatively charged anions to travel towards the anode. As a result of such migration the

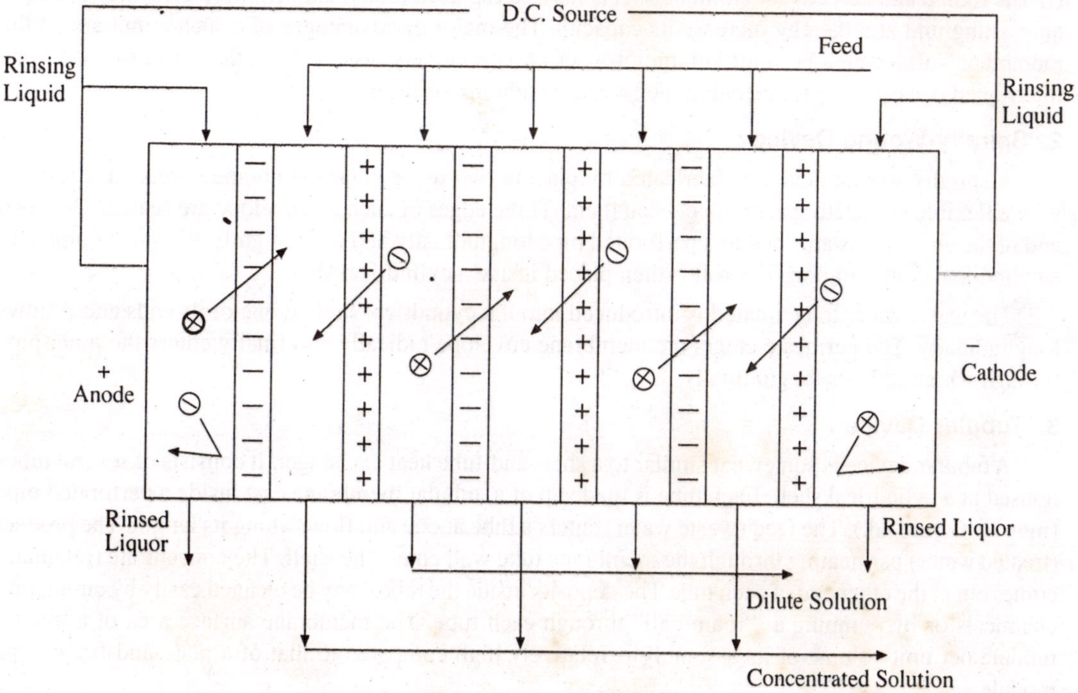

Fig. 9.43 : Schematic Diagram of An Electrodialyser.

concentration of ions (both cations and anions) increases in cell and thereby the solution flowing through the cell becomes richer in ions while the solution flowing through the neighbouring cell becomes depleted of the ions initially present it it. Figure 9.43 shows a schematic diagram of an electrodialyser assembly.

The field of application of the electrodialysis process for treatment of waste water is rather restricted. It may be used cost-effectively for recovery of metal ions from a waste water stream. For smooth operation of an electrodialyser the following factors/ aspects need proper monitoring : (i) pre-treatment of the influent stream for removal of low solubility salts and suspended solids (including colloids), (ii) pH, (iii) temperature, and (iv) flow rates of influent in the adjoining cells.

9.11.5.2 Membrane Configuration and Geometry

Polymeric membranes used are of the following types : (i) flat sheets, and (ii) tubular. Depending on membrane module configuration they are broadly classified as :

1. Plate-and-frame device,
2. Spirally-wound device,
3. Tubular device, and
4. Hollow fibre device.

1. Plate-and-Frame Device :

A plate-and-frame module is similar to a plate–and-frame filter press. It consists of several flat membrane sheets supported by plates and interspaced with frames. Two plates and a frame constitute a cell. Several of such cells are placed side by side parallelly to make up a module. The cells of a module are held together mechanically so as to prevent any leakage of liquid. A waste water stream (feed) to be treated is passed through a frame on either sides of which there are membranes. The permeate stream after passing through a membrane flows along the adjacent plate surface into a common header. The retentate stream flows out of the frame into another header. Such a set up has the following advantages : (i) The fouled and defective membrane sheets may be replaced easily, and (ii) more cells may added to an existing unit and thereby increase its capacity. The major disadvantages of a such a unit are (i) the membrane surface area per unit volume of a set up is relatively less, and (ii) the operation has to be interrupted occasionally for cleaning the fouled membrane surfaces.

2. Spirally-Wound Device :

A spirally wound device is fabricated by placing two rectangular membrane sheets back to back with a flexible permeate spacer in between them. Three edges of such an envelope are sealed. The open end of the envelope is attached to a perforated pipe longtudinally and rolled tightly around the pipe into a cylindrical configuration. The roll is then placed inside a cylindrical shell.

The waste water to be treated is introduced into the cylindrical shell at one of its ends and it flows longitudinally. The permeate enters the membrane envelope radically and finally enters the inner pipe through which it flows longtudinally.

3. Tubular Device :

A tubular device is somewhat similar to a shell-and-tube heat exchanger. It consists of several tubes housed in a cylindrical shell. Each tube is made up of a tubular membrane cast inside a perforated pipe (may be 12 mm i.d.). The feed (waste water) enters a tube at one and flows along its length. The product (treated water) permeating through the membrane tube wall enters the shell. The concentrate (retentate) comes out at the other end of each tube.The deposits inside the tubes may be cleaned easily by circulating chemicals or by pumping a "foam ball" through each tube. The membrane surface area of a tubular module per unit volume of its assembly is relatively high compared to that of a plate-and-frame type module.

Table 9.15 : Characteristics of Polymeric Membrane Based Separation Processes

Process	Membrane Type	Mechanism of Separation	Driving Force	Species Retained	Species Permeated
Micro-filtration (MF)	Isotropic micro–porous membrane.	Sieving	Pressure gradient 7–100 kPa	Particles (size 0.02 –10 μm) colloids and micro-organisms	Particle free solution.
Ultra-filtration (UF)	Anisotropic micro-porous membrane, skin thickness 0.1 to 10 μm, Porous base	Sieving	Pressure gradient 70–700 kPa	High molecular weight solutes.	Solvent and low molecular weight solutes.
Nano-filtration (NF/Loose RO)	Anisotropic porous skin with more porous thick base. skin often has negatively charged ions.	Sieving Coupled with anion repulsion.	Pressure gradient 500–1000 kPa	High molecular weight organics and anions with higher charges.	solvent, low molecular weight organics, and some ionic species.
Reverse osmosis (RO)	Anisotropic non-porous membrane, skin thickness ≈ 0.2 μm, base porous	Sorption and capillary flow.	Pressure gradient 0.8–10 MPa	Inorganic and organic solutes.	Mainly solvent and some leaked solutes.
Dialysis	Isotropic micro-porous membrane.	Pore diffusion	Concentration gradient.	Higher molecular weight solutes.	Lower molecular weight solutes.
Electro-dialysis	Isotropic cation exhange membrane and anion exchange membrane.	Ion difusion in electric field.	D.C. electric potential gradient	Solvent freed from ionic particles.	Ionic Particles.

4. Hollow Fibre Device :

Hollow fibre membrane tubles have very small diameter. Unlike tubular type membranes these tubles do not need any mechanical support. A bundle of such tubles forming an assembly is inserted in a cylindrical housing (shell). The feed (waste water) may enter the tubles and flow along their length. The permeate in such an arrangement would flow inside–out through the cylindrical surfaces of the tubles into the shell while the retentate would flow out through other end of the tubles. Alternatively the feed may be introduced at end of the shell and flow axially. The permeate in such an arrangement would enter the tubles through their outer cylindrical surfaces and flow out axially. The retentate would emerge at the other end of shell. Any deposit on the inside/outside surfaces of the tubles cannot be cleaned, hence the feed for a hollow fibre device should be freed from suspended particles and other fouling matter.

9.11.6 Ion Exchange Process

Ion exchange process is carried out by bringing a waste water stream containing some ionized species (cations and anions) in contact with some solid particles having replaceable ions. The solid particles are referred to as ion exchangers. During the process ions (of a specific type) in solution replace the ions of the same type from the exchangers. The process is a reversible one, that is, the arrested ions may be replaced with another similar type of ions subsequently. The exchanges are basically chemical reactions. The ion exchangers may be natural or synthetic zeolite having replaceable cations or synthetic resins having either replaceable cations or anions.

The cation exchangers may have either replaceable sodium ions (Na^+) or hydrogen ions (H^+), while the anion exchangers may have replaceable chloride ions ($C1^-$) or hydroxyl ions (OH^-)

The exchange reactions may be represented typically as followes :

Cation Exchanger

Zeolite Exchanger—

$$Z^= Na_2^{++} + \left.\begin{array}{r} CaCl_2 \\ MgCl_2 \\ FeCl_2 \end{array}\right\} \rightarrow \begin{array}{l} Z^= Ca^{++} + 2NaCl \\ Z^= Mg^{++} + 2\,NaCl \\ Z^= Fe^{++} + 2NaCl \end{array}$$

Synthetic Resin Exchanger—

$$(a)\quad 2R^-Na^+ + \left.\begin{array}{r} CaCl_2 \\ MgCl_2 \\ FeCl_2 \end{array}\right\} \rightarrow \begin{array}{l} \begin{matrix} R^- \\ R^- \end{matrix}\!\!> Ca^{++} + 2NaCl \\ \begin{matrix} R^- \\ R^- \end{matrix}\!\!> Mg^{++} + 2NaCl \\ \begin{matrix} R^- \\ R^- \end{matrix}\!\!> Fe^{++} + 2NaCl \end{array}$$

$$(b)\quad 2R^-H^+ + \left.\begin{array}{r} CaCl_2 \\ MgCl_2 \\ FeCl_2 \end{array}\right\} \rightarrow \begin{array}{l} \begin{matrix} R^- \\ R^- \end{matrix}\!\!> Ca^{++} + 2HCl \\ \begin{matrix} R^- \\ R^- \end{matrix}\!\!> Mg^{++} + 2HCl \\ \begin{matrix} R^- \\ R^- \end{matrix}\!\!> Fe^{++} + 2HCl \end{array}$$

Anion Exchanger

Synthetic Resin Exchanger—

(a) $2R^{+}Cl^{-} + H_2SO_4 \rightarrow \begin{matrix} R^{+} \\ R^{+} \end{matrix}\rangle SO_4^{=} + 2HCL$

(b) $2R^{+}OH^{-} + H_2SO_4 \rightarrow \begin{matrix} R^{+} \\ R^{+} \end{matrix}\rangle SO_4^{=} + 2H_2O$

The synthetic ion exchangers are classified as follows depending on their degree of ionization under the process conditions, mainly the pH.

1. **Cation Exchange Resin :**

(i) *Strong acid type :* These have sulfonated groups, $R–SO_3^- Na^+$+ or $R–SO_3^- H^+$ Over the entire pH range these are highly ionized.

(ii) *Weak acid type :* These have carboxylic type functional groups, R—COO^-H^+ and they are weakly ionized.

2. **Anion Exchange Resin :**

(i) *Strong base type :* These have strong basic functional groups. These ionize strongly over the entire pH range.

(ii) *Weak base type :* These have week basic functional groups. Their degree of ionization depends on the prevalent pH.

Each particle of an ion-exchanger would have a limited number of exchangeable ions. It is an important property of an ion exchanger. It is referred to as exchange capacity. The exchange capacity is expressed in the unit of g. eq/L or g. eq/kg. The other important properties of ion exchanger particles are their structural changes, such as swelling or shrinking and chemical degradation during use.

As the ion-exchanger particles have limited capacity they become exhausted after sometime during the (exchange) process. At that point of time those particles need to be regenerated , that is, restored to their reuse. The regeneration process is carried out by reacting those (spent particles) with appropriate inorganic chemicals (in aqueous solutions). The regeneration reactions may be represented as :

Regeneration of Cation Exchangers

Zeolite Exchanger—

$$Z^{=}Ca^{++} + 2NaCl \rightarrow Z^{=}Na_2^{++} + CaCl_2$$

Synthetic Resin Exchanger—

(a) $\begin{matrix} R^{-} \\ R^{-} \end{matrix}\rangle Ca^{++} + 2\,NaCl \rightarrow 2R^{-}Na^{+} + CaCl_2$

(b) $\begin{matrix} R^{-} \\ R^{-} \end{matrix}\rangle Ca^{++} + 2HCl \rightarrow 2R^{-}H^{+} + CaCl_2$

Regeneration of Anion Exchangers

Synthetic Resin Exchanger—

(a) $$\begin{matrix} R^+ \\ R^+ \end{matrix} \!\!> SO_4^{=} + 2NaCl \rightarrow 2R^+Cl^- + Na_2SO_4$$

(b) $$\begin{matrix} R^+ \\ R^+ \end{matrix} \!\!> SO_4^{=} + 2NaOH \rightarrow 2R^+OH^- + Na_2SO_4$$

The ion exchange processes are classified into three groups depending upon the treatment objective. These are :

(i) Softening :

The process is used where the objective is to remove cations like Ca, Mg, Fe, etc. by Na. The exchanger may be either Zealite type or synthetic cationic resin type. The treated water is suitable for domestic use, that is, use in laundries and for feeding low pressure boilers.

(ii) Dealkalization :

By this process hydroxides, carbonates, and bicarbonates of Ca, Mg, Na, etc. can be removed. The process reduces the alkalinity of water. The exchangers used are synthetic cationic type with replaceable hydrogen ions (H^+). The regenerating reagent is an aqueous HCl. The reactions may be represented as :

Dealkalization Reaction—

$$R^{=}H_2^{++} + MgCO_3 \rightarrow R^{=}Mg^{++} + H_2CO_3$$

Regeneration Reaction—

$$R^{=}Mg^{++} + 2\ HCl \rightarrow R^{=}H_2^{++} + MgCl_2$$

Dealkalizations reduces the alkalinity of water and makes it less fouling in heat exchangers.

(iii) Demineralization/Deionization :

The purpose of this process is to produce virtually cation-and anion-free water. It is generally carried out in two steps. In the first step the cations are removed and in the second step the anions are removed. However, sometimes both cations and anions are removed in a single piece of equipment. Synthetic resin is used for this process.

This process is employed for producing high pressure boiler feed water, process water for pharmaceutical industries, biochemical process industries and other chemical industries which require high purity water.

For regeneration of cationic resins an aqueous solution of HCl is used and for regeneration of anionic resins an aqueous NaOH solution is used.

The reactions taking place during exchange operation and those during regeneration operation may be represented as under :

Exchange Operation

Cationic Step :

$$2R^-H^+ + CaCl_2 \rightarrow \begin{matrix} R^- \\ R^- \end{matrix} \!\!> Ca^{++} + 2HCl$$

$$6R^-H^+ + Al_2(SO_4)_3 \rightarrow 2\left.\begin{array}{l}R^-\\R^-\\R^-\end{array}\right\rangle Al^{+++} + 3H_2SO_4$$

Anionic Step :

$$R^+OH^- + HCl \rightarrow R^+Cl^- + H_2O$$

$$2R^+OH^- + H_2SO_4 \rightarrow \left.\begin{array}{l}R^+\\R^+\end{array}\right\rangle SO_4^{=} + 2H_2SO_4$$

Regeneration Operation

Cationic Resin :

$$\left.\begin{array}{l}R^-\\R^-\end{array}\right\rangle Ca^{++} + 2HCl \rightarrow 2R^-H^+ + CaCl_2$$

Anionic Resin :

$$R^+Cl^- + 2NaOH \rightarrow R^+OH^- + NaCl$$

$$\left.\begin{array}{l}R^+\\R^+\end{array}\right\rangle SO_4^{=} + 2NaOH \rightarrow 2R^+OH^- + Na_2SO_4$$

Process Equipment

Theoretically an ion exchange process may be carried out batchwise or continuously. In practice, continuous operation is preferred since a batch operation is cumbersome, and it is not suitable for large scale operation. A continuous operation is in fact a cyclic operation, that is, an exchange operation is followed by a regeneration operation. For such a process resin particles are placed on a perforated support plate located near the bottom of a vertical cylindrical vessel. An influent freed from suspended particles is allowed to flow through the resin packed column in the downward direction. The quality of the treated effluent is monitored and once it reaches a preset limit the exchange operation is stopped. At this point the exchangeable ions of the resin particles would be almost totally replaced by the exchanged ions, hence the particles need to be regenerated, that is, to be restored to their original chemical structure.

Prior to regeneration operation the column is to be backwashed with a portion of the treated effluent for removing the accumulated suspended particles (if any) in the column and also for removing the column hold up. Then an aqueous solution of the regenerant is allowed to flow through the column till regeneration of the particles is completed. Next the resin particles are rinsed with a portion of the treated effluent in order to free the column of the regenerating solution. At this stage the column would be ready for the next cycle of operation.

Several alternative arrangements of the exchanger columns are practised in industrial units. The arrangement to be selected in a particular situation depends on the quality of the influent, the desired quality of the effluent and the scale of operation. Some of these are discussed hereunder.

(i) Monobed Arrangement

When the objective of treatment is to obtain either softened or dealkalized water and the scale of operation is relatively small, a single cationic column is used for exchange operation, while the resin particles of another (cationic) column is regenerated and made ready for reuse.

In case the influent flow rate be high, at least two resin beds should be operated in series. In such a situation the first column is referred to as the lead column, in which most of the exchange reactions would take place. The second column would act as a polishing column where the residual (undesired) ions would be removed. As and when the lead column becomes exhausted it is taken off the stream and regenerated. At this point the polishing column be used as the lead column and a freshly regenerated column would be used as a polishing column.

A monobed arrangement may also be used for production of demineralized water. For such an operation a column is charged with both cationic and anionic resin particles. During exchange operation in such a column removal of both cationic and anionic ions would take place simultaneously. When the bed becomes exhausted it needs to be regenerated. Prior to regeneration the column is to be backwashed with treated water and the resin particles are to be segregated within the column hydraulically. This step is necessary as different reagents are to be used for regeneration of the cationic and anionic resin particles.

Regeneration of one type of resin is done at a time. After both types have been regenerated the column has to be rinsed with demineralized water. The column would now be ready for reuse. The construction of such a column and its operation would be a complex one. Its operation particularly the regeneration operation would require a skilled operator.

For smooth and uninterrupted operation of such a unit two or more columns should be operated in series.

(ii) Two-Bed Arrangement

For production of demineralized water a two-bed arrangement is better than a monobed arrangement. In a two-bed unit the first bed is used for cation removal and the second bed is used for anion removal. Regeneration of such a unit can be carried out easily. The following schematic diagrams (Fig. 9.44) show different alternative arrangements of two–bed units.

Referring to the Fig. 9.44 it is to be noted that the role of a decarbonator is to remove the dissolved CO_2 present in decationized water as H_2CO_3 by air sparging. Such a column reduces the load on the anion exchanger.

For uninterrupted operation of a two-bed system there should be two or more cation exchangers and two or more anion exchangers connected in series. Since a decarbonator is not resin based more than one such column is not required.

(iii) Two-Bed Continuous System

Systems have been developed which can be operated with a single cationic exchanger, a decarbonator and a single anionic exchanger. In such units a portion of the resin particles is taken out of a column continuously or intermittently, regenerated (outside the column) and returned to the column. Such units do not require process interruption or column isolation for resin regeneration. The mechanical features of such columns would be a little complex, but the total quantity of resin in use would be much less compared to that in a multi-bed system.

The treated effluent produced in such units would contain some residual ionic species due to channelling through a resin bed and / or partial exhaustion of resin capacity. A residual concentration of ions in the treated effluent may be about 0.5% of that in the influent. Hence if a very pure treated effluent is desired, then a multi-bed system should be used.

Column Sizing

The total quantity of resin required for treatment of an influent stream depends on (a) the influent flow rate, (b) the concentration of the undesirable ions present in the influent, (c) the capacity of the resin to be used, and (d) the breakthrough period. Based on the above mentioned data/information, the theoretical quantity of resin required is estimated. The actual amount of resin to be used may be 20-30% more than the theoretically estimated amount.

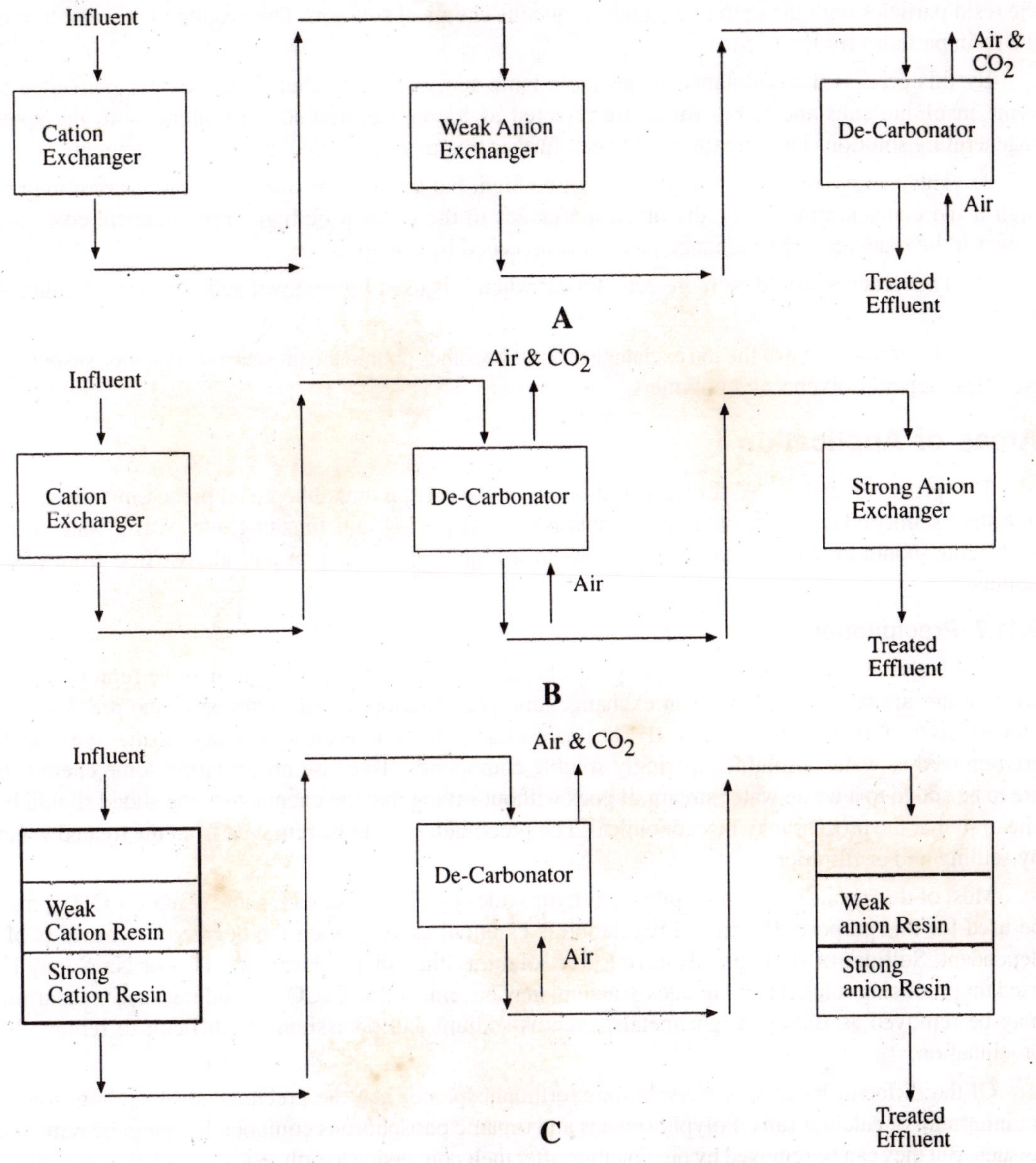

Fig. 9.44 : Alternative Arrangements of Two-Bed Ion Exchangers.

An ion exchange column diameter is calculated based on the superficial liquid velocity which is normally maintained in the range of 20–40 cm/min. The resin bed depth typically ranges between 0.75 to 2.0 m.

Process Limitations

The following needs to be noted about the limitations of the ion exchange process :

1. This process can remove only dissolved ionized constituents present in water.

2. It is a cyclic process. In the first stage the undesirable ions in solution are retained (arrested) by the resin particles, whereby water gets 'purified'. In the second stage the retained ions are stripped from

the resin particles with the help of a suitable aqueous chemical solution. This results in regeneration of the resin particles for their reuse.

By this process the pollutants (undesirable ionic species) are neither destroyed nor converted to some insoluble substances, but those are rejected as a concentrated solution along with the spent regenerating solution. This stream would need further treatment for 'final' pollution abatement.

3. The energy cost for pumping may not be high, but the reagent (for regeneration) cost may be high if the concentration of the dissolved inorganics in the influent be high. The chemical cost may, however, be reduced if ion exchange process is preceded by precipitation.

4. This process would be more economical when it is used for removal and recovery of valuable metal ions.

5. The performance of the ion exchange process becomes poor in the presence of oxidants, suspended particles, organic solvents and polymers.

Areas of Application

This process may be used for treatment of waste water from units like metal processing, electronic industry (semiconductors, printed circuit boards), metal plating and finishing, etc. Waste water from such units would contain valuable metal ions at a higher concentration and almost free from other pollutants.

9.11.7 Precipitation

The major processes by which heavy metals and some basic ions (anions) may be removed from waste water are reverse osmosis, ion exchange, and precipitation. Of these proceses the precipitation process has the following advantages : (i) The process equipment cost is the lowest, and (ii) the constituents are removed as water insoluble/ sparingly soluble compounds. To cause precipitation some chemicals are to be added to a waste water stream. It goes without saying that the chemicals to be added should be cheap so that the process may be economical. The precipitates are to be removed from the treated water by settling and or filtration.

Most of the metals can be precipitated as hydroxides by pH adjustment. Lime [$CaO/Ca(OH)_2$] may be used for this purpose. Proper pH regulation is essential as very often the degree of removal is pH dependent. Sulfides of some metals have lower solubility than their hydroxides. H_2S or Na_2S may be used for producing sulphide precipitates. Calcium may be removed as $CaCO_3$ by adding Na_2CO_3. Barium may be removed as $BaSO_4$. Light metals, such as sodium and potassium are difficult to remove by precipitation.

Of the different basic ions phosphorous (orthophosphate) may be precipitated by adding iron or aluminimum or calcium salts. Polyphosphates and organic phosphorous compounds cannot be removed as such. But they can be removed by precipitation after their conversion to orthophosphate during secondary treatment. During coagulation and flocculation some organic phosphorous compounds and polyphosphates get removed as insoluble complexes and due to adsorption onto the floc particles. A major portion of sulphate ions may be removed, as $CaSO_4$. Cloride, nitrate and nitrate ions are not amenable to precipitation.

9.11.8 Oxidation and Reduction

Oxidation

Chemical oxidation reactions are sometimes carried out for treatment of waste water in order to—

1. reduce the concentration of recalcitrant/refractory organics, such as dyes, insecticide, pesticides, etc.,

2. reduce odours and colours,

3. oxidize certain inorganic and organic compounds, which are toxic to microbes and / or inhibit microbial growth, and

4. reduce the microbial and viral population in waste water (disinfection).

The oxidants normally used are Oxygen (O_2), Chlorine (Cl_2), Chlorine dioxide (ClO_2), Ozone (O_3) and hydrogen peroxide (H_2O_2). Of these oxygen is the cheapest, but it is least reactive. Chlorine is cheap and reactive, but the residual chlorine (unreacted) beyond some concentration is toxic to living beings, hence it is not preferred as a general oxidant. ClO_2 is a strong oxidant and it is particularly effective in treating phenolic compounds. During its use a part may get converted to chlorate, which is harmful to human beings. ClO_2 is to be generated at site.

Ozone and hydrogen peroxide are good oxidants though relatively costly. They do not leave any harmful residues. To enhance the oxidation rates of ozone/hydrogen peroxide, sometimes catalysts, such as, elevated pH, titanium oxide (TiO_2), ultraviolet rays ($\lambda < 310$ nm), ultrasonic waves are used.

In the presence of these catalysts the oxidants (O_3/H_2O_2) are converted to hydroxyl radical (OH*) which is a very strong oxidant. H_2O_2 is commercially manufactured but ozone is to be generated at the site.

Some typical examples of use of chlorine as an oxidant are :

(i) Oxidation of free ammonia in waste water

$$2NH_3 + 3Cl_2 + 6H_2O \rightarrow N_2 + 6HCl + 6H_2O$$

(ii) Oxidation of cyanide compounds, such as NaCN

$$NaCN + 2NaOH + Cl_2 \rightarrow NaCNO + 2NaCl + H_2O$$

$$2NaCNO + 4NaOH + 3Cl_2 \rightarrow 6NaCl + 2CO_2 + N_2 + 2H_2O$$

The optimum pH for these reactions is 8 to 9.5.

(iii) Oxidation of ferrous salts.

$$6FeSO_4 + 3Cl_2 \rightarrow 2FeCl_3 + 2Fe_2(SO_4)_3$$

Reduction

An example of the use of reduction process for treatment of waste water is reduction of hexavalent chromium (Cr^{+6}) ions. Cr^{+6} cannot be removed by precipitation but trivalent Cr^{+3} can be.

Reduction of Cr^{+6} is carried out at an acid pH say, 2 to 3. Ferrous sulphate ($FeSO_4$)/ sodium metabisulphite ($Na_2S_2O_5$)/ sulphur dioxide (SO_2) may be used for reduction of Cr^{+6} to Cr^{+3}. The reactions are listed below :

Reaction with $FeSO_4$

$$2Na_2CrO_4 + 6FeSO_4 + 8H_2SO_4 \rightarrow Cr_2(SO_4)_3 + 3Fe_2(SO_4)_3 + 2Na_2SO_4 + 8H_2O$$

Reaction with $Na_2S_2O_5$

$$4Na_2CrO_4 + 3Na_2S_2O_5 + 10H_2SO_4 \rightarrow 2Cr_2(SO_4)_3 + 4Na_2SO_4 + 6NaHSO_4 + 7H_2O$$

Reaction with SO_2

$$2Na_2CrO_4 + 2H_2SO_4 + 3SO_2 \rightarrow Cr_2(SO_4)_3 + 2Na_2SO_4 + 2H_2O$$

9.11.9 Disinfection

After removal of inorganic and organic pollutants from a waste water stream it is finally discharged either into a water body or on a piece of land if it is not reused. If it is decided to discharge a treated waste water stream, it should be disinfected, that is, the microbes, such as, parthogens, virus, protozoa present if any, must be destroyed/ inactivated. If not properly disinfected, the discharged water may cause harm to living beings coming in contact with such water.

Disinfection may be carried out by any one of the following methods or a combination of them :

(a) Addition of Chemicals, (b) Physical Means,

(c) Mechanical Means, (d) Radiation.

The method to be employed for disinfection in a specific situation would depend on the type/types of the organisms present and their population. Viable and growing bacteria are relatively easily destroyed, whereas slime covered bacteria, bacterial spores, virus and protozoa resist disinfection. The degree of disinfection achieved in a given situation depends on the method employed, the duration of treatment, and the disinfectant concentration/intensity employed.

Chemical disinfectants affect the cell wall and cell constituents in various ways. The commonly used chemical disinfectants are Cl_2, ClO_2, O_3, H_2O_2 and phenolic compounds. Of these the first four are oxidants. They oxidize the cell wall, modify cell wall permeability and react with the various constituents of the cells including the enzymes.

Physically waste water may be disinfected by exposing it to heat or UV radiation or ultrasonic waves. On heating cell proteins coagulate and thereby cell death occurs. UV radiation is absorbed by DNA and RNA. As a result they undergo structural changes and lose their capacity to reproduce.

Mechanical means of disinection are filtration and sedimentation. During these operations the solid particles while being removed from waste water, trap some of the micro organisms and remove them. The degree of removal of the organisms depends on their size. In general the percent removal is not high.

Waste water irradiation particularly with γ rays quite effective in disinfection. However, this process is relatively costly. Of the different types of micro-organisms, virus is the most difficult to remove/ destroy. The processes which are more effective in removing/destroying virus are chlorination, reverse osmosis and UV radiation.

Cl_2, O_3 and UV radiation are more commonly used for disinfection of waste water. Of these Cl_2 is the cheapest. Ozone though costlier than chlorine is finding increasing use as a disinfectiont as it leaves no residue.

Presence of suspended particles and dissolved inorganics and organics hinder the disinfection process in general, hence those should be removed prior to disinfecting a water stream.

Chlorine on dissolution in water produces HCl and HOCl. HOCl ionizes into H^+ and OCl^-. The OCl radical is the active disinfectant. Chlorine has a strong afinity for materials, such as, Fe^{++}, Mn^{++}, NO_2^-, H_2S, NH_3 and organics. Reactions with the inorganics are very fast whereas those with the organics are slow.

The difficulties experienced in disinfection of water-borne pathogens with chlorine depend on the nature of the pathogens. Cysts are most difficult to disinfect. Virus disinfection is easier than cysts. Bacteria are easily disinfected.

The disinfection rate depends on the water temperature, pH, degree of mixing, turbidity, presence of the interfering substances and the chlorine dosage. At a lower pH the rate of disinfection is high and the chlorine dosage required for achieving a desired degree of disinfection is low. An advantage of the chlorination proces is that free residual chlorine gives post-treatment protection.

Ozone

The advantages of using ozone as a disinfectant are : (i) its high germicidal ability, (ii) its ability to oxidize most odorous and colouring substances, and (iii) it leaves behind only dissolved oxygen after treatment. It is more effective than chlorine in disinfecting virus and cysts. Its performance as a germicide is not affected by pH or ammonia. However, ozone dosage has to be increased in the presence of dissolved organic and suspended matter.

Its major disadvantages are : (i) it has to be produced at the site : (ii) it cannot be stored and transported; (iii) its relatively higher cost (compared to chlorine), and (iv) its inability to maintain germicidal action beyond the treatment unit.

Ozone and chlorine may be used in a complementary fashion. Initial treatment with ozone would oxidize phenolic compounds (if present), destroy germs quickly and improve the physical quality by oxidizing odorous and colouring substances. After ozone treatment, water may be treated with chlorine in order to provide germicidal action during transportation and distribution.

CHAPTER 10 Abatement of Some Specific Water-borne Pollutants

Waste water may contain some specific pollutants, which are toxic in nature. For abatement of a specific toxic pollutant very often a tailor-made treatment method may have to be employed. The method may be either physical or chemical or biological in nature. A physical method is incapable of converting a pollutant into an innocuous substance, whereas a chemical/biological method converts a toxic pollutant into an immobilized or a detoxified substance.

For treatment of a specific pollutant often several alternate methods are available. In order to select a suitable method in a given situation one should examine the following aspects: (i) the initial concentration of the pollutant, (ii) the desired concentration of the pollutant after treatment, and (iii) the quantity of the waste water to be treated.

The list of the toxic pollutants, which need special treatment, is a long one. An exhaustive discussion on their treatment methods is beyond the scope of this book, hence the abatement methods of only a few are listed hereunder.

10.1 Arsenic (As)

Source

Arsenic and arsenical compounds are often present in waste water produced in metallurgical, glass, ceramic, petroleum refinery and such other industries. Waste water generated in manufacturing units of dyes, pesticides, herbicides, and some other inorganic and organic chemicals may also contain arsenical compounds. Arsenic compounds have also been found in groundwater in some places.

Toxic Effects

Arsenic compounds are quite toxic. When an arsenic compound containing approximately 100 mg of AS is ingested, it causes severe poisoning. When As is ingested at a low level a considerable fraction accumulates in the body. Repeated intake leads to chronic poisoning, which is difficult to diagnose at an early stage. Progressive poisoning leads to "black-foot" disease and subsequently causes disabling and death.

The maximum limit of arsenic in treated industrial effluent is 0.2 mg/L as As, and 0.01 mg/L* in potable water.

Treatment Technology

Considerable information is available about the methods for removal of arsenite (ASO_2^-) and arsenate (ASO_4^{3-}) ions from water, but relatively less information is available about the abatement methods of other types of arsenical compounds.

The major treatment methods for removal of arsenite and arsenate from water are (1) precipitation as Sulphide, (2) complexation with polyvalent cations (Ca^{2+}, Fe^{3+}, Al^{3+}) and co-precipitation with metal oxides, (3) adsorption on activated carbon or alumina, (4) ion exchange process, and (5) membrane separation process (RO).

The removal efficiency of arsenite by the precipitation method (Sulphide or complexation) is much less compared to that of arsenate. To achieve higher removal efficiency of arsenate it should be at first oxidized (by chlorinating) to arsenate and then precipitated. Addition of sodium/Hydrogen Sulphide at pH 6 to 7 precipitates arsenic as sulphide.

Of the different complexing agents being used lime has been found to be the best. Ferric (chloride/ sulphate) has lower efficiency than that of lime. Alum has a relatively poor efficiency. The optimal pH for lime is 12, for ferric salts 8.5–9 and for alum it is 7–8. At a pH higher than the optimal the efficiency decreases sharply. Presence of heavy metals in waste water improves removal efficiency of arsenite and arsenate. During sedimentation and filtration of the heavy metal precipitates some arsenites and arsenates get adsorbed/enmeshed into the flocs whereby the overall removal efficiency increases. Finally, adsorption onto activated carbon/activated alumina removes some of the residual arsenic compounds.

It is to be noted here that the removal efficiency due to adsorption onto granular activated alumina is higher than that due to alum complexation. However, activated alumina being much costlier than alum, the former may be used only as a polishing agent.

Ion exchange process being a costlier one it may be used for removal of residual arsenite/arsenate after removing the major portion by precipitation/complexation.

Membrane separation (RO) process is capable of removing both inorganic and organic arsenical compounds. But because of its higher cost it may be used only when the methods, discussed earlier, cannot reduce the arsenic content of a waste water to the desired extent.

10.2 Cadmium (Cd)

Source

Cadmium finds its way into waste water from electroplating units, primafy batteries, standard electrochemical cells, zinc smelters and galvanizing units. In a galvanizing bath cadmium may be present as a contaminant.

Toxic Effects

Cadmium is highly toxic. Its concentration in food at about 13-15 mg/L is likely to cause serious illness. The upper limit of its concentration in treated effluent is 2 mg/L as CD. In drinking water the limit is 0.003 mg/L*.

Treatment Technology

Cadmium may be precipitated frpm waste water as hydroxide (Cd ((OH)2) at a pH 10–11. It can also be co-precipitated along with other heavy metals, such as iron. Its residual concentration can be brought down to about 0.008 mg/L, when it is precipitated as Sulphide (CdS). Cadmium is not precipitated in the presence of cyanide.

10.3 Chromium (Cr)

Source

Chromium may be present in waste water as hexavalent chromium (Cr^{6+}) and trivalent chromium (Cr^{3+}). The main sources of chromium bearing waste water are : chromium plating units, chrome tanning units and chromate treated cooling water systems.

Toxic Effects

Hexavalent chromium is toxic. It can cause cancer. Trivalent chromium is not as toxic as the hexavalent one. In treated effluent the upper limit for Cr^{3+} is 0.1 mg/L and that for total Cr is 2 mg/L when discharged into inland surface water. The limit for total chromium in drinking water is 0.05 mg/L*.

Treatment Technology

The treatment to which a chromium bearing waste water may be subjected to depend on the valency state of chromium. Hexavalent chromium Cr^{6+}, (e.g., $Na_2\ Cr_2O_7$ or Na_2CrO_4) cannot be precipitated as hydroxide directly; hence, it has to be abated by any technology other than precipitation. Trivalent chromium Cr^{3+}, (e.g., $Cr_2(SO_4)_3$) can be easily removed as hydroxide precipitate.

10.3.1 Hexavalent chromium bearing waste water may be treated by any one of the following methods :

1. reduction of hexavalent chromium to trivalent state followed by precipitation as hydroxide,
2. ion exchange process,
3. reverse osmosis,
4. carbon adsorption.

1. Reduction-Precipitation Process

When hexavalent chromium is present in a waste water stream along with some heavy metals its recovery and reuse would be difficult. Under this condition Cr^{6+} is reduced to Cr^{3+} at a pH 3.0 or below by adding a suitable reducing agent. pH is regulated by adding sulphuric acid. Any one of the following reducing agents may be used : sulphur dioxide (SO_2), sodium bisulphite ($NaHSO_3$), sodium metabisulphite ($Na_2S_2O_5$), sodium hydrosulphite ($Na_2S_2O_4$), and ferrous sulphate ($FeSO_4$).

Sulphur dioxide may be preferred as reducing agent as it is relatively cheap. When SO_2 is used as the reducing agent sulphuric acid need not be added for pH regulation. When any one of the sodium salts listed above is used as a reducing agent the TDS (total dissolved solids) of the treated effluent would increase. Use of ferrous sulphate as a reducing agent would yield more sludge, as ferric hydroxide would be co-preciptated along with chromic hydroxide. Treatment of Cr^{6+} waste containing cyanide with ferrous sulphate would produce Ferro-cyanide complexes. Subsequent treatment of such complexes would be difficult for cyanide abatement. Reduction of Cr^{6+} to Cr^{3+} should not be attempted in the presence of CN as highly poisonous HCN gas would be produced during the process.

The reduction process may be carried out in two stages. In the first stage, any one of the above mentioned reducing agents may be used whereby the major portion of Cr^{6+} would be reduced. In the second stage, the remaining portion of Cr^{6+} is reduced with hydrazine (N_2H_4). After reduction trivalent chromium (Cr^{3+}) is precipitated with lime or soda-ash as hydroxide.

2. Ion Exchange Process

When it is desired to recover Cr^{6+} from a waste water stream, the stream is first freed from suspended solid and then passed through an anion exchange resin bed. On exhaustion of the resin bed it is regenerated with sodium hydroxide (NaOH) solution. The eluted solution containing sodium chromate (Na_2CrO_4) is to be passed through a cation exchange bed, which would retain sodium ions and allow chromic acid solution to pass through. Prior to this step the Na_2CrO_4 solution concentration should be so adjusted that the chromic acid solution finally produced would not have a pH below 4.0, as at a pH below 4.0 the chromic acid produced would attack the resin particles.

3. Reverse Osmosis

Waste water containing Cr^{6+} is to first freed from suspended solids. Then it (Cr^{6+}) may be concentrated using a highly selective (cellulose acetate membrane). At a pH around 7, Cr^{6+} rejection may be around 98%. Moreover, neutral pH would prevent acid hydrolysis of the membrane.

4. Carbon Adsorption

The carbon adsorption process may be used, only when the initial concentration Cr^{6+} and other heavy metals are low.

10.3.2 Trivalent chromium may be removed from waste water either by precipitation as chromic hydroxide or by ion exchange process.

Precipitation is normally carried out by addition of lime. As an alternative soda ash may be used. The optimum pH range for precipitation is 8.5–9.5. The chromic hydroxide precipitate along with other metal hydroxides may be separated from the treated effluent by sedimentation followed by filtration.

Ion exchange may be used when trivalent chromium is present along with hexavalent chromate and dichromate, and it is desired to recover and reuse chromic acid. Waste water from a chromium plating unit is first passed through a cation exchange bed, whereby Cr^{3+} and other cations are retained and the effluent would contain chromic acid. Care should be taken during this step so that the treated effluent pH would not drop below 4.0 as otherwise chromic acid would oxidize the resin particles. The Cr^{3+} ions retained in the resin bed is to be eluted with an acid, say sulphuric acid.

10.4 Cyanide

Source

Cyanide bearing waste water is produced during metal finishing, metal plating and silver and gold extraction processes. Cyanide may also be present in discharges from plastic and fertilizer factories.

Toxic Effects

When about 50 to 60 mg of cyanide is taken as a single dose it becomes fatal. When ingested at a lower dose (say, 10 mg or less) it is converted to thiocyanate, which is not harmful. Cyanide as such may cause nerve damage or thyroid problems. Cyanide bearing waste water at an acidic pH produces HCN gas, which is extremely poisonous.

Treated effluent when discharged into an inland surface water body, should not contain more than 0.2 mg/L of cyanide (as CN) as fish get killed at a much lower concentration. Its limit in drinking water is 0.07 mg/L* as CN.

Treatment Technology

The methods which may be used for abatement of cyanide are :

(a) Oxidation,

(b) Electrolytic decomposition,

(c) Ion exchange,

(d) Reverse osmosis.

(a) Oxidation

Oxidation of cyanide with chlorine is carried out in alkaline medium. During the first stage of the reaction cyanate is produced as shown below :

$$NaCN + 2\ NaOH + Cl_2 \rightarrow NaCNO + 2\ NaCl + H_2O \quad (10.1)$$

For this reaction about 1.75 kg of Cl_2 is required per kg of CN treated. Subsequently cyanate is oxidized to CO_2 and N_2. The reaction may be represented as

$$2NaCNO + 4NaOH + 3Cl_2 \rightarrow 6NaCl + 2CO_2 + N_2 + 2H_2O \quad (10.2)$$

The total quantity of Cl_2 required for complete oxidation CN to CO_2 and N_2 is 4.3 kg per kg of cyanide. The optimum pH for chlorine oxidation of cyanide is 8 to 9.5. However, if other metals be present along with cyanide the chlorine demand will be higher as chlorine may oxidize some of metals present. Some metals such as iron, nickel when present along with cyanide form stable complexes, which are difficult to oxidize with Cl_2. These may be oxidized at pH 10^+ at about 90°C.

Ozone oxidation of cyanide takes place in two steps as in the case of chlorine oxidation. At first cyanate is produced, which is then oxidized to CO_2 and N_2. For complete oxidation of cyanide about 4.6–5 kg of ozone is required per kg of cyanide. Cyanate formation reaction is very rapid at pH 9–12, but further oxidation of cyanate is relatively slow. Metal cyanide complexes get oxidized in the presence of copper or manganese, which acts as a catalyst.

(b) Electrolytic Decomposition

Electrolytic decomposition of cyanide is carried out by subjecting it to anodic oxidation. It is a batch process. It is economical if the cyanide concentration in a spent liquor (waste water) be high and the quantity of waste water to be treated is not very large. initially cyanate is produced which is finally converted to CO_2, N_2 and NH_3. As the process goes on the bath conductivity (electrical) decreases and the process slows down. Finally, there may be some residual cyanide. However, if the waste water contains some sodium chloride (NaC1) or some NaCl is added to it, then the oxidation rate increases due to increased solution conductivity and generation of chlorine gas which takes part in the oxidation process. This process is capable of destroying metal cyanide complexes. One draw back of this process is anode scaling (fouling) in the presence of sulphate ions in the waste water to be treated.

(c) & (d) Ion Exchange and Reverse Osmosis

Ion exchange and reverse osmosis have not been found satisfactory for treatment of cyanide bearing waste water as such, as fouling occurs due to deposition of metal cyanides. The other drawback is the deterioration of the resins and the membranes by cyanide.

10.5 Fluoride

Source

Fluoride is present in natural water (ground water) in some areas. Certain industrial processes, such as phosphoric acid production, super phosphate production, aluminium production, and glass manufacturing result in generation of waste water containing fluorides. Waste water from metal finishing, electroplating, semi-conductor manufacturing and ore beneficiation units also containing fluorides. Waste water from metal finishing, electroplating, semi-conductor manufacturing and ore beneficiation units also contains fluorides.

Toxic Effects

Fluoride when present in drinking water at a concentration of more than 3 mg/L can cause dental fluorosis. Water containing 8 to 20 mg/L of fluoride, if consumed over a long priod of time, would lead to bone changes and may cause crippling fluorosis.

Drinking water having an optimum fluoride content of 0.7 to 1.2 mg/L prevents dental caries during childhood. The upper limit is 1.5 mg/L*. Treated waste water containing up to a maximum of 2 mg/L of fluoride (F) as may be discharged into inland surface water bodies.

Treatment Technology

Several methods have been developed for treatment of fluoride bearing waste water. These may be classified into two groups :

(a) precipitation/co-precipitation
(b) adsorption.

(a) Precipitation/Co-precipitation

The chemicals which have been found to be effective in abating fluoride in waste water as precipitate, are lime, dolomite and alum. The precipitate is separated by sedimentation and filtration.

On addition of lime to a fluoride bearing waste water calcium fluoride, CaF_2, is formed whose solubility in water is low. When fluorine is present as a fluoride a reaction time of 30 minutes is sufficient. But when complex fluoride is present—the complex at first gets hydrolyzed and then the fluoride ions reacts with lime to form CaF_2. The total reaction time may be 24 hours.

The precipitate formation rate is slow, hence it takes a relatively longer time for the fluoride concentration to reach its solubility limit (approximately 8 mg/L as F at 18 °C). At a higher lime dosing (than the stoichiometric amount) the residual fluoride concentration may become less than that at its solubility limit. Lime ($Ca(OH)_2$) and $CaCl_2$ are normally added. pH between 8 and 9 or above 12 minimizes the solubility of CaF_2 in water.

Addition of alum or magnesium compound in the pH range of 6.5 to 7.5 leads to co-precipitation of fluoride along with hydroxide of aluminium/magnesium. The quantity of alum required depends on the initial fluoride concentration, the desired final fluoride concentration and the pH. Under alkaline condition the alum requirement increases.

The best strategy for fluoride removal by precipitation is to treat with lime followed by alum, as lime is much cheaper than alum.

(b) Adsorption

Adsorption process may be used for removal of fluoride from waste water. The process consists of passing a fluoride bearing waste water stream through a bed of granular particles (either a weak-base type anion exchange resin or activated alumina). When an anion exchange bed is used, anions other than fluoride are also arrested. For regeneration of the ion-exchange resin particles, an alkali (NaOH)/ammonia (NH_4OH) solution may be used. An activated alumina bed would remove both fluoride and arsenic (if present). The spent alumina bed is regenerated with a caustic soda (NaOH) solution. The spent regenerant solution from ion exchange resin/activated alumina bed is neutralized with dilute sulphuric/hydrochloric acid.

The adsorption process can be cost effective for treatment of low level fluoride waste water. It is to be noted here that complexed fluoride cannot be abated by adsorption process.

Waste water having higher concentration of fluoride should be treated by a two-stage process. At first it should be treated with lime in order to bring down the fluoride concentration to about 8 mg/L and then it should be subjected to adsorption so as to have a final fluoride concentration around 1 mg/L or less.

10.6 Heavy Metals

Heavy metals normally present in waste water may be classified into the following two groups depending on their pollution potential :

1. metals having very high pollution potential, such as
   Silver (Ag), Gold (Au), Cadmium (Cd), Copper (Cu), Mercury (Hg), Lead (Pb), Antimony (Sb), Tin (Sn), Telurium (Te), Zinc (Zn);
2. metals having high pollution potential, such as
   Barium (Ba), Bismuth (BI), Iron (Fe), Manganese (Mn), Molybdenum (Mo), Titanium (Ti), Uranium (U),

It should be pointed out here that the above mentioned classification is not a complete one.

Source

Waste water produced during mining operation, ore beneficiation, metal processing, electroplating and production and use of inorganic chemicals is likely to contain one or more of the toxic metals. Groundwater at some places also contains toxic metals. Industrial operations utilizing inorganic chemicals containing toxic metals would produce waste water bearing those metals.

Toxic Effects

Heavy metals in general are toxic. Some are carcinogenic. These accumulate in human body and produce serious toxic effects. For some metals the upper limit in drinking water is as low as 0.01 mg/L or still less.

Treatment Technology

The methods which may be applied for removal of metals from waste water are :

(a) Precipitation
(b) Carbon adsorption,
(c) Ion exchange process, and
(d) Reverse osmosis.

(a) Precipitation

Of the different methods available for removal of metals from waste waters chemical precipitation is very often used, as it is the cheapest. Most of the metals can be precipitated as hydroxides or sulphides. The precipitates are separated by settling, and by sand bed or miced media filtration. The residual concentration of a metal after precipitation depends on the solubility product of the compounds formed (precipitate). For hydroxide precipitate the solubility product is expressed as $[M^{n+}] \times [OH^{n-}] = K$. In general, as pH increases the residual metal ion concentration in the treated water decreases. However, for each specific metal there is an optimum pH at which the residual concentration of the metal ion is the minimum. For some metals it is possible to reduce the residual metal ion concentration below that predicted by their respective solubility products. This may be due to adsorption of the metal ions by the chemical flocks. It must be mentioned here that when metals are present in waste water as organo-metallic compounds, their abatement by lime precipitation may not be that effective. Alum coagulation (co-precipitation along with $A1(OH)_3$ at near neutral pH values also produces some metal hydroxides. Ferric hydroxide co-precipitation of metals leads to better removal.

For some metals, sulphide precipitation reactions are more effective in reducing their residual concentration levels compared to their respective hydroxide precipitation reactions. The solubility product of a metal sulphide may be expressed as

$$[M^{m+}] \times [S^{n-}] = K$$

The residual metal concentration for sulphide precipitation reactions are pH dependent. Each metal has a specific pH at which its residual concentration is the minimum. The reagent used for sulphide precipitation is either hydrogen sulphide (H_2S) or sodium sulphide (Na_2S).

Removal of some heavy metals either as hydroxide or as sulphide may be poor, hence those are precipitated as some other sparingly soluble salts. A few specified example are mentioned below.

Removal of silver (Ag) as chloride (AgC1) is very effective as its solubility in water at 25 °C is 1.4 mg/L only. Barium (Ba) can be precipitated as barium sulphate whereby its residual concentration may be brought down to about 0.5 mg/L. Ferric (Fe) ion can be effectively removed as hydroxide, but ferrous ion has to be first oxidized to the ferric state by chlorinating and then precipitated as hydroxide. Of the different manganese (Mn) compounds mangnese oxide (MnO_2) and hydroxide are insoluble. For removal of manganous ions those are oxidized and then precipitated as oxide or hydroxide. Oxidation may be carried out with air (in the presence of copper as a catalyst) at 8.5–10 pH or with chlorine /chlorine dioxide at 9–10 pH or with ozone in the presence of lime Nickel (Ni) may be precipitated as either hydroxide or sulphide. Lead (Pb) is removed either as carbonate or as hydroxide precipitate. Selenium (Se) may be precipitated from waste water as sulphide at a pH of 6.6.

(b) Carbon Adsorption

Activated carbon adsorption process as such is not much effective in removing metal ions from waste water. However, when waste water contains dissolved organic compounds and those are removed by activated carbon adsorption process, some metal ions get co-adsorbed. As such this process is not an effective method for abatement of heavy metal ions from waste water.

(c) Ion Exchange Process

Ion exchange process may be used for removal of heavy metals present in waste water in ionic state only. The process cannot remove organo-metallic compounds. This being a costlier process may be used either for removal of the residual ions after precipitation or for recovery of metals from waste water.

(d) Reverse Osmosis

Reverse osmosis may be used for separation of heavy metals present in ionic state as well as organo-metallic compounds. It is a costlier process and hence it may be used if it is found to be economic or if the earlier discussed processes are found to be inadequate.

10.7 Mercury (Hg)

Source

The major processes which give rise to mercury bearing waste water are (i) electrolysis of brine for production of caustic soda, (ii) production of compounds containing mercury, (iii) mining recovery and purification of mercury, and (iv) production of fungicides and pharmaceuticals. Discharge of waste water from refineries also contains mercury.

Toxic Effects

Mercury is highly toxic. It damages the brain, the central nervous system and the kidney.

The upper limit for its concentration in treated waste water is 0.01 mg/L, when discharged in inland surface water. Its limit in drinking water is 1 μg/L*.

Treatment Technology

Of the different treatment technologies reported in literature the most commonly used are: (a) precipitation, (b) carbon adsorption, (c) reduction (d) ion exchange and (e) coagulation.

(a) Precipitation

Mercury present in waste water as mercuric ion can be precipitated as sulphide at an alkaline pH. Other mercury compounds need to be oxidized to the mercuric state before precipitation. The reagents, which may be used for sulphide precipitation, are sodium sulphide (Na_2S), and sodium hydrogen sulphide (NaHS).

The precipitate may be separated by flocculation, gravity settling, filtration and dissolved air floatation. The minimum achievable mercury concentration even after precipitation followed by precipitate separation and activated carbon polishing is about 10–20 μg/L. The other drawbacks of the sulphide precipitation process are: (i) the formation of soluble mercury sulphide complex in the presence of excess reagent, and (ii) the difficulty in monitoring excess sulphide content in the treated effluent.

Co-precipitation of mercuric hydroxide with aluminium hydroxide may reduce the residual mercury level to about 1–10 μg/L. Co-precipitation along with ferric hydroxide may bring down the residual level to about 0.5–5 μg/L.

(b) Carbon Adsorption

Activated carbon adsorption may be used as a polishing step. Its effectiveness depends on the following factors : (i) the initial form and concentration of mercury present in waste water, (ii) the dosage and type of powdered activated carbon used, and (iii) the contact period between the carbon particles and mercury bearing waste water. This method is more effective in removing organic mercury compounds than inorganic mercury compounds. The effectiveness of the process may be enhanced if ferric hydroxide or aluminium hydroxide precipitation is carried out simultaneously. Addition of poly-electrolyte also helps.

(c) Reduction

Mercury present in waste water as inorganic ionic mercury may be reduced to its metallic form by using reducing agents, such as aluminium, zinc, hydrazine, stannous chloride and sodium borohydrate. The metallic mercury produced may be recovered by a suitable solid separation technique. The major disadvantage of this process is that it cannot achieve a residual level of mercury much below 100 μg/L.

(d) Ion Exchange Process

Special types of resin are used for removal of mercury from waste water. When mercurous salts or organic mercury compounds are present in waste water those are oxidized with chlorine whereby negatively charged mercuric chloride complex is produced. These may be removed by using anion exchange resins. In the absence of high chloride concentration in waste water, inorganic mercury may be removed by using cation exchange resins. The ion exchange process can bring down the inorganic mercury concentration level at best to about 1–5 μg/L. This process is not much effective for abatement of organic mercury compounds in waste water.

(e) Coagulation

Aluminium sulphate, iron salts and lime have been found to be better than alum. Increase in coagulant dosage beyond 100–150 mg/L does not improve mercury removal. The coagulation process has been observed to be ineffective in methyl mercury removal.

10.8 Nutrients

A waste water stream containing nitrogen (N) and phosphorous (P) compounds when discharged into a water body promotes uncontrolled aquatic plant growth. Because of this, those compounds are referred to as nutrients.

Uncontrolled growth of aquatic plants in water bodies, such as ponds, rivers and channels often leads to eutrophication. Hence it is necessary to abate those compounds from waste water streams prior to their discharge into surface water bodies.

Sources

The major industrial sources of waste water containing nitrogen compounds are nitrogen fertilizer manufacturing units, coke oven plants, nitric acid and nitrate/nitrite salt manufacturing units, fish and meat processing units, etc.

Phosphorus bearing waste water is generated mainly during production of phosphoric acid, phosphate fertilizers, and organo-phosphorous compounds.

Toxic Effects

Waste water containing nitrogen and phosphorus compounds, when discharged into water bodies, promote growth of aquatic plants including algae. It may lead to their prolific growth, which is referred to as algal bloom. The aquatic plants utilize dissolved oxygen (DO) for respiration and thereby deplete the same. At some stage the re-oxygenation rate becomes less than the oxygen depletion rate and the DO concentration becomes too low for the aquatic plants to survive. They start decomposing. Finally, the water bodies become foul smelling and contains decomposing/decomposed organic matter. This is termed as an eutrophic condition.

In general, nitrogen and phosphorous compounds present in waste water cause the above mentioned ill effects. However, waste water from some industries may contain some specific nitrogen and phosphorus compounds which are toxic to aquatic flora and fauna. The upper limit for nitrate is 50 mg/L* (as NO_3) and that for nitrite is 3 mg/L* (as NO2) for short-term exposure in drinking water. It is to be noted here that nitrate gets reduced to nitrite due to bacterial action in the intestine. Nitrite produced combines with haemoglobin to form a complex, which reduces the oxygen carrying capacity of blood.

Treatment Technology

The methods which may be used for removal of nitrogen and phosphorous compounds frcm waste water are pollutant specific as described below :

10.8.1 Nitrogen Removal

Nitrogen may be present in waste water as ammonia (in free or combined state), nitrite, nitrate, amino acids and other nitrogenous organic compounds. Any of the following methods or a combination of some of them may be used for removal of above named compounds from a waste water stream : (a) air stripping, (b) oxidation, (c) biological methods, (d) adsorption, (e) ion exchange and (f) membrane separation.

(a) Air Stripping

This method may be used to remove free ammonia (NH_4OH) from waste water. The process consists of counter-currently contacting waste water and air in a packed column. Waste water freed from suspended solid is introduced at the top of the column in which air is injected at the bottom. The air stream leaving the column at the top would contain ammonia, and other volatile substances (if any) present in waste water.

Since the air-ammonia mixture leaving the column at the top cannot be discharged untreated into the atmosphere, it has to be subjected to any one or a combination of the following processes for recovery/destruction of the stripped constituents : cooling/scrubbing/oxidation (incineration). For removing ammonia from waste water when it is present as a salt, the waste water is to be first treated with lime and then subjected to air-stripping. Cooling/scrubbing of air-ammonia mixture leads to recovery of ammonia as a solution whereas incineration converts ammonia into N_2 and H_2O. Recovery of ammonia by air stripping may be economical when the concentration of ammonia/ammonium salts in waste water is relatively high.

(b) Oxidation

Break-Point Chlorination

Ammonia in waste water undergoes the following reaction when chlorinated at a pH 6 to 7 :

$$H_2O + Cl_2 \rightarrow HCl + HOCl \tag{10.3}$$

$$2NH_3 + 3HOCl \rightarrow N_2 + 3H_2O + 3HCl \tag{10.4}$$

Improper control of pH may lead to formation of nitrogen trichloride (gas). Dissolved hydrocarbons present in waste water may produce trichloromethane, a toxic substance. Some pollutants other than ammonia present in waste water may also react with chlorine and thereby increase the chlorine consumption, which would result in higher treatment cost.

This method is economical, only when the concentration of ammonia in waste water is initially low or has been reduced by some other treatment. It has the added advantage that disinfection takes place simultaneously. Care should be taken that the treated effluent would not contain high residual chlorine.

(c) Biological Methods

Both inorganic and organic nitrogenous compounds except the recalcitrants and non-biodegradables can be abated by the biological methods. During this process a part of the total nitrogen present in waste water is assimilated to synthesize microbes while the other part is catabolized. The process is carried out in two stages.

During the first (aerobic) stage the Nitrosomonas and Nitrobacter bacteria oxidize nitrogenous compounds to nitrite (NO_2) and nitrate (NO_3). The reactions may be expressed as

$$2NH_4^+ + 3O_2 \xrightarrow{\text{Nitrosomonas}} 2NO_2 + 4H^+ + 2H_2O \tag{10.5}$$

$$2NO_2^- + O_2 \xrightarrow{\text{Nitrobacter}} 2NO_3^- \tag{10.6}$$

Whereas during the second (anaerobic) stage nitrite and nitrate are converted to gases like N_2, NO, NO_2, N_2O, etc. Mainly, N_2 is produced. The microbes which carry out these reactions are Achromobacter, Aerobacter, Alcaligenes, Bacillus, Flabobactrium, Micrococus, Proteus, Pseudomonous, etc. The aerobic (nitrification) and anaerobic (denitrification) treatments of waste water containing nitrogenous compounds have been discussed in Sections 9.11.3.2 and 9.11.3.3. It should be pointed out here that the biological methods for treatment of nitrogenous pollutants in waste water is cost effective even when their concentration is high.

(d) Adsorption

Activated carbon adsorption method is capable of removing both inorganic and organic nitrogenous compounds. It is more effective for abatement of organic compounds including the recalcitrants and non-biodegradables.

The degree of removal is adsorbent-adsorbate specific. It is also dependent on the factors such as temperature, pH, space time and the other adsorbates (pollutants) present, if any.

Either powered or granular activated carbon may be used. On the surface and microspores of the carbon particles the adsorbates get adsorbed. Once the particles become saturated with the adsorbates the particles may be either regenerated (freed from the adsorbates) and reused or discarded. When powdered carbon is used no pretreatment of waste water for separation of suspended particles is necessary. Normally powdered carbon particles are discarded after use. Granular carbon particles are used in a packed bed through which waste water to be treated flows in the downward direction. In order to avoid chocking of the packed bed a waste water stream should be pretreated for removing suspended particles present, if any. Granular carbon particles are regenerated and reused as a rule. This method being relatively costly may be used when the pollutants are present at a low concentration or when the other methods are not effective.

Further details of the carbon adsorption process are given in Section 9.11.4.

(e) Ion Exchange Method

This method can be used for removal of ionized nitrogenous radicals such as NH_4^+, NO_3^-, NO_2^- present in waste water. Non-ionized nitrogenous compounds cannot be removed by this method.

The process is carried out by passing waste water free from suspended particles through a column containing cationic/anionic resin particles depending on the type of ions to be removed. As waste water flows through the resin bed, the ions (cations/anions) in solution are arrested and the resin particles becomes gradually saturated. Once the particles become completely saturated, no further removal of ions would take place. Before such a state is reached the process is discontinued and the resin particles are regenerated by chemical treatment. During this process not only nitrogenous ions but also other inorganic and organic ions (if present) would be retained by the resin particles and hence the load on the resin bed would be high.

The ion exchange process has been elaborated in Section 9.11.6.

(f) Membrane Separation

In this process waste water free from suspended particles but containing dissolved substances is allowed to flow over specially prepared polymer (membrane) sheet or tube. Through the sheet/tube wall water permeates to the other side whereas the solutes are retained.

This process is capable of separating both inorganic and organic solutes from water. It is not cost effective unless a wastewater stream contains solutes at low concentration. The retained solutes along with some water flow out of the unit, which is termed as a retentate.

The basic aspects and some other details of this process are discussed in Section 9.11.5.

10.8.2 Phosphorus Removal

Phosphorus may be present in waste water as metaphosphate (PO_3^-), orthophosphate (PO_4^{-3}), pyrophosphate ($P_2O_7^{-4}$), tripolyphosphate ($P_3O_{10}^{-5}$) and organophosphorus compounds. The sources of phosphorus bearing waste water are the units producing phosphoric acid, phosphoric fertilizers, various phosphorus compounds, detergents, pesticides (insecticides, herbicides, and fungicides), etc.

The major methods, which may be used, for abatement of phosphorus compounds from waste water are (a) precipitation, and (b) biological treatment. The other methods for phosphorus removal are carbon adsorption, ion exchange and membrane separation. The latter methods are relatively costly and hence may be used for removal of recalcitrant compounds only.

(a) Precipitation

Addition of metal salts or lime to waste water containing orthophosphate ions (PO^{3-}) results in the formation of sparingly soluble metal phosphates, which precipitate out. The solubility of metal phosphate is pH dependent. $AlPO_4$ has a minimum solubility at pH 6.5; $FePO_4$ has a minimum solubility at pH 5.3. Ferrous phosphate [$Fe_3(PO_4)_2$] and calcium phosphate [$Ca_3(PO_4)_2$] have low solubility at higher pH values. Lime reacts with waste water alkalinity and precipitates as $CaCO_3$. As the pH level increases beyond 10, Ca^{2+} ions react with phosphate ions and precipitate as $Ca_5(PO_4)_3OH$.

The precipitation reactions are almost instantaneous. There may be some side reactions leading to the formation and precipitation of other compounds as listed in Table 10.1

Table 10.1 : Phosphate Precipitation Reactions

Reacting Ions	Product
$Al^{3+} + PO_4^{3-}$	$AlPO_4$
$Al^{3+} + (OH)^-$	$Al(OH)_3$
$Fe^{3+} + PO_4^{3-}$	$FePO_4$
$Fe^{2+} + PO_4^{3-}$	$Fe_3(PO_4)_2$
$Fe^{3+} + (OH)^-$	$Fe(OH)_3$
$Ca^{2+} + PO_4^{3-} + (OH)^-$	$Ca_5(PO_4)_3(OH)$
$Ca^{2+} + CO_3^{2-}$	$CaCO_3$
$Mg^{2+} + (OH)^-$	$Mg(OH)_2$

It should be pointed out here that very little polyphosphate and organophosphorous compounds are removed along with phosphorous precipitates. The metal salts added (for phosphate removal) in excess of the stoichiometric amount would remain in solution as a result of which the total dissolved solid content of the treated effluent would increase.

Aqueous solutions of iron and aluminium salts are normally added for phosphate precipitation. It is easier to handle, store and dose them. The dosing rate is ascertained by laboratory trials.

Lime may be added as a slurry. Its storage, handling and dosing is somewhat difficult. Moreover, the quantity of sludge produced would be larger. Hence its use for phosphate precipitation is declining though it is cheaper than iron and aluminium salts.

If the initial concentration of PO_4^{3-} ions be high in a waste water stream, then phosphate may be precipitated during the primary treatment. The other phosphate compounds including the organo-phosphorous compounds can be removed by precipitation, only after/during the secondary treatment as those are converted to PO_4^{3-} is a result of biological reactions. The precipitate produced during the primary/secondary treatment is separated in a classifier and discarded as a sludge.

The phosphorous compounds which escape removal by precipitation may be removed by carbon adsorption and/or membrane separation process.

(b) Biological Treatment

Biological treatment of phosphorus bearing wastewater is carried out by subjecting it alternately to aerobic and anaerobic processes. During biological treatment a part of the phosphorous and nitrogenous compounds present in waste water are assimilated for synthesis of new cells.

Under aerobic condition the biodegradable phosphorous compounds including the organic ones are oxidized to orthophosphate and polyphosphate, some of which are stored in microbes as such. During anaerobic treatment the stored phosphorous compounds (orthophosphate and polyphosphate) are released into the water. The released Phosphorous compounds may either be discarded with the secondary sludge or precipitated prior to sludge separation and disposal. It may be summed up by saying that for biological phosphorus removal both anaerobic and aerobic treatments of waste water are essential.

Several commercial processes have been developed and are being used for biological phosphorus removal in which the anaerobic and aerobic steps are sequenced in different orders. Some of these have been discussed in Section 9.11.3.4. It should be pointed out here that during biological phosphorus removal processes proper sequencing of the anaerobic and aerobic steps would lead to abatement of some nitrogenous compounds as well as BOD.

10.9 Phenol

Source

Phenol (C_6H_5OH) is also known as carbolic acid. The major sources of phenol bearing waste water are : petroleum refineries, coke oven plants, synthetic phenol plants and plants producing phenolic resins, phenolic compounds and plants using phenol as a raw material.

Toxic Effects

Phenol is corrosive and it is poisonous to all living beings. When treated effluent is discharged into inland surface water bodies the concentration of phenol should not exceed 1 mg/L. In drinking water its limit is 0.001 mg/L**.

Treatment Technology

Several chemical, Physical and biological treatment methods are in use for removal of phenol and phenolic compounds from waste water. These are discussed under (i) treatment of concentrated solutions, (ii) treatment of intermediate concentration solutions, and (iii) treatment of dilute solutions.

Before attempts are made to remove phenol from a waste water stream pretreatments are necessary for removal of suspended matter, heavy metals (when present at a high concentration), oils, cyanides, etc.

(i) Concentrated Solutions

Waste water containing phenol having a concentration above 500 mg/L is considered to be a concentrated solution. Since recovered phenol has a market value, it may be recovered from waste water by solvent extraction. Commercially used processes are : Benzene-caustic dephenolization, Phenosolvan dephenolization (Lurgi), and IFAWOL dephenolization. These processes have high phenol removal efficiency (98–99%). It should be pointed out here that benzene being a carcinogenic substance, its use as a solvent needs very careful handling.

Depending upon the initial concentration of phenol in waste water its residual concentration after extraction may be 10–30 mg/L or higher. The residual phenol may be removed by any one or a combination of the following treatments : biological, activated carbon adsorption, coagulation with alum/iron salts, chemical oxidation with permanaganate/Chlorine/Chlorine dioxide/ozone.

(ii) Intermediate Concentration Solutions

Waste water having a phenol concentration in the range of 50–500 mg/L is labelled as an intermediate concentration solution. Such a solution may be treated by a suitable biological (aerobic) process, like lagoon, oxidation ditch, trickling filter, activated sludge treatment. Biological treatment may bring down the phenol concentration to about 0.5–1 mg/L.

The other alternative treatment methods are : (a) activated carbon adsorption, which is as effective as the biological method, (b) coagulation with alum/iron salts at a suitable pH—its effectiveness is rather poor, and (c) chemical oxidation.

Chemical oxidation may be carried out either with permanganate, which is a costly chemical or with chlorine and lime at pH less than 7. It is highly effective. However, a large quantity of chlorine must be used to ensure complete oxidation of phenol, as otherwise toxic chlorophenols would be produced.

Oxidation may be carried out with chlorine dioxide, which is a strong oxidant and it is quite effective in oxidizing phenol and phenolic compounds. However, its possible conversion to chlorate (which is toxic to humans) makes its use in treatment of potable water questionable.

Oxidation may also be carried out very effectively with ozone. It is a very strong oxidant and it does not produce any harmful by-product. For oxidation of 1 part of phenol about 1.5 to 2.5 parts of ozone is required. The residual phenol after ozone treatment may be as low as 3 ppb.

(iii) Dilute Solutions

Waste water containing phenol less than 50 mg/L is considered to be a dilute solution. Such a solution may be treated biologically or with activated carbon or by ozone oxidation. The major difficulty with ozone treatment is that ozone has been generated in situ.

10.10 Volatile Organic Compounds (VOCs)

Organic compounds present in waste water may be of the following types :

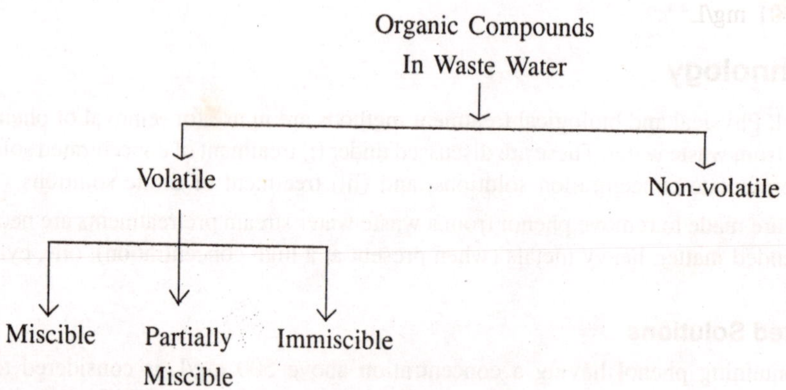

The volatile compounds may be biodegradable or non-biodegradable. The non-volatile compounds are in general non-biodegradable.

Source

The major industrial sources of waste water containing VOCs are petroleum refineries, petrochemical industries and industrial units producing different types of organic chemicals.

Toxic Effects

VOCs bearing waste water when kept in contact with air would lead to volatilization of VOCs and thereby cause atmospheric pollution. Waste water containing biodegradable VOCs if discharged untreated into surface water bodies would cause DO depletion of the receiving bodies. Some of the VOCs, such as benzene, toluene and xylene (BTX) are toxic. Benzene is a carcinogen. Its reduction in treated water below 500 ppb is a compliance requirement. The limits in drinking water for benzene, toluene and xylene are 0.01,0.7 and 0.5 mg/L* respectively.

Treatment Technology

The methods which may be used for abatement of VOCs from waste water are (a) air/nitrogen stripping, and (b) activated carbon adsorption.

(a) Air/Nitrogen Stripping

To remove VOCs from a waste water stream it may be stripped with a gas stream, such as air or nitrogen. Steam is not used for VOC stripping from waste water as a very large amount of steam would be required for heating waste water, consequently the process would be uneconomic. This process is generally carried out in a packed column. To avoid column fouling the waste water stream should be pretreated to remove suspended solid particles as well as non-volatile organic pollutants.

In a stripper, waste water is introduced at the top and the gas at the bottom, the flow being counter current. For designing a suitable column the following are to be considered : (i) waste water flow rate, (ii) the desired degree of removal of the most offensive pollutant, and (iii) the operating temperature. Since the pollutant concentration in most cases would be low, its equilibrium data may be expressed by Henry's law.

A column should be designed based on the targeted pollutant and its desired degree of removal. The extent of removal of the other VOCs present should then be estimated based on the column designed. The column dimensions would depend on the gas to liquid ratio, the mass transfer coefficient and the packing (type and size) chosen. A gas to liquid volumetric ratio around 50 : 1 is considered to be a good one. The column should be designed based on the peak hydraulic and pollutant load and not on the average load.

Air may be selected as the stripping gas when it is not desired to recover the stripped VOCs. VOC laden air should not be discharged into the atmosphere in order to avoid atmospheric pollution. It should be incinerated either in a utility boiler or a waste heat boiler or a catalytic incinerator.

As some of the pollutants present in waste water may be biodegradable, those would undergo biodegradation and produce biomass in an air stripper. The biomass thus produced may cause column fouling. To remove the accumulated biomass any one of the following biocides may be used : (i) oxidizing biocide, such as chlorine or chlorine dioxide, (ii) dilute caustic or acid solution. Each of these has some limitations.

Nitrogen may be used for stripping VOCs from waste water in a closed-loop system when it is economical to recover the stripped VOCs, such as BTX. A closed-loop system would have the following units : (i) a RH (relative humidity) modification unit, (ii) activated carbon adsorption beds (at least two, being operated alternately), and (iii) a nitrogen recirculation blower. A RH modification unit is essential as at RH 50% or more VOCs adsorption by carbon bed would be inefficient.

The process is carried out through the following steps : (i) VOCs are stripped from pretreated waste water with nitrogen gas in a packed column, (ii) the VOC laden nitrogen gas leaving the stripper may either be heated to 10–15 °C above its dew point or first cooling and condensing some water vapour and then reheating by 10–15 °C above its dew point, (iii) the RH modified gas stream is next passed through one or two carbon adsorption beds whereby most of the VOCs would get adsorbed; and

(iv) finally, the nitrogen stream emerging from the absorber is recycled back to the stripper. The recycled nitrogen stream would invariably contain some low molecular weight VOCs. To avoid building up of those, a part of the recycled gas is purged from time to time and the loss is made up with fresh nitrogen.

As and when a carbon bed reaches its breack point, it is taken off and regenerated by steam stripping. The steam-VOC mixture is condensed for VOC recovery.

(b) Activated Carbon Adsorption

Organic compounds present in waste water as dissolved substances as well as droplets can be removed by activated carbon may be used. From regeneration and reuse point of view powdered carbon is not a good choice. The most effective adsorbent is granular activated carbon (GAC). Its uniqueness lies in its high specific surface area and its pore network comprised of micro, maso and macrospores. It has a high adsorptive capacity. One major drawback of GAC is its non-selective adsorption of organic substances. It is regenerated and reused. Regeneration of GAC means desorption of adsorbed VOCs. Low molecular weight VOCs are easy to desorb, whereas high molecular weight organic substances, such as oil, grease, tar, etc., are poorly desorbable.

VOC removal by the carbon adsorption process is a cyclic one. It consists of passing a stream of waste water (containing dissolved and suspended organic substances) through a column packed with GAC. The organic substances get adsorbed on the surfaces of the carbon granules. The process continues till the surface area of all of the particles (including their pore area) are almost completely covered with adsorbed molecules. This condition is referred to as the "break point". If a column is operated beyond this point the VOC content of the effluent stream would be almost the same as that of the influent. At this stage the carbon particles are to be regenerated, that is, the adsorbed substances are to be removed, if those are to be reused.

Regeneration

The first step in regeneration would be to drain the held up water from the column. The carbon granules may then be regenerated using any one of the following methods; (i) on-site air/steam stripping, (ii) off-site heating of the particles with limited supply of air.

On-site air/steam stripping would be cheaper. However, it cannot remove most of the high molecular weight VOCs. While stripping with air, care should be taken so that the air–VOC mixture should always be below its lower explosive limit (LEL). It is very difficult, if not impossible, to remove all of the adsorbed substances. The residue left on the carbon particles after stripping is referred to as the "heel". The heel reduces the adsorption capacity of a regenerated bed. The heel would be lower if stripping be done with steam at a higher temperature.

Off-site desorption of VOCs is costlier. When high molecular weight organic compounds, such as oil, grease, etc. are adsorbed from waste water, they cannot be desorbed by air/steam stripping. They go on accumulating on the carbon granules (as heel). As a result the working (adsorption) capacity of the column would decrease progessively. To regenerate such carbon particles those are taken out of the column and heated in a chamber in a limited supply of air. This would result not only in removal (oxidation) of the adsorbed substances but also oxidation of some portions of carbon particles.

To overcome this situation a 'guard column' may be installed before the 'main adsorber'. The guard column would trap the high molecular weight pollutants whereas the main adsorber would remove lighter VOCs from a waste water stream. The main adsorber may be regenerated by air/steam stripping and the guard column carbon particles may be either regenerated by air oxidation or replaced from time to time.

During regeneration a column would have to be isolated. Hence, for continuous operations of such a system it is essential to have at least two adsorption columns operating alternately.

10.11 Pesticides

Insecticides, herbicides and fungicides are generally termed as pesticides. These may be either inorganic or organic chemicals. These are harmful to man, domestic animals as well as to useful flora and fauna. However, their use is unavoidable as man is able to reduce both agricultural and horticultural losses to some extent by using pesticides.

Source

Waste water originating from pesticide manufacturing units would contain those along with some other organic pollutants.

Run off water from agricultural fields and fruit orchards where pesticides are used would invariably contain them. The run off water contaminates not only surface water bodies but also groundwater. Potable water produced by conventional treatment of water from such pesticide contaminated sources would be hazardous.

Toxic Effects

Ingestion of large amounts of pesticides causes severe adverse health effects. Small amounts ingested may accumulate in the body and may affect the central nervous system in the long run. Different pesticides affect different organs of the human body, for example, the liver, the reproductive system, etc. The organo-phosphorus and carbamate pesticides are very poisonous.

Herbicides, in general, are less toxic than insecticides.

Pesticides should be absent in drinking water, however, in the absence of an alternative source the permissible limit is 0.001 mg/L**.

Treatment Technology

Inorganic pesticides and organometallic pesticides may be treated by any one or a combination of following methods : (i) oxidation, (ii) reduction, (iii) precipitation, and (iv) membrane separation (RO).

It should be noted that RO does not convert a pesticide present in waste water into an innocuous substance but produces a concentrated stream, which has to be further treated for converting the pesticide into a harmless substance.

The methods available for abatement of organic pesticides from waste water are (i) activated carbon adsorption, (ii) reverse osmosis (RO), and (iii) chemical oxidation.

(i) Activated carbon adsorption may carried out with GAC (granulated active carbon). The spent particles should be regenerated by air oxidation so as to destroy the adsorbate.

(ii) Reverse osmosis would produce a concentrated pesticide-rich stream, which would need chemical oxidation for pesticide destruction.

(iii) Chemical oxidation of pesticide present in waste water may be carried out with a suitable oxidant in the presence of a catalyst. Economic feasibility of this process would depend on the quanitity of waste water to be treated and the initital concentration of the pollutants present.

Note : * WHO Guideline values ((3rd edition)

** Indian Standard (IS 10500 : 1991)

APPENDICES

APPENDIX—I

A BRIEF GUIDELINE FOR PREPARATION OF ENVIRONMENTAL IMPACT ASSESSMENT REPORT

The issues to be considered and addressed while preparing an EIA Report depend on the proposed activity. For a new project the issues listed below need attention.

(i) Type of the proposed project.

(ii) Nature of the terrain, which is likely to be affected.

(iii) Natural disaster to which the area is prone.

(iv) The area (land and water bodies) likely to be affected.

(v) The size of land, which will be tied up.

(vi) Is the project a part of several other projects ?

(vii) Plans of the proponent about expansion/addition of new projects in near future.

(viii) Special features of the local flora and fauna.

(ix) Whether the historic sites and existing public utilities would be affected.

(x) How many people are likely to be displaced?

(xi) Whether the local plants, animals and migratory animals would be affected during construction.

(xii) The sources of information about the existing ecosystem.

(xiii) The extent to which the environment would be affected during the construction phase.

(xiv) Expected infrastructural inadequacy, if any, during construction and operation.

(xv) Types of wastes and pollutants, which will be generated during construction and operation of the project.

(xvi) Provision incorporated in the project for abatement and disposal of wastes and pollutants and to cope with accidents.

(xvii) Training to be imparted to the project and operators for environment monitoring and observance of safety regulations.

(xviii) The extent to which local man-power and resources would be utilized during construction and operation.

(xix) Would the local social structure be affected?

(xx) Would the local standard of living improve?

(xxi) What are the major plus points and minus points of the project ?

(xxii) Information available about EIA reports for similar projects elsewhere.

(xxii) Local, state and national regulations, which are to be abided by.

(xxiv) Views of the local people on the expected environmental impact.

(xxv) Local/outside experts' view on the expected environmental impact.

(xxvi) Expected environmental impact (EI) during construction, during operation and in the long run.

(xxvii) Possible modifications of the project to reduce EI.

(xxviii) From EI point of view should the project be shifted to a different place? Should some other project be implemented at this site ?

APPENDIX—II
SALIENT FEATURES OF POLLUTION CONTROL ACTS AND RULES IN INDIA

1. INDIAN PENAL CODE 1860 (45 of 1860)

Under this Code a polluter of environment can be punished for certain types of pollution. These types of pollution may be broadly categorized under the following heads :

A. Water Pollution

If a person voluntarily corrupts or fouls the water of any public spring or reservoir so as to render it less fit for the purpose for which it is ordinarily used, he may be punished under Section 227.

B. Pollution of Atmoshphere

If a person vitiates the atmosphere in any place so as to make it noxious to the health of persons generally dwelling or carrying on business in the neighbourhood or passing along a public way, he may be punished under Section 278.

C. General Pollution

If a person does any act or omits to do any act which causes any common injury, danger or annoyance to the public or to the people in general, who dwell or occupy property in the vicinity or which must cause injury, obstructioin, danger or annoyance to person who may have occasion to use any public right, this act or omission may amount to public nuisance. Such offenders may be punished under Sections 290 and 291. If a person unlawfully or negligently does any act, which is likely to spread the infection of any disease dangerous to life, he may be punished under Section 269. If a person causes wrongful loss or damage to the public or any person, causes the destruction of any property or any such change in any property or in the situation thereof which destroys or diminishes its value or utility or affects it injuriously, he may be punished under Sections 426, 430, 431 and 432.

2. Bengal Smoke Nuisance Act, 1905

According to this act, for erection and/or alternation of furnaces, flues, chimneys and other smoke abating units, sanction has to be obtained from the Chief Inspector of Smoke Nuisances. Initially this act was extended only up to Calcutta and Howrah. Subsequently, similar acts were enacted for some other cities in India.

3. The Factories Act, 1948

Section 12 of this act provides for the regulation of disposal of wastes and effluents from the factories. According to this act effective arrangement shall be made in every factory for the treatment of wastes and effluents produced due to the manufacturing processes carried out therein, so as to render them innocuous for their disposal.

The State Governments were authorized to make rules for implementation of this Act.

4. The Water (Prevention and Control of Pollution) Act, 1974

Acoding to Section 24 of the Act,

(a) No person shall knowingly cause or permit any poisonous, noxious or polluting matter, determined in accordance with such standards as may be laid down by the State Board to enter (directly or indirectly) into any stream or well;

(b) No person shall knowingly cause or permit to enter into any stream any other matter, which may tend either directly or in combination with similar matters, to impede the proper flow of the water of the stream in a manner leading or likely to lead to a 'substantial aggravation of pollution due to other causes of its consequences.

As per Section 25 of the act, no person shall, without the previous consent of the State Board, bring into use any new or altered outlet for the discharge of sewage or trade effluent into a stream or well, or begin to make any new discharge of sewage or trade effluent into a stream or well.

5. The Water (Prevention and Control of Pollution) Cess Act, 1977 and the Water (Prevention and Control of Pollution) Cess Rules, 1978

Section 3 of the Act (1977) states that, cess shall be payable by (a) every person carrying on any specified industry; and (b) every local authority. The cess shall be calculated on the basis of water consumed for any of the purposes listed below :

(i) Industrial cooling, spraying in mine pits or boiler feed,

(ii) Domestic purpose,

(iii) Processing whereby water gets polluted and the pollutants are easily biodegradable,

(iv) Processing whereby water gets polluted and the pollutants are not easily biodegradable and are toxic.

Metering

Under this Act (1977) and the Rules (1978) every person carrying on any specified industry and every local authority should install meters for measuring and recording the quantity of water consumed.

Furnishing of Returns

Every person and every local authority, who are liable to pay the cess, are required to submit a return every month showing the quantity of water consumed during the previous month.

Rebate

Under the Water Cess Act it is provided that where any person or local authority liable to pay cess under this Act, installs any plant for the treatment of sewage or trade effluent, such person or authority shall be entitled to a rebate of 70% of the cess payable.

6. The Air (Prevention and Control of Pollution) Act, 1981

Section 19 of this Act states that, the State Government after consultation with the State Board is empowered to prescribe any area or areas within the State as 'air pollution control area or areas' for the purpose of this Act.

According to Section 20 of the Act, the State Government is empowered to ensure that the standards for emission of air pollutants from automobiles as laid down by the State Board are complied with.

Section 21 of the Act states that, no person shall, without the previous consent of the State Board, establish or operate any industrial plant for the purpose of any industry specified in the Schedule in an air pollution control area.

Under Section 22 of the Act, no person carrying on any industry specified in the Schedule or operating any industrial plant in any air pollution control area shall discharge or cause or permit to be discharged the emission of any air pollutant in excess of the standards laid down by the State Board.

7. The Environment (Protection) Act, 1986

According to Section 6 of the Act, the Central Government may make rules in respect of—

(a) the standards of quality of air, water or soil for various areas and purposes;

(b) the maximum allowable limits of concentration of various environmental pollutants (including noise) for different areas;

(c) the procedures and safeguards for the handling of hazardous substances;

(d) the prohibition and restrictions on the handling of hazardous substances in different areas;

(e) the prohibition and restrictions on the location of industries and the carrying on of processes and operations in different areas;

(f) the procedures and safeguards for prevention of accidents which may cause environmental pollution and for providing for remedial measures for such accidents.

As per Section 7 of the Act, no person carrying on any industry, operation or process shall discharge or emit or permit to be discharged or emitted any environment pollutant in excess of such standards as may be prescribed.

Under Section 8 of the Act, no person shall handle or cause to be handled any hazardous substance except in accordance with such procedure and after complying with such safeguards as may be prescribed.

According to Section 9 of the Act, when the discharge of any environmental pollutant in excess of the prescribed standards occurs or is apprehended to occur due to any accident or other unforeseen act or event, the persons responsible for such discharge and the person in charge of the place at which such discharge and the person in charge of the place such discharge occurs or is apprehended to occur shall be bound to prevent or mitigate the environmental pollution caused as a result of such discharge and shall also forthwith intimate the fact of such occurrence or apprehension of such occurrence to the appropriate authority.

As provided in the Act the Central Government/Central Pollution Control Board/State Pollution Control Board has laid down

(a) the maximum permissible limits of emission of various pollutants from some specific industries;

(b) the maximum allowable limits of concentration of various pollutants in a discharged effluent;

(c) the ambient air quality standard.

These laid down Standards and Limits have been categorized under the following heads :

A. Maximum Permissible Limits of Discharge from Some Specific Industries.
(Appendix–IIIA) (Source : Gazette of India Notifications)

B. General Standards for Discharge of Effluents.
[Indian Standards—IS : 2490 (Part I), 1981]

C. Ambient Air Quality Standards.
(Appendix–IIIB) (Source : Gazette of India Notifications)

8. Manufacture, Storage and Import of Hazardous Chemicals Rules, 1989

These Rules have been prescribed under the Environment (Protection) Act, 1986.

Under these Rules a list of Hazardous and Toxic Chemicals has been prepared and the indicative criteria for toxic, flammable and explosive chemicals have been listed.

These Rules have specified the on-site and off-site (statutory) obligations of the exporter/importer/ occupier, who has control over an activity involving handling, storage, and processing Hazardous and Toxic chemicals. The 'Authorities' from whom permission has to be obtained or to whom reports are to be submitted are also categorically stated.

Indicative Criteria for Toxic, Flammable and Explosive Chemicals

(a) Toxic Chemicals

Those Chemicals, which have acute toxicity and which owing to their physical and chemical properties are capable of causing major accidents/hazards, are to be labelled as 'Toxic Chemicals'. The Criteria for ascertaining the toxicity of a chemical are listed in Table-1.1.

Table 1.1 : Criteria for Chemical Toxicity

Sl. No.	Degree of Toxicity	Medium lethal dose by the oral route LD_{50} (mg/kg body weight of test animals)	Medium lethal dose by the dermal route LD_{50} (mg/kg body weight of test animals)	Medium lethal concentration by inhalation route (four hours) LD_{50} (mg/lit inhalation in test animals)
1.	Extremely toxic	1-50	1-200	0.1-0.5
2.	Highly toxic.	51-500	201-2000	0.5-2.0

(b) Flammable Chemicals

(i) **Flammable gases** are defined as those chemicals, which in the gaseous state at normal pressure and mixed with air become flammable and the boiling point of which at normal pressure is 20 °C or below.

(ii) **Highly flammable liquids** are those chemicals, which have a flash point lower than 23 °C and the boiling point of which at normal pressure is above 20 °C, have been defined as highly flammable liquids.

(iii) **Flammable liquids** are those chemicals, which have a flash point lower than 65 °C and which remain in the liquid state under normal pressure, whereas at particular processing conditions, such as high pressure and high temperature, may create major accident hazards.

(c) Explosives

These are defined as those chemicals which may explode under the effect of flame, heat or photo-chemical conditions or which are more sensitive to shocks or friction than dinitrobenzene.

9. Hazardous Wastes (Management and Handling) Rules, 1989

These Rules have been framed under the Environment (Protection) Act, 1986.

The objectives of these Rules are to provide control on generation, collection, import, storage, transport, treatment and disposal of hazardous wastes. Under these rules the Central Government is empowered to lay down the procedures and safeguards for handling hazardous susbstances, which include hazardous chemicals, hazardous wastes and hazardous micro-organisms. Eighteen Categories of Hazardous Wastes have been specified.

APPENDIX—IIIA

MAXIMUM PERMISSIBLE LIMITS OF DISCHARGE FROM SOME SPECIFIC INDUSTRIES

Sl. No.	Industry	Parameter	Standards	
1	2	3	4	
1.	Caustic soda industry		Concentration not to exceed milligram per litre (except for pH and flow)	
		Total concentration of mercury in the final effluent*	0.01	
		Mercury bearing waste water generation (flow)	10 kilolitres/tonne of caustic soda produced	
		pH	5.5 to 9.0	
		* Final effluent is the combined effluent from (a) cell house, (b) brine plant, (c) chlorine handling, (d) hydrogen handling, (e) hydrochloric acid plant.		
2.	Man-made Fibres (synthetic)		Concentration not to exceed milligram per litre (except for pH)	
		Suspended solids	100	
		Biological oxygen demand, 5 days at 20 °C	30	
		pH	5.5 to 9.0	
3.	Oil refinery industry		Concentration not to exceed milligram per litre (except for pH)	quantum, kg/1000 tonnes crude processed.
		Oil and grease	10	7
		Phenol	1	0.7
		Sulphide	0.5	0.35
		Biological oxygen demand, 5 days at 20 °C.	15	10.5
		Suspended solids	20	14
		pH	6 to 8.5	

Sl. No.	Industry	Parameter	Standards
1	2	3	4
4.	Sugar industry		Concentration not to exceed milligram per litre
		Biological oxygen demand, 5 days at 20 °C	100 for disposal on land 30 for disposal in surface waters
		Suspended solids	100 for disposal on land 30 for disposal in surface waters
5.	Thermal power plants		Maximum limiting concentration milligram per litre (except for pH and temperature).
	Condenser cooling water (once through cooling system)	pH	6.5 to 8.5
		Temperature	Not more than 5 °C higher than the intake water temperature.
	Boiler blow down	Free available chlorine	0.5
		Suspended solids	100
		Oil and grease	20
		Copper (total)	1.0
		Iron (total)	1.0
	Cooling tower blow down	Free available chlorine	0.5
		Zinc	1.0
		Chromium (total)	0.2
		Phosphate	5.0
		Other corrosion inhibiting material	Limit to be established on case by case basis by Central Board in case of Union territories and State Boards in case of States
	Ash pond effluent	pH	6.5 to 8.5
		Suspended solids	100
		Oil and grease	20
6.	Cotton textile industries (composite and processing)	milligram per litre	Concentration not to exceed (except for pH and bio-assay)
	Common :		
		pH	5.5 to 9.0
		Suspended solids	100
		Bio-chemical oxygen demand, 5 days at 20 °C.	150

Sl. No.	Industry	Parameter	Standards
1	2	3	4
		Oil and grease	10
		Bio-assay test	90% survival of fish after 96 hours.
	Special :		
		Total chromium (as Cr)	2
		Sulphide (as S)	2
		Phenolic compounds (as C_6H_5OH)	5

The special parameters are to be stipulated by the Central Board in case of Union territories and State Boards in case of States depending upon the dye used in the industry. Where the industry uses chrome dyes, sulphur dyes and/or phenolic compounds in the dyeing/printing process, the limits on chromium of 2 mg/litre, sulphides of 2 mg/litre and phenolic compounds of 5 mg/litre respectively shall be imposed.

Where the quality requiremnent of the recipient system so warrants, the limit of BOD should be lowered up to 30 according to the requirement by the State Boards for the States and the Central Boards for the Union territories.

A limit on sodium absorption ratio of 26 should be imposed by the State Boards for the States and the Central Board for the Union territories if the disposal of effluent is to be made on land.

Sl. No.	Industry	Parameter	Standards
7.	Composite woolen mills.		Concentration not to exceed milligram per litre. (except for pH and bio-assay)
	Common :		
		pH	5.5 to 9.0
		Suspended solids	100
		Bio-chemical oxygen demand, 5 days at 20 °C.	100
		Oil and grease	10
		Bioassay test	90% survival of fish after 96 hours.
	Special :		
		Total chromium (as Cr)	2
		Sulphide (as S)	2
		Phenolic compounds (as C_6H_5OH)	5
8.	Dye and Dye Intermediate Industries		Concentration not to exceed milligram per litre (except for pH, temperature and bio-assay)
		Suspended Solids	100

Sl. No.	Industry	Parameter	Standards
1	2	3	4
		pH	6 to 8.5
		Temperature	Shall not exceed 5 °C above the ambient temperature of the receiving body.
		Mercury (as Hg)	0.01
		Hexavalent (as Cr) Chromium	0.1
		Total Chromium (as Cr)	2.0
		Copper (as Cu)	3.0
		Zinc (as Zn)	5.0
		Nickel (as Ni)	3.0
		Cadmium (as Cd)	2.0
		Chloride (as Cl)	1000
		Sulphate (as SO_4)	1000
		Phenolic Compounds (as C_6H_5OH)	1.0
		Oil and Grease	10
		Bioassay Test (with 1 : 8 dilution of effluents)	90% survival of test animals after 96 hours.

The standards for chlorides and sulphates are applicable for discharge into inland and surface water courses. However, when discharged on land for irrigation, the limit for chloride shall not be more than 600 milligram per litre and the sodium absorption ratio shall not exceed 26.

Sl. No.	Industry	Parameter	Standards
9.	Electroplating Industries		Concentration not to exceed milligram per litre (except for pH and temperature)
		pH	6.0 to 9.0
		Temperature	Shall not exceed 5 °C above the ambient temperature of the receiving body
		Oil and Grease	10
		Suspended Solids	100
		Cyanides (as CN)	0.2
		Ammoniacal Nitrogen (as N)	50
		Total Residual Chloride (as Cl)	1.0
		Cadmium (as Cd)	2.0
		Nickel (as Ni)	3.0
		Zinc (as Zn)	5.0

Sl. No.	Industry	Parameter	Standards
1	2	3	4
		Hexavalent Chromium as (Cr)	0.1
		Total Chromium (as Cr)	2.0
		Copper (as Cu)	3.0
		Lead (as Pb)	0.1
		Iron (as Fe)	3.0
		Total Metal	10.0
10.	Cement Plants Plant Capacity. 200 tonnes per day	Total dust (All Sections)	Not to exceed milligram per normal cubic metre. 400
	Greater than 200 tonnes per day	Total dust (All Sections)	250

The Central and State Pollution Control Boards may fix stringent standards, not exceeding 250 milligram per normal cubic metre for smaller plants and 150 milligram per normal cubic metre for larger plants if the industry is located in an area which, in their opinion, requires more stringent standards.

Where continuous monitoring integrators are provided on dust emission lines, the integrated average values over a period, to be fixed by the Central and State Boards but not exceeding 72 hours shall be considered instead of momentary dust emission values for conformity to standards.

Sl. No.	Industry	Parameter	Standards
11.	Stone Crushing unit	Suspended Particulate matter.	The Suspended particulate matter measured between 3 metres and 10 metres from any process equipment of a stone crushing unit shall not exceed 600 microgram per cubic metre.
12.	Coke Ovens		Concentrations in the efluents when discharged into inland surface waters not to exceed milligram per litre (except for pH).
		pH	5.5–9.0
		Bio-chemical Oxygen Demand (5 days at 20 °C)	30
		Suspended Solids	100

Sl. No.	Industry	Parameter	Standards
1	2	3	4
		Phenolic Compounds (as C_6H_5OH)	5
		Cyanides (as CN)	0.2
		Oil & grease	10
		Ammoniacal Nitrogen (as N)	50
13.	Synthetic Rubber		Concentration in the effluents when discharged into inland surface waters not to exceed milligram per litre (except for colour and pH).
		Colour	Absent
		pH	5.5–9.0
		Bio-chemical Oxygen Demand (5 days at 20 °C)	50
		Chemical Oxygen Demand	250
		Oil and Grease	10.0
14.	Small Pulp and Paper Industry		Concentration not to exceed milligram per litre (except for pH and sodium absorption ratio).
	*Discharge into inland surface water	pH	5.5–9.0
		Suspended Solids	100
		BOD	30
	Disposal on land surface water	pH	5.5–9.0
		Suspended Solids	100
		BOD	100
		Sodium Absorption Ratio	26
15.	Fermentation Industry, Distilleries, Maltries and Breweries)		Concentration in the effluents not to exceed milligram per litre (except for pH and colour & odour)
		pH	5.5–9.0
		Colour & Odour	All efforts should be made to remove colour and unpleasant odour as far as practicable

Sl. No.	Industry	Parameter		Standards
1	2	3		4
		Suspended Solids	100	
		BOD (5 days at 20 °C)		
		-disposal into inland waters	30	
		-disposal on land	100	
		** - disposal on land using it as secondary treatment system.	500	

* (1) Waste water generation shall not exceed 250 metre cube per tonne of paper produced.

** (2) This limit of 500 mg/L is entitled only in case land application is envisaged as a secondary treatment system for further removal of BOD. It is to be noted that controlled and properly designed land treatment system has to be adopted for this purpose, taking into account soil and crop characteristics. Approval of the concerned State Pollution Control Board is necessary prior to adopting this system.

(3) The drainage water from the land after the secondary treatment system, as mentioned in the note (2), has to satisfy a limit of 30 mg/L of BOD and 10 mg/L of nitrate, expressed as N. The net addition to the groundwater quality should not have a BOD more than 3 mg/L and nitrate, expressed as N more than 10 mg/L.

(4) It has been further stipulated that the BOD level may be raised up to 700 mg/L for land application as a secondary treatment system, considering hydraulic loading and other soil characteristics, if regular and careful monitoring of run off and leachate satisfies the concerned State Pollution Control Board that the BOD level higher than 500 mg/L can be allowed in the effluent.

(5) Where land applicatioin as a secondary treatment system is adopted implying higher BOD in the treatment effluent, referred to in notes (2) and (4) domestic waste should be excluded from the effluent or disinfection should form a part of the treatment prior to application of the same for land treatment.

(6) The 500 mg/L of BOD shall be applicable with effect from the 30th June, 1990. The BOD for disposal of effluent on land has been permitted up to the upper limit of 1000 mg/L till the 29th June, 1990.

(7) In case of distilleries against which cases are pending in courts of law on the basis of standards notified earlier and are consistent with any orders passed by any of these courts of law, the standards specified in the Environment (Protection) Amendment Rules, 1990, shall not be applicable.

Sl. No.	Industry	Parameter	Standards			
1	2	3	4			
16.	Leather Tanneries		Concentration in the effluents not to exceed milligram per litre (except for pH and per cent sodium)			
			Inland Surface Waters	Public Sewers	Land for irrigation	Marine Coastal areas
			(a)	(b)	(c)	(d)
		Suspended Solids	100	00	200	100
		BOD (5 days at 20 °C)	30	350	100	100
		pH	6.0–9.0	6.0–9.0	6.0–9.0	6.0–9.0
		Chlorides (as Cl)	1000	1000	200	—
		Hexavalent Chromium (Cr^{6+})	0.1	0.2	0.1	1.0
		Total Chromium (as Cr)	2.0	2.0	2.0	2.0
		Sulphides (as S)	2.0	5.0	—	5.0
		Sodium percent	—	60	60	—
		Boron (as B)	2.0	2.0	2.0	—
		Oil & Grease	10	20	10	20

Sl. No.	Industry	Parameter	Standards	
17.	Fertilizer Industry		Concentration in the effluents not to exceed milligram per litre (except for pH)	
		Effluents—Straight Nitrogenous Fertilizers, excluding Calcium Ammonium Nitrate, and Ammonium Nitrate Fertilizers	Plants Commissioned January 1, 1982 onwards	Plants Commissioned prior to January 1, 1982
			(a)	(b)
		pH	6.5–8.0	6.5–8.0
		Ammoniacal Nitrogen	50	75
		Total Kjeldahl Nitrogen	100	150
		Free Ammoniacal Nitrogen	4	4
		Nitrate Nitrogen	10	10
		Cyanide as CN	0.2	0.2
		Vanadium as V	0.2	0.2
		Arsenic as As	0.2	0.2
		Suspended Solids	100	100
		Oil and Grease	10	10
		* Hexavalent Chromium as Cr.	0.1	0.1
		* Total Chromium as Cr	2.0	2.0

Sl. No.	Industry	Parameter	Standards	
1	2	3	4	
		Straight Nitrogenous Fertilizers, including Calcium Ammonium Nitrate, and Ammonium Nitrate Fertilizers	Plants Commissioned January 1, 1982 onwards (a)	Plants Commissioned prior to January 1, 1982 (b)
		pH	6.5–8.0	6.5–8.0
		Ammoniacal Nitrogen	50	75
		Total Kjeldahl Nitrogen	—	150
		Free Ammoniacal Nitrogen	4	4
		Nitrate Nitrogen	20	20
		Cyanide as CN	0.2	0.2
		Vanadium as V	0.2	0.2
		Arsenic as As	0.2	0.2
		Suspended Solids	100	100
		Oil and Grease	10	10
		* Hexavalent Chromium as Cr	0.1	0.1
		* Total Chromium as Cr	2.0	2.0

* To be complied with at the outlet of Chromate removal unit.

Complex Fertilizers excluding, Calcium Ammonium Nitrate, and Ammonium Nitrophosphate Fertilizers	Plants Commissioned January 1, 1982 onwards (a)	Plants Commissioned prior to January 1, 1982 (b)
pH	6.5–8.0	6.5–8.0
Ammoniacal Nitrogen	50	75
Free Ammoniacal Nitrogen	4	4
Total Kjeldahl Nitrogen	100	150
Nitrate Nitrogen	10	10
Cyanide as CN	0.2	0.2
Vanadium as V	0.2	0.2
Arsenic as As	0.2	0.2
Phosphate as P	5	5
Suspended Solids	100	100
Oil and Grease	10	10
* Fluoride as F	10	10
** Hexavalent Chromium as Cr	0.1	0.1
** Total Chromium as Cr	2.0	2.0

Sl. No.	Industry	Parameter	Standards	
1	2	3	4	
		Complex Fertilizers, including Calcium Ammonium Nitrate, and Ammonium Nitrophosphate Fertilizers	Plants Commissioned January 1, 1982 onwards (a)	Plants Commissioned prior to January 1, 1982 (b)
		pH	6.5–8.0	6.5–8.0
		Ammoniacal Nitrogen	50	75
		Free Ammoniacal Nitrogen	100	100
		Nitrate Nitrogen	20	20
		Cyanide as CN	0.2	0.2
		Vanadium as V	0.2	0.2
		Arsenic as As	0.2	0.2
		Phosphate as P	5	5
		Oil and Grease	10	10
		Suspended Solids	100	100
		* Fluoride as F	10	10
		** Hexavalent Chromium as Cr	0.1	0.1
		** Total Chromium as Cr	2.0	2.0

* To be complied with at the outlet of fluoride removal unit. If the recipient system so demand, fluoride as F shall be limited to 1.5 mg/L.

** To be complied with at the outlet of Chromate removal unit.

	Straight Phosphate Fertilizers		
	pH	7.0–9.0	
	Phosphate as P	5	
	Oil and Grease	10	
	Suspended Solids	100	
	* Fluoride as F	10	
	** Hexavalent Chromium as Cr	0.1	
	*** Total Chromium as Cr	2.0	
Emission			
Phosphatic Fertilizers (Fluorides and particulate matter emission)	Phosphoric Acid Manufacturing unit Granulation, mixing and grinding of rock phosphate.	25 milligram per normal cubic metre as total Fluoride, 150 milligram per normal cubic metre of particulate matter.	

Sl. No. 1	Industry 2	Parameter 3	Standards 4
	Urea (Particulate Matter emission)	Prilling Tower Commissioned prior to 1-1-1982	150 milligram per normal cubic metre or 2 kilogram per tonne of product.
		Commissioned after 1-1-1982	50 milligram per normal cubic metre or 0.5 kilogram per tonne of product.
18.	Aluminium	Particulate Matter Emissions	
		— calcination	255 milligram per normal cubic metre
		—Smelting	150 milligram per normal cubic metre.
19.	Calcium Carbide	Particulate Matter Emission	
		—Kiln	250 milligram per normal cubic metre.
		—Arc Furnace	150 milligram per normal cubic metre
20.	Carbon Black	Particulate Matter Emission	150 milligram per normal cubic metre.
21.	Copper, Lead and Zinc smelting	Particulate Matter Emission in concentrator.	150 milligram per normal cubic metre.
		Emission of Oxides of Sulphur in Smelter and Convertor.	Off-gases must be utilized for sulphuric acid manufacture. The limits of sulphur dioxide emission from stack shall not exceed 4 kilogramme per tonne of concentrated (one hundred percent) acid produced.
22.	Nitric Acid (emission of oxides of nitrogen)	Emission of Oxides of Nitrogen.	3 kilogram of oxides of Nitrogen per tonne of weak acid (before concentration) produced.
23.	Sulphuric Acid (emission of sulphur dioxide & acid mist)	Sulphur dioxide Emissions.	4 Kilogram per tonne of concentrated (one hundred percent) acid produced.
		Acid mist	50 milligrams per normal cubic metre.
24.	Iron & Steel (Integrated)	Particulate Matter Emission	
		—Sintering Plant	150 milligram per normal cubic metre.
		Steel Making	
		—during normal operations	150 milligram per normal cubic metre.

Sl. No.	Industry	Parameter	Standards
1	2	3	4
		—during oxygen lancing.	400 milligram per normal cubic metre.
		— Rolling Mill	150 milligram per normal cubic metre.
		—Carbon monoxide from coke oven.	3 kilogram per tonne of coke produced.
25.	Thermal Power	* Particulate Matter Emissions :	
		—generation capacity 210 MW or more.	150 milligram per normal cubic metre.
		—generation capacity less than 210 MW.	350 milligram per normal cubic metre.

* Depending upon the requirement of local situation, such as protected area, the State Pollution Control Boards and other implementation agencies under the Environment (Protection) Act, 1986, may prescribe a limit of 150 milligram per normal cubic meter, irrespective of generation capacity of the plant.

Sl. No.	Industry	Parameter	Standards
26.	Natural Rubber Industry		Concentrations in the effluents not to exceed milligram per litre (except for pH) 44 °C.
	—Discharge into inland surface waters.	Colour and Odour	Absent
		pH	6.0–9.0
		BOD	50
		COD	250
		Oil and Grease	10
		Sulphides	2
		Total Kjeldahl Nitrogen	100
		Dissolved phosphate (as P)	5
		Suspended solids	100
		Dissolved solids (inorganic)	2100
		Ammoniacal Nitrogen as (N)	50
		Free ammonia (as NH_3)	5
	—Disposal on land for irrigation	Colour and Odour	Absent
		pH	6.0–8.0
		BOD	100
		COD	250
		Oil and Grease	10
		Suspended solids	200
		Dissolved solids (inorganic)	2100

Sl. No.	Industry	Parameter	Standards
1	2	3	4
27.	All types of Asbestos manufacturing units (including all processes involving use of Asbestos).	Emissions :	
		—Pure Asbestos material	4 Fibre */cc
		— Total Dust	2 mg/m^3 (normal)
28.	Chloro Alkali (Caustic Soda)	Emissions :	Concentrations in mg/m^3 (normal)
	(a) Mercury Cell	Mercury (from hydrogen gas holder stack)	0.2
	(b) All processes	Chlorine (from hypo tower)	15.0
	(c) All processes	Hydrochloric acid vapours and mist (from hydrochloric acid plant)	35.0
29.	Large pulp and paper	Emissions :	Concentration in mg/m^3 (normal)
		Particulate matter	250**
		H_2S	10

* Fibre of length more than 5 micrometre and diameter less than 3 micrometre with an aspect ratio of 3 or more.

** This standard of 250 mg/m^3 (normal) shall apply only for a period of 3 years with effect from the date on which the Environment (Protection) Second Amendment Rules, 1989 came into force. After three years the standard to be applicable is 15 mg/m^3 (normal).

Sl. No.	Industry	Parameter	Standards
30.	Integrated Iron and Steel Plants :	I. Emissions :	
	(a) Coke Oven	Particulate matter	50
	(b) Refractory material plant	Particulate matter	150
		II. Effluents :	Concentration in mg/L except for pH
	(a) Coke Oven By-product Plant	pH	6.0–8.0
		Suspended solids	100
		Phenol	1.0
		Cyanide	0.2
		BOD (5 days at 20 °C)	30
		COD	250
		Ammoniacal nitrogen	50
		Oil and Grese	10
	(b) Other plants such as sintering plant, blast furnace, steel melting and rolling mill	pH	6.0–9.0
		Suspended solids	100
		Oil and Grease	10

Sl. No.	Industry	Parameter	Standards
1	2	3	4
31.	Re-heating (Reverberatory) Furnaces :	Emissions :	Concentration in mg/m^3 (normal)
	Capacity : All sizes		
	Sensitive area	Particulate matter	150
	Other area	—do—	450
32.	Foundries	Emissions :	
	(a) Cupola		
	Capacity (Meltling rate) :		
	Less than 3 Mt/hr	Partuiculate matter	450
	3 Mt/hr and above	—do—	150

Note : It is essential that stack is constructed over the cupola beyond the charging door and emissions are directed through the stack which should be at least six times the diameter of cupola.

Sl. No.	Industry	Parameter	Standards
	(a) Arc Furnaces		
	Capacity : All sizes	Particulate matter	150
	(c) Induction Furnaces		
	Capacity : All sizes	—do—	150

Note : In respect of Arc Furnaces and Induction Furnaces provision has to be made for collecting the fumes before discharging the emissions through the stack.

Sl. No.	Industry	Parameter	Standards
33.	Thermal Power Plants	Stack height/limits	
		Power generation capacity :	
		—500 MW and above	275
		—200 MW/210 MW and above to less than 500 MW	220
		— Less than 200 MW/210 MW	$H = 14 (Q)^{0.3}$, where Q is emission rate of SO_2 in kg/hr, and H is stack height in metres.
		Steam generation capacity :	1/2 times the neighbouring
		— Less than 2 ton/hr	building height or 9 metres (whichever is more)
		—More than 2 ton/hr to 5 ton/hr	12
		—More than 5 ton/hr to 10 ton/hr	15
		—More than 10 ton/hr to 15 ton/hr	18
		—More than 15 ton/hr to 20 ton/hr	21
		—More than 20 ton/hr to 25 ton/hr	24
		—More than 25 ton/hr to 30 ton/hr	27
		—More than 30 ton/hr	30 or using formula $H = 14 (Q)^{0.3}$ (Whichever is more), Q is emission rate of SO_2 in kg/hr and H is stack height in metres.

Sl. No.	Industry	Parameter	Standards
1	2	3	4
34.	Small Boilers Capacity of Boiler	Emissions * Particulate matter	
	—Less than 2 ton/hr.		1600
	—2 to 5 ton/hr.		1200
	— More than 15 ton/hr		150
35.	Oil Refineries (Sulphur dioxide)	Emissions* —Distillation (Atmospheric plus vacuum)	0.25 kg/Mt of feed**
		—Catalytic Cracker	2.5 kg/Mt of feed
		—Sulphur Recovery Unit	120 kg/Mt of Sulphur in the feed.
36.	Aluminium Plants : (a) Alumina Plant :	Emissions	
	(i) Raw Material Handling	Primary and Secondary Crusher Particulate matter.	150

* All emissions normalized to 12 per cent carbon dioxide.

** Feed indicates the feed for that part of the process under consideration only.

Sl. No.	Industry	Parameter	Standards
	(ii) Precipitation Area —Calcination	Particulate Matter	250
		Carbon Monoxide	1% max.
		Stack height	$H = 14\ (Q)^{0.3}$, where Q is emission rate of SO_2 in kg/hr and H is stack height in metres.
	(b) Smelter Plant	Particulate Matter	
	(i) Green Anode Shop	—do—	150
	(ii) Anode Bake Oven	—do—	150
		Total Fluoride (F)	0.3 kg/Mt of Aluminium
	(iii) Potroom	Particulate Matter	150
		Total Fluoride (F)	
		VSS	4.7 kg/Mt of Aluminium produced.

Sl. No.	Industry	Parameter	Standards
1	2	3	4
		HSS	6.0 kg/Mt of Aluminium produced.
		PBSW	2.5 kg/Mt of Aluminium produced.
		PBCW	1.0 kg/Mt of Aluminium produced.
		Stack height	$H = 14 (Q)^{0.3}$, where Q is emission rate of SO_2 in kg/hr and H is stack height in metres.

Note : VSS = Vertical Stud Soderberg, HSS = Horizontal Stud Soderberg, PBSW = Prebacked Side Worked, PBCW = Prebacked Centre Worked.

Sl. No.	Industry	Parameter	Standards
37.	Stone Crushing Unit	Suspended Particulate Matter (SPM)	The standards consist of two parts : (i) Implementation of the following Pollution Control measures : (a) Dust containment cum suppression system for the equipment. (b) Construction of wind breaking walls. (c) Construction of the metalled roads within the premises. (d) Regular cleaning and wetting of the ground within the premises. (e) Growing of a green belt along the periphery. (ii) Quantitative standard for the SPM : The suspended particulate matter contribution value at a distance of 40 metres from a controlled isolated as well as from a unit located in a cluster should be less than 600 mg/Nm^3. The measurements are to be conducted at least twice a month for all the 12 months in a year.

Sl. No.	Industry	Parameter	Standards
1	2	3	4
38.	Petrochemicals (Basic & intermediates)	Effluents :	
		pH	6.5–8.5
		*BOD (5 days at 20 °C)	50
		◊ Phenol	5
		Sulphide (as S)	2
		COD	250
		Cyanide (as CN)	0.2
		♣ Fluoride (as F)	15
		Total suspended solids	1000
		Hexavalent Chromium (as Cr)	0.1
		♦ Total Chromium (as Cr)	2.0

* State Board may prescribe the BOD value of 30 mg/L if the recipient system so demands.

◊ The limit for phenol shall be conformed to at the outlet of effluent treatment of phenol plant. However, at the final disposal point, the limit shall be less than 1 mg/L

♣ The limit for fluoride shall be conformed to at the outlet of the chrome removal unit. However, at the disposal point fluoride concentration shall be lower than 5 mg/L.

♦ The limits for total and hexavalent chromium shall be conformed to at the outlet of the chromate removal unit. This implies that in the final treated effluent, the total and hexavalent chromium shall be lower than the amount prescribed herein.

Sl. No.	Industry	Parameter	Standards
39.	Pharmaceutical Manufacturing and Formulation Industry.	Effluents :	
		1. pH	5.5–9.0
		2. Oil and Grease	10
		3. Total Suspended solids	100
		4. BOD (5 days at 20 °C)	30
		5. Bio-assay test	90% survival of fish after 96 hours in 100% effluent.
		6. Mercury	0.01
		7. Arsenic	0.20
		8. Chromium (Hexavalent)	0.10
		9. Lead	0.10
		10. Cyanide	0.10
		11. Phenolics (as C_6H_5OH)	1.00
		12. Sulphides (as S)	2.00
		13. Phosphates (as P)	5.00

Sl. No.	Industry	Parameter	Standards
1	2	3	4

Notes :

(1) Parameters listed as 1 to 13 are compulsory for Formulators. However, the remaining parameters (6 to 13) will be optional for others.

(2) State Board may prescribe limit for Chemical Oxygen Demand (COD) correlated with BOD limit.

(3) State Board may prescribe limit for total dissolved solids depending upon uses of recipient water body.

(4) Limits should be complied with at the terminal of the treatment unit before letting out of the factory boundary limits.

(5) For the compliance of limits, analysis should be done in the composite sample collected every hour for a period of 8 hours.

Sl. No.	Industry	Parameter	Standards
40.	Pesticide manufacturing and Formulation Industry.	Effluents :	
		1. Temperature	Shall not exceed 5 °C above the receiving water temp.
		2. pH	6.5–8.5
		3. Oil and Grease	10
		4. BOD (5 days at 20 °C)	30
		5. Total suspended solids	100
		6. Bio-assay test	90% survival of fish after 96 hours in 100% effluent.
		7. (a) Specific Pesticides :	
		Benzenyl Hexachloride	10
		Carbonyl	10
		DDT	10
		Endosulfan	10
		Diamethoate	450
		Fenitrothion	10
		Malathion	10
		Phorate	10
		Methyl Parathion	10
		Phenathoate	10
		Plyrethrums	10
		Copper Oxychloride	9600
		Copper Sulphate	50
		Ziram	1000
		Sulphur	30
		Paraquat	2300
		Proponil	7300
		Nitrogen	780

Sl. No.	Industry	Parameter	Standards
1	2	3	4
		(b) Heavy Metals :	
		Copper	1.00
		Manganese	1.00
		Zinc	1.00
		Mercury	0.01
		Tin	0.10
		Any other metal like Nickel, etc.	Shall not exceed 5 times the drinking water standards of BIS.
		(c) Organics :	
		Phenol and phenolic compounds as C_6H_5OH	1.0
		(d) Inorganics :	
		Arsenic (as As)	0.2
		Cyanide (as CN)	0.2
		Nitrate (as NO_3)	50.0
		Phosphate (as P)	5.0

Notes :

(1) Limits should be complied with at the end of the treatment plant before any dilution.

(2) Bio-assay test should be carried out with available species of fish in receiving water.

(3) State Boards may prescribe limits of total dissolved solids (TDS), sulphates and chlorides depending on the uses of recipient water body.

(4) State Board may prescribe COD limit correlated with BOD limit.

(5) Pesticides are known to have metabolites and isomers. If they are found insignificant concentration, standard may be prescribed for these in the list by Central or State Board.

(6) Industries are required to analyse pesticides in waste water by advance analytical method such as GLC/HPLC.

(7) All the parameters will be compulsory for formulators. For others, the 7th will be optional.

Sl. No.	Industry	Parameter	Standards
41.	Tannery (after primary treatment) Disposal : Channel/Conduit Carrying waste waters to secondary treatment plants Type of Tanneries —Chrome tanneries/ combined chrome & vegetable tanneries.	Effluents :	
		pH	6.5–9.0
		SS	Not to exceed 600
		Chromium concentration after treatment in the chrome waste water stream.	45

Sl. No.	Industry	Parameter	Standards
1	2	3	4
	—Vegetable tanneries	pH	6.5–9.0
		SS	Not to exceed 600

Note : The above standards will apply to those tannery units, which have made full contribution to a Common Effluent Treatment Plant (CETP) comprising secondary treatment. Those who have not contributed will be governed by earlier Notification No. S.O. 42 dated January 18, 1988.

Sl. No.	Industry	Parameter	Standards
42.	Paint Industry	Effluents :	
	Waste water discharge	pH	6.0–8.5
		Suspended soilds	100
		BOD (5 days at 20 °C)	50
		Phenolics as C_6H_5OH	1.0
		Oil & Grease	10.0
		Bio-assay test	90% survival in 96 hours.
		Lead as Pb	0.1
		Chromium as Cr Hexavalent	0.1
		Total Chromium	2.0
		Copper as Cu	2.0
		Nickel as Ni	2.0
		Zinc as Zn	5.0
		Total heavy metals	7.0
43.	Inorganic Chemical Industry (Waste water discharge)	Effluents :	
	Part I (metal compounds of Chromium, Manganese, Nickel, Copper, Zinc, Cadmium, Lead and Mercurty)	pH	6.0–8.5
		Chromium as Cr Hexavalent	0.1
		Total Chromium	2.0
		Manganese as Mn	2.0
		Copper as Cu	2.0
		Nickel as Ni	2.0
		Zinc as Zn	5.0
		Cadmium as Cd	2.0
		Lead as Pb	0.1
		Mercury as Hg	0.01
		Cyanide as CN	0.2
		Oil & Grease	10.0
		Suspended Solids	30.0

In addition to the above, total heavy metals are to be limited to 7 mg/L.

Sl. No.	Industry	Parameter	Standards
1	2	3	4
44.	Bullion Refining (Waste water discharge)	Effluents :	
		pH	6.5–8.5
		Cyanide as CN	0.2
		Sulphide as S	0.2
		Nitrate as N	10.0
		Free Cl_2 as Cl	1.0
		Copper as Cu	2.0
		Nickel as Ni	2.0
		Zinc as Zn	5.0
		Arsenic as As	0.1
		Cadmium as Cd	0.2
		Oil & Grease	10.0
		Suspended soilds	100
45.	Dye and Dye Intermediate Industry (Waste water discharge)	Effluents :	
		pH	6.0–8.5
		Colour Hazen Unit	400.0
		Suspended soilds	100.0
		BOD (5 days at 20 °C)	100.0
		Oil & Grease	10.0
		Phenolics as C_6H_5OH	1.00
		Cadmium as Cd	0.2
		Copper as Cu	2.0
		Manganese as Mn	2.0
		Lead as Pb	0.1
		Murcury as Hg	0.01
		Nickel as Ni	2.0
		Zinc as Zn	5.0
		Chromium as Cr Hexavalent	0.1
		Total Chromium	2.0
		Bio-assay test	90% survival in 96 hours.

46. Noise Limits for Automobiles (Free Field) at one meter in dB (A) at the manufacturing stage to be achieved by the year 1992.

(a)	Motorcycle, Scooters & Three-wheelers.	80
(b)	Passenger Cars	82
(c)	Passenger or Commercial Vehicles up to 4 Mt	85
(d)	Passenger or Commercial Vehicles above 4 Mt & up to 12 Mt	89
(e)	Passenger or Commercial Vehicles exceeding 12 Mt	91

Sl. No.	Industry	Parameter	Standards
1	2	3	4
47.	Domestic Appliances and Construction Equipment at the manufacturing stage to be achieved by the year, 1993.		
	(a) Window Air Conditioners of 1 ton to 1.5 ton		68
	(b) Air Coolers		60
	(c) Refrigerators		46
	(d) Diesel generators for domestic purposes		85–90
	(e) Compactors (rollers) Front loaders, Concrete mixers, Cranes (Movable), Vibrators and Saws		75
48.	Glass Industry	Emissions	
	A. Sodalime & Borosilicate and other special Glass (other than Lead)		
	(a) Furnace Capacity :		
	(i) Up to a product draw capacity of 60 Mt/day	Particulate Matter	2.0 kg/hr
	(ii) Product draw capacity more than 60 Mt/day	—do—	0.8 kg/Mt of product drawn
	(iii) For all capacities	Stack height	$H = 14 (Q)^{0.3}$, where Q is the emission rate of SO_2 in kg/hr & H is Stack height in metres
		Total Fluorides	5.0 mg/Nm^3
		NOx	Use of low NOx burners in new plants.

(b) Implementation of the following measures for fugitive emission control from other section :

(i) Raw materials should be transported in leak-proof containers.

(ii) Cullet preparation should be dust-free using water spraying.

(iii) Batch preparation section should be covered.

B. Lead Glass

(a) Furnaces :

All capacities	Particulate matter	50 mg/Nm^3
	Lead	20 mg/Nm^3

(b) Implementation of the following measures for fugitive emission control from other sections :

(i) Batch mixing, proportioning section and transfer points should be covered and it should be connected to control equipment to meet the following standards :

Particulate matter	50 mg/Nm^3
Lead	20 mg/Nm^3

(ii) Minimum stack height should be 30 metres in lead glass units.

Sl. No.	Industry	Parameter	Standards
1	2	3	4
	(c) Pot Furnace at Firozabad		
	Furnace :	Particulate matter	1200 mg/Nm^3

Note : Depending upon local environmental conditions, State/Central Pollution Control Board can prescribe more stringent standards than those prescribed above.

Sl. No.	Industry	Parameter	Standards
	Glass Industries (for all categories)	Effluents :	
		pH	6.5–8.5
		Total suspended solids	100 mg/L
		Oil & Grease	10 mg/L
49.	Lime Kiln Capacity	Stack Height	
	Up to 5 t/day	—do—	A hood should be provided with a stack of 30 metre height from ground level (including kiln height).
	Above 5 t/day	—do—	$H = 14 (Q)^{0.3}$, where Q is emission rate of SO_2 in kg/hr and H = stack height in metres.
	More than 5 t/day and up to 40 t/day	Particulate matter	500 mg/Nm^3
	Above 40 t/day	—do—	150 mg/Nm^3
50.	Slaughter House, Meat & Sea Food Industry Category	Effluents	Concentration in mg/L
	A. Slaughter House		
	(a) Above 70 TLWK	BOD (5 days at 20 °C)	100
		Suspended Solids	100
		Oil and Grease	10
	(b) 70 TLWK & less	BOD (5 days at 20 °C)	500
	B. Meat Processing		
	(a) Frozen Meat	BOD 5 days at 20 °C	30
		Suspended Solids	50
		Oil and Grease	10
	(b) Raw meat from own Slaughter House	BOD (5 days at 20 °C)	30
		Suspended Solids	50
		Oil and Grease	10
	(c) Raw meat from other sources.		Disposal via screen and septic tank
	C. Sea Food Industry	BOD (5 days at 20 °C)	30
		Suspended Solids	50
		Oil and Grease	10

Sl. No.	Industry	Parameter	Standards	
1	2	3	4	

Note : (i) TLWK—Total Live Weight Killed, (ii) In case of disposal into municipal sewer, where sewage is treated, the industries shall install screen and oil and grease separation units, (iii) The industries having slaughter house along with meat processing units will be considered in meat processing category as far as standards are concerned.

Sl. No.	Industry	Parameter	Standards	
51.	Food and Fruit Processing	Effluents	Concentration not to exceed mg/L except pH	Quantum gm/Mt of product
	Category			
	A. Soft Drinks			
	(a) Fruit based/Synthetic (More than 0.4 Mt/day)			
	Bottles and tetrapack	pH	6.5–8.5	—
		Suspended Solids	100	
		Oil and Grease	10	
		BOD (5 days at 20 °C)	30	
	(b) Synthetic (Less than 0.4 Mt/day)		Disposal via septic tank	—
	B. Fruit & Vegetables			
	(a) Above 0.4 Mt/day	pH	6.5–8.5	—
		Suspended Solids	50	
		Oil and Grease	10	
		BOD (5 days at 20 °C)	30	
	(b) 0.1–0.4 Mt/day (10 Mt/year)		Disposal via septic tank	—
	C. Bakery			
	(a) Bread and Bread & Biscuit			
	(i) Continuous process (more than 20 t/day)	pH	6.5—8.5	—
		BOD (5 days at 20 °C)	200	25
	(ii) Non-continuous process (Less than 20 Mt/day)		Disposal via Septic Tank	
	(b) Biscuit Production			
	(i) 10 t/day & above	pH	6.5–8.5	—
		BOD (5 days at 20 °C)	300	35
	(ii) Below 10 t/day		Disposal via septic tank	

Sl. No.	Industry	Parameter	Standards
1	2	3	4
D.	Confectioneries	Effluents	
	(a) 4 t/day and above	pH	6.5–8.5
		Suspended Solids	50
		Oil and Grease	10
		BOD (5 days at 20 °C)	30
	(b) Below 4 Mt/day		Disposal via septic tank

Note : To ascertain the category of 'unit fails' the average of daily production and waste water discharge for the preceding 30 operating days from the date of sampling shall be considered.

Sl. No.	Industry	Parameter	Standards
52.	Jute Processing Industry	Effluents	Concentration in mg/L except pH and water consumption
		pH	5.5–9.0
		BOD (5 days at 20 °C)	30
		Suspended Solids	100
		Oil and Grease	10
		Water Consumption	1.60 m^3/Mt of product produced.

Notes : 1. Water consmption for the Jute processing industry will be 1.5 m^3/Mt of production from January, 1992.

2. At present no limit for colour is given for liquid effluent. However, as far as possible colour should be removed.

Sl. No.	Industry	Parameter	Standards
53.	Large Pulp & Paper, News Print/Rayon Grade Plants of capacity above 24,000 Mt/annum.	Effluents	Concentratioin in mg/L except pH and TOCL
		pH	7.0–8.5
		BOD (5 days at 20 °C)	30
		COD	350
		Suspended Solids	50
		*TOCL	2.0 kg/Mt of product
		Flow (Total waste-water discharge)	
		∇ (i) Large Pulp & paper	200 m^3/Mt of Paper produced
		(ii) Large Rayon Grade News Print	150 m^3 /Mt of Paper produced
54.	Small Pulp and Paper Plant of capacity up to 24,000 Mt/annum.	Effluents	

Sl. No.	Industry	Parameter		Standards
1	2	3		4
	Category :			
	A. ◊ Agrobased	Total waste water discharge,	200 m^3 /Mt of paper produced	
	B. ● Waste paper based	—do—	75 m^3 /Mt of paper produced	
55.	Common Effluent Treatment Plants :	Efluents (Inlet effluent quality for CETP)		(Concentration in mg/L)
	A. Primary Treatment	pH		5.5–9.0
		Temperature in °C		45
		Oil & Grease		20
		Phenolic Compounds (as C_6H_5OH)		5.0
		Ammoniacal Nitrogen (as N)		50
		Cyanide (as CN)		2.0
		Chromium hexavalent (as Cr^{6+})		2.0
		Chromium (total) (as Cr)		2.0
		Copper (as Cu)		3.0
		Lead (as Pb)		1.0
		Nickel (as Ni)		3.0
		Zinc (as Zn)		15
		Arsenic (as As)		0.2
		Mercury (as Hg)		0.01
		Cadmium (as Cd)		1.0
		Selenium (as Se)		0.05
		Fluoride (as F)		15
		Boron (as B)		2.0
		Radioactive Materials		
		Alpha emitters, He/ml.		10-7
		Beta emitters, He/ml		10-8

* Standards for total organic chloride (TOCL) will be applicable from January 1992.

∇ Standards with respect to total waste-water discharge for the large pulp and paper mills to be established from 1992, will meet the standards of 100 m^3/Mt of paper produced.

◊ Agro based mills to be established from January, 1992 will meet the standards of 150 m^3/Ton of paper produced.

● Waste paper mills to be established from January, 1992 will meet the standards of 50 m^3/Mt of paper produced.

Notes : 1. These standards apply to the small scale industries, i.e., total discharge up to 25 kL/day.

2. For each CETP and its constituent units, the State Board will prescribe standards as per the local needs and conditions; these can be more stringent than those presribed above. However, in case of clusters of units, the State Board with the concurrence of CPCB in writing, may prescribe suitable limits.

1	2	3	4
	Into Inland surface waters (a)	On land for Irrigation (b)	Into Marine coastal areas (c)
B. Treated Effluent Quality of Common Effluent Treatment Plant Concentration in mg/L except pH and temperature.			
pH	5.5–9.0	5.5–9.0	5.5–9.0
BOD (5 days at 20 °C)	30	100	100
Oil & grease	10	10	10
Temperature	Shall not exceed 40 °C in any section of the stream within 15 metres downstream from the effluent outlet.	—	45 °C at the point of discharge.
Suspended Solids	100	200	(a) For processed waste water 100 (b) For cooling water effluents 10 percent above total suspended matter of influent cooling water.
Dissolved Solids (Inorganic)	2100	2100	—
Total residual Chlorine	1.0	—	1.0
Ammoniacal Nitrogen (as N)	50	—	50
Total Kjeldahl Nitrogen (as N)	100	—	100
Chemical Oxygen Demand	250	—	250
Arsenic (as As)	0.2	0.2	0.2
Mercury (as Hg)	0.01	—	0.01
Lead (as Pb)	0.1	—	1.0
Cadmium (as Cd)	1.0	—	2.0
Total Chromium (as Cr)	2.0	—	2.0
Copper (as Cu)	3.0	—	3.0
Zinc (as Zn)	5.0	—	15
Selenium (as Se)	0.05	—	0.05
Nickel (as Ni)	3.0	—	5.0
Boron (as B)	2.0	2.0	—
Cyanide (as CN)	0.2	0.2	0.2
Chloride (as Cl)	1000	600	—
Fluoride (as F)	2.0	—	15
Sulphate (as SO_4)	1000	1000	—
Sulphide (as S)	2.8	—	5.0
Pesticides	Absent	Absent	Absent
Phenolic compounds (as C_6H_5OH)	1.0	—	5.0

Sl. No.	Industry	Parameter	Standards
1	2	3	4

Note : All efforts should be made to remove colour and unpleasant odour as far as possible.

56. Dairy

Effluents	Concentration in mg/L, except pH	Quantum per product processed
pH	6.5 – 8.5	—
* BOD (5 days at 20 °C)	100	—
** Suspended solids	150	—
Oil and Grease	10	—
Waste water generation	—	3 m^3 per kL of milk

Note : * BOD may be made stringent up to 30 mg/L if the recipient fresh water body is a source for drinking water supply. BOD shall be up to 350 mg/L for the chilling plant effluent for applying on land provided the land is designed and operated as a secondary treatment system with suitable monitoring facilities. The drainage water from the land after secondary treatment has to satisfy a limit of 30 mg/L of BOD and 10 mg/L of nitrate expressed as 'N'. The net addition to the groundwater quality should not be more than 3 mg/L of BOD and 3 mg/L of nitrate expressed as 'N'. This limit for applying on land is allowed subject to the availability of adequate land for discharge under the control of the industry, BOD value is relaxable up to 350 mg/L, provided the waste water is discharged into a town sewer leading to secondary treatment of the sewage.

** Suspended solids limit is relaxable up to 450 mg/L, provided the waste water is discharged into town sewer leading to secondary treatment of the sewage.

57. Tannaries

Effluents	Concentration in mg/L, except pH	Quantum per raw hide processed
pH	6.5 – 9.0	—
* BOD (5 days at 20 °C)	100	—
Suspended solids	100	—
Sulphide (as S)	1	—
Total Chromium (as Cr)	2	—
Oil and Grease	10	—
Waste water generation	—	28 m^3/Mt

* For effluent discharge into inland surface water BOD limit shall be made stricter to 30 mg/L by the concerned State Pollution Control Board.

58. Natural Rubber Processing
● Industry

	Centrifuging and creaming unit (a) for disposal into inland surface water	Centrifuging and creaming unit (b) for disposal on land for irrigation	Crape and crumb units (a) for disposal into inland surface water	Crape and crumb units (b) for disposal on land for irrigation
	(Concentration in mg/L, except pH & quantum of waste water generation)		(Concentration in mg/L, except pH & quantum of waste water generation)	
pH	6 – 8	6 – 8	6 – 8	6 – 8
Total Kjeldahl Nitrogen (as N)	200(100*)	▲	50	▲

Sl. No.	Industry	Parameter		Standards	
1	2	3		4	
	Natural Rubber Processing ● Industry	Centrifuging and creaming unit		Crape and crumb units	
		(a) for disposal into inland surface water	(b) for disposal on land for irrigation	(a) for disposal into inland surface water	(b) for disposal on land for irrigation
		(Concentration in mg/L, except pH & quantum of waste water generation)		(Concentration in mg/L, except pH & quantum of waste water generation)	
	Ammoniacal Nitrogen as (N)	100 (50*)	▲	25	▲
	BOD (5 days at 20 °C)	30	100	30	100
	COD	250	▲	250	▲
	Oil and Grease	10	20	10	20
	Sulphide (as S)	2	▲	2	▲
	TDS	2100	NP ■	2100	NP ■
	SS	100	200	100	200
	Quantum of waste water generation	5 lit/kg of product processed	8 lit/kg of product processed	40 lit/kg of product processed	40 lit/kg of product processed

* To be achieved in three years.

■ Not prescribed in case effluent is used for rubber plantation of their own. In other cases, suitable limit, as necessary, may be perscribed by the State Board

▲ Not specified.

● These standards supersede the standards notified at Serial No. 26 vide notification no. S.O.8 (E), dated 3rd June, 1989.

Sl. No.	Industry	Parameter	Standards
59.	Bagasse-fired Boilers	Emission	(Concentration in mg/L)
	(a) Step grate	Particulate matter	250
	(b) Horse shoe/pulsating grate	Particulate matter	500 (12% CO_2)
	(c) Spreader stroker	Particulate matter	800 (12% CO_2)

Note : In the case of horse shoe and spreader stroker boilers, if more than one boiler is attached to a single stack, the standard shall be fixed based on added capacity of all the boilers connected with the stack.

Sl. No.	Industry	Parameter	Standards
60.	Man-made fibre industry (Semi-Synthetic)	Effluents	(Concentration in mg/L except for pH)
		pH	5.5 – 9.0
		Suspended solids	100
		BOD (5 days at 20 °C)	30
		Zinc (as Zn)	1

Sl. No.	Industry	Parameter	Standards
1	2	3	4
61.	Ceramic Industry	Emission	(Concentration in mg/Nm^3)
	A. Kilns		
	(a) Tunnel, top hat, chamber	Particulate matter	150
		Fluoride	10
		Chloride	100
		Sulphur dioxide	**
	(b) Down – draft	Particulate matter	1200
		Fluoride	10
		Chloride	100
		Sulphur dioxide	**
	(c) Shuttle	Particulate matter	150
		Fluoride	10
		Chloride	100
		Sulphur dioxide	**
	(d) Vertical shaft kiln	Particulate matter	250
		Fluoride	10
		Sulphur dioxide	**
	(e) Tank furnace	Particulate matter	150
		Fluoride	10
		Sulphur dioxide	**
	B. Raw Material Handling, Processing and operations		
	(a) Dry raw materials handling, and processing operations.	Particulate matter	150
	(b) Basic raw material handing, processing operations.	Particulate matter	*
	(c) Other sources of air pollution generation.	Particulate matter	*
	C. Automatic Spray Unit		
	(a) Dryers		
	(i) Fuel fired dryers	Particulate matter	150
	(ii) Heat recovery dryers	Particulate matter	*
	(b) Mechanical finishing	Particulate matter	*
	(c) Lime/Plaster of Paris manufacture capacity :		
	Up to 5 Mt/day	Stack height	A hood should be provided with a stack of 30 metre height from ground level (including kiln height)

Sl. No.	Industry	Parameter	Standards
1	2	3	4
	Above 5 Mt/day	—do—	$H = 14 (Q)^{0.3}$ Where Q is emission rate of SO_2 in kg/hr and H = stack height in metre.
	Upto 5 Mt/day	Particulate matter	500 mg/Nm^3
	More than 5 Mt/day and up to 40 ton/day	—do—	150 mg/Nm^3

Note : Oxygen reference level for particulate matter concentration calculations for kilns mentioned at A (c) is 18% and for those at A (b), A (d), and A (e) is 8%.

* All possible preventive measures should be taken to control pollution as far as practicable.

** The standard for sulphur dioxide in terms of stack height limits for kilns with various capacities of coal consumption shall be as indicated below :

Coal consumed per day	Stack height
More than 8.5 Mt	9 m
More than 8.5 to 21 Mt	12 m
More than 21 to 42 Mt	15 m
More than 42 to 64 Mt	18 m
More than 64 to 104 Mt	21 m
More than 104 to 105 Mt	24 m
More than 105 to 126 Mt	27 m
More than 126 Mt	30 m or using formula $H = 14 (Qg)^{0.3}$, (whichever is more)

Note : In this notification

H - Physical height of the stack, meter

Qg - Emission of sulphur dioxide in kg/hr

Mt - Metric ton

m - Meter.

Sl. No.	Industry	Parameter	Standards
62.	Viscose Filament Yarn (Sub-sector of man-made fibre semi-synthetic industry)	Effluents	(Concentration in mg/L except for pH)
		pH	5.5 – 9.0
		Suspended solids	100
		BOD (5 days at 20 °C)	30
		Zinc (as Zn)	5

Note :

Principal rules were published in the Gazette of India vide Notification S.O. No.. 844(E) dt. the 19th November 1986. Amending rules were published vide S.O. No. 433(E) dt. 18.04.1987, S.O. No. 64(E) dt. 18.01.1988, S.O. No. 12(E) dt. 08.01.1990, S.O. No. 8(E) dt. 03.01.1989, S.O. No. 190(E) dt. 15.03.1989, G.S.R. 913(E) dt. 24.10.1989, G.S.R. 742(E) dt. 30.08.1990, S.O. No. 23(E) dt. 16.01.1991, G.S.R. 93(E) dt. 21.02.1991, G.S.R. 95(E) dt. 12.02.1992, G.S.R. 329(E) dt. 13.03.1992, G.S.R. 475(E) dt. 05.05.1992, G.S.R. 797(E) dt. 01.10.1992, G.S.R. 386(E) dt. 28.04.1993, G.S.R. 422(E) dt. 19.05.1993, and G.S.R. 801(E) dt. 31.12.1993.

APPENDIX—IIIB

NATIONAL AMBIENT AIR QUALITY STANDARDS IN INDIA
CENTRAL POLLUTION CONTROL BOARD
NOTIFICATION
New Delhi, the 18th November, 2009

No. B-29016/20/90/PCI-I.—In exercise of the powers conferred by Sub-section (2) (h) of Section 16 of the Air (Prevention and Control of Pollution) Act, 1981 (Act No. 14 of 1981), and in supersession of the Notification Nos. S.O. 384 (E), dated 11th April, 1994 and S.O. 935(E), dated 14th October, 1998, the Central Pollution Control Board hereby notify the National Ambient Air Quality Standards with immediate effect namely :

NATIONAL AMBIENT AIR QUALITY STANDARDS

Sl. No.	Pollutant	Time Weighted Average	Concentration in Ambient Air		
			Industrial, Residential, Rural and Other Area	Ecologically Sensitive Area (notified by Central Government)	Methods of Measurement
(1)	(2)	(3)	(4)	(5)	(6)
1.	Sulphur Dioxide (SO_2) $\mu g/m^3$	Annual*	50	20	–Improved West and Gacke
		24 hours **	80	80	—Ultraviolet fluorescence
2.	Nitrogen Dioxide (NO_2), $\mu g/m^3$	Annual*	40	30	—Modified Jacob & Hochheiser (Na-Arsenite)
		24 hours**	80	80	—Chemiluminescence
3.	Particulate Matter (size less than 10 µm) or PM_{10} $\mu g/m^3$	Annual*	60	60	—Gravimetric —TOEM
		24 hours **	100	100	—Beta attenuation
4.	Particulate Matter (size less than 2.5 µm) or $PM_{2.5}$ $\mu g/m^3$	Annual*	40	40	—Gravimetric —TOEM
		24 hours**	60	60	—Beta attenuation
5.	Ozone *O_3) $\mu g/m^3$	8 hours**	100	100	—UV Photometric —Chemiluminescence
		1 hour**	180	180	—Chemical Method
6.	Lead (Pb) $\mu g/m^3$	Annual*	0.50	0.50	—AAS/ICP method after sampling on EPM 2000 or equivalent filter paper
		24 hours**	1.0	1.0	—ED-XRF using Teflon filter

Contd.

THE GAZETTE OF INDIA : EXTRAORDINARY

(1)	(2)	(3)	(4)	(5)	(6)
7.	Carbon Monoxide (CO) mg/m^3	8 hours** 1 hour **	02 04	02 04	—Non Dispersive Infrared (NDIR) spectroscopy
8.	Ammonia (NH_3) $\mu g/m^3$	Annual* 24 hours**	100 400	100 400	—Chemiluminescence —Indophenol blue method
9.	Benzene (C_6H_6) $\mu g/m^3$	Annual*	05	05	—Gas chromatography based continuous analyzer —Adsorption and desorption followed by GC analysis
10.	Benzo(α) Pyrene (BaP)–particulate phase only, ng/m^3	Annual*	01	01	—Solvent extration followed by HPLC/GC analysis
11.	Arsenic (As), ng/m^3	Annual*	06	06	—AAS/ICP method after sampling on EPM 2000 or equivalent filter paper
12.	Nickel (Ni), ng/m^3	Annual*	20	20	—AAS/ICP method after sampling on EPM 2000 or equivalent filter paper

* Annual arithmetic mean of minimum 104 measurements in a year at a particular site taken twice a week 24 hourly at uniform intervals.

** 24 hourly or 08 hourly or 01 hourly monitored values, as applicable, shall be complied with 98% of the time in a year. 2% of the time, they may exceed the limits but not on two consecutive days of monitoring.

Note : Whenever and wherever monitoring results on two consecutive days of monitoring exceed the limits specified above for the respective category, it shall be considered adequate reason to institute regular or continuous monitoring and further investigation.

Sant Prasad Gautam, Chairman
[ADVT-III/4/184/09/Exty.]

Note : The notifications on National Ambient Air Quality Standards were published by the Central Pollution Control Board in the Gazette of India, Extraordinary vide notification Nos. S.O. 384(E), dated 11th April, 1994 and S.O. 935(E), dated 14th October, 1998.

REFERENCES

Aiba, Shuichi, A. E. Humphry, and N. F. Millis,
Biochemical Engineering, 2nd ed., Academic Press Inc., New York, 1973

Bailey, J.E., and D. F. Ollis, Biochemical Engineering Fundamentals, 2nd ed.,
Mc Graw-Hill, New York, 1986

Bailey, R. A., H. M. Clark, J. P. Ferris, S. Krause, and R. L. Strong,
Chemistry of the Environment, 2nd ed.,
Academic Press, San Diego, 2005

Bortman, M. P., etal, eds.,
Environment Encyclopedia, Volume 1 & 2, 3rd ed.,
Thompson-Gale, Detroit, 2003

Bosanquet, C. H., etal,
Proc. Institute of Mechanical Engineers (London), 162, 355 (1950)

Burden, F. R., ed.,
Environmental Monitoring Handbook
Mc Graw-Hill, New York, 2002

Celinkaya, B., etal,
Control FCC Flue-gas Emissions,
Hydrocarbon Processing, page 55-62,
July 2000

Cheremisinoff, P. N., and R. A. Young,
Air Pollution Control and Design Handbook, Pt. 1 and 2,
Marcel Dekker, New York, 1977

Compendium Environment Guideline,
Department of Environments,
Government of West Bengal, India, 1987

Conneli, D. W.,
Basic Concepts of Environmental Chemistry, 2nd ed.,
CRC Taylor & Francis, 2005

Corbitt, R. A.,
Standard Handbook of Environmental Enginnering, 2nd ed.,
Mc Graw-Hill, New York, 1999

Davis, W. T, ed.,
Air Pollution Engineering manual, 2nd ed.,
John Wiley, New York, 2000

Davis, M. L, and D. A. Cornwell,
Introduction to Environmental Engineering, 3rd ed.,
WCB Mc Graw-Hill, Boston, 1998

De, A. K.,
Environmental Chemistry, 4th ed.,
Wiley Eastern Ltd., New Delhi, 2001

Drbal, L. F, (Managing Ed.),
Black & Veatch
Power Plant Engineering,
CBS Publishers & Distributors,
New Delhi, 1998

Environmental Engineering,
A special supplement to February, June, October, 1993,
Chemical Engineering,
Mc Graw-Hill

Environmental Acts, Rules & Notifications,
Department of Environments,
Government of West Bengal, India, 1999

Evans, F. L, Jr.,
Equipment Design Handbook for Refineries and Chemical Plant, 2nd ed.,
Gulf Publishing, 1980

Fair, G. M, J. C. Geyer, and D. A. Okum,
Water and Waste Water Engineering, Vol. 1 & 2
John Wiley & Sons, New York, 1966, 1968

Flagen, R. C, and J. H. Seinfield,
Fundamentals of Air Pollution Engineering,
Prentice-Hall, New Jersey, 1998

Fleagle, R. G, and J. A. Businger,
An Introduction to Atmospheric Physics,
Academic Press, 1963

Hammer, M. J, and M. J. Hammer, jr.,
Water and Waste Water Technology, 3rd ed.,
Prentice-Hall of India, New Delhi, 1998

Heinsokn, R. J, and R. K. Kabel,
Sources and Control of Air Pollution,
Prentice-Hall, New Jersey, 1999

Henry, J. G, and G. W. Heinke,
Environmental Science and Engineering, 2nd ed.,
Prentice-Hall of India, New Delhi, 2004

Humenick, M. J., Jr.,
Water and Waste Water Treatment Calculation for Chemical and Physical Processes,
Marcel Dekker, Inc, New York, 1977

Johnson W. A.,
Chemical Engineering, 79, 87-92 (1972)

Kiely, G.,
Environmental Engineering,
Irwin Mc Graw-Hill, Boston, 1998

Kohl, A. L, and F. C. Riesenfeld,
Gas Purification 4th ed.,
Gulf Publishing, Houston, 1985

Leslie Grady, C. P., Jr. and H. C. Lin,
Biological Waste Water Treatment Theory and Application,
Marcel Dekker, New York, 1980

Licht, W.,
Air Pollution Control Engineering—Basic Calculation for Particulate Collection, 2nd ed.,
Marcel Dekker, New York, 1988

Liptak, B. G, ed.,
Environmental Engineer's Handbook, Vol. 1 & 2,
Chilton Book Company, Radnor, Pennsylvania, 1974

Marchello, J. M.,
Control of Air Pollution Sources,
Marcel Dekker Inc., New York, 1976

Manahan, S. E.,
Environmental Chemistry, 8th ed.,
CRC Press, Boca Raton, 2005

Metcalf & Eddy, Inc
Revised by G. Tchobanolous, etal.,
Waste Water Engineering, Treatment & Reuse
Tata Mc Graw-Hill, New Delhi, 2003

Nathanson, J. A.,
Basic Environmental Technology, 4th ed.,
Prentice Hall of India, New Delhi, 2002

Nemerow, N. L.,
Industrial Water Pollution-Origins, Characteristics and Treatment,
Addision-Wesley, Reading, Massachusets, 1978

Newman, S. A., ed.,
Acid and Sour Gas Treating Processes,
Gulf Publishing, Houston, 1985

Noel de Nevers,
Air Pollution Control Engineering,
Mc Graw-Hill, New York, 1995

Nonhebel, G., ed.,
Gas Purification Processes for Air Pollution Control,
Newnes-Butterworths, London, 1972

Palmer, T.,
Understanding Enzymes, 2nd ed.,
Ellis Horwood, Chichester, England, 1985

Patnaik, P.,
Handbook of Environmental Analysis
CRC, Lewis Publishers, Boca Raton, 1997

Peavy, H. S., etal.,
Environmental Engineering,
Mc Graw-Hill, New York, 1985

Rao, C. S.,
Environmental Pollution Control,
New Age Industrial (P) Ltd., New Delhi, 2006

Rao, M. N. and A. K. Datta,
Waste Water Treatment-Rational Methods and Industrial Practices, 2nd ed.,
Oxford & IBH Publishing Co. (P) Ltd., New Delhi, 1978

Reible, D. D.,
Fundamentals of Environmental Engineering,
Springer, Lewis Publishers, Boca Raton, 1999

Roy, S.,
Environmental Science-A Comprehensive Treatise on Ecology and Environment,
Publishing Syndicate, Kolkata, 2003

Salvato, J. A.,
Environmental Engineering and Sanitation, 4th ed.,
John Wiley & Sons Inc., New York, 1992

Sawyer, C. N., etal.,
Chemistry for Environmental Engineering and Science, 5th ed.,
Tata Mc Graw-Hill Publishing Co. Ltd., New Delhi, 2003

Schnelle, K. B., Jr., and C. A. Brown,
Air Pollution Control Technology Handbook,
CRC Press, Boca Raton, 2002

Spellman, F. R. and N. E. Whiting,
Environment Engineer's Mathematics Handbook,
CRC Press, Boca Raton, 2005

Spiro, T. G. and W. M. Stigliani,
Chemistry of Environment, 2nd ed.,
Prentice-Hall of India Pvt. Ltd., New Delhi, 2002

Stern, A. C., ed.,
Air Pollution, Volume 1 to 5, 3rd ed.,
Academic Press, New York, 1977

Stern, A. C., etal.,
Fundamentals of Air Pollution, 2nd ed.,
Academic Press, Orlando, Florida, 1984

Strauss, W.,
Industrial Gas Cleaning, 2nd ed.,
Pergamon Press, Oxford, 1975

Wilson, F.,
Design Calculation In Waste Water Treatment,
E & F. N. Spon Ltd., London, 1981

INDEX

A

Abiotic environment 2
Absorber design 90
Absorption of
  Gaseous pollutants 87
  VOCs 92, 101, 139
Activated carbon 92
  granular 92
  powdered 92
Adiabatic 17
  sub-adiabatic 17
  super-adiabatic 17
Adsorber design 94
Adsorption of
  gaseous pollutants 92, 140
  break point 94, 95
  chemical 101
  physical 93
  VOCs 101, 140
  Water-borne pollutants
  methods 170
Aerobic treatment 225
Aerosol 12
  dispersion 12
  condensation 12
Air pollutants 13
  classification 13
  effects on animals 14, 21
  human beings 14, 21
  land 24
  materials 24
  tropospheric properties
  vegetation 20
  invisible injury 20
  visible injury 20
  water bodies 24
Air sampling 38
Anaerobic treatment 256
Analysis 39
  gaseous pollutants 40
  particulate matter 38
  waste water 155
Anoxic process 276, 280
API separator 209
Alkalinity waste water estimation 158
Arsenic waste water abatement 299
  sources 298
  toxic effects 298
Atmosphere 8
Atmospheric chemical 10
  chemistry 21, 25
  stratospheric 24
  pressure 8
  temperature 8, 16
  Catalytic incineration 104
Automobile exhaust 139
Autotrophes 4

B

Bacteria 1, 213
Bacteriological assessment
  waste water 163
Bag house 70
Bioassay 163
Biological effects on 21
  gaseous pollutants 23
  particulate matter 23
Biological methods for
  BOD removal 211
  nitrogenous compound removal 274, 308
  nutrient removal 274, 307
  phosphorus compound removal 279, 311
Bio-oxidation of gaseous pollutants 106
Biosphere 2
Biotic community 2
BOD estimation 160

C

Cadmium in water 299
 abatement methods 299
 sources 299
 toxicity effects 299
Carbon cycle 31, 34
Carnivores 4
Chemical treatment of gaseous pollutants 101
Chemosphere 10
Chlorine and chloride abatement 138
Chlorofluorocarbons (CFC) 24
Chromium in water 300
 abatement methods 300
 sources 300
 toxic effects 300
CO abatement 139
Coagulants 206, 208
 inorganic 206
 polyelectrolyte 207
Coagulation jar test 207
COD
 waste water estimation 162
Colour
 waste water estimation 157
Comminution 176
Conductivity waste water estimation 157
Cooling & condensation of gaseous effluent 84
Coriolisis force 19
Cyanide in waste water 301
 abatement methods 301
 sources 301
 toxicity 301
Cyclone separator 59

D

De-emulsification 208, 209, 210
Disinfecting agents 295, 297
 chemicals 296
 heat 296
 ultrasonics 296
 UV radiation 296
Disposal of
 Gaseous effluents 106
Dissolved air floatation (DAF) 199
Dissolved residue waste water estimation 156
Dissolved oxygen (DO)
 waste water estimation 159
Drinking water standard 150
Dust 12

E

Ecology 2
Ecosystem 4
Effects of pollution 21
 in stratosphere 24
 in troposphere 15
 animals 21
 human beings 14, 21
 land 24
 materials 24
 vegetation 20
 water bodies 24
EIA report 3
Emulsified oil removal 209
Environment inventory 4
Equalization 169
 basin sizing 171
Eukaryotes 214

F

Fabric filter 67
Filter for separation of
 gas-borne particles 67
 water-borne particles 203
Filtration 203
 granular filter 204
 rotary filter 205
Final polishing treatment 166, 169
Fixed solids waste water
 estimation 156
Flare stack 102, 141, 143
Flocculation 193, 206, 208
Fluoride in water 302
 abatement methods 303
 sources 302
 toxic effects 303
Fluorine & Fluoride
 abatement 138, 303
Fly ash 12
Fog 12, 15

Food chain 4
Food web 4
Fossil fuel 1, 122
Free settling velocity 52, 55, 177
Fugitive emission control 142
Fumes 12
Fungus 214

G

Gas-borne pollutant 47
classification 47
gaseous pollutant 12
classification 12
primary 12
secondary 12
sinks 26
sources 13
monitoring 39
treatment methods 47
areas of application 48, 49
biological method 47, 106, 132, 137
bio-oxidation 106
chemical 101
catalytic incineration 104
thermal incineration 101
physical method 47
absorption 87, 140
adsorption 92, 140
particulate matter 49
abatement devices 49
cyclone separator 59
E S P 71
filters 67
fabric 67
gravel 67
gravity settler 50
scrubbers 78
baffle plate 80
bubble cap 80
fiber bed 80
packed bed 80
sieve plate 80
spray type 81
impingement 81
mechanically aided 82
venturi 81
Gaseous effluent disposal
flare stack 102, 141, 143
stack 4, 106, 111, 117
Gaseous effluent
liquid droplet removal 82
Global warming 18
Grease removal 208
Green house gases 18
Grit removal 176

H

Hardness-waste water estimation 158
Haze 12, 15
Heavy metal removal 294, 304
abatement methods 294, 304
sources 304
toxic effects 304
Herbivores 4
Heterosphere 10
Homosphere 10
Human activities 1, 2, 3
Hydrocyclone 187
Hydrogen sulphide (H_2S)
abatement 132
dry processes 132
wet processes 133
Hydrological cycle 29, 30
Hydrosphere 2

I

In situ analysis gaseous pollutants 40
Inversion 16, 17
Ion exchange processes 288, 309
anion exchange 289

K

Kinetics 218, 223
effects of temperature 225
enzymatic 218
microbial growth 221
parameters 225
Kyoto protocol 18

L

Lapse rate 8, 116

Liquid droplet removal 82
Liquid waste 6

M

Mass conservation troposphere 29
Membrane separation 282
  electrodialysis 285
  microfiltration 283
  nanofiltration 284
  reverse osmosis 284
  ultrafiltration 284
Mercury in water 305
  Fundamentals of microbes
  anaerobes 217
  cryophilic 217
  eukaryotes 214
  facultative 217
  mesophilic 217
  thermophilic 217
  prokaryotes 213
  growth kinetics 223
  inhibition 219
  physiology 216
Mist 12
  removal 82
Monod equation 223, 229
Montreal protocol 25

N

Nitrogen cycle 31, 33
Non-viable particulates 12
NOx
  abatement methods 136
  production control 137
Nutrients in water 307
  abatement methods 307, 310
  sources 307
  toxic effects 307

O

Odor-waste water estimation 157
Odorous compound abatement methods 143
Oil de-emulsification 209
Oil, fats greases-waste water estimation 158
Oxidation-reduction 294
Oxygen cycle 29, 32
Ozone depletion substances 24
Ozone effects on
  human beings 22, 23
  plants 22
Ozone formation 24
Ozone layer 10, 24

P

Particulate 11
  monitoring 38
  non-viable 12
  viable 11
Pesticide in water 315
  abatement methods 315
  sources 315
  toxic effects 315
pH-waste water 158
  estimation 158
  regulation 173
Phenol in waste water 311
  abatement methods 311
  sources 311
  toxic effects 311
Physical treatment 47
  gaseous pollutants 47
Pitot tube 39
Plant nutrients in waste water 162, 274, 307
  abatement methods 274, 307
  nitrogen 162, 274, 276, 307
  phosphorus 163, 279, 309
  estimation 162
Plume
  dust deposition 120
  pollutant contration distribution 112
  profile 107
  rise 115
Pollutants 3, 11
  concentration units 36, 155
  ppb 36, 155
  ppm 36, 155
  μg/L 36, 155
  gaseous 12
  abatement methods 49, 87
  effects 14, 21

monitoring 39
primary 11
secondary 11
sinks 26
sources 13
TLV 23
Particulate abatement methods 49
effects 23
monitoring 38
sinks 23
sources 13
Pollution
control legislation in India 7
regulation approach 6
Population pyramid 5
Precipitation 15, 294, 304
heavy metal 294, 304
phosphorus 294, 310
Primary 4
consumer 4
producer 4
Primary treatment-waste water 174
circular tank 190, 195
colloid removal 206
coagulation 206, 208
inorganic coagulant 206
jar test 207
comminution 176
dissolved air 199
floatation (DAF) 199, 200
flocculation 206, 208
grease removal 208
API separator 209
trap 209
grit removal 176
proportional weir 177, 179, 184
rectangular chamber 177, 181
sutro weir 177, 179
trapezoidal chamber 179, 184, 185
hydrocyclone 187
screening 175
sedimentation 187
thickening 187
Protists 212
Protozoa 214

R

Respirable Particulate matter (RPM) 23
Reverse osmosis 284

S

Sample-gas 36
collection 36
preservation 43
storage 43
Sampling 36
isokinetic 38, 39
stack 38
train 37
waste water 154
Scour velocity 19, 177
Secondary consumer 4
Secondary pollutants 13
Secondary treatment 211
aerobic treatment 225
activated sludge processes 234, 239
CAS 235
CMAL 228
lagoon 228
nitrification 274
oxidation ditch 237
rotary biological contractor 250
trickling filter 245
anaerobic treatment 258
denitrification 276
digester 262, 269
single stage 263
two stage 265
methane production 257, 258
expanded bed 266
facultative lagoon 258
fluidized bed 266
imhoff tank 260
packed bed 265
septic tank 259
sludge blanket 265
SO_2 abatement methods 122
dry processes 123
wet processes 126
Segregation processes 169, 170
Smog 12

Smoke 12
Spray 12
Stack design 111, 117
  flare 102, 141, 143
Stratopause 9
Stratosphere 9, 24, 28
Sulfur cycle 31, 35
Suspended solids-waste water estimation 156

T

Temperature-waste water estimation 158
Tertiary consumer 4
Tertiary treatment-waste water
  methods 166, 169, 270
  adsorption 280, 308, 314
  air stripping 272, 313
  disinfection 295
  filtration 271
  ion exchange 288, 309
  membrane separation 282, 309
  oxidation-reduction 294
  precipitation 294, 310
Threshold limit value (TLV) 23
  human beings 21, 23, 24
  plants 21, 23, 24
Total solids-waste water estimation 156
Tropopause 9
Troposphere 9, 11, 15, 25, 29
  mass conservation 29
Tropospherical dry air composition 11
Turbidity-waste water estimation 157

V

Viable particulate 11
Virus 212
Visibility 15
VOC in gas
  abatement methods 139
  absorption 140
  adsorption 140
  combustion processes 141
VOC in water 312
  abatement methods 280, 313
  sources 312
  toxic effects 312

Volatile solids-waste water estimation 156

W

Waste 1, 3
  disposal 5
  handling 5
  gas 5
  liquid 5
  treatment 5
Waste water analytical methods 155
  classical 155
  colourimetric 155
  instrumental 155
  sampling 154
  treatment methods 166, 167, 168
  classification 165
  biological 166, 168, 308
  chemical 166, 167
  physical 166, 167
  control strategy 169
  primary treatment 166, 169, 174
  equalization 169, 171
  neutralization 169, 173
  segregation 169, 170
  secondary treatment 166, 169, 211
  aerobic 225
  anaerobic 256
Water
  availability 144
  availability in India 145
  consumption-Indian industries 145
Water-borne pollutants 147
  classification 147, 165
  effects 148
  biological 150
  chemical 149
  physical 149
  physiological 149
  toxic 149
  sources 148
  tolerance limits-Indian standards 150
Wind
  direction 18
  rose 19
  velocity 18

Some exciting gifts are up for grabs with this book!!

AIR AND WATER POLLUTION CONTROL ENGINEERING

Prof. D N Ghosh and Prof. S K Ghosh

FREE Gifts Rs. 1000/-

DEAR READERS

By now you must have gone through this book in the entirety. So we invite your assessment on this title with absolute impartiality and candid observations. After all, we publishers blindly depend on your benchmarking. Friends, please fill up the open spaces below with CAPITAL LETTERS. You may add some extra sheets of paper if the space provided is not sufficient for you.

i. What are the important topics of your syllabus which are not adequately covered in this book?

ii. In which chapters and on what topics the treatment of the subject-matter by the author is not satisfactory and why?

iii. Have you come across the typos, factual inaccuracies, inconsistencies, and other forms of mistakes in the book? If yes, then please specify the mistakes and page numbers.

iv. Name top three books on the same subject, which, in your consideration, are better than this book. Could you provide some reasons?

Your 1st Preference: ....

Your 2nd Preference: ....

Your 3rd Preference: ....

v. Any suggestion to improve the quality of illustrations, diagrams, etc.?

vi. How did you like the cover design? Any suggestion on colours?

vii. Suggestions for further improvement of production-standard:

viii. Who recommended you this book:

☐ Teacher ☐ Friend ☐ Parents ☐ Bookseller ☐ Librarian

ix. Name of the person who has recommended:

Designation: ....

Address: ....

Phone No.: ....

e-mail: ....

x. Name and address of the bookseller from whom you have purchased this book:

....

....

....

xi. Name and address of the library where you would like to find the book:

....

....

xii. Name and address of your institution (Please mention the University or Board):

....

....

xiii. Your name, e-mail, and complete postal address:

....

....

....

xiv. A few other titles published by us that you would like to read:

....

....

The best assessment will be rewarded half-yearly. The award will be in the form of our publications, as decided by the Editorial and Marketing Operations Division, amounting to Rs. 1000/- (Rupees one thousand) only.

....

Please mail the filled up coupon at your earliest to :

Editorial & Marketing Operations Division

NEW CENTRAL BOOK AGENCY (P) Ltd

8/1 Chintamoni Das Lane, Kolkata 700 009

West Bengal, INDIA

Phone + Fax: 033 + 2241 8411, 2241 8573, 2241 9094

e-mail: ncbapvtltd@eth.net, ncba@cal2.vsnl.net.in

Website: www.centralgroup.com